AF394576

Stalin's Plans for
Capturing Germany

Stalin's Plans for Capturing Germany

Bogdan Musial

In collaboration with Oliver Musial
Translated by Oliver Musial

Pen & Sword
MILITARY

AN IMPRINT OF PEN & SWORD BOOKS LTD.
YORKSHIRE – PHILADELPHIA

First published in Great Britain in 2023 by
Pen and Sword Military
An imprint of
Pen & Sword Books Ltd.
Yorkshire - Philadelphia

Copyright © Bogdan Musial, 2023

ISBN 978 1 39906 813 0

A CIP catalogue record for this book is available from the British Library.

Typeset in INDIA by IMPEC eSolutions
Printed and bound in England by CPI Group (UK) Ltd.

Pen & Sword Books Ltd incorporates the imprints of Pen & Sword Books
Archaeology, Atlas, Aviation, Battleground, Discovery, Family History, History,
Maritime, Military, Naval, Politics, Railways, Select, Transport, True Crime,
Fiction, Frontline Books, Leo Cooper, Praetorian Press, Seaforth Publishing,
Wharncliffe and White Owl.

For a complete list of Pen & Sword titles please contact

PEN & SWORD BOOKS LIMITED
47 Church Street, Barnsley, South Yorkshire, S70 2AS, England
E-mail: enquiries@pen-and-sword.co.uk
Website: www.pen-and-sword.co.uk

or

PEN AND SWORD BOOKS
1950 Lawrence Rd, Havertown, PA 19083, USA
E-mail: Uspen-and-sword@casematepublishers.com
Website: www.penandswordbooks.com

Table of Contents

Introduction

It is common knowledge that the German surprise attack on the Soviet Union on 22 June 1941 was an ideologically-motivated, meticulously-planned and unprovoked war of aggression with the goal of claiming *Lebensraum* – living space – for the German people. This is backed up by countless pieces of evidence, including from Hitler himself. Understandably, this aspect was always emphasized in Soviet propaganda during and after the war. What Soviet, and now Russian, propaganda neglects is that the Soviet Union had been in an economic and political alliance with Nazi Germany for nearly two years when Germany attacked, and that the Soviet Union had its own plans to attack its ally – which the Germans were oblivious to. Recent findings in Soviet archives in Moscow show that the Soviet Union had in fact been aggressively preparing for its own ideologically motivated attack on the rest of Europe beginning in the late 1920s, especially after the start of the Great Depression in the autumn of 1929.

The goal of the planned Soviet invasion was to spread communism across Europe – and then the world. Key to these plans was Germany, which was located strategically in the heart of Europe, had a very powerful industry, and whose very numerous proletariat could potentially be transformed into well-disciplined soldiers of the revolution. Once Germany had been secured, Europe was bound to fall. However, both anti-communist and anti-German Poland stood in the way.

Already in 1930, the famed general Mikhail Tukhachevsky had drawn up his plans for a great invasion of the West with a gigantic army with 50,000 tanks, 40,000 aircraft, and the "massive use of chemical weapons". He soon managed to convince Stalin of the merit of his ideas and beginning in early 1931, the entire Red Army was reorganized in accordance with Tukhachevsky's vision. However, the Soviet armaments industry was very weak in the 1930s and tank production especially was virtually non-existent. To realize Stalin and Tukhachevsky's grand plans, the entire Soviet economy and society was subordinated to that one goal. This enormous simultaneous industrialization and armaments program was flanked by an unprecedented terror campaign that was targeted mostly at the still-independent peasantry and claimed millions of lives.

Despite all these great efforts, sacrifices and crimes, however, the armament program did not go according to plan – it was marred by frequent and often spectacular setbacks that Stalin and his comrades attributed to sabotage and wrecking. After six years of failure after failure, it was Tukhachevsky's turn to fall and in June 1937, he and his closest associates were executed. Still, progress remained sluggish and when Germany attacked on 22 June 1941, the Soviet Union was still in the midst of the gigantic armaments program it had embarked on in the late 1920s.

For both leaders, the Hitler-Stalin Pact of 24 August 1939 was nothing more than a temporary arrangement. Hitler needed Soviet resources and non-intervention in his war against Poland, while the Soviet Union got to move its borders to the west, spreading communism and gaining new forward deployment areas. Furthermore, Stalin wanted Hitler to start a great war in Europe that pitted the continent's greatest powers against each other. Once they were exhausted, the Red Army would move in and brush aside its weakened foes. Both Stalin and his closest associates readily talked about this. As late as 4 June 1941, Zhdanov, a key member of Stalin's inner circle, declared that by invading Poland alongside Germany in September 1939, the Soviet Union was now on the path of "offensive policy", i.e. the path of the revolutionary wars of conquest.

Following the annexation of most of its western neighbors, the only thing that remained to the west of the Soviet Union was Germany. In early 1941, Stalin and his comrades thus began to intensively prepare for their planned invasion of Germany. Indeed, Stalin was so preoccupied with his invasion of Germany that he failed to take heed of the many warnings of the impending German attack. It was thus in the midst of these offensive preparations that the Germans struck the Soviet Union on 22 June 1941. However, it has to be noted that the Germans did not know of Soviet war preparations until after the invasion; they were "not aware" as Goebbels put it in his diary on 19 August 1941. The strength and size of the Red

Army grossly exceeded German expectations and despite its great initial successes, the advance of the Wehrmacht was ultimately ground to a halt. Instead of crushing the Soviet Union in a matter of weeks or a few months, the Red Army would go on to defeat the Wehrmacht and take Berlin on 2 May 1945.

This book shows in great detail the genesis and the progress of the Soviet war preparations based on a host of contemporary documents from Soviet archives. Unfortunately, the current state of research on this issue has not been particularly good, and in some cases even repeats the Soviet propaganda of its defensive or even "peace-loving" foreign policy without due criticism. Likewise, the exceedingly aggressive Soviet military thinking is still frequently characterized as "forward defense", an old Soviet rhetorical trick many scholars have fallen for. Richard Overy, for example, wrote that "despite the many attempts to show that Stalin was planning revolutionary wars of conquest in the 1930s and 1940s, the bulk of evidence still suggests that he took on a defensive, reactive posture."[1] However, he is far from the only one. I myself believed so as well[2], until I was able to access the Moscow archives.

So far, a proper, source-based debate on the motives and plans of Stalin has not taken place. A major reason for this is that this question is being assigned very high political and ideological importance. This is never good for debate as political interests and ideological beliefs take center stage, not the facts. In addition to that, the debate has also suffered from a lack of sources from Russian archives, which have become increasingly closed in recent years. This has made factual debate hard and ideological speculation easy. Finally, past debates, especially the one surrounding the book *Icebreaker* (1988) by Viktor Suvorov (Vladimir Rezun). In the book, Suvorov had claimed that the German invasion of the Soviet Union had been a pre-emptive strike with which Hitler aimed to avert an imminent Soviet attack. In the 1990s, this debate had triggered what some described as "a kind of political-ideological religious war".[3]

As a former Red Army officer and as someone who had worked in Soviet military intelligence, Suvorov was intimately familiar with the communist system and was well aware of the expansionist nature of Soviet communism. Lacking access to the relevant archives, he based his thesis on published memoirs, newspaper reports, and other printed sources. While his general idea that the German attack on the Soviet Union in 1941 was a pre-emptive strike is clearly wrong – the Germans were completely unaware of Soviet war preparations[4] – he was nevertheless right about the general goals and plans of Stalin.

Sources

As mentioned earlier, the debate surrounding the thesis of the pre-emptive strike involved only a few sources from the relevant Soviet archives. Instead, the dispute revolved around a handful of individual documents – how to interpret them and if they were even genuine. For a brief time in the 2000s, however, the old Soviet archives became temporarily more accessible in spite of the still-restrictive archival policy of the Russian state. This account is based on a host of contemporary Russian-language documents retrieved during that thaw, and presents for the first time many of these documents that have been analyzed.

The most important of these sources are the secret Politburo protocols which represent the key to understanding Soviet history. They have been formally accessible only since the late 1990s, and individual protocol points still remain blocked. Nevertheless, the available protocols have been analyzed by various historians asking various questions,[5] but this is the first account to examine these documents regarding Soviet war preparations.

Also important are the notes of the Soviet leaders, chief among them Stalin himself. Furthermore, the notes from other high-ranking Bolsheviks such as Molotov, Zhdanov, Mikoyan, and Malenkov have been publicly accessible since the 2000s; in addition, there are also plenty of documents from Trotsky, Dzerzhinsky, Voroshilov, or Lenin's own secretariat. Other important sources are the documents from various Soviet institutions such as the Revolutionary War Council, the Politburo, the Central Committee, or the Party or State Control. Particularly important as well are the holdings of the Committee for Defense. It was the Committee for Defense that exclusively focused on war preparations.

The key documents for this topic are located in the former party archive, the Russian State Archive of Socio-Political History (RGASPI). While this is no military archive, it does contain a wealth of political-historical material with a strong emphasis on military, economic, and social aspects, which is what this work is ultimately about. Most importantly, the RGASPI holds the documents of the Politburo, the Central Committee, and individual party leaders, which in turn offer great insight into the inner workings of the Soviet Union, because it was precisely these people and their party organizations that controlled the entire state, including its military.

Another important source are various Russian-language publications which have been published since the late 1990s, among them two large multi-volume source editions on Soviet village policy, the six-volume document collection on the history of the gulag, the source editions for the Chief War Council of the Red Army, the session protocols of the War Council at the People's Commissar for Defense from 1937 to 1938, a document collection on the Finnish-Soviet Winter War, the correspondences between Stalin and Molotov, as well as between Stalin and Kaganovich, or the several-volume collection of intelligence reports and communications delivered to Stalin. Key were also the diaries of Georgi Dimitrov, the chief of the Komintern, as well as the often-ignored speeches and articles published by both Lenin and Stalin.[6]

With these sources, it is possible to draw a detailed picture of Soviet domestic and foreign policy, its goals, and their implementation outside of the realm of Soviet propaganda. In many cases, the most important documents were often not the ones made in the standard reporting process, but the ones made by special inquiries, which took stock of existing problems and then sought to solve them. Particularly vital were the various memoranda on the state of war preparations of the Red Army and the armaments industry, as well as related ones that dealt with questions such as military doctrine and ideology, which were directed primarily at Stalin and his closest associates. Likewise key are the contemporary protocols and notes of the various sessions, meetings, and discussions. In combination with the other contemporary sources, they make it possible to accurately reconstruct the progress of Soviet war preparations as well as the motivation behind them.

This work primarily focuses on the years between 1919 and 1941 and is divided into two parts. The first part covers the period from 1919 to the summer of 1929, and deals with the prelude of the gigantic war preparations of the 1930s, the Bolshevik ideology of world revolution, and the decisive role of Germany in these plans, as well as the failed breakthrough into Western Europe during the Polish-Soviet War of 1920, which would haunt the Soviet Union for the next two decades.

Following their defeat at the gates of Warsaw in the summer of 1920, the Bolsheviks turned inwards and sought to solidify their power at home. However, despite their victory in the Russian Civil War, they soon faced a series of anti-communist uprisings; although they were able to bloodily suppress them, they were forced to compromise in the end and renege on their most radical policies in favor of the much more moderate New Economic Policy in 1921. While armed resistance was thus more or less defeated by force of arms and concessions in 1921/22, the Soviet economy was in complete disarray after nearly a decade of constant warfare. After an initial recovery immediately after the introduction of the NEP, the country was headed towards another economic and social crisis by 1924. By the second half of the 1920s, the Kremlin even feared a new round of uprisings.

The situation abroad was even more disheartening and Moscow was forced to watch as the supposedly irresistible revolutionary momentum was quickly evaporating before their eyes. In particular, the failure of the German communists to stage a revolution in the autumn of 1923 was a painful blow to the Bolsheviks, which was made even worse by the fact that the German economy began to recover quickly afterwards, together with the rest of Europe. The end of the post-war economic and political crises now made another proletarian revolution in Europe a distant prospect. The economic and social crisis was thus joined by an ideological one.

Amidst this crisis, Lenin – the undisputed leader of the Bolsheviks – died on 21 January 1924. His death immediately triggered a vicious power struggle in which Stalin and his faction emerged victorious. By 1927, Stalin had fully consolidated his power and began to build a completely unrestrained dictatorship that allowed him to implement his vision of Socialism in One Country. The goal of his policy was to strengthen the Soviet Union and in particular the Red Army in such a way that it was able to spread the flames of revolution abroad on its own with force of arms – even if the local communists were to fail once again. For this, both the Red Army – but especially the armaments industry – had to be built up significantly, since both were in a very poor state throughout the 1920s. At the same time, the Bolsheviks had to pacify their own hinterland ahead of the coming revolutionary war, which in practice meant destroying the rebellious peasantry.

The first part closes with a review of the state of war preparations in July 1929. These were far from satisfactory for Moscow, but just when all hope was nearly lost, a ray of light appeared – the Great Depression. Seeing the capitalist West being thrown into a great economic crisis, Stalin and his comrades believed that a new "imperialist war" similar to the First World War was now inevitable, which they would seek to exploit for their own cause. The second part thus focuses on war preparations after the start of the Great Depression, which quickly took on gigantic proportions.

In order to finance this enormous armaments program, Stalin sped up the collectivization of agriculture which gave him full access to the peasants' harvests he could then sell abroad. As the peasants generally refused to join the collective farms voluntarily, the Bolsheviks unleashed a massive terror campaign against the peasantry that broke their resistance once and for all. A separate chapter will examine the famine caused by excessive grain requisitions that killed millions in 1932/33.

This is followed by a description of Mikhail Tukhachevsky's concept of war of annihilation, with which he won over Stalin in 1930. It was thus in accordance with Tukhachevsky's vision that the Soviet armed forces were restructured and expanded, with a particular focus on the air force and tanks, which in turn necessitated great investments to build up a modern heavy industry capable of producing enough aircraft and tanks. However, this did not go to plan, and unwilling to admit failure, the Bolshevik leadership began to search for scapegoats, which led to the execution of countless industrial experts and officers, including Tukhachevsky himself.

Although the Soviet Union frantically prepared for the great "imperialist war", it refused to materialize for the time being. Most of the developed capitalist West remained relatively stable. Things had looked promising in Germany, but instead of a revolution, it was Hitler who – with ample support from Moscow and the German communists – rose to power and turned the country into a decidedly anti-communist dictatorship in a matter of months while also building up the country's military. During that time, Stalin repeatedly misread Hitler's anti-communist statements, believing them to be a mere ploy to "lull" France, which Stalin thought was Hitler's true target. While he was wrong, the events of 1938 and 1939 did seem to prove Stalin right as Hitler made his move against France and its allies.

A key development was the Hitler-Stalin Pact of 1939, which had major economic, military, and political implications for the Soviet Union and seemed to have finally ushered in a new age of irresistible Bolshevik advances. However, these hopes were quickly dampened during the botched invasion of Finland in 1939/40, which showed that despite over a decade of intensive modernization, the Red Army was still unable to successfully attack and overwhelm an organized, determined enemy.

Roiled by this setback, the Red Army was once again reorganized, rearmed, and expanded to turn it into the greatest invasion army the world had ever seen. Beginning in late 1940, Stalin was explicitly preparing the Red Army for its attack on Germany, a process that only intensified in early 1941. In the midst of these preparations, however, the German attack caught the Soviets by complete surprise. In this context, the question of how much Hitler knew of Soviet preparations will be discussed, as well as Suvorov's thesis of the German invasion having been a pre-emptive war.

In this work, I use terms such as "communist", "Bolshevik", or "Soviet" instead of "Russian" when writing about Soviet policies and crimes, even though these are often interchangeable in everyday use. The reason for this is that unlike, for example, Nazi Germany, the Soviet Union was not a nation-state at all – it was a multiethnic empire whose leaders saw themselves as communists and were in many cases not ethnically Russian. At the same time, the Soviet terror machine also targeted ethnic Russians, who in the sheer number of casualties only came second to Ukrainians. Especially in the first years of communist rule, the Bolsheviks specifically targeted Russian nationalists and patriots as they saw them as key pillars of the anti-communist resistance. Instead of Russian nationalism or imperialism, it was their unshakable belief in the ideals of communism that inspired Lenin, Stalin, and the others to do what they did.

The Russian-language sources were translated by me and my translators, and we are responsible for any translation mistakes. The bibliography only includes works cited in the book and does not claim to be exhaustive.

In my research, I was assisted by many people. In particular, the archivists in Moscow were very helpful. Furthermore, Jan Szumski and Andrej Zamoiski greatly supported me in my research; aside from their assistance, their knowledge of Soviet everyday life greatly helped me understand many otherwise incomprehensible aspects of Soviet history. In addition, Jan Szumski was able to decipher a great many barely legible handwritten documents. Finally, I would also like to thank Christopher Casson and Nicholas Siekierski for their assistance in editing and translating the book.

This book was first published in 2008 under the German title "Kampfplatz Deutschland. Stalins Kriegspläne gegen den Westen" [Battleground Germany. Stalin's War Plans against the West]. Since then, not much has changed regarding our knowledge of Soviet war preparations in the 1920s and 1930s. Indeed, the state of research has even regressed somewhat, both in German[7] and in English.[8] However, the situation is even worse in Russia, where Vladimir Putin has taken up as his duty to revive the old Soviet narrative of the peace-loving Soviet Union whose wars and annexations of 1939 and 1940 were purely defensive.[9] The purpose of this maneuver became clear on 24 February 2022, when Putin ordered the Russian army to launch an unprovoked attack on Ukraine. Like Stalin's earlier conquests, this war was and still is being presented as a defensive action, designed to protect Russia from an imaginary threat.

Note

The translation for this work was financed by the Polish National Foundation.

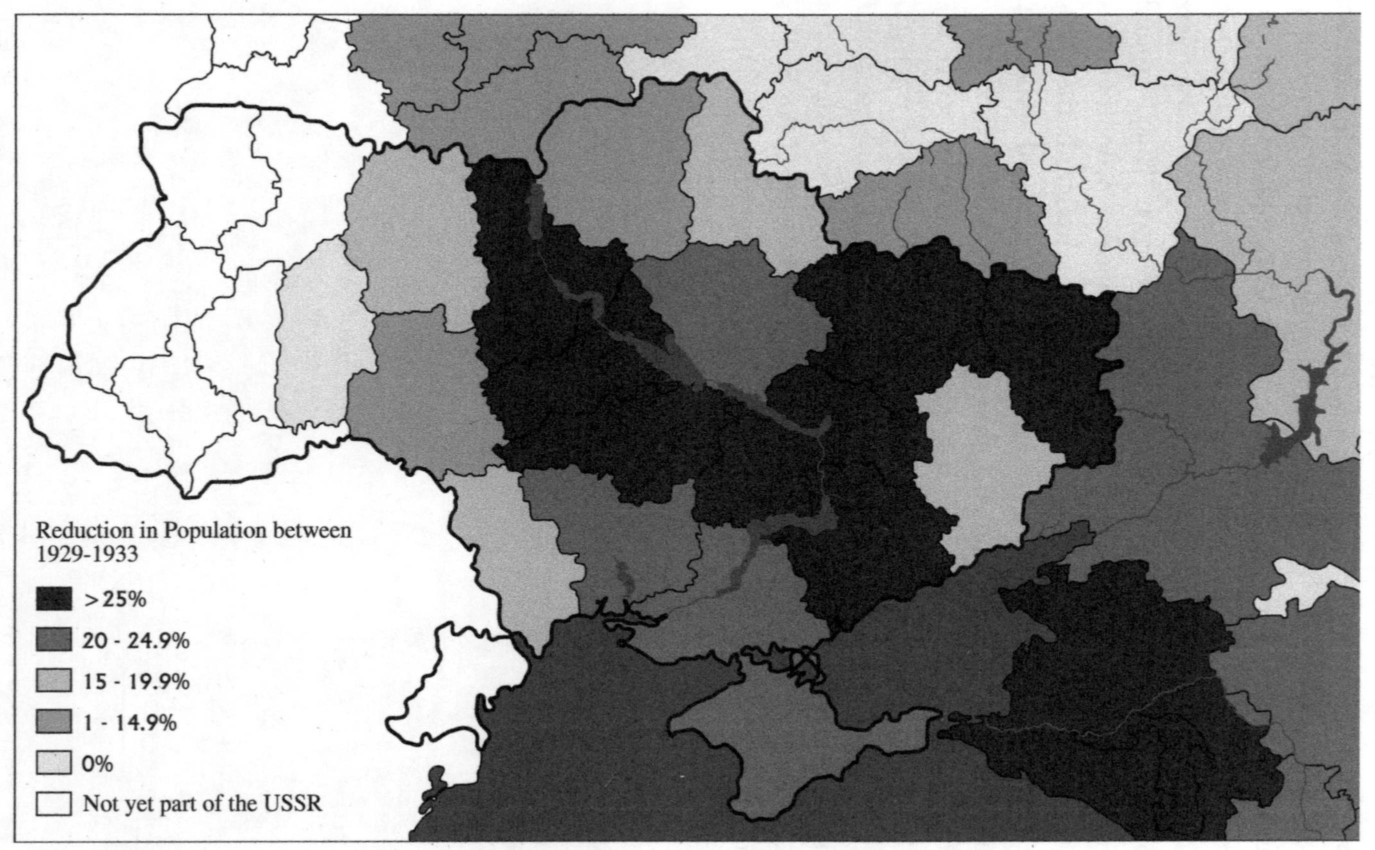

Depopulation of Soviet Ukraine as a result of famine and mass terror against peasants

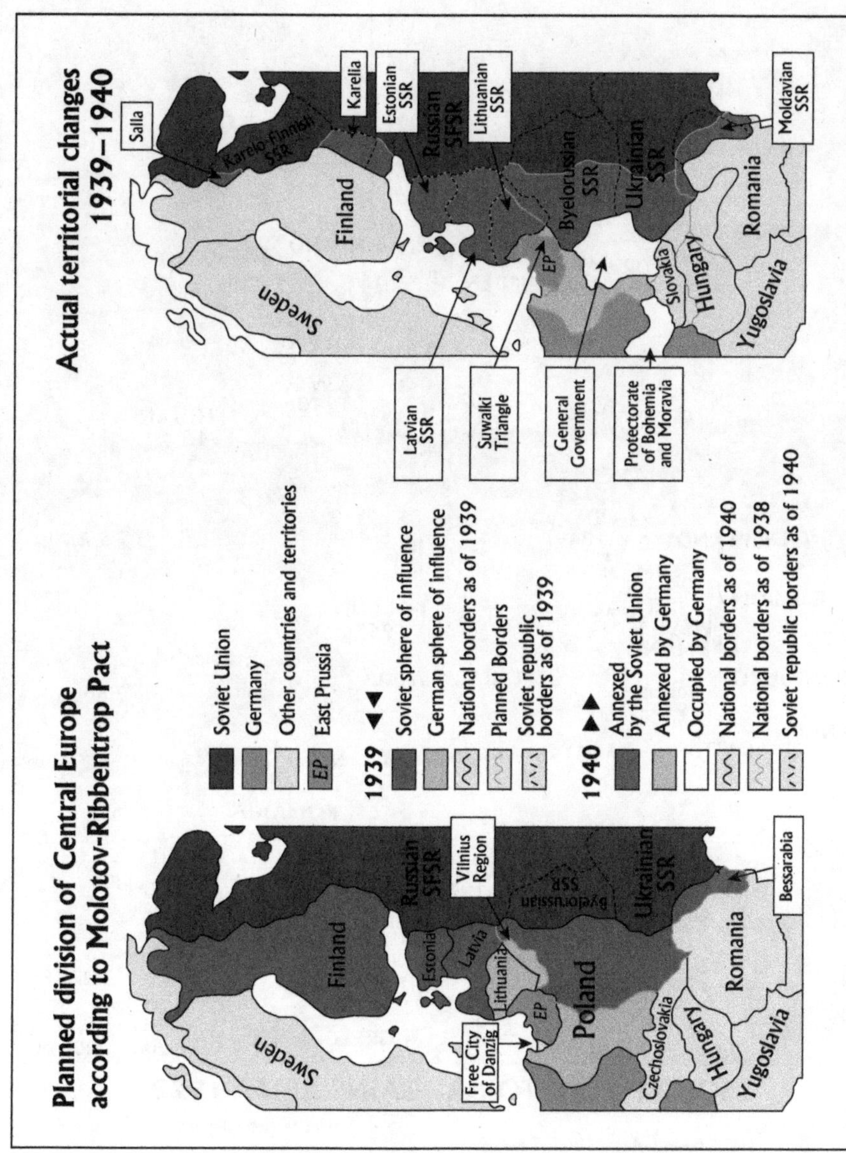

The division of Central and Eastern Europe between Germany and the Soviet Union 1939-1940

Soviet territorial expansion under Stalin

Part I

Great Hopes and Great Setbacks

Chapter 1

The October Revolution in Russia: The Beginning of the Bolshevik World Revolution

When Lenin and his fellow Bolsheviks took control over Russia in October 1917, they were absolutely convinced that they had ignited the flames of the world revolution which would soon set ablaze all of Europe and then the world, ushering in a new chapter of human existence. Once the Bolsheviks were finished consolidating power in Russia, they could realize Russia's true purpose: To become "the centre of the world socialist conflagration" – as Lenin put it – and to carry abroad the world revolution.[1]

This was Lenin's guiding ideal. In a speech held on 6 November 1920, he explained: "We knew at that time that our victory would be a lasting one only when our cause had triumphed the world over, and so when we began working for our cause we counted exclusively on the world revolution."[2] A few months earlier, on 1 March 1920, he had said: "When, over two years ago, at the very beginning of the Russian revolution, we spoke about this approaching international, world revolution, it was a prevision, and to a certain extent a prediction."[3]

Initially, Lenin had hoped that the rest of Europe would quickly follow Russia's example and would see their own communist revolutions. At the time, Lenin and his Bolsheviks still had to contend with their enemies in the Russian Civil War, which forced him to limit himself to supporting various European revolutionaries with money, propaganda materials and political instructions. That, he hoped, was enough to help his European comrades overthrow the old order.[4]

The Russian Civil War also left Lenin unable to immediately assert his role as the intellectual leader of a global movement. With war raging across his newly conquered empire, he did not find the time to work on his planned treatise "The Experiences of the Russian Revolutions of 1905 and 1917" with which he hoped to inspire other communists outside of Russia. On 30 November 1917, he complained that "apart from the title, however, I had no time to write a single line of a chapter; I was 'interrupted' by a political crisis—the eve of the October revolution of 1917. Such an 'interruption' can only be welcomed [...]. It is more pleasant and useful to go through the 'experience of revolution' than to write about it."[5] This lack of intellectual guidance soon became noticeable. Three years later, Trotsky sent this letter to Lenin, asking for guidance:

In our party-military circles there is currently raging a debate regarding military doctrine. [...] In particular, the Red Army stands accused that its 'military doctrine' (this entire quarrel flared up because of this puffed-up little phrase) does not include the idea of the revolutionary offensive war. I am currently working on a series of articles or a brochure in which I want to summarize that the party has spoken about revolutionary wars at different points in time – before and after October. Could You [...] tell me what You have written about it? Was there not a resolution in the matter? Your Trotsky.[6]

Lenin replied immediately. On 23 November 1921, he sent a letter to Trotsky, saying: "It does look like there was no specific article. On the sidelines, plenty [...], especially in the years 1914-17."[7] In the months and years following the October Revolution, Lenin and his comrades had been simply too busy to dedicate their time to theoretical-ideological debates about world revolution and revolutionary warfare. Instead, Lenin, Trotsky, Zinoviev and the others knew they were shaping the course of world history itself. The lack of theoretical discussions notwithstanding, the Bolsheviks – and the other communists all over Europe – were convinced that the First World War and the crises that followed it had created the conditions for a Europe-wide communist revolution that would destroy bourgeois society once and for all.[8]

For Lenin and his comrades, Russia was just the first step, the ember that would ignite the blaze of world revolution. This was not an optional goal or even a mere propaganda claim: Indeed, world revolution was a

Marxist article of faith, and in March 1919, Lenin sponsored the creation of the Third Communist International (Comintern) in Moscow, whose sole purpose it was to lead and coordinate the world revolution.[9]

At the time, political events appeared to prove right the predictions of a coming wave of communist revolutions. Both the German and the Austro-Hungarian empires had been decisively defeated and were in complete chaos; in the case of Austria-Hungary, the entire country had been dismantled. Communist revolutionaries immediately tried to fill the vacuum and in March 1919, much to the delight of Moscow, they turned Hungary into a Soviet republic. In April 1919, Zinoviev wrote: "The movement is developing with such a dizzying speed that one can safely say that in a year, we will begin to forget that there was a struggle for communism in Europe, because in a year, all of Europe will be communist. And the struggle for communism will be carried into America, perhaps also into Asia and other parts of the world."[10]

Four years later, a wearier Zinoviev looked back on his and his comrades' enthusiasm: "Bolshevism expected the victory of the world revolution immediately after the victory of the Revolution in Russia. Capitalism, however, proved to be more viable and flexible. As far as concrete time tables for the world revolution are concerned, Bolshevism has already admitted its partial miscalculations in that area"[11]

Germany – The Heart of Europe

Right from the beginning, Germany played a central role in Bolshevik plans for world revolution. Lenin himself had proclaimed "again and again that Soviet power would be lost if the German worker would not provide aid: '... we will without doubt perish despite all conceivable fortunate events, if the German revolution does not happen...'"[12]

Although the country had been industrializing rapidly, when the First World War broke out in 1914, Russia was still a largely agrarian and relatively backward country. With casualties mounting and major centers occupied, Russia was thrown into a deep economic, social, and political crisis that the Bolsheviks used to wrestle power from a weakened central government, which in turn triggered a bloody civil war that claimed millions of lives and worsened the crisis even more. At the same time, the

Western powers directly intervened against the Bolsheviks, embargoing them and actively supporting their enemies in a bid to halt or at the very least weaken the revolution. The embargo hit the Bolsheviks especially hard, and of all the major capitalist countries, Germany was the only one that had objected to it.[13]

Thus the only country that could provide any form of tangible economic aid to the Bolsheviks was Germany. Aside from trade considerations, Germany was seen as essential for the success of the world revolution due to its great industrial potential and because it housed Europe's largest force of industrial laborers, which made it the "primary core of the international proletariat" in the mind of the Bolshevik revolutionaries.[14]

The German communists shared this sentiment. On 4 November 1918, a week before the German Revolution and the surrender of Germany, Karl Liebknecht sent this telegraph to his Russian comrades: "In Germany, the flames of the sacred fire are shooting out simultaneously in hundreds of places. The revolution of the German proletariat has begun. This revolution will save the Russian Revolution from all blows and overthrow the foundations of world capitalism."[15]

For the German and Russian communists to link up, however, there needed to be a direct land border between Bolshevik Russia and Germany. This had been the case traditionally, but now the re-emergence of an independent Poland in the wake of the German collapse had changed things. All of a sudden, there was a several-hundred-kilometer-wide barrier separating them.

Poland – The Barrier

As the re-emergence of an independent Poland had cut off Bolshevik Russia from Germany, thus threatening the survival of the revolution itself, one of the main geopolitical goals of the Bolsheviks was to restore direct, unfettered access to Germany. Unfortunately for them, Poland refused to embrace communism. Communist parties and groups had traditionally been of lesser importance in Poland, and Pilsudski, the leader of the socialists, had taken up the mantle of independence, vehemently opposing foreign – including Bolshevik – domination. At the same time, Poland also received support from France, which had become continental Europe's preeminent military power following the defeat of Germany.

To make matters worse, the ongoing Russian Civil War further forced the Bolsheviks to fight on other, more pressing fronts, which gave Polish forces time to consolidate. Thus the Soviet Western Army which was facing off against the Poles received only relatively small reinforcements in early 1919, forcing them to remain on the defensive. For now, the Western Army's task was to occupy a line along the Niemen (Memel), Szczara (Shchara), and Pripyat (today in Western Belarus) rivers, which the Bolsheviks wanted to become the new Bolshevik-Polish border.[16]

This border had been decided upon by the Supreme Soviet on 3 December 1918[17] and would have effectively ensured direct land access to Germany via East Prussia as German Freikorps were operating in the borderlands in the vicinity of Kaunas at the time.[18] However, the lack of manpower and resources did not allow the Western Army to fulfill its task. On the contrary, through March and April 1919, the still not fully organized Polish army advanced into the area and pushed back the Bolshevik Western Army.[19]

In April 1919, Polish soldiers and volunteers ejected the Bolsheviks from Vilnius (Polish: Wilno) and the surrounding lands, where they had fought side-by-side with the Lithuanians.[20] Lithuania laid claim on Vilnius as it had been the historical capital of Lithuania for centuries. By the early 20th century, however, Vilnius was a mostly Polish and Jewish city, while the countryside was dominated by Poles, with significant Jewish and Belarusian minorities. Lithuanians were very few and far between.

The Polish advance continued in the following months and by summer 1919, Polish troops had pushed back the Soviet Western Army all the way to the Berezina River in what is now eastern Belarus. The fighting was dominated by small-scale skirmishes, from which the Poles usually emerged victorious. Throughout the conflict, Bolshevik troops were demoralized, poorly armed and plagued by crippling supply difficulties, which prevented them from launching any sort of large counterattack.[21]

Nevertheless, the situation on the Polish side was not much better and the Polish army soon reached its limits. Compared to their Bolshevik counterparts, the Polish army was even more poorly armed and their logistics were not much better as the Polish army was still in the process of formation. Where the Poles had the edge, however, was in soldier morale and discipline, as well as military leadership. This proved decisive. Still, logistical and organizational issues made further advances impossible. At the same time, the Polish political leaders in Warsaw were more than happy with the current state of the border and did not want to push any further, especially since much of Ukraine and southern Russia were held by the anti-communist White general Denikin. While his main enemies were the Bolsheviks, he also insisted on the restoration of Russia to its pre-1914 borders, which would mean the annexation of most of Poland, including Warsaw and Łódź. Under these circumstances, Warsaw was not intent on helping Denikin by launching an attack on the Bolsheviks.[22]

While the Bolsheviks had been beaten in the west, they were succeeding elsewhere, winning decisive battles against their enemies over the course of 1919. With their allies beaten, the Western powers intervening in the conflict retreated and the Bolsheviks were left in control of most of Russia.[23] In November 1919 alone, the Red Army "liberated" 1,359,500 square kilometers and around 15,880,000 people.[24] Bolstered by the string of victories, Lenin explained to the assembled delegates at the VII All-Russian Congress of the Soviets on 5 December 1919: "*Our main difficulties are already behind us.* [...]. *We can say that the Civil War which we conducted with such tremendous sacrifices has ended in victory.*"[25]

The situation only improved over the next few months and on 16 January 1920, the Western allies decided to lift the economic blockade against the Bolsheviks. Lenin was overjoyed: "Lifting the blockade is a fact of major international significance showing that a new stage in the socialist revolution has begun. For the blockade was in fact the principal, really strong weapon with which the imperialists of the world wanted to strangle Soviet Russia."[26]

Even though the military situation seemed advantageous at that moment, Bolshevik Russia was heading toward total economic collapse. On 1 March 1920, Lenin stated: "The bloody war is over and we are now waging a bloodless war, a war against the economic chaos, ruin, poverty and disease to which we have been reduced by four years of imperialist war and two years of civil war. You know that the economic chaos is terrible. [...] We are now trying with great difficulty to secure aid from abroad. [...] How are we going to restore industry when we cannot exchange manufactured goods for grain because there isn't any?"[27]

Only Germany, Europe's industrial powerhouse, was able to provide the economic help the Bolsheviks needed, but the advancing Poles had severed the direct land connection to Germany. In a speech on 2 October 1920, Lenin complained: "The Versailles Peace has turned Poland into a buffer state which is to guard against German contact with Soviet communism."[28] Additionally, the Bolsheviks believed that Germany was close to experiencing its own revolution and that it only needed a small push from outside. In his opening speech at the IX Party Congress of Russian Communist Party (Bolsheviks) RCP(b) on 29 March 1920, Lenin declared:

From the international standpoint, our position has never been as favorable as it is now; and what fills us with particular joy and vigor is the news we are daily receiving from Germany, which shows that, however difficult and painful the birth of a socialist revolution may be, the proletarian Soviet power in Germany is spreading irresistibly. [...] Not only is it one more absolute confirmation of the correctness of the line, but it gives us the assurance that the time is not far off when we shall be marching hand in hand with a German Soviet government.[29]

On the same day, he elaborated in his report to the Central Committee of the RCP(b):

The new phase, the new stage of the revolutionary upswing in Germany [...] proves clearly [...] that the will to fight of the workers is ever-growing. [...] We know that each passing month strengthens our powers enormously and will strengthen them even more. [...] We have received a formal peace offer from Poland. [...] Because we know that our enemy [the Polish bourgeoisie] is in an incredibly difficult situation – an enemy who does not know what he wants, what he will do tomorrow – so we have to tell ourselves with all certainty that despite the peace offer, a war is possible.[30]

Chapter 2

The Polish–Soviet War of 1920 –
The Breakthrough into Europe Fails

As the Bolsheviks were emerging as the undisputed victors of the civil war, they turned their gaze toward Germany and Poland. After the Polish military had ceased its advance in Belarus in the early summer of 1919, the northern section of the border with Poland had been more or less quiet. In the south, the Poles had defeated the Ukrainians and moved the borders 200 km east of Lwów, making contact with the Bolshevik South-Western Front.[1] From the Bolshevik perspective, the only thing separating them from Germany now was several hundred kilometers of Polish territory.

On 8 December 1919, the Red Army was given the explicit task to scout out the Polish forces.[2] Bolshevik spies received decisive help from local communists, who repeatedly urged the Bolsheviks to invade. On 24 December 1919, Julian Marchlewski[3], a German communist of Polish origin, presented the results in a memorandum addressed to the Central Committee of the RCP(b), in which he described in detail the political and economic conditions as well as the state of the Polish army.[4]

Marchlewski reported that Poland was divided into two political camps, one led by Józef Piłsudski (the provisional head of state and commander in chief), and the other by the National Democrats. Piłsudski, said Marchlewski, had no intention of starting a war against Bolshevik Russia or aiding the Whites, because he believed that a victory of the "counterrevolution" would mean the end of Polish independence. At the same time, he was said to be afraid of the spread of communism to Poland, which is why he was pushing for the creation of buffer states, namely Lithuania and Belarus. The National Democrats, meanwhile, wanted to join the Entente in supporting Denikin in the war against Bolshevik Russia, Marchlewski stated.

He further explained that Poland was in the middle of a catastrophic economic and financial crisis, and that while Polish soldiers and especially the officers were highly motivated, the equipment of the Polish army was in a horrible state. Marchlewski's conclusion: "Therefore, I think that an attack of the Polish army is possible in the near future." To prevent this, Marchlewski called for the strengthening of the Western Front but added that Denikin had to be defeated first before the Red Army could take any action against Poland.[5]

Preparing for the War against Poland

Marchlewski's memorandum was received with much enthusiasm in Moscow, where Bolshevik leaders were already preparing to march against Poland. The news about the economic hardships Poland faced as well as the poor equipment of the Polish military emboldened Lenin and his comrades, and in early 1920 war preparations began in all earnest.

In January 1920, Boris Shaposhnikov, a former Tsarist staff officer turned chief of the operative administration of the Red Army, began to draw up his plans for the invasion of Poland.[6] That same month, the Revolutionary Military Council ordered two divisions to be transferred to the Polish border.[7] On 17 February 1920, the Polish Bureau at the Central Committee of the RCP(b) sent out a telegram calling on the political departments of the various armies and fronts to send all of their Polish-speaking political workers (*politrabotniki*) to the Western Front. Likewise, Polish communists working in various agencies were supposed to be delegated to the Polish Bureau.[8]

Just a day later, on 18 February 1920, an American journalist asked Lenin if Soviet Russia was planning to attack Poland and Romania. Lenin responded: "No. We have declared most emphatically and officially [...] our peaceful intentions. It is very much to be regretted that the French capitalist government is instigating Poland (and presumably Rumania, too) to attack us."[9] Despite these words, Soviet war preparations continued unabated. On 27 February 1920, Trotsky sent Lenin a telegram from his armored train, which reached Lenin the next day. In it, Trotsky wrote:

I fully agree with you that it is necessary to carry out open agitation for the war preparations against Poland, which is threatening us.

It is necessary to […] publish a manifesto with our motives and Poland's counter-activities, aimed at the working people. […] I will select volunteers here with whom I shall go to the Western Front after the [party] congress. I ask for an immediate resolution of the Politburo.[10]

Lenin reacted immediately. At the session of the Politburo on 28 February, the minutes included under item 22 the "telegram of comrade Trotsky and the presentation of comrade [Karl] Radek about Poland". The Politburo resolved:

22: a) Approved is the resolution on the organizational bureau on the delegation of all Polish-communists from the other fronts and the inner governorate to the Western Front; b) Take measures so that Comrade Radek and the commission for Polish issues [which was] created by him receives broad access to all libraries. Make sure that Comrade Radek can call on all specialists he deems necessary to work for the commission; c) Make available all necessary material means to the Polish Bureau at the Central Committee to support the movement in Poland; […] g) to give Comrade Radek leadership over the entire agitation in the press and to inform public opinion from the Russian perspective and that of the Polish government in such a way that the possible outbreak of war with Poland will be correctly understood by the Russian and Polish masses, namely as an attack of imperialist Poland on peace-desiring Soviet Russia on behalf of the Entente.[11]

At the same time, Lenin continued to publicly declare that Soviet Russia only sought peace with Poland. On 1 March 1920, Lenin said: "We declare to them that we shall never cross the line on which our troops are now stationed […]. We are proposing peace on this basis".[12] This peace offer was not a serious one; its purpose was merely to mislead Poland and the world about true Bolshevik plans. That same day, Trotsky sent another telegram from his armored train:

I think that the recent peace offers to Poland were unnecessary. I concur with the opinion of Litvinov that this conveys an impression of weakness. I think it is absolutely necessary to lead a broad campaign at home that is in and of itself important for the preparations, it can also stop the Poles.[13]

Lenin took heed. Just a few days later, on 6 March 1920, he said:

> We must preserve, develop and strengthen our military preparedness, so as to accomplish the task that confronts the working class. If, in spite of all our efforts, the Polish imperialists […], embark on a war against Russia, if they launch their military venture, they must receive, and will receive, such a rebuff that their fragile capitalism and imperialism will fall to pieces.[14]

By early March, the preparations for the invasion of Poland were running at full speed. On 8 March, the Revolutionary War Council (RVSR) ordered the stockpiles of bread to be increased on the Western Front, so that they could last for two weeks. On 14 March, the RSVR called for the military to speed up this process. Furthermore, trains and wagons were supposed to be repaired with the aim of using them to transport "marching provisions".[15] Moscow expected an easy victory.

On 12 March 1920, Josef Unszlicht, a member of the War Council of the Western Front, notified Lenin:

> The haste of work requires: 1) The immediate dispatch of communists – Poles, Belarusians, Lithuanians for the work behind the demarcation line. 2.) Red officers to wage war together with the insurrection movement (regarding that I have send the Central Committee a report on 24 February). 3.) An order to the Smolensk Polygraphic Department concerning the manufacture of printed materials without question. 4.) 100 pud [1 pud = 16.38kg] of, printed materials in Polish […] 2000 pud of newsprint.[16]

Five days later, on 17 March 1920, the Politburo discussed Unszlicht's request and resolved to "telegraphically notify Unszlicht about the steps taken."[17] Unszlicht's had the task of spreading Bolshevik propaganda behind Polish lines and to incite a guerrilla war.[18]

On 19 March, the RVSR issued an order to provide the Western Front with horses as quickly as possible; the cavalry army was to be reorganized so that it would be in a good state once transferred to the west. Commanders were also ordered to pay special attention to discipline.[19] A week later, on 26 March, the RVSR declared that the Western Front was now the most important front and that provisioning them with two weeks' worth of supplies was of utmost priority; for this, additional trains were to be provided. Furthermore, the transfer of troops to the front was to be further accelerated since some units experienced delays on the railways.[20]

On 6 April, the RVSR ordered a great number of communist activists to be transferred to the Western Front. At the same time, Polish commanders were to be removed because "they possibly could have ties to White-Polish elements"; this was to occur on all fronts, not just the Western Front.[21] The Bolshevik fears that commanders of Polish origin would defect to the Poles were not entirely unfounded. Many did just that, as did commanders of other ethnic backgrounds, having been forcibly conscripted into the Red Army in the first place. In order to combat desertions and defections, the Bolsheviks arrested the families of former officers, keeping them as hostages.[22]

Within the Red Army, the task of dealing with deserters and "counterrevolutionaries" was given primarily to the political commissars, however the so-called special detachments (*osobye otdely*) were involved too, as were party members and communist sympathizers. By 1 October 1919, the Red Army had 5,200 political commissars in its ranks, of whom 3,212 were serving in units on the various battlefields. At the same time, the number of communists among the deployed units stood at 61,681 in total and 11,460 on the Western Front.[23] These people kept the 447,000 strong Red Army motivated.[24]

As Moscow was redeploying its troops to the Western Front, the Politburo attempted to incite a guerrilla war behind Polish lines. From the minutes of the Politburo session from 8 March 1920: "The development of partisan activities in Tarybskaya Litva [Lithuania in the borders of 1920, i.e. without Vilnius] and in the areas under Polish occupation [current-day central and western Belarus] is extremely encouraging."[25] Once the preparations were done, the partisan war began in early April 1920 with Bolshevik partisans launching attacks against Polish institutions, landowners and police.[26]

To further improve their chances of success, the Bolsheviks also reached out to potential allies abroad. Lithuania was one of the two natural allies; after all, Poland and Lithuania had fought over Vilnius just a year earlier. On 8 March, the Politburo therefore decided to begin "peace talks" with Lithuania while also halting all preparations for a communist takeover of the country for the time being.[27] The goal was to win over "capitalist" Lithuania as an ally in the war against Poland since the success of a communist revolution in Lithuania was far from assured, and taking such a great risk just before the planned invasion of Poland was deemed undesirable from a strategic standpoint.[28]

The second potential ally was Germany. In mid-April 1920, Viktor Kopp, the unofficial Bolshevik ambassador in Germany, contacted the expert for Russia at the foreign ministry, Adolf Georg von Maltzan. Kopp wanted to see "if the possibility existed to combine the [German] army with the Red Army for the purpose of a joint fight against Poland." During the talks, von Maltzan pointed out the fact that the Communist Internationale had just issued a call to arms to the German proletariat, encouraging it to overthrow the German government. Such appeals, he continued, "would make such a far-reaching understanding rather illusory at the moment."[29]

Poland Attacks

Despite Moscow's repeated interventions, the preparations for the invasion of Poland were behind schedule, with many of the troops being still en route in mid-April. On 16 April, there were 65,682 infantry and 4,248 cavalry stationed on the Western Front, with an additional 35,700 men, including 1,000 cavalry, scheduled to arrive soon, pushing the total number to over 100,000. The South-Western front meanwhile only had 17,410 infantry and 2,200 cavalry stationed there, with an army of 9,940 cavalry en route. According to Bolshevik intelligence, they were facing 51,000 infantry and 7,000 cavalry in the West, and 30,200 infantry and 4,840 cavalry in the South-West.[30]

Although the Bolsheviks significantly outnumbered the Poles on both fronts, Moscow was particularly concerned about the insufficient political reliability of the soldiers stationed on the Western Front. Composed of fresh recruits, the Bolsheviks feared that they would not be willing to fight for them. On 23 April, Trotsky sounded the alarm:

> The work of building up the Western Front proceeds extremely slowly. The mobilization of party activists for the Western Front has hardly shown any results. By now, we are in great danger. Poland has cut its telegraph connection lines abroad this week. It is evident that there are [troop] transfers and regrouping happening in that country. We have transferred considerable forces to the Western Front, but they mostly consist of politically unshaped masses. Only the timely arrival of a considerable number of hard communists to the troops on the Western Front can secure the stability of the Front, which is receiving raw second-rate troops in great numbers.[31]

Trotsky called for quick and decisive action to ferry as many communists as possible to the Western Front. However, his warnings came too late. Just two days later, on 25 April 1920, Polish troops launched a surprise attack in the Ukrainian sector of the Polish-Bolshevik front. This attack was not a military adventure but a deliberate pre-emptive strike.[32]

The Polish side had been fully aware of the Bolshevik war preparations from the beginning. As early as summer 1919, Polish cryptologists had deciphered the Soviet codes and where thus able to intercept thousands of classified telegraphs. Poland therefore was very well-informed on the state of the Red Army, the progress of the civil war, and the transfer of troops. Beginning in January 1920, Polish intelligence picked up on suspicious troop movements on the Bolshevik Western and South-Western Fronts, which only intensified in March 1920. By April, Warsaw was convinced that the Red Army was preparing a full-scale attack on the Western Front.[33]

It was in this context that Piłsudski, the Polish supreme military leader and head of state, decided to take the initiative and attack the not-yet-battle-ready units of the Red Army, even though the Polish army was at a significant numerical disadvantage. At the same time, the Poles lacked both equipment and manpower reserves. Poland was therefore unable to sustain a prolonged war, unlike Soviet Russia.

Nevertheless, the Polish army began its attack on 25 April 1920. The Bolshevik units of the 12th Army on the South-Western Front were caught by surprise and had to fall back. However, the Poles knew that this was not the main invasion army; Trotsky had been gathering most of his forces in the northern section of the front, in modern-day Belarus. The goal of the "Kyiv Operation" was thus not to take out the Bolshevik invasion force, but to push back the weaker Bolshevik units behind the Dnieper and to re-establish the Ukrainian People's Republic in Kyiv. The Ukrainians would then aid the Poles in their war, forcing the Bolsheviks to divert troops from the main invasion force to the south. Only after the anti-Bolshevik Ukrainian buffer state had been established would the Polish army seek to destroy the Bolshevik forces in the north.[34]

This operation was a success initially. Kyiv fell on 7 May and Polish forces soon crossed the Dnieper east of Kyiv. The front line now ran from Chernobyl just to the north of Kyiv to Trypillia in the south of it; from there, the front followed the river Dnieper to the south-east, stopping shy of Bila Tserkva and Volodarka. There, the Polish troops halted and let the shattered and demoralized units of the 12th Army retreat without giving further chase.[35]

Piłsudski then transferred the victorious Polish units to the north in order to face the numerically superior Bolsheviks there. The early victories in the south led many on the Polish side to underestimate the remaining Bolshevik forces. Piłsudski was not one of them, however, and he knew full well that the main Soviet force would be waiting for them in Belarus.[36]

The Soviet Advance: To Germany, through Poland

Despite the initial setbacks, the Bolshevik military and political leadership did not lose heart. On the contrary, the buildup of troops in eastern Belarus was further intensified. On 14 May, the 15th Army under the command of Mikhail Tukhachevsky began its attack. The Polish troops stood firm, however, and by late May, the Red Army had been thrown back to its positions at the start of the offensive.[37]

Just prior to the offensive, on 10 May, Tukhachevsky had suggested to ask the Lithuanians to attack Polish-held Vilnius no later than 18 or 20 May. Such a flanking attack would have forced the Poles to divert troops from the Belarusian front, boosting the Red Army's chances of success. Once the Lithuanians launched their attack, the Red Army would assist them with a flanking maneuver on their own on 23 May.[38] Trotsky passed Tukhachevsky's proposal on and Soviet Russia indeed made this offer to the Lithuanian government. The Lithuanians were skeptical however, and preferred to watch how the situation developed.[39]

Lithuanian assistance would have been more than welcome, since despite preparing for months, the Red Army was not yet ready for its main thrust. The situation was particularly dire in the 16th Army. On 9 May, Trotsky raised the alarm: "The Western Front is very neglected." For this, Trotsky blamed the communists who supposedly had been stationed on the Western Front for so long that they got used to civilian life. He therefore asked for better political activists such as Smilga, Pyatakov, Myaznikov and others to be sent to the west.[40]

More political commissars were not the only thing that was needed to motivate the unwilling Red Army soldiers, however. On 15 May, Trotsky appealed to the Central Committee: "Detachments for special duties and blocking units will play nearly the same role [in increasing combat readiness on the Western Front]. To set up blocking detachments one needs time, however."[41] The role of these blocking units was to force unwilling soldiery, which was composed of "defectors, prisoners and locally mobilized recruits"[42], into battle and to crack down on desertion. Desertion was indeed a major problem and a fair number of deserters banded together to form armed groups that destabilized the rear areas. Many such raids apparently also had a clear political, anti-Bolshevik motivation.[43]

While the Belarusian sector of the Western front remained in crisis, the Bolsheviks managed to launch a successful counterattack in the Ukrainian sectors. In June, Polish troops had to evacuate Kyiv and by the end of the month, the Polish army had more or less retreated to their initial positions from 25 April.

The Polish troops in the Ukrainian section had been weakened as many Polish units were hastily transferred to the north to fend off the Bolshevik attacks in Belarus between early May and late June. While they managed to beat back the Soviet advance, the Polish forces were nevertheless exhausted from the fighting.[44] Meanwhile, the Red Army was able to amass more and more troops on the Western Front, while the troops already stationed there were being disciplined to make them ready for combat. The process took time, however, and Soviet leadership grew restless.[45]

After months of delay, Tukhachevsky's main assault finally began on 4 July 1920. This time, his soldiers emerged victorious – as did the men on the South-Western Front.[46] On 11 July, Yegorov, the commander of the South-Western Front, informed the Red Army's high command: "On the entire Polish front, the enemy fully retreats in front of the armies of the Western and South-Western Fronts."[47] With the Polish army in full retreat, it seemed as if there was nothing that could hold back the advance of the Red Army towards Warsaw and the German border.

The Polish government immediately recognized the severity of the situation and asked the Western Allies to help negotiate a truce. The British government offered to mediate – under the condition that Poland was to accept the so-called Curzon Line as its new border. Named after the British foreign minister, the Curzon Line would have left Lviv, Vilnius, as well as the regions of Lida and Grodno, outside of Poland's borders even though they had Polish majorities or at least pluralities.[48] Left without much of a choice, the Polish government begrudgingly accepted these conditions.

The Bolsheviks, however, rejected this proposal and continued to sabotage peace talks by making demands they knew were unacceptable, such as even further territorial losses and near-total disarmament.[49] After all, this was not a minor border conflict – the goal was to turn Poland into a communist dictatorship and to establish a direct land connection to Germany. On 17 July, Trotsky issued the following guidelines to the War Councils of the South-Western and the Western Fronts, led by Stalin and Smilga, respectively:

We have […] rejected Curzon's attempt at mediation. One must now expect massive military aid for Poland and Wrangel and perhaps also attempts to get Romania, Lithuania and Finland involved in the war [against the Soviet Union]. Against the backdrop of the situation in general and the decisions made, we are facing the following tasks: 1.) Inform the troops of the Western and South-Western Fronts about the goals of the English maneuver and the pivotal character of the present moment. Therefore, it is imperative to not only keep up the pressure, but to increase it in order to crush White Guard Poland more quickly and help the Polish workers and peasants with *the establishment of a Soviet Poland.* 2.) Agitation against chauvinism is to be intensified, cruel treatment of captured workers and peasants as future Polish Red Army soldiers is to be severely punished. 3.) Commanders and commissars shall ensure considerate and friendly treatment of the local working population as a whole and of the Polish in particular. If confiscations are unavoidable, they shall be made from rich kulaks, and they shall be shared with the poor. 4.) Intensify agitation in the Polish language by all means. In particular, the names and biographies of well-known Polish communists (comrades Dzherzhinsky, Marchlewski, Radek, Unszlicht, and others) are to be popularized. […] Perhaps it is necessary […] to organize a conference of the most experienced front and army activists in order to work out agitational and organizational measures for a quicker advance as well as for the *Sovietization of Poland*.[50]

On 23 July 1920, the Politburo formed the provisional revolutionary committee of Poland under the leadership of Julian Marchlewski. In early August, the communist Polish government arrived in Bialystok and prepared for the imminent communist takeover of Poland.[51] Things looked good for them – the Red Army had advanced deeper and deeper into Poland and on 10 August, Polish troops had fallen back behind the Vistula and Wieprz rivers in the Polish heartland, where Piłsudski intended to make his last stand. The fall of independent Poland seemed inevitable.[52]

In Moscow, Lenin was ecstatic. At the Second Comintern Congress held between 23 July and 7 August 1920, he proclaimed: "Soon we will have Germany. We will reconquer Hungary. The Balkans will rise up against capitalism, Italy will shake. Bourgeois Europe is caught in a storm and trembles."[53]

The question of Germany remained a key issue in the war against Poland. On 19 July, Lenin explained at an internal party conference: "For Russia, an alliance with Germany, regardless if the revolution there succeeds or not, opens up gigantic economic prospects."[54] With the Bolshevik victory over Poland seemingly imminent, the Politburo asked Grigory Chicherin to arrange a peace conference with Germany in order to revive trade.[55] A few days later, on 5 August, Chicherin sent a telegraph Adolf Yoffe in Riga, writing: "It was decided to make You the leader of our delegation at the conference in Berlin regarding a treaty with Germany, this is urgent and secret for the time being."[56] These preparations highlight the Bolshevik's chief goal in this war: Poland itself with its meager industry was not the main target. Instead, Poland was to serve as the bridge to the heart of Europe – Germany – with its great industry and powerful proletariat.

In their quest to reach Germany, the Bolsheviks relied heavily on German aid. For good reason – aside from harboring a strong communist movement, Germany was also aggressively anti-Polish. When Poland re-emerged as an independent state in 1918, Polish revolutionaries had taken over traditionally Polish territories that had been in German hands for centuries, such as the Danzig Corridor, Poznan and parts of Upper Silesia. Especially in Upper Silesia, a series of Polish uprisings triggered a Polish-German civil war that lasted until 1921. However, even before these conflicts, anti-Polish sentiments had been very strong in Germany, particularly in the east.[57]

By 1920, anti-Polish emotions had reached such heights that the anti-communist German national conservatives began to see Soviet Russia as their most important ally against the Poles. In Early 1920, the commander of the German armed forces, General von Seeckt, penned the memorandum "Germany and Russia" in which he wrote, among other things: "Only with a firm embrace of a Greater Russia does Germany have the prospect of regaining its status as a world power. [...] and whether current-day Russia in its internal structure appeals to us or not, it matters not. [...] This [Greater Russia] is what we need, a united, strong empire with a broad border at our side."[58]

For the German military leadership, it was clear that a new partition of Poland was the way for Germany to reclaim its lost geopolitical position.[59] The Soviets were perfectly aware of this and Lenin even noted in the summer of 1920 that "the German bourgeoisie fundamentally supports us".[60] In early August 1920, Trotsky sent a telegraph to Chicherin: "It is imperative to issue appeals in German [and to distribute them] in East Prussia and Germany in general, in which our demands to the Polish government are detailed, together with an appeal to the German workers, to not let any troops or supplies pass through to Poland. That appeal could perhaps come from the Comintern."[61]

Indeed, Germany – but also Czechoslovakia – blocked arms shipments to Poland even without the Bolsheviks asking for it. In the meantime, communist agents tried their best to sabotage the Polish hinterlands. They were particularly successful in the conflict-ridden industrial region of Upper Silesia, where both Gliwice and Katowice saw German anti-Polish riots on 16 August 1920.[62]

The first half of August continued to be fortuitous for the Bolsheviks, and on 13 August, the Politburo felt confident enough to establish – on Trotsky's initiative – a direct train connection to Germany with the aim of importing weaponry for the Red Army.[63] At the same time, Trotsky began to ask for German communists to be sent to the Western Front. On 10 August, the Politburo discussed this question and agreed to "order the Comintern to send Comrade Bulich, to whom around 100 German communists capable of conducting Soviet and organizational work are to be made available, to the German border."[64] The German communists heeded the call. On 13 August, Unszlicht reported to Trotsky and the Central Committee from Minsk:

> Every day, dozens of German workers cross over from the German border, some of them equipped with papers from the Spartacists... They come to us with the request to form a special brigade from their ranks and to transfer them to the German border, so that at a suitable political moment they can march into East Prussia to spark an uprising. Some of them come with weapons, they are also intending to bring artillery. I believe that we can gather up to 3,000 former soldiers with their own officers.[65]

By setting up the German brigade, the Bolsheviks thus took the first step to intervene in Germany. Despite the setbacks in the previous year, Lenin still believed that the prospects for a revolution in Germany were good in the summer of 1920. In an internal party speech in September 1920, he elaborated:

> All Germany began to seethe when our forces approached Warsaw. In that country a situation arose very much like that which could be seen in Russia in 1905, when the Black Hundreds aroused and involved in political life the largest and most backward sections of the peasantry, which were opposed to the Bolsheviks one day, and on

the next were demanding all the land from the landed proprietors. In Germany too we have seen a similar unnatural bloc between the Black Hundreds and the Bolsheviks. There has appeared a strange type of Black-Hundred revolutionary, like the backward rustic youth from East Prussia who, as I read in a German non-Bolshevik newspaper the other day, says that the Kaiser will have to return because there is no order, but one has to follow the Bolsheviks.[66]

The Bolsheviks were readying themselves for the march on Berlin. But before then, they had to finish off Poland first.

The Disaster on the Vistula

In early August 1920, the Bolsheviks were confident that they would take Warsaw in a matter of days, likely by 16 August. From the Western Front, Ivar Smilga at the Revolutionary War Council of the 7th Army informed Lenin and Trotsky about the progress of the war on 12 August:

I have returned from the inspection of the [Western] Front. Due to the immense advance, the troops are very spread out. The supply train lags behind dreadfully, the march beyond the Vistula will plunge us into a catastrophe, because a strong revolutionary movement has failed to materialize in Poland. Morale among the troops is good so far. In Bialystok, we were well received and in the rest of Poland – satisfactorily or cautiously. [...] We are in an extraordinarily complicated situation. Because I do not know the most recent decisions at all, it is very difficult for me to work now. I think that one should summon me to Moscow today so that I can return in time for the expected capture of Warsaw on 16 August.[67]

Indeed, the soldiers on the Western front advanced around 700 km in just five weeks; daily marches of over 40 km were not a rarity. These rapid, arduous marches and the frequent skirmishes with Polish forces thinned out the ranks of the advancing Red Army. Aside from minor causalities, the Bolsheviks had to leave behind large numbers of men to garrison the newly conquered lands. Furthermore, the Red Army was plagued by severe supply problems, which were made worse by the fact that many roads and bridges had been destroyed by the retreating Poles. As a result, the men were lacking virtually everything, ammunition in particular, although there was plenty of food looted from the local population. The situation was made even worse by the fact that during the advance, many units were repeatedly transferred from one sector of the front to another, which often resulted in the units losing contact with their staff. "Ultimately, the army arrived at Warsaw exhausted, tired and disorganized."[68]

The high command of the Red Army was perfectly aware of this and in early August 1920, it decided to transfer three armies of the South-Western Front to the Western Front in current-day Belarus and eastern Poland. However, this was easier said than done, and in a telegraph from 8 August, Tukhachevsky, the commander of the Western Front, noted that reorganizing the troops in such a way would be difficult.[69]

After much discussion, the high command of the Red Army ordered the 1st, 12th and 14th Cavalry armies to be transferred from the South-Western Front to the Western Front in order to secure the open southern flank of the Western Front against a possible Polish counterattack.[70] However, Stalin in his position as head of the War Council of the South-Western Front disagreed. He argued that having these armies split off during the ongoing assault on Lwów (Lviv) to march them north was pointless. This may have been possible three days earlier, Stalin continued, but now that the preparations had been concluded and the attack had begun, he could only send away these men after the city was taken. The supreme commander Sergey Kamenev was baffled and immediately reported Stalin's refusal to obey orders to Trotsky.[71]

While this was happening, units of the Western Front were already engaging Polish troops a few kilometers from Warsaw. Meanwhile, the Polish forces under Piłsudski prepared for their counterattack by transferring troops to the unprotected southern flank of the Bolshevik Western Front, encouraged by intelligence reports confirming that it was poorly protected. On 16 August, the Polish army launched its decisive counterattack – with overwhelming success. The Bolshevik forces to the north had to break off their assault on Warsaw and retreat to the north and north-east in order to evade encirclement. When Budyonny's 1st Cavalry Army belatedly tried to reinforce the Western Front from the south, his forces were defeated at Zamosc on 29 August – he and his men only narrowly escaped total annihilation. In a matter of just a few days, the triumphal advance had thus turned into a panicked rout.[72]

It took a few days until Moscow realized the severity of the situation. Still, on 19 August – three days after the devastating Polish counterattack had begun – the Politburo debated about the state of the war, with both Trotsky and Stalin talking about the situation on the Polish front. Yet during that session, the Politburo declared the Wrangel front to be Soviet Russia's most important front.[73] In April 1920, the former Tsarist general Pyotr Wrangel had managed to gather the remnants of the shattered Volunteer Army in Crimea and continued his war against the Bolsheviks. By late July 1920, Wrangel's troops were on the advance in southern Russia (Kuban) and southern Ukraine. Stalin warned that the Polish front was in danger as long as Wrangel's troops were still in the field.[74]

At the same meeting, the Politburo also decided to speed up the mobilization of the Belarusians. Additionally, there was to be another push to mobilize communists, of whom 55% were to be sent to the Wrangel front, with the rest destined to the Polish front.[75] Only a day later, on 20 August, Smilga notified Lenin and Trotsky: "The failure [at Warsaw] is turning into a great defeat. It is evident that in a few days, the war will move onto Belarusian territory. For the second time I insist for Danichevsky [the Soviet chief negotiator during the Polish–Soviet ceasefire negotiations] to offer the Poles a ceasefire, and if they reject it, to chase them away. [...] We will do everything to salvage the situation."[76]

A few days later, on 26 August, Karl Radek reported to the Politburo on the situation in Poland.[77] Slowly, Lenin and his comrades began to realize that Warsaw had not been a mere setback, but that the entire Soviet front was unraveling. On 1 September, the Politburo recognized that the war had been lost and issued a number of measures designed to control the damage coming from their defeat. The Politburo designated Adolf Yoffe as the leader of the Bolshevik delegation at the ceasefire negotiations with Poland. Furthermore, the Politburo decided to shift attention away from Wrangel, ordering 60% of mobilized communists and recruits to be sent to the Polish front.[78]

Point 19 of that Politburo session concerned "Comrade Stalin's request to be relieved from his military duties." The decision of the Politburo:

"Comrade Stalin is to be relieved of his function as a member of the Revolutionary War Council of the Republic."[79] It is very likely that by dismissing Stalin, the Politburo was drawing the consequences from Stalin's earlier acts of insubordination. Just two weeks earlier, on 14 August, Stalin had refused to send three armies from the South-Western Front to protect the southern flank of the advancing Western Front. Two days later, the Poles attacked - thanks to Stalin - the unguarded flank and routed the Western Front, turning the war on its head.

The final out of the 24 items was the "Proposal by Comrade Lenin to take measures to make ciphers more elaborate and to protect encrypted messages more strictly."[80] Apparently, it was only now that Moscow began to suspect that the Poles had been intercepting their encrypted communications and thus had detailed knowledge of the Red Army's ongoing operations. By that point, it was more than suspicious that the Polish counterattacks always happened in precisely the sections of the front that were particularly fragile at the moment. Recent Polish research has shown that the materially considerably weaker Polish forces managed to emerge victorious in large part due to their intelligence intercepting and deciphering the Red Army's messages. It was thanks to these intercepted messages that the Poles were aware of Stalin's insubordination and therefore knew that they did not have to fear a counterattack from the south-east.[81]

The Military Implications of the Disaster at Warsaw

The defeat at Warsaw was a devastating military – and especially political – setback for the Bolsheviks, which they noticed very quickly. Already on 4 September 1920, Yuri Pyatakov, a member of the Revolutionary War Council of the 16th Army, wrote a report on the defeat which he sent to the Central Committee and to Trotsky. He began his report as follows: "On the western front of the republic, a catastrophe has occurred. The front armies are shattered and the front staffs are in confusion. [...] The history of this catastrophe I cannot describe in detail. But I can say one thing, the republic has never experienced anything like this."[82]

Indeed, the entire front had fallen apart and Pyatakov's 16th Army was no exception. By 1 August, it had swollen to encompass five divisions and

27,872 infantry, of whom only around 11,500 reached the approaches of Warsaw. When the retreat began, the army only numbered 7,500 men – 86% of the army had disappeared in the span of just two weeks.[83] As the retreat turned into a rout, losses continued to mount and by 1 September, the 16th Army only had 2,016 men left.[84] Many other armies fighting on the Western Front, such as the 15th fared similarly[85]; while the situation on the South-Western Front was not as bad, losses were significant there as well.[86]

The Red Army leadership tried to stem the tide, but to no avail. For example, the 27th Division, which had been part of the 16th Army and had suffered 4,000 casualties in August, had already been reconstituted with raw recruits by early September. However, these freshly mobilized soldiers refused to fight and immediately deserted, leaving the division unable to fight.[87]

Seeing their enemy disintegrate before their eyes, the Poles continued their offensive and pushed deep into Belarus and eastern Galicia. On 12 October 1920, a ceasefire was proclaimed and on 18 March 1921, the Treaty of Riga brought the war to a close. Poland received Western Belarus, Volhynia, and Galicia, as well as reparations for the economic exploitation of Poland under the Russian Empire and the removal of industrial plants and railways during the First World War. At the same time, Soviet Russia had to return cultural goods that had been looted during the Bolshevik advance.[88]

The Emergence of the Soviet Poland-Complex

While the military losses were significant, the Bolsheviks were able to quickly re-fill the ranks of the ravaged divisions with fresh recruits and restore order through violent Bolshevik disciplinary action. In contrast, geopolitical damage could not be recovered as easily. Indeed, the outcome of this war would hamper the progress of the communist world revolution and development of the Soviet Union over the next two decades.

On 22 September, with the war still raging, Lenin brought up the political implications of the war in a speech at the All-Russian Conference of the RCP(b):

Our army's close approach to Warsaw has incontestably shown *that the centre of world imperialism's entire system* […] *lies somewhere very close to the Polish capital*. Poland, the last anti-Bolshevik stronghold fully controlled by the Entente, is such an important element in that system that when the Red Army threatened that stronghold the entire structure was shaken.[89]

A few days later, on 2 October 1920, he repeated his assessment: "The Versailles Peace has turned Poland into a buffer state which is to guard against German contact with Soviet communism and is regarded by the Entente as a weapon against the Bolsheviks."[90] This became the Poland-complex of the Bolsheviks. As Lenin repeatedly proclaimed, Poland was seen as the bulwark against the Bolshevik's march towards Germany, and as such, this obstacle had to be removed. This line of thought would remain a mainstay of Soviet geopolitical considerations until the Second World War.

Cut off from Germany and its vital industry, the Bolsheviks were on their own, and instead of continuing their irresistible march west, they now found themselves on the defensive. Already on 21 November 1920, Lenin complained about the "delay of the socialist world revolution" caused by the defeat at Warsaw.[91] Stalin thought so as well, and on 23 April 1923 he said this at the II Party Congress of the RCP(b):

You know, comrades, that by the will of history we, the Soviet federation, now represent the advanced detachment of the world revolution. […] You know that in our advance we got as far as Warsaw, that we then retreated and entrenched ourselves in the positions we considered strongest. […]from that moment we took into account the slowing down of the international revolutionary movement, and from that moment our policy changed from the offensive *to the defensive*.[92]

Indeed, this trauma would remain with the Bolsheviks until the end of the Soviet state. Still in 1983, Roman Werfel, a Soviet communist looked back and said: "After the defeat at Warsaw, Russia had to build up socialism on its own. To this day I am convinced that history would have turned out differently and that we would not have had to make the terrible experiences of the 1930s [...] had the Red Army broken through to Berlin."[93]

The defeat also convinced the Bolshevik leadership that Poland was not ready for communism because of the strength of Polish nationalism, even among workers and peasants. In March 1923, Stalin wrote in *Pravda*:

> This was the situation in 1920 during the war against Poland, when we, underestimating the power of the nationalist momentum in Poland and being carried away by the easy successes of a sensational advance, took on a task beyond our power, *to break through into Europe via Warsaw*, turning the vast majority of the Polish population against the Soviet troops, thereby creating a situation that nullified the successes of the Soviet troops at Minsk and Zhytomyr and damaged the prestige of Soviet power in the west.[94]

In a speech held on 31 January 1925, Dmitri Manuilsky, a close associate of Stalin who was then dealing with the issue of national minorities, located the strength of Polish nationalism in Poland's "terrible national oppression in the past", when it was partitioned by its neighbors in the eighteenth century, only to re-emerge as an independent country after 123 years in 1918. Like Stalin, he also blamed Polish nationalism for the loss: "The proletarian revolution was smashed by the Polish peasant. This is an indisputable historical fact." Manuilsky continued: "As long as Polish workers and peasants do not get tired of nationalism, the task of revolution in Poland will be extraordinarily difficult."[95]

The defeat at Warsaw also instilled the Bolsheviks with a great deal of respect for the Polish army and its leader Józef Piłsudski, who had laid the foundations for it as early as 1914 with the creation of the Polish Legions who had fought in the First World War. Internal Red Army reconnaissance reports also remarked on the quality of the Polish officer corps and the high morale of the soldiers, which oftentimes compensated for their poor equipment, as well as the role of Polish paramilitary organizations.[96] While this was true to some extent, the main reason was the weakness of the Red Army.

At any rate, the war had shown the Bolsheviks that Poland was fighting "with the courage of despair" and even attack if threatened. As Zinoviev explained in a secret speech in September 1923, when a communist revolution in Germany seemed imminent: "The reason that the Polish bourgeoisie will be the worst enemy [of the German revolution and therefore Soviet Russia] is not only that French imperialism tends to use Poland in particular as the tool of its counterrevolutionary ideas, but also that the Polish bourgeoisie recognizes very well the difficulty of its future position between a Soviet Germany and a Soviet Russia and will fight *with the courage of despair*."[97]

Germany: The Natural Ally of Soviet Russia

Following its defeat in the First World War, Germany was forced to sign the humiliating Treaty of Versailles, according to which it was forced to disarm, pay substantial war reparations, and admit that it held sole responsibility for the war. To make matters worse, Germany lost all of its overseas colonies and even some core German lands. Among the most painful were the loss of Alsace-Lorraine to France and the loss of parts of western Prussia, Upper Silesia, and Greater Poland to Poland, while Danzig became semi-independent. In the east, the losses cut off East Prussia from the rest of the country. All this was unacceptable for Germany and it immediately moved to regain at least some of its territories, especially vis-à-vis Poland. The Bolsheviks in Moscow quickly picked up on the German revisionist desires and before long, Germany emerged as Soviet Russia's natural ally, in particular against "nationalist" Poland, even though Germany was still capitalist and firmly anti-communist at home. However, this did not matter since the Bolsheviks needed Germany's support against Poland, and the aid of German industry was needed to revive Russia's ruined economy. Furthermore, Soviet Russia needed a land border with Germany to help the German communists once the time came.

Already on 2 October 1920, Lenin lectured on the consequences of Versailles for Germany:

You know that, after defeating Germany, the Allied imperialists— France, Great Britain, America and Japan—signed the Peace of Versailles, which, to say the least, was far more brutal than the infamous Peace of Brest-Litovsk [...]. One of the pillars of this monstrous peace is Poland's cutting across Germany, since Polish territory stretches to the sea. Relations between Germany and Poland are at present strained to the utmost. [...] It is robbing Germany of coal [from Upper Silesia], robbing her of her milk herds, and is reducing her to an unparalleled and unprecedented state of servitude.[98]

Lenin frequently spoke along similar lines. On 21 December 1920, for example, he elaborated:

Germany is, aside from America, the most progressive country. [...] And this country, gagged by the Treaty of Versailles, finds itself in an impossible situation. Such a situation naturally pushed Germany into an alliance with Russia. [...] The German bourgeois government harbors a furious hatred against the Bolsheviks, but the international situation forces them, against their own will, into peace with Soviet Russia.[99]

This overlap in interests would be vital for the economic recovery of Soviet Russia – and for German capitalists. On 6 December 1920, Lenin thus explained the importance of Germany in this regard:

Germany [...] possesses incredible economic possibilities. Germany in its economic development is the second country in the world, if one regards America as the first. Experts even claim that the electric industry of Germany is higher than that of America. And they know what a gigantic importance the electric industry has. [...] To restore the world economy, one needs Russian resources. One cannot get around relying on them, this is economically correct.[100]

Five days later, on 21 December, Lenin declared that the alliance with Germany would be the "foundation of the entire economic situation and our foreign policy"[101] Despite the remarkable rapprochement between the Bolsheviks and capitalist Germany, the Bolsheviks still continued to work towards a communist revolution in Germany that would inevitably crush their capitalist friends there. The reason was simple: Germany was the country "in which the chances for a revolution are the greatest", Lenin said in a speech on 6 November 1920.[102] This assessment would not change anytime soon and as late as July 1924, Stalin declared that "if a revolutionary upheaval commences anywhere in Europe it will be in Germany."[103]

Despite mutual distrust, both the Germans and the Bolsheviks would work together to undermine the order established by the Treaty of Versailles. Poland in particular drew the ire of both parties, with Germany trying to reclaim former territories and the Bolsheviks seeking to restore direct land access to Germany in order to help the communist revolutionaries there.

As a result of these overlapping interests, Germany did its best to support the Bolsheviks in their war against Poland, and when that failed, tried to sabotage the peace talks between Poland and Soviet Russia. With German-Polish tensions mounting over the plebiscite in Upper Silesia, the Germans approached the Bolsheviks in the autumn of 1920 and suggested a joint war against Poland. Feeling that the German communist movement was going nowhere, the Soviet emissary to Berlin, Viktor Kopp, saw this as the opportunity to destroy Poland and sent a report to Trotsky on 6 November 1920.[104]

In the report, Kopp mentioned that he had met General von Seeckt, the chief of staff of the German military, a few days before:

The concrete proposal by von Seeckt who [...] is firmly convinced that we will use to our advantage the Polish–German conflict, amounts to the following. For us, the German staff holds ready weapons for purchase and export from Germany. German military specialists (pilots, specialists for different combat arms, designers and captains of submarines) are ready to come to us and help us. The German general staff wants to send representatives to us to establish a liaison and to settle all these practical questions. Regarding the first point, I will do everything possible once the necessary funds are available. The proposed technical assistance is to be absolutely accepted in my opinion, but of course with the utmost caution. Likewise, I would suggest authorizing the entry of von Niemeyer, von Seeckt's personal adjutant, as military attaché.[105]

While the open German-Polish war did not materialize in the end, the secret German-Soviet military cooperation von Seeckt had proposed did in fact come true. It would formally begin in 1921 and last more or less until 1933, when Hitler took over.[106]

Chapter 3

The Imperative of Economic Recovery

The failed advance into the heart of Europe forced the Bolsheviks to rethink their strategy. Without access to Germany's industry, they were forced to rebuild their own, and for this, they needed peace. By the autumn of 1920, Lenin and his comrades thus knew that they had to bring the war with Poland to a swift end – even if it meant territorial losses – and crush the remnants of the White forces under Wrangel.

For the Bolsheviks, it was clear this peace would only be temporary. Once they had fully recovered, they would once again go on the attack with renewed vigor. At the time, however, the devastated country was simply too poor to support an army powerful enough to do that. On 2 October 1920, Lenin complained in a speech:

> Our chief difficulty in the present war is not manpower—we have enough of that—but supplies. The chief difficulty on all the fronts is the shortage of supplies, the shortage of warm clothing and footwear. Greatcoats and boots—that is the main thing our soldiers lack, and it is on that account that quite successful advances have so often failed. That is the difficulty which prevents us from rapidly utilising for a victorious advance the new units, which we possess in sufficient numbers, but which, without sufficient supplies, cannot be formed and cannot be of any real combat value.[1]

Lenin was not wrong. By late 1920, the industry of Soviet Russia was indeed in terrible shape. On 6 December 1920, Lenin reported that "Russia is in a state of industrial ruin; she is ten times or more worse off than before the war."[2] Iron production had fallen by a stunning 95%. Coal, meanwhile, was more abundant as production had fallen by 70%, but even that was nowhere near enough to fuel the economy. As a result, locomotives were now being fueled with wood, which cut their power in half. Agriculture had suffered as well. In 1920, around a quarter of agricultural lands remained unused and overall grain production had dropped by 48%. The shortage of food, coal, and industrial goods depopulated the cities as millions of people moved back to the countryside to survive. Out of its 1.2 million inhabitants in 1914, Moscow lost 700,000 while Petrograd lost 1.3 million of its original 2 million inhabitants. The other great cities, Kyiv, Odessa and Kharkiv also suffered immensely and their population dropped to around 250,000.[3]

As the first step towards recovery, the Bolsheviks focused on achieving peace as soon as possible. Once a truce had been signed with Poland on 18 October 1920, the Red Army under Frunze wheeled around and attacked Wrangel's remaining forces, who had fortified themselves in Crimea. With his defenses overrun, Wrangel decided to evacuate his troops. On 16 November 1920, the last of his ships landed in neutral Constantinople. Now that Wrangel was defeated, *Pravda* announced the Bolshevik victory and the end of the Russian Civil War on 15 December 1920. A week later, the Eighth All-Russian Soviet Congress proclaimed the beginning of a period of peaceful development and with it, a new economic policy.[4]

At the Eighth All-Russian Congress, the Bolshevik leadership also decided to radically shrink the Red Army. While it was not announced, it does strongly suggest that the Bolsheviks were serious about preserving peace with Poland, thus ignoring the proposal of von Seeckt, who had wanted Germany and Soviet Russia to join forces and attack Poland.

At the time, the Red Army was the largest army in the world. For the war against Poland and the planned march into Western Europe, the Bolsheviks had mobilized a grand total of 5.3 million men by the autumn of 1920.[5] In December 1920, the Red Army numbered 55 infantry divisions (1,972,000 men), 23 cavalry divisions (228,000 men); 648,000 men served various internal service troops, while another 600,000 were deployed in reserve units. In addition, the Red Army also included 187,000 auxiliary and technical troops, 30,000 men active in various training agencies and 115,000 in training units. The number of medical troops stood at 500,000 and the remaining 1,020,000 were employed in various agencies, administrative offices, and other institutions.[6]

It has to be emphasized that little over half of the 5.3 million Red Army soldiers were in combat units, and that even among them, most were non-combat soldiers employed in administration, various agencies, or were in fact the relatives and family members of the soldiers, in other words – camp followers. Thus only a small fraction of this great army, less than 10%, was composed of combat troops. This frequently raised eyebrows. On 17 November 1920, Shtrodakh, a member of the staff of the 15th Army, penned a memorandum on the issue of camp followers in the Red Army. In it, he estimated that the real, operating army consisted of around 50 divisions with around a million men, much less than the over 5 million the Red Army had officially. Shtrodakh further wrote: "This is an awe-inspiring number. However, in this army of millions, we have all in all only around 130,000 bayonets [soldiers who take part in battle with rifle in hand], 213,000 other soldiers and around 493,000 non-combat soldiers up to the divisional level; in the army agencies, around 180,000, which leaves us with 673,000 non-combat soldiers in total."[7]

This bloated Red Army was far too large to be properly supplied by the Soviet economy while also not being able to beat Western armies. It was simply a drain on the economy and the Bolshevik leadership thus decided to radically shrink and reorganize the Red Army in December 1920. The Red Army was to be downsized in four stages to a more manageable 1,370,000 men by December 1921, including 644,228 operational troops (infantry) and 91,200 cavalry. The rest was to be employed in various other areas such as military administration, agencies, training or the medical service.[8]

Commercial Concessions

Lenin and his comrades very quickly realized that the economic recovery would be impossible without foreign capital, technology, and equipment. In a speech held on 21 December 1920, Lenin declared:

> If we want to trade with foreign countries—and we do want to, because we realise its necessity—our chief interest is in obtaining as quickly as possible, from the capitalist countries, the means of production (locomotives, machinery, and electrical equipment) without which

we cannot more or less seriously rehabilitate our industry, or perhaps may even be unable to do so at all, because the machinery needed by our factories cannot be made available.[9]

The precondition for such trade was the normalization of relations with the developed capitalist countries of the West, such as the USA, Germany, or Great Britain, for it was them who had the capital, technology, and modern equipment Moscow so desperately needed. However, this was easier said than done, especially since Soviet Russia outright refused to assume and pay off the 20 billion gold rubles of debt their Tsarist predecessors had accumulated.

After much consideration, Lenin believed he had found the solution in late 1920: concessions. In a speech on 6 December, he addressed the issue:

> They say, let us trade in grain; but we cannot give them grain. We therefore propose to solve the problem by means of *concessions*. [...]. Without concessions, we shall not be able to carry out our programme and the electrification of the country; without them, it will be impossible to restore our economic life in ten years; once we have restored it we shall be invincible to capital.[10]

The Kremlin was willing to grant several types of concessions: forestry concessions in the endless taiga of the Far North, grain concessions in Northern Russia where foreign investors were to cultivate farmland in return for modern machinery, and mining concessions in resource-rich Siberia. On 23 November 1920, the Soviet government thus issued the Decree on Concessions, and with the legal basis established, a broad information campaign soon began. At that time, the Bolsheviks had high hopes for this program as they were convinced that the lure of high profits was enough to attract foreign investors.[11]

After intense negotiations, Soviet Russia soon cleared another hurdle by re-establishing commercial ties to the West, which had been severed during the Russian Civil War. On 16 March 1921, Soviet Russia concluded a trade agreement with Great Britain, on 6 May with Germany, on 7 December with Austria, and on 26 December with Italy. The signing of commercial treaties continued over the following year, with trade agreements being signed with Sweden on 1 February 1922 and with Czechoslovakia on 5 July. Foreign investors were now free to come.[12]

However, only a few did so. Despite the possibility of high profits, foreign investors remained wary. After all, the Bolsheviks had thoroughly expropriated foreign and domestic capitalists alike, frequently even killing the latter, just a few years prior. One exception was the German company Junkers, which bought a concession and in 1922 began the production of aircraft in the former Second "Russo-Balt" automobile plant in Fili, at which Tupolev would later develop his famous aircraft.[13] Instead of setting up factories and sending expensive equipment to Soviet Russia, the rest of the capitalists preferred to produce at home and saw Russia as a market where they could sell their goods.[14]

On 16 February 1923, a frustrated Trotsky wrote a memorandum in which he condemned the previous attempts at industrializing the country as "administrative partisanism", i.e. as disorganized, improvised, and above all unsuccessful. He continued: "As long as our state industry does not receive foreign capital, our development is closely tied to the development of agriculture."[15]

Feliks Dzerzhinsky replied to Trotsky's devastating memorandum – and agreed with it. Dzerzhinsky, too, saw that the concessions program had not brought the desired results and that the rebuilding of Soviet industry was failing: "Hope for an influx [of foreign capital] into state industry is weak and without any basis."[16] He went on to specifically attack at length the idea that concessions could be a panacea for the Soviet economy:

This attitude had brought us immeasurable misery, it disorganized our Soviet industry, *all* of the former owners and hundreds of thousands of their henchmen, with whom our former chief committees [administering the individual industrial sectors] were filled with and with whom our trusts and syndicates are filled with, organized themselves against them [the concessions]. A correct idea, wrongly implemented, brought us ruin. I would formulate my stance towards the concessions as such: 'For us and the capitalist countries, the participation of foreign capital in the form of concessions and joint ventures is a necessity. That requires mutual interests. If foreign countries and capitalists do not want to participate, then we have to build up our economy *by ourselves*, albeit at a slower pace and with great sacrifices.'[17]

Following these devastating reviews, the Politburo decided to discontinue the program on 25 February 1923. However, this was done gradually, as the Politburo did not want to deal with the international consequences of breaking the contracts it had signed after just one or two years.[18]

The New Economic Policy

While the concessions program aimed to attract foreign capital to Soviet Russia with the promise of profits, the vast majority of people there were subjected to War Communism, which was based on forced requisitioning of grain from the peasantry without any compensation. War Communism had been implemented shortly after the start of the Russian Civil War, but continued even after it had been officially concluded. Thus it had been the peasantry that had to carry the burden of the civil war, for it was them who had to feed the bloated Red Army as well as the remaining urban population, while also having to provide the manpower the Bolsheviks needed in their campaigns. In return, the peasants received neither money nor industrial goods, which were a rarity as industry was in ruins. Naturally, War Communism was extremely unpopular.

In order to collect grain from the unwilling peasants, the Bolsheviks unleashed requisitioning commandos (units) looted the countryside, which further enraged the rural population. To mention but one example, here is a report from the Pugachev district (Samara governorate, in the Volga region) from 18 January 1921:

In several localities [in the Pugachev district] in December [1920], the mood among the population was tense due to the collection of the [grain] levy. For example, in the villages of Mosty, Tyaglo-Ozerskoye and Mikhaylo-Ovsyanka there had been women's uprisings, which were liquidated; the attitude towards the local authorities is unfriendly. The reason: seed grain was not left behind and other objects were confiscated due to the non-fulfillment of the levy. For a more speedy collection of the levy, 36 co-workers have been sent to the rayon and the collection is satisfactory overall.[19]

This was a common occurrence in Soviet Russia under War Communism.[20] Further exacerbated by the devastation of the civil war, the demands of the Polish-Soviet War and the build-up of the Red Army, this predatory policy critically disrupted the already suffering agricultural sector and by the winter of 1920/21, the specter of famine loomed over the countryside.

In 1921/22, over 26 million people were suffering from hunger according to contemporary estimates. Particularly affected were the rich agricultural lands of the Volga region, the nearby Kama region, Bashkiria, the Urals, southern Ukraine, the Crimea, the middle Don region, Azerbaijan and Armenia, as well as parts of Kazakhstan and western Siberia. In the Saratov governorate, 69% of the population was facing hunger in July 1921, while just to the south, in the Samara governorate, that number was at nearly 90% on 1 September. It is estimated that around five, maybe even six million people died as the result of the famine of 1921/22.[21]

Aside from mass starvation, War Communism also triggered widespread peasant resistance, which ranged from peasants refusing to work all the way to veritable peasant uprisings. The Bolsheviks responded with violence, bloodily suppressing several rebellions, but in the end, they were forced to relent and abolish War Communism. The peasants had won – for now.

In place of the hated policy of War Communism, the Bolsheviks introduced the New Economic Policy (NEP), which was much less intrusive and reintroduced several free market elements into the Soviet economy. It replaced grain confiscation with a simple tax deliverable in kind; with the rest of the harvest, the peasants could dispose of as they wished, including selling their surpluses on the market. At the same time, the NEP also allowed for the leasing of state enterprises to private entrepreneurs, albeit under strict government oversight.[22]

This opening of the economy was extended to capitalists from other countries as the Bolsheviks hoped to attract foreign investment via the ultimately unsuccessful concessions program. As Lenin stated in a speech on 6 January 1923: "And the practical purpose of our New Economic Policy was to lease out concessions".[23]

The NEP immediately made its mark. The catastrophic state of the economy suddenly improved considerably, stimulating the growth of agriculture, as well as small industrial and commercial enterprises. In particular, light industry made a comeback, once again supplying the villages with industrial goods. Still, the rest of the economy and especially large businesses remained in the hands of the state via various trusts and syndicates, and already beginning in 1922, private entrepreneurship was slowly being restricted again. This trend continued and between 1923 and 1928, the NEP was gradually liquidated. Nevertheless, the NEP did revive the dying Soviet economy. By the end of 1922, agricultural production was at 37% of what it had been in 1913, while industrial production had bounced back to 25% of its pre-war levels. Aside from a rise in productivity, living standards improved as well, especially for peasants with large and medium plots of land, but also for small traders, craftsmen and entrepreneurs.[24]

Chapter 4

Anti-Communist Resistance in the First Years after the Russian Civil War

I n the devastating Russian Civil War, the Bolsheviks may have more or less prevailed over their White enemies by late 1920, but this did not mean that their newfound subjects were inclined to accept their new overlords. Even after 1920, resistance to Soviet rule was common throughout the entire empire; Russians, Ukrainians, Belarusians, Caucasians, Turkic peoples, Siberians, and many others continued to oppose the Bolsheviks throughout the 1920s and well into the 1930s in all kinds of ways.

By 1921, the highly unpopular policy of War Communism had managed to trigger a series of large-scale peasant uprisings all over the country. While the Bolshevik rulers managed to crush most of the uprisings, they were ultimately forced to relent and replace War Communism with the NEP to appease the incensed peasantry. Still, some of them continued well into the mid-1920s. The situation was tense in the cities as well, and the Bolsheviks had to brutally put down countless revolts, riots, and strikes. Looking back in November 1922, Lenin recounted that this had been the worst internal crisis Soviet Russia had ever faced:

> In 1921, after we had passed through the most important stage of the Civil War and passed through it victoriously – we felt the impact of a grave – I think it was the gravest – internal political crisis in Soviet Russia. This internal crisis brought to light discontent not only among a considerable section of the peasantry but also among the workers.[1]

In late 1920, the situation was particularly dire in Ukraine, the agricultural heartland of pre-war Russia. On 15 October 1920, Lenin complained that "not a single [pud] can be expected from Ukraine, because of the bandits there."[2] In late 1920, Soviet authorities estimated that in Ukraine alone, the number of "bandits" fighting against communist rule stood at 40,000 men.[3]

In December 1920, a special commission for combat against "banditry" in Ukraine was created under the leadership of Mikhail Frunze, who was assisted by other high-ranking Bolsheviks such as Dzerzhinsky and Kamenev. The fight against the Ukrainian "bandits" was of very high priority for Moscow and all available troops were mobilized for this task, including internal troops, the Cheka and even the Red Army; in 1921, at least 35,000 Red Army soldiers were fighting the "bandits", including an entire cavalry and an infantry division. Despite these efforts, this was by no means an easy fight. In the winter of 1920/21, the Bolsheviks were even forced to resort to partisan warfare against the "bandits" who had more or less full control over much of the region.[4]

In the end, the reinforcements helped to turn the tide and on 7 February 1921, Mikhail Frunze was able to bring back good news. He reported that his forces had been able to reduce the number of "bandits from 40,000 in late October 1920, to just 6,500." Still, he remained cautious: "Banditry is declining now. That is a fact. However, in spring we have to expect it to strengthen."[5] Future events would prove him right.[6]

While the situation in Ukraine was bad enough, the events that unfolded in the Tambov governorate in the Volga region were even worse. There, the greatest peasant uprising in the history of the Soviet Union broke out on 19 August 1920. A Bolshevik requisitioning commando had been thoroughly looting the village of Khitorovo, taking not only grain but all kinds of valuables, even pillows and cooking utensils, while savagely abusing the villagers. To add insult to injury, the looted grain was brought to the railway station where it was not properly stored and was left to rot. The incensed villagers quickly organized themselves and overwhelmed the Bolsheviks. Encouraged by the success of the people of Khitorovo, many other villages followed suit and the rebellion spread rapidly.[7]

By September 1920, the rebellion had swollen to more than 14,000 fighters, most of whom were deserters with military training. Together, they had managed to kill or at least drive off all Soviet functionaries in three districts in the Tambov governorate. As the Bolsheviks failed to quickly suppress the rebellion, it continued to grow. Before long, the now 50,000 rebels found themselves under the leadership of Alexander Antonov, a Social Revolutionary who had broken with the Bolsheviks in 1918. Antonov continued to push back the Bolsheviks, who found themselves confined to just the city of Tambov and a few other towns – the countryside had been lost completely. This rebellion enraged Moscow and on 19 October 1920, Lenin reprimanded Dzerzhinsky: "This movement has to be put down in the quickest and most exemplary way. [...] Show more energy."[8]

However, Dzerzhinsky did not have sufficient forces to contain, let alone defeat the rebels. By early 1921, the rebellion had spread south into the Lower Volga region and east, into western Siberia. The increasingly desperate Bolsheviks were now forced to send in Red Army units they considered to be unreliable, which did not always go well; in the Samara region, for example, entire Red Army units simply deserted in the winter of 1921. With the rebels running rampant, the Politburo turned to Mikhail Tukhachevsky on 27 April 1921; the man who had lost at the gates of Warsaw in August 1920 was thus given the opportunity to redeem himself against the rebels of Tambov.[9]

Tukhachevsky was given command of a 100,000-man-strong army, with heavy artillery and even aircraft. Eager to impress, he proceeded with utmost ruthlessness, taking hostages and carrying out executions; over the coming months, his army robbed and murdered its way through the region, exterminating entire villages suspected of "banditry". In the rear areas, the Cheka set up a network of concentration camps, in which at least 50,000 people were imprisoned by July 1921; mostly children, women and the elderly. On 12 June 1921, Tukhachevsky even ordered the use of poison gas: "The remnants of the defeated bands as well as individual bandits continue to gather in the forests. [...] The forests, in which the bandits are hiding, are to be cleared with poison gas. Everything is to be calculated in such a way that the gas cloud enters the forest and destroys everything that hides there." With this order, he went too far, however. Several Bolshevik party leaders intervened and a week later, he withdrew it.[10]

In 1920, Tukhachevsky had failed to defeat the outnumbered and outgunned Polish army, but in 1921 he was able to overcome Russian peasant rebels with overwhelming force. On 16 July 1921, he was thus able to report his victory to Lenin:

There were up to 21,000 bandits. The uprising began in September 1920 and the local peasant population and bandits called it their revolution. […] The causes for this uprising are the same as for the entire Russian Federation of Soviet Republics, i.e. unhappiness about the duty to deliver [grain] and its clumsy as well as extremely brutal implementation by local confiscation commandos. […] Plan of the campaign. The forthcoming activities had to be planned not as a more or less large operation but as a proper campaign, if not a war. The destruction of the armed forces of the bandits was not a difficult task thanks to their weak fighting capabilities. The main difficulty was to conquer the territory, to occupy and Sovietize the areas from which the bandits hailed. For the occupation, primarily military and political forces were deployed, and for the operative-tactical operations, only three cavalry brigades. […] As the result of systematic operations, the peasant uprising in the Tambov governorate was liquidated within 40 days. […] Soviet power was established everywhere. Of 21,000 bandits, less than 1,200 sabers remained by 11 July. Most bandit leaders were annihilated.[11]

To this day, Tukhachevsky enjoys a splendid reputation as one of the greatest Soviet generals and strategists. He is even widely considered to be an innocent victim of Stalin's purges, since in 1937 he was arrested and executed following a show trial. His gratuitous massacres in the Russian Civil War and especially in the Tambov governorate are generally omitted in this narrative.

As Tukhachevsky had hinted at in his report to Lenin, similar peasant unrest and uprisings were occurring all over Soviet Russia in 1921.[12] In response, the Cheka and the Red Army were unleashed upon the rebels, "pacifying" entire regions. Like in Tambov, hostages were taken and executed, family members and supposed sympathizers of the "bandits" were abducted, and entire villages were razed in order to intimidate the population.[13]

While it was the villages that remained the hotbeds of anti-Soviet resistance, unrest also spread to the cities and the military as well. The most well-known incident is the Kronstadt Rebellion. On 28 February 1921, navy soldiers mutinied on two armored cruisers stationed at

Kronstadt, a naval base on an island close to Petrograd. The mutineers were quickly joined by around 2,000 Bolsheviks stationed in Kronstadt, while the striking workers in Petrograd sympathized with them, as did most of the city's civilian population. Now controlling the naval approaches to Petrograd, the mutineers issued a series of political demands to the government in Moscow, including an end to Bolshevik terror, new elections to the councils as well as the liberation of political prisoners. The Bolsheviks could not accept this and moved to crush the rebels. In early March, the Cheka conducted mass arrests among the strikers, but not among unarmed workers of Petrograd in an attempt to confine the rebellion to the naval base alone.[14]

With the rebels cleared from Petrograd, the Bolsheviks now geared up to crush the mutineers' headquarters on the island of Kronstadt. Command of the Bolshevik forces, mostly fresh Red Army recruits and seasoned Cheka men, was given to Tukhachevsky – the later butcher of Tambov – who ordered a direct assault on the island fortress on 8 March 1921. After the initial attacks over the frozen bay were beaten back with heavy casualties, the Bolsheviks ultimately managed to overcome the rebels on 18 March. Of the rebel force, around 8,000 were able to flee to Finland. Once the fierce fighting was over – both sides had lost several thousand men – the Bolsheviks exacted their revenge. Hundreds were summarily executed, and between April and June 1921, a further 2,102 people were sentenced to death and 6,459 sent to prison or to one of the concentration camps.[15]

The unrest and uprisings that rocked Soviet Russia in 1921 were so intense that the Bolsheviks were forced to postpone the planned troop reductions. In the summer of 1921, the Bolsheviks thus fielded a total of 192,000 Red Army soldiers, both infantry and cavalry, who were supposed to have been demobilized according to the troop reduction plan from December 1920. Instead of returning to civilian life, they were now sent out to kill the very peasants and workers they officially protected.[16]

Aside from Red Army soldiers, the Bolsheviks frequently employed Cheka troops like at Kronstadt and also mobilized all communists capable of bearing arms. On 24 March 1921, the Central Committee issued a resolution according to which all party members and candidates, as well as members of the Komsomol (Young Communist League), were to be mobilized and organized into special detachments. This order applied to everyone between the ages of 17 and 60, including women. As with everything, there were exceptions. Party members with health issues were exempted, as were high-ranking party members and functionaries. Many women, too, were allowed to stay behind for "family reasons". The party members who were already serving in the Red Army, the Cheka, the militia or in the fire brigades, were to remain within their respective organizations and form special detachments there.[17]

By the summer of 1921, these desperate measures had paid off and the most dangerous uprisings had been brutally crushed. But even then, thousands of "bandits" carried on fighting the Bolsheviks, oftentimes motivated by hunger. As a military dispatch from 1 September 1921 reported: "The bands in the starving territories of the Zavolzhye Military District [Eastern Volga Region] attack Sovkhozes [state farms], grain delivery points, railways. They kill communists and Soviet functionaries, who the population, its senses clouded by hunger, blames for the natural catastrophe [famine]."[18]

In the second half of August 1921, the Red Army reconnaissance administration reported that there were 1,975 "bandits" operating in Soviet Belarus, 2,675 in Soviet Ukraine, 2,000 in the Zavolzhye Military District, 700 in the Tambov governorate, 300 in the Voronezh governorate, 5,165 in the Northern Caucasus, and in Turkestan – a staggering 16,745.[19] Two months later, on 11 November 1921, things had not improved by much. While their number had slightly decreased in Zavolzhye (1,460) and Turkestan (15,240), it had stayed more or less the same in the Northern Caucasus, where 5,173 "bandits" were active, most of them on horseback (4,350). At the same time, the situation in the west had deteriorated considerably, with the amount of "bandits" in Soviet Ukraine nearly tripling to 6,752. In Soviet Belarus, reconnaissance now reported 9,427 "bandits" – nearly four times as many – of whom nearly 7,500 were considered "foreign bandits" with their supply bases being in Polish Belarus from where they launched cross-border raids.[20]

According to similar estimates, around 40,000 people were carrying on the armed fight against the Bolsheviks by the end of 1921. While this was far from optimal, this was nevertheless a great improvement – after all, Antonov's rebels in Tambov alone had numbered around 50,000 fighting men. On 27 December 1921, Trotsky felt confident enough to announce his triumph over "counterrevolutionary bandits" at the 9th Soviet Conference: "The first half of the year was a time of unprecedented growth of banditry. The year began with Kronstadt, Tambov, with the bandit movement in Siberia, in the Caucasus, in Transcaucasia and in Ukraine. The second half of the year brought with it a radical, decisive change of the situation. Certainly, there are bands here and there, but they are bands. Banditry as a broad social phenomenon, as armed detachments of broad masses of kulaks and parts of the medium peasant masses, belongs to the past."[21]

Trotsky was right. While there were indeed many thousands of "counterrevolutionary elements" who continued to fight Soviet rule in strikes, riots, and outright uprisings, the resistance never again grew as dangerous as it had been in 1921. Additionally, there was also a geographic shift. In 1921, the heartland of anti-Soviet resistance had been in the rural, ethnically-Russian central regions of Soviet Russia. With the Russian peasants pacified by terror and the abolition of War Communism, the situation in the non-Russian periphery came to the forefront in the second half of 1921. In the Caucasian mountains, the rebels were able to find refuge in remote mountain valleys, while in the border regions, such as Karelia, Ukraine, Belarus, Siberia, and Turkestan, rebels regularly crossed the border to evade their Soviet enemies, only to return once the Bolsheviks had left. This made crushing them much harder.

By August 1922, 39 governorates, oblasts and autonomous republics were officially in a state of war. That number remained unchanged in October, but in December 1922 it decreased, but only marginally, to 38.[22] The last large-scale rebellion was to occur in January 1924 in the Soviet Far East.[23]

Chapter 5

The Stabilization of Soviet Rule

Following their victory in the Russian Civil War and the brutal suppression of the peasant uprisings that followed it, the Bolsheviks had cemented their hold over Russia. With peace more or less restored, the New Economic Policy helped agricultural production rebound, which in turn improved the living standards of the population, especially in the countryside. While agricultural production would not reach pre-war levels, it was nevertheless a very welcome development. As Lenin stated in a speech on 13 November 1922:

In one year the peasants have not only got over the famine, but have paid so much tax in kind that we have already received hundreds of millions of poods of grain, and that almost without employing any measures of coercion. Peasant uprisings, which previously, before 1921, were, so to speak, a common occurrence in Russia, have almost completely ceased. […] Nobody questions the fact that the peasants are a decisive factor in our country. And the position of the peasantry is now such that we have no reason to fear any movement against us from that quarter. […]The peasantry may be dissatisfied with one aspect or another of the work of our authorities. They may complain about this. That is possible, of course, and inevitable, because our machinery of state and our state-operated economy are still too inefficient to avert it; but any serious dissatisfaction with us on the part of the peasantry as a whole is quite out of the question.[1]

The industrial sector was on a much more difficult footing, however. A handful of exemptions aside, foreign capitalists did not invest in the country and did not transfer much technology either. At the same time, the state-owned industrial sector suffered from countless structural issues, such as a bloated bureaucracy, the tendency to organize fruitless but time-consuming debates between countless commissions, as well as mismanagement, dilettantism, nepotism and corruption.[2] These problems severely hampered the industrial development of the Soviet Union and would continue doing so until its very end. As a result, industrial recovery was painfully slow, especially in the armaments and heavy industries. In contrast, light industry strongly benefited from the more liberal environment of the NEP. Many factories were leased out or fully privatized; private investors even ventured to build new factories. As light industry was now dominated by private entrepreneurs, factories worked in a profit-oriented manner, which helped these businesses grow quickly. At the same time, light industry simply did not require as high initial investments as heavy industry, which further increased the gap between light and heavy industry. On 13 November 1922, Lenin stated:

> The third question is that of heavy industry. I must say that the situation here is still grave. […] The economic history of the capitalist countries shows that heavy industry in backward countries can only be developed with the aid of long-term loans of hundreds of millions of dollars or gold rubles. We did not get such loans, and so far have received nothing. All that is now being written about concessions and so forth is not worth much more than the paper it is written on.[3]

The weakness of heavy industry was an existential problem for the Bolsheviks, because without a powerful heavy industry and therefore a powerful armaments industry, Moscow would not be able to wage a great revolutionary war against the rest of the world. This problem was further exacerbated by the fact that the financial situation of the Soviet Union was very poor, and without the necessary funds, the Bolsheviks could not finance major projects. As a result, the Soviet armaments industry as well as the Red Army would suffer from serious underfunding for years to come. The world revolution would have to wait.

Chapter 6

The Red Army After 1920

It had been the Red Army that won the Russian Civil War for the Bolsheviks and it was the Red Army that was to spread war abroad as well. However, although it did defeat its Russian foes, it failed to overcome Poland in 1920, which ended Bolshevik hopes of revolutionary conquests for the time being. Since the 5.3 million-man army was a nightmare to supply, the Bolshevik leadership decided to demobilize nearly 4 million soldiers to save money at the end of 1920. As mentioned earlier, this had to be partially postponed due to the revolts and peasant uprisings of 1921.

Nevertheless, the strength of the Red Army had been reduced to just 1,370,000 men by December 1921, not counting the weak Red Fleet. Among the nearly 1.4 million soldiers were 644,228 infantry and 91,200 cavalry. The rest served in the military administration, training units, or in one of the many military agencies.[1] In addition to that were the 270,000 soldiers of the Cheka, the Red Fleet, guard troops, as well as the troops for special use.[2] The troops of the Cheka/OGPU (Joint State Political Directorate) numbered 126,300 men in early 1922.[3]

Despite the reduction of the Red Army by well over 70%, the dire financial situation forced the Politburo to further cut troop numbers. On 2 August 1922, the Central Committee thus resolved to cut the armed forces down to just 800,000 men, a number that included the Red Fleet, troops for special use, as well as training units. Likewise, the troops of the GPU were to be reduced as well, as was the number of guard troops and the border guard. However, even this was not enough, and the Central Committee tasked Trotsky with devising another plan to further reduce the strength of the Red Army in the coming year.[4]

However, the next round of cuts arrived even earlier, in November 1922. This time, the Red Army was to be reduced to just 610,000 men, a number that included the Red Fleet but not the GPU troops. By May 1923, the

Red Army had reached the desired size of 610,000 men, which included: 273,000 infantry, 63,000 cavalry, 76,000 technical troops, 11,500 fortress troops, 79,000 in training units and facilities, 23,000 in the administration, 8,000 as troops for special use, and 25,000 in the Red Fleet.[5]

Although the troops of the GPU were not included in this round of cuts, their number was drastically reduced as well. On 22 June 1922, the Soviet government decided to cut the number of GPU troops in half, reducing it from 126,300 to just 56,400, and to devise measures to "improve the situation in the other units".[6] On 1 October 1922, the troops of the GPU were given the task to patrol the land and sea borders of Soviet Russia. For that purpose alone, a new GPU border guard corps was created that numbered 50,000 men, a sixth of them cavalry.[7]

With funds remaining scarce in Moscow, more proposals came in to cut the Red Army even further. In June 1923, it was thus suggested to the Politburo that the Red Army should be shrunk to 100,000 or even 50,000 men – to save costs. However, this would not happen. In August 1923, a serious crisis broke out in Germany and the country came close to having its own Bolshevik revolution. While it did ultimately fail, it convinced the Politburo to change course, and instead of further cutting the Red Army, it was now being enlarged again.[8]

The State of the Red Army

Despite these successive troop reductions that cut the size of the Red Army by nearly 90%, from 5.3 million to 610,000, the Red Army together with the 100,000-strong troops of the GPU still remained one of the largest militaries in the world. Only France, which fielded a similar number of troops, and China whose army numbered 1,370,000 men in 1922, could rival the Soviet Union in this regard.[9]

Table 1: Size of the Soviet Union's Rivals' Armies[10]

Year	France	Great Britain	Poland	Romania	Italy	Japan	USA
1922	802,600	398,566	254,678	192,063	250,000	300,000	144,748
1924	639,000	281,000	241,800	143,425	250,000	236,000	135,000

The Soviet Union had thus a military larger than all of its neighbors to the west. Countries like Finland (1922: 30,000, 1924: 28,000), Estonia (14,000), Latvia (1922: 19,500, 1924: 35,000) and Lithuania (1922: 45,000, 1924: 35,000) were insignificant militarily, and further west, Germany's once feared army was now not allowed to exceed 100,000 men under the Treaty of Versailles.[11]

Even though the Red Army was very large, it was not particularly effective. On the contrary, it was in a truly catastrophic state in nearly every regard. The Red Army and its commanders were poorly armed and poorly supplied. They also suffered from poor accommodations and low morale. In 1921, the Red Army had even struggled to suppress the peasant revolts on its own, and many Red Army soldiers – most of whom were peasants themselves – deserted instead of fighting the rebels. The Bolsheviks were therefore forced to rely more on the generally reliable troops of the Cheka and mobilized communists.

Particularly noticeable was the lack of heavy armament. In 1923, the units of the Red Army had on average 3.3 artillery pieces per battalion. In comparison, in the French army that ratio was 15.5 artillery pieces per battalion, in the Polish army 11.9, and in Romania 6.2. Even disarmed Germany was better equipped artillery-wise with 3.9 artillery pieces per battalion. The Soviet air force was similarly weak. Of its 611 aircraft, only 54% were operational. At the time, France had over 2,000 aircraft, Poland over 960, Romania over 500 and Finland over 100. At the same time, the Red Army had a grand total of 59 tanks, which were both obsolete and poorly maintained, as well as 186 armored cars, which were in a similarly poor condition.[12]

In regards to the infantry and cavalry, an in-depth report on the state of the Red Army from 17 May 1923 had this to say: "The infantry units of the Red Army are poorly armed in most military districts. There are many issues: Available weapons are in need of repair, there is a lack of revolvers (common issue) and there is a lack of weapons in general."[13] Here are a few examples from the report:

Moscow Military District: In the 14th division, weapons are rusty because there is a lack of preservatives. [...] In regiment 54 of the 18th infantry division, 50% of weapons are unusable. [...] *Petrograd*

Military District: Lack of weaponry and ammunition in regiment 32 of the 11th division, in regiment 166 of the 56th division, in regiments 46 and 47 of the 16th division and in regiment 167 of the 56th division, 70% of the ammunition is missing. […] *Ukrainian Military District*: […] In regiment 43 of the 15th division, 50% of rifles are in need of repairs. In regiment 45 of the 45th division, 16 out of 26 machine guns are defective. […] *The Independent Caucasian Army*: In the 1st division, 50% of all rifles are completely unusable, 20% are in need of repairs. Of 233 machine guns, 33 are unusable, 85 are in need of repairs. […] In the Azerbaijani division, 90% of all weapons need to be repaired. […] Cavalry. Cavalry troops are not better armed than the infantry. […] North Caucasian Military District. In the units of the 4th division, there are 704 rifles missing, 6 'Maxim' machine guns [heavy machine guns], 1620 revolvers, 1770 sabers, 625 pikes, 446 cartridge belts for the 'Maxim' […]. In the Northern Donetsk Regiment 33 of the 6th division there are missing 63% of rifles, 51% of revolvers, 166 sabers, 86 pikes, 2 'Maxim' machine guns, 11 'Lyunsa' machine guns, 28,556 rifle bullets. [14]

Aside from a lack of equipment, both infantry and cavalry were plagued by poor tactical training and were not combat-ready. Again, however, it was the artillery that was in particularly poor shape, lacking lubricants, spare parts, ammunition, and equipment in general, which seriously hampered gunnery training and practice.[15]

Even the food supply was not entirely secured; especially sugar, cheese and meat were scarce. To make matters worse, the Red Army also suffered from a severe lack of uniforms and boots. In 1923, it only had 44% of the boots it needed, and 78-88% of the uniforms.[16] Another report described the situation as such:

Red Army soldiers often run around barefoot and without clothing [uniforms]. It is not uncommon that Red Army soldiers, who leave the barracks, wear the boots of soldiers staying in the barracks. In all infantry units and other combat arms there is an acute lack of bedding. Overall, the situation regarding uniforms is the same in all other combat arms. It has been noted that many cavalrymen are equipped with half-shoes instead of cavalry boots. On average, 25% of Red Army soldiers do not have uniforms across the military districts.[17]

The lack of boots and uniforms did not go unnoticed among the neighbors of the Soviet Union. On 3 August 1922, the political administration of the Revolutionary War Council of the Republic reported: "Regiment 3 of the 1st Border Guard Division reports that Polish soldiers taunt Red Army soldiers over their lack of boots and uniforms and insult them, calling the Red Army soldiers hobos."[18]

Three weeks later, the same office reported: "Red Army soldiers of the 1st Border Guard Division are begging at the junction of our and the Polish railroad in front of the passing foreigners. Barefoot and ragged, the Red Army soldiers are photographed by the foreigners who think that the entire Red Army is like that."[19] Six days later, on 30 August 1922, the political administration of the Revolutionary War Council reported that in the Petrograd Military District, 22% of Red Army soldiers did not have uniforms, further saying that "Red Army soldiers remind one of typical hobos and in this state they are often photographed by foreign agents at the border posts. The delivered uniforms are of low quality, they wear out quickly and are the source of epidemic diseases."[20]

As mentioned above, the Red Army also lacked housing. In 1923, only 55% of soldiers were stationed in proper barracks; the rest had to live in makeshift accommodations or were quartered in civilian housing. Others, especially cavalrymen, were quartered in villages. Not only was there a lack of barracks, the existing barracks were in horrible shape. Only 10% had intact roofs, while the vast majority – 75% in total – had barely patched up roofing; in 15% of cases, the roofs were leaking. At the same time, only around 30% of windows in the barracks had panes, a problem that was made worse by the fact that the rooms were poorly if at all heated due to a lack of fuel. The Red Army also had issues with its horses; out of the 145,000 horses it was supposed to have on paper, it only had 133,000 on 1 February 1923, a deficit of 12,000 (8.3%) horses. Even worse, the horses were in very poor shape; many were old and suffering from neglect. The lack of fodder was particularly harmful.[21]

On 2 July 1923, several high-ranking commanders of the Red Army, including Kliment Voroshilov, then the commander of the Northern Caucasian Military District, thus penned a secret memorandum in which they criticized further budget cuts. Stalin then sent this report to all members and candidates of the Central Committee as well as the members of the Presidium of the Central Control Commission of the Party. The memorandum stated among other things:

Barracks are falling apart. Roofs have not been painted in the last 10 years [metal roofing], they are corroded and leak; walls, ceilings, floors, foundations and ovens are falling apart. Window frames are rotting, do not have glass panes, lavatories overflowing, water pipes damaged, no light, darkness everywhere, moisture and decay everywhere. Ammunition depots and store rooms are in an even worse state. The explosions that have occurred over the past 1-2 years have cost the state many million gold rubles. [...] The second issue: Fuel, wood and coal are insufficient to cook food and water. Under these circumstances (poorly clothed, without bedding, cold, unheated and damp barracks) one can imagine what kind of mood and feelings towards this climate of the NEP are rampant among the Red Army soldiers, commanders, political workers, students and their family members.[22]

Although the cuts were averted for the time being, the material standing of the Red Army soldiers did not improve over the coming years. The political administration of the Revolutionary War Council of the Republic thus stated in its report for the month of February 1924:

Over the past month, the food supply situation was abnormal in many units. Poor baking of bread and distribution – raw and rotten – (22nd Division, 14th Cavalry Division, 19th Division). In some units of the 14th cavalry division, the situation during the distribution of bread is extremely tense. [...] *Barracks*: Lack of fuel, coldness in the barracks – lack of fuel took on particularly dire proportions. It was rare that units were fully supplied with fuel. Most units did not have enough fuel. The distribution quota for fuel is inadequate. A part of the distributed fuel is of poor quality – wood is not dry and is rotten. […] In many units, the temperature in the barracks is below 10 degrees […], in some it was not higher than 4-5 degrees, and there are barracks in which temperatures fell below 0 degrees (regiment 167 of the 56th division). These circumstances forced Red Army soldiers to cover themselves with all of their clothing at night so that they do not freeze to death. In many units, Red Army soldiers jump out of their beds at night and run through the barracks to warm themselves up. In the 4th Cavalry Division, the steam bath maintained by Regiment 2 ceased to function due to the lack of fuel, the laundry stopped working, water froze in the sinks. The supply of fuel is particularly tight among the units of the Western Front; the 33rd Division could not supply itself with firewood, because it lacked warm clothing (felt boots, etc.); Red Army soldiers searched for wood with tears in their eyes. There were cases of frostbite. Due to the cold in the barracks, [soldiers] caught the cold (27th Division). […] *Sanitary situation*: In the 44th Territorial Division it was recorded that 80% of the Red Army soldiers there had lice. One of the reasons for this is that no soap has been made available to wash their clothing. The political administration of the Leningrad Military District emphasizes that if current regulations for medical examination were to be strictly observed, for example in the 4th Cavalry Division, there would remain no more than 40-50 men in each regiment.[23]

The terrible state of the Red Army was made even worse by the "massive theft and mismanagement", reported Genrikh Yagoda, who then headed the special detachment of the GPU at the Red Army, in May 1923. He further lamented:

The results of the fight of the special detachment against various economic crimes show that it is *these crimes and the mismanagement that not rarely are the primary and decisive reason for the material grievances for one or other sphere of army life*. […] [several examples of millions being embezzled follow]. In late 1921 (October), 18 'Halberstadt' planes had been bought via the company 'Sablatnik'.

[...] When they were received, the aircraft were operational, some of them were air-tested. After they arrived in Petrograd (10 aircraft) and Moscow (8 aircraft), it turned out that the aircraft were not operational. The commission that was established last year found that all of the planes are not operational and that they have to be completely overhauled. [...] These aircraft were bought for 240,000 gold rubles; the damage for the republic stands at 117,320 gold rubles. [...] Five large explosions in ammunition depots between 1919 and 1922 have caused the Republic 150,000 gold rubles in damages. [...] The five aforementioned explosions destroyed around 5,000 wagons of ammunition – in the ammunition depots there are 90,000 wagons of ammunition.[24]

Yagoda went on to complain that great quantities of clothing, boots and other items were being stolen from military warehouses and then sold. He estimated the losses incurred from that alone to be in the dozens of millions of gold rubles.

It comes thus as no surprise that both morale and discipline in the Red Army were very low. To make matters worse, the Red Army was not at all imbued with the spirit of equality and democracy the Bolsheviks had promised at the start. Instead, the common soldiers were treated very poorly by their superiors and abuse was normal. The aforementioned report from 17 May 1923 went into detail on this issue as well:

In the Petrograd Military District, the mood among the Red Army soldiers cannot be described as good. [...] The divide between the commanders, members of the administrative and economic agencies on the one side, and the Red Army soldiers on the other is growing ever wider. The reasons for this are firstly arrogance, coarse and presumptuous behavior that includes beatings. Second, drunkenness and chumminess among the commanders. Third, abuse of positions and theft, which in recent times has reached the state of a chronic disease and which has a fatal effect on the mood of the masses of the Red Army. They subvert and infect the Red Army soldiers and undermine the authority of the commanders and the members of the political agencies.

> Siberia: The material undersupply, coarseness and isolation [of the commanders] from the mass of the Red Army soldiers cause dissatisfaction among the latter. This leaves fertile ground for the activities of sects, especially the Baptists. [...] These factors have a negative effect on the mood among the Red Army soldiers.[25]

Despite this and other reports, the situation in the Red Army and therefore the mood among the Red Army soldiers did not change much over the coming years. For example, the political administration of the Revolutionary War Council wrote in its report for the month of February 1924 that among others, the soldiers received their pay late and, in some cases, not at all. At the same time, the soldiers were incensed by letters from home in which their friends and families complained about the Bolshevik's high taxes making life hard. Aside from the common soldiers, lower-ranking commanders and even some higher-ranking ones were deeply dissatisfied with their standards of living. Discipline also suffered and orders were not followed. At the same time, the report also noted that the commanders of some of the units were caught drunk on the job.[26] These issues provided fertile ground for "counterrevolutionary agitation". On 29 February 1924, the political administration thus reported: "The number of kulaks in the individual units is rather high. In Regiment 90 there are 115 kulaks, which is 10% of the units. The most eager kulaks are creating such a mood with their 'shouts' and their demagogic agitation that order can be maintained only with the greatest difficulty."[27]

By December 1924, the situation had deteriorated even further, the OGPU reported, which was largely due to the letters the Red Army soldiers received from their home villages in which their friends and families complained about the dire economic situation. This in turn spurred into action the "counterrevolutionary elements" (kulaks, traders, dismissed students) among the Red Army soldiers. With the divide growing between soldiers from urban and rural backgrounds, discipline was further breaking down. Many Red Army soldiers even began to openly complain about the oppression of the villagers: "In Regiment 105 of the Siberian Military District some Red Army soldiers declared: 'Soviet power is no power, but looting. When the war comes, we will wage war against the communists, and if they do not go to war, then we will kill them and will not fight.'

In the 3rd Division, a Red Army soldier, son of a trader, agitated among the Red Army soldiers against the 'unfair' treatment at the hands of the commanders: 'We do not serve the Red Army, this is red oppression.'"The report then went on to summarize: "Dissatisfaction due to poor material and living condition is rife in all military districts."[28]

Things stayed more or less the same in 1925, with the GPU reports again highlighting poor material and living conditions of the Red Army soldiers, who were suffering from a lack of uniforms, poor food, poor discipline, and abuse, and thus often harbored strong anti-Soviet attitudes.[29]

This was not confined to the lower ranks, and many commanders were deeply dissatisfied as well, because they also had to serve under horrible conditions. In the report for the month of May 1924, the political administration of the Red Army stated the already meager salaries for low and medium-ranked commanders were paid out only irregularly. As a result, many commanders had gone into debt with local merchants and then often ended up unable to repay these loans in time. Furthermore, their living quarters were not much better than those of the common soldiers; this was particularly a problem in Turkmenistan. These issues disproportionately impacted married commanders who could barely support their families.[30]

The report of the Revolutionary War Council for the month of April 1924 also highlighted the low salaries the commanders received and the resulting horrible economic hardships their families were facing.[31] In the organization's earlier report from 29 February 1924, the authors also pointed out that the commanders' poor economic situation undermined their authority among the soldiers.[32] Faced with the prospect of low pay and horrible living conditions, few wanted to become commanders. In October 1925, the OGPU thus reported that among those who took part in various courses in the battalion schools, which were specifically targeted at training lower-ranking commanders, only a few wanted to remain in the military. This was the case across all military districts. Some apparently failed their exams on purpose so they could be demobilized. Overall, many already serving lower-ranking commanders wished to leave the military as well.[33]

A grim phenomenon accompanying the crisis of the Red Army was suicide, which was particularly prevalent among the commanders. In the units of the 5th Army, the political administration of the Red Army reported a total of 24 suicides, the reasons being: psychological disorders (60%), incurable illnesses (20%), professional problems (10%) and fear of punishment (5%). The report continued: "The ratio of suicides of commanders to Red Army soldiers [in the 5th Army] is at 8:1, which in part hints at the very difficult material situation of the commanders."[34]

In the Moscow Military District, the suicide rate soared by 250% between 1922 and 1923, even though the number of men fell by 21.3%. In total, there were 65 confirmed suicides in the year 1923, with 67.7% of the suicides being commanders, administrators, and trainees. Most of the suicides were due to the poor material conditions the commanders faced, the report stated.[35]

Finally, there was also the issue of ethnic tensions between the various peoples of the Russian-dominated but still multicultural empire. In November 1921, 80.3% of the Red Army was composed of ethnic Russians, 10.9% were Ukrainians, 2.6% Tatars, 1.6% Jews, 1.1% Poles, 0.7% Latvians, 0.6% Germans, 0.4% Bashkirs and the remaining 2.8% belonged to other ethnic groups.[36] Especially problematic were the tensions between ethnic Russians and Ukrainians, and between Jewish and non-Jewish soldiers.

The report by the administration of the Red Army for the month of February 1924 had this to say: "Over the past month there were many cases of ethnic antagonisms between Russians and Jews (21st Division: 'For the Jews there is respect everywhere, but we are forced to toil') and Russians and Ukrainians (30th Division). In the latter case, the antagonism was created by the chauvinistic agitation of the 'Ukapists'."[37] The "Ukapists" were Ukrainian communists who agitated for the independence of Soviet Ukraine from Soviet Russia.[38]

On 19 February 1924, the political administration of the Red Army reported that parts of the political agencies of the 7th Cavalry Division on the Western Front refused to conduct political propaganda and training in the Ukrainian language, even though that had been introduced following the creation of national units within the Red Army. In the 1st Brigade, the political administration noted the proliferation of anti-Semitism, reporting that Red Army soldiers were caught saying: "Jews have spread across the civilian administration but not in the army." In the first squadron of regiment 38, a Red Army soldier was asked during a political training session: "What duties does a Red Army soldier have in battle?" to which he replied: "To beat the Jews."[39] During the Russian Civil War, the Red Army had been involved in countless pogroms against Jewish communities.

In its monthly report for May 1924, the political administration of the Red Army once again brought up the issue of anti-Semitism: "Anti-Semitism appeared among a number of troops (Baltic Fleet, Black Sea Fleet, Ukrainian Military District), especially among the troops of the Kharkiv Garrison, where one of the Red Army soldiers proposed during a rayon conference to 'ban the Jews from serving in the Red Army'. He justified this with the low number of Jews in tactical units."[40] Following this wave of reports of anti-Semitism, the political leadership of the Red Army decided to take measures against it. In a report of the political administration from 10 May 1924, it said: "Against the background of the increase of the anti-Semitic mood among the troops [of the Ukrainian Military District], the political conference decided, in order to fight these occurrences, to conduct planned agitation and a regrouping of the political apparatus according to ethnic background."[41]

With the Red Army in complete disarray, it comes as no surprise that the Red Army leadership was also singled out for severe criticism. Mikhail Tukhachevsky, who had become the commander of the troops on the Wester Front in 1924, penned a particularly scathing memorandum on 23 January 1924. In the piece, addressed to the Central Committee, he criticized the army in general and the top leadership in particular. Already in the introduction, Tukhachevsky stated that "in many respects, the state of the Red Army appears in a very dark light, especially in recent times. I currently see no indications [...] that the situation will change for the better." Among others, he criticized:

Strategic leadership: It exists only in a formal, lifeless fashion, if at all. [...] High command and staff have no defined idea of operative leadership. We see neither preparations nor strategic questions about the war, nor any kind of training for it by the staff responsible. This is especially important for the different specialists. The work of some fronts in this area even triggers condescending ridicule. My opinion: The Red Army is in a barbaric state when it comes to strategic preparation.

Organization and mobilization: There is no guiding idea, no guiding plan. The organizational structures of the army are adapting to the constant changes in the budget without any kind of system. Stocks are in constant flux. Nobody knows the current organizational structure of the army. [...] Training lags behind. It is already 1924 and we still do not have any field service regulations, even though all other foreign armies (including Poland) have had them since 1921. [...]

Military Doctrine: It died in early 1922, when the persecution of the scientific approach began. It was declared that there was no such thing as military doctrine, that the 'red generals' and their strategy were not needed and that the primary task of the Red Army was to shine boots. [...]

Commanders and members of the political apparatus: In general, the strongest commanders remained with the army at the end of the civil war. When it comes to the members of the political apparatus, [...] the quality has fallen considerably, because the better forces were taken to the economic front. These two circumstances have led to the fact that the relations between the commanders and the members of the political apparatus have considerably worsened when the commanders are communists. And their percentage is very high.[42]

Tukhachevsky further elaborated that the political apparatus within the army had become something of an opposition to the military commanders, undermining the principle of unified command. This had to change, he continued: "Without these measures we will face the progressive dissolution of the leadership of the Red Army." Tukhachevsky continued, calling for a radical reorganization of the high command.[43]

The Bolshevik leadership was very well-aware of the issues the Red Army faced. After all, the aforementioned reports and memoranda had been written primarily for them. Already in March 1923, Trotsky held a speech at the plenum of the Central Committee in which he lamented the poor state of the Red Army. According to Trotsky, the main issue was the high fluctuation within the military:

Over the past 3 years, the army has lived through two serious processes – *continuous demobilization and reorganization*. Year after year, the older cohorts had to be discharged.[…] This together with the continuous reorganization has led *to an incredible fluctuation in the personnel of the army, which has been very harmful for the state of training and supply of the troops*. […] The army is currently composed of young, poorly-trained soldiers, and *the army's uniform plan has failed due to giving clothes to the demobilized*."[44]

In response to these complaints, the Central Committee set up a special commission on 30 March 1923. Composed of high-ranking Bolsheviks such as Trotsky, Rykov, Dzerzhinsky, Pyatakov, Bogdanov, Sokolnikov, Frunze, and Voroshilov, the commission was to work out a new defense plan.[45] On 3 May 1923, Trotsky presented the results at a session of the Politburo, suggesting building up the Red Army over a period of five years. The Politburo approved the idea and tasked the commission with devising such a plan.[46] However, nothing would come of this in the end.

On 3 February 1924, the Central Committee once again discussed the state of the Red Army. Among others, Sergey Gusev, the chief of the political administration of the Red Army, reported that the Red Army was in a very poor state, suffering from massive personnel fluctuations but also from dismissed Tsarist specialists not getting replaced, as well as poor security in ammunition depots that had repeatedly led to great explosions.[47] Again, the Central Committee set up a commission to save the Red Army, and on 19 February 1924, Mikhail Frunze was put in charge of it.[48]

In the end, all these plans and proposals this and the previous commissions had come up with proved to be for naught, because the Soviet Union simply did not have the funds to pay for them. Even the current level of spending was a great strain on the state budget. As Dzerzhinsky wrote in a memorandum on 9 July 1924: "Furthermore, we absolutely have to review our spending on the Red Army. It is unsustainable for us, it destroys us economically."[49]

In the summer of 1924, the Revolutionary War Council of the Republic asked for 427 million rubles for the Red Army, Red Fleet, and the armaments industry for the 1924/25 budget year. However, the Politburo only approved 380 million rubles. Dismayed, the War Council warned that this budget cut would make a further shrinking of the Red Army inevitable, this time by a third. It then pointed out: "Such an army, amputated by a third, can under no circumstances fulfill the task of defending the country when one considers the real forces of the possible enemies."[50]

While the Red Army was not in fact reduced by a third, the cuts were still devastating. In light of the shortage of funds, Mikhail Frunze proposed to shrink the Red Army on 5 July. The number of divisions was to be lowered from 107 to 90, with the number of soldiers falling from 610,000 to 594,000. Reducing the size of the Red Army in this way would free up enough funds to better supply the remaining divisions with rifles, machine guns and ammunition ("the greatest problem"); Frunze estimated that this would improve the supply situation by 20%. At the same time, this was to guarantee the military training of around 33% (225,000-250,000) of the yearly cohorts (700,000 able-bodied recruits per year).[51] Unlike the previous plans, this one was actually implemented, at least in part, and over the next three years, the number of divisions in the Red Army shrank to 90.[52]

However, these measures failed to noticeably improve the state of the Red Army. This became painfully obvious in September 1926, when the Soviet government rehearsed a mobilization in four military districts to test the combat readiness of the country. Five regiments of infantry and two regiments of artillery took part, as well as a cavalry squadron and an intelligence company. The results were catastrophic in every respect. Neither civilian nor military authorities were prepared for such a mobilization, and the resulting chaos paralyzed the mobilization effort to such an extent that the entire action was cancelled prematurely.[53]

It was found that the commanders were not at all prepared for leading the army under wartime conditions; the reservists had not been trained properly and did not shoot well. At the same time, the supply lines were in complete chaos, as was the organization of the rear areas. Even the horses taken from the peasants were inadequate for they were too weak and not used to military service.[54]

In the end, even the OGPU began to investigate the Red Army. In July 1926, an OGPU commission under Genrikh Yagoda drew up a list of issues that undermined Soviet war preparedness and how to take care of them. Unsurprisingly, the Red Army was carefully examined as well.[55]

According to the commission, the entire army had to be reorganized. However, in order to devise a workable mobilization program, all reorganization efforts had to stop for the time being. The report criticized the current mobilization plans as completely unrealistic; in some sectors, such as chemical warfare and the air force, the situation was very dire. The commission also demanded measures to strengthen the party organizations within the Red Army while also lowering the chasm between the commanders and the common soldiers.[56]

Furthermore, proper discipline needed to be restored since the Red Army had veered into two extremes – excessive democratization and excessive reliance on corporal punishment – simultaneously. The report also lamented the rations the soldiers were given, stating that if they further declined in quality, it would trigger mass unrest within the army. Therefore, the quality of the rations had to be increased, primarily through improving the output of the workers in the supply chain, as well as by stamping out mismanagement with the help of the OGPU. The material standards of living of the reserve commanders had to be raised as well. [57]

Finally, in a sign of what was to happen in the 1930s, the commission also called for the tougher punishment of political crimes. It was necessary, said the commission, for the OGPU and in particular the special detachments to focus on former Tsarist officers and "Whites", as well as on the slow spread of "peasant sentiments" into the ranks of the commanders and common soldiers.[58] Later reports did indeed pay special attention to "peasant sentiments" within the Red Army and found that, indeed, continuously radicalizing anti-Soviet sentiments were seeping into the Red Army from the countryside.[59]

Throughout the early and mid-1920s, the Red Army was ill-prepared for war: It was terribly equipped, poorly fed and housed, and discipline was low, as was morale.

The Armaments Industry

To the Bolsheviks, it was clear from the beginning that one of the main roots of the Red Army's weakness was the weakness of the Soviet armaments industry, which struggled to properly equip the army. In early June 1923, Smirnov, a member of the Central Commission's national defense committee, wrote a memorandum in which he lamented: "While we can […] mobilize masses of people relatively quickly and then organize them around a core of 600,000 men and raise a great army, the issue of arming these millions is considerably harder." He also pointed out that in the coming revolutionary war, the Soviet Union could not rely on its capitalist enemies to arm itself and instead had to make do with its own industrial potential.[60]

However, the Soviet armaments industry of the early 1920s was far too weak for that. Due to its vital importance in the wars, the armaments industry had suffered less than the civilian sector, which saw its production decline by 75% between 1914 and 1923.[61] Nevertheless, it was still deeply affected by the war. For example, only two factories making rifles survived the civil war, one in Tula and one in Ishevsk. Between 1914 and 1920, rifle production had declined relatively moderately from 525,000 to 426,984 in 1920, but with the official conclusion of the civil war and the beginning of the demobilization, rifle production plummeted to 216,688 in 1921, before rebounding somewhat to 245,301 in 1922 and 250,000 in 1923. Even with this moderate recovery, production was still only 48% of what it was in 1914. This was nowhere near enough to properly equip an army as large as the Red Army.[62]

The situation was even worse when it came to machine guns. In 1923, the Red Army lacked a grand total of 50,000 heavy machine guns. However, the Soviet armaments industry was only able to produce 150 heavy machine guns per month. Part of this was due to the shortage of funds, but even if the funding had been there, production would still be only 250 heavy machine guns per month. Nevertheless, this was still higher than the production of light machine guns, which stood at 100 per month, and of which the Red Army lacked 200,000.[63]

Ammunition production was in a poor state as well. In 1914, Russia produced 900 million rounds of ammunition; by 1919, that number had fallen to 350 million, then to 318 million in 1922 and finally to just a planned 300 million in 1923.[64] In contrast, the two foundries in Perm and Moscow were able to meet the Red Army's demand for artillery pieces and even had the capacities to further increase production if need be. In 1922, the foundry in Moscow had produced 102 artillery pieces, with a further 165 planned for 1923, while the foundry in Perm had produced

408 artillery pieces in 1922, and was planning to increase production to 440 in 1923.[65] While this looked good on paper, it has to be noted that the Red Army of the time relied very little on artillery and thus had relatively few pieces.

Even though the Red Army had enough artillery for its current needs, it was in dire need of explosives. According to the mobilization plans for 1923, the Red Army required 121,000 pud of TNT monthly, but Soviet industry was only able to produce 61,500 pud of TNT per month, half of what was needed.[66] The still fairly new Soviet aviation industry was in terrible shape as well and had fallen far behind its rivals. Due to the shortage of funds, it was impossible to import advanced technology from abroad and to expand already-existing factories. Even worse, the Soviet Union simply did not have enough experienced aircraft construction specialists who could design and build modern aircraft. As a result, the Soviet aviation industry was far from meeting the needs of the military, being able to deliver only 240 of the planned 528 aircraft and just 80 of the planned 660 aircraft engines in 1923.[67]

The Red Fleet played a very marginal role during the Civil War and would continue to do so afterwards. Of the 60,567,205 rubles the military spent on equipment and weaponry in the 1922/23 budget year, only 1,800,000, or 2.97%, were spent on naval purchases. Aside from a lack of interest and funds, there was also a lack of capacity in the early 1920s, as there was just a single armaments factory in the entire Soviet Union dedicated to the production of naval equipment.[68] Production capacity was even more of a limiting factor for armor; in the 1920s, the Soviet Union had a grand total of zero tank factories and the handful of tanks that were produced were built in small-scale workshops.

When the state of the Red Army was intensely debated in the summer of 1923, the Politburo also devised a Five Year Plan to specifically build up the armaments industry. For this purpose, the Red Army and the Red Fleet would see their budget for the purchase of military equipment soar from 339,237,205 rubles in 1923/24, to 382,630,800 rubles in 1924/25, and all the way to 463,947,000 rubles in 1927/28.[69]

However, like with the other plans for the Red Army, this project too failed in the face of budget cuts. For the 1924/25 budget year, the Politburo set the budget of the Red Army, the Red Fleet, and the armaments industry at just 380 million rubles.[70] The combined military budget was therefore 2,630,800 rubles lower than what the planners had in mind for the armaments industry alone. On 7 May 1924, a frustrated Trotsky held a speech at a Red Army academy in which he said:

> We tried to realize a five year plan, a two year plan for the buildup [of the Red Army], but they [the plans] failed. We had made a great many attempts, they failed not because of internal defects of the plans, but because these plans were not sufficiently coordinated with the economic and financial plans of our country. [...] The economic plans of our country [...] were and are in a rudimentary state, [...] we are very poor in technical and especially organizational respects, therefore we can set ourselves great tasks only in a perspective of many years.[71]

While both the Red Army and the armaments industry supporting it were in a truly catastrophic state, this curiously had no impact on contemporary debates on military strategy and the war of the future.[72] Despite the technological and industrial backwardness of the Soviet Union, it was assumed that in the future, it would be able to sustain both a long and highly technologically advanced war. For Trotsky, the decisive role in that war would be played by aircraft and chemical weapons, which would usher in an era of total war, negating the traditional distinction between the military and civilians. On 19 May 1924 Trotsky held a speech in which he outlined his vision:

> Air squadrons with enormous carrying capacity and range transport [chemical weapons] deep into rear areas and thereby not only exterminate the [traditional] front, [...] but also erase the distinction between the army and the civilian population. We have said more than once that in the future war, not only the army will fight, but the entire people.[73]

Even though the use of chemical weapons played an ever-increasing role in Soviet military thinking after its successful use in the Tambov Rebellion, the Soviet chemical industry remained in very poor shape.

Like everywhere else, there was a shortage of specialists, the factories and facilities were technologically behind, and the lack of funds prevented modernization. The state of the chemical industry not only affected the production of chemical weapons, but also slowed down the production of other military goods such as ammunition and explosives, further weakening the Soviet Union. In 1925, the chief of the chemical industry warned Felix Dzerzhinsky of the dismal state it was in: "Together with other important branches of industry, the chemical industry belongs to the most disorganized ones." According to him, the main issue was the lack of funds.[74]

On 28 May 1926, confronted with countless similar reports, Dzerzhinsky wrote to his closest associates, Kraval and Shtern, complaining about the terrible state of all sectors of the armaments industry. Among others, Dzerzhinsky identified as main problems a bloated workforce, both in regards to workers and clerks, "ridiculous work quotas" and "extremely confusing finances". He then told his associates: "I ask each of you to compile available information from each of your sectors and to present me with a project to save the armaments industry."[75]

This was not the only probe into this issue. At the same time, either in May or June 1926, the secret Rykov commission for defense also gave the order to examine the work of the administration of the armaments industry in general as well as that of the individual factories.[76] Four members of the commission personally visited 18 factories, half of all armaments factories in the Soviet Union; for the rest, they relied on data provided by the administration of the armaments industry. Their findings were as devastating as they were expected: Machines were in very poor condition, for the most part obsolete (in many cases older than 35 years), and in many factories, up to 60% of these machines were completely worn out. Furthermore, the probe also criticized the extremely poor organization, horrible work discipline and mismanagement in all sectors.[77]

On 5 July 1926, the Rykov commission discussed this report and began to draw up a plan to revive the armaments industry. In its proposal, the commission stated:

The work of the defense plants and the defense industry suffers from colossal defects both in regards to financial-economic policy as well as in regards to labor organization. In the factories of the defense industry there is an enormous surplus of clerks and in some cases a surplus of workers, especially of unskilled workers. Labor productivity, work quotas and discipline are inadequate in the factories, and in some cases there is no discipline at all. It has been noted that the factories are not fully utilized with armaments orders, there is no scheduled work. The production of civilian and military products shows enormous defects, in particular in regards to planning and production technology. Significant defects have been noted both in civilian and military products, large backlogs in reporting in all factories, [...] and finally, the lack of any organization of the administration, both at the center and locally. All these above-mentioned defects can be explained in part by objective causes, which slow down the recovery of the defense industry and its parts. However, a significant part of these defects could be remedied.[78]

The commission proposed to reorganize the administration of the defense industry and the merger of the different armaments factories into just five different trusts, for each of the five major branches of the defense industry. The thus reorganized defense industry was to employ 84,215 workers in total, while the central administration was to be shrunk down to just 400. Furthermore, the commission also suggested a number of smaller organizational changes to revive the ailing defense industry.[79]

On 8 July 1926, the Politburo discussed the proposal of the Rykov commission and confirmed the proposed measures. It then set up another commission consisting of Dzerzhinsky, Voroshilov, and Tomsky, and tasked it with the implementation of this plan. At the same time, the Politburo dismissed two of the leading functionaries in the defense industry, Berezin and Sharko, after the Rykov commission had pinned the blame for the problems on them.[80] With the defense industry reorganized and the worst functionaries punished, the Politburo hoped that the Soviet defense industry was now on the path of recovery. However, this did not happen.

Chapter 7

The German Red October of 1923 and the Bolsheviks

When one considers the catastrophic state that the Red Army and the Soviet armaments industry found themselves in during the early 1920s, one would expect that the Soviet Union would have sought to avoid open conflict with its neighbors at all costs. However, this was not the case. Still wedded to their idea of world revolution, Soviet leaders remained committed to an expansionist foreign policy.

The Red Army's defeat at the gates of Warsaw in August 1920 did nothing to dissuade Lenin and his comrades from trying to bring about world revolution. If anything, Warsaw was merely a setback during which the Soviet Union would catch its breath. Lenin was intent to use this hopefully brief break to consolidate communist power within the Soviet Union and to rebuild the country's ravaged economy, so that it would be better prepared for the next stage of the world revolution than it was in the summer of 1920. Time was on his side. After all, Lenin and his fellow communists knew that the communist world revolution was inescapable. For them, the inevitability of the collapse of capitalism and the resulting imperialist wars between the capitalist states were genuine articles of faith. For example, on 6 March 1920, Lenin explained in a speech:

> The fall of the capitalist governments is unavoidable, because everybody can see that another war like the last one is inevitable if the imperialists and the bourgeoisie remain in power. [...] *Wars are inevitable* because of private property. War is inevitable between Britain, which has acquired colonies through plunder, and France, which considers herself robbed of her full share. No one knows where and how it will break out, but everybody sees, knows and says that war is inevitable, and is being prepared again.[1]

Nine months later, on 21 December 1920, Lenin stated in a speech: "The respite will be temporary. The experience of the history of revolutions and great conflicts teaches us that wars, a series of wars, are inevitable."[2] Stalin was animated by the same spirit, stating that the inevitability of military confrontations was a law of history.[3] On 3 December 1927, he elaborated:

> Partial stabilisation is giving rise to an intensification of the crisis of capitalism, and the growing crisis is upsetting stabilization – such are the dialectics of the development of capitalism in the present period of history. […] The only 'way out' left open for capitalism is a new redivision of colonies and of spheres of influence by force, by means of armed collisions, by means of new imperialist wars. Stabilisation is intensifying the crisis of capitalism.[4]

The numerous political, economic, and social crises in post-war Europe and indeed the world seemed to prove right the Bolsheviks' vision of world history. Thus their strategy was to stoke conflict among the "imperialist" powers to trigger civil wars or even a greater "imperialist" war. In that case, the Bolsheviks would intervene at an opportune time and unleash a true revolutionary war on their enemies, trying to replicate their success in Russia in 1917.

Despite the setback in 1920, Germany remained a key feature in these plans. After all, Germany still had both a powerful industry and a large population base, and the ongoing turmoil meant that the Bolsheviks still saw it as the most promising candidate for the next major communist revolution. The communists' chance came in 1923. After the German government defaulted on its reparations payments, French and Belgian troops occupied the heavily industrialized Ruhr valley on 11 January 1923.

The occupation triggered a political and economic earthquake. The German government issued a call for passive resistance in order to drive out the French and Belgians, and both German workers and civil servants went on strike, with many engaging in acts of sabotage as well. By the summer of that year, strikes and unrest had spread to the rest of Germany as the economic disruptions made both unemployment and inflation skyrocket. Both hit the working classes particularly hard and the mood turned sour. The German communists immediately stepped in and vigorously supported the passive resistance. As a result, their influence grew immensely.[5]

The events in Germany captivated the party leadership in Moscow – the long-awaited German revolution was finally at hand. "The most important and decisive period in the history of our [Bolshevik] revolution" was approaching, rejoiced Zinoviev on 21 September 1923.[6] Already on 31 July he had written to Stalin:

> The crisis in Germany is evolving very fast. A new chapter of the German revolution is beginning. Soon we will face grand challenges. The NEP will open up new possibilities. The minimum that we currently require is the question of: 1) supplying the German communists with a great number of weapons; 2) the progressive mobilization of around 50 of our best party members of the armed workers' group for their gradual transfer to Germany. The time of gigantic events in Germany is approaching. The time approaches in which we have to make decisions of world-historical importance.[7]

As the German crisis continued to escalate, the Politburo summoned Zinoviev, Trotsky and Bukharin to Moscow on 8 August 1923. Later that month, on 21 August, the Politburo set up a special commission that included prominent Bolsheviks such as Zinoviev, Kamenev, Trotsky, Radek, and Stalin, whose task it was to deal with the German question. The very next day, the commission presented the Politburo with several proposals, which were accepted: "On the basis of the information available to the Central Committee, in particular thanks to letters from leading comrades in the German communist party, the Central Committee judges that the German proletariat stands immediately before the decisive power struggles."[8]

The Politburo further resolved: "a) The working masses of the [Soviet] Republics are to be prepared for the coming events. b) The combat units of the Union are to be put into a state of mobilization. [...] c) The German workers are to be supported economically."[9] To support the German revolutionaries, the Soviet government issued an order in September, according to which 60 million pud of grain were to be transported immediately to the border as well as to Petrograd. At the same time, a reserve fund was to be created for the revolutionaries. Furthermore, 20,000 Soviet communists had been chosen to be sent to Germany in case of a revolution, Grigory Bessedovsky wrote in 1930. The Red Army transferred troops to the Western border with Poland as well, especially cavalry units.[10]

On 23 August, the Executive Committee of the Comintern – which was under the firm control of the Politburo – decided "to convene – on 20 September at the latest – a conference on the topic of 'The German Revolution' to which not only members of the [German] KPD but also delegations of the French, Belgian, Czechoslovak, and Polish parties were invited."[11] This secret conference did indeed take place in Moscow on 25 September 1923. Aside from members of the executive of the RCP(b) and a contingent from the KPD, further delegations from the communist parties of France and Czechoslovakia were also in attendance. During the conference, its chairman – Zinoviev – told the foreign guests: "The German revolution is not a local revolution, but the start of an international revolution, and all parties have to understand what this is about."[12]

Just three days earlier, on 22 September, Zinoviev had presented his "theses on the coming 'German revolution' and the tasks of the Russian communists" at a secret meeting of the Central Committee, in the course of which he laid down the Soviet strategy:

> As of now it has become completely clear that a proletarian revolution in Germany is not just inevitable, but that it has moved very close – extremely close. [...] What wonders of energy the 20 million German proletarians – the principal core of the international proletariat – will unleash is very hard to foretell, however. [...] The proletarian revolution in Germany already gains in its beginnings an even greater international significance than was the case with the Russian one. It lies precisely in the center of Europe. [...] Germany has a powerful proletariat that will shake every equilibrium in the rest of Europe when it stretches its limbs. [...] Within days, Soviet Germany will enter the most cordial alliance with the USSR. This alliance will grant the working masses in Germany and the USSR untold benefits. The USSR with its leadership in agriculture and Germany with its leadership in industry will complement each other perfectly.

An alliance between Soviet Germany and the USSR will very soon become the greatest economic power. [...] The agricultural sector of the USSR would benefit from such an alliance to an extraordinary extent, because our villages would – under good conditions – gain access to the necessary agricultural machinery, fertilizers and such. The industry of Soviet Germany would benefit in a non-minor way, because it would secure great amounts of raw materials and access to markets. The most dangerous weak points of the NEP in the Soviet Union would be neutralized most effectively. The alliance between Soviet Russia and Soviet Germany will usher in a new phase for the NEP in Russia, speed up the development of socialist state industry of the USSR and cement it [...]. The coming [...] proletarian revolution in Germany will help Soviet Russia emerge victorious at the decisive front of the socialist buildup of the economy once and for all, and thereby create an unshakable basis for the socialist economic system in all of Europe. The alliance between Soviet Germany and the USSR will have a no less powerful military base. [...] The coming German revolution brings us – to the highest degree – closer to the revolution in Europe and then also the world revolution. The principal slogan of the Bolsheviks, that of the 'world revolution' is taking shape for the first time in flesh and blood.[13]

The rest of the Politburo agreed with Zinoviev's assessment. Already two days earlier, on 20 September, Stalin had written to August Thalheimer, the editor of the communist newspaper *Rote Fahne* and a senior KPD leader: "The coming revolution in Germany is the most important world event of our days. The victory of the revolution in Germany will be of greater importance for the proletariat in Europe and America than the Russian revolution six years ago. The victory of the German proletariat will without a doubt shift the center of the World Revolution from Moscow to Berlin."[14]

For the Bolshevik leadership, the German revolution not only heralded the beginning of the World Revolution, but also represented the solution to all the economic, political and social problems that were plaguing the Soviet Union. They came to see the success of the German Revolution as the key for the Soviet Union's continued existence. As Stalin put it during a Politburo debate on 21 August 1923:

It appears to me that it is clear that the main question that we are confronted with now is the *question of the existence of our federation.* Either the revolution fails in Germany and slays us, or the revolution succeeds there, everything goes well and the situation is secure. There is no other choice. The behavior of the RCP is important. And the basis of the question is a great exertion of our military strength.[15]

For the Bolsheviks, it was obvious that a German revolution would trigger a war which in turn would force the Soviet Union to intervene. Therefore, troops were mobilized, propaganda campaigns were launched, and revolutionary activists were sent to Germany. Karl Radek himself became the representative of the Politburo in Germany.[16]

For the communists in Moscow it was clear that as the first step in the event of a successful German revolution, they had to find a way to supply their German comrades with weapons and food. The second step was also clear: a war against Poland, because without a land border, a proper military-economic alliance between Soviet Germany and Soviet Russia was unthinkable. On 19 August, Stalin responded to earlier comments by Zinoviev on the German Revolution, which the latter had made during a session of the Politburo on 15 August:

In the theses one has to say loud and clear that a revolution in Germany and our aid in the form of food, weapons, people and so on means that there will be a war between Russia and Poland and perhaps against other buffer states as well, because it is clear that without victory in a war – at least against Poland – we will not be able to send food to Germany or to maintain contact with Germany (to hope that Poland will remain neutral in the case of a workers' revolution in Germany and will provide access via the Polish corridor and Lithuania means to hope for a miracle; the same has to be said about Latvia, and even more about England, which will not permit shipments by sea). I am not even talking about other pillars of military assistance given by us to revolutionary Germany. If we really want to help the Germans – and we want to and need to help – then we have to prepare for war, in all seriousness and on all fronts, because at the end it will be about the existence of the Soviet federation and the fate of world peace for the near future.[17]

Two days later, Stalin explained the international situation during a Politburo debate:

> For us, a shared border with Germany is very important and necessary. One has to tear down one of the bourgeois buffer states and create a corridor to Germany. Preparations have to be concluded by the time of the revolution. As of now, it is not clear how to do that, but the issue has to be worked on.[18]

The other Bolshevik leaders thought the same. Unfortunately, however, the Red Army was in a catastrophic state and even though it was the numerically strongest army in Europe, it was poorly led, equipped and trained. Even worse, most of the recruits were peasants, many of whom were not eager to shed blood for a regime they hated. The Polish army meanwhile was again significantly outnumbered, but in the years after 1920 it had received better armaments and training, and was better motivated as well. This did not deter everyone. One of the more enthusiastic Bolsheviks was Sergey Gusev, the chief of the political administration of the Red Army, who wrote to Zinoviev:

> Comrade Zinoviev! Did you not consider that in the case of a revolution in Germany and our war against Poland and Romania[19], our attack [nastupleniye] on Eastern Galicia (where instigating an uprising is not difficult) and our 'accidental' breakthrough into Czechoslovakia could be of decisive significance? There [in Czechoslovakia], with the strong communist party, a revolution is absolutely possible (with the 'support' of two to three of our divisions). That way we would 1.) find ourselves in the rear of Poland and Poland's fate would be sealed, 2.) we would create a 'corridor' to Soviet Germany, 3.) we would have a Czechoslovak Red Army.[20]

Guzev's idea was far too bold for Stalin, who knew about the poor state of the Red Army and urged caution: "The plan is also problematic in and of itself. Not these questions are decisive today, but a different one, namely: Under which legal pretext are the soldiers to be mobilized so as to preserve the appearance of being peace-loving, or at least defensive."[21]

Nevertheless, the Politburo took Guzev's ideas seriously. Among others, on 13 November 1923, the Politburo decided to fund armed Ukrainian organizations in Polish Eastern Galicia and to infiltrate Soviet agents in order to take control of them. Additionally, 2,000–3,000 Galician fighters were to be brought from Czechoslovakia to Soviet Ukraine, where the GPU would then "carefully filter" them.[22]

While the Politburo prepared for a new attack on Poland, Trotsky argued that the Politburo should try to pressure the Polish government first. In a letter from 3 October, directed at the members of the Politburo and the Central Control Committee, he urged his comrades to demand from Poland mutual non-intervention in German affairs as well as allowing the free transit of Soviet grain and German industrial goods if Poland wished peace.[23] Even the doves were eager to threaten war.

Although others, including Stalin, were rather skeptical of Trotsky's attempt at diplomacy,[24] the Politburo did decide to give negotiations a chance and ordered the People's Commissariat of Foreign Affairs to mellow its posture towards Poland in order to facilitate talks. A few days later, on 18 and 13 October, Polish and Soviet emissaries met for negotiations in which the Soviets also demanded military access on top of commercial transit. Disappointingly for Moscow, the Polish emissary made it clear that his government would certainly refuse such a deal.[25]

The Politburo remained undeterred and on 18 October resolved to send its emissary to Warsaw to "carefully" lead negotiations.[26] The emissary, Kopp, arrived in Warsaw in early November and immediately sought to initiate talks. In order to convince the Polish side to indeed allow the transit of goods – and a few Red Army cavalry brigades[27] – the Politburo was ready to make wide-ranging concessions towards Poland. Bessedovsky, who worked at the Soviet legation in Warsaw at the time, reported: "In return, Poland was offered from the Soviet side [...]: 1.) free transit of Polish goods to The Middle and the Far East through Soviet territory; 2.) the payment of 30 million gold rubles which had to be delivered as indirect payment according to the Treaty of Riga; 3.) freedom of action in Eastern Prussia."[28]

In other words – the Soviet Union offered Poland all of East Prussia if it only gave them commercial and limited military access. Bessedovsky was not the only one to mention this. On 2 November 1923, Trotsky wrote a letter to Chicherin in which he confirmed that he hoped Poland could be coaxed into an agreement with the Soviet Union if it was given East Prussia.[29] According to Bessedovsky, Kopp had claimed that:

Politically, Moscow believed it to even be beneficial for the future Soviet Germany to lose East Prussia temporarily. For the first period of existence of Soviet power in Germany, East Prussia would only become the cradle of the Vendee. But once Soviet Germany had grown in strength, the reconquest of East Prussia would cause no great difficulties.[30]

Despite making some headway, these negotiations came to nothing as Kopp was suddenly ordered back to Moscow. The reason for this was simple: While Moscow was plotting to intervene in Germany, the revolutionaries within Germany had failed at their task and any such deal was pointless now.[31]

In Germany, the political establishment had sensed the existential crisis the country was in and in August 1923, the major parties had come together to form a new, stable government that was supported by a grand coalition. On 26 September 1923, the new chancellor Stresemann was thus able to finally end the disastrous policy of passive resistance in the Ruhr area, which had triggered the entire crisis in the first place. This action immediately exacerbated the domestic crisis in the immediate aftermath: Inflation soared to dizzying heights, unemployment rose, and in October and November 1923, a series of separatist, communist, and far-right rebellions tried to overthrow the government. The most well-known of these attempts was Hitler's miserably-planned and executed Beer Hall Putsch in Munich on 9 November 1923, which local authorities quashed with ease. Once these threats were eliminated, however, Stresemann's efforts gradually stabilized the country both economically and politically.[32] The time for revolution was over.

This was devastating for the German communists, whose own attempt at revolution had failed in late October 1923. On 22 October, communist groups in Hamburg attacked 13 police stations and captured around 100 rifles which they handed out to roughly 120 rebels. Although the barricades went up as planned, Hamburg's workers refused to stage a general strike.

The insurrectionists were able to beat back a police counterattack on 24 October, but without the support of the workers their struggle was hopeless so in the night, they abandoned their barricades and their cause.[33]

The German communists were thoroughly disillusioned. On 26 October 1923, the head of military operations at the KPD headquarters concluded: "Because the fighting did not trigger a mass movement among Hamburg's workers or have any repercussions in the country, it is evident that our functionaries […] with their assertions 'that the masses can no longer be controlled' misjudged the situation."[34]

Nevertheless, it took a while before Moscow and the KPD realized that the German revolution was over before it had even begun. As soon as the realization came, so began the search for those responsible for this disaster. The German historian Friedrich Firsow described the scenes that unfolded:

> Of course, the fantastic plans of the RCP(b) that were forced onto the Komintern and the KPD were not seen as the cause of the defeat. The leadership of the KPD had known that very little had been done to prepare for the uprising, but still had dutifully taken Zinoviev's and Stalin's instructions. In the new, official narrative, the failure to follow the directives from Moscow in the face of the betrayal by leftwing social democrats was considered the main reason for the defeat.[35]

The fallout of the failed revolution also triggered a veritable struggle in Moscow between the Troika (Stalin-Zinoviev-Kamenev) on one side, and Trotsky, Pyatakov, and Radek on the other. While both agreed that the primary issues were mistakes by the KPD and the "betrayal" of the social democrats, backed by the Politburo and Central Committee, Stalin's tight grip on the party bureaucracy allowed the Troika to pin some of the responsibility on their rivals as well.[36]

The failure of the German revolution in the autumn of 1923 thus became a key turning point for the Soviet Union. Domestically, it cemented the power of Stalin, Zinoviev, and Kamenev just months before Lenin's death in January 1924, while simultaneously diminishing the standing of Trotsky, who used to be the second man in Bolshevik Russia. In Germany, meanwhile, the economic and the political situation continued to stabilize like in the rest of Europe – before long, the Roaring Twenties were in full swing. And with prosperity returning, the prospects of revolution were waning. The Soviet Union was isolated and would remain so for the time being.

Crisis of Faith

The events of 1923 triggered a veritable ideological crisis among the Bolsheviks as their prophecies of a German revolution failed to manifest. Indeed, their entire strategy since the conclusion of the Russian Civil War had hinged upon the success of the KPD, which would then allow them to continue their irresistible advance west. Even worse, they also depended on a Soviet Germany to save the Soviet Union from its enormous economic, social, and political troubles. Now they had to deal with all of that on their own. On 19 April 1924, Trotsky wrote in *Pravda*:

> And in the second half of last year, the German revolution became more and more apparent each day. Therein we saw a fundamental fact of geopolitical development. Had the German revolution been successful, the balance of power of the world would have changed completely. The Soviet Union with its 130 million strong population, with its countless resources on the one side, and Germany with its technology, its culture and its working class on the other side, would create an unbeatable block and a powerful alliance which would very quickly influence the development in Europe and in the entire world.[37]

While Trotsky lamented what he called the "German catastrophe,"[38] Stalin had not given up hope yet. As late as 3 July 1924, he proclaimed in a speech: "If the revolutionary conflagration begins at one corner of Europe, it will surely be in Germany."[39] Before long, however, even he had to admit that it was over: "It is also beyond doubt that in Germany, in the center of Europe, the period of revolutionary upsurge has come to an end."[40]

In his book, Bessedovsky recalled the mood when he travelled back to Moscow in the summer of 1924:

The atmosphere in Moscow was bad. The collapse of the German revolution triggered mood swings and pessimism in wide party circles. Everyone understood that the last revolutionary trump card of an entire historical epoch had been beaten. One looked for culprits for the failure and everything was blamed on Radek, the unlucky emissary-in-chief of the Komintern. In the circles close to Trotsky there was a saying that there simply had not been enough courage to deploy the waiting Red cavalry and let it move into Germany. [...] One could sense that within the party, a wide-ranging crisis was brewing and that new, fierce fighting lay ahead.[41]

With the revolution in the West stalled, the Bolsheviks now turned towards Asia and Africa, where they sought to use the "growth and consolidation of the national-liberation movements in India, China, Egypt, Indonesia, North Africa, etc., which are undermining capitalism's rear", as Stalin wrote in *Pravda* on 22 March 1925.[42] By pressuring the European empires abroad, they hoped to destabilize the situation back in their European mainland.

The place where the Bolsheviks were the most active and also the most successful was China, where they had begun their work as early as 1920 and brought about the founding of the Communist Party of China on 23 July 1921. After nearly three decades of struggle, the CPC under the leadership of Mao Tse-Tung would manage to take more or less full control of the Chinese mainland in 1949. During the rule of Mao Tse-Tung alone, up to 70 million Chinese were killed as a result of his policies.[43] Despite these efforts, it was clear that Europe was still the primary focus of the communist revolutionary efforts; the hinterland of capitalism – China, India, North Africa – were only of secondary importance.

Chapter 8

Poland – The Testing Ground of Revolutionary Irredentism

Poland's continued refusal to let the Red Army march through its lands to Germany ensured that it remained a thorn in the side of Soviet leaders. Aside from ideological issues, economic considerations played a key role as well. On 19 October 1923, when the Soviets were still waiting with bated breath for the seemingly imminent outbreak of the German Revolution, Trotsky held a speech at the 3rd Moscow conference of the All-Russian Metalworkers Union:

> The German proletariat controls the industrial goods that we need. Between Germany and the Soviet Union there should be an exchange of goods. The geographic key to this exchange of goods lies in Poland's hands. For us, Poland can either be a bridge or a barrier. In the case that Poland serves as a transit bridge for us, we shall pay them in cash. If we cannot transport our grain to the German workers in exchange for necessary industrial goods, *we suffocate economically*. Therefore, Poland will be pressured immensely if it becomes a barrier between us and Germany. We are prepared to pay a high price for peace, but we will not permit *our economic death* and the starvation of the German proletariat.[1]

The events of autumn 1923 once again showed the Bolsheviks that Poland would remain uncooperative on the transit question as the consensus in Poland saw Germany and the Soviet Union as the chief enemies of Poland's newly-won independence. The Polish point of view was further reinforced by the German-Soviet Treaty of Rapallo from 16 April 1922, which was primarily directed against Poland. In that treaty, both countries agreed to establish official diplomatic ties, renounced reparations claims against one another, and signed a trade deal, giving each other most-favored-nation treatment. Furthermore, they also established secret military cooperation.[2]

Germany's Reichskanzler Joseph Karl Wirth explained the necessity of Rapallo to Count Brockdorff-Rantzau, the later German ambassador to Moscow: "… and this I tell you unapologetically: Poland must be finished off. My policies are geared towards this goal. […] I do not sign treaties that could strengthen Poland. […] For this reason, I have signed the Treaty of Rapallo."[3] Poland's fears were not unfounded, and aside from keeping the Soviet Union and Germany apart from each other, Poland also worked together with other European powers – with France against Germany, and with Romania against the Soviet Union.

With the German Revolution having ended in complete failure, the focus of the Bolsheviks' subversive activities shifted towards Poland. There, the main role was given to the GPU-infiltrated Communist Party of Poland (KPP), which was both financed and led by Moscow. On 11 August 1924, Pavel Lapichinsky, a Soviet communist, wrote a letter to Felix Dzerzhinsky in which he detailed the negative consequences of the GPU infiltration of the KPP. Aside from spying, Soviet agents also systematically perpetrated terrorist attacks within Poland while relying on the KPP for aid:

> Broad party circles and even party functionaries are being used for work in both areas [communist organization and Soviet terrorist attacks in Poland] contrary to the guidelines. In many cases one cannot differentiate any more where the party structures end and where our counterintelligence [Soviet agency] begins. […] Nearly the entire Ukrainian organization is literally from the bottom to the top inextricably intertwined with counterintelligence.[4]

On 28 August 1924, the Politburo decided to increase its subsidies to the KPP by 140,000 gold rubles for the next six months.[5] One of the goals was for the KPP to organize a party conference, which did occur in late January 1925 – in Moscow. Ahead of the conference, on 3 January 1925, the Politburo created a commission that was tasked with dealing with the "Polish party conference". That commission was headed by Zinoviev and also included other high-ranking communists such as Dzerzhinsky, Unszlicht, Rykov, Bukharin and Stalin. Clearly, the Politburo assigned it very high importance. The conference was to "verify all information on the state of the [communist] movement in Poland, in particular on the borders of Poland, and to inform the Politburo of the Central Committee about the result."[6] In the course of the conference, the leaders of the KPP received detailed instructions which had been prepared by Dmitri Manuilsky, a close associate of Stalin who dealt with the issue of nationalities on behalf of the party and the Komintern.[7] On 30 January 1925, Manuilsky presented his ideas about how the KPP should operate to the assembled Polish comrades:

> The original role of contemporary Poland is to act as a barrier to halt the spread of communist ideas to the West. This is the first and most important conclusion when characterizing the international role of Poland. [...] Therefore, the destruction of bourgeois Poland and the transformation of it into a proletarian-peasant and Soviet Poland is the task of the entire international proletariat at the moment.[8]

In his presentation, Manuilsky also brought up the issue of the German minority in Poland. Until then, the KPP had claimed that this was not an issue at all. Manuilsky vehemently rejected their stance, pointing at the results of the referendum in Upper Silesia on 20 March 1921,[9] especially in the cities of Kattowitz and Königshütte, where a majority of the urban population had voted to stay in Germany but found itself in Poland. Manuilsky went even further, suggesting that the assertion of the KPP that there was no German question in Poland could be interpreted as a sign that Polish nationalism had taken root in its Central Committee.[10]

While the idea to destabilize Poland by stirring up ethnic hatred was not new, it gradually began to emerge as the primary weapon in the fight against Poland in 1923/4. After all, the abysmal state of the Red Army and the Soviet armaments industry made a successful invasion of Poland virtually impossible. Instead, Poland became the primary field of experimentation for Soviet attempts to subvert countries by fomenting ethnic conflict during this period of "revolutionary ebb". The lessons of the activities in Poland were to be then transferred to other countries in Southern and Eastern Europe, such as Czechoslovakia or Yugoslavia.

As Zinoviev expounded in his theses about the German Revolution from 20 September 1923, the "Polish bourgeoisie" was the primary enemy of the German and Russian Revolutions and that it would fight the revolutionaries tooth and nail. "However," Zinoviev continued "one cannot underestimate the importance of national conflicts that will break out within Poland when war comes. The national moment (Ukrainians, Lithuanians, Belarusians, Germans, Jews) causes great difficulties for the Polish ruling clique."[11]

Aside from strategic considerations, Poland also seemed ripe for the picking at the time. While most other European countries had more or less recovered after the chaos of the post-war era, Poland remained mired in deep economic crisis, internal political conflicts as well as social and ethnic strife. The situation worsened considerably in 1925, when Germany began a customs war with Poland that resulted in the breakdown of Polish international trade. The resulting economic crisis triggered political turmoil and Poland found itself facing imminent disaster by the end of the year. Józef Piłsudski, one of the pre-eminent figures of Polish independence, saw himself forced to return to the political scene which he had abandoned just 3 years earlier. His return was far from universally welcomed, however, and in early 1926 Poland was sliding towards civil war between Józef Piłsudski and his supporters, and the government.[12]

This was exciting news for Moscow, since a civil war could result in a partition of Poland between the Soviet Union and Germany – Poland would have been turned from a barrier into a bridge. On 25 March 1926, the Politburo created a commission for Polish issues, headed by none other than Zinoviev; Dzerzhinsky, Chicherin, Voroshilov, and Bogucki (KPP) also participated.[13] In their session on 30 March 1926, the commission gave Chicherin the task to intensify exploratory talks with Piłsudski's camp and other Polish political groupings.[14] In a letter to Bogucki on 17 April, Dzerzhinsky laid down the aims of the communists in the Polish crisis: "I favor that our party [intervenes] in the fight raging between the National Democrats and Piłsudski, throwing its entire weight against National Democrats and the PPS [Polish Socialist Party] and supporting Piłsudski, to force him to the left and to ignite a peasant revolution."[15]

The crisis came to a head on 12 May when Piłsudski and military units loyal to him took over Warsaw. In accordance with the instructions from

Moscow, the KPP supported the coup, hoping to help spark a civil war. On 19 May, Zinoviev issued further guidelines for the KPP with the aim of "growing the movement among the masses and the exacerbation of the civil war between Piłsudski and his enemies."[16]

However, the government had surrendered on 14 May after short, but bloody fighting that claimed the lives of 379 people. A new government was quickly formed. Formally, the minister of defense and chief of the army, Piłsudski was now the most powerful man in Poland. With his power secured, the constitution remained largely in place, aside from a weakening of the parliament.[17] The crisis was over.

Moscow soon realized what had happened. On 20 May 1926, the Politburo came to the conclusion that having the KPP support Piłsudski had been a serious political mistake, for which Stalin later blamed Zinoviev personally.[18] On 20 May, the Politburo approved of the new policy towards Piłsudski that the Polish commission had formulated:

c) An open, exposing campaign against Piłsudski and his government is to begin; one has to show that in reality, Piłsudski has entered an alliance with the fascists against the workers and peasants. [...] e) The criticism, decisive exposing and struggle against the government have to be fought in a very broad fashion, in which especially the matters of peace with all neighbors are to be highlighted.[19]

Disheartened by Piłsudski 's success in restoring order in Poland, the Politburo ordered a wide-ranging propaganda campaign against him and his government in which he was to be denounced as a "fascist" and "warmonger". The results of this propaganda campaign are still noticeable to this day.[20]

Since Piłsudski commanded a great degree of respect in Poland, his takeover soon stabilized the volatile political situation. As Poland began to regain its economic footing as well, the window of opportunity for an imminent civil war or even a Polish "peasant revolution" closed once again.[21]

The head of the GPU, Felix Dzerzhinsky, realized it by late June 1926. On 25 June, he wrote to his deputy Yagoda: "It becomes clear to me that Piłsudski's coup turns out to be the work of the nationalist forces in Poland

– which are fully backed by England – that are aimed against 'Russia', i.e. against us. Because of this, it is imperative to use all of our forces to make defensive preparations. The target of their attack will be Belarus and Ukraine – Minsk and Kyiv as key cities."[22] Piłsudski's supposed war plans in 1926 became a main rallying cry to mobilize both the party and Soviet society in general over the coming years. Naturally, Poland never planned or even intended to attack the Soviet Union in 1926 or at a later point.[23]

Chapter 9

The Social, Economic and Ethnic Crisis of the Soviet Union in the Mid-1920s

By 1924, most European countries had recovered from the post-war chaos and their economies were booming once again. The newfound calm and prosperity helped defuse social tensions, much to the chagrin of the Bolshevik leaders in Moscow. On 18 December 1925, a frustrated Stalin reported to the assembled party members at the XIV Party Congress:

> Capitalism is emerging, or has already emerged, from the chaos in production, trade and in the sphere of finance which set in, and in which it found itself, after the war. The Party called this the partial, or temporary, stabilisation of capitalism. [...] In the main, if we take Europe as a whole, production and trade are making progress, although they have not yet reached the pre-war level. [...] Coal output in Britain in 1925 amounts to 90 per cent of the pre-war level, in France to 107 per cent of the pre-war level, in Germany to 93 per cent. Steel production in Britain amounts to 98 per cent of the pre-war level, in France to 102 per cent, in Germany to 78 per cent. Consumption of raw cotton in Britain is equal to 82 per cent of the pre-war level, in France to 83 per cent, in Germany to 81 per cent. [...] The level of European trade as a whole, taking 1921, was 63 per cent of the pre-war level, but now, in 1925, it has reached 82 per cent of that level. The budgets of these countries balance in one way or another, but the balance is obtained by imposing a frightful burden of taxation upon the population. There is a fluctuation in the currency in some countries, but, in general, the former chaos is not observed. The general picture is that the post-war economic crisis in Europe is passing away, production and trade are approaching the pre-war level.[1]

On the other side of the Atlantic, the economy of the USA was in excellent shape as well and it became the world's dominant economic power in the 1920s.[2] Stalin continued:

That country [USA] is growing in every respect: as regards production, as regards trade, and as regards [capital] accumulation. I shall quote some figures. The production of grain in North America has risen above the pre-war level; it is now 104 per cent of that level. Coal output has reached 90 per cent of the pre-war level, but the deficit is compensated for by an enormous increase in the output of oil. And it must be pointed out that the oil output of America amounts to 70 per cent of world output. Steel production has risen to 147 per cent – 47 per cent above the pre-war level. The national income amounts to 130 per cent of the pre-war level – exceeding the pre-war level by 30 per cent. Foreign trade has reached 143 per cent of the pre-war level and has an enormous favourable balance in relation to the European countries. Of the total world gold reserve amounting to 9,000 million, about 5,000 million are in America.[3]

As the economies of Europe and the rest of the world recovered to the benefit of their citizens, the Soviet Union was headed for a new economic, social, ethnic, ideological, and political crisis. The main reason was the horrible state of the economy. On 2 March 1923, Lenin wrote in *Pravda*:

Economic necessity, especially under NEP, keeps the productivity of labour of the small and very small peasants at an extremely low level. Moreover, the international situation, too, threw Russia back and, by and large, reduced the labour productivity of the people to a level considerably below the pre-war level. [...] Thus, at the present time we are confronted with the question—shall we be able to hold on with our small and very small peasant production, and in our present state of ruin, until the West-European capitalist countries consummate their development towards socialism? But they are consummating it not as we formerly expected.[4]

Lenin himself pointed out that it had been the Bolsheviks themselves who had created the small and marginal peasantry when they broke up the large landholdings.[5] In October 1923, Trotsky warned that Soviet Russia desperately needed industrial goods from Germany: "If we cannot transport our grain to the German workers in exchange for industrial goods from Germany via Poland, we will suffocate economically."[6]

But even if Poland had been willing to be a bridge between Germany and the Soviet Union, Soviet grain production was just too low for it to be exported in large quantities. This was a serious problem, since grain was the chief good the Soviet Union could have sold on the world markets at the time. Before the war, Russia exported on average 600-700 million pud, sometimes even up to 900 million pud. In 1923, when the Soviet Union once again began to export grain, it only sold 50 million pud on the world markets, or less than 10% of the pre-war numbers.[7] Grain exports did not recover in the following year. On the contrary, a bad harvest forced the Soviet Union to import 83 million pud.[8] In 1925/6, the Soviet Union once again exported grain – 123 million pud. The next year, exports increased to 153 million pud before collapsing to just 27 million pud in 1927/8.[9]

The low export of grain was due to the low economic productivity of the small and marginal peasantry, which – as Lenin had observed earlier – had been created when the Bolsheviks broke up the large landholdings. Before the war, it was primarily these large landholdings that had been producing the grain that was being exported.[10] During a speech on 28 May 1928, Stalin explained the low grain production in the following terms:

> The reason is primarily and chiefly the change in the structure of our agriculture brought about by the October Revolution, the passing from large-scale landlord and large-scale kulak farming, which provided the largest amount of marketable grain, to small- and middle-peasant farming, which provides the smallest amount of marketable grain. The mere fact that before the war there were 15,000,000 to 16,000,000 individual peasant farms, whereas at preset there are 24,000,000 to 25,000,000 peasant farms, shows that now the basis of our agriculture is essentially small-peasant farming, which provides the least amount of marketable grain.[11]

Aside from the fragmentation of the large landholdings, Stalin also identified "the extreme backwardness of our agricultural technique and the exceedingly low cultural level in the countryside" as a key cause of the agricultural sector's weakness in a speech on 3 December 1927.[12] In 1925, 32% of all farms did not have draught animals, and 53.4% had only one draught animal.[13]

In 1928, Soviet peasants were cultivating nearly as much land as they did before the war – 95%. However, yields were only at 50% of the pre-war levels. And because of the low productivity, grain exports were severely limited, complained Mikoyan, the People's Commissar for External and Internal Trade, at a Politburo session in June 1928.[14].

In addition to fragmentation, technological backwardness and "the exceedingly low cultural level", Soviet agriculture was further plagued by the so-called scissors crisis, in which industrial goods were overpriced while agricultural goods remained underpriced. In 1913, gross production in the Russian agricultural sector stood at 11.79 billion rubles but due to the war it had fallen to just 6.9 billion in 1921/2. It took half a decade to reach pre-war levels, with a gross production of 12.775 billion rubles in 1926/7, equivalent to 108.3% of pre-war production. The situation in the industrial sector was similar: By 1921/22, gross industrial production had fallen to 1.344 billion from a peak of 6.391 billion in 1913. It gradually increased in the years after the war. In 1924/5, it stood at nearly 5 billion rubles and two years later it was at 100.9% of pre-war production.[15]

Unsurprisingly, foreign trade also suffered from the sluggish recovery. By 1924/5, it had risen to 1.282 billion rubles – around 27% of pre-war levels. Two years later, it had risen to 1.483 billion rubles, or just 35.3% of pre-war levels. Meanwhile, the government budget recovered slowly but still comparably fast: In 1925/6, it stood at 5.024 billion rubles or 72.4% of pre-war levels. A year later, it had soared to nearly 7 billion rubles, somewhere between 110% and 112% of pre-war levels.[16]

The primary cause of this malaise was the Bolsheviks themselves. Foreign capital shied away from investing in the anti-capitalist Soviet Union. As a result, industry lacked the capital it needed to develop. The only way out of this was to export raw materials and agricultural goods, mainly grain, as Trotsky elaborated in a speech on 3 July 1923. He was certain that grain production would rise in the coming years, allowing the Soviet Union to import machinery and entire industrial plants.[17] However, Soviet grain production failed to meet expectations and only minor amounts of grain could be exported. With the government left unable to buy foreign machinery in sufficient quantities, Soviet industry continued to fall behind.

The failure of this policy soon attracted criticism. On 3 December 1925, Felix Dzerzhinsky, in his function as Chairman of the Supreme Soviet of the National Economy, wrote a letter to Stalin in which he lamented the abysmal state of the Soviet economy. Among others, Dzerzhinsky took issue with the "mistake of state planning regarding the grain procurement plan. [...] there are many other possibilities to accelerate the export of other goods instead of grain. Without increasing exports, industry will suffocate (without imports). [...] one has to find money for the import of raw materials and industrial plants, and one has to find means for the internal financing of our industry."[18]

The lack of capital was far from the only reason for the Soviet Union's lack of industrial growth. In the same letter – which he never sent – Dzerzhinsky further elaborated:

> Against the backdrop of the conditions that prevail in industry and at the Supreme Soviet of the National Economy, I feel compelled to ask the Central Committee for my dismissal, because successful industrialization is impossible under the given circumstances. We have neither a proper nor a unified plan for the entire Soviet economy, nor coordination between the various branches of industry. That way, we are quickly moving towards crises in individual sectors, which will continue to spread, proliferate everywhere, which can then turn into a serious crisis unless the party does not immediately take the necessary measures. Personally, I am not a politician and I am unable to ask the question in time so they can be discussed and decided upon by the party (I had submitted them multiple times and nearly every time they were forwarded for further analysis, votes, etc. and in the end these questions are being worked on until today.[19]

In particular, Dzerzhinsky pointed to the general chaos in the economy, the fight between artisans and light industry against heavy industry, the lack of coordination between individual economic agencies and the chaos in the credit and financial system. Consequently, he continued, a sprawling bureaucracy began to engulf everything, as the standard response to any problem was to establish yet another institution, agency, or commission, which had to coordinate every action among themselves. The overgrown bureaucracy succeeded in suffocating economic initiative and undermined the general effectiveness of the economy. "Our agencies became more and more bureaucratic and out of touch."[20]

A few months later, on 3 July 1926, a desperate Dzerzhinsky wrote to Valerian Kuibyshev, complaining about the system of economic planning in the Soviet Union:

We have people who we could give responsibility to. However, they are currently drowning in votes, reports, papers, commissions. The capitalists in contrast had their own means and were themselves responsible. Here, it is the Council for Labor and Defense and the Politburo that are responsible for everything. We cannot compete with private entrepreneurs and capitalism like that. Here, there is no work, just pure torture. The existing commissariats and their competences, this is the paralysis of life and the life of the civil servant-bureaucrat. We cannot get out of this paralysis without a surgical intervention, without courage, without thunder. Everyone expects this surgical intervention. [...] Now we are stuck in the swamp. Discontent and expectations are everywhere. [...] I myself and my work friends are incredibly tired of these conditions. Total powerlessness. [...] I protest with my entire being against [these conditions] [...]. I fight with everyone. Without success. Therefore, I believe that only the party and your unit are able to accomplish this task, because my actions could strengthen those who would without a doubt lead the party and the country into disaster, these are Trotsky, Zinoviev, Pyatakov, Shlyakhtunov. [...] I am completely convinced that we can deal with all enemies when we find and follow the correct course of action in leading the state and in the economy, when we accelerate the lost tempo that today trails behind the necessities of life. If we do not find and follow this course of action, our opposition will grow and our country will find its dictator-gravedigger of the revolution, regardless of how great his accomplishments for the revolutions are. Nearly all of today's dictators are former Reds – Mussolini, Piłsudski. I am too exhausted by these contradictions. With such thoughts and torments that plague me, I cannot remain the chairman of the Supreme Soviet of the National Economy.[21]

At a meeting in July 1926, Dzerzhinsky wrote on a piece of paper: "I am tired of having to always play the role of the strict 'master'. I really cannot stay at the VSNKh [Supreme Soviet of the National Economy] any longer. I beg all of you to dismiss me and appoint a man, i.e. someone who will not be met with as much resistance in all questions."[22]

At the common plenum of the Central Committee and the Central Control Committee on 20 July 1926, Dzerzhinsky once again ranted against the supposed anti-party activities of the "Trotsky-Zinoviev Block". Three hours later – at 4:40 pm local time – he suddenly died.[23] With him, one of the most fanatical and murderous leading Bolsheviks had fallen victim to the terrible state of the Soviet economy.

The Price Scissors

Throughout the mid-1920s, the Soviet civilian economy was plagued by a deliberate policy of the Politburo that resulted in overly expensive consumer goods while prices for agricultural goods were overly low.[24] Aside from the general weakness of Soviet light industry, the so-called Price Scissors had been intentionally created by the Politburo as a form of alternative taxation or tribute in order to finance the build-up of industry. On 11 July 1928, during a speech at the plenum of the Central Committee of the CPSU(b), Stalin explained:

What was the dispute about yesterday? First of all, about the "scissors" between town and country. It was said that the peasant was still overpaying for manufactured goods and being underpaid for his agricultural produce. It was said that these overpayments and underpayments constitute a supertax on the peasantry, something in the nature of a "tribute," an additional tax for the sake of industrialisation, a tax which we must certainly abolish, but which we cannot abolish at all once unless we intend to undermine our industry, undermine a definite rate of development of our industry, which works for the whole country and which advances our national economy towards socialism.[…] Of course, 'supertax,' and 'additional tax' are unpleasant words, for they hit hard. But, in the first place, it is not a question of words. In the second place, the words fully correspond to the facts.[25]

An unwanted consequence of the Price Scissors was that many peasants were not inclined to sell their underpriced products in return for overpriced consumer goods, assuming they were available in the first place. Consequently, many peasants preferred to consume their own goods instead of selling them, and the economy remained at a relatively primitive level and the consumption of industrial and consumer goods lagged far behind pre-war levels.

Table 2: Per capita consumption of basic necessities in Russia and the Soviet Union. (1 pud =16.38kg; 1 arshin = 0.71 m^2)[26]

Consumption of	1913	1922/23	1924	Percentage of 1913
Petroleum (in pud)	0.379	0.116	0.147	39%
Salt (in pud)	28.06	14.93	20.15	72%
Wrought Iron (in pud)	1.7	0.15	0.24	14%
Steel (in pud)	1.79	0.27	0.4	22%
Cotton (in arshin)	17.3	5.3	6.8	39%
Pairs of galoshes per 1000 persons	178	38	52	30%
Matches (in boxes)	31.6	10.4	13.2	61%
Sugar (in pounds)	19.3	3.2	6.4	33%
Tobacco (in smoking units)	313	120	147	47%
Paper (in pounds)	6.6	1.7	2.4	36%

By 1926, per capita consumption of commodities had only reached 28% of pre-war levels. In 1913, the average peasant paid 34 gold rubles and 22 kopeks for consumer goods including vodka; by 1926, expenses had dropped to 16 rubles and 50 kopeks (48.2%) even though prices had nearly doubled in the meantime.[27] It has to be noted that in 1926, peasants were not buying much vodka from the state. Instead, they distilled their own alcohol or bought bootlegged alcohol on the black market.

The acute hunger for commodities only became worse over the following years,[28] and together with the Price Scissors, this led to a great deal of speculation on the black market. In the 1920s and even beyond, it was primarily this black market that dominated everyday economic life and the economic relationship between the cities and the countryside.[29]

The Vodka Monopoly to Finance the Build-up of Soviet Industry and the Red Army

One of the main ways in which the Soviet Union raised the funds needed to finance the Red Army and the expansion of its industry was through the production and sale of vodka. Over time, the sale of vodka even became one of the primary sources of income for the Soviet state as a whole. While Tsarist Russia did have a long history of alcoholism,[30] the Soviet vodka policy that emerged in 1923-25 escalated the situation in the long term, with devastating consequences for the country that are painfully visible even to this day.

The production and consumption of homemade alcohol, so-called *samogon*, was already common before the war, but during the chaos of the Civil War and the early 1920s, it experienced a true golden age. Since samogon was homemade and the government did not profit from it, Soviet leaders soon raised the alarm. On 13 January 1923, Trotsky approached the Politburo via Stalin: "The samogon question is of immense importance. If things continue as they are, we will achieve neither socialist nor capitalist accumulation." Trotsky demanded that severe measures had to be taken against samogon before issuing the reminder that "the budget question is intimately tied to the samogon question."[31]

In an OGPU report for the Pskov governorate from 2 September 1924, the authors complained about the scope of samogon production in the countryside – up to 35% of the population in certain communities were involved in the production of samogon. According to the report, "the reasons for this are historical, the so-called '[Price] Scissors', low prices for grain play a large role in the development of the samogon industry." The cost of producing a bucket of samogon was estimated to be around 2 rubles, which in turn sold for 11 rubles in the Pskov county – a profit margin of over 450%. The dispatch noted that profits were even higher in other counties of the governorate. It was estimated that in the Pskov governorate alone, around 500,000 pud of grain were being used to make samogon, all while the government was desperately searching for more grain to export.[32]

Aside from the fact that the samogon industry used up valuable grain – the Soviet Union's main export item – the Soviet government also resented that it did not receive a cut from the trade, since it happened exclusively on the black market. Additionally, it had severe health repercussions and also led to crime. The above-referenced report mentions that over 50% of prison inmates in the Pskov governorate were murderers, "where as a rule, the murders had been committed against the background of samogon." The report further stated: "[…] aside from the destruction of a great quantity of grain, crime rises in connection with samogon, not to talk about the dangerous dimensions for the health of the population."[33]

The debate around the vodka policy of the Soviet Union began as early as 1921, perhaps even beforehand. For Soviet leaders, the main point of concern was not crime or public health, but rather how to harness the vodka monopoly for the state budget. The otherwise not very squeamish Lenin decidedly rejected this idea, however. In a speech on 27 May 1921, he explained: "I think that we should not follow the example of the capitalist countries and put vodka and other intoxicants on the market, because, profitable though they are, they will lead us back to capitalism and not forward to communism."[34] Ten months later, on 28 March 1922, Lenin intervened once again: "If under present conditions the peasant must have freedom to trade within certain limits, we must give it to him, but this does not mean that we are permitting trade in raw brandy. We shall punish people for that sort of trade."[35]

Citing Lenin, Trotsky was a decided enemy of the "vodka budget" as well. In a letter to his friend Pyatakov from 23 July 1923, he wrote: "Just heard from Vladimir Ilich [Lenin], who certainly does not tend towards abstract moralization, in verbatim the following: 'You understand, if one were to create a [alcohol] monopoly, one could save oneself from the deficit, however, too many moral-political arguments speak against it."[36]

Naturally, not everyone agreed with Lenin and Trotsky. As Lenin grew increasingly sick, his influence began to wane while the power of the Stalin-led "vodka faction" began to wax. Ironically, they also invoked Lenin. On 13 August, 1923, a rather unhappy Trotsky wrote to Nikolai Semashko, the People's Commissar of Public Health of the RFSR:

The existence of a large and powerful faction whose program is solely to have the budget be based upon vodka is an undeniable fact. This faction invokes Vladimir Ilich [Lenin] in doing so, which is not right in my opinion. But that is not the question here. Considering our slow and weak [economic] recovery, the attempt to base our budget on vodka resembles the behavior of a starving man who cuts out his most important muscles to satisfy his hunger. As of now, the supporters of the drunken budget are on the retreat as far as I can tell. That is the result of the party's first reaction to the rumors about the alcoholization of the Soviet build-up.[37]

In his letter, Trotsky also called for a broad campaign against alcoholism, especially against samogon "and not as competition for legal drunkenness, but against an acute social evil."[38]

It soon turned out that Trotsky's assertion that the supporters of the "drunken budget" were on the retreat was not quite true. On 23 July 1923, just a few weeks earlier, Trotsky had stated in a letter to Pyatakov that the local party bureaucracy ("Party-Soviet-Secretary-Bureaucracy") heavily relied on the "restoration of alcoholism" for financing. Trotsky continued: "I was told the phrase that we are supposedly no romantics, no vegetarians, no moralists, but 'sober' realists, which is why we are for a drunken budget."[39]

The same day, Trotsky wrote to Serebryakov (People's Commissar for Transport), asking him about the state of the debate in Ukraine. Apparently, most supported the principle of the "drunken budget".[40] Three days later, an angry Trotsky wrote to Rykov:

Yesterday, Voroshilov told me that in the South-Western oblast 20% [40 proof] vodka is being sold that is produced by a company belonging to the Supreme Soviet of the National Economy. Do you know anything about that? Was the question discussed in the Central

Committee? […] I remember well when in early autumn of last year it was suggested to establish a commission about the vodka question, and You together with me voted against handing the question to the commission, because it was believed that any step towards the legalization of vodka should not be permitted.[41]

Indeed, it took nearly two years until a majority of the Politburo voted with Stalin's vodka faction. On 19 March 1925, the Politburo resolved under Point 9:

a) The question of the production of vodka and spirits shall be submitted to the provisional decision of the Council for Labor and Defense with a duty to report to the Politburo; b) the possibility of increasing the strength of the vodka to 40% is to be permitted; […] c) the orientation price for a bottle of vodka is to be set at 1 ruble.[42]

The sale of vodka by the state began as a trial to explore the possibility of using the revenue to build up the country's industry, especially metallurgy.[43] Considering that Stalin frequently defended that decision, it was very likely that he was the driving force behind the "vodka budget". On 18 December 1925, he wrote in the annual political report: "A word or two, by the way, about one of the sources of reserves – vodka. There are people who think that it is possible to build socialism in white gloves. That is a very gross mistake, comrades."[44]

In a letter from 20 March 1927, Stalin justified himself to a certain Shinkevich after he had pointed out that Lenin had ruled out that practice:

You refer to what Lenin said against vodka […]. The Party's Central Committee is familiar, of course, with what Lenin said. And if it agreed to introduce vodka, nevertheless, it was because it had Lenin's consent to this, given in 1922. Lenin did not consider it excluded that we might, with certain sacrifices on our part, arrive at a settlement on the debts with the bourgeois states and receive a substantial loan or substantial long-term credits. That was what he thought at the time of the Genoa Conference.[45] With such an arrangement, there would have been no need, of course, to introduce vodka. But as that arrangement did not materialise, and as we had no money for industry, and without a certain minimum of monetary funds we could not count upon any satisfactory development of our industry – on the development of which the fate of our entire national economy depends – we, along with Lenin, came to the conclusion that vodka would have to be introduced. Which was better: enslavement to foreign capital or introduction of vodka? – that was the question that faced us. [...] The question came up for discussion in the Central Committee of our Party in October 1924. Some members of the Central Committee objected to the introduction of vodka, without, however, indicating the sources from which we could derive the funds needed for industry. In reply to this, seven C.C. members, myself among them, submitted the following statement to the plenum of the Central Committee: 'In the summer of 1922 and the autumn of the same year (September), Comrade Lenin said several times to each of us that, since there was no hope of receiving a loan from abroad (failure of the Genoa Conference), it would be necessary to introduce a vodka monopoly, and that this was particularly necessary in order to create a minimum fund for the maintenance of the currency and the maintenance of industry. We consider it our duty to make a statement about all this in view of the fact that some comrades refer to earlier statements of Lenin on this subject.' The plenum of the Central Committee of our Party decided to introduce a vodka monopoly.[46]

Contrary to Stalin's assertions, it is likely that Lenin had not in fact approved of the "drunken budget" just a few months after categorically ruling it out in March 1922. It is also rather telling that the Politburo only approved of it once Lenin had died.

Stalin himself believed the sale of vodka to be a provisional measure that was to be discontinued eventually. As he explained in a speech on 3 December 1927: "Lastly, we have liabilities like vodka in the budget [...]. I think that it would be possible to start gradually to reduce the output of vodka and, instead of vodka, to resort to sources of revenue such as the radio and the cinema. Finally, we have minus items such as vodka in the state budget."[47] Regardless of his initial statements, vodka production was never wound down during his tenure – on the contrary.

Incensed by the Five Year Plan foreseeing the increase of the production – and consumption – of vodka by a whopping 227%, the party opposition under Trotsky and Zinoviev complained that "per-capita consumption has risen over the past few years, from 0.6 bottles in 1924/5 to 2.9 bottles in 1925/6 to 4.3 bottles of vodka in 1926/7. The brandy industry emerges as the 'leading' branch of industry under this Five Year Plan."[48]

The 227% increase in vodka production was a tremendous achievement, but Stalin needed more. In a letter to Molotov on 1 September 1930, while discussing the necessity of growing the Red Army from 640,000 to 700,000 men, he wrote: "Where do we get the money from? In my opinion we have to increase vodka production (*by as much as possible*). We must rid ourselves of the false feeling of shame and directly and openly aim for a *maximal* increase of vodka production in order to fully ensure a truly solid defense of our country."[49] Stalin further added that this decision was to be included in the official government budget for 1930/33.

Unsurprisingly, the Politburo complied. On 15 September 1930, it resolved to take the "necessary measures for a rapid increase of vodka production. [...] a program for the distillation of 90 million buckets of alcohol in the years 1930/31 is to be adopted."[50] On 30 October, the Politburo then accepted a proposal to produce 92 million buckets of alcohol, for which, among other things, 596,000 tons of grain were allocated.[51] A few weeks later, on 10 November, the Politburo ordered the expansion of the Red Army to 700,000 men by 1 October 1931.[52]

In order to firmly establish the new vodka monopoly, the Soviet government not only increased production but also cracked down on the underground samogon industry. That task was handed over to the OGPU, the militia and local party organizations. In a dispatch from the governorate of Penza, for example, for the month of July 1924, the OGPU reported: 7,126 searches, the confiscation of 1,225 distillation apparatuses, 1,783 arrests; 2,196 persons were put on trial.[53] The same day, the OGPU announced similar successes from the Pskov governorate, where the agency reported to have conducted 7,803 searches, including 5,345 with "results" as well confiscation of 2,634 distillation apparatuses and 520 buckets of samogon.[54]

Despite these numbers, the fight against samogon was not very successful overall. In February 1925, the OGPU reported that both the production of samogon and drunkenness steadily increased in all of Soviet Russia and Ukraine, and that local agencies failed to act sufficiently.[55] Thus the battle against samogon continued for years. When reporting on grain procurement in June 1928, Mikoyan, the People's Commissar for External and Internal Trade, proposed to continue the "fight against [unsanctioned] liquor distillation". The Politburo commission approved of this.[56]

The fight against samogon was crucial for the economy of the Soviet Union. After all, samogon production used up much-need grain while also depriving the state of revenues from the sale of vodka. With the sale of vodka, the Soviets sought to "to extract cash surpluses from the countryside" as Stalin put it on 13 February 1928.[57] In the end, only violent collectivization appears to have broken the back of the illicit samogon industry.

Skyrocketing vodka production was a godsend for the Soviet budget. However, it did have predictable social and economic side effects. In an OGPU report on the political situation in the USSR for October 1925, the authors wrote:

> Concurrently with the sale of 40% [80 proof] vodka one can register a strong rise of drunkenness among the workers. In the early October days and especially on paydays, drunkenness reaches mass character. In connection with drunkenness one can register an extraordinary rise in idleness at work and cases of people showing up at work drunk. In the 'Tsaryad' factory, 1,300 workers were not at work three days after payday. [...] An increase in worker idleness was recorded in many factories in Moscow, Leningrad and elsewhere. Drunkenness is accompanied by other amoral occurrences: Family conflicts and scandals, wifebeating, rowdiness, etc. In the counties of the Moscow district, groups of drunken workers beat up militiamen. Because of drunkenness, one can also observe a strong pauperization of workers (Bryansk district).[58]

Naturally, the opposition around Trotsky and Zinoviev continued to criticize the "drunken budget" and the resulting social and economic issues. On 10 November, several prominent leaders signed a manifesto in which they criticized the Five Year Plan, including its provisions on the sale of vodka:

The sale of vodka by the government was initially introduced as an experiment and a method to use most of the profits to finance industrialization, in particular the build-up of the metalworking industry. In reality, however, industrialization loses out from the sale of vodka. The experiment has to therefore be described as very unsuccessful. In the Soviet economic system, not only does the private sector lose out, as it did under the Tsars, but for the most part the public sector does too. The damages caused by the increase in idleness, damage to machinery, increase in accidents, fires, physical altercations, cases of assault, etc. go go into the millions each year. Government industry does not lose less than the budget gains from vodka, and in many cases loses more than the industry gets from the budget. A reduction of vodka sales will automatically, in a short period of time (2-3 years), raise the material and mental resources for industrialization.[59]

Trotsky had been at the forefront of in the battle against the "drunken budget" from the start and continued his struggle after it had been implemented. In the manuscript of an unfinished book he worked on in 1927, Trotsky brought up the issue of vodka:

Vodka became the scourge of the industrial proletarian instead of becoming a weapon against samogon in the villages. The 'lowering of the prices' [for vodka] lowers the standard of living of the worker and worsens his diet. […] the supporters of this theory [Socialism in One Country] say: 'One cannot demand the improvement of the lot of the workers when there are no means for it; one cannot demand a quick development of industry and rise in wages, because this would put the economic system into question; one cannot forsake vodka, otherwise one cannot sustain the budget.' […] Socialism demands the increase of the cultural level of the proletariat, and vodka lowers it.[60]

By 1928, however, Stalin had finally vanquished his opposition and forced Trotsky into exile. With them gone, criticism of the vodka policy fell silent. Over the next few decades, the revenues from the sale of vodka remained one of the Soviet Union's chief sources of income while vodka turned from a "scourge of the industrial proletariat" into a scourge of the entire Soviet society, especially in the *kolkhozes* (collective farms). These side effects may have been unfortunate, but for Stalin and his followers, the build-up of Soviet heavy industry and the expansion of the Red Army were of much greater importance.

Social Tensions and the Radicalization of Anti-Soviet Sentiment

The catastrophic state of the Soviet economy created a great deal of resentment among the population, and the Bolshevik policy of prioritizing the Soviet heavy and armaments industries at the expense of everything else made matters only worse. Years earlier, the Civil War with its countless massacres of enemies, real or imagined, the bloody suppression of peasant uprisings, and the ruthless punishment meted out on the rebels and their families, as well as the general Bolshevik terror that never really stopped, had all but put an end to the active armed and organized resistance. However, this did not mean that the population had resigned itself to its fate. On the contrary, dissent remained common and gradually radicalized in the face of economic crisis, Soviet mismanagement, arbitrariness, and the short-sighted plunder policy. With each passing month, the atmosphere became increasingly tense, both in the countryside and among the city dwellers.

Workers

In 1926, around 2.5 million workers were employed in the Soviet Union's light and heavy industries, with 1.55 million of them working in state-owned factories.[61] That was not much for a country of 147 million of whom 120.66 million (82%) lived in the countryside and 25.74 million (17.5%) in towns and cities. [62]

For the workers, the situation in the 1920s remained considerably worse than it had been in the booming pre-war years, and their standard of living fell even further behind that of other European workers. This issue raised concern among Soviet leaders and in 1927, Trotsky was working on a book about the state of the working class in the Soviet Union. Even though he never published it, the surviving fragments are an important source as Trotsky had easy access to key documents, including the OGPU report.[63]

Already in the introduction, Trotsky surmised: "Numerous facts from recent years bear witness to a *considerable deterioration of the situation of the workers in state enterprises*. To hide these facts, to paint them over with phrases about the necessity of sacrificing the interests of individual sectors in the name of class interest, means nothing other than the refusal to defend the interests of the working class."[64] The budget of the working family, Trotsky continued, had fallen by 3.8% in real terms between 1927 and 1926. An average worker's family spent 22.7% on housing (including related expenses); before the war, it was 17% and in Western countries, it was even lower. In Germany, housing only accounted for less than 10% of a worker's family budget.[65]

At the same time, the size of workers' accommodations began to shrink significantly. Before the war, the standard was 14 m² per person; by 1923, it had fallen to 12.05 m² and to just 11.57 m² per person in 1927. Urban working families were hit particularly hard. In 1925, the average living area per person in eight major cities (Rostov, Sevastopol, Armavir, Yaroslavl, Smolensk, Arkhangelsk, Tver, and Penza) was only 6.3 m² for workers, further declining to 5.2 m² the following year. Other urban groups were doing somewhat better, such as salaried workers (6.8 m² in 1925, 6.5 m² in 1926), artisans (5.7 m² in 1925, 7.6 m² in 1926) and the self-employed (10.9 m² in 1926). The situation was similar in Leningrad and Moscow, with workers in Leningrad being slightly better off with 6.99 m² in 1925 and 6.51 m² in 1926, whereas the opposite was true for Moscow's workers who lived on just 4.55 m² in 1925 and only 4.46 m² the following year.[66]

Trotsky also noted that the conditions of female workers as well as teenagers had deteriorated too. However, even their plight paled in comparison to that of agricultural workers, Trotsky surmised: "No part of the working class finds itself in such a poor situation as the agricultural workers." These agricultural workers numbered roughly one million, in addition to two million "'half' agricultural workers", i.e. poor farmers who had to work as agricultural workers to make ends meet, as well as their family members, possibly several million. Furthermore, there was the issue of unemployment, which began to rise. In October 1925, there were 920,000 people registered as unemployed. Their number had grown to 1.163 million by October 1926, reaching 1.46 million in April 1927.[67]

Workers' wages had recovered from the war and were on average at 100-102% of pre-war levels. However, the marginal wage gains evaporated as they had to pay more for food and accommodation, which were not only more expensive but also of poorer quality.[68] Meanwhile, worker productivity was only 16-20% of pre-war levels, mostly due to wear and tear of equipment and the worsening quality of raw materials but also because of poor discipline, bureaucracy, and incompetence.[69]

Faced with abysmal standards of living and mismanagement, the Soviet working class slowly became more radical and anti-Soviet. In the political situation report of the OGPU or April 1925, the authors stated that the question of the workers was the primary concern. The number of labor disputes was on the rise and while the number of strikes in April had been the same as in March – 24 – they had been larger and more aggressive. These conflicts were caused by low wages, poor working conditions and rising labor quotas, the report noted:

> The mood among the workers is characterized by rising discontent. [...] The rising discontent caused by the difficult economic situation and the pressure to increase labor productivity [...] is being instrumentalized by various anti-Soviet elements, including former members of the RCP, to spread discontent with Soviet power among the masses. Among [...] textile workers, there are rumors that foreign workers live better than Soviet ones. [...] in a needle and shoe last factory in the Volyn district, Polish workers were agitating, saying that 'in Poland, the workers live better; that everyone feels free there. While there are landowners in Poland, Russia has communists, who are like landowners.'[70]

Over the coming years, the tone of the OGPU reports did not change at all – the workers were restless.[71] A telling indicator of the growing discontent and radicalization among the workers was the number of labor conflicts which rose sharply after 1924, despite local efforts to hide them from the capital.[72] In 1926, the OGPU registered 4,999 labor conflicts during wage negotiations in state-run enterprises in which 4,059,000 workers took part, many of them multiple times. A year earlier, there had only been 2,357 labor conflicts involving 1,585,000 workers. Within a single year, the number of conflicts thus had risen by 112% and the workers involved by 156%. Wage negotiations were far from the only issue triggering labor disputes; in 1924/25, poor working conditions triggered 6,523 labor conflicts involving 250,000 workers. In 1925/26, the number of such labor disputes had skyrocketed to 19,115, with 552,000 workers involved.[73]

The Peasantry

Thanks to recently published documents from Russia, it is possible to paint an accurate picture of the mood in the villages. For the Soviet authorities, the situation looked grim. Like the urban workers, the villagers were not happy with the state of the economy at all. Anti-communism was rife among them, and much more so than in the cities.

The vast majority of the Soviet population lived in villages and therefore the OGPU closely monitored them and regularly – at least once a month – sent reports to Soviet leaders. Once the peasant uprisings in 1921/22 had been brutally put down and Soviet power had been fully established, peace and quiet returned to the Soviet village. However, this was not to last and beginning in late 1924, discontent was on the rise again. The OGPU was alarmed and in 1926 directed its local agencies to gather information on anti-Soviet sentiment in the villages. Based on these and similar reports from between 1925 and 1927, the OGPU composed a detailed dossier on anti-Soviet activities in the rural Soviet Union in 1928.[74]

In the introduction, the authors state that beginning in late 1924, new forms of anti-Soviet resistance were recorded. Previously, anti-Soviet activities had been conducted by anti-Soviet parties (Social Revolutionaries, monarchists, etc.), a broad "bandit movement" and outright rebellions. However, these had been more or less wiped out by 1924. In their stead emerged:

1). Counterrevolutionary agitation (its especially aggressive forms are defeatist and anti-Semitic agitation); 2.) Spread of anti-Soviet leaflets; 3.) Agitation of farmers' associations; 4.) Kulak and other anti-Soviet groups; 5.) Kulak terrorism and political hooliganism; 6.) Takeover of the lower Soviet and cooperative agencies by anti-Soviet elements; 7.) Mass rallies.[75]

According to the report, the most common form of anti-Soviet agitation in the countryside was "counterrevolutionary agitation", i.e. "private conversation among small groups of peasants, open appearances at meetings, conferences, congresses, agitation at places, where peasants gather (tea rooms, markets, reading rooms, etc.)." There, "anti-Soviet elements" criticized the Soviet system, high taxation, called for resistance and even uprisings, as well as for boycotts of measures by the government, such as grain requisitions, taxes or elections.[76]

Parallel to the increase in anti-Soviet agitation, anti-Semitic agitation rose as well and became more radical. Especially in Ukraine and Belarus, anti-Semitism became a serious issue, the authors lamented, as did "defeatist agitation". With "defeatist agitation", the OGPU was referring to voices that were anti-war and called for mass-flight to the "bandits" in case of war and mass mobilization. Slogans included: "The communists and workers should go to war! – For whom should we even fight?" The anti-war sentiment was spurred on by a massive but baseless propaganda campaign about a looming attack on the Soviet Union by the capitalist countries, especially Poland.[77]

In 1926/7 alone, the OGPU registered 7,269 incidents of "defeatist agitation" which was just the tip of the iceberg. 75% of incidents had been caused by kulaks and only 25% by average and poor peasants. Among the 705 cases of "defeatist agitation" in the west (mostly Belarus), 167 had been perpetrated by Poles; in the Northern Caucasus, around half of all the 1,803 incidents had been carried out by "Cossack kulaks" and 20% by members of the intelligentsia and anti-Soviet elements.[78]

The distribution of anti-Soviet leaflets was a minor issue at first; in 1926, the OGPU registered only 83 incidents and 163 in 1927. Only a few of them came from abroad. However, between January and August 1928 alone, the number of instanced skyrocketed to 506. That very few of the leaflets came from abroad strongly suggests that foreign agitation had very little influence on anti-Soviet sentiment in the countryside. Furthermore, the leaflets were for the most part written by hand and distributed in very small numbers; oftentimes they were riddled with mistakes,[79] again underlining the spontaneous nature of this form of resistance.

A topic of particular concern for the OGPU was the "agitation for the organization of farmers' associations". The Bolsheviks saw these as attempts to create a peasants' party powerful enough to challenge the dictatorship of the proletariat, i.e. the Bolsheviks themselves. At the same time, they saw it as the attempt of average and poorer peasants to improve their own economic and socio-cultural situation, similar to unions for urban workers. The report included this passage:

> *Farmers' associations.* The farmers' association is the most widespread and popular slogan of the anti-Soviet agitation, which resonated in virtually all strata in the village. The popularity of the idea of the farmers' associations favors both leaders and followers of the agrarian movement of 1905-1907, who are present in the village, as well the role of the peasants' organizations, where they had been the leaders of the rebellious anti-Soviet movement.[80]

With much concern, the OGPU stated that this form of peasant organization began to re-emerge after 1924, and that this idea was very popular among Russian but also non-Russian peasants.[81]

While the OGPU registered only 139 cases of "agitation for farmers' associations" in 1924, that number nearly quadrupled to 543 in 1925, only to triple again the next year to 1,676. In 1927, the OGPU reported 2,312 such incidents. These farmers' associations were particularly common in the regions surrounding important industrial centers as well as the parts of the country with the most developed and productive agricultural sector. The initiatives differed widely in their aims. Poor and average peasants generally called for the creation of associations similar to workers' unions that would advocate for the economic and social interests (insurance, etc.). In very agrarian regions, complaints about the Price Scissors were key, as was opposition to the requisition of agricultural goods. Some of them even called for direct trade with foreign countries; richer peasants played an especially important role in this respect.[82]

According to internal OGPU statistics, the primary aims of calls for famers' associations in 1927 were: The establishment of an openly political organization like a peasants' party at 22.6%; 33.1% wanted the prices of grain and industrial goods to be regulated; in 30.7% of cases, the goal was to form the equivalent of a workers' union; 11.5% were about protesting tax policies; the rest – 0.2% – were about direct trade with foreign countries and other issues.[83]

In 1926, the OGPU recorded 2,207 persons who were active in farmers' associations; in 1927, their number had risen to 2,844. The initiators of the farmers' associations were by and large average peasants (51.2% in 1926, 52.5% a year later), who promoted them in private conversations with groups of peasants but also increasingly at public gatherings and conferences. Between 1926 and 1927, the percentage of public appearances rose from 30% to 40.9% of all incidents.[84]

The OGPU clearly shows that peasant discontent with Soviet rule was rapidly rising and radicalizing. Contrary to what Soviet propagandists claimed, it was not just the wealthy peasants but also the average and poor peasants who were hostile to communist rule. By founding farmers' associations, they sought to advocate for their self-interests in a legal way.

A different – similarly illegal – method of resistance was the "infiltration" of the lower, publicly-accessible Soviet apparatus by "anti-Soviet elements" by way of elections. This was especially the case for village councils and cooperatives. When the OGPU examined the composition of village soviets in Ukraine in early 1928, they found that for 6,085 of their members, "compromising information" was available at the OGPU. Many of them had previously been involved in anti-Soviet activities or had an otherwise "anti-Soviet" past. The authors of that report concluded the OGPU had to purge the lower Soviet state apparatus of such anti-Soviet and subversive elements.[85]

Another common phenomenon was the creation of "Kulak and anti-Soviet organizations" as the OGPU called them. These groups were mostly small, illegal organizations whose aim was to organize resistance to Soviet measures, fight Soviet activists in the villages and to have their own members infiltrate the lower Soviet state apparatus. Between 1 November 1925 and 1 November 1928, the OGPU reported that it had managed to expose 2,161 such organizations. Some of them were apparently insurrectionary as well, especially in Ukraine and the Northern Caucasus. Worryingly, virtually all of them had ties to the Red Army or were in the process of establishing them.[86]

At the same time, public rallies began to spring up everywhere. In October 1928, the OGPU reported that 564 mass rallies had occurred between February and August 1928, a sharp rise from just 63 rallies in 1926 and 1927. In the vast majority of cases – 448 to be exact – the public rallies occurred in connection with what the OGPU termed the "crisis of food distribution". Fifty-six happened during the requisition of grain, and the rest during tax collection and similar events. The OGPU analysis recommended that "our blows should not be against the greater mass of participants, but against the anti-Soviet heads that organize them."[87]

While peasant resistance was largely peaceful, violence erupted from time to time, which the OGPU termed "kulak terror" and "political hooliganism". This included violent threats, acts of arson, assault and even murder. The targets were rural Soviet activists – mostly members of the lower Soviet state apparatus – as well as members of the party and the youth-wing, the Komsomol. Attacks often occurred during grain requisitions and tax collection, but also during electoral and propaganda campaigns.[88]

These violent acts too were on the rise after 1924. While the OGPU reported 339 incidents in 1924, the number rose to 902 in 1925. They fell slightly to 711 in 1926, before rebounding to 901 the next year; in the first seven months of 1928, the number of violent attacks rose to 1,049. Among the 711 incidents of "kulak terror" in 1926, the OGPU registered 110 murders (15.5%), 240 attempted murders (38%) and 290 violent assaults (40.8%). A plurality of the attacks was directed against members of the lower Soviet state apparatus; 33.3% in 1926, 34.6% in 1927 and 44.9% in the first eight months of 1928. The second most targeted group were members of the party and the Komsomol; attacks on them made up 21.1% of registered attacks in 1926, 29.2% in 1927 and 17.3% in the first eight months of 1928. Village correspondents were also singled out, with 8.6% of attacks being directed against them in 1926, a number that fell to 3.1% the next year. In addition to these groups, other activists and "members of the village underclass" who actively supported the Soviet government, also faced violence.[89]

Aside from attacks on activists, the OGPU also monitored "political hooliganism" – attacks on the "political and cultural work of our party in the countryside", i.e. Soviet propaganda. The agency lamented that such incidents were becoming much more common beginning in 1926. Groups of "rowdies" – primarily made up of "kulak youths" and "criminal elements" who were frequently drunk – disrupted meetings, defaced revolutionary posters and monuments, damaged and even destroyed cultural and educational institutions.[90] The fact that these attacks mostly targeted Soviet propaganda, seems to confirm that they were indeed politically motivated for the most part.

The anti-Soviet mood in the villages was not contained to the countryside. Since the vast majority of recruits came from villages, the Red Army soon found itself exposed to an anti-Soviet "peasant mood" as some reports put it. This had serious consequences. In a resolution of the Revolutionary War Council of the USSR about the moral-political state of the Red Army from 27 June 1928, the Red Army was chided, among other reasons, for its poor discipline: "In connection with this, one has to point out the radicalization of the 'peasant mood' that is tied to the grain procurement measures and the bread shortages in 1927/28 as well as with the intensification of the class struggle in the village."These factors, the report continued, influenced the soldiery and resulted in attempts by kulaks to take leadership over the barracks; current state policy had a long-term impact on the atmosphere in the military.[91] The OGPU came to similar conclusions regarding the radicalization of the "peasant mood" within the Red Army.[92]

Like in the cities, the Soviet system was increasingly met with outright hostility in the countryside. Thanks to the frequent OGPU reports, Soviet leaders were clearly aware that the majority of peasants were not communists at all. Nevertheless, their propaganda continued to assert the exact opposite. During a speech on 9 July 1928 on the topic of "industrialization and the grain issue", Stalin told the members of the Central Committee:

> Those comrades were perfectly right who said here that the peasant today is not what he was six years ago, say, when he was afraid that he might lose his land to the landlord. The peasant is already forgetting the landlord. He is now demanding new and better conditions of life. Can we, in the event of enemy attack, *wage war* against the external enemy on the battle front, and at the same time *against the muzhik* [peasant] *in the rear* in order to get grain urgently for the army? No, we cannot and must not.[93]

In autumn 1927, Grigory Bessedovsky traveled to Ukraine where he talked to numerous party functionaries but also to villagers. One of the villagers he talked to had joined the Bolsheviks in 1917, even becoming a communist functionary before returning to the countryside where he now lived the life of an ordinary peasant. This man told Bessedovsky: "The peasants are already beginning to hate us just as much as they used to hate the nearest landlord or Count K. A little time will pass and they will forget that we have given them the land. Then will begin a new war with the peasantry. I have to say quite openly that I will be on the side of the peasants this time."[94] Bessedovsky continued: "These sentiments from the village have long leaked into the district and urban organizations of the communist party."[95]

Stalin and his closest comrades knew perfectly well that they could not rely on the peasantry – Russian and non-Russian alike – to lead the fight for world revolution. The peasants were openly hostile to the Bolshevik cause and therefore it was imperative to crack down on them. In 1927, the OGPU ordered its local units to systematically gather records on the "anti-Soviet elements" in the villages. At the same time, the OGPU began "operative work against anti-Soviet elements" in several rayons.[96] The stage for the war against the peasantry was set, although the Bolsheviks would wait until January 1930 to unleash the terror.

The Failure of the Bolshevik Minority Policy

Like Imperial Russia, the Soviet Union was a not uniform nation-state but a multicultural empire with countless ethnic minorities. According to the census of 1937, the Soviet Union was home to 162 million people, of whom only 94 million were Russians (58%); by far the most numerous minority group were the Ukrainians with 26.4 million (16.3%), followed by 4.8 million Belarussians (2.9%), 4.55 million Uzbeks (2.8%), 2.86 million Kazakhs (1.76%), 2.7 million Jews (1.6%), 2 million Georgians (1.23%), 1.15 million Germans (0.7%), 636,000 Poles (0.39%) and many other smaller groups.[97]

Managing such a multicultural empire was not an easy task and it remained an issue throughout the existence of the USSR and beyond. The Bolsheviks immediately recognized the importance of that question and gave Stalin the task of dealing with it. As the People's Commissar for Nationalities, Stalin played a key role in shaping Soviet policy towards the Soviet Union's ethnic minorities, often butting heads with Lenin. In the summer of 1922, Stalin argued for the direct annexation of the other Soviet republics – Ukraine, Belarus, Azerbaijan, Armenia and Georgia – into the Russian Soviet Federative Socialist Republic (RSFSR). Lenin was horrified and instead argued for a union of Soviet republics in Europe and Asia. Despite these disagreements, both ultimately wanted the same thing: a multinational one-party state with only one ideology – communism.[98]

In the end, Lenin won the argument with Stalin and when the new constitution was ratified on 31 December 1922, the Soviet Union was created as a federal state. However, this was nothing more than a façade and it was the Politburo of the Russian Communist Party that called the shots.[99] Despite the unquestioned dominance of Moscow, the Bolsheviks initially refused to continue the hated Russification policies of the Tsars. On the contrary, Stalin and the Politburo promoted linguistic and cultural autonomy in the other Soviet republics in order to strengthen the emerging communist system with indigenous cadres whose numbers were very low in the beginning. Stalin himself warned about the issue of "Greater Russian chauvinism" spreading within the party, which he saw as a danger to the establishment of communism in the other, non-Russian republics.[100]

In March 1923, Stalin wrote a memorandum about the ethnic issue during the process of building the party and the state. He complained that the non-Russian republics had very few if any indigenous Old Bolsheviks who were familiar with local customs. As a result, Russian activists dominated not only the central party structures but also those in the non-Russian republic. This was a problem since they rarely even spoke minority languages and also had a tendency towards "Greater Russian chauvinism".[101]

To combat this trend, Stalin suggested a series of measures designed to promote the emergence of young minority cadres in the national republics. Marxist circles involving local communists were to be founded, communist writings and "party literature" were to be translated and disseminated, while the universities of the eastern peoples were to be strengthened along with their subsidiaries. At the same time, Stalin called for the intensification of "educational party work" and youth work in general in the ethnic republics.[102]

In June 1923, Stalin even suggested creating a special unit in the Red Army exclusively made up of ethnic minorities in the Red Army, numbering 30,000 men in total. However, Trotsky vetoed this idea, pointing out that due to ongoing financial problems, the Soviet Union had to shrink the Red Army – adding another 30,000 men was thus out of the question.[103] Instead, a number of already existing units were transformed into ethnic units, with the relevant minority language becoming the language of command. By July 1924, these ethnic units (Belarusian, Ukrainian, Armenian, etc.) numbered 13,225 men.[104] Four years later, that number had risen to 34,054, the target being 47,876 men.[105] The expansion of the ethnic units was stopped in June 1929 and they were gradually dissolved by the late 1930s.[106]

Also beginning in 1923, the Politburo made an effort to promote local functionaries in the party and state apparatus in the national republics. The various minority languages were made official languages locally, next to Russian. In Belarus, for example, Belarusian became the official language – together with Russian but also Yiddish and Polish. Local cultures and languages also received government support provided that they produced pro-Soviet content. The goal of this so-called *korenizatsiya* ("putting down roots" – indigenization) policy was to entrench Soviet power in the national republics by having local activists run them. These local activists had a better chance of reaching the non-Russian population and winning them over to the communist cause than Russians, thus was the calculation.

Unfortunately, this experiment did not deliver the expected results. Instead of ushering in a peaceful, multicultural Soviet society, the program of indigenization set free the centrifugal forces of political, ethnic, cultural and even economic division that threatened the very existence of the Soviet Union.

A primary example was Ukraine. In September 1922, Stalin's colleague Dmitry Manuilsky had stated that "the Ukrainian peasant" did not care about the ethnic question.[107] Six years later, the situation was unrecognizable. When the OGPU issued its secret report on rural anti-Soviet movements in October 1928, the authors lamented that – in particular in Ukraine, Belarus and the Cossack regions – the wealthy but also many of the poorer villagers were spreading "national-chauvinist ideas and slogans". "Chauvinism is the direction in which the ideologues and organizers of the rural anti-Soviet movement try to steer it", the authors continued. Responsible for this was the national intelligentsia that – unlike its Russian counterpart – had close ties to the villages, because they had hailed from there. As a result, the national intelligentsia enjoyed a high degree of respect and therefore influence among the peasants and the petit bourgeoisie.[108]

The report stated that the number of kulaks and wealthy peasants was relatively high in Ukraine and that it was they who were the most aggressively anti-communist. Furthermore, the rural anti-Soviet movement also affected the petit bourgeoisie in the cities: "The Ukrainian Peasants' Party, peasant organizations, the creation of the Sugar Beet Cooperative and a number of other organizations are examples of the activities of the [Ukrainian] national intelligentsia and their attempts to organize in the village." The national intelligentsia also overlaid the economic and political demands of the kulaks and "capitalist elements" with "chauvinistic phrases about national liberation. National liberation is the general slogan for all counterrevolutionary organizations in Ukraine and Belarus, it is the binding agent that can bring together divergent and sometimes opposing groups for the general struggle against the dictatorship of the proletariat [i.e. the Bolsheviks]."[109]

In many cases, it was members of the former nationalist and anti-Soviet parties that were involved in the anti-Soviet agitation in the towns and in the countryside. Outside of the USSR, these parties had remained intact and continued to maintain contact with their home countries, with émigré nationalists playing an important role. The report continued:

Aside from the well-developed anti-Soviet movement in the countryside, one has to take note of the insurrectionary character of many emerging organizations. Insurrectionary organizations founded by students or the national intelligentsia attempted to enter the Red Army in order to involve it in the fight against Soviet power.[110]

The authors concluded their report on the situation in Ukraine as follows:

This all proves that in Ukraine, the anti-Soviet movement in the countryside is entering a state in which it attempts to transform from an isolated and unorganized movement into a unified one, seeking a single goal and the armed struggle against Soviet power. The participation of a significant portion of the urban national intelligentsia in this movement, and its close ties to the village, proves that one cannot separate the fight against the anti-Soviet movement in the countryside and the anti-Soviet groups and organizations in the towns, after all, the latter almost exclusively rely on rural anti-Soviet activities. Therefore, the fight of our agencies has to be conducted against both sectors of the revitalizing counterrevolution, and namely as a unified task.[111]

The situation was similar in the Cossack areas in the Urals, Siberia, the Far-East and especially in the Northern Caucasus where anti-Soviet activities were skyrocketing both among Cossacks and non-Cossacks. It was noted, however, that in promoting Cossack interests, the Cossacks frequently turned against nearby non-Cossacks, which had resulted in numerous clashes and therefore played into the hands of the Bolsheviks. Nevertheless, in the Kuban, the OGPU had detected attempts by anti-Soviet elements to establish contacts with anti-Soviet forces in Ukraine,[112] while both in the Kuban and the Don region, anti-Soviet Cossacks were agitating for secession from the USSR.[113]

Anti-Soviet and nationalist sentiments were an issue in all national republics and ethnic regions.[114] However, it was not only the ethnic minorities that were restive – Russians, workers and peasants alike, felt they were being disadvantaged by the Soviet minority policy. According to a party report from August 1926, these feelings led to an increase in anti-Semitism. Especially problematic was the Soviet policy of settling Jews in the Russian or Ukrainian-dominated countryside; not only did the Bolsheviks take away land from Russian and Ukrainian peasants to give it to the Jews, Jews also became more visible in the local Soviet agencies. This enraged the peasants and turned them against the Jews who were seen as Soviet agents, and the Soviet Union as a Jewish organization. This contributed to the anti-Soviet mood among the Russian majority, the report stated.[115]

The policy of indigenization sought to create indigenous communist cadres whose knowledge of local languages and customs would help the

Russian-dominated Soviet Union put down roots in the national republics. However, the exact opposite occurred and nobody was to blame but Stalin, who came up with the idea and oversaw its implementation.

Instead of being grateful for the Soviets funding their schools and cultural programs, ethnic minorities – like nearly everyone else in the Soviet Union – were furious at the horrible economic and social situation, the ever-present but primitive propaganda, and above all, Soviet misrule and terror. This was made even worse by the often poor implementation of the policy, which created conflict between the many ethnicities in the Soviet Union. As a result, anti-Soviet and nationalist, even secessionist sentiments proliferated. The situation was particularly bad in Ukraine, where Moscow feared that a nationalist uprising was imminent.

Naturally, Soviet leaders did not blame themselves for these problems. The OGPU and the party were adamant that it was the national intelligentsia and the kulaks that were entirely responsible for these problems. After all, it was they who spread nationalist, anti-Soviet propaganda that resonated among the peasants and the youth. For Stalin and his colleagues, the solution was simple: These troublemakers had to be exterminated.

Chapter 10

"Socialism in One Country" – The New Path to World Revolution

While the Soviet Union hurtled towards chaos, Europe had been recovering quickly. With the economy once again reaching pre-war levels and then surpassing them, social and political unrest soon calmed down as well. By 1924, even Germany – a hotbed of revolutionary activism and the Bolshevik's greatest hope – was on the path of recovery, as was Poland following Pilsudski's coup in May 1926. With the supposedly shaky capitalist states entering a newfound period of stability, the prospects of world revolution began to wane. This called into question the viability of the communist project which was predicated on the spread of worldwide revolution. In a speech on 9 May 1925, Stalin explained:

The new feature that has revealed itself lately, and which has made an impression upon the international situation, is that the revolution in Europe has begun to ebb, that a certain lull has set in. [..]What is the ebb of the revolution, the lull? Is it the beginning of the end of the world revolution, the beginning of the liquidation of the world proletarian revolution? [...] No, it is not. The epoch of world revolution is a new stage of the revolution, a whole strategic period, which will last for a number of years, *perhaps even a number of decades*. During this period there can and must be ebbs and flows of the revolution. [...] After the October victory we entered *the third strategic period*, the third stage of the revolution, *in which the aim is to overcome the bourgeoisie on a world scale*. How long this period will last is difficult to say. *In any case, there is no doubt that it will be a long one.*[1]

In a speech held in front of the Central Committee on 1 August 1927, Stalin again lamented "… the absence of that profound revolutionary crisis [in the capitalist countries] which revolutionizes the masses, brings them to their feet and turns them abruptly towards communism."[2]

If anything, it was the Soviet Union that was moving closer towards a revolution – albeit an anti-communist one. With the economy in shambles and both urban workers and peasants turning against communism once again, the OGPU was warning of a renewed wave of anti-communist uprisings. To make matters worse, improvement was not in sight. When Anastas Mikoyan took over the post of People's Commissar for Internal and External Trade from Lev Kamenev in August 1926, Kamenev warned him of the looming economic crisis, even going so far as to claim that "we are heading towards a catastrophic break-up of the revolution."[3]

In addition, the Soviet Union was also confronted with a deep crisis of leadership. In May 1922, the undisputed leader of the communist movement, Lenin, had fallen severely ill, and even though he tried to continue to participate in Soviet politics as best as he could, his frequent absences created a power vacuum at the top. Despite the best efforts of his doctors, Lenin never recovered and died in his country estate in Gorky, near Moscow, on 21 January 1924, aged just 53.[4]

With sickness gradually incapacitating Lenin, a small, influential group began to emerge among Lenin's companions that soon took control over the party and the country. Its main members were Stalin, Zinoviev, Trotsky, and Kamenev. At Lenin's behest, Stalin had been named secretary general of the communist party on 3 April 1922, but following Lenin's illness, Stalin was able to use what had originally been a purely administrative post to expand and solidify his power within his party through a series of careful appointments.[5] He was thus able to install his own loyalists in key positions in the party, the government, and in the Red Army. These people continued to play an important role over the coming years and decades, such as Vyacheslav Molotov, Sergo Ordzhonikidze, Kliment Voroshilov, Semyon Budyonny, Lazar Kaganovich, Sergey Kirov, and Andrey Andreyev.[6] In addition, Stalin also paid close attention to the mid-level cadres as well. On 7 November 1937, Stalin looked back and explained to his closest confidantes the way he had won the struggle for power in the Soviet Union:

Why did we defeat Trotsky and the others too? It is known that Tr[otsky] was the most popular man in the country after Lenin. Bukharin, Zinoviev, Rykov and Tomsky were also popular. And we were barely known. Myself, Molotov, Vor[oshilov], Kalinin… back then. During Lenin's time we were the practitioners, his fellow fighters. But we were supported by the mid-level cadres, they explained our views to the masses… Trotsky however did not pay any attention to these cadres.[7]

On 6 September 1924, Isaac Levin, a clearly well-informed Western correspondent in Moscow, reported: "The unlimited power of Lenin was transferred to three people who are now the dictators of Soviet Russia. The most powerful among them is Stalin, the son of a shoemaker." Levin attested a Lenin-like willpower to him, strength, toughness but also modesty, vision, and boldness. The other two "dictators" Levin had in mind were Zinoviev and Kamenev, who formed the "troika" that controlled the Soviet Union after Lenin's death. Levin had fewer positive things to say about them, however, writing that they were "soft" in comparison to Stalin. Finally, Levin also emphasized the enmity between Stalin and Trotsky, who was a heretic in Stalin's eyes.[8]

Nevertheless, Trotsky remained an influential figure, and as the founder of the Red Army and Lenin's deputy during the civil war, he felt that it was he who was Lenin's "natural" successor. An intense power struggle was inevitable. However – thanks in large part to Stalin's political acumen – it was Trotsky who gradually saw his power and influence wane. By the end of the decade, Stalin had emerged as Lenin's undisputed successor and the Soviet Union's absolute ruler, with his rivals within the party marginalized and humiliated – and soon to be murdered on his orders.[9]

While the inner-party conflict was certainly a power struggle, it was also an ideological conflict over strategy, the future of the Soviet Union and the world revolution, and the ideological-political legitimacy of the newly-established communist system. The repeated failures of the revolution in Germany had shaken the Bolsheviks' confidence in the immanence of the world revolution. Anastas Mikoyan described this mood in his recollections from the 1960s:

> In the first years of the revolution we were convinced that the world revolution would soon emerge victorious. Therefore, we never discussed the question: What do we do when the world revolution does not emerge victorious, will we manage to build socialism? When the revolutionary wave in Europe had receded, when the revolutions in Hungary, in Germany suffered defeat, this question became pressing. At this time, Trotsky came up with the explanation that the victory in a separate county, in Russia, was not possible. From this emerged the question, what are we building and what are we dealing with?[10]

For Trotsky and his supporters, the situation was clear – building socialism was an impossible task in such a backward country as the Soviet Union. In 1927, Trotsky wrote: "The theory of building Socialism in One Country – in the epoch of imperialism, based on the division of labor – is a reactionary fantasy. […] It is false that one can build Socialism in One Country without the victory of the world revolution."[11]

Stalin vehemently disagreed. On 17 December 1924, he wrote: "There can be no doubt that the universal theory of a simultaneous victory of the revolution in the principal countries of Europe, the theory that the victory of socialism in one country is impossible, has proved to be an artificial and untenable theory. The seven years' history of the proletarian revolution in Russia speaks not for but against this theory."[12]

Stalin and his supporters went even further, saying that it was not only possible to build socialism in Russia, but that this was indeed their duty to do so in order to revive the fortunes of the floundering world revolution. The general idea was to build up the armaments industry and the military of the backward Soviet Union so that the Red Army would be able to prevail in the coming revolutionary war. That there would be such a revolutionary war was an undisputed fact for the Bolsheviks, it was only a question of time. As Stalin explained in a speech on 3 November 1926, the numerous systemic antagonisms between the "imperialist countries" were so great that "this cannot but lead to sharp conflicts and gigantic wars between the imperialist groups".[13]

In the great ideological struggle that followed, it was Stalin and his followers that ultimately triumphed over Trotsky. In this, Stalin not only benefited from his shrewd personnel policy but also from long-forgotten Leninist slogans. As Mikoyan later stated, Bukharin – the editor-in-chief of *Pravda* – came to Stalin's aid and denounced Trotsky for defeatism as well as for going against Lenin himself:

> Bukharin cited Lenin's well-known slogan from 1916 on the possibility of victory in a single country. Sadly, we had forgotten that slogan. Many of us had not read it and did not know it. This great, genius prediction by Lenin turned out to be a great aid not only in the struggle against Trotsky but also in the solidification of our ideological positions. And there was also the Lenin essay on cooperatives (1922) in which he said that everything one needed to build socialism in Russia was Soviet power + electrification and cooperatives. Such statements by Lenin questioned every one of Trotsky's concepts. Stalin too, like all of us, acted in the spirit of Leninist principles.[14]

Mikoyan was slightly mistaken – Lenin had formulated that guiding principle in 1915 and not in 1916. It read as follows:

> Uneven economic and political development is an absolute law of capitalism. Hence, the victory of socialism is possible first in several or even in one capitalist country alone. After expropriating the capitalists and organizing their own socialist production, the victorious proletariat of that country will arise against the rest of the world – the capitalist world – attracting to its cause the oppressed classes of other countries, stirring uprisings in those countries against the capitalists, and in case of need *using even armed force* against the exploiting classes and their states.[15]

Lenin's idea that it was possible to build up socialism in just a single country in order to – if need be – use it as a base from which to wage war on the capitalists with the goal of spreading the revolution, became the "basic article"[16], the ideological and political basis of Bolshevik policy after 1925. It remained in place until at least June 1941 – the eve of the German invasion of the Soviet Union.[17]

Unsurprisingly, Stalin himself was very fond of this principle and referenced it frequently.[18] During a polemic against Trotsky from 1 November 1926, he brought up "Lenin's thesis that "the victorious proletariat of that country (that is, of one country – J. St.), having expropriated the capitalists and organised socialist production, [will] stand up against the rest of the world, the capitalist world."[19]

In another instance, on 7 August 1927, Stalin sent a resolution of the XV Party Congress on the intra-party opposition and the opposition to building Socialism in One Country to the members and candidates of the Central Committee and the Central Control Committee. One of the points of critique was: "The party assumes that our revolution is a socialist revolution, that the October Revolution is not only a signal, trigger and starting point for the socialist revolution in the West, but also, first and foremost, the basis for the further development of the world revolution."[20]

The resolution also alleged that the Trotskyists, i.e. the internal opposition, believed that the dictatorship of the proletariat in the Soviet Union would collapse from the inevitable conflicts between the "workers" i.e. the Bolsheviks themselves, and the peasants if the socialist World Revolution was delayed. To refute the Trotskyists, the resolution included Lenin's article from 1915 on the viability of building socialism in one country – until the time was right to export the revolution by force of arms. Citing one of his statements from before the revolution, in August 1917, Trotsky was further denounced for supposedly believing that a revolutionary Russia stood no chance against a reactionary Europe.[21]

The resolution continued further: "The party assumes that the progressive capitalist countries are experiencing temporary stabilization in general and in particular, and that the current time is a period between revolutions, which obliges the communist parties to prepare the proletariat for the future revolution."[22]

Considering the nature of these discussions, the thesis that Socialism in One Country meant the end of Bolshevik attempts to carry the flames of revolution beyond the borders of the Soviet Union remains untenable, despite the assurances of some researchers.[23] On the contrary, Socialism in One Country was meant to be a mere stepping stone to the ultimate goal of World Revolution. With the capitalist states having largely recovered and the post-war window of opportunity gone, Bolshevik strategists had to change their plans. Now, it was the Soviet Union that was to become the staging ground for the world revolution, which it would spread by any means possible, even by war.

This new strategy was intimately linked to Stalin himself and his rise to the all-powerful ruler of the Soviet Union. To legitimize and enforce his vision, Stalin habitually invoked the authority of Lenin. On 26 January 1924 – just after Lenin's death – Stalin held a speech at the II Soviet Congress in which he solemnly swore to uphold Lenin's legacy: "*Departing from us, Comrade Lenin enjoined us to hold high and guard the purity of the great title of member of the party. We vow to you, Comrade Lenin, that we shall fulfill your behest with honour!*"[24] Stalin repeated this vow six times in his speech and further stated:

The third basis of the dictatorship of the proletariat is our Red Army and our Red Navy. More than once did Lenin impress upon us that the respite we had won from the capitalist states might prove a short one. More than once did Lenin point out to us that the strengthening of the Red Army and the improvement of its condition is one of the most important tasks of our Party. [...] Let us vow then, comrades, that we shall spare no effort to strengthen our Red Army and our Red Navy.[25]

Following Lenin's death, the Bolsheviks began to rename schools, factories, streets, and squares after him. Even the former imperial capital and the starting ground of the revolution, Petrograd – until 1914, St. Petersburg – was renamed Leningrad. After all, that was where the October Revolution had begun. In the capital of Moscow, the body of Lenin was embalmed and displayed in a new mausoleum on Red Square, right in front of the Kremlin. In the words of the German historian Jörg Barberowski:

After his death, Lenin was given the status of a revolutionary saint, his writings were canonized and sacralized. They could be cited, but not criticized. Lenin was posthumously given the status of a prophet. Whoever wanted to make himself heard within the party, had to make his case by referring to Lenin's works. And it was Stalin, who as general secretary and great manipulator, finally decided what was to be said and how. Now came the talk of Leninism. It referred to a canon of articles of faith, to which every member of the party had to submit unconditionally. Whoever spoke against Stalin and his followers, violated the commandment of unity.[26]

Stalin continuously invoked Lenin's legacy even decades after his death and even in private meetings. On 7 November 1940, during a reception for his closest colleagues, he held a lengthy address during which he talked himself into a rage, crudely insulting his confidants and threatening them. Naturally, he invoked Lenin: "You do not like to learn, you live complacently. Giving away the inheritance of Lenin with both hands."[27]

However, he also brought up Lenin when he was in a good mood. On 4 February 1941, he raised a toast at the birthday party of Voroshilov: "Lenin has created us, he is our ancestor. We owe everything to him. Be like Lenin. We are all 'chicks' compare to Lenin."[28] In the evening of 22 June 1941 – the day of the German surprise attack on the Soviet Union – when the first shocking reports of the catastrophic situation on the front arrived in Moscow, when Stalin's mood had hit rock-bottom, Mikoyan recalled that Stalin said self-critically: "Lenin had left us a great inheritance. We – his heirs – have fucked up everything!"[29]

Chapter 11

Preparing for the Revolutionary War: The Committee for Defense

The explicit belligerence of Socialism in One Country was not limited to mere words and in 1927, Stalin's Soviet Union began to ready itself for war – despite the absence of any direct threat. The primary emphasis lay on mobilization and armament programs to prepare the Red Army, and indeed the entire country, for a long and total war. At the same time, the government embarked on a campaign to "pacify" the restive population at home, in other words a crackdown on the peasantry and other "unreliable" groups.

From 1927 until late 1930, it was the top-secret Administrative Session of the Council for Labor and Defense (RZ STO) that played the key role in war preparations. Headed by Rykov, it was formally subordinated to the Council of Labor and Defense, but in reality it took directions directly from the Politburo. It was then the Politburo itself that disestablished the RZ STO on 23 December 1930, replacing it with the Committee for Defense, which was composed of Molotov, Voroshilov, Kuibyshev, Ordzhonikidze, and Stalin himself.[1] The RZ STO and later the Committee for Defense were tasked with centrally organizing, coordinating, and overseeing war preparations. Due to its secretive nature, not much is known about the work of these organizations.[2]

Already in early 1925, the Politburo had established the precursor to the RZ STO and the Committee for Defence, the secret Commission for Defense, which was also headed by Rykov and was thus often called the Rykov Commission. Like its successors, its focus lay on the armaments industry and military mobilization.[3] However, the committee had not achieved much by late 1926, aside from concluding that after years of neglect, neither the Red Army nor the Soviet armaments industry were ready for war. On 26 December 1926, Soviet political leadership was confronted with the committee's report on the Staff of the Red Army; on the same day, the Chief of Staff – none other than Tukhachevsky – repeated the key findings of the report at the session of the Politburo: "Neither the Red Army nor the country are prepared for war. Our material mobilization stocks are so low that they will barely be sufficient for the first phase of the war."[4]

This was unacceptable to Stalin and he personally took the initiative and ordered that Voroshilov, his close confidante and also the People's Commissar for Military and Naval Affairs, work out a "defense plan". At the Politburo meeting on 13 January 1927, Stalin brought up that issue and the Politburo resolved: "For mid-February of this year, a date for a closed session of the Politburo is to be set, to listen to the presentation of Comrade Voroshilov on the danger of war and the plan of defense in case of war."[5] At the same time, the Rykov Commission was dissolved only to be replaced by a new commission on 24 February, which was soon renamed to the above-mentioned RZ STO.[6] While it was similarly short-lived, its successor, the Committee for Defense, was active for over a decade, from late 1930 all the way until the German invasion of the Soviet Union in June 1941.[7]

Voroshilov proved rather energetic and on 17 March 1927, a month after his initial presentation, the Politburo discussed his "defense plan" and resolved to take action: "To review the resolution-project presented by Comrade Voroshilov, a commission is to be established, consisting of Comrades Voroshilov, Rykov, Stalin, Kuibyshev, Ordzhonikidze and Tolokontsev. [...] The commission shall be tasked with listening to the Voroshilov report and to prepare operative plans."[8]

Naturally, these preparations were not defensive in nature. By 1927 "capitalist" Europe had been gripped by a wave of pacifism and serious talks were under way to hold a disarmament conference in Geneva at the end of 1927. As a result, Stalin and his comrades knew that their preparations for war had to be conducted in secret – word could not be allowed to leak abroad.

To prevent any leaks, the Politburo decided at Stalin's behest to establish yet another commission, which was to "devise radical measures to ensure maximum secrecy in the handling of secret documents."[9] The commission then presented its proposal to the Politburo, which approved it on 5 May 1927.[10]

Every document that had to do with these war preparations was classified as top-secret at the very least, meaning that only members of the Politburo were allowed to view them. Even the Central Committee, which formally supervised the Politburo, was barred from seeing such documents, as was the Council of People's Commissars, formally the Soviet Union's government. Furthermore, the decisions of the Politburo dealing with war preparations were sent only to individual leaders charged with very specific tasks, and only in narrow excerpts, not as entire documents. As a result, only a small number of Politburo members had an overall view of the entire plan and state of war preparations. This fragmentation makes it hard for historians to fully reconstruct the totality of the Soviet war preparations after 1927.[11]

As with Rykov's earlier commission, the new one also highlighted the catastrophic state of the Soviet armaments industry and the Red Army. When Voroshilov reported on the problems within the armaments industry in April 1927, he focused especially on the planned wartime demand and the existing production capacities.[12]

Table 3: Mobilization demands and war production in case of war (April 1927)[13]

	Mobilization Demand	Production in the First Year of the War	Production in the Second Year of the War
Rifles	900,000	50%	75%
Machine Guns	18,000	30%	45%
Rounds of Ammunition	3,250,000	29%	50%

The table demonstrates clearly that the Soviet armaments industry was indeed nowhere near ready for war. The most impactful bottleneck was in the production of gunpowder – the Soviet armaments industry could only satisfy 41% of wartime demand. Tank production was absent, and the aircraft industry was both too backward and rudimentary to supply the Red Army with modern planes. The production of chemical weapons was in a similarly poor state.[14] All in all, the Soviet Union was economically unable to wage a great revolutionary war.

Table 4: Spending for Military Purposes and on the People's Commissariat for Military and Naval Affairs 1923/4 – 1928/9 (in thousand rubles)[15]

1923/24	1924/25	1925/26	1926/27	1927/28	1928/29
444,660	471,005	644,829	779,489	1,056,238	1,148,455

Having realized the disastrous effects of underfunding, the Politburo began to drastically increase military spending beginning in the fiscal year 1925/6. In May 1927, the Red Army was the largest army in Europe, with 607,125 men, including 32,722 in the navy. In case of mobilization, the Red Army could count on 2.6 million men. However, this army was very poorly equipped. In the event of war, it could muster 1,046 aircraft, 90 tanks – organized in three tank battalions with 30 tanks each, 99 armored vehicles and 7,034 artillery pieces. Poland, Romania, the Baltic states, and Finland – the countries which the Red Army would have to fight in the first stage of the revolutionary war – could mobilize up to 3.1 million men, 1,190 aircraft, 401 tanks and 5,620 artillery pieces.[16]

To make matters worse, the Soviet tanks and aircraft were not only few in number, but were also obsolete. The tanks the Red Army had in 1927 were the ones that had been captured in the Civil War or were copies of the French Renault tanks that had been captured in 1919.[17] Soviet aircraft was on a similarly low technological level as the tanks, as were chemical weapons, which were seen as one of the "main weapons" of the coming war alongside aircraft, tanks and artillery, as Voroshilov confidently stated in a report on 10 January 1933.[18]

When the Five Year Plan (1928-1932) for the expansion of the Red Army was being drafted in 1927/8, Soviet planners consequently put much emphasis on ensuring the army's supply of modern equipment. Furthermore, the plan also foresaw the numerical expansion of the Red Army to 630,500 men in peacetime and 3.5 million men in case of mobilization, as well as a million horses. The goal was also to stockpile ammunition, equipment, weaponry, fuel and food, enough to last for the first stage of war, or 1.5 years. Additionally, the economy of the country had to be reorganized so that it would be able to completely fulfill wartime demand in just 1.5 years.[19] This was a very ambitious program, and was to be implemented gradually. On 21 July 1927, the Politburo took the first step and ordered the peacetime strength of the Red Army to be moderately increased from 612,000 to 617,000. At the same time, the number of tanks was to rise to 2,510, from just 90 in May; the number of aircraft was to increase to 4,522 and the number of artillery pieces to 13,650.[20] In the month before, the Red Army had only been able to field just over 1,000 aircraft and 7,000 artillery pieces.

The Soviet planners also thought about the rear areas of the future front against the West, i.e. the Belarusian and the Ukrainian SSRs. Here, the Bolsheviks focused on: a) the implementation of a general military mobilization, the 'b) fight against desertion, c) fight against banditry and rebellions", d) protection of institutions important to the state and e) general measures to protect the revolutionary order. In the fight against "bandits" and rebels, it was the OGPU and the "troops for special use" who would see action as well as the militia and – if necessary – the Red Army too.[21] These precautions demonstrate how afraid the Soviet rulers were of their own subjects – they not only had to fear desertion but also outright popular rebellions. This was not surprising considering that the Soviet Union had to face several large uprisings earlier that decade.

This ambitious armament program went counter to the overall climate of political stabilization, economic growth, and pacifism that prevailed in Europe following the chaos of the immediate post-war years. The erstwhile pinnacle of the international disarmament movement was the Geneva Conference of 1927, held between 30 November and 3 December. Preliminary talks began in 1925 and it soon became clear that the goal of the conference was to reduce both the participant countries' standing armies and armaments industries, and to establish international commissions to oversee the disarmament. This was unacceptable to the Kremlin, for it would put an end to its ambitious armament program and thus preclude the very opportunity of a grand revolutionary war.

On 12 December 1925, the League of Nations invited Chicherin to participate in the preparations for the conference. Thus prompted, the Politburo responded on 7 January 1926, declaring that in principle, the Soviet Union was willing to take part in the preliminary talks.[22] As the negotiations progressed, the Politburo became more reserved. When it debated the matter again on 14 June 1927, it resolved among other things: "4a) to take no initiative on the question of the participation of the USSR in the disarmament conference, nor to hold exploratory talks in this matter; 4b) given the possibility of being asked to by the League of Nations, to task the People's Commissariat for Foreign Affairs to conduct preparations."[23]

By 3 November 1927, the Politburo felt it had no other option than to attend and it officially confirmed its participation in the conference beginning later that month. However, it did not intend to play a constructive role, instructing Litvinov, the leader of the Soviet delegation, to insist on a "broad disarmament program up to the complete abolition of standing armies" – an unpalatable proposal for most participants.[24] Two weeks later, on 17 November, the Politburo issued detailed instructions to the Soviet delegation, among others demanding that on the topic of chemical and biological arms control, "public oversight" was to be replaced with "workers' oversight", yet another motion clearly designed to derail the conference.[25]

Over the following days, the position of the Politburo further crystallized. On 28 November – a mere two days before the start of the conference – Litvinov received a telegraph with last-minute instructions for him and his delegation:

> We order you to insist by all means possible on complete disarmament. [...] In voting against practical proposals brought forth by other states, argue not only on the grounds that these proposals are inconsistent with complete disarmament, but also with factual objections showing that these proposals have no practical meaning for disarmament and peacekeeping.[26]

The telegraph reveals the true intention of Stalin and his comrades: The goal was to sabotage the disarmament negotiations, and in this, they were successful. On 30 November, during the opening of the IV Session of the Commission of the League of Nations in Geneva, the Soviet delegation read out its declaration, requesting to implement a program of total disarmament. As expected, the Soviet proposal was immediately rejected, and the entire conference was effectively derailed.[27]

The contemporary Western press rightfully recognized the Soviet conduct as insincere.[28] Stalin, meanwhile, dismissed the idea of disarmament as "bourgeois" and even "imperialist pacifism" aimed at "lulling the working class".[29]

As the Politburo was busy sabotaging the disarmament talks, the Soviet government embarked on a broad propaganda campaign warning of an immediate invasion of the Soviet Union. Top party leaders eagerly participated, repeatedly invoking the threat of foreign invasion, especially by Poland. The campaign had its desired effect at home and as rumors of an immediate war spread throughout the country, the population began to hoard supplies while peasants held back grain, many hoping that war would put an end to the hated communist system.[30]

Soviet propaganda about an imminent invasion did not reflect reality, however. As the Russian historian N.S. Simonov puts it:

> International historians have now shown convincingly that neither in the middle nor at the end of the 1920s was anybody preparing to attack the USSR. Public opinion in the countries which had been the victors in World War I was generally pacifist. Germany, where there was a strong revanchist mood, did not, under the terms of the Versailles peace treaty, have armed forces capable of conducting an aggressive war. The closest neighbours of the USSR did not have strategic and operational plans coordinated at general staff level for a surprise attack and destruction of the 'first socialist state in the world'.[31]

Why then was there a war scare? The answer is simple: The war scare was engineered to confront growing internal unrest by mobilizing both party and country, as well as to give the Bolsheviks a pretext for the grand war preparations. Stalin himself had repeatedly expressed such sentiment. Already in 1923, when the possibility of an attack on Poland was being discussed behind closed doors, Stalin raised the all-important question: "under which legal pretext can soldiers be mobilized, how can one preserve the appearance of love for peace or at least defense?"[32] The answer was: A war scare.

Years later, on 1 September 1930, Stalin wrote to Molotov: "The Poles are certainly forging (if they have not already done so) a bloc of Baltic states (Estonia, Latvia, Finland) to wage war against the USSR. I think that as long as they do not have this bloc, they will not start a war with the USSR, which means that *as soon as they have this bloc*, they will go to war (a reason can always be found)." This imagined threat – he knew very well that there were no such plans and that these countries had much smaller militaries than the USSR – Stalin took as justification to increase the size of the Red Army by "at least 40 to 50 divisions more than under our *current guidelines*."[33]

Stalin was far from the only one who thought that way. Felix Dzherzhinsky was also an eager follower of this tactic. On 11 July 1926, he wrote to Stalin: "A whole number of indicators show that without a doubt (for me) and in full clarity that Piłsudski is preparing an attack on us to take Belarus and Ukraine from us. […] Meanwhile, in large parts of the country there is a completely complacent mood."[34] At the time, Poland had just managed to avert a civil war and was still suffering from severe political and economic turmoil. Poland was in no shape to attack anyone, least of all the Soviet Union, and the Bolsheviks knew that very well, having intervened in the crisis themselves.

As Dzherzhinky noted, the war scare was also thought to be a means with which to fight against the "complacent mood" as well as against domestic foes. In the same letter, Dzherzhinsky further elaborated: "Piłsudski looks at our territorial divisions with complete contempt and is counting on the disruption of our party in connection with our conflict at the XIV Party Congress. I fear that his opinion in this regard may lead him to attack earlier than it is thought among us (in the Revolutionary War Council, they were talking about 1927)."[35]

Stalin and his supporters also used their manufactured war scares against Trotsky in a bid to discredit him. In the resolution project of the united Plenum of the Central Committee and the Central Control Committee from 8 August 1927, it read: "In the moment of a war threat, the central task of the party is to strengthen our own hinterland. And the main prerequisite for this is to increase war readiness and discipline the party. The opposition meanwhile pursues its own factional interests, subverts party discipline and thus promotes the development of anti-Soviet forces in our country."[36]

A year later, on 1 August 1928, Stalin called on his comrades in the Central Committee and the Central Control Committee: "Comrades, we are faced by two dangers: the danger of war, which has become the threat of war; and the danger of the degeneration of some of the links of our Party. In setting out to prepare for defense we must create iron discipline in our Party. Without such discipline defense is impossible. […] Only thus, only in this way shall we be able to meet war fully armed."[37]

Stalin would re-use this tactic time and time again. In the summer of 1932, in the early stages of the famine, parts of the Ukrainian party apparatus spoke out against the grain levies. Outraged at this attempt at insubordination, Stalin immediately invoked the danger of foreign invasion. In a letter to Kaganovich, he bitterly complained about the local party apparatus and the GPU in Ukraine, and warned: "If we do not tackle the improvement of the situation in Ukraine [via purges of the party apparatus] now, we risk losing Ukraine. Do not forget that Piłsudski does not sleep and that his agencies are stronger in Ukraine than Redens [chief of the OGPU in Ukraine] and Kosior [party chief in Ukraine] think."[38] The made-up threat of a Polish invasion was thus used to justify a new wave of terror in Ukraine.

"Pacifying" the "own hinterland" and purging it of "anti-Soviet elements" was a key priority for the Bolsheviks. After all, it was impossible to win a great revolutionary war with active resistance behind the front paralyzing the entire state – the Soviet Union needed a "strong revolutionary rear". Stalin elaborated on this idea on 28 July 1927, writing in *Pravda*:

It can scarcely be doubted that the main issue of the present day is that of the threat of a new imperialist war. It is […] the real and actual threat of a new war in general, and of a war against the USSR in particular. […] The task is to increase the defensive capacity of our country, to expand our national economy, to improve our industry – both war and non-war […]. The task is to strengthen our rear and cleanse it of dross, not hesitating to mete out punishment to 'illustrious' terrorists and incendiaries who set fire to our mills and factories, because it is impossible to defend our country in the absence of a strong revolutionary rear.[39]

The necessity of "pacifying" the hinterland and "cleansing it of dross" to win the future war was not a new development. As early as May 1920, during the war with Poland, Stalin had written about it in *Pravda*:

> No army in the world can be victorious (we are speaking of firm and enduring victory, of course) without a stable rear. The rear is of prime importance to the front, because it is from the rear, and the rear alone, that the front obtains not only all kinds of supplies, but also its man power – its fighting forces, sentiments and ideas. An unstable rear, and so much the more a hostile rear, is bound to turn the best and most united army into an unstable and crumbling mass.[40]

On 3 December, Stalin elaborated in his speech at the XV Party Congress: "For waging war, increased armaments are not enough, the organization of new coalitions is not enough. For this it is additionally necessary to strengthen the rear in the capitalist countries. Not a single capitalist country can wage an important war unless it first strengthens its own rear, unless it curbs 'its' workers, unless it curbs 'its' colonies."[41] This statement may have been about the capitalist states, but given the all-pervasive anti-Soviet mood in the Soviet countryside, it also applied to the USSR.

Who were the primary enemies in the hinterland? For Stalin and his comrades, these people were by and large the wealthy peasants – the kulaks – who riled up the villages, and the bourgeois specialists who allegedly sabotaged the build-up of Soviet industry. On 13 April 1928, Stalin exhorted his party comrades: "The fight against the kulaks must not be regarded as a trifling matter. In order to defeat the machinations of the kulak speculators without causing any complications in the country, we need an absolutely united party, an absolutely firm rear and an absolutely firm government"[42] In the same speech, Stalin also denounced the "bourgeois specialists" for trying to lead an "economic counterrevolution" and trying to destroy the Soviet Union's growing industry.[43]

Naturally, it was not just the kulaks and the bourgeois specialists who were discontent with Soviet rule, and the Bolsheviks knew this all too well. After all, the OGPU had been reporting on the widespread anti-Soviet sentiment in the Soviet hinterland; some areas were even judged to be close to an open insurrection. On 15 June 1928, Moissey Frumkin, a member of the inner party opposition, sent a letter to the Central Committee, in which he wrote that it was not just the kulaks but also the majority of average and poor peasants – the supposed bastions of Bolshevik rule in the countryside – who were deeply opposed to the Soviet Union, and that "this sentiment is already beginning to spread to the working-class centers".[44] While Stalin heavily denounced Frunkin's ideas, he did have to admit that: "Undoubtedly, the kulak is furious with the Soviet Government: it would be strange to expect him to be friendly towards it. Undoubtedly, the kulak has an influence on a certain section of the poor and middle peasants."[45]

With widespread rural discontent threatening the revolutionary hinterland, Stalin and his comrades were convinced that they had to "pacify" the countryside sooner rather than later if they wanted to win the coming revolutionary war. On 23 October 1927, he elaborated: "What does peace in the countryside mean? It is one of the fundamental conditions for the building of socialism. We cannot build socialism if we have bandit activities and peasant revolts."[46] As detailed earlier, "building socialism" meant preparing for the revolutionary war.

On 9 July 1928, Stalin explained at a session of the united Plenum of the Central Committee and the Central Control Committee: "Can we, in the event of enemy attack, wage war against the external enemy on the battle front, and at the same time against the *muzhik* [peasant] in the rear in order to get grain urgently for the army? No, we cannot and must not."[47] Unwilling to face such a two-front war, Stalin and his comrades resolved to "pacify" the countryside during preparations for the revolutionary war.

The Red Army itself was another point of concern. The OGPU reported that the anti-Soviet "peasant mood" had spread widely among the common soldiers and even affected many commanders. Stalin knew full well that he could not count on such an army to fight in the coming great revolutionary war. On 1 August 1927, Stalin talked about this issue at length at the united Plenum of the Central Committee and the Central Control Committee on the international situation and the defense of the USSR, citing parts of a speech he had given on the state of the Red Army several years earlier, on 21 March 1919:

I must say that those non-working-class elements – the peasants – who constitute the majority in our army will not voluntarily fight for socialism. A whole number of facts bear this out. The series of mutinies in the rear and at the fronts, the series of excesses at the fronts show that the non-proletarian elements comprising the majority of our army are not disposed to fight for communism voluntarily. Hence our task is to re-educate these elements, infusing them with a spirit of iron discipline, to get them to follow the lead of the proletariat at the front as well as in the rear, to compel them to fight for our common socialist cause, and, in the course of the war, to complete the building of a real regular army, which is alone capable of defending the country.[48]

These words may have been about the state of the Red Army in 1919, at the height of the civil war, but much of it still applied in 1927. According to a survey from 1 April 1926, the vast majority of ordinary Red Army soldiers were of peasant stock – 80.9%, whereas 14.1% were workers and 5% came from other backgrounds. The commanders – 47,822 in total – were more proletarian, but even among them, peasants accounted for 50% of the force, with 22% of commanders coming from working-class backgrounds and 28% from other backgrounds.[49]

The Failure of the Mobilization Plans of 1927/28

It was with the Mobilization Plans of 1927/28 that the Bolsheviks tried to revive the ailing Red Army. Years of neglect had seen the Red Army fall far behind the armies of Western Europe which it was designed to fight; even agrarian Poland's army had better, more modern equipment. In 1929, Soviet intelligence estimated Poland to have around 1,000 aircraft and 300 tanks. In addition, the Polish military was also much more mobile than the Red Army, mainly due to Poland having a better developed railway system that allowed troops and equipment to be transferred quickly.[50]

From the start, the top leadership of the Red Army, chief among them Tukhachevsky, who was the Chief of Staff until March 1928, called for the total economic mobilization of the Soviet Union. By putting the Soviet economy on a permanent war footing, the Red Army could be transformed into a modern mechanized army. This would also ready the yet-unprepared Soviet economy for the coming revolutionary great war, which Tukhachevsky assumed would be long and bloody, similar to the First World War. The lack of both financial and economic resources, as well as internal circumstances, made this impossible, however.[51]

In its Five Year Plan, the Politburo instead opted for a scheme that was somewhat less ambitious but nevertheless far from modest, seeking to equip the Red Army with 2,510 tanks, 4,522 aircraft and 13,650 artillery pieces.[52] Still, it soon became clear that even this downsized plan was doomed to failure as neither the civilian economy nor the armaments industry was able to cope with the demands.

In a bid to restore war readiness, the Politburo ordered a range of measures to be taken on 27 June 1927. Among others, it tasked Rykov with taking care of the defense industry.[53] On 11 July, the Politburo then ordered the RZ STO to devise and implement its own series of measures as well.[54] Four days later, Rykov wrote to Molotov: "The preparations for the defense of a series of larger factories and entire industrial sectors are still in a rudimentary condition. A complex administration system, many intermediate instances, frequent paper war – they all hinder the quick implementation of measures to prepare the factories and plants for wartime work."[55]

Rykov further said that a special working group – the so-called Institute – had been established. Composed of party functionaries, it was tasked with inspecting key factories, particularly in Leningrad, in regard to war readiness and overall performance. Over the following six months, it was to find the reasons behind the delay in the mobilization effort in the individual factories and to eliminate them. Rykov also emphasized that they were not to lead a "political campaign" but to focus on the task at hand.[56]

By February 1928, the first working group presented its findings. Summarizing them on 9 February 1928, Rykov reported that the group had found that "civilian factories often do not know which products they should make in case of mobilization. There is a lot of paper war in mobilization work. It was noted that there was negligent handling and storage of equipment and mobilization stores. The construction of war factories occurs without the necessary interest on the part of the managers of the factories and trusts. Management only seldom takes the initiative in such cases." As a result, Rykov ordered the working group to go back to work for another six months.[57]

However, this did not change much, and the activities of the working groups and the commissions did not yield a great deal. On 26 March 1929, the RZ STO set up another commission to examine the progress of war preparations, which presented the devastating results in early July.[58] On 15 July 1929, the Politburo once again discussed the state of the Soviet armaments industry and found that the issues were so severe that they compromised the entire armament program of the Red Army as well as the mobilization plans of the economy.[59]

Despite all the efforts of the past years, it was found that the wartime capacities of the defense industry had in fact shrunk and that it would take the factories 1 to 1.5 years to reach their full wartime capacity. This in turn necessitated the accumulation of great stores of military equipment with which to supply the Red Army until industry was producing at full capacity in case of war.[60]

Furthermore, the Politburo also criticized the many supply bottlenecks in the defense industry which often led to the non-fulfillment of production plans. For example, there was a general lack of chemical components for the production of explosives, which in turn paralyzed ammunition production. Similarly, there was a lack of special steel needed for the manufacture of artillery pieces, rifles, and machine guns. Electricity was in short supply as well in most factories and many chemical factories also lacked enough steam engines.

The Politburo found that overall, the defense industry was not able to design new types of equipment and weapons systems and to mass-produce them. This was not only the case for advanced weapon systems such as tanks, but also more traditional ones such as artillery or even rifles. Additionally, the repair network was wholly inadequate, and the factories in the hinterland that were to serve as fallback manufacturing hubs for artillery parts were not properly prepared to pick up production in case of a war. This was a major problem because the main factories were "close to the front" in places like Leningrad, Bryansk or Kyiv, and therefore vulnerable to attack.[61]

Finally, there were serious organizational problems as well. Although the machinery already present was not being fully utilized, foreign machines were still being bought abroad for a lot of money. At the same time, the production processes were outdated and needed to be modernized. The Politburo had already found a scapegoat for these problems, namely the old bourgeois experts who had been in charge until 1928/29. However, once they and the counterrevolutionary organizations they had supposedly been part of were eliminated, industry was suffering from a shortage of skilled experts. This was the final nail in the coffin of the Soviet defense industry, and it was clear that in its current state, it would not be able to fully supply the Red Army with anything.[62]

After this devastating survey, the Politburo issued a series of orders designed to turn things around. Aside from setting up another commission to examine the situation further, the Politburo also called for the hunting down of saboteurs beyond the bourgeois experts who had already been eliminated, as well as "wreckers". At the same time, new weapons systems were to be designed and then mass-produced, while the delivery of resources and parts to the armaments factories was to be improved, which in turn had to make better use of their already existing production capacities. The Politburo then gave the RZ STO the task of implementing these measures.[63]

At that session on 15 July 1929, in addition to the state of the armaments industry, the Politburo also discussed the state of the Red Army and its war readiness. Voroshilov had prepared a report on these two issues and already sent a copy of the report to Stalin on 13 July.[64] The rest of the Politburo received it two days later and after discussing it, the Politburo adopted it as a decision.[65] In its decision, the Politburo thus diagnosed a whole host of issues with the Red Army and its lack of war readiness:

a) The technical basis of the armed forces is still very weak overall and lags far behind the technology of modern bourgeois armies;
b) the material supply of the mobilized army is very insufficient overall according to the existing mobilization plan;
c) the material defense reserves (imported as well as domestic) are extremely unsatisfactory;
d) the preparations of the entire industry, including the armaments industry, to meet frontline demand, is extremely unsatisfactory.[66]

Furthermore, the Politburo stated: "The Five Year Plan for the Development of the National Economy offers favorable conditions to remedy the listed shortcomings and to significantly increase the defensive preparedness of the USSR in terms of quantity and quality."[67]

The Politburo then resolved to order a series of changes to create "a modern military-technical basis for defense". First, the portion of the technical troops within the Red Army was to be further increased, while the number of auxiliary and service troops was to be cut. By the end of the Five Year Plan in 1932, the size of the Red Army was to increase to 643,700 men, and its war readiness and tactical training were to improve. The Politburo also criticized the poor housing conditions negatively affecting morale and educational efforts within the army; to change this, the Politburo ordered the remedy of the existing shortcomings and to accelerate the construction of barracks for common soldiers and apartments for commanders.[68]

The Politburo also found that the technological backwardness of the Soviet economy had seriously slowed down plans for the re-tooling of the military. Artillery and tank production was particularly affected, and targets could not be met. The Politburo responded by ordering the speed up of the modernization of modern weapon systems, as well as to develop and then mass-produce new models. For this, foreign technology was to be relied on; especially weapons systems that had already proved themselves were to be bought abroad.[69]

It was clear to the Bolsheviks that without Western technology, the Red Army could not be modernized. Vassili Litunovsky, a close associate of Voroshilov and the man responsible for the modernization of the Red Army, expressed this sentiment in a letter to Voroshilov:

> For me it is completely clear that we are not able to implement our technological program in the given timeframe. We have fallen back technologically to such an extent, wrecking activities have eaten up our cadres to such an extent that only in five years' time will we train young forces [...]. We cannot avoid hiring foreign technicians and engineers, buying technological secrets and proven models. For money, we can buy second-rate technological goods in America. Good, new inventions and good engineers, however, we can only buy in Germany.[70]

The air force was another weak point even though it had been one of the key areas the armaments program of 1927 had focused on: "It has to be said that it [the air force] is lagging behind in terms of quality, which negatively impacts its combat capabilities."[71] Particularly problematic was the manufacturing of engines; and without modern engines, newer aircraft could not be produced, which in turn prevented the modernization of the air force. The Politburo gave the RZ STO the order to specifically address this issue, instructing it to rely on foreign technology. Aside from hiring leading foreign experts and buying successful aircraft models, domestic research and design capabilities were to be improved as well, especially in the area of engine production.[72]

On 10 August 1929, roughly a month after this resolution, Litunovsky wrote another letter to Voroshilov in which he complained that the flurry of directives, resolutions, and plans had no noticeable impact on the aviation industry. He continued: "In the design work [in the aviation industry], a decisive and radical breakthrough is necessary. Otherwise, all of our resolutions and the Five Year Plan will only remain on paper. Otherwise, we will be misled, and even worse, we will mislead the higher agencies."[73]

In the aforementioned resolution from 15 July 1929, the Politburo also decided to expand the Red Army in general to a larger extent than they had planned initially in 1927. The strength of the mobilized army was to be increased from 2.6 million to 3 million by the end of 1931, while the Red Army was to receive even more modern equipment. Thus, the number of combat-ready aircraft was to be raised from 1,032 or 2,000, with a reserve of 1,000 additional aircraft to be mobilized in times of war. By the end of 1931, the Red Army was to have in its possession 9,348 pieces of light and heavy artillery as well as anti-air guns, and another 3,394 small-caliber guns, in addition to 1,500 combat-ready tanks and another 1,500-2,000 in reserve. Trotsky may have been pushed out already, but new chemical weapons were still to be developed as well. Finally, the mobilization stores were to be raised accordingly, which included a mobilization reserve of 150,000 to 160,000 motor vehicles.[74]

This armament program targeted only the army and air force. After all, the coming revolutionary war was to be fought as an offensive war on the Central European Plain, in what was then Poland and Germany. The navy was far less important for such a land war and while the budget of the Red Army was raised significantly on 15 July 1929, the Red Fleet faced devastating cuts and saw its budget fall from 284.5 million rubles to just 200 million rubles, with the savings going to the Red Army.[75]

The Politburo also put a lot of emphasis on logistics. For example, the railway system was to be improved and new roads were to be built "especially in the BSSR and the UkSSR" – the deployment areas for the future revolutionary war. At the same time, the Politburo embarked on a campaign against "negative phenomena" in the Red Army that hampered the "building of socialism" such as "kulak" sentiment, anti-Semitism, poor discipline and bureaucratism.[76]

Chapter 12

Strengthening the Hinterland: The Hunt for Wreckers, Saboteurs, Spies and Counterrevolutionary Elements

As other communist states would later emulate, the beginning of the great industrialization and armament program in 1927/28 went hand in hand with a new, far-reaching wave of communist terror. This time, it not only targeted religious authorities but all former members of the old ruling class, the *byvshe lyudi* – the former people. At first, they were dismissed from their posts in the ministries, councils, schools, and universities.[1] In 1929 and 1930 alone, 164,000 officials were purged from the Soviet administration; many of them were arrested, deported, and even executed. The purge also affected the family members of these "socially alien elements" and for example, their children were barred from universities.[2]

This terror wave was directly connected to the war preparations and was to pacify the still-hostile "own hinterland" ahead of the coming revolutionary war. Thus, the focus lay not only on the persecution of "bourgeois" specialists in the defense industry who could sabotage the armaments program from within, but also on the "White guards", ethnic minority intelligentsia and the kulaks in the countryside.

On 3 March 1927, following a speech by the chief of the OGPU Vyacheslav Menshinsky, the Politburo found that the most important armaments factories as well as many otherwise defense-relevant factories were not sufficiently protected from enemy agents. The Politburo, therefore, set up a commission headed by the very same Menshinsky that was to devise measures to secure these factories from potential bomb attacks, arson and sabotage in general, but also from other issues that slowed down the work.[3]

On 31 March, the commission presented its result to the Politburo, which adopted its suggestions with minor amendments.[4] From now on, there was to be a permanent OGPU commission watching over the armaments industry, fighting against fires, explosions, accidents, and other disturbances caused by enemy agents and negligence. Local party organizations, as well as factory workers, were to participate in this struggle, and the managers were now personally liable if something went wrong. Furthermore, armament factories, railway installations, important government agencies and factories, as well as other strategically important installations were to be guarded by troops of the OGPU or the Red Army itself.[5]

The Politburo also ordered the removal of anyone living without permission on the property of important state facilities and of ammunition and bomb depots – from the looks of it, lack of housing had led people to squat there. Carelessness and a failure to adhere to safety standards were to be punished more stringently by the OGPU and the party. The OGPU was even given the right to punish such offenders without the involvement of courts, up to and including the death penalty and the publishing of the executions in local newspapers. Additionally, foreign defectors were barred employment in armaments factories, military depots, in the railway system and in key industrial sectors. In general, the borders were closed to foreign defectors, and they were also banned from Soviet Ukraine, Belarus, the Caucasus, the Moscow and Leningrad Military districts, as well as from the chief railway lines and industrial centers elsewhere. Only the OGPU was able to issue exemptions. At the same time, the Politburo also ordered a purge of unwanted elements from the railway system in Belarus, Ukraine, and the Leningrad Military District over the next six months.[6] In addition to protecting key industries from enemy action, these measures also served to keep the ongoing war preparations secret. The Politburo sought to enhance secrecy even further and also ordered stricter confidentiality regulations to be drawn up.

Before long, the purges began in earnest as well. On 7 June 1927, a White Russian émigré assassinated Pyotr Voykov, the Soviet emissary to Poland. Never one to miss out on a golden opportunity, Stalin sent an encrypted telegram to Molotov the next day: "The murder of Voykov presents us the opportunity to smash the monarchist and White guard cells in the entire USSR with all revolutionary means. This is what our task of strengthening our own hinterland requires."[7]

These were no empty words. Already on 8 June, the Politburo passed a series of measures against "White guards", including a broad, OGPU-led propaganda campaign seeking to "educate" the population on the White guards' supposed nefarious activities and the danger they posed. Additionally, the OGPU was to conduct mass searches and arrests of White guards, and twenty well-known White guards were to be executed and their executions to be made public. To fulfill its task, the OGPU was given extra reinforcements in both materiel and personnel, and also gained the right to enact extrajudicial punishments, including executions.[8] In an effort to further justify this terror wave, the Politburo also issued a "call of the Central Committee on the growing danger of war and the attempts of the White guards to disorganize our hinterland" on 27 June.[9]

The next group was the "bourgeois specialists". Due to the lack of qualified personnel, throughout the 1920s the Bolsheviks had allowed former Tsarist technicians, engineers, designers, as well as administrators, professors, lawyers and similar specialists back into their former professions. As a result, these people now played a key role in the Soviet Union, including in industry, where most leadership positions in factories and in the administration were held by former Tsarist professionals. However, the Bolsheviks deeply mistrusted them on an ideological basis and in 1928, they declared these "bourgeois experts" to be responsible for virtually all problems the Soviet Union faced while building socialism, i.e. its war preparations.

The pretext for this became the Shakhty Trial of 1928. In this show trial, Bolshevik authorities uncovered serious instances of mismanagement in the coal mines around Shakhty in the Donets Basin, for which they blamed the managers and engineers. As coal was not only the basis of energy generation and railway transport but was also a key material for the heavy and chemical industries, this trial put a spotlight on the supposed sabotage of the Soviet war preparations.

In the course of its investigations, the OGPU found that much of the machinery and equipment that had been bought in the West for a lot of money was rusting away in the open air. If it was utilized it was misused and poorly maintained which in turn led to countless accidents.

At the same time, safety precautions were routinely ignored and workers were intimidated; beatings were even reported. The miserable working conditions triggered frequent strikes and walkouts, and as a result, the production plans could not be fulfilled in time, which in turn had a cascading effect on the rest of the Soviet economy.[10]

These issues were not uncommon at all. In fact, they were a hallmark of the Soviet economy and administration - and would remain so until the very end. Still, the Bolsheviks declared these problems to be part of the "economic counterrevolution" led by the "bourgeois specialists" who were conspiring with foreign enemies, usually from Poland and Germany. Stalin himself showed great personal interest in this trial and aside from purging the bourgeois specialists, he also spearheaded a campaign to create a "red intelligentsia" to replace the old one.[11]

Stalin soon widened his search for "wreckers" and "saboteurs" from the coal mining industry to other industrial sectors and the transport system, which were also suffering from disastrous mismanagement.[12] On 16 June 1928, Stalin forwarded an OGPU report on wrecking activities in the railway sector to several party leaders. In the accompanying letter, he stated:

> Two months ago, an OGPU report on wrecking activities in the railway transport sector had been compiled. Now the second related OGPU report on wrecking activities in the railway transport sector is being sent around with new materials. [...] Considering the special importance of the question regarding both the development of our industry, and especially regarding the defense of our country, I ask you to *personally* read the report and to store it as a *highly classified document*.[13]

Together with economic difficulties and the criminality that came with it, the terror wave led to a massive increase in convictions. In 1926, 570,000 people had been convicted of all crimes. That number jumped to 709,000 in 1927, 909,000 in 1928, and in 1929 alone, a grand total of 1,178,000 people were convicted. However, the prisons had not been expanded sufficiently, and had only enough room for 150,000 prisoners. To cope with the soaring numbers of fresh convicts, the Politburo issued a decree under which shorter prison sentences were to be replaced with unpaid labor "in factories, on construction sites or in forestry" with the expressed hope to "reeducate" the convicts.[14] On 27 June 1929, the Politburo went a step further and decided that all prisoners who had been sentenced to three or more years now had to serve their sentences in labor camps. This became the legal basis for the infamous gulag system.[15]

Chapter 13

The "Pacification" of the Village and Financing War Preparations

The hunt for saboteurs and wreckers within industry and administration remained a top priority for the Bolsheviks, but the main focus of these purges was the rural hinterland, which accounted for around 80% of the Soviet population in 1927. There, the majority continued to be hostile to the Bolshevik cause and in some areas such as Ukraine and the Cossack lands, there was a real danger of an insurrection. That the rural population was already restive under the status quo presented the Bolshevik leadership with a serious problem, because the means needed to finance the Soviet Union's ambitious industrialization and war preparation program had to be taken from the peasantry. However, the peasantry had already rebelled once over the Bolsheviks' high taxation in 1920/21, which had brought Soviet Russia to the brink of collapse and had forced Lenin to accede to their demands and end War Communism.

The taxes the Bolsheviks planned to impose on the peasantry were enormous, because developing Soviet heavy industry to be able to support the armament effort was exceedingly costly. This was especially the case for the mechanical engineering sector, "the principal nerve of industry in general".[1] Stalin knew this all too well. In a speech on 13 April 1926, he declared that "in order to renovate our industry on the basis of new technical equipment, we need considerable, very considerable, amounts of capital. And we are very short of capital, as you all know."[2]

Stalin continued to explain that the way forward was "to find funds for industry out of our own savings, the way of socialist accumulation, to which Comrade Lenin repeatedly drew attention as the only way of industrialising our country."[3] He was not entirely wrong. Although the USSR was able to take out a German loan worth 300 million marks to buy

German industrial equipment and machinery, the loan had to be repaid within four years, and the 9.5% effective interest rate was painfully high. At the same time, German manufacturers oftentimes sold their equipment at inflated prices and did not always deliver on time. Despite these issues, the Bolsheviks continued to search for further loans abroad, including a 600 million mark loan from Germany to be repaid within ten years in 1929, but these efforts remained unsuccessful.[4]

Anastas Mikoyan, who had just been appointed People's Commissar of Internal and External Trade in August 1926, was now given the task of raising the necessary funds for the purchase of industrial equipment and machinery through the export of raw materials and agricultural products. Decades later, Mikoyan looked back on that period: "We exported all kinds of foodstuffs that we needed for ourselves to finance imports, Siberian butter, eggs, pork, agricultural raw materials like linen, hemp and others." According to Mikoyan, this was a key priority for Stalin, who demanded to personally oversee questions of trade.[5]

Even though grain exports would soon play a key role, they were relatively marginal at the beginning. In the third quarter of the 1927/28 budget year, grain and related products only accounted for 2.5% (4.766 million rubles) of total exports, which stood at 187.972 million rubles. The share of grain rose in the 1928/29 budget year, but out of the total exports of 910 million rubles, grain still only accounted for a meager 4.4%. Much more important was the export of wood, which stood at 20.5 million rubles in the third quarter of 1927/28, and at 45 million in the third quarter of 1928/29, eggs (18 million and 20 million, respectively), butter (10.5 and 15.5 million, respectively) and linen (4.5 and 14.5 million, respectively).[6] The export of grain only began to play an outsized role after 1929. By 1929/30, grain accounted for 14.5% of exports (total: 895 million rubles), which further rose to 21% in 1930/31 (total: 1.089 billion rubles).[7]

This was no coincidence that Stalin and his comrades had identified the export of grain as one of the key pillars of "socialist accumulation". In June 1928, Mikoyan prepared a memorandum on the grain procurement policy; Stalin personally read and then edited it, before sending it to top party leaders on 30 June. In it, Mikoyan emphasized the importance of grain: "It is on the scope of exports of agricultural goods and especially grain products that the scope of imports of means of production for industry depends upon, it creates a certain limit for the speed of industrial development."[8]

Mikoyan also pointed out that even though the area under grain cultivation was at 95% of pre-war levels, grain production was just under 50% of what it was before the war. As a result, the export of grain – which had amounted to 600-700 million pud a year – had more or less ceased. To remedy this, Mikoyan and Stalin declared that it was necessary to finally implement the decision of the XV Party Congress, turning small-scale peasant farms into large collectives equipped with modern technology. Only that way, they argued, could grain production be sufficiently raised. Furthermore, new government-owned farms, the sovkhozes, were to be set up while the existing ones were to be expanded.[9]

On 3 December 1927, at the above-mentioned XV Party Congress, Stalin had proclaimed that the way to increase agricultural productivity rapidly was "to turn the small and scattered peasant farms into large united farms based on cultivation of the land in common, to go over to collective cultivation of the land on the basis of a new and higher technique."[10] At the time, collective and state farms only accounted for around 2% of agricultural production, Stalin claimed.

The trigger for this collectivization campaign was the grain procurement crisis that began to unfold in the autumn of 1927. In November 1927, Soviet authorities noticed that the amount of grain levied from peasants had fallen, even though the harvest had been good. The shortfalls further increased over the course of December, and by the end of January 1928, the peasants had only delivered 4.8 million tons of grain, 7.81 million tons less than planned. This threatened to throw the entire Soviet economy into disarray. The reasons for this were manifold: the prices the government offered for the peasants' grain were too low, the prices for industrial goods had increased rapidly, rumors of war – spread by the Bolsheviks themselves – had convinced peasants to store food, while a lack of organization in the agencies responsible for grain procurement slowed down grain collection. Officially, however, the reason was far simpler: A "kulak strike".[11]

Labelling the grain procurement shortfalls a result of enemy sabotage, Stalin and his comrades fully broke with the NEP and instead resorted to the old methods that had been pioneered under War Communism a decade earlier. Travelling directly to Siberia, Stalin personally organized a forced grain procurement campaign in January 1928, while his closest associates did the same in the other grain-growing regions of the Soviet Union. The Politburo ordered local authorities to arrest all kulaks, speculators, and other "disruptors of the market and the price policy". Thousands of communists were thus organized into special commandos which were then unleashed onto the villages of the Russian and non-Russian countryside. There, they searched farms, confiscating grain, meat, and all kinds of household possessions. Peasants and their families were attacked and handed over to various security agencies for punishment. At the same time, the taxes on the wealthy peasants were repeatedly increased; within just two years, they rose tenfold. Markets were closed as well in order to prevent trade in agricultural products.[12]

Naturally, these acts of plunder enraged the rural population, and even Stalin had to publicly admit that the anti-Soviet and anti-urban sentiment in the villages was radicalizing rapidly. On 13 July 1928, Stalin held a speech at a party conference in Leningrad, in which he lamented that the "renewed recourse to emergency measures, the arbitrary administrative measures, the infringements of revolutionary law, the house-to-house visitations, the unlawful searches and so on [...] worsened the political situation in the country and created a threat to the bond [between the working class and the peasantry]."[13]

Although the grain procurement crisis of 1927/28 did trigger serious unrest, it also provided Stalin and his comrades with a pretext to deal with the kulaks and the other anti-Soviet elements in the countryside once and for all. It also marked the beginning of the great collectivization campaign to secure grain procurement in the future. It also marked the start of the dekulakization campaign, the deliberate annihilation of the wealthier peasants, which would peak between 1930 and 1932.[14] Already in January 1928, Stalin had declared:

But there is no guarantee that the kulaks will not again sabotage the grain procurements next year. Moreover, it may be said with certainty that as long as there are kulaks, there will be sabotage of the grain procurements. In order to put the grain procurements on a more or less satisfactory basis, other measures are required. What measures exactly? I have in mind developing the formation of collective farms and state farms. [...] We cannot allow our industry to be dependent on the caprice of the kulaks. We must therefore see to it that in the course of the next three or four years the collective farms and state farms, as deliverers of grain, are in a position to supply the state with at least one-third of the grain required.[15]

Stalin sought to remake the countryside and replace the villagers' individual farms with grand, collectively or state-owned "grain factories", as he put it on 13 April 1928.[16] In this, he was trying to emulate the example of the mechanized, large-scale corporate farms in the USA.[17] However, because the Soviet farms would be directly controlled by the state, Stalin intended to take the grain without paying market prices, increasing profit margins and thereby fueling the extremely costly war preparations. For Stalin, this was a return to War Communism. In a speech on 5 July 1928, he defined it as such:

> War communism is a policy forced upon the proletarian dictatorship by a situation of war and intervention; it is designed for the establishment of direct product-exchange between town and country, not through the market but apart from the market, chiefly by measures of an extra-economic and partially military character, and aims at organising such a distribution of products as can ensure the supply of the revolutionary armies at the front and of the workers in the rear.[18]

Although the Soviet Union was not at war or even under threat of an invasion, by manufacturing successive war scares, the Soviet Union was able to justify the reintroduction of this modernized version of War Communism in 1928 and 1929. The NEP was over.[19]

Initially, the collectivization campaign progressed rather slowly as Soviet authorities tried to convince the peasants to join the kolkhozes and sovkhozes – which accounted for only 2% of agricultural production at the end of 1927[20] – through largely administrative means such as high taxation as well as intimidation. Frustrated by the slowness of the campaign, the Bolsheviks ramped up the pressure on the peasantry in the second half of 1929, which finally brought the breakthrough, especially in the key grain-growing regions.[21]

Between June and September 1929, the number of kolkhozes thus nearly doubled from around one to nearly two million. The collectivization in the North Caucasus and the Lower Volga Region was particularly rapid, where 19% and 18%, respectively, had been collectivized.[22] By December 1929, 124 rayons (5.3% of all rayons), reported collectivization rates of over 70%, 117 rayons (4.9%) reported rates of 50-70%, 266 (11.2%) reported rates of 30-50%, 461 (19.4%) rayons claimed to have collectivized 15-30% of all farms. However, in 59.2% of rayons (1,405 in total), collectivization rates were still below 15%.[23]

In response to the forced grain requisitions, collectivization, and the terror in general, the already tense situation in the countryside began to escalate immediately. Among others, this was documented in the reports of the OGPU, which noted a drastic increase in mass protests and "acts of terror" beginning in early 1928.

Table 5: "Acts of Terrorism" and Mass Protests in the Countryside, 1926-1929[24]

	1926	1927	1928	1929
"Acts of Terrorism"	711	901	1,027	9,137
Mass Rallies	63[25]		703	1,307

In particular, the OGPU recorded attacks (including killings) and arson, targeting Soviet activists who went out to terrorize the villages. The forced grain requisitions also triggered mass protests, as did the closing of churches. In 1929, the OGPU reported that despite the terror, 300,000 people – most of them women – took part in such mass protests.[26]

However, all the attacks on Soviet activists paled in comparison to what these activists were unleashing on the peasantry. According to the OGPU, 95,208 people were accused of being counterrevolutionaries and then arrested in the Soviet countryside. During these arrests, the OGPU claimed to have destroyed 225 counterrevolutionary organizations, 6,769 counterrevolutionary groups and 281 active bands, which had virtually all been formed in response to the "grain procurement campaigns" and displayed an "insurrectionary spirit".[27] Even though the terror campaign of 1928/29 had been extremely destructive in its own right, it was just the prelude to the total war against the peasantry that Stalin and his comrades would unleash upon the countryside in January 1930.

Part II

Stalin Prepares for Total War

Chapter 14

The Great Depression and Its Consequences

Throughout the 1920s, the Bolshevik leaders in Moscow looked on in horror while their dreams of world revolution faded away as the capitalist countries of Europe continued to recover economically and stabilized politically. Still, they were convinced that this period of stabilization was just temporary. Sooner or later, the internal contradictions of capitalism were bound to trigger another crisis that would plunge the "imperialist" countries into another fratricidal great war. This would in turn present the Soviet Union with the perfect opportunity to launch a grand revolutionary war against the weakened capitalists and finally realize the dreams of World Revolution. It was for this purpose that Stalin and his comrades began to massively expand the Soviet armaments industry and to "pacify" the hinterland in 1927/8, which stood in stark contrast to the general pacifist mood globally.

The communist parties in the various capitalist countries were given the task to exploit the coming crisis as well. Moscow wanted them to turn the "imperialist" wars into civil wars in order to trigger the "profound revolutionary crisis which revolutionises the masses, brings them to their feet and turns them abruptly towards communism."[1] To train communist party leaders for this purpose, a special school was set up in Moscow in 1928 to which, at first, only Polish communists were invited. On 14 January 1929, Leon Purman, the representative of the Communist Party of Poland [KPP], contacted the Politburo:

In accordance with the decision of the Central Committee of the KPP, a party school is to begin operations in Moscow in February of this year [1929] whose task it is to raise the theoretical level of our party activists. Due to the danger of war, this school shall, in accordance with the revolution of the VI Congress of the

Communist International, give special attention to all questions relating to the struggle against attacking troops as well as to the preparation of our party activists to turn the imperialist war into a civil war. A similar school had been operating for six months last year [1928].[2]

Purman then asked the Politburo for permission to launch such a school. Molotov forwarded the plea to Voroshilov who fully endorsed the idea, offering the support of Soviet military agencies – after all, the courses from 1928 had yielded promising results. At the same time, Voroshilov emphasized the necessity of utmost secrecy.[3]

The courses for the Polish communists must have been a success as well and on 25 October 1929, the Politburo backed a proposal by Voroshilov's deputy, Josef Unszlicht, that aimed to set up similar courses for communists from other countries also. From the protocol of the Politburo session:

1) Polish instruction courses with a training period of 9 months and 30 participants are to be established.
2) For groups of German-speaking attendees, courses with a training period of 5 months for 50 persons are to be established.
3) Such groups are also to be formed for French-speaking attendees, 30 persons, 5 months each.
4) The program of the already existing Leninist courses is to be expanded to include new military disciplines.
5) Military disciplines are to be added to the six-month courses of the Youth Communist International.
6) For next year, English groups are to be prepared for Great Britain and the USA; [...] To set the budgets [for these schools], provided will be:
a) For the training of Westerners in special courses 151,750 rubles, 28,800 US-Dollars;
b) For the training of Easterners [Chinese, Mongols] [...] 469,652.70 rubles, 10,800 US-Dollars;
c) For the training of three Germans at the military academy 10,521,4 rubles.[4]

Of course, training activists was just a small part of the revolutionary struggle. How exactly Moscow expected communists to transform a war into a revolutionary war, can be seen in the contemporary Manchuria policy. On 7 October 1929, Stalin wrote to Molotov:

> By the way, I believe that it is time for us to get ready to *organize* a *revolutionary* insurrectionary movement in Manchuria. The individual units we sporadically send to fulfill individual tasks in Manchuria are of course a good thing, but *they are not the correct thing to do.* We should plan to do *something greater.* We need to organize two brigades, consisting of two regiments each, which are mostly made up of Chinese, supply them with everything they need (artillery, machine guns, etc.) and put Chinese at the heads of these brigades. We need to infiltrate them into Manchuria with the task of triggering a revolt among the Manchurian troops, to draw reliable soldiers from these units (to send the rest back home, after removing the leadership beforehand), to consolidate them into divisions, to take Harbin, and, when one has gathered sufficient forces, to declare Zhang Xueliang to have been deposed, to establish revolutionary power (massacre the landlords, win the peasantry, establish councils in the cities and villages, etc.).[5]

Ever since the fall of the imperial Qing dynasty in 1912 and the death of Yuan Shikai in 1916, China had been politically fractured and in a state of ongoing civil war between the various factions of warlords that dominated the country. In other words: It was a country ripe for revolution – unlike contemporary Europe. Nevertheless, Stalin was completely convinced that capitalism would collapse and the seemingly stable European order with it – the prophesies of Marx and Lenin were inescapable, after all.[6]

By 1927, Stalin was claiming that the crisis of capitalism was about to occur any moment now. On 23 October, he said: "Only the blind can deny that the elements of the crisis of capitalism are growing and not diminishing."[7] This would inevitably lead to collapse, as he pointed out a little more than a month later, on 3 December: "The stabilization of capitalism is becoming increasingly rotten and unsteady. While one could and should talk about a subsiding of the revolutionary waves in Europe two years ago, we now have all reason to claim that Europe is clearly entering *the phase of a new revolutionary upsurge*." This would wash away the established order of Europe, Stalin elaborated: "Partial stabilization is giving rise to an intensification of the crisis of capitalism, and the growing crisis is upsetting stabilization—such are the dialectics of the development of capitalism in the present period of history."[8] This could easily lead to war, after all "that is how things were before the last imperialist war, when the assassination in Sarajevo led to war. That is how things are now."[9] Naturally, this became the official line of the Comintern.[10]

By that time, Stalin was the only senior party leader who still believed in the world revolution and eagerly awaited the coming crisis of global capitalism, Grigori Bessedovsky claimed. Bessedovsky had been a high-ranking Soviet diplomat with ties to the highest party circles before he defected to the West in 1929, and his defection became the topic of intense discussions in the Politburo session on 7 January 1930.[11] As Bessedovsky wrote in 1930:

Stalin is the only one among the old October Guard who still believes in the world revolution. He does not notice the ill effects of his economic policy on the country and does not acknowledge them. He is ruthless towards people. He strongly believes that he will be able to maintain the party apparatus until the day that, despite all obstacles and hindrances, the world revolution finally flares up. How could he maintain this belief? How can one believe this in the face of the evidence to the contrary? His belief is being affirmed by representatives from abroad and by emissaries in particular. From Berlin, from Tokyo, from Stockholm, from Rome and of course Paris [...] the representatives are reporting to the Politburo of the unstoppable advance of the 'revolutionary process'. It is necessary to lie. If the emissary tells the truth, he will not be believed; he will be suspected of 'alienation' and deposed. If the facts do not match the 'ideological attitude' set in Moscow, the worse for the facts. It is because of that, for six years already, the legations first ask about the attitude in Moscow before they compile their reports on the political situation in the specific country. [...] However, Stalin is not only being misled intentionally, because people fear his wrath and disfavor. Sometimes, this occurs unconsciously and the effect of such 'unconscious reports' is even more damaging. Stalin puts more faith in them than in official reports. [...] The Soviet dictatorship is thus upheld by Stalin's firm belief in the world revolution.[12]

Black Friday – The Visions Come True

For years, Stalin had prophesied the next great crisis and for years, nothing happened. On the contrary, the economies of the West continued to reach hitherto unknown heights and with prosperity fostering a climate of stability, the prospects for world revolution grew increasingly dimmer. This all changed in October 1929, when Wall Street crashed. American investors hastily withdrew the money they had invested abroad in the previous years and the contagion quickly spread across the globe, including to Europe. In the following years, industrial production contracted significantly, as did both international and domestic trade. Mass unemployment emerged once again and with it came political instability. This was a godsend for Stalin.

As the epicenter of the crisis, America was the hardest-hit major industrial economy in the world, with industrial production falling by an astounding 47% between 1927/28 and 1932/33, and national income by 52%. European countries were heavily affected as well, including the European industrial powerhouse of Germany, which saw industrial production drop by a slightly lower but still staggering 43% between 1927/28 and 1932/33, with national income falling by 40% between 1929 and 1932. Other European countries were hard-hit as well. Between 1929 and 1932, industrial production fell by 46% in Poland, 39% in Austria, 36% in Czechoslovakia, 33% in Italy, 31% in France and Belgium; the effects were relatively mild in Great Britain and Finland, with industrial production dropping by "only" 17% there.[13]

The most pressing issue was mass unemployment, which had grown to around 15 million in Europe and 12.06 million in the USA by late 1932.[14] In Germany, the number of unemployed had jumped from 1.9 million (9.6%) in 1929 to 3 million (15.7%) in 1930. Over the coming years, it only continued to rise, to 4.52 million (23.1%) in 1931 and then to an astronomical 5.575 million (30.8%) in 1932. In 1933, it fell to 4.804

million (26.3%), which was still extremely high.[15] The result was visible immediately – as political and social tensions escalated, German cities were rocked by bloody clashes and street riots claiming the lives of hundreds of people. In the end, the Weimar Republic was unable to weather this storm. The economic crisis and the political and social chaos that followed in its wake, led directly to Hitler's takeover of power in 1933.[16]

When news of the crisis reached Moscow, it immediately electrified the Bolshevik leadership – the long-awaited capitalist crisis that was bound to throw the established order into chaos had finally arrived. Already as early as 26 October 1926, the day after Black Friday, the old Bolshevik and Comintern functionary Iosif Pyatnitsky turned to Stalin with the idea to convene an expanded presidium of the Comintern in February 1930 that was to include members of the presidium currently staying abroad. At that meeting, two points were to be discussed: "1.) the approaching international economic crisis and the tasks of the C.I. [Communist International]; 2.) the financial policies of the sections of the C.I." Pyatnitsky went on to say that Manuilsky also wanted to have the various sections of the C.I. discuss their progress in fulfilling the guidelines set at the X Plenum of the Comintern, which referred to "mass struggle and labor in the factories".[17] Stalin quickly granted this request.

This was far from the only initiative that was being launched. On 17 December 1929, the secretariat of the Comintern organized a conference on the topic of the Great Depression. Manuilsky personally opened the conference and a host of Soviet economic experts and Comintern functionaries gave talks trying to analyze the developing situation. Eugen Varga, a Hungarian communist and Comintern functionary, made the main presentation in which he described the crisis as the explosion of the contradiction of capitalism. Varga went on to predict: "In terms of depth, breadth and dimensions of unemployment, this crisis will without a doubt break all contemporary 'records' of capitalism by far and result in an intense worsening of the social-political struggle."[18]

When the expanded plenum of the Comintern met in Moscow between 18 and 28 February, Stalin personally attended. Placing a fair deal of importance on that meeting, he and his inner circle had discussed – and set – the various resolutions and points of discussion of the plenum just a few days before on 14 February. Point 1 of the resolution of the presidium referred to "the developing world economic crisis, mass unemployment and labor struggle". In terms of geopolitical analysis, the resolution attested to the "acceleration of the collapse of capitalist stabilization", a "deepening and broadening of the revolutionary movement of the world proletariat", as well as the "maturing of the anti-imperialist revolution in the colonial countries". To facilitate the course of events, the presidium also called for general strikes.[19]

To organize these general strikes, Moscow sought to have communist agents infiltrate already established Western trade unions and repurpose them for the communist cause. On 3 January 1930, the Politburo decided to establish "an international school for the labor union movement" under the auspices of the Profintern, the Red International of Labor Unions.[20] Officially independent, the Profintern was in fact part of the Comintern which in turn was under the firm control of the Politburo.[21]

As the Great Depression continued to unfold, the seemingly vindicated Stalin grew increasingly triumphant. At his speech at the VI Party Congress on 27 June 1930, he looked back: "Recall the state of affairs in the capitalist countries two and a half years ago. Growth of industrial production and trade in nearly all the capitalist countries. Growth of production of raw materials and food in nearly all the agrarian countries. [...] And what is the picture today? Today there is an economic crisis in nearly all the industrial countries of capitalism. Today there is an agricultural crisis in all the agrarian countries."[22]

In accordance with Marxist-Leninist teachings, Stalin remained convinced that the Great Depression would turn into an imperialist war in the future. In the speech, he continued:

A most important result of the world economic crisis is that it is laying bare and intensifying the contradictions inherent in world capitalism. a) It is laying bare and intensifying the contradictions between the major imperialist countries, the struggle for markets, the struggle for raw materials, the struggle for the export of capital. [...] Means of struggle: tariff policy, cheap goods, cheap credits, regrouping of forces and new military-political alliances, growth of armaments and preparation for new imperialist wars, and finally – war. [...] b) It is laying bare and will intensify the contradictions between the victor countries and the vanquished countries. Among the latter I have in mind chiefly Germany. Undoubtedly, in view of the crisis and the aggravation of the problem of markets, increased pressure will be brought to bear upon Germany, which is not only a debtor, but also a very big exporting country. [...] To think that the German bourgeoisie will be able to pay 20,000 million marks within the next ten years and that the German proletariat, which is living under the double yoke of 'its own' and the 'foreign' bourgeoisie, will allow the German bourgeoisie to squeeze these 20,000 million marks out of it without serious battles and convulsions, means to lose one's mind.[23]

Stalin also pointed towards the increasing contradictions between the imperialist countries and their colonies and dependent states, as well as the contradictions between the bourgeoisie and the proletariat within the capitalist countries. He continued: "It is not surprising that these circumstances are revolutionising the situation, intensifying the class struggle and pushing the workers towards new class battles." Stalin then concluded: "What do all these facts show? That the stabilisation of capitalism is coming to an end. That the upsurge of the mass revolutionary movement will increase with fresh vigour [...] This means [...] that in the sphere of foreign policy the bourgeoisie will seek a way out through a new imperialist war. It means, lastly, that the proletariat, in fighting capitalist exploitation and the war danger, will seek a way out through revolution."[24] Believing that capitalism was on its way out, Stalin and his comrades tried their best to make the Great Depression even worse and to turn it into a greater socio-political struggle.

The Intensification of War Preparations: Total Mobilization of the Economy and Society

Moscow's activities were not limited to capitalist countries. On the contrary, the main focus lay on the Soviet Union itself, which had barely been affected by the Great Depression in any way thanks to its economic isolation. After all, the entire idea of Socialism in One Country had been to enable the Soviet Union to spread the revolution by way of arms. The repeated failures of the German communists between 1919 and October 1923, had convinced Stalin that he could not rely on communist activists alone. This time, the Red Army would assist the revolutionaries.

Once it was clear that the crisis in America had turned into a global crisis with no end in sight, Stalin and his comrades took a series of measures that raised the pace of Soviet war preparations. Chief among them were new armament plans that – if successful – would enable the Red Army to sweep away all opposition. At the same time, the persecution of domestic enemies – real and perceived – reached hitherto unknown dimensions as Moscow sought to secure its hinterland. Millions of people, most of them peasants, were directly affected by the waves of terror that washed over the country in the years to follow.

The Armament Plans after Black Friday

In early July 1929, the Politburo extensively reviewed the state of the armaments industry and the armed forces. The results were devastating – the ambitious armament plans from 1927/28 had failed completely. At the end of this review, on 15 July 1929, the Politburo devised new plans and ordered the existing issues to be taken care of. However, this did not result in any tangible initiatives by the time of the Wall Street Crash. On 5 November, the RZ STO alarmed Shaposhnikov, the Chief of Staff of the Red Army: "The question of war preparations remains unresolved to this day, because the staff of the Red Army has not yet submitted its final plans, even though it had promised to do so in July [1929]."[25] The situation was similar for the defense industry – nothing had been done since July 1929.[26]

However, this was soon to change as the unfolding world economic crisis spurred the Politburo into frenzied activity – the Red Army had to be well-armed to spread the flames of revolution abroad. The Politburo first turned its gaze towards tank production, because tanks were seen as the weapon of the future. On 25 November 1929, the Politburo established a commission that was to review the state of Soviet tank production.[27] Headed by Sergo Ordzhonikidze, one of Stalin's most trusted confidantes, the commission worked quickly and presented its results at the Politburo meeting ten days later, on 5 December. After some discussion, the Politburo adopted the commission's proposal.[28]

With the proposal, the Politburo acknowledged that the only tank model the Red Army had at the moment was the T-18, which was being produced at only one site, the "Bolshevik" factory in Leningrad. The T-18 had the following parameters: 12 km/h top speed, a 37mm caliber cannon and two machine guns, as well as 16mm armor. With these characteristics, the T-18s did not meet the requirements for modern warfare, the Politburo concluded. Furthermore, the Politburo criticized the lack of coordination between tractor and tank production, and that Soviet factories were unable to make the powerful tractors the Red Army needed. The production of both tank armor and engines had not been fully secured yet and the tank factories were suffering from a shortage of skilled designers. Finally, the Politburo pointed out that despite its resolution calling for a wide-ranging tank building program from 15 July 1929, no concrete plans for an expansion of tank factories had been drawn up.[29]

On 5 December 1929, the Politburo thus decided to take a series of measures to turn things around. First, the development of all aspects relating to the production of tanks and tractors (armor, engines, steel, etc.) had to be sped up considerably. The development of new and better tanks was to be sped up as well. Due to the backwardness of domestic designs, the Politburo resolved that an expert commission was to be sent abroad by 20 December 1929 at the latest. By 1 April 1930, these experts were required to select and buy several tank models, especially medium and heavy tanks, while also inquiring about the possibility of acquiring technical aid and recruiting foreign designers. At the same time, the Politburo decreed that the tank production program from 15 July 1929 was to be completed by late 1932/33, with the production targets for 1929/30 (300 T-18 tanks, 30 T-12 tanks and 10 armored reconnaissance vehicles) having to be met by October 1930.[30]

At least the procurement of foreign tanks was a success, and in 1930 and 1931, the Soviet Union bought the two tank models that would go on to become the foundation of the new Soviet tank industry. The first foreign tanks to be acquired were the Christie tanks. On 15 April 1930, the Politburo decided to import two of these tanks from the USA as well as technical assistance for their production. The modified Christie tanks – now termed BT tanks – entered mass production the following year. On 5 November 1930, the Politburo also decided to mass-produce a British model, a light Vickers tank, in the "Bolshevik" factory in Leningrad; however, these were to be modified by, among other things, switching them to Ford engines. A few months later, in January 1931, the Politburo also wanted to have a medium Vickers tank produced under the name T-26.[31]

While the expansion of the tank arsenal was one of the key components of the renewed armaments campaign, it was far from the only change. Already on 28 November 1929, the Politburo had increased the overall military budget by a relatively cautious 22 million rubles, and two days later, it approved Voroshilov's proposal to expand the Red Army by 15,000 men.[32] The total budget of the People's Commissariat for Military and Naval Affairs for 1929/30 now stood at 995 million rubles. In addition, the troops of the OGPU were assigned 66.85 million rubles; the medical administration was given 29 million rubles, while the armaments industry was given a budget of 128 million rubles.[33] Three months later, on 1 March 1930, the RZ STO further raised the 1929/30 budget of the People's Commissariat for Military and Naval Affairs to 1.017 billion rubles.[34] The ever-increasing budget now also included 550,000 rubles and 750,000 US-Dollars for "special work" abroad as well, approved by the Politburo a few months earlier, on 15 December 1929.[35]

At the same time, the Soviet Union also sought to import great numbers of tractors. On 20 December 1929, the Politburo thus ordered the export of an additional 25 million pud (1.526 million tons) of grain to finance the import of 8,000 to 10,000 tractors by the following spring. Indeed, the Soviet Union imported a grand total of 21,488 tractors between January and March 1930 alone. Also on 20 December 1929, the Politburo resolved to build up its domestic tractor industry by seeking technical support from abroad, preferably from the USA; if that proved impossible, from Canada or even Mexico. Negotiations had to be initiated with German firms producing tracked tractors as well. This was accompanied by instructions to the Highest Economic Council to draw up plans for the construction of tractor factories in the USSR.[36]

Shortly afterwards, on 7 January 1930, the Politburo decided on the composition of the expert committee that was to oversee the purchase of tractor technology from abroad, as well as the guidelines according to which it was supposed to operate. Specifically, the group under Ossinsky was to direct the purchase of the equipment, licenses, and technical aid needed to build two tractor factories - one in Chelyabinsk and one in Kharkiv - as well as two combine harvester factories. The plan was to have these plants built according to Western standards, by Western engineers and foremen, who were then to train local workers to operate and maintain the factories.[37]

The establishment of a Soviet tractor industry was important as it would certainly boost Soviet agricultural output, which would allow the government to finance an even larger military. However, that was far from the only reason. Also very important was the fact that it would greatly help in establishing a Soviet tank industry. After all, the technology was not too dissimilar – interwar Germany initially disguised its tank production as tractor production – and it was impossible to buy up entire tank factories from abroad. Only a few countries such as the USA, France, Italy, and the UK even had a tank industry to speak of, and none of them would willingly export their technology, especially not to the Soviet Union.

On 20 January, Ordzhonikidze's commission for tank production turned to the Politburo and suggested a range of new guidelines for the expert group overseeing the purchase of tractor models abroad. First of all, the commission had to be reorganized to meet the Red Army's demand for tanks. Ossinsky's group was to be given the task of buying individual models of both fast and slow tractors as well as engines, and to familiarize themselves with the production processes. Ordzhonikize's men were to draw up plans for the production of tanks in tractor and car factories in the meantime.[38]

As the Great Depression set in, Stalin and his comrades also turned their attention to the question of wartime mobilization. On 30 December 1929, Ordzhonikidze thus reported to the Politburo on the state of the mobilization plans and in response, the Politburo ordered a closed session to be held in which the responsible agencies were to report on the issue at length. In addition, Ordzhonikidze was also given the task of preparing a report on the state of the artillery.[39]

The Politburo discussed both topics on 15 January 1930.[40] At this session, the RZ STO report on the mobilization readiness of industry was adopted by the Politburo as its own decision. At the beginning, the report stated that between 1924 and 1 January 1930, around 600 million rubles had been spent on the build-up of the armaments industry to meet the army's basic demands in case of war. However, the Supreme Soviet of the National Economy (VSNKh) had so far failed to prepare a realistic plan for the mobilization of Soviet industry; if war were to break out between then and 1 July 1930, the Soviet armaments industry would be forced to operate without a mobilization plan.[41]

The plans that already existed foresaw the production of 11 million artillery shells and 2.2 billion rifle bullets for the first year of the war. This was nowhere near enough. In particular, the planned production of artillery shells lay below the real number in 1915, when Tsarist Russia produced 11.3 million artillery shells, which were further augmented by imports from abroad. The situation was particularly dire for heavy artillery. As a result, the Politburo promptly decided to increase the numbers; for the first year of war (beginning on 1 July 1930), the new plan foresaw the production of 19 million artillery shells, 3 billion rifle bullets, 53,500 light and heavy machine guns, as well as a number of artillery pieces in accordance with the plan of the RZ STO from 23 August 1928.[42]

At the same time, the Politburo passed several measures to raise the level of preparedness of Soviet industry. The armament factories still under construction were to be finished in time, and to achieve this, they were to be given the resources and equipment they needed from abroad. Furthermore, mobilization plans were to be drawn up for individual sectors of industry. Naturally, the Politburo naturally ordered these preparations to remain completely secret. Finally, it also criticized the fact that its resolutions on the armaments industry from July 1929 had been largely ignored. The RZ STO was thus given the task of overseeing the implementation of these measures; in case of non-compliance, those responsible were to be held accountable.[43]

Given the disastrous state of Soviet artillery, the Politburo paid special attention to it. The Revolutionary War Council was ordered to immediately being radically modernizing and rearming the army with the help of experts from abroad (Germany, USA, Italy). In the meantime, the Supreme Soviet of the National Economy was to accelerate its efforts to build up the armaments industry as well. To ensure compliance, the Central Committee ordered the Revolutionary War Council to report on its activities in three months' time.[44]

Thus spurred into action, the Revolutionary War Council discussed the modernization of armaments on 23 January 1930. After some deliberation, the War Council came to the conclusion that one of the main reasons the earlier modernization plan from January 1929 had failed was the administration of artillery. The sluggish pace of industrial production was seen as another factor, caused in part by an inexperienced and disorganized workforce. To remedy this situation, the Revolutionary War Council issued a series of orders to speed up the pace of modernization of individual weapons (such as the 7.62 mm rifle, the "Maxim" heavy machine gun and the 76 mm cannon of the MS-1 tank) as well as other equipment.[45]

The air force and the aviation industry also came into the spotlight and in January and February 1930, the Politburo created a special commission to investigate these sectors as well. Perhaps unsurprisingly, this commission also found many serious issues. While the Soviet air force was quite large at 1,628 military aircraft, only France (2,750) and the USA (2,040) had more, the quality and the flight parameters of the Soviet planes was considerably inferior. As a result, the report stated that the Soviet air force was weaker than the Polish one, even though it outnumbered it 3 to 1. The French, American, Italian, and British interceptors were able to reach speeds of up to 252-280 km/h at 3,000m and 246-280 km/h at 5,000m. The Polish planes were inferior, but they still managed to go as fast as 230 km/h at 3,000m and 225 km/h at 5,000m.[46] In contrast, the Soviet planes were only able to reach speeds of 180-220 km/h at 3,000m; at 5,000m, they were unable to even engage aircraft at all. Soviet interceptors were also too slow to gain altitude. It took them up to 25 minutes to reach 5,000m. In comparison, their American, French, Italian and British counterparts only needed 9 to 13 minutes to reach such heights, the Polish ones needed 13 to 16 minutes. The maximum altitude was also much lower, at just 5,700m for the Soviet interceptors. The Polish planes could reach heights of up to 7,000-8,000m and the Western ones even 8,000-9,000m.[47]

Based on this report, Ordzhonikidze drew up a proposal regarding the aviation industry and presented it to the Politburo on 5 March 1930, which accepted it. Like the report that had inspired it, the adopted resolution lamented the catastrophic state of the aviation industry. The plans for the previous years had not been fulfilled, and even though new licenses for engines had been bought in the West a year and a half beforehand, no new aircraft models or even engines had been developed. As a result, the quality of aircraft had stagnated. The Politburo sought to improve the situation by resolving to establish new commissions; new engines and aircraft were to be designed and mass-produced, while engineers from other industrial sectors were to be sent to work in the aviation industry. Foreign experts were to be recruited as well, especially engineers and master craftsmen. Furthermore, "more than a few" aircraft engines were to be bought abroad, with the goal of having them mass-produced domestically.[48]

To finance all of these new initiatives, the Soviet Union needed foreign currency. On 25 January 1930, the Politburo thus discussed the export and import plan for the second quarter of the fiscal year 1929/1930 (the fiscal year began in October and ended in September), ultimately deciding to increase the export of wood and petroleum products. At the same time, the import of goods that the Soviet Union could manufacture domestically was to be limited or even stopped entirely. To facilitate the substitution of imports, the equipment and machinery necessary to build up domestic production was to be imported from abroad.[49]

Stalin and his comrades anticipated that the Great Depression would play in their favor. On 25 January 1930, the Politburo discussed the planned purchases in the USA, mostly modern equipment and machinery, which the Soviet Union sought to finance with a five-year loan of 200 million dollars.[50] Due to the ongoing financial crisis, the Politburo hoped that it could get such a loan on favorable terms.[51] Less than a month later, on 15 February 1930, the Politburo ordered credit negotiations to commence with Great Britain as well, again to finance the import of modern equipment and machinery. The Soviet Union had also been leading credit negotiations with Germany since December 1929,[52] but these talks went nowhere.

Aside from assessing the situation and issuing new armament plans, Stalin and his comrades also turned to the question of why the earlier plans had failed. Before long, they had identified the culprits – the very same bourgeois experts and wreckers who had supposedly conspired to sabotage the earlier mobilization and armament plans. This was not a new development. Already in its resolution on the state of the armaments industry from 15 July 1929, the Politburo had ordered an intensive search for wreckers and saboteurs.

On 20 February 1930, Kuibyshev wrote a report for the Politburo about how the liquidation of wrecking was progressing within the armaments industries, which was adopted by the Politburo with only minor amendments on 25 February 1930.[53] Among others, the resolution declared:

> Having heard the report of the OGPU on the liquidation of the consequences of wrecking activities in the armament factories, the Central Committee of the VKP(b) notes that to this day, no sufficient measures had been taken to liquidate the consequences thereof and that to this day, there are deliveries of poor quality military goods from all armament factories. The existing *situation is explained largely by the fact that the heads of the factories, trusts, GVPU* [Chief Administration of the Armaments Industry] *underestimate the full extent of the disruption within the armaments industry*, [...] Wrecking undermined not only the supply base of the Red Army but also inflicted direct damage to the perfection of military technology, it slowed down the rearmament of the Red Army and worsened the quality of war stocks. *Heroic efforts are necessary to make up for these failures.*[54]

The resolution further criticized the fact that production in virtually every sector of the armaments industry was plagued by serious quality issues in the last quarter of 1929. Design was a particular weak spot as technical experts and designers were still too few in number. Another problem was the lack of technical improvement to the production processes which contributed to the malaise of the armaments industry. "All this shows that the resolutions of the Politburo from 15 July 1929 were by and large not implemented. [...] All of this obliges the heads of the factories, the heads of trusts, the GVPU and VSNKh to mobilize all available forces and means to liquidate the effects of wrecking in armaments production as soon as possible."[55]

The Politburo thus ordered the industry to establish special commissions to deal with the alleged problem of wrecking. This was supposed to be a broad process said to include both communist and nonpartisan activists. Indeed, the entire industrial workforce was urged to raise its vigilance and help detect acts of wrecking. Within factories, their directors and heads of trusts were held liable not only for their management, but also for the technical sector. Naturally, the OGPU was to help in this process as well; it was to step up its ongoing campaign to eliminate wrecking so that it would be completely eradicated by 1931.[56]

As the aviation industry was diagnosed to be in a very poor state, Stalin and his comrades assumed that it was a hotbed of wrecking activities and therefore had to be purged. In its final report, the commission for the aviation industry stated: "The very difficult situation in the air force is caused by the activities of a large counterrevolutionary organization that operated within the aviation industry and the administration of the air force of the Red Army, and which has already been exposed by the OGPU."[57]

Who were these wreckers? Traditionally, they were thought to be old bourgeois engineers and technical experts. However, as a Politburo resolution form 5 March 1930 attested, wreckers had also infiltrated the ranks of industrial workers. That was the case for the aviation industry, but other sectors were similarly affected and were thus purged of supposed wreckers with the help of the OGPU.[58] The same report also lamented the very inadequate use of foreign specialists and skilled workers.[59]

Indeed, the lack of skilled workers throughout the armaments industry had been an ongoing problem that was only made worse by the purges. The Politburo quickly recognized that and on 25 February it resolved to "more decisively draw on foreign assistance (recruitment of measurement specialists from Germany)". At the same time, engineers from civilian industries were to be mobilized for the armaments industry, in particular designers and metallurgists, while the military technical universities and technician schools were to be expanded significantly. The organizational bureau of the Central Committee was given the task of finding fifty suitable party activists, including engineers and technicians, for the armaments industry as well as twenty military specialists within a month. Local agencies were also urged to mobilize party activists for the armaments industry who were to oversee the implementation of the Politburo decrees.[60]

The program of recruiting foreign specialists was initially a success. Between 1929 and 1931, thousands of foreign experts arrived in the USSR, mostly from Germany but also from other countries such as the USA and Austria. Even scientists and artists were recruited. In the electricity conglomerate in Moscow, Elektrozavod, alone, 180 foreigners were employed in 1932, 80% of them Germans. Even though many of the foreign experts had come as communists or at least communist sympathizers, they quickly became disillusioned with life under real, existing socialism. The first wave of returns began in 1931/1932 and most followed soon thereafter. The German experts who did not leave voluntarily by 1937, were either extradited that year, or put in concentration camps or even executed.[61]

But in 1930, very few anticipated this turn of events and the Soviet Union eagerly welcomed them. After all, the lack of skilled workers did indeed cripple the armaments industry. For example, when Vassily Litunovsky inspected the Rybinsk aviation factory in summer 1930, he was thoroughly shocked and reported back to Kliment Voroshilov:

The Rybinsk factory – a marvelous factory. It is said that there is no such plant in Europe, and only 1-2 in the USA. [...] The factory is excellently equipped. And one has to wonder why only 30 engines have been produced so far. One has to answer thusly: Only because of unqualified technical and general leadership, only because of the lack of skilled labor. An old German who works at the factory told Comrade Uborevich: 'The workers are useless, their work is sloppy, [...]. Give the factory efficient leadership, give it many technicians and engineers, give it young Red Army soldiers who are not qualified either, but are disciplined and have gone through elementary political schooling, and in the next year we will have 875 BMW UI of our own.'[62]

Unfortunately for the old German worker at the Rybinsk factory, this was not to happen. On the contrary, the purging of "bourgeois" experts made the skills shortage even more acute. Already in 1931, the Politburo was forced to reverse course and to release and re-employ many of the "remorseful specialist-wreckers" it had just purged.[63] Between May and November 1931 alone, the OGPU released 1,087 previously sentenced experts and allowed them to go back to work.[64]

Many of the leading Bolsheviks may have been very educated and well-read men, but they had precious little knowledge of the complexities of modern industrial development. Instead, Stalin and his comrades seemed to have been genuinely convinced that they could enforce maximum productivity via resolutions and commissions, terror and propaganda. They completely underestimated the power of positive motivation that flows in large part from material incentives and a good work environment. It is hard to imagine that the poorly paid Soviet workers who were forced to subsist on meager food rations and live in cramped, run-down housing were eager to work for a government they hated and which conducted frequent purges in their workplaces. If anything, the horrible working and living conditions as well as the widespread discontent led to horrible work performance in the factories. The situation was further exacerbated by the all-pervasive mismanagement of the administration of the factories, whose leadership was appointed not according to expertise, but political reliability.

The poor work performance was especially devastating in processes that required a great deal of precision. Precision work is of key importance in the manufacture of tools and machines and was thus crucial for the Soviet armament plans. Such work requires very motivated and highly qualified personnel that needs to be trained for years by experienced teachers in specialized technical schools. However, these were completely absent in the Soviet Union. When the Soviet Union bought expensive modern machinery from abroad, it lacked the trained personnel that could operate it properly – the foreign specialists were too few in number.

Such considerations did not seem to have crossed the minds of Stalin and his comrades. Instead, they believed the inevitable setbacks to be the result of deliberate sabotage, which had to be rooted out with terror. The rulers of the Soviet Union may not have been the most technically competent, but they certainly were ruthless in implementing their communist vision of the World Revolution, to achieve heaven on earth.

Aside from the lack of technical expertise on the side of the Bolsheviks, another likely reason for the purges was probably the need to find scapegoats for the failures that were ultimately their own. Stalin and his comrades were not at all willing to admit responsibility for their actions; doing so would have forced them to correct their mistakes. Even worse, there was always the danger of losing power.

Forced Collectivization: The Annihilation of the Free Peasantry

Throughout the first decade of the USSR, the free peasantry had been a thorn in the side of the Bolshevik rulers in Moscow. The Bolsheviks may have portrayed themselves as friends of the peasantry, but their policies quickly alienated the peasants and they remained hostile to communism. Before long, they were seen as the primary enemy at home. Already on 6 March 1920, Lenin had commented on the widespread resistance to the violent grain requisitions and declared that "when the peasant acts as a property-owner holding a surplus of grain not required by his household, and acts towards us as a property-owner, as a well-fed man towards a hungry man, such a peasant is our enemy, and we will fight him with the utmost determination, the utmost ruthlessness."[65]

With the Great Depression spreading around the world, Stalin and his comrades decided that now was the time to annihilate the free peasantry once and for all. The Politburo's ambitious armament plans had to be financed somehow, and since the Soviet Union was a largely agricultural nation, it had to do so by exporting grain. As the free peasantry would certainly object to such plans, it had to be dealt with if the armament program was to stand a chance of success. Thus at the turn of the year 1929/1930, the Politburo worked out an elaborate strategy to annihilate the free peasantry once and for all. The peasants were to be made serfs once again, the fruits of their labor sold abroad to finance Stalin's plans for a great revolutionary war, which they were expected to fight in as well.

Another issue was the fact that Soviet power remained immensely unpopular in the Soviet countryside. As the Politburo gradually increased the pressure on the Soviet peasantry, the situation continued to deteriorate. Soviet repressions only further hardened peasant resistance, and attacks on Soviet activists spreading communist terror in the villages rose, as did mass rallies and "women's uprisings". Such conditions were intolerable, especially when the Soviet Union was expecting to fight a great revolutionary war in the near future. Giving in to the peasants' demands would represent a loss of face and – more importantly – jeopardize the armament plans, so the pressure on the peasantry was increased and collectivization sped up significantly.

On 5 December 1929, the Politburo listened to a report on the progress of collectivization in the Volga German Autonomous Soviet Socialist Republic. Local party agencies reported that collectivization had progressed at a very fast pace; until late November, up to 60% of all small and medium farms had been collectivized in the Lower Volga region. The Politburo was encouraged by this report and set up a commission under Yakovlev that was to propose a series of measures to speed up the pace of collectivization in the rest of the country.[66]

Stalin in particular was excited about this news. Still, on 5 December 1929, he wrote to his friend "Molotstein" i.e. Molotov: "The kolkhoz movement grows rapidly. Of course there is a lack of machinery and tractors (where would that come from!); but even a simple collection of peasant tools brings with it a colossal increase in the area under cultivation (in some rayons up to 50%!). In the Lower Volga already 60% of all farms have been transformed into kolkhozes (already transformed!)"[67]

When Yakovlev presented his proposals on 22 December 1929, Stalin was less pleased. In another letter to Molotov, sent on 25 December, he wrote: "In a few days we want to pass a resolution on the pace of the expansion of the kolkhozes. The Yakovlev commission has put forward a proposal. The proposal is not suitable in my opinion. You probably have it already. Telegraph me your opinion."[68] Naturally, Molotov agreed with Stalin and proposed changes, without going into details, however. Stalin was happy that Molotov shared his opinion and wrote that Yakovlev's proposal would have to be cut in length and limited to operational instructions only.[69]

Stalin sat down with Yakovlev and together the two men got to work on 3 January 1930. The proposal, which had been revised multiple times already, was again heavily edited. Stalin cut out entire points and completely rewrote others, and in the end, the proposal was much shorter than it had been originally. The next day, Stalin sent the revised proposal to the other members of the Politburo.[70] At the Politburo session on 5 January 1930, Stalin's revised proposal was adopted as a resolution and published the following day.[71] The resolution called for a decisive acceleration of the collectivization campaign. Initially, the plan had been to collectivize around 20% of the farms in the grain-producing regions by the end of the Five Year Plan in late 1932. Now, however, this goal had to be met in less than a year. The Lower and Middle Volga regions as well as the Northern Caucasus had to reach the 20% mark by autumn 1930 or by spring 1931 at the latest; in the other grain-growing regions, the target had to be met by spring 1931 or spring 1932 at the latest.[72]

The revised draft from 5 January 1930 did not include any measures against the kulaks, even though that had been a major part of Yakovlev's original proposal; there had even been a sub-commission dedicated specifically to that issue, which was headed by Karl Baumann, a communist from Latvia. On 14 December, the said sub-commission presented its results in a memorandum, writing, among other things, that "the kulak as an economic category is doomed to destruction in the nearest historical term, the earlier, the better. [...] We can and should re-open the question of the struggle against the kulak in the fully collectivizing rayons." While indeed necessary, the sub-commission did not believe that the complete expropriation of kulaks was enough. Instead, it proposed that the kulaks that offered resistance should be deported, while the others should become laborers deprived of any rights in the new kolkhozes. Baumann and his colleagues were nothing but gracious, however, and went on to suggest that this would only be temporary; former kulaks would be allowed to become regular kolkhoz members after three to five years, granted that they behaved themselves.[73]

The sub-commission estimated that these measures would affect somewhere between five and six million people. According to a different estimate, also from December 1929, there were 1.5 million kulak farms (5%) in the Soviet Union, where about seven to eight, maybe even nine million people lived. Six months later, on 1 July 1930, the OGPU reported that there were 622,562 kulak farms still remaining in the USSR; over 300,000 of them had been liquidated already.[74]

As the resolution from 5 January 1930 was meant for public consumption. Stalin felt the need to cut the parts about expropriating the kulaks and deporting those resisting – repressions that would affect millions of people.[75] Nevertheless, this did not mean that Stalin and his comrades distanced themselves from the idea that the kulaks should be annihilated. On the contrary, just a few days later, on 11 January 1930, the deputy chief of the OGPU, Genrikh Yagoda, turned to his staff: "Considering the worsening of the situation in the village (class struggle during the restructuring of agriculture), the kulak question is so very pressing that it is necessary to immediately take a whole range of measures to purge the village of the kulak element. The kulaks as a class have to be annihilated."[76]

Yagoda predicted that the kulaks would violently resist collectivization "which is what we see in the village as well". After all, the kulaks knew that collectivization would spell their end. The kulaks would therefore take part in insurrectionary plots, form counterrevolutionary kulak organizations, and engage in arson and even terrorism. Yagoda continued:

> They [the kulaks] will even set grain and kolkhozes on fire, which is what they are doing already, they already murder activists and government representatives. If we do not deliver a quick, decisive blow against the kulaks like we did during the time of the grain requisitions, we will be faced with broad uprisings during the spring sowing campaign and the campaign will fail. We need to finish off the kulaks by March/April [1930] and *break their backs* once and for all.[77]

To break the kulaks, Yagoda ordered the OGPU to "work" the regions in question, to arrest, deport or send the kulaks to concentration camps immediately. The procedure was as follows: "1.) Particularly malicious ones are to be sent to the camps, their families are to be deported; 2.) Kulaks engaging in anti-Soviet agitation are to be deported." Those who were deported were sent to the freezing regions of the Russian north, to the Kazakh steppe and other inhospitable places.[78]

Yagoda was serious and gave his senior subordinates fourteen days to gather information on the number of arrested in the course of grain requisitions in the last six months as well as about particularly unsafe rayons. He further inquired about the capacity of the concentration camps, ideas on where to establish new camps, and for places where the kulaks could be put to work without needing constant supervision.[79] On the same day, the OGPU headquarters sent out an order instructing its branches to report on the number of recorded kulaks, White, and bandit elements in the individual rayons by 14 January 1930. The directive further stated that "the center" – i.e. Stalin and his comrades in the Politburo – needed this kind of information in connection with preparations for the most serious political question – the final blow against the kulaks.[80]

Then, the Politburo sprang into action again. On 15 January 1930, it established a commission under the leadership of Molotov with the aim of "devising measures against kulak-dom".[81] The commission began its work immediately and presented the Politburo with a draft on the "measures for the liquidation of the kulak farms in the fully collectivized rayons", which the Politburo adopted on 30 January 1930.[82]

This resolution opened a new chapter in the history of Bolshevik terror and surpassed all earlier campaigns in terms of ruthlessness, planning, and sheer size. No longer did the Bolsheviks seek to break active and passive resistance, now they wanted to completely eliminate a whole social group numbering up to nine million people while also intimidating the rest of the rural population into compliance.

The first step was the complete expropriation of all kulaks who were to lose not only their lands, but also their tools, their livestock, their farm buildings and their houses. Even fodder and seeds were to be confiscated. At the same time, the kulaks were divided into three distinct categories:

1) The kulaks of the first category – "the counterrevolutionary kulak activists" – were to be immediately liquidated by sending them to the concentration camps. Those who had helped organize terrorist attacks, counterrevolutionary rallies, and insurrectionary organizations were to be executed instead.

2) The second category included the rest of the kulak activists, especially the wealthy. They were to be deported to remote regions within the USSR.

3) The kulaks of the third category referred to all the other, less "dangerous" kulaks who were to be resettled within their rayons and who were supposed to be conscripted for various types of work (road construction, forestry, etc.) outside of the kolkhozes.[83]

The number of kulak farms to be liquidated was to vary from rayon to rayon, depending on the number of kulaks living there. In its guidelines, the Politburo recommended that 3-5% of farms should be classified as kulak farms. Between February and May 1930, the OGPU was ordered to send 60,000 kulaks to the concentration camps and deport 150,000 kulaks along with their families. Of them, 70,000 were to be sent to the north, 50,000 to Siberia, 20,000 to the Urals, and 25,000 to Kazakhstan. Naturally, there were exceptions and the families of Red Army soldiers and commanders were to be spared.[84]

The question of who belonged to the first category, who was to be sent to the camps and who was not, lay with the local OGPU branch, while it was the local party that decided on who belonged to the second and third categories. To facilitate the mass arrests and deportations, the Politburo ordered the OGPU enlarged by 800 men, while the troops of the OGPU were to be augmented by 1,000 "bayonets" and "sabers". At the same time, 2,500 party activists were to be mobilized to participate in this wave of terror.[85]

The OGPU and local party organizations had anticipated this order and had already been slowly preparing for such action in advance, but on 30 January they intensified their efforts significantly. The OGPU further specified and widened the individual kulak categories, adding to the first category other groups such as "White guards", "rebels", "former bandits", "former White officers", religious activists and sect members. The family members of these people were added to the second category. On top of that, the headquarters of the OGPU established OGPU troikas in the individual rayons which were to decide on the sentences for the "kulaks" of the first category – concentration camps or immediate execution. Meanwhile, the local party organization drew up lists of those who were to be expropriated, deported or resettled within the rayons. Yagoda issued the final order on 2 February 1930. According to the plan, the operation was to begin on 10 February and would last until April 1930.[86]

The expanded OGPU made it clear that the operation was not merely targeting wealthy peasants, but also all real and imagined enemies of the Soviet system in the countryside. Collectivization was very unpopular, after all, and Soviet pressure to force the peasants into the kolkhozes was radicalizing peasant resistance to Soviet rule. By eliminating the imagined pillars of resistance – former White officers and landowners, religious activists and sect members, along with their families – Stalin and his comrades hoped to nip rural resistance against collectivization in the bud.

Stalin's fears were not unfounded. Collectivization essentially meant the expropriation of all peasants, who were turned into serfs who had to work for the communist bureaucracy, which oversaw everything they produced. Every peasant who joined had to hand over all of his property to the kolkhoz – his land, any facilities and tools, his horses and cattle and all of his supplies. In theory, the members of a kolkhoz were to decide communally on everything, under the leadership of a kolkhoz chairman.

In reality, however, the kolkhoz chairmen were often the same workers and members of the collectivization brigades that forced the peasants into the kolkozes. Most of them were not peasants and knew little of agriculture, but that was not a problem. After all, they only had to follow orders from the party bureaucracy, which kept a close watch over them. Indeed, it was the party bureaucracy that decided what was to be grown and how much was to be harvested. The kolkhoz farmers were thus nothing more than forced laborers.

Considering their position in the kolkhozes, it comes as no surprise that the peasantry was not eager to join voluntarily. As a result, the local party organizations had to resort to a wide range of measures to intimidate them into joining. One of them was the creation of special collectivization brigades, the so-called "25,000-ers", who were made up of young, indoctrinated, fanatical – and armed – urban workers, who forced the peasants into the kolkhozes.[87] Being volunteers, the "25,000-ers" were paid for their work and later played a key role in the administration of the kolkhozes, often as their chairmen.[88]

An OGPU report from 5 January 1930 described the activities of a collectivization brigade in the county of Usman, near Voronezh, as follows: "The eleven man brigade that arrived in the Annenskoye rayon literally terrorized the population." The brigade herded the peasants into meetings in which they were told to join the kolkhozes and threatened them with reprisals if they refused. When the peasants were collecting signatures asking for the release of a number of recently arrested peasants, the brigade promptly arrested seven people. In the village of Berezovke, they told the assembled peasants: "Whoever is against Soviet power, for him we will find a place in Solovki [an infamous concentration camp near the Arctic Circle][89] and the kolkhoz will get his property." Then they asked: "Who is against the kolkhoz?" Thoroughly intimidated, the peasants remained silent, which the brigade proclaimed as their agreement to join the kolkhoz. The next day, the peasants staged a protest in front of the chairman of the local executive party committee. The chairman was unmoved and threatened to arrest them, telling the peasants that there were enough ropes to tie them all up.[90]

In many other villages, the brigade began its collectivization campaign with arrests and then declared: "We have come to build the kolkhoz, whoever is against the kolkhoz, we will launch to the moon!" Most peasants would then leave the meeting and the remaining peasants all voted for joining the kolkhoz – "unanimously". Once that was done, the brigade went through the houses of the peasants and assessed their property which they had to bring with them to the kolkhoz. If a peasant dared to protest, he was arrested. According to incomplete records, the collectivization brigades arrested 144 persons – 80% of them poor and average peasants – between 24 December 1929 and 5 January 1930 in the rayon. That way, the percentage of collectivized farms in the rayon soared from 26% to 82.4% in just 10 days.[91]

However, not all peasants were intimidated by such attempts and many even resisted forced collectivization. In early May 1930, the OGPU reported:

Late 1929-early 1930, especially the last four months were characterized by a strong rise in counterrevolutionary kulak activities in the village. White guards, bandits, sect members, church activists, social democratic elements [...] etc. [...] had formed a united front with the kulaks and led a persistent and bitter struggle against Soviet power and its measures, especially against collectivization.[92]

In many cases, the resistance turned into open insurrection, the report continued. In all of 1929, the OGPU had counted a total of 2,390 anti-Soviet leaflets; in just the first three months of 1930, the number of anti-Soviet leaflets was at 2,295, nearly eclipsing the previous year's total. The number of recorded "acts of terror" against Soviet activists rose as well, with 4,449 attacks occurring between 1 January and 10 April 1930. In all of 1929, their number had been at 9,137. Mass protests also proliferated. In 1929, the OGPU had counted 1,307 anti-Soviet mass rallies with around 300,000 participants. Both numbers were easily surpassed between January and April 1930, with 6,117 mass protests occurring, attended by 1,755,300 people.[93]

Naturally, the OGPU did not stand by idly. In the same report, it boasted of having liquidated 206 "counterrevolutionary organizations", arresting 8,790 members in the process – just between January and April 1930. In addition to that, it also reported the destruction of 6,827 "counterrevolutionary groups" and the arrest of 50,009 persons in this context, as well as 229 "gangs (armed detachments in kulak rebellions)" leading to the arrest of 8,913 "gang members". Outside of this, the OGPU also detained 73,062 individuals, putting the total of arrested persons at 140,774, of whom 34,270 were released after questioning. During these actions, 2,686 "leaders and active members" were killed, while 7,310 surrendered. In total, 5,533 firearms and blank guns were confiscated.[94]

The agents of the OGPU were not the only ones to note the extent of the peasant resistance to collectivization. As a party activist from the Vassiliyevskaya Terekhkovka rayon in the Gomel district in Belarus said at a public meeting: "Our peasants are not going to join the kolkhozes voluntarily. It is necessary to shoot 20 people and only then will our cause [collectivization] proceed."[95] Stalin and his comrades also knew what was going on; in fact, the very campaign to exterminate the kulaks themselves had been primarily aimed at breaking the anti-collectivization resistance in the countryside.

The terror quickly left its mark. Between February and April 1930 alone the Bolsheviks launched their first wave of deportations targeting the kulaks of the second category. By the end of April, the OGPU and party agencies reported that they had deported a grand total of 501,290 people (98,000 families) to far-off, inhospitable regions – and they were not finished yet. A total of 19,945 persons (3,900 families) were about to be deported, with the Soviet agencies aiming to deport 631,000 persons (121,000 families) altogether.[96]

By far the largest group – 230,065 persons, 46,562 families – was sent to the northern reaches of the Soviet Union, the rest were sent to the Ural Oblast (85,134 persons, 17,835 families), Siberia (80,305 persons, 16,061 families), with many others being deported to the Far East and Kazakhstan. Others were resettled within the Ural (66,115 persons, 13,708 families) and Leningrad Oblasts.[97] By the end of 1930, Soviet agencies had deported 550,558 persons (112,828 families) belonging to the second kulak category.[98]

Sent into internal exile, the deportees were forced to work for the Bolsheviks. For most, that was logging, for others it meant cattle herding and fishing, while others were sent to work in various mines, extracting coal, iron ore and gold.[99] One of the many who was deported to the north, complained in a letter from late June 1930: "Our work here is horrible, many people were killed by pine trees [while logging], many have died, and many people get edema from hunger and many are losing their minds, so it is terrible to watch this all. You ask how we are being fed – worse than a dog. A good owner feeds his dog better than we are being fed here."[100]

As the deportations targeted entire families, most of the deportees ended up being women and children. This was particularly the case for the kulaks of the first category, where the men were sent to concentration camps instead – or executed outright. Stranded in a strange, inhospitable land, the women and children did not fare well. As a deportee described in a letter: "There are many disabled people, widows and orphans here, the forest kills them and they also die on their own. Mothers suffocate their children, drown themselves in the rivers together with them, they die from hunger like flies."[101] According to the OGPU, among the 371,645 people who had been exiled to other regions in 1930, there were 134,185 children (36.1%), 113,653 (30.5%) women and 123,807 (33.4%) men.[102] The deportees lived under abysmal conditions, in barracks or earthen huts and suffered from hunger. Many got sick as a result and mortality rates were very high, especially among children.

In April 1930, the People's Commissar for Internal Affairs, V. Tolmachev wrote a report on the situation of the deportees in the north, which was then forwarded to Stalin on 21 April. Tolmachev stated that 45,000 "kulak families" numbering 158,000 persons had been exiled to the north. Among them, there were around 25-35% poor and average peasants, as well as others who had been deported "illegally" – likely peasants who had resisted collectivization. Among the exiles, there were around 36,000 able-bodied men who were immediately put to work. The vast majority – 122,000 persons in total – was made up of women, children and men who were not able to perform hard labor. They were sent to live in just 750 unheated barracks along the Vologda-Archangelsk and Vyatka-Kotla railway lines. There, the exiles lived in "unbelievably cramped conditions", sometimes on only 1m^2 per person, and diseases spread rapidly:

This, all together with the scarcity of food, many do not get anything, causes a lot of disease and a very high mortality rate among the children. [...] In the city of Arkhangelsk, 6,007 out of 8,000 children fell ill in March and in the first 10 days of April, among them: scarlet fever – 199 cases, measles – 1,154, flu, pneumonia – 4,238, diphtheria – 21, 597 children have died. In the Severodvinsk District, 784 persons have died up to 12 April 1930, including 643 children. In the Vologda District, 4,850 children fell ill between 29 March and 15 April, 677 of them died, on 12 and 13 April alone, 162 children died. The percentage of children who fell ill is at 85%. Mortality among children is at 7 to 8%. The mortality of sick children is between 24% (in the Arkhangelsk District) and 45.5% (in the city of Arkhangelsk), and it is primarily the youngest children who fall ill and die.[103]

The extreme mortality rates persisted over the coming months and years and by 1 December 1930, 21,213 exiles sent to the north had died – 9.12% of the total. The north was no exception in this regard and mortality rates were similarly high elsewhere. However, Tolmachev's intervention did likely see some results as 35,400 children who had been deported to the north were returned to their homes. Additionally, 580 of the 1,390 "illegally" deported were allowed to return as well, while 26,500 people who had been deported to the north "illegally" were released and allowed to settle freely within the north, but not return back home.[104]

In addition to the 550,000 deported kulaks of the second category, 44,900 families – or around 220,000 persons assuming an average family size of 5 people – were "resettled" within their own rayons as kulaks of the third category. For the latter, home was close and consequently many immediately fled. In some places, up to 50% of all deportees fled their places of banishment.[105] This was relatively common among deportees of the second category as well, with an average of 16.4% attempting to flee. However, 46% of them were quickly tracked down.[106]

Despite the extreme hardships the deportees – around 780,000 in 1930 alone – had to face, they were still relatively lucky compared to the kulaks of the first category, who were either killed immediately or sent to concentration camps. Considered to be the most dangerous kulaks and anti-Soviet elements, the OGPU pursued them with special vigor. Between

January and 15 April 1930, the OGPU reportedly arrested a grand total of 140,724 people in the course of the so-called Kulak Operation. Among them were 79,330 kulaks (56.3%), 5,028 religious activists, 4,405 were former land and factory owners and 51,961 belonged to various other anti-Soviet elements. In the next five months, from 15 April to 1 October, the OGPU arrested another 142,993 kulaks of the first class; this time, kulaks were nowhere near the majority – only 45,559 (31.9%) of the arrestees were kulaks, while 97,343 were classified as various other anti-Soviet elements. Most of the arrested were then sent to concentration camps.[107]

Given that only 44.2% of the 283,717 supposed kulaks arrested until 1 October 1930 were even kulaks, suggests that the goal of the operation was not just to facilitate collectivization, but also to "pacify" the countryside by crushing all kinds of anti-Soviet groups. As the terror wave continued, it became less and less focused on kulaks. On 25 October 1925, the OGPU headquarters ordered its local agencies to round up and arrest all former "White officers" who had a "counterrevolutionary attitude". In the course of the mass arrests, the OGPU had come to the conclusion that it was the former officers who were the link between the kulaks and the urban intelligentsia and that it was "White officers" who headed the most active anti-Soviet organizations.[108]

It is not entirely known how many people died over the course of the Kulak Operation, be it in exile through hunger, cold, and disease or through outright execution. What is known is that the Kulak Operation directly affected at least 1.05 million people, most of them women (around 30%) and children (around 35%).

Despite the extraordinary brutality and scope of the terror the Bolsheviks unleashed on the countryside, the peasant resistance was far from broken, and there were frequent reports of attacks on Soviet activists who had come to terrorize the locals. Between January and September 1931, the OGPU still recorded 1,835 mass rallies with 242,000 participants, 6,173 acts of terrorism and 1,704 instances of leaflets being distributed, some of them calling for an insurrection.[109]

In early February 1931, the OGPU thus prepared a report on the kulak counterrevolution, i.e. peasant resistance, in which it concluded that another blow against the kulaks was absolutely necessary to advance the cause of collectivization.[110] On 15 March 1931 the Politburo established a commission headed by Andreyev which was to organize a second great Kulak Operation. On 25 March 1931, the Andreyev commission had finished its work and its proposal was accepted by the Politburo, which ordered the "resettlement" of 190,000 kulak farms, i.e. families; 40,000 were to be sent to northwestern Siberia while the remaining 150,000 were to be deported to Kazakhstan.[111]

The first stage of the operation had already begun on 20 March 1931, five days before the Politburo resolution, and it lasted until 25 April. It was followed by a second wave that lasted from 10 May to 13 September. A grand total of 787,341 people (162,962 families) were deported over the course of this operation, with women (223,834 or 28.42%) and children (320,731 or 40.73%) again making up the majority of exiles.[112] They were joined by an additional 103,208 families (469,470 people) who were deported to inhospitable areas within their own rayons and regions. By the end of September 1931, 265,795 families or 1,243,860 people had been deported.[113]

Life in exile remained as grim as it was in 1930. Like those who had come before them, the newly deported people had to contend with horrible living conditions and as a result, thousands died from the cold, starvation, and disease, with epidemics such as typhus and smallpox running rampant. Again, it was the children who suffered the most, especially children under the age of 8. In some regions, their mortality lay at 10% – per month.[114]

Seeing this, the Politburo moved into action and on 23 December 1931, it passed a series of measures to lower the number of deaths among the deported children in the Narymsk region of western Siberia. New clinics and hospitals were to be established, as well as special supply points for young children that were to provide them with food over the next six months. For the 2,000 weakest children under 8 years old, a food supply was to be ensured for eight months. A month later, on 28 January 1932, the Politburo implemented similar measures for the other places of banishment in the USSR.[115]

By then, the deportations had become somewhat routine and around the turn of 1931/32 both OGPU and party organizations assumed that another series of deportations would follow, and thus already drew up lists of kulak families that had not been deported yet. On 27 January, the chief of the secret political department of the OGPU forwarded the question of several local OGPU agencies who wanted to know if there would in fact be another wave of deportations and if it was to occur, when and to what extent. After all, OGPU agencies in 15 oblasts had reported the presence of 145,742 kulak farms, i.e. families. By 10 March 1932, the number of reported kulak farms had risen to 208,723.[116]

As expected, the Politburo did pass another resolution ordering yet another wave of deportations on 10 April 1932. This time, 30,000 to 35,000 kulak families who had been expelled from the kolkhozes or who had been dekulakized beforehand, were to be banished.[117] The OGPU quickly worked out a deportation plan according to which 38,300 kulak families were to be deported by 15 August 1932; the plan was presented to the responsible Politburo commission on 26 April and was adopted by the Politburo on 4 May.[118] A few days later, however, the Politburo changed its mind and on 16 May, it stopped this mass deportation, instead ordering the OGPU to "remove" particularly "malicious" anti-Soviet elements in the countryside via individual arrests.[119] The Politburo revised its position again before long and by October 1932, the OGPU once again began to systematically deport people. In the deportation action that lasted until May 1933, 33,785 families or 147,283 people were sent into internal exile.[120]

It is hard to find the exact number of people who were sent to concentration camps or outright executed as part of the pacification actions of 1931/32. What is clear, however, is that their numbers were in the hundreds of thousands. Beginning with the first anti-kulak actions in January 1930, the number of concentration inmates rose rapidly. On 1 February 1929, the concentration camps in the RSFSR had 76,523 inmates in total. Many of them had been sent to the concentration camp complex on the Solovetsky Islands in the White Sea that had been established in 1923 on the initiative of Dzerzhinsky, but in May 1929, the OGPU had begun to establish a new concentration camp in the Ukhta region.[121]

Parallel to its resolution on the liquidation of the kulaks from 30 January 1930, the Politburo also ordered the establishment of new concentration camps in Siberia and northern Russia which were to hold the kulaks of the first category who had not been executed immediately.[122] Of the approximately 280,000 kulaks of the first class who had been arrested in 1930, most were sent to concentration camps, both old and new. On the

Solovetsky Islands alone, the number of inmates jumped from around 22,000 in 1929 to 71,363 in December 1930.[123]

The Soviet concentration camp system continued to grow rapidly and by 1 January 1934, 510,309 people were imprisoned there. Just ten months later, the number stood at 685,000 and in 1935, it was 788,675. In addition to that, there were also 278,848 people who had been deported to prison colonies (labor camps for prisoners serving three years or less), while the "ordinary" prisons had 161,142 inmates. In 1935, the Soviet Union thus officially had 1,222,675 people incarcerated in its many camps and prisons. Most of the imprisoned were peasants.[124]

By early 1933, the Bolsheviks believed that they had finally vanquished the active peasant resistance. On 11 January, Lazar Kaganovich felt confident enough to announce at the Plenum of the Central Committee and Central Control Committee of the VCP(b) that the kulaks as a class had been destroyed. Still, he cautioned that the kulaks were still acting from behind the shadows, disguising themselves as ordinary kolkhoz farmers and wrecking the Soviet economy. It was them, Kaganovich continued, who were responsible for all of the problems the kolkhozes faced, such as theft and mismanagement. Kulak sabotage supposedly took such a serious toll on the kolkhozes that the gains in grain collection of the years 1930 and 1931 had been reversed in 1932. Therefore, the fight against the kulaks had to continue.[125]

The lower party and OGPU organs took Kaganovich's words to heart and began to plan yet another round of mass deportations, sending their proposals to the Central Committee and the Council of People's Commissars in April 1933. The plans foresaw the immediate deportation of around 100,000 peasant families (around 500,000 people), but this time, these proposals went too far, even for Stalin. On 5 May 1933, he and Molotov issued a directive to all party and Soviet functionaries as well as to all OGPU agencies and the justice system, in which he stated among other things:

The past three years of our work in the countryside represented the struggle for the liquidation of kulak-dom and the victory of the kolkhozes. In these three years we smashed our class enemies in the countryside and once and for all solidified our Soviet-socialist positions in the village. […] The Central Committee and the Council of People's Commissars believe that thanks to our successes in the countryside, the time has come when we no longer need the mass repressions, which as we know not only hit the kulaks but also individual peasants and part of the kolkhoz farmers.[126]

From now on, the Soviet Union would only deport families whose heads had actively participated in the fight against the kolkhozes as well as the sowing and procurement campaigns. Instead of the approximately 100,000 households the party and the OGPU wanted to deport, Stalin and Molotov set the quota at "just" 12,000 households for the near future.[127]

While Stalin did not halt the deportations completely, the deportations between 1933 and 1935 never reached the proportions of 1930/31. By July 1933, 8,766 families (41,875 people) were exiled[128], while in the first half of 1935, Stalin and his comrades ordered the deportation of 24,541 families (around 115,000 people)[129] in what would be the last great deportation wave for the time being.

With the kulaks more or less broken by 1933, the focus of communist terror shifted towards "former kulaks", "wreckers", "saboteurs", "thieves", etc. who were supposedly undermining the success of the kolkhoz system from the inside. As a result, many thousands of kolkhoz farmers and their families were deported, sent to concentration camps or outright executed. While this campaign had already begun much earlier, it accelerated in 1933 and reached its peak in 1937.[130]

At this time, a new problem arose. On paper, the deportees were to remain in exile for a period of five years – or just three, if they had been sent to work in the gold or platinum mines.[131] However, as the return date for the first major batch of deportees approached in early 1935, Soviet leaders began to have second thoughts. On 17 January 1935, Yagoda turned to Stalin, writing that the return of the deportees was not only economically harmful but also "politically undesirable". Stalin agreed and on 25 January 1935, the Central Executive Committee of the USSR decreed that the deportees were not allowed to return home even after they had regained their full civil rights.[132]

Nevertheless, thousands returned home anyway and sought employment in kolkhozes and factories. For Stalin and his comrades, they – as well as the countless fugitives who had fled their places of banishment beforehand – were a critical danger to the Soviet system as they had managed to defy it and were spreading anti-Soviet sentiment, "inciting" the population against communism. So on 2 July 1937, the Politburo ordered the returned "kulaks" and "criminals" to be arrested and tried in front of NKVD troikas. The most troublesome were to be executed and the rest to sent to the concentration camps.[133]

In the weeks that followed, the Politburo set quotas for the various regions on how many "anti-Soviet elements" were to be shot and how many were to be sent to concentration camps.[134] The NKVD, the successor of the OGPU, then began to work out Operative Order No. 00447, which became the blueprint for the unprecedented massacre that was about to take place.[135] In January 1938, it reported on the progress of the campaign:

> Until 1 January 1938, a total of 555,641 people were arrested. In addition to that, the NKVD in the Novosibirsk Oblast and the Altai region arrested 22,108 people in connection with the liquidation of the counterrevolutionary organization "ROVS". Among those arrested under Order 00447, there are: 248,271 former kulaks, 116,506 criminals, 162,594 other counterrevolutionary elements, for 28,270 people there is no data. […] Up to 1 January 1938, a total of 553,362 people were sentenced. […] Among those sentenced under Order 00447, there were:
>
> a) First category [execution] 239,352 people, among them former kulaks – 105,124, criminals – 75,930, other counterrevolutionary elements – 78,237, no data – 19,828.
>
> b) Second category [5-10 years in a concentration camp] 314,110, among them former kulaks – 138,588, criminals – 75,930, other counterrevolutionary elements – 83,591, no data – 16,001.[136]

On 31 January 1938, the Politburo approved the supplementary plan worked out by the NKVD which foresaw the persecution of additional former kulaks, criminals, and other active "anti-Soviet elements".

According to the plan, 48,000 people were to fall under the first category [shooting] and 9,700 under the second [concentration camp]. Naturally, the Politburo again set the quotas for the various republics and districts, which the NKVD had to fulfill by 1 April 1938.[137] However, there was still more to come and a few weeks later, on 17 February 1938, the Politburo further increased the execution quota for Ukraine from 6,000 to 30,000.[138]

Together with the so-called National Operations, Operative Order 00447 was one of the campaigns of the Great Terror that claimed the lives of hundreds of thousands until Stalin put an end to it in November 1938. It is estimated that between 1937 and 1938, around 1,575,000 people were arrested by the NKVD, 85.4% of them (1,345,000) were convicted, and around 51% (681,692) of those convicted were executed.[139]

Forced Collectivization, Grain Procurement and the Great Hunger

Overall, the terror was a great success and allowed Stalin and his comrades to finally remove one of their greatest internal foes – the free peasantry. With the countryside pacified and resistance to collectivization broken, more and more peasants joined the kolkhozes. While only a million farms had been collectivized in 1929, their number jumped to six million (23.6% of all farms) in 1930 and 13 million (52.7%) in 1931. Collectivization slowed down afterwards, but continued at a steady pace, with 14.9 million (61.5%) kolkhozes in 1932 and 15.2 million (65%) in 1933.[140] By 1 July 1934, 71.4% of all farms had been collectivized and by 1937 – 93%.[141]

Table 6: Percentage of collectivized farms in the USSR between 1933 and 1938[142]

	1933	1934	1935	1936	1937	1938
Share of collectivized farms	65.6%	71.4%	83.2%	92.5%	93%	93.5%
Share of collectivized farmland	83.1%	87.4%	94.1%	98.2%	99.1%	99.2%

Over the course of the 1930s, the Bolsheviks replaced the traditional village with the kolkhoz and turned the entire country into a great plantation worked by serfs and their families, over 70 million people in total.[143] Even though the active resistance had been largely broken through sheer terror, the dispossessed and disenfranchised peasants were far from happy with their lot and sought to flee to the cities. The Politburo quickly moved to keep their serfs on their plantations and former "kulaks" out of the cities. On 15 November 1932, the Politburo instituted a passport system that only allowed people with a valid pass to register in the cities.[144]

Since individual and kolkhoz farmers were not given such passes,[145] they were effectively banned from leaving their place of residence. Now bound to the land, the Soviet peasant had become a serf once again, lorded over by party functionaries who cared only for the plans their superiors laid out, no matter the cost.

The forced collectivization allowed the Soviet bureaucracy to directly access Soviet agricultural production without paying market prices. These cheap agricultural goods, mostly grain, were then to be sold on world markets at a significant profit. That way, Stalin and his comrades sought to finance their gigantic armament and industrialization program by exporting huge amounts of grain. In the 1920s and early 1930s, the Bolsheviks had employed other methods as well, such as forced requisitions. However, robbing the peasants took a lot of effort and was quite risky, and did not pay off in the long term. In the kolkhozes, meanwhile, the serfs were at the complete mercy of the Bolshevik bureaucracy, which was able to simply take whatever it wanted.

Such a policy went against everything communist and socialist revolutionaries had fought for under the Tsars that ruled Russia until just over a decade earlier. While most Bolsheviks did go with the times, there was some internal dissent as well. In autumn 1932, the OGPU searched the house of Christian Rakovsky, a prominent member of the internal opposition, and found a memorandum titled "Return to the Party Program, to the Soviet Constitution, to Leninism". In it, the unnamed author criticized Stalin and pointed to the horrible state of the USSR, in particular Ukraine, the desperate situation of the deported Cossacks and kulaks, the hunger in Ukraine and among other things concluded: "Our declaration [i.e. that of the internal opposition] from October 1928 [...] that the collectivization and industrialization conducted by the bureaucracy, would not liberate the working masses but enslave them, has come true."[146]

However, enslavement was not the worst that happened. In 1932 and 1933, millions of freshly enserfed peasants starved to death in a great famine that was directly caused by Stalin's collectivization policy. It became the single largest mass crime in 20th century Europe and was only surpassed by Mao's Great Leap Forward in China in which Mao – himself having been helped into power by Stalin – sought to emulate Stalin's collectivization two decades later.

The origin of the great famine of 1932/33 lay in Stalin's desire to industrialize the Soviet Union by importing expensive Western technology and equipment, paid for by grain exports. Furthermore, large quantities of grain were stockpiled for the war the communists thought was about to break out in the near future. Stalin himself pushed to raise grain collection and export to a new level. In late August 1930, Stalin wrote to his friend Molotov:

We still have maybe one to one and a half months left for the export of grain: In late October (maybe earlier), American grain will arrive on the markets in great quantities, against which we will not be able to persist. If we do not export 130 to 150 million pud of grain in these one and a half months, our foreign exchange situation will be downright desperate later. Again: *The export of grain has to be intensified with all our might.*[147]

In another letter from 24 August 1930, Stalin wrote to Molotov: "Mikoyan reports that the procurement [of grain] is rising and that we export 1 to 1.5 million pud of grain each day. I think this is *too little*. The daily export quota has to be (immediately) raised to 3 to 4 million pud."[148] Six days later, on 30 August 1930, the Politburo then passed a resolution, declaring: "Based on the need to push forward the export of grain immediately and as best as possible, the People's Commissariat for Trade shall be instructed to guarantee grain exports of not less than 3 to 4 million pud per day."[149]

For the year 1930/31, the Soviet Union planned to export 280 million pud (17.1 million tons) of grain, including 163 million pud of wheat, 25 million pud each of rye and oats, 55 million pud of barley, as well as 6 million pud each of corn and legumes. Meanwhile, domestic demand was expected to be 951 million pud compared to 673 million pud the previous year,[150] when the USSR was able to export just 30.8 million pud of wheat and rye.[151]

The grain procurement plan for 1929/30 had foreseen the collection of only 997 million pud – of which just 78.8% were collected – the plan for 1930/31 foresaw the procurement of 1.504 billion pud. These plans were very optimistic to say the least, but thanks to collectivization, the Soviet bureaucracy was able to deliver. By 15 November 1930, it managed to collect 1.074 billion pud of grain, 304 million pud more than in the previous year. Of the just over a billion pud it managed to collect, 61.8% came from individual farms and 36.4% from kolkhozes.[152]

From the perspective of Stalin and his comrades, the collectivization and the terror that accompanied it were thus a roaring success. The Soviet Union was now able to export much more grain and was able to import much more foreign technology and machinery in return. In 1930/31, the profits from the revived grain export covered over 20% of the imports of new equipment. In 1929/30, most of the machinery and equipment came from Germany (45%) and the USA (42.8%), with the UK (6.5%), Sweden (3.8%), Italy (1.4%), and Norway (0.4%) supplying relatively minor amounts.[153]

While the USSR had bought technical and electrical equipment for 538 million rubles, the plan for 1930/31 foresaw only a mild increase to 547 million rubles. However, things did not quite go to plan and the Soviet Union had to pay 571.2 million rubles for foreign equipment, with total imports being just above one billion rubles.[154] This was evidently too much and by 1931, a serious financial crisis was looming over the Soviet Union. To avert the impending crisis, Stalin and his comrades were forced to radically cut imports, from a billion rubles in 1931 to just 386.4 million rubles in 1932.[155]

This seriously jeopardized industrialization plans and the Bolsheviks had to desperately search for a way out. They soon found it in increased grain exports. On 15 October 1931, the Politburo issued a series of guidelines for trade talks with Germany with the aim of raising grain exports to finance the import of technical equipment. From the 1931/32 harvests, the Politburo aimed to export 800,000 tons of grain (wheat, barley, corn, oil, fruit), and from the 1932/3 harvests – 1.7 million tons. In addition, other goods such as lumber and petroleum products were to be exported as well.[156]

In early September 1931, it looked like everything was going according to plan. In a letter from 6 September, Lazar Kaganovich wrote to Stalin that 378,834,000 pud of grain had been collected by 1 September, 27% of the yearly plan and 176 million pud more than in the previous year.[157] The Politburo was thus able to approve the resolution of the foreign exchange commission on the storage of 560,000 tons of grain as import collateral.[158] However, things were about to change. Already on 16 September, Kaganovich rang the alarm – over the past ten days, the procurement of grain had slowed down "frighteningly". As a result, only 306 million pud were collected in September 1931 – 450 million pud had been planned.[159]

The problems persisted over the coming months and especially Ukraine, Kazakhstan, and the Far East failed to meet expectations.[160] Nevertheless, the Soviet Union desperately wanted Western machinery. On 25 November 1931, the Politburo instructed Mikoyan, the People's Commissar for Internal and External Trade, to make sure the grain export plan was fulfilled.[161] Five days later, on 1 December, the Politburo set the grain export target for that month at 250,000 tons. The Politburo remained anxious for these goals to be met and on 25 December once again reminded Mikoyan to meet the target for December at all costs, in addition to 500 tons of butter, timber and 10,000 tons of petrol.[162]

On 16 January 1932, the Politburo issued the foreign exchange, import and export plan for that year, which foresaw the export of 704 million rubles' worth of goods (including 168 million rubles from the export of grain) and the import of goods of similar value. This plan was soon revised, however, and on 28 January 1932, the Politburo increased the grain export target for the first quarter of 1932 by 200,000 tons. Most of that grain came from the stockpiles allocated for domestic consumption and as a result, the Politburo reduced the shipments of wheat flour to domestic consumers by 164,000 tons.[163]

Aside from diverting grain from domestic consumption, Stalin and his colleagues also resorted to the tried and tested method of violent grain requisition. Sent directly from Moscow, Stalin's associates mobilized the local Soviet and party apparatus and set up requisition commandos that went directly into the villages, harassed their inhabitants and often took all of their crops.

Of the 1.482 billion pud of grain the Bolsheviks wanted to collect in 1931/32, 510 million pud were to come from the fertile fields of Ukraine. However, by 25 December 1931, only 401 million pud of grain had been collected there, a deficit of over 20%.[164] This was unacceptable and Stalin immediately dispatched Molotov to deal with the situation.

Molotov went to Ukraine on 28 December 1931 and remained there until 3 January 1932, during which he organized the grain requisition campaign. He immediately called for a meeting of the Ukrainian Politburo in Kharkiv and together they drew up a detailed plan on how to take "their" grain from the Ukrainian peasants.[165]

According to the plan, Ukraine was divided into six rayon groups, to which the various members of the Ukrainian Politburo were assigned. There, they were to be assisted by 300 leading activists and functionaries mobilized precisely for that purpose; if need be, they were to fall back on the local party, Komsomol, or Soviet activists as well. Thus organized, they were to "lead the battle for grain", with each operative group being given detailed instructions on how much grain was to be requisitioned in which rayon.[166] Already on 30 December, the orders were telegraphed to all rayons and the requisitioning campaign began immediately.[167]

Molotov justified the violent requisitioning campaign to his Ukrainian comrades as follows:

When we decided to declare metals, energy, machine construction and transport to be the primary economic task, we assumed that there would be grain here, that we would have grain. That is the premise from which we started [...], and it appears to me that we were right; if there is no grain in our hands, then there should be, it must be. [...] Without grain, the Five Year plan cannot be fulfilled in four years. Even more, Lenin said that the struggle for grain means the struggle for socialism. [...] It is about the kolkhozes that are led by the party, and not the kulaks; about kolkhozes that are fulfilling the state grain collection plan, and about kolkhozes that do not fulfill the plan and do not want to fulfill it. [...] If we really want to defend the USSR, if we truly want that the Red Army is truly invincible, leave it [the Red Army], Comrades, not without grain, do not leave it in the condition in which the Soviet state is at the moment. We are fulfilling the Five Year Plan in four years, we are achieving great things in the areas of metal, coal, machine construction and transport. But if there will be no grain, if we do not immediately collect grain, then we are destroying our army and if our enemy attacks us, we will become defenseless. [...] Do not forget that our Red Army is a powerful army. We are supplying it with heretofore unseen quantities of aircraft, machine guns, artillery pieces, projectiles, chemical weapons. We are doing very much in this area, it is all being done [...] if there is grain. If we do not have grain according to the minimal plan, then we are destroying our work, we are undermining the Red Army. [...] The rifles must be ready to fire.[168]

Relatively little is known about how exactly the requisitioning campaign proceeded in Ukraine, but what is known is that it was absolutely devastating for the Ukrainian population. When the requisition commandos pillaged the farms and kolkhozes, they took everything, even the seed grain. Before long, rumors of famine in Ukraine reached Moscow. In early April 1932, the OGPU reported: "In a number of townships (in the oblasts of Kharkiv, Kyiv, Odessa, Dnipropetrovsk, Vinnitsa) a supply emergency and instances of hunger in kolkhoz families have been recorded. According to incomplete data, there have been 83 cases of hunger edema, 6 deaths from starvation, instances of cannibalism in 17 families and 4 cases of child abandonment."[169] In March 1932 alone, the OGPU recorded 17 revolts sparked by hunger. Large crowds of up to 500 people attacked grain depots and distilleries to take the grain stored there. At the same time, the OGPU also noted the mass death of horses as people were eating their fodder.[170]

Ukraine was by no means the exception and the entire country was gripped by hunger. However, it was not only the grain-growing regions of Ukraine but also southern Russia and the Volga region that were hit particularly hard, as was Kazakhstan. Between December 1931 and 10 March 1932, the OGPU reported 1,219 deaths from starvation and 4,304 people suffering from hunger edema in these regions, with most of the affected being kolkhoz farmers. The situation was dire, but the worst was still to come. As the requisition commandos had taken even the seed grain, many farmers were unable to plant their crops for that year.[171]

Local party leaders soon recognized the gravity of the situation and on 17 March 1932, the General Secretary of the Central Committee of the Ukrainian communist party, Stanislav Kosior, asked the Politburo in Moscow for seed grains for the upcoming sowing season. The Politburo accepted his plea and sent 10,000 tons of oats as well as 100,000 pud (6,105 tons) of barley as "seed loans", a quantity that was further increased two days later by 1.35 million pud of barley.[172] However, this was nowhere near enough and Kosior once again turned to the Politburo, asking for more seed grain. Again, the Politburo agreed to ship grain to Ukraine – 5,000 tons of oats and 3,000 tons of barley in "seed aid" were approved on 26 March, with another 20,000 tons of wheat and barley on 4 April – "as an exception". The next day, another 20,000 tons of wheat and barley were approved – again "as an exception". On 19 April, a shipment of 5,000 tons of millet and 6,000 tons of buckwheat were approved "as an exception", as well as 3,000 tons of millet as "food aid" for kolkhoz farmers. This trend continued and on 28 April, the Politburo approved of yet another grain shipment to Ukraine, this time 4,000 tons of millet and 5,000 tons of buckwheat as "seed loans".[173]

Beginning in March 1932, the Politburo found itself confronted with a wave of similar requests from other parts of the country to which it responded by sending shipments of grain to the affected regions.[174] However, these shipments were nowhere near enough to save the spring sowing season and local agencies all over the country warned of the impending catastrophe.[175] The Politburo was clearly alarmed and on 25 May it set up a commission "regarding the critical state of the spring sowing in Ukraine", which set out to Ukraine the very next day with the mission to "take all necessary measures to maximally increase spring sowing". The commission itself was headed by the same Molotov who had organized the forced requisitions that had caused the shortage in the first place; he was assisted by Mikoyan, Yakoviev, Markovich, and Odintsov.[176] This time, Molotov and his comrades were not able to work their magic. It was already late May and the spring sowing season had already passed, meaning it was far too late to increase sowing. With the sowing season ruined, there was no hope for the coming harvest and the Soviet Union was headed towards a full-blown famine.

Aside from minor grain shipments, mostly to guarantee sowing, Stalin and his comrades in Moscow took no serious steps to avert the crisis they had unleashed upon the country. Even though he was constantly bombarded by reports of famine, Stalin simply refused to send sufficient grain to Ukraine or the other regions. On 15 June, Stalin wrote to Kaganovich: "In my opinion, Ukraine has gotten more than it deserves. To give more grain is useless, and where should we get it from, anyway."[177] As the famine unfolded, Stalin insisted on continuing grain exports. In March 1932 alone, grain and grain products worth 6.5 million rubles were to be exported, including 30,000 tons of wheat, 70,000 tons of rye, 20,000 tons of barley and 50,000 tons of corn – much more than Ukraine had received in the same timeframe.[178]

In the second quarter of 1932, the Politburo decided to change course somewhat and reduced grain exports to 70,000 tons. Other foodstuffs were exported too, such as eggs (2,792 wagons), butter (14,700 tons), chicken (25 wagons), game (20 wagons), bacon and pork (1,700 tons), as well as fish and various fish products worth 2,166 rubles. Food exports were adjusted downwards and in the third quarter of 1932, the Politburo planned to export only 15,000 tons of flour as well as bacon worth 11,392 rubles. For Ukraine, the Politburo decided to lower the grain collection plan by 40 million pud on 17 August 1932; the grain quota for kolkhozes in the "particularly affected" areas was to be cut in half, that for individual peasants by a third.[179]

Instead of stopping food exports and importing food to save millions of people from starvation, Stalin and his comrades continued to sell food abroad, albeit at reduced volume. The Politburo did not deviate from that course of action, even when many thousands were dying each day. On 9 December 1932, at the very peak of the famine, the Politburo decided to export 100 million pud (6.1 million tons) of grain from the 1932 harvest, including 49 million pud of wheat and rye. In total, the Politburo planned for the collection of 1.212 billion pud of wheat for 1932/33, just 33.360 million pud less than in the previous year, when there was no famine.[180] From the 1.376 billion pud of grain the Politburo planned to collect in 1933, 100 million pud were to be sold abroad, and as the famine slowly subsided, the Politburo once again began to increase its grain exports. On 19 December 1933, the Politburo decided to increase grain exports for the first half of 1934 from 1.3 million tons to 1.59 million tons.[181]

Throughout 1932 and 1933, party leaders in Ukraine (Kosior and Chubar) repeatedly asked Moscow to reduce or at least delay the grain procurement plans in light of the unfolding hunger catastrophe. However, Stalin and his comrades continued to insist that the targets they had set were to be met in full and on time. Instead, the Politburo put the blame for the famine on anti-Soviet elements within the Ukrainian peasantry as well as leadership failures of the local communist party.[182]

The harvest of 1932 did not relieve the starving population. On the contrary, due to the lack of seed grain during the sowing season, many fields had gone untilled, while much of the grain that was eventually harvested was immediately confiscated by Bolshevik requisitioning commandos. On 22 October, the Politburo sent two special commissions to speed up grain collection; the one headed by Molotov went to famine-stricken Ukraine, while the one led by Kaganovich travelled to the also starving North Caucasus. Molotov and Kaganovich immediately got to work. Following Kaganovich's visit to the Northern Caucasus, 5,000 local communists were arrested for supposedly sabotaging the requisitioning campaign in the month of November 1932 alone, as were a further 15,000 kolkhoz farmers. In December 1932, a wave of mass deportations hit the Northern Caucasus, in which not only individual families but also entire villages were resettled. In Ukraine, Molotov's special commission undertook similar measures as well.[183] On 14 December 1932, the Politburo issued the order to fulfill the grain collection plan for 1932/33 by the end of January 1933 for the famine-stricken regions of Ukraine, Northern Caucasus and Western Russia. All "kulaks" as well as local communists who dared to "sabotage" the requisitions were to be deported.[184]

As a result of these harsh measures, the famine reached its height in the winter of 1932/33 and the following spring. News of the famine was extensively reported back to Moscow on a regular basis by the OGPU, which did not have the habit of exaggerating the situation.[185] In one of its many dispatches, the secret political department of the OGPU reported on 23 June 1933 that 58 of the 64 rayons in the Ukrainian Kharkiv oblast were suffering from a "supply shortage", with 23 rayons hit particularly hard. At the same time, the number of "begging" elements and homeless children in the city of Kharkiv had skyrocketed. In May 1933 alone,

11,403 of them had been apprehended, among them 4,439 adults and 6,378 children and youths. For them, mortality rates were very high; in the month of May 1933 alone, 992 bodies were picked up from the streets and markets of Kharkiv. Nevertheless, the peasants in the surrounding villages continued to send their starving children to the city of Kharkiv in the hope that they might survive there.[186]

In the Donbas, the Starobielshchin region was hit particularly hard by that "supply shortage". Between 1 January and mid-June, 5,335 people starved to death in the Novo-Pskovsk rayon, 2,211 in Rubeshansk, 2,289 in Starobelsk, 2,130 in Troitsk and around 5,000 in Belodutsk. In the entire region, hunger claimed over 40,000 people in just half a year.[187]

At the time, the OGPU report from 23 June 1933 continued, up to 50% of the Ukrainian population was suffering from hunger. Kolkhoz farmers suffered the most by far, but people were also dying from hunger in the cities. There were also reports of cannibalism coming from the rayons that were hit particularly hard. Between February and 15 April 1933, 206 instances of cannibalism and 113 instances of people eating corpses were recorded in Ukraine. These numbers rose over the coming months, and between 15 April and 1 June, 315 cases of cannibalism and 368 cases of people eating corpses were registered. The report further elaborated that in most cases of cannibalism, the victims had been children who were killed for food. In the border regions, the OGPU also noted "emigration tendencies", i.e. many kolkhoz peasants tried to flee across the border into Poland, together with their families.[188]

Perhaps not surprisingly, the organizers of this famine did not keep detailed, comprehensive statistics on the number of deaths from hunger – at least none that are accessible today. What is known, however, is that most of the victims were farmers and their families, mostly children and the elderly. Modern scholarship is divided on the exact number of deaths. Robert Conquest, the first Western historian to study the famine in detail, estimated a number of around seven million victims in 1986, five million in Ukraine, a million in the Northern Caucasus and a million in other parts of the country.[189] Others, such as Nicolas Werth, estimate the number of deaths to have been at around six million, four million in Ukraine, a million in Kazakhstan and a million in the Northern Caucasus and Southern Russia. [190]

Based on now accessible demographic data from the 1920s and 1930s, in particular from the censuses in December 1926 and January 1937, one can make a relatively reliable overall estimate for the number of victims of the famine as well as the terror.

Table 7: Births, "natural" deaths and population growth in the USSR in the years 1927-1939 (in thousands)[191]

Year	Population at the Start of the Year	Births	Deaths	Population Growth	Population Growth in %
1927	148,656	6950	3984	2955	1.97
1928	151,622	6944	3878	3066	2.00
1929	154,687	6876	4132	2745	1.76
1930	157,432	6694	4284	2410	1.52
1931	159,841	6510	4510	2009	1.25
1932	161,851	5837	4786	1051	0.65
1933	162,902	5545	11,450	-5905	-3.69
1934	156,787	4780	3140	1369	0.87
1935	158,167	5249	3282	1967	1.24
1936	160,134	5589	3223	2366	1.47
1937	162,500	6549	3557	2992	1.82
1938	165,429	6516	3483	3033	1.82
1939	168,625				

These numbers are a testament to the greatest peacetime demographic tragedy in Europe after the Middle Ages. In 1927/28 and 1937/8, the population of the USSR was growing by around 3 million people annually.[192] Had this trend continued between 1929 and 1936, the population of the USSR in 1937 would have been around 178 million people – meaning a deficit of 16 million. However, it has to be noted that this number not only includes the direct population losses via death, but also passive population loss via fewer births and such.[193]

Rather tellingly, Stalin also relied on similar figures when on 26 January 1934 he proudly announced the "increase of the population in the Soviet Union from 160.5 million in late 1930 to 168 million in 1933". He was estimating that the population was growing by 2.5 million annually.[194] In reality, however, there were only 156.7 million people in the USSR at the beginning of 1934, 11 million fewer than Stalin had announced.

The number of "natural" deaths continuously rose with the beginning of the forced collectivization in 1929, which is without a doubt related to the food shortages.[195] Overall recorded mortality reached its peak in 1933 with 11,450,000 deaths. However, it has to be noted that this was not complete data. If one takes the yearly death rate of 1927 and 1928 as a baseline, the number of "surplus" deaths between 1929 and 1933 stands at 9.62 million. In the years 1932 and 1933 alone, there were 8.346 million more deaths than in 1927 and 1928. With the end of the famine in 1933/34, the mortality rates began to fall significantly. This was likely due to the fact that the famine and the diseases that accompanied it had primarily claimed the lives of the weak, namely children and the elderly.[196]

Despite the reduction in deaths, people continued to die from hunger even after the famine was over, albeit on a much smaller scale.[197] Young children were particularly affected, and child mortality remained high as a result, mostly due to poor nutrition and sanitary conditions.

Table 8: Infant Mortality in the USSR between 1933 and 1939[198]

Year	Infant Mortality (below the age of 1)	Share of infant deaths in overall mortality
1933	718,700	14.4%
1934	537,500	20.4%
1935	706,000	27.5%
1936	938,100	31.5%
1937	1,031,300	34.4%
1938	1,023,300	34.6%
1939	1,053,600	35.4%

According to official numbers, mortality among the youngest children even rose after 1934. However, this could be due to more accurate official records, since it is likely that a lot of newborns who died at the height of the famine had not even been registered in the first place.

While hundreds of thousands of Soviet children continued to die each year from malnutrition and associated diseases, Stalin and his comrades

Collectivisation. The expulsion of a peasant family from their home in Donetsk Oblast (now Ukraine), 1930.

Dekulakization (looting) of peasant P. Emez in Grishinsky district, Donetsk Oblast (now Ukraine), 1930s.

Collectivisation. The expulsion and looting of peasant P. Masjuk and his family from their home in Udachnye, Donetsk Oblast, 1934.

Dekulakization of a peasant family in Udachnye Donetsk Oblast, 1930s.

Children picking frozen potatoes from a collective farm field in Udachnye, Donetsk Oblast, 1933.

Starved peasants on a street in Kharkiv, 1933.

Tukhachevsky in 1936.

Stalin with Voroshilov, 1 May 1935.
(Mikhail Mikhaylovich Kalashnikov)

Iron soldiers in single file line up in front of Russia's biggest tractor factory, in Chelyabinsk. Surround these American-designed machines with armor and guns and you have tanks. Chelyabinsk remained unscathed in the Urals while war devastated Leningrad, Kharkiv and Stalingrad, and other tractor centers. Under the Tsars, the town was a stopover for exiles. *(Cassinam)*

Maintenance of the T-26 mod. 1931. Summer, 1934.
(Russian State Archives of Motion Picture Documents (RGAKFD)).

A T-26 operated by Spanish Republican forces during the Battle of Belchite, 1937.

First prototype of a T-35 tank.

Stalin and Ribbentrop shake hands after signing the Non-Agression Pact. Moscow, 24 August 1939.
(Bundesarchiv, Bild 183-H27337 / CC-BY-SA 3.0)

Vyacheslav Molotov, the People's Commissar for Foreign Affairs, signs the Non-Agression Pact between the USSR and Germany, with Stalin looking on from behind.
(Mikhail Mikhaylovich Kalashnikov)

The Reich Minister for Foreign Affairs, Joachim von Ribbentrop, signs the treaty. To his left is the Soviet Russian ambassador in Berlin, Shkarzew; behind them (from right) Stalin, Foreign Commissar Molotov and the Chief of Staff of the Soviet Russian Army, Stapostnikov. *(Bundesarchiv, Bild 183-S52480 / CC-BY-SA 3.0)*

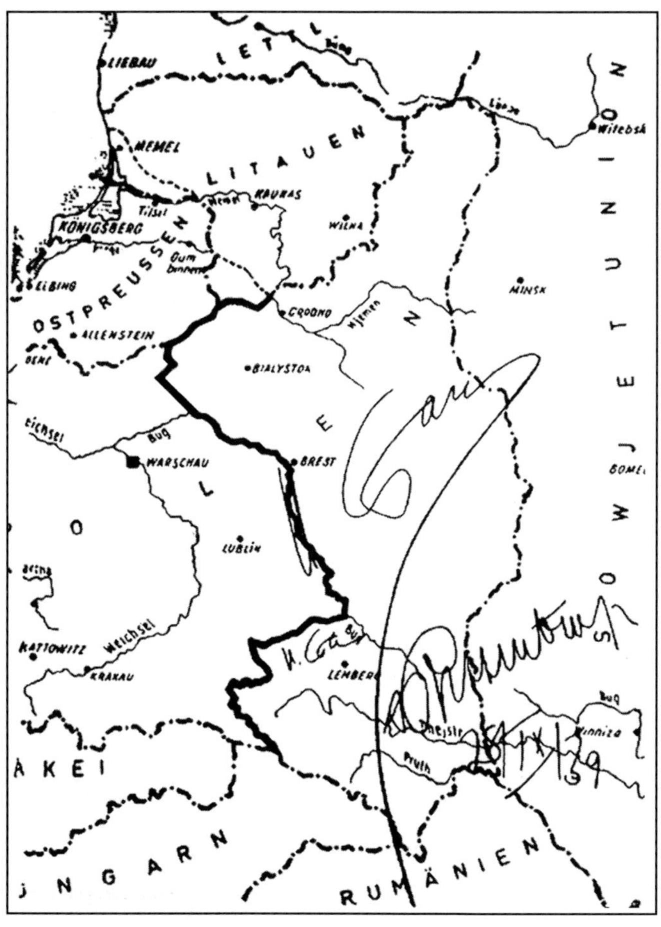

Map dated 28 September 1939, with the signatures of Stalin and Ribbentrop. Stalin's smaller signatures indicate coordinated minor changes to the line. This image of the document was made in 1946 by the defence of von Ribbentrop and Herman Göring at the Nuremberg Trials.

A sketch from *The Washington Star*, 9 October 1939.

German and Soviet soldiers meet in Poland, 20 September 1939.
(Bundesarchiv, Bild 101I-121-0008-25 / Ehlert, Max / CC-BY-SA 3.0)

The Nazi-Soviet joint military parade in Brest-Livosk, Poland, on 22 September 1939. The parade marked the withdrawal of German troops to the demarcation line secretly agreed to in the Molotov–Ribbentrop Pact, and the handover of the city and its fortress to the Soviet Red Army. *(Contando Estrelas)*

German General Heinz Guderian and Soviet Combrig Semyon Krivoshein holding a joint victory parade in Brest, 28 September 1939. *(Bundesarchiv, Bild 101I-121-0011A-23 / CC-BY-SA 3.0)*

A German and a Soviet officer shaking hands at the end of the invasion of Poland. September 1939.

Parade of Wehrmacht and Red Army in Brest at the end of the invasion of Poland. In the centre is Major General Heinz Guderian, with Brigadier Semyon Krivoshein on his left. *(Bundesarchiv, Bild 101I-121-0011A-22 / Gutjahr / CC BY-SA 3.0 DE)*

Twin-turreted T-26 mod. 1931 with riveted hull and turrets, armed with the 37-mm Hotchkiss gun (PS-1) in the right turret. Battle of Tolvajärvi, December 1939.

Soviet oil pumped into tanks for Germany, Przemyśl, July 1940.

were gravely concerned with the plight of hungry children abroad. After all, the Bolsheviks always were more than eager to project a good image by impressing progressive Westerners with their generosity. Furthermore, sending food aid abroad helped to dispel any rumors of domestic food shortages. On 23 September 1936, the Politburo thus approved a large food shipment to help Spanish children suffering from the effects of the civil war that had just broken out. That shipment included 500,000 pud of wheat and flour, 100,000 pud of sugar, 30,000 pud of butter, 750,000 cans and 1,000 crates of eggs.[199] On 14 May 1937, the Politburo greenlit the admission of 1,000 Spanish children into the Soviet Union, where they were allowed to stay in various vacation homes, including ones operated for NKVD personnel, for rest and recuperation. Three days later, the Politburo then sent another shipment of 3,500 tons of wheat to needy women and children in Spain.[200]

The number of famine deaths estimated above does not include the many deaths in the concentration camps and prisons, or the deaths of the deportees or those who were executed by the OGPU or its successor, the NKVD. It is estimated that until 1937, somewhere between 1 and 1.5 million people perished in the various concentration camps, prisons and in exile.[201] As the NKVD kept more or less accurate records on the amount of people it executed, the number of execution victims is relatively well known. According to its own data, the NKVD arrested 1,565,041 people between 1 October 1936 and 1 November 1938, of whom 668,305 were immediately executed; the rest were sent to various concentration camps. It is unclear how many were executed up to 1 October 1936, but the number is probably in the tens of thousands.[202]

Taken together, one can assume that Soviet terror and mismanagement claimed the lives of at least 12 million people between 1929 and 1937, with the vast majority of victims succumbing to famine. Most famine deaths occurred in Ukraine, a fact that is backed up by all studies dealing with this catastrophe.[203] Again, however, it is not entirely clear how many exactly died in Ukraine.

In the 1920s, the renowned Ukrainian demographer M. Ptukh studied demographic trends in Ukraine, and in 1930, he published his work. In it, he estimated that the population of the Ukrainian Soviet Republic would grow as follows in the course of the 1930s as follows:

Table 9: Population Growth Forecast for the Ukrainian Soviet Republic for the Years 1930-1939 (in thousands)[204]

1930	1931	1932	1933	1934	1935	1936	1937	1938	1939
30,652	31,127	31,641	32,157	32,689	33,235	33,786	34,333	34,868	35,397

According to Ptukh's estimates, the population of Soviet Ukraine should have been around 34.3 million people in 1937. However, the Soviet census conducted in 1937 only counted 28.3 million people living there – six million fewer than Ptukh had forecast. Even more worryingly, the population had shrunk compared to 1927, when the census had counted just below 29 million people living in Soviet Ukraine, a drop of nearly 700,000. Here it has to be noted that there had been migration to Ukraine during that time period; in late 1933 alone, over 100,000 kolkhoz farmers from Belarus and Russia were resettled in Ukraine.[205]

Of the six million "missing" people, only a few managed to flee the Soviet Union. Hundreds of thousands were deported, tens of thousands were executed, but the vast majority of them – more than five million – died a slow, agonizing death from hunger and disease. As Ukraine and the famine-stricken regions in particular there were heavily ethnically Ukrainian, the victims were in fact ethnic Ukrainians for the most part.

Ukrainians not only lived in Soviet Ukraine, but were spread out all across the Soviet empire. In December 1926, the Soviet Union was home to 31.2 million ethnic Ukrainians, of whom only 23 million lived in Soviet Ukraine. The rest lived in the Russian provinces as well as in the cities. By the time of the census of January 1937, the number of Ukrainians living in the Soviet Union had dropped to just 26.4 million, a fall of 4.8 million people. However, this drop occurred during a period of high birth rates. Assuming a normal average population growth rate of 2% per year, the number of Ukrainians living in the USSR should have been around 37.5 million in 1937 – 10 million fewer than the census reported.[206] While much of this gap was the direct result of Bolshevik terror and famine, it was also the consequence of intense Bolshevik efforts to Russify the Ukrainian minority.[207]

While famine and terror did in the end break the resistance of the peasantry in Ukraine, as it did in the rest of the country, the Bolsheviks failed in their design to turn Ukraine into a fortress of the Soviet Union, as Stalin put it in a letter to Kaganovich on 11 August 1932.[208] Instead, the peasants in Ukraine - but also in much of the rest of the Soviet Union - silently hoped for a quick end to the Soviet Union. Many desperate Ukrainians continued to wish for a foreign invasion to liberate them from the Soviet yoke, and in the late 1930s, the most "promising" foreign invader was Nazi Germany.[209] The willing collaboration of thousands of Ukrainians, but also Russians, Belarusians, Tatars, Chechens, and many other groups with the invading Germans between 1941 and 1944, cannot be properly understood without taking into account the scale of death and terror the Bolsheviks unleashed on their subjects in the 1930s. Unfortunately, this often gets ignored in Western debates.

To impose their agenda on the unwilling populace, the Bolsheviks relied exclusively on violence, terror, forced labor, and primitive propaganda. However, this course of action did not yield immediate results and it took years until the kolkhoz system was fully consolidated. On 28 May 1939, Andreyev, Stalin's man for the collectivization, reported to the Plenum of the Central Committee on the "Measures to Protect Kolkhoz Lands from Squandering". Dimitrov subsequently noted in his diary:

[Andreyev] reported on the displacement of kolkhozes by individual farms on the basis of numerous facts). A series of secretaries painted a distinctively pessimistic picture. *I[osif] V[issarionovich] [Stalin] took the floor. He pointed out the kolkhoz order has been secured. 60% of kolkhoz farmers are honest and love to work. 10% are lazy and speculators.* If we now take measures to remove such elements from the kolkhozes, it will be easier to fix the issue.[210]

Before the passes were introduced, masses of peasants tried to flee the kolkhozes to find a better life in the cities. Between 1928 and 1932 alone, around 12 million people moved from the countryside into the cities.[211] However, even there, the situation was dire. Real wages in the cities were even lower than they had been in the 1920s and as the urban population exploded, construction could simply not keep up and the housing situation deteriorated. At the same time, urban workers – similar to the kolkhoz peasants – were bound to their factories through draconian disciplinary laws.[212] The Soviet Union of the 1930s had thus become the world's greatest labor camp.

The Ethnic Component in the Communist Mass Terror

As shown earlier, the Politburo and the entire Soviet bureaucracy waged their war on the free peasantry with the goal of "pacifying" the restive hinterland ahead of the coming revolutionary war, while also turning them into the slave cattle that was to pay for the extravagant armament program. As such, the mass terror was primarily directed against the peasantry and all other real and imagined anti-Soviet elements. Even though ethnic Russians were massively targeted as well, the Soviet terror of the 1930s also did have a clear ethnic dimension to it.

Already on 20 February 1930, the Politburo specifically ordered the persecution of supposed "kulak activists" belonging to the various peoples living in the Caucasus and in Asia, of which the most "malicious" were to be executed. In Dagestan, 350 people were to be shot; 1,300 in Uzbekistan, 200 in Turkmenistan, 100 in Kyrgyzstan, 500 each in Georgia and Azerbaijan, 200 in Armenia and 100 in Buryatia. As with other "kulak activists", the families of the executed were to be deported. The rest, the less "malicious" ones, were to either be deported to somewhere far away or resettled within their respective rayons. In total, the Politburo ordered 2-3% of all farms in these regions to be dekulakized, i.e. expropriated and the people living there either executed or deported. In the eyes of the Politburo, these only vaguely defined groups were particularly disruptive to the process of collectivization and building a new communist order. Therefore, they had to be eliminated and their destruction was to serve as a reminder to the rest of the population.[213]

Another ethnic group that drew the ire of the Bolsheviks were the Poles, even though there were many high-ranking ethnic Poles in their ranks.[214] For example, none other than the founder of the Cheka, Feliks Dzerzhinsky (Dzierżyński) came from a Polish family, while another Pole, Stanislav Kosior, was the General Secretary of the Central Committee of the Communist Party of Ukraine; his brother Iosef Kosior meanwhile was the Deputy People's Commissar for Heavy Industry between 1932-37. Nevertheless, the Bolshevik leadership had developed a special hatred towards Poland after the country had defeated the Bolsheviks in their drive to the West in 1920. Bolshevik-Polish relations remained abysmal throughout the interwar years and this did have an effect on the Polish minority in the Soviet Union, which became a hostage of Moscow.

The beginning of the war against the free peasantry also marked the beginning of the ethnic persecution of the Polish minority in the Soviet Union. As early as 1927, Kaganovich had suggested to ethnically cleanse the Polish minority after a visit to the Ukrainian-Polish border region; in his mind, the local Poles were too "anti-Soviet" and "defeatist".[215]

What Kaganovich had suggested in 1927, was soon put into practice by Stalin and his comrades – including Kaganovich himself. On 5 March 1930, the Politburo thus decided to de-polonize the border regions. The entire Polish population living there was to either be deported or killed. During this action, it was not social class that was the decisive factor, but ethnicity. In addition to the Poles, people who had in the past been convicted of "banditry", espionage, as well as counterrevolutionary and professional smuggling, were to be "removed" as well.[216]

For Soviet Belarus, the Politburo set a quota of 3,000-3,500 families, and for Soviet Ukraine 10,000-15,000 families, that were to be deported as kulaks of the first or second category, with kulaks of the first category facing concentration camps or outright execution while their families were deported, and kulaks of the second category being deported together with their families. In addition, there were deportations of "gentry" i.e. Polish families that were resettled within Soviet Ukraine and Belarus, away from the borer. Many of these "noble" families were in fact quite poor and would not have been considered kulaks under normal circumstances. Nevertheless, they were to be deported as well, although the Politburo did not set specific quotas for them, letting local party and GPU agencies decide on their own. Furthermore, local government agencies in the borderlands were to be purged of supposedly counterrevolutionary Poles also. These deportations were to happen on top of the deportations decided upon a month earlier, on 30 January 1930.[217]

On 5 April 1930, a month after the start of the deportation of Poles in the border regions, the Politburo resolved to develop the region economically and culturally. New kolkhozes were to be established and provided with seed grain, agricultural machinery, and even tractors, while also improving local hospitals, schools, and libraries. On top of that, the Poles that had been just deported were to be replaced by more loyal "red partisans" and demobilized Red Army soldiers.[218] Two weeks later, on 20 April 1930, the Politburo dealt in great detail with the issue of developing the western border regions of Soviet Ukraine and Belarus and also of the Leningrad Oblast. There, kolkhozes and light industry were to be particularly promoted and for this purpose, the Politburo set aside 26 million rubles for 1930 alone, while for the resettlement of demobilized Red Army soldiers, the Politburo allocated 1.5 million rubles in Soviet Ukraine and Belarus, and half a million rubles in the Leningrad Oblast.[219]

Ahead of ethnically cleansing the borderlands, Stalin and his comrades were deeply concerned about resistance by "Polish kulak elements" which the Polish government could potentially use as a justification for "meddling" in the affairs of the Soviet Union. To preclude this from happening, the Politburo issues a series of special directives designed to prevent any unrest. The local party apparatus was to be strengthened by functionaries from other regions, while the operative OGPU units were assigned extra personnel for the duration of this operation. Furthermore, the arrests and deportations were to be carried out as swiftly as possible and "without noise". At the same time, these directives were to remain top secret, with only the Ukrainian and Belarusian Politburo, as well as the chiefs of the OGPU in Ukraine (Balitsky) and Belarus (Rappoport) receiving access.[220]

The operation went according to plan and on 6 May 1930, the operative group of the OGPU announced the success of this action. In Soviet Ukraine, the OGPU reported that it had deported 14,894 individuals of "special designation" (*osobogo naznacheniya*, the term the OGPU used for the deported Poles in internal reports), including 32 families, to Siberia. In Soviet Belarus, 3,589 individuals were deported, including 183 families, who were in turn sent to the Far East.[221] How many Polish families were "resettled" within Soviet Ukraine and Belarus in the course of that action remains unclear, however.

The deportation of the Polish minority from the western border further supports the thesis that the Soviet rulers were preparing for an offensive war against the West, especially against Poland. As the western borderlands would undoubtedly be the main deployment area in their initial push west, they had to remove all unreliable elements beforehand, which ethnic Poles would likely have been in case of a war against Poland. It has to be noted that this operation was not the end of the anti-Polish operations, but just the beginning. Just a few months later, on 30 October 1930, the Politburo ordered the purge of Poles and anti-Soviet elements in general within the railway and road transportation systems in the western borderlands. Like the earlier operation, this too was to be carried out secretly.[222]

When the Politburo re-examined the issue in late 1931, it came to the conclusion that the purges and deportations in the borderlands had not produced the desired results and were still not entirely consolidated politically. On 1 December 1931, the Politburo thus initiated another purge. Within the next six months, the borderlands were to be cleansed of kulaks, anti-Soviet elements, saboteurs, and spies working for "fascist" Poland. Special attention was to be paid to the local Soviet, cooperative, and kolkhoz organizations, where they were to be replaced by more politically reliable elements. At the same time, the region had to be developed further economically, with a focus on light industry and craftsmen, but not heavy industry. Furthermore, schools, hospitals, and various other instructions were to be expanded and receive additional equipment and personnel.[223]

However, this was not enough, and in March 1933, the OGPU launched yet another broad purge in the western border regions of Soviet Ukraine and Belarus as well as in the Leningrad Oblast targeting the local Finns and Karelians. In the course of this action, the OGPU arrested 18,802 people, 14,391 as suspected members of insurgent or sabotage organizations, and 4,441 as supposed spies and their contacts. Most of these arrests occurred in Belarus and Ukraine. In 1933, the OGPU also reported on the activities of the Polish Military Organization (POW), whose alleged aim was to spy on the Soviet Union and conduct sabotage operations. Indeed, many of the arrests happened in connection to this supposedly active organization.[224]

The purges continued throughout 1934 and on 23 December 1934, Stanislav Kosior reported to Stalin that somewhere between 10,000 and 11,000 families (around 50,000 people) had been deported from the Ukrainian border region that year. 2,000 families had been exiled to the north, while the vast majority – 8,000-9,000 families – was deported to the Far East. The targets of this deportation campaign were supposed anti-Soviet elements, mostly individual and kolkhoz farmers of mainly

Polish but also German descent. At the same time, the party dissolved Polish village councils and replaced them with Ukrainian ones. The same happened to most Polish schools in Ukraine.[225]

The first half of 1935 saw another wave of purges of the borderlands, this time everywhere, not just in the west. Between 1 and 9 February 1935, the NKVD and the party deported 2,000 families – 8,678 people in total – including 681 Polish families, 615 German families, 589 Ukrainian ones as well as 115 families belonging to other ethnicities (mostly Czechs, Moldovans, Bulgarians and Jews). In Soviet Belarus, 2,000 families were to be deported between 1 and 7 August 1935, most of them likely Polish. The deportations in the Leningrad Oblast were scheduled to take place between 6 April and 1 May 1935, during which 5,100 families, or 22,511 people, were sent into internal exile. In the Northern Caucasus, 1,553 families, or 7,867 people, were deported, mostly Chechens, Ossetians and Dagestanis.[226]

While the Polish minority had been persecuted from the beginning of the terror campaign, the German minority was only targeted beginning in 1934. The reason for this was the changed geopolitical situation in Europe following Hitler's rise to power, which turned Germany from a potential ally against Poland, and indeed the West, into a determined enemy. In the mind of Stalin and his comrades, the German minority in the Soviet Union now had to pay for Hitler's recalcitrance, like the Polish minority had to pay for the resistance of the Polish government. The newfound community of fate was underlined by the next wave of deportation when on 24 April 1936, the Politburo ordered the deportation of 15,000 Polish and German families (around 45,000 people) to Kazakhstan.[227]

The erstwhile highpoint of the persecution of the Polish and German minorities were the so-called Polish and German Operations, which were part of the more general National Operations of the NKVD targeting most ethnic minorities living in the USSR. On 20 July 1937, Stalin ordered Yezhov, the head of the NKVD, to arrest and deport all Germans working in the Soviet armaments industry. The terror quickly escalated and soon everyone who was merely suspected of being German could be arrested, deported, or even shot. Within a year, 42,000 people were killed in the course of the German Operation.[228]

As a result of the terror of the 1930s, the German minority shrunk from 1.23 million in December 1926 to 1.15 million in January 1937.[229] This occurred despite otherwise high natural growth rates. Assuming a population growth of 2% annually, the German population in the Soviet Union should have risen by around 250,000 people in that timeframe, meaning that there was a deficit of around 330,000 people. And that was before the German Operation.

While the German Operation was bloody, the Polish Operation was even worse. On 11 August 1937, Yezhov sent out a top secret memorandum about supposed Polish intelligence networks in the USSR, which allegedly engaged in fascist insurrectionary activities, as well as espionage, sabotage, wrecking, and terrorism. Yezhov further asserted that Polish spies and saboteurs had infiltrated all levels of Soviet society, from the party and the military to the economy and even the security agencies. These elements all supposedly were part of the dreaded Polish Military Organization and had been responsible for countless setbacks and even for the defeat at the gates of Warsaw in 1920, once again highlighting the anti-Polish complex of the Bolsheviks.[230]

This memorandum served as the starting point of the Polish Operation. On 14 September 1937, Yezhov informed Stalin on the progress of the operation, boasting that 23,216 people of Polish heritage had been arrested for spying for the Polish state. On the margins of the report, Stalin commented: "To Comrade Yezhov. Very good! Beat and remove this Polish spy-filth in the future as well. Exterminate it in the interest of the USSR, I. Stalin. 14.IX.37."[231] Yezhov took Stalin's encouragement to heart and the Polish Operation continued.[232]

In the course of the Polish operation, over 150,000 people were arrested, around half of whom were immediately executed.[233] In his quest to root out any Polish influence, Stalin even had the Communist Party of Poland dissolved and executed most of its leadership, even though that organization had loyally supported his reign of terror and had done its best to undermine Poland from the inside.

Due to the terror, the Polish minority in the Soviet Union shrank from officially 792,000 people in December 1926 to 627,000 people in 1939.[234] Assuming a 2% annual growth rate, the Polish minority should have numbered around a million in 1937 – meaning there was a deficit of nearly 400,000 people. Particularly hard-hit were the Poles in Soviet Ukraine and Belarus; in Soviet Ukraine, the number of Poles declined by around 30% despite high overall birth rates.[235]

In Soviet Belarus meanwhile, the Polish minority, which had numbered around 300,000 people in the 1920s, was virtually annihilated. On 4 August 1938, just as the mass terror slowly began to wind down in the rest of the country, the First Secretary of the Central Committee of the Communist Party of Belarus, Panteleimon Ponomarenko, proposed to Stalin that one should deport "from the border regions of the BSSR the families of the repressed [i.e. those who had previously been sent to concentration camps or shot], of counterrevolutionary and insurrectionary elements, as well as people who had close familial ties to Poland and Latvia".[236] Stalin agreed and on 18 August, local Belarusian authorities wrote to Molotov that this deportation was to include 11,732 families, 50,019 people in total, including 25,000 children. In their stead, demobilized border guards and Red Army soldiers were to be resettled in the local kolkhozes.[237]

It is not clear if this operation was indeed carried out and how many people were deported, but when the invading German troops arrived in eastern Belarus in the summer of 1941, they found only a few Poles there. On 19 September 1941, the 221 Security Division, which had the order to "pacify" the region, reported: "In the current operational area of the division, the Poles are a barely noticeable minority. […] Additionally, Poles made an appearance only very sporadically over the reporting period."[238] Soviet authorities were concerned about the near-complete disappearance of the Polish minority as well and in order to cover up their destruction, Soviet agencies promptly counted local Russians and Belarusians as Poles in the statistics.[239]

Aside from the Polish and German Operations, Stalin and his comrades launched a number of National Operations against several other ethnic minorities, such as the Latvians, Chinese, Kurds, Iranians, and Koreans. Between summer 1937 and November 1938, the NKVD thus arrested over 350,000 people (150,000, or nearly half of them, in the course of the Polish Operation), of whom around 250,000 were executed.[240]

Due to the Bolshevik hatred of Poland, it was the Polish minority that was the first ethnic group to be systematically persecuted by the Soviet

Union. Before long, however, the communists broadened the scope of their terror and many other groups went on to share a similar fate, such as the Germans, the Crimean Tatars, and the Chechens. As Poles were one of the main Catholic groups in the Soviet Union, the Catholic Church was severely hit by these purges too, as well as by the general anti-religious terror. In the 1920s, the Soviet Union was home to 1.6 million Catholics, as well as 500 churches and 370 priests. In the late 1930s, after the worst of the purges, only two Catholic churches were still in service, one in Moscow and one in Leningrad.[241]

Chapter 15

The Creation of a Modern Soviet Armaments Industry and the Reorganization of the Red Army, 1930-1941

In early 1930, the violent pacification of the countryside was still in full swing. Yet Stalin and his comrades had already moved on to the next two projects, namely the creation of a modern Soviet armaments industry of gargantuan size as well as the expansion and reorganization of the Red Army. The trigger for this was the Wall Street Crash of 1929 that took place in the autumn of that year. As outlined earlier, Soviet leadership had already decided on an ambitious armaments program in 1927/28. However, by the summer of 1929, it was clear to Stalin and his comrades that their initial goals could not be met. Stalin attempted to remedy this by issuing a number of orders on 15 July 1929, but by the end of the year, they had not even begun to be implemented. Thus the Red Army was in no shape to wage a major war in early 1930.

Table 10: Peacetime Strength of the Soviet Armed Forces 1930-1939[1]

Date	Army	Airforce	Navy	Other	Total
01.01.1930	567,729	27,297	36,592	–	631,616
01.01.1931	567,838	33,030	38,915	–	629,783
15.01.1932	675,513	55,178	44,689	–	775,519
01.03.1933	835,683		64,229	–	899,912
01.01.1934	836,043		71,568	125.959	1,033,570
01.01.1935	986,934		98,239	–	1,085,173
01.01.1936	868,493	111,157	101,763	137.912	1,219,325
01.01.1937	1,145,563	159,603	127,893	212.924	1,645,983
01.01.1938	1,232,536	191,702	–	157.829	1,582,057
24.02.1939	1,720,296		–	211.666	1,931,962

The Wall Street Crash changed everything. Convinced that the capitalist world order was about to face a serious crisis, Stalin decided that it was time to turn things around and ensure the Red Army would be able to take advantage of the coming chaos and launch a successful invasion of the crumbling West. Therefore, the Red Army had to be transformed into a powerful offensive force. In order to achieve this, Stalin had to build up the Soviet Union's armaments industry. At the same time, he had to acquire state-of-the-art military technologies from abroad. The documents that are available today indicate that despite how grandiose Stalin's plans appeared to be at first, they seemed to have been quite successful indeed.

Table 11: Yearly Tank and Aircraft Production 1930-1940[2]

	1930	1931	1932	1933	1934	1935	1936	1937	1938	1939
Tanks	79	847	2585	3509	3582	3061	3981	1610	2386	3107
Aircraft	1149	1489	2490	4116	4354	2529	4270	6039	7727	10362

Table 12: Arms Supplied to the Red Army 1933-1937[3]

Weapon Type	1933	1934	1935	1936	1937 (Planned)
Artillery Pieces	1,797	5,164	4,895	6,923	7,073
Rifles	241,000	319.600	220,603	442,558	553,182
Machine Guns	32,700	29,500	29,789	34,496	39,135
Artillery Shells	2,135,000	1,991,000	2,389,000	5,675,000	8.382,000
Rifle Ammunition	225,000,000	259,000,000	450,000,000	800,000,000	1,740.000,000
Bombs (in Tons)	284,000	216,000	200,000	600,000	975,000
Aircraft Engines	5,785	7,600	5,658	5,350	15,675

Table 13: Mobilization Plans of the Red Army 1930-1934[4]

	Mob.-Plan No. 10 (1930)	Mob.-Plan No. 11 (1932)	Mob.-Plan No. 15 (Dec. 1932	Mob.-Plan No. 15 (May 1933)	Mob.-Plan 1934
Force Strength	3,175,325	3,536,250	4,710,500	4,467,000	4,800,000
Horses	1,223,750	1,787,000	1,537,.000	1,537,400	
Infantry Divisions	105 ½	144	150	150 I.D. und 2 Brigades	149

Armored Troops		14 Battalions			4 Brigades
Airforce		74 Squadrons 52 Detachments			32 Brigades
Cavalry	15 ½ Divisions	14 Divisions 7 Brigades	21 Divisions	22 Divisions 3 Regiments	22 Divisions
Aircraft	1420	1923	3515	3740	3500
Tanks	429	1444	4115	8463	9000
Artillery Pieces	6936	11600	12000	10657	

Table 14: Mobilization Plans of the Red Army for 1937 and 1938, According to General Staff Figures from November 1937[5]

	Mobilization Plan 1937	Mobilization Plan 1938
Infantry	2,608,000	4,194,800
Cavalry	352,000	289,700
Armored Units	153,200	230,100
Artillery	183,300	343,000
Airforce	304,900	387,000
Navy	215,000	261,000
Total	5,300,000	8,645,000

The tables above show how impressive these results were – on paper. However, the majority of scholars have to date neglected to examine the state of the Red Army and how prepared it was to wage war. Most works tend to merely note how the initial goals regarding plane and tank production had been much higher and were only partially fulfilled.[6]

Considering the peculiar nature of Soviet reporting – it was very inaccurate and overly optimistic, to say the least – it is imperative to look beyond the façade. Only by looking at classified internal reports is it possible to get an accurate picture of how these plans were implemented in reality. This chapter will analyze in detail the progress made on tank and plane production. Both tanks and planes were crucial to Stalin's plans as the concept of modern Soviet offensive warfare relied upon them. Additionally, they also were to play a key part in the Second World War and it was in large parts thanks to overwhelming Soviet superiority in this area that Nazi Germany was eventually defeated. In order to understand the Soviet armament program of the 1930s, one first has to understand the role of Mikhail Tukhachevsky, who shaped the development of the Red Army between 1930 and 1936 like no one else.

Tukhachevsky's Idea: War of Annihilation

It was the future marshal Mikhail Tukhachevsky who was the driving force behind the effort to turn the Red Army from a backward military into a force to be reckoned with. Born in 1893, he had risen to the position of commander of the Leningrad Military District by 1930. Before that, he had been in charge of teaching strategy at the country's military academy, where he used his spare time to read up on the newest developments in military technology and strategy in the West.[7] Beginning in 1929, he penned a series of memoranda in which he called for a radical reorganization of the Red Army as well as an overhaul of Soviet military strategy.

On 17 August 1929, he sent a memorandum to the People's Commissar for Defense, Kliment Voroshilov, in which he highlighted the role of transportation infrastructure in modern warfare. Tukhachevsky argued that the road system was in such poor condition that in a future war, the Red Army should rely on planes to supply its frontline troops with ammunition. Therefore, it was imperative to create an air transport fleet modeled after the American one.[8] A few days later, he sent a letter to famous aircraft designer Oleg Antonov in which he wrote about the rising importance of air transport for the postal service. Tuhachevsky further suggested that these postal planes could also be used for military purposes.[9]

Two months later, on 19 October 1929, Tukhachevsky penned yet another memorandum, this time about the horrible state of the Soviet railways. He complained that in a future war – one that he clearly thought was going to be an offensive one – the railway system would not even come close to being able to supply the Red Army. A comprehensive reorganization of the Soviet railway system was therefore inevitable. He further went on to claim that he had inspected the combat readiness of the Red Army's railway regiments in the summer of 1929, but to his great shock had found that both equipment and facilities used had been obsolete for decades already. Tukhachevsky also emphasized that new railway bridges had to be built and that the process of building bridges and railway tracks had to be mechanized.[10]

On 11 January 1930, Tukhachevsky penned arguably his most impactful memorandum. It was about the warfare of the future and it arrived in Moscow at the same time as Stalin and his comrades were frantically coordinating their activities regarding the Great Depression. In his memorandum, Tukhachevsky forcefully argued for a radical re-organization of the Red Army, which would also have to be expanded significantly. Tukhachevsky stated in his introduction: "In the Five-Year Plan for the Build-up of the Armed Forces, which was devised by the staff of the Red Army on the basis of the Five-Year Plan of the USSR, it has been noted that neither the state of industry nor the social structure of the village allowed it to constructively begin the organizational reconstruction of the armed forces."[11] However, Tukhachevsky argued, this had changed in the meantime and thus he submitted a proposal for a re-organization of the armed forces.

Tukhachevsky was very clear about who he saw as the target of that war: "This memorandum is mostly aimed at our Western neighbors and the great imperialists of Europe who support them." He continued:

> The extermination of the kulaks as a class and the collectivization of the means of production in the fully collectivized rayons allow us without a doubt to use the peasant masses in war, especially via the creation of territorial militias on a large scale. These could then – thanks to the mechanization of agriculture – be trained not only as riflemen and cavalrymen, but also find use in mechanized units. [...] Our resources enable us, thanks to the successful completion of the Five-Year Program, to engage in: a) massive development of the army; b) increase of its mobility; c) increase of its offensive capabilities.[12]

Tukhachevsky put a lot of hope in the capacity of the Soviet armaments industry and genuinely believed that the development of Soviet industry as foreseen in the Five-Year Plan would enable it to produce a grand total of 122,500 planes and 100,000 tanks. At the same time, he complained about the reduction of the size of the Red Army in 1924, which was due to a lack of equipment, as well as the Five-Year Plan of 1926, which included only a moderate increase in the number of divisions. In his words: "Today, the future of industrial development allows us to settle the question in a way that meets the requirements of the coming great war."[13]

Tukhachevsky argued that the reorganization and expansion of the Red Army had to reach the following benchmarks: 260 divisions of infantry and cavalry, 50 divisions of "ARGK" [artillery reserve of the high command] + large-caliber artillery and grenade launchers, 225 PRGK [machine-gun reserve of the high command] battalions, 40,000 combat-ready planes and 50,000 combat-ready tanks. This enormous amount of soldiers and materiel was necessary to fulfill his strategic vision: the massed use of tanks and aircraft in a simultaneous attack on a 450 km wide front that would destroy enemy formations 100 to 200 km away from the initial frontline. A depth of up to 200 km was supposed to be achieved thanks to paratroopers landing far behind enemy lines. This would allow the Red Army to completely annihilate enemy forces that were technologically inferior. Tukhachevsky's plan also foresaw the "massive use of chemical weapons" (*massovym primenenyem khimicheskikh sredstv borby*).[14]

Tukhachevsky was no naïve theorist. In the summer of 1920, Tukhachevsky had led the main Soviet force invading Poland on its push to Warsaw. Already then he was a major proponent of the "revolution from abroad" that was to be imposed onto unwilling countries.[15] In 1921, he and his Red Army had failed in their push West, but this time around, Tukhachevsky wanted to leave nothing to chance. This included the use of gas, which he also had first-hand experience with; after all, he had personally ordered the use of poison gas against the rebel peasants of the Tambov Uprising in the summer of 1921.

In this memorandum from 11 January 1930, Tukhachevsky was arguably one of the first to fully formulate a coherent plan for a "Blitzkrieg"-like war of annihilation. The Soviet Union would not need the 50,000 tanks and 40,000 aircraft Tukhachevsky wanted to defeat Poland and its potential allies (Romania, Latvia and Estonia), which taken together – according to contemporary Soviet estimates – could only field up to 1,000 tanks and 2,240 planes.[16] It was for a follow-up war with Germany that the Soviet Union would need such a great amount of materiel, given that France would likely oppose both the destruction of Poland and the Sovietization of its German neighbour.

Tukhachevsky submitted his memorandum to Voroshilov and sent copies to the Chief of Staff, Shaposhnikov, and the Chief of Armaments of the Red Amy, Uborevich; the latter two posts had just been created two months earlier, in November 1929.[17] Voroshilov ordered Shaposhnikov to analyze Tukhachevsky's proposal and to formulate a response. His assessment was devastating. Shaposhnikov lambasted the plan for being completely unrealistic. Unlike Tukhachevsky, he did not believe the Soviet armaments industry would be able to produce such a gigantic amount of tanks, planes and other kinds of equipment. Additionally, he pointed out that the Red Army did not have a sufficient number of qualified technical and military specialists to deal with such a dramatic expansion of the army and its technical troops.[18] A few days later, the general staff finalized its own assessment of Tukhachevsky's memorandum, which was mostly based on Shaposhnikov's earlier analysis. This assessment highlighted that Tukhachevsky completely overestimated the future expansion of Soviet industry. Furthermore, the number of able-bodied recruits was too low, as was the number of technical specialists, commanders, and pilots. All in all, the general staff surmised, Tukhachevsky's project was not economically viable.[19]

Voroshilov forwarded the general staff's assessment to Stalin on 5 March, adding the following comment: "Tukhachevsky wants to be original and 'radical.' It's bad that there are people in the Red Army who take this radicalism at face value. I ask you to read both documents and to let me know your opinion."[20] Stalin did in fact read both documents attentively, as evidenced by his very liberal use of his trademark blue pen. On 23 March, Stalin sent out his reply. His assessment, too, was damning. Like the others before him, Stalin accused Tukhachevsky of ignoring the country's economic, financial and cultural circumstances. He saw the entire plan as unrealistic and outright fantastic, and asked:

How could such a plan emerge in the head of a Marxist who went through the school of the Civil War? I think that the 'plan' of Comrade Tukh-sky [that is how Stalin abbreviated Tukhachevsky's name] resulted from the fashionable enthusiasm for 'leftwing' phrases, from the enthusiasm for bureaucratic office-maximalism. Thus, in the plan, analysis was *replaced* by 'playing around with numbers' and a Marxist perspective of the development of the Red Army with a fantastical one. To realize such a 'plan' would doubtlessly doom the economy of the country and the army. This would be worse than any counter-revolution.[21]

These assessments remained confidential and Tukhachevsky was initially not aware of the hostile response his ideas received. Thus he continued to author memoranda in which he further elaborated on his ideas of a future offensive war. On 23 February 1930 – when the general staff was still contemplating his earlier proposal – Tukhachevsky sent his next memorandum to Voroshilov. This time, Tukhachevsky criticized the state of mobilization of Soviet industry, which he saw as wholly inadequate. He wrote that the Soviet armaments industry was not integrated enough with civilian industry and that preparations for the coming war followed what Tukhachevsky called the "one-shot principle," meaning that they only targeted the armaments industry and were not geared towards waging a long war.[22]

Tukhachevsky was not finished. On the contrary, he penned two more memoranda in March 1930. On 8 March, he wrote about the production of artillery pieces and shells as well as recent developments in artillery technology and tactics. In it, he explained how the Soviet Union would need around 20,000 artillery pieces for the next war, as well as 180 million artillery shells per year during wartime. This was to go hand in hand with a massive expansion of the Soviet artillery corps, from 41,000 soldiers in 1930 to 131,000 soldiers in 1932/3, with the combat engineer corps being given special attention. Furthermore, Tukhachevsky called for the rapid expansion of the chemical industry in order to build up the needed capacities to manufacture explosives for the artillery shells required.[23]

On 16 March 1930, he wrote his second memorandum of the month, this time on the topic of engineer units. Tukhachevsky argued that it was their task to build roads and bridges as it would be very likely that the retreating enemy would systematically destroy the existing ones. This would "put the activities of the assault army in a difficult logistical situation in narrow sections of the front." Therefore, the engineering corps had to be expanded. Tuhachevsky was entirely focused on offense and the memorandum did not even mention possible defensive tasks of the engineer corps, such as constructing fortifications.[24] Two months later, he expanded on his earlier thoughts in yet another memorandum, in which he wrote about provisional motorways that could be constructed quickly from pre-fabricated parts. Like in the memorandum from March, the focus was on offense as these quickly assembled roads would enable advancing units to bypass damaged roads.[25]

Tukhachevsky wrote and sent out all these memoranda completely unaware of the scathing reception of his ideas, upon which he continued to build. It was only on 13 April 1930 that he was informed about how Stalin received his memorandum from 11 January when Voroshilov read out Stalin's criticism during an enlarged meeting of the Revolutionary War Council, which Tukhachevsky personally attended. A week later, he was also confronted with the criticism levied against his ideas by the general staff. Despite this great humiliation, Tukhachevsky held on to his vision and formulated a response, which he eventually sent to Stalin – together with the memoranda he had penned in the meantime.[26]

After nearly two months of deliberation, Tukhachevsky sent out his reply on 19 June. In it, he argued that the general staff ignored information that backed him while also misrepresenting his ideas in a bid to discredit him and his ideas. For example, he wrote that he had stated that in a single war year, 50,000 combat-ready tanks were needed, as well as an additional 50,000 for spare parts. He explained that not all of these were supposed to be standard combat tanks; a large portion was to be made up of tractors that could quickly be converted into tanks. Even though these makeshift tanks would not hold up against enemy armor, Tukhachevsky saw them as powerful enough to hold their ground against infantry and thus included them in his plans for the second and third attack waves, after the first-rate tanks had already destroyed the enemy's armor and artillery. This line of thinking also permeated his vision for the air force and he proposed to build up the Soviet civilian air force in such a way that civilian planes too could be quickly converted into planes capable of fulfilling military duties. At the same time, Tukhachevsky forcefully denied being delusional.[27]

His vigorous defense of his vision did pay off and he was given a second chance at the XV Party Conference held in Moscow in late June 1930, where

Tukhachevsky managed to talk to Stalin personally. In the conversation, Stalin admitted that he had based his scathing critique of Tukhachevsky on the evaluation of his general staff and promised that he would read Tukhachevsky's response to it as well as his other memoranda.[28] That was not an empty promise. Stalin did indeed read all of the memoranda with great care as evidenced by the ample comments and underlines he left on the document.[29]

Stalin slowly began to change his mind and started to toy with Tukhachevsky's ideas. In the autumn of 1930, Stalin began to work on his plan for a massive expansion of the Red Army. On 30 November 1930, the Politburo announced the expansion of the Red Army for the next year. In case of war, it would be able to field 102 infantry divisions, 29 corps, 12 cavalry divisions, 7 cavalry brigades, 24 artillery regiments, 23 large-caliber artillery battalions, 1,535 combat aircraft, 830 light and medium tanks, 400 armored cars, 8,864 medium and large-caliber artillery pieces as well as 3,585 small-caliber pieces.[30] The same day, the Politburo decided that by spring 1932, an additional 4,000 armored cars, 13,800 light and 2,000 medium tanks were to be produced for the Red Army.[31]

Even though this was not quite what Tukhachevsky had in mind, he felt encouraged all the same. On 30 December 1930, he sent Stalin another memorandum regarding the expansion of the armored forces. He was motivated to do so after Stalin's decision to significantly expand the Red Army as well as to reorganize the civil aviation sector. Tukhachevsky was particularly happy about the latter development and noted that Stalin's reforms went above and beyond what he himself had proposed.[32]

The year 1930 had begun poorly for Tukhachevsky, but luckily for him, things turned around in the second half of that year. This trend was to continue and 1931 represented a breakthrough in Tukhachevsky's career. On 10 May 1931, the Politburo had Tukhachevsky's main critic, Shaposhnikov, relieved of his post of Chief of the Red Army. He was succeeded by Ion Yakir, who resigned soon after, in turn succeeded by Alexander Yegorov on 10 June.[33] On the same day, Stalin appointed Tukhachevsky to the posts of Vice-Chief of Armaments of the Red Army as well as Vice-People's Commissar for Military Affairs and the Fleet. These were highly influential posts and Tukhachevsky remained in these positions until his downfall in 1937. This allowed him to realize his plans for the coming lightning war of annihilation with little to no opposition.

Stalin had Tukhachevsky's back and not only distanced himself from his earlier attacks on Tukhachevsky's ideas, but even apologized for these remarks. In a letter dated 7 May 1932, which he sent to Tukhachevsky but also forwarded to Voroshilov, Stalin wrote: "Today, after two years, after some issues that seemed to be unclear to me have become clearer, I have to admit that my judgement was too harsh and that not all of my statements were correct."[34] He continued that despite this, he still believed that Tukhachevsky's idea of having an army numbering 11 million soldiers was unrealistic. Stalin believed that not even expanding the military to "just" 8 million service members was realizable in the short term; he thought that this could only be achieved within 3 or 4 years. However, Stalin explained, the deciding factor in the upcoming war would not be the number of divisions, but their quality and their equipment. He continued: "I think You would agree with me that a six million man army, well equipped and reorganized, is completely sufficient to guarantee the independence of our country on all fronts, without exceptions."[35] In the end, this was the benchmark that Tukhachevsky had to reach in his quest to reorganize the Red Army.

Building Tanks and Expanding the Armored Corps

As outlined above, the Politburo decided to embark on a large-scale tank building program on 30 November 1930. The program foresaw the construction of 4,000 new armored cars, 13,800 light and 2,000 medium tanks by early 1932.[36] Encouraged by these developments, Tukhachevsky began to work on his own plan for the mass production of tanks, copies of which he sent to Stalin and Voroshilov on 30 December 1930. In it, he made clear that he was building on his memorandum from 11 January 1930.[37]

Tukhachevsky argued that a modern war with modern equipment – the kind he had described in his memorandum from 11 January 1930 – required a wide array of different tank types. The tanks destined to take part in the first attacking wave were to be powerful enough to break through the enemy front. As such, they had to be of the highest quality. They also had to be very well armored in order to withstand enemy anti-tank fire. This, however, was not true for the tanks used in the following attack waves. Tukhachevsky believed that their main purpose was to destroy the remnants of the overrun enemy forces, i.e. already weakened infantry armed with rifles and maybe machine guns. For this purpose, tanks of poorer quality and with much weaker armor were more than enough.[38]

Unfortunately, the Soviet Union did not have the means to mass-produce the high-quality tanks needed to achieve breakthroughs, Tukhachevsky cautioned. This was not the case for the tanks of the second type, however. Tuhachevsky believed that modified cars and tractors were good enough, and that these could be mass-produced with relative ease. Thus he argued that the Soviet Union could dramatically increase its number of tanks in a short period of time. Additionally, this would also allow the Soviet Union to diversify the types of tanks it produced to fulfill various roles. According to Tukhachevsky, these were the following: overcoming enemies in fortifications, combat against enemy anti-tank artillery, overcoming entrenched enemies, as well as fighting opponents armed with machine guns. He pointed out that capitalist countries approached their tank-building programs with similar considerations in mind.

Naturally, mass-producing even second-rate tanks was easier said than done. Soviet engineers and designers first had to find a suitable type of car or tractor onto which the guns and armor could be mounted. Tukhachevsky believed that he had already found suitable models in the USSR, namely the "Carden-Lloyd" tank as well as smaller armored cars that were built using Ford technology and were able to reach speeds of up to 40 km/h. For the slower tanks, tractors were sufficient to serve as a basic model. According to Tukhachevsky, the first prototypes had already been produced and tested in the Leningrad Military District, but unfortunately these had proven to be too weak. However, he continued, the "Krasny Putilovets" factory would begin producing a new type of tractor in March 1931 and that these tractors could be modified into good light tanks. For this to happen, the Soviet Union needed an ample supply of tank hulls that could be punched [metal cutting process]. Tukhachevsky claimed that the "Lenin" and "Stalin" factories located in Leningrad had both the technology and the production capacities to punch these tank hulls. Thus, he argued, every tractor and every car could be easily modified into a tank if the need arose. This was quite significant as the production of cars and tractors in the Soviet Union was rapidly increasing at the time and the country was importing them in large numbers as well. By 1933, the number of cars in the Soviet Union was projected to reach 203,000 and the number of tractors 166,300.

Taking this into consideration Tukhachevsky claimed that it was perfectly feasible to build up a force of 75,000 tanks by 1933. Most of these tanks would be equipped with machine guns, as only the tanks of the first attack wave were intended to have proper tank guns. Tukhachevsky argued that the drivers of the second-rate tanks were to be recruited from among tractor drivers, who would receive special training. He went on to criticize the alleged conservatism of the general staff which he felt was stuck in the mindset of the First World War with its static battles and overuse of artillery. Tukhachevsky instead was a harbinger of a different kind of warfare; one based on maneuver and massed use of tanks.[39]

Tukhachevsky's talk about modern maneuver warfare struck a chord with Stalin, who – judging by his many underlines – had read the memorandum with great care. Stalin and the Politburo had already issued guidelines calling for the purchase of tractor factories as well as modern technology in order to adapt it for the Soviet Union's future tank production. On 10 January, less than two weeks after Tukhachevsky sent out his memorandum, Voroshilov set up a commission tasked with overseeing the tank building program. Naturally, Tukhachevsky became part of the commission.[40]

On 20 February 1931, the Politburo passed a decree on the tank building program, which was ultimately a product of his memorandum from 30 December 1930. The decree specified the following: the T-27 tankette, which was to use the Ford motors Tukhachevsky had mentioned earlier, was to be produced in Automobile Factory No. 2. For 1931, the plan foresaw the production of 400 tankettes, which could be increased to 2,000 in times of war. A second factory producing T-27s was to be built near the already existing automobile factories in Nizhny Novgorod. Meanwhile, the light tank of choice was the T-26 (Vickers), which was to be built in the "Bolshevik" factory in Leningrad. For 1931, the plan was for 400 to be produced. However, the plan also included a significant expansion of the factory so that it would be able to produce 1,500 of these tanks. Additionally, the tractor factories in Stalingrad were to produce a grand total of 12,000 T-26 tanks per year beginning in early 1932. The guidelines for the medium tanks were much more modest in comparison. The first T-G tanks were to be produced in the tractor factory in Kharkiv. Only 50 to 75 were to be built in 1931. That number was scheduled to rise dramatically, and with the setup of a second factory in the Urals, the number of T-G tanks produced annually was scheduled to reach 2,000.[41]

The decree of 20 February 1931 also specified that the production of infantry support tanks was to be organized along the same lines as the automobile and tractor industry up to 1932/33. This would, according to the decree, allow the Soviet Union to reach "satisfactory results for the assimilation of the T-27 tankette with the Ford AA as well as preliminary results with the armor and armament of the tractors 'Communard' and 'Caterpillar' tractors, thus with their modification to tanks for the purpose of infantry support." Furthermore, the Politburo decided to organize the production of motors and the steel necessary for tanks.[42]

Naturally, the Politburo did not forget the cadres, and a few days later, on 25 February 1931, issued a decree calling for the mobilization of 7,000 communists who would enter training in several military academies to become commanders in the air force, the tank force and the artillery. However, the duration of the training was to be shortened to 1 ½ to 2 years.[43] Half a year later, on 5 July, the Politburo judged that it was necessary to additionally increase the political reliability as well as the military training of the commanders – including those belonging to the reserve – so that they would be able to handle modern military hardware.[44]

The Politburo decree of 20 February 1931 strongly suggests that Stalin and his comrades were aiming to be ready for war in 1933 and that they were preparing for a major war in 1933/34. This is further supported by the resolution of the Revolutionary War Council from September 1931, which painted the newly-created motorized units as the "armored fist of motorized units" for the war of the future that could break out in 1933/34. Until then, the Politburo aimed for the production of 10,000 tanks, including 3,000 light tanks, 5,000 armored cars and 2,000 medium tanks."[45]

The goal of producing 10,000 tanks remained the target throughout and was reaffirmed by the Committee of Defense on 10 January 1932 at Stalin's behest. However, Stalin's ambitions did not end there. Already in July 1931, Tukhachevsky had been given lead of a team tasked with drawing up another "great tank program" that was to be realized beginning in 1932. This program envisioned, among other things, a massive expansion of the automobile factories in Nizhny Novgorod, which were to produce 28,000 to 35,000 armored cars in a single year during wartime. The tractor factories in Stalingrad were to be greatly expanded as well, with the goal of producing 12,000 light tanks (T-26) a year.[46]

In early 1932, Stalin and his closest colleagues – chief among them Tukhachevsky – closely monitored the expansion of the mechanized units of the Red Army, with a special focus on the armored units. On 21 January 1932, Tukhachevsky wrote to Stalin and Voroshilov, telling them that planned mass production of tanks would allow the Red Army to turn infantry divisions stationed in the Western border regions of the BSSR and the UkrSSR into fully-fledged mechanized brigades and corps. These new units would then be able to conduct Tukhachevsky's "deep operations" (i.e. the campaigns of annihilation) against countries like Poland, Romania and Latvia.[47]

Later plans were even more ambitious. When the new Five Year Plan for 1933-1938 was announced in March 1932, it included the creation of a tank industry capable of building 62,500 tanks, including 20,000 tankettes, 12,000 light tanks and 500 heavy tanks as well as 20,000 makeshift tanks to be used for the second wave of attack. Furthermore, the Red Army was to receive 350,000 trucks and 19,000 tractors. In May and June 1932, Chief of Staff of the Red Army, Yegorov, devised a plan that by 1938 saw the Red Army expand to 32,000 aircraft, 40,000 tanks, 20,000 armored cars, 100,000 tractors, 500,000 trucks, 84,500 artillery pieces and 75 million artillery shells.[48] If these targets were to be reached, Tukhachevksy's memorandum from 11 January would have become reality.

The Soviet plans were truly gargantuan by the standards of the day and doubly so for a largely agrarian country like the Soviet Union. So how were they implemented? On 16 November 1932, Voroshilov in his capacity as the People's Commissar for Military Matters and the Fleet issued a detailed report on the state of the Red Army's preparations for war in 1931/32. In the introduction, he stated:

> The year 1932/3 was the year with the largest organizational expansion of the Red Army following the Civil War. In the course of this year, 10 new infantry divisions were raised, 117 armored and mechanized units were in the process of being raised; the raising of 58 aerial units has been practically completed; raised were also two large units – kolkhoz and railway corps, etc.[49]

Eighteen thousand commanders of the reserve had been mobilized to lead the new units and 13,000 commanders as well as political commissars had been transferred within the military. Commanders and political commissars had received schooling and new soldiers were trained as well. Nevertheless, Voroshilov warned: "The Red Army is still far away from meeting the demands of the new technology, the new [...] organizational structure and in many ways, the transformed character of modern battle and operations."[50]

Voroshilov blamed the Red Army's leadership for these deficiencies. He lamented that until 1930, the Red Army did not have a proper staff system, which is why a lot of attention was given to the strengthening of the staff as well as the training of the staff commanders in 1932. Voroshilov went on to say that military intelligence was one of the major weaknesses of the staff system as it was unable to properly analyze incoming information and reports. The administration in the rear areas was also criticized as being inadequate. Additionally, he complained about the state of training regarding preparatory shelling among the artillery but also the cavalry and infantry.[51]

Voroshilov's report further stated that the level of education was very low among the commanders; many did not receive more than a primary education. This represented a challenge for the military academies, which in 1932/33 were expected to train 10,700 and 17,700 commanders the following year. Among the mid-level military academies, it was the technical academies that played the most important role. In 1932, 34,750 aspiring commanders were enrolled in technical academies.

Cavalry and infantry academies meanwhile only accounted for 10,180 students.[52]

This comes as no surprise as the mechanized formations represented not only the newest branch of the Red Army, but also the one undergoing the largest expansion. In 1930, there were only 43 independent mechanized units. By 1931, their number had risen to 79 and by 1932 to 193. In 1932, 200,000 soldiers were trained to serve in the new mechanized formations, as well as 9,000 low-ranking commanders, around 4,000 high-ranking commanders as well as 4,000 technical personnel. Despite this – Voroshilov lamented – the Red Army had difficulties finding suitable men for its mechanized units. These difficulties were exacerbated by the shortened training duration as well as the lack of vehicles. According to him, the mechanized units "are characterized by a new form of organization as well as a lack of combat experience for tank and mechanized units." Even worse, the men had problems driving their own tanks.[53]

Throughout his report, Voroshilov highlighted the decisive role Tukhachevsky's ideas had in the military build-up of 1931 and 1932. It was Tukhachevsky's new strategy, which Voroshilov called "deep tactic" in his report, that guided the overall thrust of the armament program. The strategy called for a massive attack by armored units – supported by the air force, artillery and infantry – that was to occur simultaneously along a wide front. In theory, this would guarantee a quick breakthrough and allow for the annihilation of enemy forces on an operative level. Voroshilov argued that this theory had achieved partial success during training exercises in 1932. At the same time, he cautioned that the use of artillery to break through enemy lines was an idea that had not proven itself in the battles of the previous world war.[54]

Voroshilov again noted that there had been severe difficulties in supplying the new armored units with the tanks they needed. In fact, it was clear already in the summer of 1932 that the tank building program could not meet its target of 10,000 tanks for the year. Up to August 1932, only 440 T-26 tanks had been built and the Red Army had received 264 of them. In October 1932, the yearly targets were corrected downwards to 4,700 tanks, less than half of the initial plan. However, the factories failed to meet this target as well.[55]

Table 15: The Tank Construction Program and its Implementation[56]

Model and Production Site	Plan 1932 (February 1932)	Adjusted Plan (October 1932)	Delivered to the Red Army	Only Assembled	Of which	
					Lacked Turrets	Lacked Tracks
T-26, light tank, at the "Voroshilov" Factory	3,000	1,600	911	1,409	500	–
Medium Tank BT, at the Kharkiv Locomotive Plant	2,000	600	239	600	300	290
T-27 Tankette at Factory No. 2 in Moscow;	5,000	1,800	1,370	1,618	–	–
Factory in Nizhny Novogrod		300	65	87		
Total	10,000	4,300	2,585	3,714	800	290

By the end of 1932, the Red Army had received only 2,585 tanks, or around 25% of the tanks it should have. To make matters worse, many of the delivered tanks had not been built according to specifications. For example, Soviet factories failed to deliver the tank turrets needed for the medium BT tank. Thus, the original 44 mm tank gun had to be replaced with a much weaker 37 mm tank gun. This was only supposed to be temporary; once strong enough tank turrets were available, the weaker BT tanks were to be modified to fit the original specifications.[57]

The reasons for the failure of the plan were manifold: Abysmal organization, delayed construction of factories, as well as lack of steel and other vital materials. The factories in Stalingrad, for example, did not even come close to fulfilling their quotas for the production of tank hulls as they only received 250 of the 1,000 tons of steel they needed. In the tractor factories of Kharkov and in the "Voroshilov" factory in Leningrad, there were over 700 that remained only partly assembled due to crippling material shortages. In the summer of 1933, Tukhachevsky raised the alarm: The factory halls and workshops were filled with unfinished tanks, which would begin to decay with the onset of winter.[58]

The situation did not improve much in the following years. As part of the Second Five Year Plan, the Red army received 3,640 tanks and assault guns. That number fell to 3,340 in 1934 and 3,061 in 1935 before rising to 3,939 in 1936; for 1937, the target was set at 2,145 tanks and assault guns.[59] This was a far cry from the initial 10,000 tanks per year target of the tank building program of 1932 and demonstrates the grossly over-optimistic nature of the plan that vastly overshot the capacities of the Soviet armaments industry.

Nevertheless, even with its failure, the plan had left the Soviet Union with a very large number of tanks compared to its capitalist rivals. According to Soviet estimates, France had 3,500 tanks in 1933, Great Britain and the USA had 1,000 tanks each, and Japan somewhere between 400 and 500.[60] The Red Army meanwhile had received 3,640 new tanks and assault guns in that year alone. Thus the Soviet Union fielded more tanks than all other European powers combined by the end of 1934.

Table 16: Number of Tanks in the Red Army 1934-1941[61]

01.01.1934	01.01.1935	01.01.1936	01.01.1937	01.01.1938	01.01.1939	01.05.1940	01.01.1941
7,574	10,180	13,339	17,280	18,839	21,110	21,982	23,307

However, this gigantic tank army was nothing more than a paper tiger. On 2 August 1936, Voroshilov reported on the armored units that had been raised in 1932 and 1933: "Tanks, with which we could go to war, were non-existent."[62]

There were many reasons for this. First of all, the quality of the tanks was abysmal. Additionally, the tanks had seen intensive use – without being properly maintained as the army lacked repair workshops, spare parts, and skilled mechanics. Already on 1 August 1933, the OGPU sent out a special report to Stalin, Molotov, Voroshilov and Ordzhonikidze, in which it condemned the massive delivery of defective weapons to the Red Army. The special report also included following remarks: "A large part of the tanks delivered to the Red Army show very serious defects, including the [presence] of foreign objects in the tank mechanisms and the engines. [...] The above-mentioned defects not only lower the combat ability of the tanks but also create a climate of distrust among the personnel of the motorized units regarding the reliability of the tanks."[63]

The report noted that this was a problem in many other arms of the Red Army. These issues were mostly blamed on the shoddy work of the technical quality control in the armament factories. Naturally, the OGPU suspected sabotage and soon claimed to have uncovered entire networks of counterrevolutionaries, intent on supplying the Red Army with defective weaponry. The OGPU thus ordered a range of measures to improve the process of quality control in the armaments industry.[64] These measures, however, had only limited effect and in November 1933, Molotov in his capacity as the Chairman of the Council for Labor and Defense, issued a resolution designed to improve the quality of military hardware produced. Among the measures taken were the expansion of the administration of the quality control department by 50 engineers and making the quality control inspectors financially and professionally independent from factory management.[65]

With Anvil and Iron Bars

Molotov's efforts failed to bring about the desired results. The quality of the weapons and equipment produced remained abysmal. The situation was especially dire for the mechanized units due to the fact that the Politburo, Tukhachevsky, and the rest of the planners had failed to establish a network of repair bases. In the end, it was the units themselves that had to repair the often unusable tanks they had been given. As they were neither properly equipped nor trained for this task, the repairs remained rather rudimentary.

It was not until the summer of 1933 that a plan was drawn up to secure the repair of combat and transport vehicles in times of peace and war. After delays of several months, the Soviet government finally issued a repair plan on 28 November 1933 that was to affect 1,300 tanks and 500 tank engines in the coming year. Nevertheless, the Chief of the Administration for Tank Armament, Khalepsky, raised the alarm just a few days later, on 1 December 1933: "If we do not take immediate action regarding this question now," then only 17% of all tanks in the Red Army would be combat ready within a year. He continued to complain that the People's Commissariat for Heavy Industry refused to do anything to set up a supply base for the repair of M-5 engines used in the BT tank or even supply spare parts for these engines. Khalepsky then asked the Vice-Chairman of the Council of People's Commissars, Kuibyshev, to order the People's Commissariat for Heavy Industry to set up a network of tank repair bases.[66]

These calls for action remained largely unanswered and the creation of a network of repair workshops progressed at a very sluggish pace. On 19 August 1934, the Council of People's Commissars ordered the construction of workshops in the BSSR that would be capable of repairing 2,995 combat vehicles and 2,800 Ford AA trucks. This was quite important as the BSSR was the main staging area for an invasion of Poland and was thus of vital strategic value. Construction was to begin in the last quarter of 1934, but by March 1935, nothing much had happened.[67]

The year 1935 saw marked improvement in this area, especially regarding the repair of tanks, but the situation on the ground was still lagging far behind the plans. In the first half of 1935, the Soviet armaments industry was able to fulfill 71.8% of its quota for the complete overhaul of broken combat vehicles, but only 33.8% of its quota for the production of spare engines. A report from 19 July 1935 stated that the supply of spare parts to the repair workshops had improved throughout 1935. Nevertheless, the supply of ball and roller bearings remained a major weakness as they were barely delivered at all.[68]

As early as 1932, the People's Commissariat for Heavy Industry had been ordered to guarantee the supply of every type of ball bearing used in Soviet tanks. The initial plan had been to rely on imports at first before switching to domestically produced ball bearings by 1934. This did not happen, however, and by 1 November 1936, the production of eleven types of ball bearings needed for tank production had not been secured. While the other types of ball bearings were already being produced, their production numbers were not even high enough to satisfy peacetime demand. As a result, there were not enough ball bearings to fulfill the production quota for T-26 and BT-7 tanks, let alone to supply the repair workshops with spare parts.[69] To make things worse, the quality of domestically-produced ball bearings was considerably worse than the ones produced abroad, meaning that the Soviet Union had to continue to rely on imports.[70]

The situation regarding the repair of tanks did not improve in 1936, with the reasons remaining the same, namely the lack of spare parts as well as the chaotic work processes within the individual repair workshops.[71] Another issue was that the repair workshops also lacked the highly specialized machinery needed to repair tanks. As a report from 15 April 1936 put it: "The factories are to be outfitted with special equipment for the repair of tanks, and the tank repair work with craftsman-like methods, with 'anvil' and 'iron bars', is to be ceased."[72] This was of course easier said than done and by the time the Second World War broke out, the tank repair workshops remained in a very poor state.[73]

The abysmal state of tank maintenance was the main reason the Soviet Union had so few combat-ready tanks in the early years of its grand armament program. This was compounded by the lack of training. Between the years 1931 and 1933, the newly raised armored units had reached their planned number of personnel in time. However, the fact that they did not receive anywhere near the planned number of usable tanks in time meant that the few tanks that were useable were overused during training and combat exercises. This resulted in them wearing down very quickly, a process that was accelerated by the aforementioned lack of proper maintenance. Looking back in August 1936, Voroshilov complained that in 1933, the Red Army did not possess any combat-ready tanks.[74]

Voroshilov responded to this emergency by limiting the use of available tanks. According to the guidelines he issued in 1933, 50% of combat vehicles in the Red Army were not be used more than 100 hours in a single year; the other 50% were only allowed to be in use for a maximum of 50 hours a year. Voroshilov touted this as a success, and in August 1936 he claimed that the percentage of combat-ready tanks had increased from close to zero to around 40-50%. Unfortunately, this was only temporary as the lack of repair workshops and spare parts meant that the tanks could not be properly maintained even at such a reduced level of usage. As the number of combat ready tanks began to decline again, Voroshilov ordered a further clamp-down on the usage of tanks in 1935. According to these new regulations, 30% of tanks were allowed to see a maximum of 50 hours of use each year. The remaining 70% were to be in use for only up to 15 hours in a single year.[75]

However, even these measures failed to ensure combat-readiness of the Red Army's tanks. At the beginning of 1936, the Soviet Union had by far the largest tank army in the world with 13,000 tanks, but only a small fraction of them were ready for war. The troubles did not end there. Perhaps unsurprisingly, there were serious issues with the commanders and ordinary soldiers of the new tank armies. As the visibly shaken Mikhail Tukhachevsky reported to Stalin on 9 July 1936:

> After familiarizing myself with the state of war preparedness among the mechanized units, I see it as my duty to inform you that the state of preparedness is extraordinarily critical. Due to shortcomings in the organization of the repair system and the lack of spare machines, it is hardly possible to conduct even less than satisfactory training of the tank drivers. The tactical preparation of tank units barely happens at all. For example, I wanted to conduct a brigade maneuver with the mechanized "Kalinovsky" corps but was unable to do so, because of a lack of tanks (they were being repaired after the May parade, etc.). One had to conduct this maneuver with a battalion each from the third and fourth brigades. It turned out that over the course of the last two years, there had been no battalion maneuvers. The only [maneuvers to take place] had been commander maneuvers, i.e. [maneuvers] with the participation of the battalion commander and three tanks of the company commanders. Naturally, one cannot talk about satisfactory battle preparations under these circumstances. Both the corps commander and the brigade commanders said that given the current deliveries of tank engines, it would not be possible to ensure satisfactory combat preparedness.[76]

Due to the severely limited repair capacities, Tukhachevsky continued, tanks were allowed to see only 15 hours of use per year for operative preparations (for the so-called first group) and 10 hours of use per year for parades. However, this was not the case for the "Kalinovsky" corps. There, tanks were used in parades for 20 hours each year. This came at the cost of training and exercises, and according to Tukhachevsky, this was the final nail in the coffin of the unit's combat preparedness.[77]

Tukhachevsky argued that in order to ensure a modicum of combat preparedness, tanks should be in use for at least 65 hours per year. At the same time, he stated that "it would therefore be desirable to restrict the use of all kinds of tank troops in parades." In order to increase the use of tanks in the Red Army, he also pointed out that the Red Army would need additional tanks, namely 300 BT, 900 T-26 and 500 T-38 tanks. Additionally, a further 800 BT, 1,800 T-26 and 1,000 T-38 tanks would have to reach the Red Army to achieve the war target stock. Tukhachevsky then concluded:

> All this shows that the state of the mechanized units is dangerous. First, combat preparedness cannot be satisfactory, and secondly [...] the tank units in the country are not setting up enough repair bases in the case of war and will therefore be out of action after the first engagement.[78]

This was the result of the greatest tank building program the world had ever seen. After five years of incredible organizational, financial, and economic exertions, after millions of deaths from hunger and after ten of millions of people had been forced into a modern system of slavery, the vaunted "armored fist" of the Soviet Union was nothing more than a paper tiger. Stalin was not happy. Despite the advice of his generals and his initial suspicions, Stalin had trusted Tukhachevsky and his extremely ambitious vision against all odds. He even apologized for his earlier doubts. Countless resources were wasted, millions of lives lost and – most importantly – Stalin's own reputation was in danger of being tarnished. This was too much. Within less than a year of him writing that devastating memorandum, the high-flying Tukhachevsky was accused of treason and executed.

In order to restore some semblance of combat readiness, the Committee for Defense issued new guidelines on 9 August 1936 that increased the average use of tanks to 88 hours per year. This was further affirmed on 19 September 1936 by a decree from the Council for Labor and Defense. This did not address the underlying issue of the lack of maintenance and repairs, and unsurprisingly, this measure had a catastrophic effect on the tanks. Voroshilov once again raised the alarm on 9 July 1937: in order to ensure the combat readiness of armored units, he proposed setting up a special tank fleet for the sole purpose of training. He suggested setting aside nine tanks per tank battalion and mechanized regiment, as well as four tanks for each tank training company. The operating time for these machines was set at 225 hours per year. In total, this tank fleet was to number 3,618 tanks; in case of war, they would be treated as a source of spare parts for the tanks that were seeing combat. The tanks designated for combat purposes, meanwhile, were to not be used for more than 20 hours per year.[79]

Another serious problem was the combat capability of the tanks – even when they were not defective. According to Soviet plans, the newly produced tanks were supposed to be equal to Western tanks in terms of armor, armament, and speed.[80] However, the commanders on the ground did not quite agree. During a session of the War Council at the People's Commissariat of Defense on 21 November 1937, the Commander of Kyiv Military District 1, Fedko said this regarding the state of the armored troops:

> Here as well the enemy had acted with much effect. What did the people's enemy, Fesenko, say regarding the preparedness of the armored troops: 'The tank troops are completely unprepared (here he is exaggerating [according to Fedko]), they shoot poorly […] the tanks are only driving in flat terrain and can overcome obstacles only with great difficulty when the terrain becomes a bit more difficult.' The latter is completely true, however.[81]

For example, T-26 tanks were only able to move at speeds of 1.5 to 2 kilometers per hour in desert terrain. Due to their weak engines, they reached the same breathtaking speeds in the mountains. The "light" T-26 tank was thus practically stationary in difficult terrain and quite literally a sitting duck for enemy anti-tank weapons.[82]

Voroshilov disagreed with Fedko in his closing remarks on 27 November 1937 and claimed that the combat readiness of the armored units was high. Voroshilov went on to say that he had observed the new tanks during many maneuvers and that they had left a positive impression on him. This was not the case for the crews, however, Voroshilov admitted. Both the common soldiers and the commanders were said to have been very poorly trained. According to Voroshilov, this was backed up by the experiences of Soviet tank troops fighting in the Spanish Civil War. He referenced an incident in which a Soviet unit had attacked the enemy with 40 tanks, of which it lost half during the very first engagement.[83]

It is thus not surprising that the Soviet leadership felt the need to re-examine the state of its armored units the following spring. In April 1938, the Chief War Council of the Red Army passed a number of measures designed to make its armored wing more effective. Most of the attention was focused on refitting the tank fleet; many tank types were to be modernized while others were to be replaced entirely. Among the ones slated for replacement were the existing breakthrough tanks, which were deemed to be obsolete. The new breakthrough tanks were to have armor 60 mm thick and were to be equipped with M-34 gasoline engines with the possibility of having them replaced with diesel engines. Despite weighing up to 55 tons, they were supposed to reach speeds of 25 to 30 km/h and have dimensions allowing them to be transported by rail.[84]

The remaining tanks of the types T-26, BT, T-28 and T-35 were scheduled to receive a wide range of upgrades, improving their armor, speed, and armament. The BT tanks were to receive diesel engines as well. Upgrades notwithstanding, the T-28 and T-35 tanks would cease to be produced once a new breakthrough tank was introduced. Additionally, two new types of fast tanks were to be developed, one with just tracks and the other one with sprockets and tracks. Protected by 30 mm of armor, these lighter tanks were to be equipped with a 45 mm gun and three machine guns. A diesel engine would then be able to propel the tanks weighing 13-14 tons (tracks) and 15-16 tons to speeds of up to 50-60 km/h. Furthermore, new tank tracks were to be produced; whereas the old ones had to be exchanged after 1,000-1,500 km, the new ones were to last for up to 3,000 km. Finally, the plan also foresaw the introduction and mass production of new types of specialized fast tanks as well as an amphibious tank.[85]

These new tanks, especially the light tanks, were only really usable in the flat terrain of Central and Western Europe, with its extensive network of good roads. Therefore, these plans from April 1938 hint at greater Soviet plans to wage campaigns on German or French soil. Given that the Soviet Union was far away from either of these states, such campaigns would likely be the result of an offensive war.

The breakthrough tank was being designed over the following months. In August 1939, the first prototypes of the new heavy KV (Kliment Voroshilov) tank had been assembled, and it entered testing the following month. Only a few months later, in December 1939, the KV tank saw action for the first time in the Winter War against Finland. The KV tank passed these tests with flying colors and was scheduled to enter mass production in 1940. By 1 June 1941, on the eve of the German invasion, the Red Army had 504 KV tanks in its ranks. The first prototype of the new medium tank, the iconic T-34, was developed mere months after the KV tank, in autumn 1939. However, this tank was to enter mass production only in early 1941 and by 1 January 1941, the Red Army had 97 T-34 tanks. This number had risen to 892 tanks by the beginning of June 1941. The KV tank and especially the T-34 tank earned themselves quite a good reputation in the history of the Second World War.[86]

In early 1941, these modern tanks were still plagued by a host of technical issues, however. The KV had major problems with its cannon, the armor was found to be too weak, and the diesel engines were not powerful enough.[87] On 4 April 1941 the Politburo addressed these issues by ordering the improvement the armor of the tank by putting additional shielding on the tank's weak points; the tank gun was also to be replaced with a new, more powerful model.[88]

By that time, the mass production of KV tanks had just begun. Between January and June 1941, the plan was to produce 745 KV tanks; the number was to rise to 1,200 by the end of the year.[89] Mass production of the T-34 medium tank only began in May 1941. For this month, the production quota was set at 200 tanks; the target gradually increased to 230 for June and 260 for July of that year. By the end of 1941, Soviet planners wanted to have 2,800 new T-34 tanks.[90] The tanks of the 1930s meanwhile ceased to be produced by the end of 1940. In early 1941, the Soviet tank industry only mass-produced four tank models, namely the KV, the T-34 as well as the T-40 and the T-50, the latter two being new light tanks.[91]

The German surprise attack on the Soviet Union on 22 June 1941 hit the Red Army just as it was beginning to refit its armored units and the vast majority of Soviet tanks in use were still outdated ones. Even worse, most of them were light T-26 and BT tanks that had not been modernized yet. M. Danchenko complained about this in a memorandum on 3 August 1940, and further warned his colleagues that the opening campaigns of the Second World War in Western Europe and in Poland had shown that it would be the medium and heavy tanks, the "modern heavy cavalry" as he put it, that played the deciding role in modern warfare. Danchenko specifically highlighted the successes of German tanks, which he thought were achieved thanks to their superior speed and maneuverability compared to French models. This, Danchenko argued, showed the need to continue development on the T-34 and KV tanks so they could enter mass production as soon as possible.[92]

As mentioned above, however, this process was in its early stages at the time Germany invaded the Soviet Union. In June 1941, the Red Army could call upon masses of obsolete and mostly light tanks, among them 10,055 T-26, 7,549 BT, 1,129 T-28, and 2,331 T-38 tanks. Together, these light tanks made up 82% (20,974) of the entire Soviet tank fleet (25,508).[93] The armor of the T-26 and the T-28 (nominally a medium tank), was so weak that it could even be penetrated by small-caliber weaponry.[94] These tanks were no match for the German military in the summer of 1941 and they were swept away with ease as the Wehrmacht advanced deep into Soviet territory.

The Airforce and The Aviation Industry

Aside from tanks and poison gas, Tukhachevsky had identified the air force as one of the key components of modern warfare. In his memorandum from 30 January 1930 in which he had laid out his vision of his lightning war of annihilation, he called for the creation of an air force numbering a grand total of 40,000 combat aircraft that would be capable of overwhelming any enemy. At that time, the Soviet air force only had 1,678 combat aircraft. Of them, 1,100 were actually deployed, with the remaining either being repaired or held in reserve.

The Soviet air force was not small. In fact, it was the third largest air force on the planet, after France (2,750) and the USA (2,040). Technology-wise, however, things did not look as good as the planes were horribly outdated.

In 1930, even agricultural Poland had better planes.[95] This was a glaring weakness and Tukhachevsky was not the only one to notice it. Already in March 1930 – when Tukhachevsky's proposals were still being met with outright hostility – the Politburo ordered a wide-ranging program of expansion and modernization of the air force. This also applied to Soviet civilian aviation. As the Soviet aviation industry was very outdated, foreign technology was to be imported on a large scale.

The task of devising the program was given to a commission headed by Kuibyshev, which presented its extremely ambitious plan in late 1931. On 11 January 1932, the Council for Labor and Defense approved the plan and ordered it to be implemented under the straightforward name "The development of the aviation industry in the years 1932-1935." According to this plan, the air force was to be expanded massively; by late 1935, it was to number 34,300 aircraft, including 3,500 interceptors, 8,000 scouting planes and light bombers, 1,800 close air support aircraft, 4,000 training planes, 12,000 smaller planes, 3,800 bombers, 700 naval aircraft and 500 special aircraft.[96] Soviet leadership genuinely believed these goals to be achievable at the time. When the Chief of Staff of the Red Army, Yegorov, drew up the mobilization plan for the years 1933 to 1938 in the summer of 1932, he expected the number of available combat aircraft to be at 10,400 in 1933. For 1938, he expected the air force to have 32,000 combat aircraft, including 5,800 interceptors, 9,500 light bombers and 8,000 heavy bombers.[97]

Officially, this project was a great success initially. On 10 January, Kliment Voroshilov reported at the Joint Plenum of the Central Committee and Central Control Commission of the VKP(b) about the supposedly great results of the expansion of the Red Army in the course of the First Five Year Plan (1928-1932). The modernization of the air force proceeded just as smoothly, Voroshilov claimed. According to him, the number of planes had nearly quadrupled compared to 1928. At the same time, the technical quality and combat abilities of the air force had been improved considerably. In 1928, the air force was dominated by scouting planes (49% of all aircraft); bombers and close air support (27%) and interceptors (24%) were much less common. By 1932, things had reversed: Bombers and close air support aircraft made up 43% of all planes in the air force, while interceptors and scouting planes accounted for 27% each.[98]

This report was a classic Soviet success story that only grazed against reality tangentially. Although it is likely that the raw number of planes was more or less accurate, the quality of the planes produced was a serious issue, both in terms of technology and overall combat ability.[99] Additionally, the original production targets had not been fulfilled either.

On 25 September 1933, for example, Korolev, the chief administrator of the Aviation Industry, reported that factories were beginning to lag behind the plan for that year. The initial target had been to produce 4,495 aircraft and 7,472 engines, but by the end of August, only 2,852 aircraft and 4,172 engines had been produced. These were quite impressive numbers on paper, but only represented 80.7% and 87.2% of the envisioned production numbers until that point. Furthermore, most of the delivered planes were light R-5 scouting planes (817 aircraft) and U-2 planes (785), which were used for training – and not the needed modern combat aircraft. Korolev blamed the lack of materials for the delay, especially the shortage of non-ferrous metals (lead, brass, and aluminum in particular), calibrated steel, and magnetos. Additionally, design errors and subsequent changes to the design of planes also slowed down production considerably.[100]

Just a few days later, on 9 October 1933, the OGPU finished its own report on the production of aircraft. Like in Korolev's report, the OGPU also found serious shortcomings. In the first 9 months of the year, only 80% of the production target had been reached. Their conclusion was not the same, however. While the OGPU report did blame shortages as well, the main focus in their report was on the poor organization at the factory level, both at the factories assembling the planes as well as in the factories manufacturing the individual parts. The report further criticized the factory managers' obsession with churning out as many aircraft as possible, as quickly as possible in order to please the planners. This, the authors lamented, led to an unacceptable reduction in quality. In some cases, the planes delivered to the air force had not even been properly assembled and came without interior equipment. In another case, at Factory No. 1, rotten wood had been used in the assembly of some of the planes. Furthermore, there was a lack of parts such as coolers and wheels which – while delivered – had turned out to be defective or even completely unsuited for assembly. Likewise, the delivered engines suffered from many shortcomings as well.[101]

These reports spooked the Committee of Defense during its session on 9 October 1933 and as usual in such cases, a commission was created to investigate these issues and to find a way to remedy them.[102] On 25 October, the Council for Labor and Defense (STO) passed a resolution regarding the state of the aircraft production program for 1933 and submitted it to Stalin, Voroshilov and Ordzhonikidze. The authors came to the conclusion that the industry was plagued by such enormous problems that the entire production plan for 1933 was virtually impossible to achieve. Factories No. 1, 29 and 31, for example, had only fulfilled 68.5% of their production quotas for planes and only 54% of their quota for engines.[103]

Furthermore, the STO report – like the one by the OGPU before it – complained about serious manufacturing defects that were all too common among the delivered aircraft. Most of the planes were too heavy; many of the coolers and the fuel cocks were leaking; connecting parts wore down too quickly; the screws in the cylinders of the N-17 engines broke off; cracks appeared in the casings of the M-34 engines; the oil pressure inside the M-22 engines was too low at low speeds.[104]

Additionally, the newly improved brakes had not been introduced yet even though the STO had ordered that to happen several times before. There was also a lack of rust-resistant steel and several kinds of vital alloys necessary to produce quality aircraft, since these had not entered mass production yet. As a result, the STO argued that for 1933, the production quota would have to be reduced by 216 planes. The STO also ordered, due to rapid technological advancements in the areas of photography, radio communications and navigation, that a lot of effort should be put into keeping up with these developments. Furthermore, the STO declared that any new component used in aircraft construction would only be able to enter mass production after intensive testing.[105]

Aside from poor manufacturing, the mass-produced Soviet planes lagged behind foreign planes in terms of technology, even though Stalin and his comrades put a lot of emphasis on the modernization of the aviation industry and the planes it produced. On 9 June 1934, a certain Kurchevsky penned a memorandum in which he informed Stalin and Ordzhonikidze about the state of the Soviet aviation industry. Stalin read the memorandum and sent it to the members of the Committee for Defense (Molotov, Kaganovich, Voroshilov, Kuibyshev, and Ordzhonikidze) with the following comment: "In spite of the overly bold tone of the memorandum by Comrade Kurchevsky, I see it as necessary to examine the presented proposals."[106]

What did Kurchevsky write? He began by saying: "Today [...] we are faced by the fact that the air force, when it comes to engines whose dimensions are larger than anywhere else in the world, is not equipped with modern aircraft." Kurchevsky blamed what he saw on the lack of a clearly formulated doctrine for this problem. It is likely that this assertion had irritated Stalin. After all, it had been Stalin himself together with his friend Sergo Ordzhonikidze who had formulated the current doctrine that Kurchevsky so derided.[107]

Kurchevsky primarily criticized the fact that the aircraft factories were producing already obsolete planes (I-5, I-7 and R-5) and did not have any plans for what to do in 1934/5. He lamented that according to the plan for 1935, engine factories such as Factory No. 26 were producing their modern M-17 engines as stock, because there were no modern machines in which these engines could be installed. He also felt that the question of aircraft armament had been neglected. Soviet planes were only equipped with small-caliber machine guns. This was a problem, as he believed the future of aerial warfare belonged to planes with powerful cannons that could hit targets at significant distances. Kurchevsky further wrote that modern Western designs were already adapted to this new type of aerial warfare, meaning that Soviet aircraft would be grossly outmatched. Even worse, Soviet planes were easy to shoot down. The BT-3, for example, could be downed by a single incendiary 7mm caliber round from a machine gun. However, nobody cared about this fact, Kurchevsky wrote.[108]

Up to 1935, the Soviet Union's aviation industry did not produce any planes that could match Western planes, even on paper. In 1933, a grand total of around 4,000 planes had been produced (the plan foresaw 4,432 planes), but 85% of them (3,450 planes) were either already obsolete as they rolled out of the factory, or not combat aircraft at all (R-5, U-2, I-5, ASh). The situation improved somewhat in 1934. Out of the 4,500 delivered aircraft, "only" 75% (3,150 planes) were outdated or non-combat aircraft.[109]

In order to tackle these issues, a new wide-ranging rearmament plan was drawn up for the air force and implemented for 1934/5. A grand total of 13 newly developed and – most importantly – modern airplane models were to begin mass production in late 1934 and 1935 alone. Among them were interceptors such as the I-15 and the IP, both of which were outfitted with M-25 engines; the I-16 planes had M-25 engines as well, but were also additionally outfitted with M-22 engines. On paper, these interceptors were just as good as contemporary Western planes. Their maximum speed at an altitude of 3,000m was between 367 and 455 km/h and between 360 and 445 km/h at a height of 5,000m, with the planes being able to reach altitudes of 8,000 to 9,800m. The IP Model was especially well armed; it had a proper cannon whereas the other two models were only equipped with machine guns. According to Soviet plans, 3,062 of these new models were to be produced in 1935 – just after entering mass production.[110]

Like the earlier plans, the revised plan could not be fulfilled either. On 5 October 1935, Khakhanyan and Berezin had to admit their failure to Molotov and Stalin. Only in regards to the interceptors had the first steps been undertaken; for the rest, the targets had been missed by a great margin. Of the 150 heavy TB-3 bombers equipped with M-34-R engines that were supposed to have been produced by 1 October 1935, a grand total of zero had been finished. 15 planes of this type had been partly-assembled by the end of September. However, they still lacked their guns, their propellers, and their coolers. Another 60 partially-assembled planes also lacked engines. A smaller number of TB-3 bombers used a different kind of engine with a reduction gear, but there too the production numbers fell far short of the target with only 6 out of the scheduled 23 having been assembled. The situation was just as dire for the other aircraft models and only a few planes were delivered.[111]

A rare exception was the interceptors. However, even though the situation there was much better, the mass production of these planes was still hampered by serious difficulties. By 1 October 1935, only 50 of the planned 125 I-15 interceptors had been produced. Additionally, these machines were plagued by design and production flaws of such severity that the air force had to cancel all flights with these planes. The production of the I-16 interceptors with their M-22 engines was delayed as well. At Factory No. 21, the production quota for I-16 interceptors for 1934 was only reached in July 1935, and of the planned 150 I-16s that were to be assembled in July and August 1935, only 52 had actually been built. Unlike with the I-15, the report noted that the I-16's flying characteristics were satisfactory. However, fuel pipes suffered from construction errors that made the planes prone to bursting into flames. Another issue was that in winter, the I-16 could only reach speeds of 310 km/h even though it was supposed to be able to go up to 360 km/h at 3,000m and 340 km/h at 5,000m. For all of 1935, it was estimated that around 500 I-16s were to be delivered to the air force.[112]

Khakhanyan and Berezin further wrote that the factories would not fulfill their production quotas for the year 1935 as they were still working on the previous year's quota. As an example, they mentioned Factory No. 22; even though it was only September, it was clear that the factory would not be able to meet its targets for 1935, because it still had to build the planes that were scheduled to have been finished the previous year. Additionally, many of the planes that had been delivered in 1934 were riddled with serious defects, and fixing these issues took up much of the factory's production capacities in 1935. Khakhanyan and Berezin concluded that the momentous task of repairing the defective aircraft that were produced in 1934 called into question the viability of the entire production plan for 1935.[113]

The production plan for 1935 had been an abject failure.[114] Of the planned 4,062 planes, including 3,062 modern aircraft, only 2,529 or 62% had been finished by the end of 1935.[115] According to data from the state controller, the air force received only 1,516 planes, however. A year earlier, the number had stood at 3,655 and in 1933 the air force had received 3,492 planes.[116]

The precipitous drop in the number of aircraft produced went hand in hand with a decline in quality. In March 1936, Boris Shaposhnikov, who had been the commander of the Leningrad Military District in 1935, informed Voroshilov about the horrendous quality of the newly-delivered aircraft. Shaposhnikov complained that the planes the units in his district had received in late 1935 were plagued by many production and design defects and that such defects were much more common than before. The new I-16 interceptors with the M-22 engines even posed a danger to pilots, he continued. The new SSS close air support aircraft that were produced in Factory No. 1 were not much better in this regard. Meanwhile, the TB-3 planes equipped with M-34-R engines had to spend the entire summer of 1935 under repair only to need to be repaired again half a year later. Voroshilov read this letter and forwarded it to Stalin, Ordzhonikidze, Kaganovich, and Meshlauk.[117]

The refitting of the Soviet air force proceeded very slowly over the coming years. On 1 July 1940, the Soviet air force numbered 21,377 aircraft, of which 3,401 were not operational. The air fleet included 3,428 obsolete training aircraft of the types U-2, R-5, and R-6. The latter were particularly common and accounted for nearly all training aircraft, numbering around 3,000 planes. The combat arm of the air force was dominated by the planes introduced in 1934/5 in all respects: bombers (TB-3: 527 planes, DB-3: 981 planes, SB: 981 planes), close air support (I-15bis: 1,105 planes), and interceptors (I-15bis: 599 planes, I-16: 3,981 planes, I-153: 1,336 planes).[118]

Although these new planes had been – at least on paper – roughly equivalent to Western planes in 1935, they were already obsolete when the Second World War broke out. The Soviet aviation industry was unable to compete globally and fell behind. During a reception at the Kremlin on 7 November 1940, Stalin remarked: "We defeated the Japanese at Khalkhyn Gol. But our planes were behind the Japanese, both in speed and altitude. We are not prepared for an aerial war the likes of which Germany and England are waging. It has turned out that our planes can remain in the air for only 35 minutes, whereas the German and English ones can do so for several hours! [...] Now one has to seriously work on the air force and air defense."[119]

The standard Soviet interceptor at the time, the I-16, of which the air force had over 3,891 units on 1 June 1940, had the following flight characteristics: a top speed of 470 km/h at an altitude of 3,000m, a maximum altitude of 9,800m, a range of 700 km; in terms of armament, it had two 7.62 mm machine guns and a single 12.7 mm machine gun. The other interceptor, the I-153 (1,336 planes on 1 June 1940) was a biplane with these characteristics: At an altitude of 5,100 m, it could reach speeds of up to 427 km/h. It could reach altitudes of up to 10,600m and had a range of 800 km. Like the I-16, it had two 7.62 mm machine guns. Additionally, it was armed with two 20 mm FF automatic cannons.[120]

At the session of the Grand War Council on 4 May 1940, Division Commander Alekseev spoke on the subject of airpower, stating, among other things, "In fighter planes we have fallen far behind. We have a speed of 470 km/h, a range of 560 km, and a [maximum] flight time of 45-60 minutes, that is, half of foreign ones."[121]

In the second half of 1940, Stalin declared the aviation industry and air defenses to be his top priority. Likely under the impression of the aerial Battle of Britain that began in the summer of 1940, Stalin consulted aircraft designers and other experts. During the aforementioned reception at the Kremlin on 7 November 1940, he complained to his inner circle: "I had invited designers and asked them: Can we arrange for our planes to stay in the air for longer? They answered: *We can, but nobody has given us this order!* This deficiency will be removed now."[122]

From then on, Stalin received regular updates about the design and production processes of the new aircraft models and engines. He then went on to personally suggest modifications that the designers had to elaborate upon and which carried into serialized production.[123] An example of this can be found in a letter he sent to the management of Factory No. 22 on 5 December 1940:

> We care very little about the production of the SB planes with the 105 engines, and even less about the ones with the 103 engines. Such aircraft are not suited for serious combat; they kill our pilots in unequal fights, because they are too slow. Such planes have now become a burden for the state and a trap for pilots. We are interested in two-engine planes with a lesser range, which are capable of reaching speeds of up to 530 km/h, 500 km/h and in extreme cases of up to 480 km/h, but not any less.[124]

Of the 15,693 combat aircraft the Soviet air forces had on 1 June 1940, 3,717 (23.7%) were light and medium SB bombers, i.e. the ones Stalin saw as a "burden for the state and a trap for pilots." The other planes in the air forces arsenal were not much better: the I-15, the I-16, the I-153, the DB-3, and the TB-3 were all obsolete. At Stalin's initiative, the Politburo issued a series of orders in April 1941 that envisioned a complete refitting of the air force with new planes within the same year. Between 10 and 23 April, the Politburo ordered the following measures: the beginning of mass-production of the MiG-3 interceptor, between May and the end of the year, 4,295 of these planes were to be produced; ceasing production of the DB-3 bombers in favor of beginning the mass production of Il-2 bombers and Er-2 close air support; beginning mass production of Yak-3 interceptors, with a goal of 250 being produced by the end of 1941; the production of 1,100 Yak-1 interceptors, 2,386 Pe-2 bombers, and 2,455 LaGG-3 interceptors by the end of the year.[125]

Furthermore, the Politburo decreed that additional new aircraft prototypes had to be designed and tested, and that many already existing programs should be continued, especially for bombers, interceptors, and close air support. At the same time, however, a grand total of 24 different projects that had been worked on since 1939/40 were cancelled altogether.[126]

The refitting was accompanied by a radical reorganization of the air force. On 10 April 1941, Stalin ordered the creation of 54 air force garrisons in the border regions, mostly in the West. Additionally, 539 air fields were to be built or expanded in 1941/2, including 255 in 1941 alone.[127] In February 1941, Stalin established new pilot schools and had new training courses devised to train pilots how to operate the new aircraft models.[128]

Plane Crashes

The frequency of serious plane accidents is generally a good indicator for the technical quality of planes as well as the quality of personnel. After all, accidents – especially serious ones like plane crashes – are rather hard to hide from one's superiors. Hiding problems is an issue in all militaries, but was particularly endemic in the Soviet Union. In terms of aircraft accidents, the 1930s were absolutely horrendous for the Soviet air force. In that decade alone, thousands of planes were lost in accidents and hundreds of pilots were killed.

While the Soviet air force had always struggled with accidents, the situation truly deteriorated after the reforms began in 1930. In that year alone, the air force recorded dozens of catastrophic plane crashes killing many pilots. Some of the fault lay with the pilots themselves.[129] In the summer of 1930, the Revolutionary War Council thus issued an order to combat the rise in accidents, and as a result, the number of crashes declined precipitously – and remained relatively low for one and a half years. The situation changed again in early 1932, as the new generation of pilots left the flying schools. In order to expand the Soviet air force at the desired rate, training hours had been cut significantly. The results were immediately noticeable: Between 1 April and 23 June 1931, 89 accidents were recorded, including 5 catastrophic accidents. During the same period following year, 136 accidents were registered, including 23 catastrophic accidents. These accidents resulted in the total destruction of 42 planes and the deaths of 50 pilots.[130]

This was a serious crisis and demanded immediate action. During a session of the Politburo on 3 July 1932, Voroshilov brought up the issue and proposed a resolution to improve flight safety. After a series of changes by Molotov, Kaganovich, and Voroshilov himself, the resolution was signed by Stalin and Molotov on 5 July. The resolution blamed the dramatic rise in accidents primarily on poor military discipline within the military. Furthermore, lack of training on the side of the pilots was identified as another main cause, as it resulted in the improper use of planes and equipment. Several commanders were found guilty of causing these issues and were tried in front of military tribunals. Aside from personal faults within the military, the issue of poor production quality of the aircraft was also raised, although the aviation industry was blamed for that.[131]

Two months later, on 16 September 1932, the Politburo revisited the issue of plane accidents.[132] This time, the emphasis lay on problems with the production and design of the planes being delivered to the air force. In the resolution, the Politburo stated that the abysmal quality of planes produced by the Soviet aviation industry was a direct cause of many plane crashes. Out of 80 accidents that occurred in May and June 1932, 17% were caused exclusively by the poor production quality of the planes. Instead of promptly fixing any defects that arose, the factories did not do anything and sent out the faulty planes to the air force, the Politburo complained. In some cases, defects were even hidden before delivery. For example, the leaking coolers in the TB-3 No. 2213 had been provisionally closed up with a sealant instead of being soldered shut. In some of the delivered aircraft, the engines were found to contain various harmful pollutants such as sand and filings. To combat this, the Politburo ordered a number of organizational measures. Additionally, the OGPU was assigned to investigate these incidents and to hunt down those responsible. Aside from the OGPU, the Communist Party was also ordered to help in both the factories and the military.[133]

As mentioned earlier, the quality of the produced aircraft did not improve in spite of all these measures, and even dropped after 1935. Unsurprisingly, plane accidents remained common. In an order issued in June 1936, Voroshilov bitterly complained that the resolution from 5 July 1932, which had as its goal a great reduction in accidents, was not "not fulfilled to this day."[134] In 1934, 384 accidents were recorded. There had been 64 catastrophic accidents, and 106 airmen had been killed. A year later, the number of accidents stood at 340, 58 of them catastrophic, with 90 dead and 29 injured. No improvement was in sight: between January and May 1936, there were 107 accidents and 25 catastrophic accidents that claimed the lives of 40 people.[135]

In the summer of 1936, Stalin and his comrades felt the need to act again and issued a number of orders in order to reduce the number of aircraft accidents.[136] These measures appear to have been somewhat successful at first, and the number of accidents dropped to 250 (including 42 catastrophic accidents) compared to 398 the year before. However, this trend reversed in 1937 and in the first nine months of 1938, the number of accidents was higher than ever before.[137]

Table 17: Plane Crashes between January 1934 and October 1938[138]

Year	Accidents	Crashes	Total
1934	384	64	448
1935	340	58	398
1936	208	42	250
1937	321	60	381
1938 (9 Months)	364	139	503

The losses the air force suffered from accidents were enormous. Well over 2,000 aircraft had been destroyed and around 1,000 pilots had died in crashes. On 29 November 1938, Voroshilov held the concluding speech at a meeting of the War Council at the People's Commissar for Defense, in which he also brought up the problem of aircraft accidents:

You have to consider that in three years [1936 to October 1938] a total of 1,134 aircraft were lost. You know, not a single one of our neighbors even dares to dream about having such a number of planes. Indeed, this is a giant air fleet. And how many people were killed? In this year, 266 have died. Now, when you try and imagine 266 pilots, we have lost an entire regiment of pilots. Was that necessary? [...] When you say: we have flown more. No; that's not it. While over the course of last year, there was one crash for every 2,000 landings, this year, there were 960 landings per crash, that means the guys worked only half as much and there were 2.5 as many crashes.[139]

Despite all efforts by both military and civilian authorities, flying accidents remained extremely high. Between 1 January and 15 May 1939, 70 pilots were killed in 34 crashes. There were a further 126 less severe accidents in which 91 planes were completely destroyed. Voroshilov reacted in the familiar way and issued a special order on 4 June 1939, introducing several measures designed to prevent plane accidents.[140]

Blame for the accidents was still assigned to the abysmal quality of the planes and the poor training and discipline within the air force. During the meeting of the War Council of the People's Commissar for Defense that took place between 21 and 29 November 1938, the divisional commander Ovchkin declared: "A high percentage of accidents in the air force is caused by the poor level of training of the pilots and navigators."[141] Another serious issue was bravado. At the same meeting, Voroshilov remarked on 29 November: "Among the pilots we have a lot of great men, many heroes, but I am afraid that we have even more braggarts and try-hards."[142]

Naturally, accidents were not the only issue. In Order No. 0019 of the People's Commissar for Defense from 14 December 1937, the air force was criticized for its low level of combat readiness. Among other things, the order stated that the coordination with the ground forces was abysmal; the accuracy of the bombers was exceedingly poor, and that the pilots were overwhelmed by flying under difficult conditions, especially at night or in clouds. The order also pointed out the high rate of aircraft accidents, which it blamed on the following factors: poor organization on the side of many commanders and political commissars, poor discipline among a large part of the flying and technical personnel, as well as a lack of control exerted by commanders.[143]

On 16 May 1939, as the Chief War Council of the Red Army once again discussed the problem of airplane accidents, Marshal Budyonny declared: "The schools train the people poorly. They graduate people who were not properly trained, these are second-rate rejects and you believe they are pilots."[144] During the session, the Chief of the Head Office for Propaganda of the Red Army, Lev Mekhlis, proposed to assign additional political commissars to the air force in order to lower the number of accidents by political means ("party work"). Stalin emphatically rejected this idea:

> What is party work supposed to do here? The pilot refuses to consider the laws of physics and meteorology. The case of Brayansky – he flew with a large plane, to look for the plane 'Rodina' [which had gone missing]. He stared at the ground and did not look to the side, as a result, two planes crashed mid-air. [...] The cause – he did not understand the laws of physics. Or a not uncommon case that the pilots do not inform themselves about difficult meteorological circumstances. You learn about the weather first, and then you fly, not like an idiot. For what do you need party work here? [...] The aviation culture is on a low level. In the air force, the laws of physics are being ignored; one is not prepared to submit to them, one distrusts the equipment. And in the air, it is often a second that decides the fate of the pilot.[145]

Despite all the orders, regulations, and appeals, the number of airplane accidents remained high over the following years. In early 1941, there were an average of two to three accidents a day, the Central Committee complained in a resolution on 9 April 1941. The same resolution further criticized that discipline had not improved whatsoever, even though it was a common cause for accidents. Even worse the leadership of the air force tried to hide accidents from the government. At the same time, the people responsible for these issues were not punished.[146]

Throughout the 1930s and the early 1940s, the Soviet Union had poured enormous resources into building up the best air force in the world. However, despite the grand plans and the great sacrifices, the Soviet air force was not capable of fighting a modern air war on the eve of the German attack – and the Soviet leadership knew this all too well.[147]

Other Parts of the Red Army

Given the state of the air force and the tank forces, it should not come as a surprise that the situation was not much better in the rest of the Red Army. There are countless reports on the catastrophic conditions that plagued every aspect of the Soviet military, but in the following section we will focus on just a few of them. The first one to be examined here is the issue of chemical weapons. Although a detailed analysis is impossible due to the fact that the relevant archives are still closed, there is nevertheless enough information available to judge the general state of affairs.[148]

Alongside the massed use of tanks and aircraft, chemical warfare was a key component of Mikhail Tukhachevsky's vision of the war of annihilation. Tukhachevsky was not the first Soviet advocate of chemical warfare, however, as leaders such as Leon Trotsky had done so before. Trotsky in particular believed in the broad use of chemical weapons and believed that they would play a decisive role in the war of the future. On 19 May 1924, Trotsky gave a speech in which he prophesied that aircraft and chemical weapons would spell the end of the traditional mode of warfare, in which opposing military forces would fight each other while ignoring the civilian population for the most part. The war of the future, in contrast, was to be a total war in which there was no difference between combatants and non-combatants: "Aircraft squadrons with enormous carrying capacity and range, transport [chemical weapons] deep into the hinterland and annihilate thereby not only the [traditional] front, [...] but also negate the difference between the army and the civilian population."[149]

In 1925 – a year after Trotsky's speech – the Soviet Union began to develop its own chemical arsenal, and by 1929, the Red Army was in possession of several new chemical weapon systems "for defense and attack" as a secret report by Voroshilov put it in June 1929.[150] However, it was noted that the condition of the chemical weapons was rather poor, which was bad news since they were a key component in the future war, Voroshilov complained at the plenary assembly of the Central Committee on 12 January 1933. Nevertheless, Voroshilov assured his comrades that the situation had improved considerably by late 1932. Tukhachevsky was not convinced by Voroshilov's assessment whatsoever and shook his head throughout Voroshilov's speech. After all, it was Sergo Ordzhonikidze and not Voroshilov who had been tasked with overseeing the development of chemical weapons.[151]

Tukhachevsky was right. Voroshilov's statements from 12 January 1933 were a standard Soviet success story. Not even two months earlier, on 16 November 1932, the same Voroshilov had raised the alarm on the same issue, declaring that the state of combat readiness among the chemical units was not satisfactory.[152]

In the Second Five Year Plan (1933-1938), 482.7 million rubles or 3.5% of all spending on military equipment (13,835 million rubles) was allocated to the production and purchase of new chemical weapons. Soon afterwards, the plan was adjusted and the spending on military equipment was increased to a grand total of 20,745 million rubles, an increase of nearly 50%. It is unknown how much of it went to the chemical weapons budget, but it is fair to assume that it saw a significant increase as well. In terms of volumes delivered, the Red Army received 1,000 tons of chemical weapons in 1933. Between 1934 and 1937, another 8,000 tons were to be delivered. However, these numbers were the peacetime stockpile; the mobilization plan foresaw the production of 63,000 tons of chemical weapons each year.[153]

In 1934, there were three factories that produced chemical weapons in the Soviet Union. Chemical Factory No. 1 in Moscow produced chemical weapons; Factory No. 102 in Chapaevsk produced chemical weapons as well as chemical grenades. Another factory in Stalingrad specialized in the production of chemical mines and bombs.[154] Just like in the rest of the Soviet armaments industry, the quality of the delivered weapons was often lacking. In 1930, for example, it was found that the rubber components of the chemical rounds that had been produced in 1929 had to be replaced. This problem affected 300,000 rounds of ammunition. Additionally, these projectiles had been leaking.[155]

Artillery

Even though Tukhachevsky had repeatedly warned about the overreliance on artillery in the coming war, it nevertheless played a large role in Soviet war plans alongside tanks, planes, and chemical weapons. This is reflected in the extremely ambitious plans for the expansion of the artillery corps.[156] The Second Five Year Plan (1933-1937) foresaw the delivery of 28,700 artillery pieces to the Red Army, excluding the navy. Like the goals for the production of tanks and planes, the production target for artillery pieces was far too ambitious and the armaments industry failed to meet it. The years 1932 and 1933 were particularly bad in this regard. Out of the planned 6,078 pieces of artillery that the Red Army was supposed to receive in 1932, only 1,882 had been produced and just 771 had been delivered to the Red Army, with many artillery pieces being defective. In the first quarter of 1933, 410 guns were supposed to have been produced. In reality, only 225 pieces of artillery were produced of which the Red Army received a grand total of 25.[157]

Table 18: Planned and Realized Deliveries of Artillery to the Red Army, Excluding the Navy, 1933-1939[158]

	1933	1934	1935	1936	1937	1938	1939
Planned	5200	5600	6900	7800	8400	-/-	-/-
Delivered	1797	5164	4895	6923	5368	11,534	18,269

The quality of the delivered artillery pieces was horrible. An OGPU report from 1 August 1933 criticized that a large number of the delivered guns were of such low quality that their service lives were drastically reduced; in many cases the newly arrived guns were not even usable. The "Maxim" heavy machine guns were plagued by similar problems, as were the light "Degtyaryov" light machine guns and rifles. Even bayonets suffered from serious production defects that often rendered them completely unusable.[159]

The delivered artillery shells were in poor shape as well. The 45mm anti-tank shells in particular had a habit of exploding in the barrels of the artillery pieces firing them. This triggered an in-depth probe in 1934 that found that there were serious production faults with the projectiles as well as the fuses. As a result, new fuses had to be designed, but their development was slow and was not finished in 1935.[160]

The level of training was also exceedingly poor. There were many complaints about the insufficient coordination with infantry, tanks, and bombers, and a lack of precision and poor handling of equipment during combat. Especially dire was the state of the anti-aircraft artillery. These complaints continued right up to the outbreak of the Second World War.[161]

Logistics, Rations and Accommodations

Another area where the Red Army suffered from massive deficits was logistics. Between 13 and 15 July 1935, a conference of Red Army logistics troops took place in Moscow, which Stalin and other members of the Politburo also attended. In a session on the first evening of the conference, Stalin took the floor and lectured the others on the necessity of self-critique: "We have to correct ourselves – because it will be too late if the war corrects us; even if the results of the probe by the CPC [Commission for Party Control] and the CSC [Commission for Soviet Control] are only 20-30% accurate, they demonstrate in what a poor state the question of supply of the Red Army is." The last word was had by Voroshilov, who supposedly admitted "that 'we did not pass the exam' and that he did not expect that such a bad state of affairs could be found in the Red Army."[162]

There were a lot of issues with military construction as well. As a result, there was a general lack of barracks, accommodations, military warehouses, and other buildings the rapidly-expanding Red Army needed, while the buildings that were there were usually in very poor condition. In many cases, individual units had to build their own barracks, accommodation and other necessary buildings. In his autobiography, the later victor of Stalingrad, Georgi Zhukov, described how when his division was redeployed to Slutsk (Belarus) in 1932, nothing had been prepared for their arrival. The soldiers and commanders, therefore, had to build the barracks, stables, and other buildings all by themselves. This whole process took 18 months and kept them away from training.[163]

This was by no means an exception and this remained a major issue throughout the 1930s and beyond; it even caused problems during the Second World War. During a meeting of the War Council of the People's Commissar for Defense on 29 November 1938, Voroshilov lamented:

The state of military construction is very bad. We failed in this regard last year as we did this year. Simply put, it is a catastrophic situation. Is it not a disgrace that we have divisions in the Belarussian Military District in which three soldiers sleep in two bunks; is it maybe not a shame that around 90,000 men under Shtern [commander of the 1st Independent Army of the Red Banner] live like prehistoric cavemen in earthen dwellings? And these, who live in barracks, dwell in horrible conditions, sleeping in three-tier beds. Can you imagine the air and the conditions in general under which these people live; no light, no water? Horrible conditions. [...] I have told you only about the soldiers, and under what conditions do the commanders live? We have around 40,000 families of commanders who are completely homeless. Is this perhaps okay, should one tolerate things like that, should one come to terms with this? No. And what will you do? One has to give these people accommodations; one has to build these accommodations. Build them for us. I do not even talk about depots and all the other things, these are also necessary.[164]

Aside from a lack of buildings, the Red Army also suffered from a dire shortage of food. The situation was so bad that in 1932, the leadership of the Red Army felt the need to order individual divisions to set up their own agricultural operations in order to improve their food supply. The Revolutionary War Council thus set the following agricultural guidelines for each division: 400 cows, 3,200 pigs, 20,000 rabbits as well as 1,000 hectares on which rye, wheat, fruit and vegetables were to be grown. The agricultural work was supposed to be done by the soldiers themselves, which naturally came at the expense of training.[165]

While the Red Army moved away from this model shortly after it had been implemented, parts of it were still in place as late as late 1938. On 26 November 1938, Lev Mekhlis complained about this during a session of the War Council of the People's Commissar for Defense: "Today there are still many soldiers who are being assigned to do all kinds work completely unrelated to preparation for combat. Some districts are still slowly liquidating their side-operations, especially the Baikal Military District. One division in the Baikal Military District has up to 670 hectares of farmland, a herd of cows and 1,000 sheep."[166]

Training, Combat Preparedness and Political Functionaries

Construction work and farm labor were not the only activities that competed with military training. The Red Army also put a lot of emphasis on political propaganda. In 1934, around 15,000 people worked in the political administration of the Red Army as political commissars of various ranks. It was their duty to indoctrinate 700,000 soldiers in communist ideology.[167]

As the soldiers were busy doing other tasks, there was very little time for weapons and tactical training and the level of training was therefore very low for both soldiers and commanders. The results were disastrous. As mentioned earlier, a large proportion of equipment was damaged or even outright destroyed by improper handling. In the mechanized units, somewhere between 5% and 7% of all cars were damaged in accidents or breakdowns in 1938 alone.[168] Between January and September 1937, 78 soldiers were killed in car accidents and 695 were injured.[169]

Combat readiness was understandably abysmal as well. During a conference of the War Council of the People's Commissar for Defense that took place between 21 and 27 November 1937, the commander of the Kyiv Military District, Fedko, complained bitterly about the state of the artillery, singling out their inability to hit their targets and to coordinate with infantry and tanks. Fedko also criticized the poor shooting skills of the soldiers and commanders, and went on to say that the previously reported results that had been very good were manipulated. In some cases, it was found that even the commanders of entire squads and companies did not know how to load their own rifles. It was necessary to energetically fight the widespread tendency to misreport unwelcome results within the Red Army, Fedko surmised.[170]

At the same conference, another issue was raised as well, namely that many commanders were struggling to properly communicate via radio. At the same time, they were also often unable to use military equipment and advanced weapons systems the right way. There had been a number of training exercises and maneuvers in 1937 that laid bare the following shortcomings: the inability of individual commanders to rely on their staff in the heat of combat; insufficient coordination of the artillery with the infantry, cavalry and tanks; poor scouting; bad management of the rear areas; disorganized field repair of both equipment and weapons systems; poor organization in the face of attacks by tanks, aircraft and chemical weapons; a low state of physical, technical and engineering preparedness among soldiers and commanders alike.[171]

At the following meeting that took place between 21 and 29 November 1938, the attendees concurred that the combat readiness of the Red Army had not improved much. Lev Mekhlis said in his presentation: "The combat readiness of the troops of the 1st and 2nd Armies and of the Baikal Military District is at a low level." He then went on urge his comrades: "The new world war is about to break out, we have won a temporary respite in the Far East, therefore, the preparations for war should be the priority now."[172] In the final speech on 29 November Voroshilov said:

> A few words, Comrades, about the problems that the Red Army is facing in the area of extraordinary events. We have talked a lot about it already. […] We are losing men, we are destroying equipment. This is not just in regards to the air force; we are losing men in the tank units as well and are destroying technical equipment. There is a lot of nonsense everywhere. It is a disgrace for us as commanders, political commissars, as chiefs of the Red Army.[173]

As mentioned earlier, the Red Army of the 1930s was struggling with a serious lack of competent specialists. There was a shortage of tank drivers, mechanics, radio operators, aircraft mechanics, and commanders, especially in the lower and mid ranks. The lack of specialists and commanders remained a great problem until the outbreak of the war.

The principal reason for this was the expansion of the Red Army, which was so rapid that the recruitment of specialists just did not keep pace. The bloody purges within the military further compounded the situation, especially at their height in 1937 and 1938. At the end of 1937, the Red Army was missing 39,100 commanders, falling 34.4% below its own benchmark. However, even nearly a decade into the expansion, the military schools and academies could not meet the demand of the army, and between June and November 1937, only 15,400 commanders and political workers (*politrabotniki*) finished training. Nevertheless, these newly-trained leaders accounted for a majority of commanders in the Red

Army by 1937. In the infantry, 60% of commanders had been trained in the 1930s; for the motorized units, the number stood at 45% and in the air force at 25%.[174]

In order to speed up the training process, training hours had been cut drastically. As a result, many of the new, inadequately-trained commanders were not particularly effective, which hurt the Red Army. This led Voroshilov to say this during a meeting of the War Council of the People's Commissar for Defense on 29 November 1938: "We have to […] teach our men [the commanders] organizational skills, to complete their tasks in a smart, thorough and accurate way. *As an organization, we are still weak, very weak.*"[175]

It thus comes as no surprise that the Red Army's first major skirmish in the 1930s, the opening stages of the Battle of Lake Khasan in 1938, ended in complete disaster. On 26 November 1938, at the same conference, Mekhlis reported: "In the course of the events at Lake Khasan, the 7th Mechanized Brigade and the 34th Infantry Division sent riflemen to the front who could not shoot with their rifles, who could not even open their rifle locks."[176] A few days later, Rychagov, the commander of the air troops of the 1st Independent Army of the Red Banner, complained at the conference: "In the first skirmishes [at Lake Khasan], many men died. We condemn pilots, we condemn tank drivers for broken tanks, but there, nearly two regiments of men died."[177]

Discipline and Morale in the Red Army

Much to the chagrin of its leadership, the Red Army of the 1920s was imbued with a "peasant mentality" which was strongly anti-Soviet. This did not change much over the course of the 1930s, which is not really a surprise considering the state of the Red Army and the Soviet Union in general, with its campaign of terror against the peasantry and the deeply-unpopular forced collectivization. Already in 1930, special units in the Red Army warned about the corrupting influence of the "Kulaks" within the ranks of the army. The OGPU investigated and sent a special report to Stalin and Voroshilov. As most soldiers came from peasant families, they were deeply concerned about the news of mass arrests, deportations, and forced collectivization. In February 1930, Voroshilov issued an order to teach the soldiers about the necessity of "dekulakization" but this measure does not appear to have met much success.[178]

Voroshilov simultaneously banned Red Army troops from being used in these "dekulakization measures."[179] Yagoda, the architect of this operation, did the same in his order on the liquidation of the kulaks from 2 February 1930: "Under no circumstances are units of the Red Army to be used in this operation [i.e. deportations and arrests]."[180]

Nevertheless, the communist terror against the peasantry did have a devastating effect on morale. On 22 May 1932, the political administration of the Red Army noted a "certain exacerbation of the negative mood among a part of the soldiery of the Red Army and among individual commanders, as well as an intensification of efforts of the class enemy to affect the Red Army from outside and from within." The cause for this development was located with the forced grain collection in early 1932 and the hunger that followed it, as well as with a recent escalation of the conflict between Japan and the Soviet Union in China. As a result, many Red Army soldiers, commanders, and even some communists criticized the policy of the communist party, the report warned.[181]

Among such "kulak remarks" were statements such as this one by a certain Novoseltsev, a soldier at an air force workshop who participated in a course: "The subject taught here does not enter my head, because they take away my father's grain and my family is suffering from hunger. And this is not just the fate of my family, but that of all peasants. The peasants do not work for themselves, but for strangers. They live worse than under the Tsars. [...] The grain that they got from the kolkhoz was taken away." Another soldier said: "The government is plundering the kolkhozes, it demands bread, it demands meat. The people are angry. When war comes, the communists will be killed."[182]

In early 1933, the special units of the OGPU noticed a rapid uptick in "negative incidents" in the Independent Army of the Red Banner. In a report from 4 May 1933, the authors concluded: "Between December of last year and March of this year, we observed an increase and radicalization of the negative political mood within the army." In December, 2,338 cases of such remarks were counted. In January, the number rose to 3,082 and in February to 3,120. The reasons for this were the collectivization as well as news about "hunger in the villages."

The report continued: "Against this backdrop, individual Red Army soldiers declared that in case of war [...] they would not defend the Soviet Union." This was followed by a list of examples of such statements and of other "negative occurrences," as well as of the formation of "counterrevolutionary groupings" among Red Army soldiers, of which 24 had been discovered in the previous three months. This report was addressed to Yagoda and Stalin himself.[183]

Considering the low morale in the Red Army, it is understandable that many soldiers chose to desert. In 1930, 1,116 desertions had been recorded, or 22.9 desertions per 10,000 men. In the following year, that number had risen to 1,677 desertions, or 32.9 desertions per 10,000 men. The suicide rate was similarly high: in 1930, it was at 9.8 suicides per 10,000 soldiers and rose to 10.4 suicides per 10,000 soldiers in 1931. Suicide rates were higher in the navy: the Baltic Fleet suffered from 12.3 suicides per 10,000 in 1930 and 14.4 suicides per 10,000 in 1931. For the Black Sea Fleet, the numbers stood at 10.2 and 15.3, respectively.[184]

The leadership reacted with a combination of intimidation, terror, and intense albeit primitive propaganda sessions. However, the latter did not convince many, especially not those who came from the countryside. During a meeting, Budyonny handed his friend Voroshilov a note in which he described such an incident: "E[fremovich] K[liment]! During a political class, the Red Army soldiers asked one of the political commissars this question: 'Why do we export grain to other countries, while we have a shortage. We have seen with our own eyes how in the harbor of Novorossiysk, grain was loaded onto ships.' The commissar replied: 'It just appeared like that to you.'"[185]

Naturally, such "arguments" did not convince many soldiers of the superiority of the new communist order. This anecdote also exemplified the low quality of the "political specialists" or political commissars. Many of them were poorly educated; most of them had gone through six or seven years of primary school, and then through a few quick party courses.[186]

Considering these circumstances, it comes as no surprise that the Red Army suffered from horrible discipline and soaring rates of crime, insubordination, desertion, and suicide. This was the case for both ordinary soldiers and commanders. The military leadership regularly complained about this and tried to counteract it, but their efforts were usually in vain.[187]

Another major issue was the excessive consumption of alcohol among the troops, especially drunkenness among the commanders, which had a devastating effect on discipline. In the closing speech at the conference of the War Council of the People's Commissar for Defense that took place between 21 and 29 November 1938, Voroshilov said this: "Two words about drunkenness. Comrades, this kind of nonsense has not occurred for the first time in our army this year, but the degree drunkenness has reached in 1938, did not exist earlier, it seems to me. We have to end this."[188]

A few weeks later, on 29 December 1938, Voroshilov in his capacity as the People's Commissar for Defense issued Order No. 0219 in the fight against drunkenness in the Red Army. At the beginning, he stated that the issue of drunkenness had reached dangerous dimensions recently, especially among commanders. In the first nine months of 1930 alone, over 1,300 incidents had been recorded in the Red Army. Drunken soldiers and commanders provoked brawls, committed crimes such as robbery, caused accidents, and destroyed military equipment. "Drunkenness has become a true scourge within the army," Voroshilov concluded. A significant portion of accidents and other disturbances was directly caused by alcohol. Against this backdrop, Voroshilov ordered his subordinates to take decisive action against drunkenness in the army.[189]

Over the course of the 1930s, Stalin had managed to assemble the largest army on the planet. However, this army was neither disciplined nor motivated – or even particularly effective. The war against Finland (waged between November 1939 and March 1940) and the battles against Germany in the summer of 1941, demonstrate that all too well. In the first six months of the German invasion of the Soviet Union, over a million Red Army soldiers and thousands of commanders deserted. Many others had to be forced to fight for Stalin and his party by political commissars and special detachments.[190]

The Red Army of the 1930s was mostly composed of unwilling soldiers who in many cases were deeply hostile towards communism. At the same time, the commanders, pilots, tank drivers, mechanics, and even the political commissars, were all poorly trained. While the Red Army did possess large quantities of weapons, ammunition and equipment, it was of very poor quality and was outright unusable in many cases. Stalin and his comrades were perfectly aware of this.

Chapter 16

The Great Purge – The Hunt
for Scapegoats

The spectacular failure of the latest – and by far the greatest – of the armament programs presented a serious problem for the Kremlin. Over the previous decade, the Bolsheviks had sacrificed millions of lives and even risked their own hold on power, but it had all been for nothing. In the face of this disaster, Stalin and his comrades reflected on what had gone wrong. As usual, the fault lay not with them or their grandiose plans, but with someone else.

In the late 1920s, it had been the bourgeois specialists who were blamed for supposedly sabotaging the Soviet armament and industrialization plans of 1927/28. For this, they had been vigorously persecuted, sent to concentration camps, deported, or executed. Their vacant positions were filled with communist activists and fresh graduates. What they had in loyalty, they lacked in experience and by 1931, "remorseful" specialists who had been convicted of sabotage were allowed to return to their posts in the Soviet economy, although they still remained at risk of being blamed if things did not go well.[1]

However, things continued to not go according to plan, and it soon became clear that the new armament plans from 1930 and 1932 could not be met. With failure looming in the summer of 1933, the OGPU handily uncovered a supposed spy organization that had deliberately sabotaged the Soviet armament effort. Founded and led by "German National Socialists", a group of 12 freshly recruited specialists was accused of having wreaked havoc in both the central administration of the armaments industry as well as in the individual factories themselves.[2] There, these saboteurs had bought foreign equipment that was either incomplete or superfluous, and as a result, equipment worth 11 million rubles, including foreign equipment worth 9 million gold rubles, was poorly stored in various warehouses, slowly rotting away. Through "sabotage" actions like these, this spy organization managed to foil the restructuring and expansion of the Soviet armaments industry.[3]

The OGPU investigation continued even after its reorganization into the NKVD in February 1934.[4] Special OGPU/NKVD units were closely observing the Soviet economy and transport system and before long, they emerged as the most important source of accurate economic information for the Politburo. Unlike official channels, through which the Soviet establishment inflated its achievements and covered up its failures, the undercover agents were relaying the truth about all the setbacks, accidents, and catastrophes.[5] Aside from gathering information, the OGPU/NKVD also tried any real and imagined saboteurs and wreckers they found. The so-called troikas that held these trials had the authority to impose any penalty they deemed fit, including the death penalty, although in this case, they needed approval from headquarters.[6]

While the purges succeeded in getting people killed and spreading terror, productivity did not improve. On the contrary, the situation in the Soviet armaments industry remained in a horrible state. Stalin and his comrades knew very well what was happening and knew that they had to act if they wanted their grand plans to succeed.

On 29 March 1934, the Politburo thus set up a commission headed by none other than Andrey Zhdanov, a close confidante of Stalin and an expert on propaganda and ideology, which was to investigate the personnel policy in the armaments industry. In particular, the commission was to look at the hiring practices of both blue- and white-collar workers ("who is hiring and who is firing"), and how they were being put to use in the factories.[7] Zhdanov and his men immediately set to work and soon reported back to the Politburo. On 4 May 1934, the Politburo adopted Zhdanov's proposals. Among others, the hiring practices were overhauled for the armaments industry. From now on, the individual factories had to organize special departments overseeing the hiring and firing of workers. Tellingly, these departments were to be led by NKVD men.[8]

The purpose of this change was of course to purge the armaments industry of "unwanted elements". Zhdanov and his commission had drawn up a list of 68 factories producing weaponry, ammunition, and equipment for the Red Army that were to be purged in this fashion.[9] On 14 June

1934, the NKVD and the People's Commissariat of Heavy Industry issued Order No. 004 on the protection of the 68 most important factories in the armaments industry, which took Zhdanov's list and carried out the purge there. Foreigners, former pre-revolutionary elites, and "Whites" were to be fired, as were people who had been previously dismissed from other factories and kolkhozes for disciplinary issues and theft. Naturally, people convicted of "counterrevolutionary" activities were to be dismissed also.[10]

On 26 July 1934, the NKVD followed up with Order No. 012, according to which the entire personnel of the armaments industry was put under special review in order to remove any "unwanted elements" still working there. The people fired as part of this purge were to not be informed of the reason for their dismissal; instead, they were to be fired under seemingly innocuous pretexts such as disciplinary offenses. The NKVD created a file for every person it investigated in the course this operation, which included everyone working in the armaments industry, and furthermore took away their passports. That way, the workers were effectively bound to their factories as the peasants were bound to their kolkhozes.[11] The workers' state had turned the very workers it supposedly sought to liberate into nothing more than industrial serfs.

As the ever-expanding armaments industry employed a great number of workers, this investigation took a lot of time, but Yagoda made sure to regularly brief Stalin on the progress of the operation. On 14 June 1935, Yagoda reported that out of the 70,385 engineers and technicians working in the 68 factories, the NKVD had finished investigating 44,616. Among them, the NKVD had found 5,416 "socially alien elements" and 2,580 people had been dismissed. Of the 398,949 workers employed in these 68 factories, 319,739 had been investigated. In the process, 30,060 "socially alien elements" had been detected and 25,059 workers had been fired. Furthermore, the NKVD had vetoed the hiring of 11,497 people trying to work in the armaments industry.[12] Yagoda also reported that a number of factory directors had been punished for violating the new hiring practices. He then took the opportunity to suggest that the list of factories subject to the special hiring practices was to be expanded further, and in mid-1936, Yagoda's proposal was accepted and now over 100 factories had their hiring process overseen by the NKVD.[13]

The armaments industry was not the only key sector that was to be purged at the time. In April 1933, Stalin ordered a comprehensive purge of the party, which by then had swollen to 3.2 million members, including 2 million full members and 1.2 million membership candidates. In the previous two-and-a-half years alone, the party had accepted 1.4 million new members, nearly doubling in size. However, the Politburo complained in its resolution that many of the membership applications had been reviewed only superficially and that many unreliable elements had joined the party as a result.[14] As the party purge ramped up in 1933, over 18% of them were either expelled from the party or left of their own volition to avoid being dismissed. Nevertheless, the purge continued over the next few years. In 1935 alone, 43,000 communists lost their party membership. In a report from late 1936, Yezhov, the new chief of the NKVD, informed the Central Committee that 33% of party members dismissed between July and December 1935 had been "spies", "White guards", and "Trotskyists".[15]

Another institution that faced repeated purges was the Red Army. Already in 1929/30, over 10,000 commanders had been dismissed from the military as part of an earlier purge, and over 2,600 were arrested. Following on its tail was Operation "Vesna" (Spring), which lasted from 1930 to 1932, during which around 3,000 commanders, mostly former Tsarist officers, were arrested and convicted. In 1933, however, the Bolsheviks reversed course and released many of them from the prisons and concentration camps; similar to the bourgeois experts, many of them were readmitted into the Red Army.[16] This thaw did not last for long and in 1934, a renewed purge hit the Red Army that lasted until early 1937. By 25 May 1937, 4,855 commanders had been dismissed as part of the operation, including 1,474 for political reasons. The number of arrests stood at 162, although the data on the arrests is not complete.[17] When this purge ended in May 1937, it was immediately succeeded by another, much more intense purge that eclipsed all earlier purges within the Red Army.

In the armaments industry, the NKVD soon realized that all the investigations and purges were not having the desired effect. The armaments industry still failed to fulfill the Politburo's plans and continued to deliver flawed weaponry, ammunition, and equipment. The mobilization preparations did not fare better.[18] As in the years before, the blame was put on the activities of supposed wreckers and saboteurs. With only a few old specialists and members of the former elite left in the armaments industry, the NKVD had to find new culprits among the ranks of party members and newly-trained specialists, who were now accused of being Trotskyists or German, Polish, or Japanese spies.

Particularly suspicious were the children of the old bourgeois experts and other "socially alien elements" who had managed to find their way into the party, government agencies and Soviet industry. Throughout the 1930s, ethnicity began to play an increasingly important role and Poles especially were persecuted, as were Germans after 1933. These two groups were the main targets of the internal purges between 1933 and 1936.

Still, both the armaments industry and the Red Army remained in a horrible state. Of particular note is Tukhachevsky's memorandum from 9 August 1936, in which he complained about the catastrophic condition of the Red Army's armored units. By pointing out in detail the failure of his personal flagship policies, Tukhachevsky likely sealed his own fate as well as that of his staff, who – having planned, initiated and overseen the operation – were blamed for this disaster.

In September 1936 at the latest, Stalin decided to thoroughly purge the party and government. With the usual suspects of former Tsarist officials and "socially alien elements" more or less gone, Stalin had to pivot to a new enemy – Trotskyists. Already in the summer of 1936, the Old Bolsheviks and former Trotsky supporters Kamenev and Zinoviev had been arrested, put before a show trial and executed. On 25 September 1936, while on vacation, Stalin and Zhdanov sent out a telegraph to Molotov and Kaganovich in which they demanded the dismissal of Genrikh Yagoda. As the chief of the NKVD and the person in charge of the previous purges, Yagoda had proven himself incapable of crushing the Trotsky-Zinoviev bloc, they argued. This move spelled the end of Yagoda's career and he was soon tried and executed. On 11 October 1936, he was succeeded by Nikolai Yezhov, a close associate of Stalin from his time as the general secretary of the Central Committee, who had also distinguished himself during earlier party purges.[19]

Yezhov immediately set to work and filled the NKVD with functionaries from the Central Committee bureaucracy, turning the organization into an instrument of the secretariat of the Central Committee and Stalin himself.[20] While Yezhov was busy preparing for the great upcoming purge of the party, government, and industry, Stalin and his comrades worked on the resolution proposals for the purges in the various individual sectors of Soviet society, which were then approved at the plenum of the Central Committee between 23 February and 5 March 1937. Ordzhonikidze dealt with Soviet industry, Kaganovich with the transport system, while the plans for the party were drawn up by none other than Stalin himself. The goal of this operation was to show that the issues plaguing these sectors were the work of one great Trotskyist conspiracy – made up of functionaries in the party, state and economy – that sought to spy and sabotage on behalf of Germany and Japan.[21]

In his draft on wrecking activities in Soviet industry, Ordzhonikidze wrote in early February 1937 that Trotskyists had managed to gather all anti-Soviet elements under their banner. Trotskyists such as Pyatakov, Radek, Serebrakov, and Sokolnikov had thus deliberately taken up key economic posts with the sole aim of dealing a devastating blow to Soviet heavy industry, targeting factories that were vital to the defense of the Soviet Union. Particularly affected were coal mining and the chemical industry. The leaders responsible for this had already been arrested in late 1936, and the show trials had already taken place in January 1937.[22]

It had to be noted that unlike the grand Trotskyist conspiracy, the severe problems these sectors of the economy faced were not made up at all. Indeed, the coal mining sector had been plagued by abnormally frequent fires and explosions and a host of other disasters that claimed countless lives. Operational disruptions were commonplace and great quantities of coal were lost through both workers and management disregarding basic rules of coal extraction. At the same time, there were considerable delays everywhere, from the construction of new mines to preparatory work in already existing ones.[23]

These problems were of course not caused by Trotskyist saboteurs but rather by the communist Strakhanovite movement and the purges themselves. Holding up the mythologized example of Strakhanov, an unusually productive coal miner, Soviet authorities aggressively pushed for competitions among workers to raise individual output in all sectors of the economy. In order to over-fulfill targets, management and workers regularly disregarded safety regulations and established production processes, and overloaded equipment and machinery while also neglecting "unproductive" maintenance. The results were devastating: frequent and deadly accidents, rapid degradation of equipment and very poor production quality. The situation was particularly noticeable in construction, where many buildings, factories, power plants and even entire dams had to be immediately torn down due to critical construction faults.[24]

In his proposal from February 1937, Ordzhonikidze put the blame for all of this on the Trotskyists whose malicious plots had remained undetected due to carelessness. The frequent accidents in the coal mines had traditionally been deemed to be of an "objective character", while the explosions in the chemical factories had been explained by material fatigue and ordinary operational errors. However, this was not true, Ordzhonikidze claimed. Instead, the trials against the Trotskyists had shown that these disasters were the result of acts of sabotage, carried out on the orders of the Trotskyist wreckers Pyatakov and Rataichak. Indeed, it was due to Trotskyist wrecking that work and production discipline was so low, with catastrophic consequences in the more advanced industries in particular.[25]

To remedy the situation in the chemical industry, Ordzhonikidze proposed to strictly enforce production discipline. Furthermore, all accidents, machine breakdowns, and operational disruptions were to be thoroughly investigated while eventual perpetrators were to be punished severely. At the same time, Ordzhonikidze called for better training for the workers. He also proposed the creation of a dedicated commission to investigate the situation in the military-chemical industry in more detail. Overall, Ordzhonikidze's ideas to save the chemical industry were rather matter-of-fact, as were his recommendations for the coal mining sector, even though both were laced with the expected slogans about Trotskyist wreckers who were at fault for everything.[26]

Roughly at the same time, Kaganovich submitted his ideas for the Soviet railway system. Like the rest of the Soviet economy, the railway system was also plagued by frequent accidents and plans were rarely met. In contrast to Ordzhonikidze, Kaganovich was much more aggressive in his attacks on the Trotskyists who were supposedly part of a secret German-Japanese organization dedicated to espionage and sabotage. His recommendations reflected that and he called for a comprehensive purge of the railway system to root out these Trotskyist wreckers.[27]

Kaganovich's aggressive approach was easily surpassed by Stalin himself, who had turned his gaze towards "our party organizations", which had supposedly been infiltrated by Trotskyist "fascists" as well. This could not stand and he thus demanded a decisive purge of Trotskyists from the party. Stalin also noted that there was much "discontent and bitterness in parts of the party", which had been caused by the heartless treatment of former party members that had been expelled earlier.[28]

Stalin rallied his associates in a speech on 3 March 1937. Afterwards, Dimitrov noted in his diary: "After the speech, it became easier."[29] While it is not clear whether or not Stalin genuinely believed the grand Trotskyist conspiracy, other leading Politburo members certainly had their doubts. Ordzhonikidze was most likely one of them, and according to Mikoyan, Stalin had to repeatedly tell Ordzhonikidze to be much more aggressive in his proposal for purges in heavy industry. However, Mikoyan later wrote, Ordzhonikidze never believed in the conspiracy, especially after his own brother, who had been a leading economic functionary in Georgia, was arrested and executed for allegedly being part of this conspiracy. Perhaps fearing to meet the fate of his brother and the other supposed Trotskyists who had been convicted in the earlier show trials, Ordzhonikidze shot himself on 18 February 1937, just days before the plenum where he was to present his plans for the purge of heavy industry.[30] The fears were not entirely unfounded. After all, Ordzhonikidze had been the People's Commissar for Heavy Industry since 1932 and as such had overseen this catastrophe. Mikoyan claimed that Ordzhonikidze was motivated by moral considerations, being unwilling to participate in the purge, but this is probably not true considering that Ordzhonikidze himself was a ruthless communist who until then had eagerly taken part in countless massacres.

Stalin and his comrades were not entirely wrong in their belief that it was specific individuals who were responsible for the disastrous state of the Red Army, the economy in general, and heavy industry in particular. Chief among them were, of course, Stalin and the Politburo who through their over-ambitious and disorganized efforts had thrown the entire economy into utter confusion. However, they could not admit this and instead began to search for suitable scapegoats while continuing their tried-and-failed policies. When Stalin wrote about the "discontent and bitterness in parts of the party" in early 1937, he likely feared losing his grip on power.

On 11 November 1937, Stalin told Dimitrov in a private conversation that many party members had not "digested" the collectivization and the extermination of the kulaks. Many of these people had not accepted the party line and instead they "went into *illegality*. They themselves being powerless, they joined forces with external enemies."[31]

One of the people who apparently resented Stalin and the Politburo was Yagoda himself, the deposed chief of the NKVD who had overseen the most recent purges. On 20 June 1937, L. Mironov, a close associate of Yagoda, claimed that Yagoda hated Stalin and the party leadership. Yagoda allegedly also said that "to us Chekists, it was clearer than to all others that the discontent in the country is rising, that one cannot take control of the situation with arrests. [...] one had to change the policy of the Central Committee of the CPSU(b) fundamentally."[32]

Stalin evidently thought otherwise and continued to rely on mass terror to fix, or at least contain, all of the problems the Soviet Union faced as result of his ambitions. In any case, criticism was absolutely taboo. On 11 February 1937, he ordered Dimitrov to educate the "European workers" about the conflict with Trotsky and the supposed activities of the great, imaginary, Trotskyist conspiracy that was cooperating with Imperial Japan and even Nazi Germany. Dimitrov was to explicitly cite "what Lenin said about the opposition: 'Any opposition within the party under the conditions of Soviet power, which insists on its errors, drifts into White Guardism.'"[33]

With the ideological ground thus prepared, Stalin unleashed his terror upon the previously, largely unscathed, leadership class of the country – high-ranking government and economic officials, top party cadres, and the commander-corps of the Red Army. At the plenum of the Central Committee that lasted from late February to early March 1937, Stalin also ordered wide-ranging purges among the lower ranks of the party, state and economic apparatus as well as the NKVD.

Immediately following the plenum, the communist terror machine accelerated rapidly. Unlike the earlier purges, this one also targeted the communist leadership, just as Stalin had promised. As a result, tens of thousands of beneficiaries and pillars of the communist system, as well as perpetrators of earlier mass terror campaigns were executed. Still, communists only made up a negligible share of the victims of the terror of 1937/38. Like before, most victims were real or imagined enemies of the communist system, mostly peasants.[34]

The Red Army Purges of 1937/38

At the plenum of the Central Committee from 23 February to 5 March 1937, the wrecking activities within the Red Army played only a minor role. When Voroshilov was asked about the issue, he replied with caution: "At the moment, not many enemies have been exposed, luckily. I say 'luckily' in the hopes that there are not many enemies at all within the ranks of the Red Army." Nevertheless, it has to be noted that quite a few high-ranking commanders had already been arrested. In 1936 alone, military tribunals had arrested and convicted 380 commanders of "counterrevolutionary agitation" and arrests continued well into early 1937.[35]

Molotov vehemently disagreed with Voroshilov's assessment and responded at the very same meeting: "The defense ministry is a very important matter, this matter will not be dealt with at the moment, but a little later, and it will be investigated very intensively. […] Until now, only few symptoms of enemy activity have been found there. […] But I think that one will find more there as well if one investigates it in depth."[36] This was not an empty threat.

On 29 March 1937, the Politburo ordered the removal of all commanders previously expelled from the party on political grounds.[37] The months of March and April also saw the arrests of several high-ranking commanders in the Ural and Ukrainian military districts, as well as in the Kalinin oblast.[38]

By April 1937 at the latest, the NKVD turned its gaze onto Tukhachevsky, the man whose concept of the revolutionary war of annihilation against the West had guided the Soviet armament efforts over the past several years. On 23 April 1937, the Politburo decided to not have Tukhachevsky represent the Soviet armed forces at the upcoming coronation of George VI in London, likely because they feared he could use this opportunity to flee to the West. Officially, however, the Politburo was afraid of Polish–German terrorist groups seeking to assassinate him.[39]

Over the next few days, the noose around Tukhachevsky and his closest associates began to tighten. Voroshilov, who had been previously humiliated by Tukhachevsky's meteoric rise, personally oversaw and coordinated the investigations. On 10 May 1937, he sent his investigation report to Stalin and Molotov, in which he wrote: "In fulfilment of the resolution of the plenum of the Central Committee of the VCP(b), in accordance with the presentations of Molotov and Kaganovich, I submit a project of measures for the liquidation and prevention of wrecking activities and espionage in the Red Army. I ask for confirmation."[40]

The report was 20 pages long and there were only three copies, one for Stalin, one for Molotov and then one copy for Voroshilov himself. While the document itself remains inaccessible to the public to this day, it is very likely that it put the blame for the disastrous state of the Red Army on Tukhachevsky and his closest associates. Stalin was clearly anticipating this report and acted as soon as he received it. The very same day, Tukhachevsky was dismissed from his post of Deputy People's Commissar for Defense.[41] Two days later, the first of his associates began to be arrested, and on 22 May 1937, he himself was put under arrest. All were brutally tortured and confessed to having been Trotskyist and German agents who had systematically wrecked the Red Army from the inside.[42]

Just over a month after Voroshilov's damning report, on 11 June 1937, the show trial against Tukhachevsky and seven high-ranking Red Army commanders took place. Everyone was sentenced to death and the sentences were carried out the next day. Stalin himself declared the executed as the chief conspirators.[43] However, this was just the beginning of the great purge within the Red Army, which eclipsed everything that came before and after. When the purge finally ended in late 1938, thousands of commanders had been executed.

The upper ranks were hit particularly hard. On 31 December 1936, the Red Army had 1,651 senior commanders above the rank of brigade commander, equivalent to a brigade general, within its ranks, across all branches. According to research by Pawel Wieczorkowicz, 87% of them lost their position between 1936 and 1939, with nine committing suicide and 1,433 being dismissed. Going by the documents available today, 1,179 of the 1,433 dismissed commanders were arrested. Of them, 715 were subsequently executed, while 71 died in prison or in the gulag. In total, nearly half (48%) of all senior commanders died between 1936 and 1939.

Hundreds more were sent to prisons and concentration camps, while others were demoted or left the service "voluntarily" to avoid persecution.[44]

The purge was even more devastating at the War Council of the People's Commissariat of Defense. On 22 November 1934, it had 80 members and a year later – 85. With the onset of the terror campaign, the number of its members began to shrink. In 1937, 26 were shot and in 1938, another 36 were executed. In other words, 73% of all members of the War Council had been executed by late 1938. On top of that, two had evaded arrest through suicide, while another one had died in prison; another four were still in prison and would be executed in 1939.[45]

In comparison, the Stalinist terror was much less drastic among the lower ranks in relative terms, although the absolute number of victims was much higher. In 1938, the Red Army had around 179,000 junior and medium commanders in its ranks. According to modern estimates, around 63,000 commanders were directly affected by the purges between 1935 and 1939. 14,775 of them were arrested directly before or after their dismissal, with some of them being sent to prison or to one of the concentration camps, while others were executed. At least 4,467 of them were executed, although the data is incomplete.[46]

This purge was absolutely devastating for the senior leadership of the Red Army. To put things into perspective, around 6.3% of Soviet generals were killed during the exceedingly bloody German-Soviet war between 1941 and 1945. In contrast, nearly 50% of them were killed in just over a year of the purge.[47] Rokossovsky, a famous Soviet general who himself had been imprisoned and repeatedly tortured between 1938 and 1940, remarked: "This is worse than artillery fire against one's own troops."[48] He was not wrong. After the purges, the morale and effectiveness of the officer corps were at an absolute low point.[49]

As a result of the mass arrests and dismissals, the Red Army was missing somewhere between 80,000 and 90,000 commanders at the end of 1938, so many of the recently dismissed commanders were quickly reinstated. Of the 12,000 lieutenants and first lieutenants that had been dismissed, 30-35% eventually rejoined the Red Army. Additionally, military schools and academies were expanded, and in November 1938, 15,000 men were in the process of being trained as commanders. However, the purge had further exacerbated the lack of skilled instructors, which lowered the quality of training.[50]

The purge also had a devastating effect on troop discipline, as the massacres had completely eroded the authority of their superiors. Already in the second half of 1937, in the early stages of the purge, cases of drunkenness, sleeping on guard duty, brawls between soldiers, disputes with commanders and even outright insubordination began to skyrocket. This directly led to the resignation of many commanders, including divisional commanders. Poor discipline also led to the exaggeration or even invention of great successes during combat preparations.[51] When Zhukov took over command of the Kyiv military district in 1939, he noted the "collapse of discipline to the point of willful abandonment of duty and desertion". To restore order, new and much harsher service regulations had to be introduced which also included physical punishment, which the commanders were more than eager to use.[52]

Unsurprisingly, it was the arrested and executed commanders who were blamed for the disastrous effects of the purge. On 21 November 1938, at a session of the War Council at the People's Commissar of Defense, N. Vashugin from the Leningrad military district explained:

> The troops of the Leningrad military district are not sufficiently prepared to fulfill the order of the People's Commissar of Defense to win victory with little bloodshed. [...] Enemies of the people, who had been active in the Leningrad military district for a long time, inveterate enemies of the people obstructed the war preparations of the troops of the Leningrad military district by any means, and attempted to derail the military preparedness of the troops.[53]

Given the magnitude of the purge that followed the trial and execution of Tukhachevsky and his closest associates, one would assume that the new leadership would move away from Tukhachevsky's vision of an offensive war of annihilation. However, this was not the case at all. On 26 November 1938, Boris Shaposhnikov, a former Tukhachevsky-skeptic who was now the Chief of the General Staff of the Red Army, had this to say at a session of the War Council of the People's Commissar of Defense: "Our army will not be attacked first, however, if it is threatened by an attack, it will deal devastating blows to the enemy. We must prepare it for this.[54]" Voroshilov interjected: "It will deal blows". Shaposhnikov then continued: "Yes, exactly – it will deal blows, and for that one has to prepare our army in tactical exercises. Because of that, our entire system of war preparations in the year 1939 has to be primarily guided by the idea of offensive operations and not by defense."[55] This trend was to continue well past 1939 and the Red Army continued to focus on preparing for offensive operations over the coming years.[56]

Chapter 17

Europe in the 1930s and Stalin's War Preparations

With the onset of the Great Depression, Stalin and his comrades anticipated a period of intense conflict between the great imperialist powers. Eager to take advantage of the coming chaos, Moscow embarked on a gigantic armament program and ambitious army reform to turn the Red Army into the greatest attacking force the planet had ever seen, capable of overrunning the capitalist states of the West and – with the help of local revolutionaries – carrying the flames of revolution into the world.

Many of Stalin's closest associates, such as Dmitri Manuilsky, regularly assured him that the Western countries were just about to buckle under the irresistible pressure of the looming proletarian revolution. In the case of Manuilsky, Stalin himself grew skeptical of his enthusiastic reports and in April 1934, he complained to Dimitrov that at one point, Manuilsky had gleefully informed him about an insurrection in a place that did not even exist.[1] Manuilsky was not the only one. On 2 March 1931, a certain D. Bogolepov sent Stalin his report on the agricultural crisis in the West, which had worsened to such an extent over the past years that a collapse was coming. At the same time, Bogolepov complained that communist parties in the West were underestimating and therefore neglecting the peasant question, and that one had to change course to turn the agricultural crisis into a true social revolution. In his opinion, the best way to achieve this was by championing collectivization.[2]

Stalin personally read Bogolepov's report and judging by the notes he left on it, he took these unrealistic theses rather seriously, even sending a copy to Manuilsky and asking him for his opinion.[3] Manuilsky's may have been overly optimistic in his own reports, but even he realized that Bogolepov's strategy was not going to work. While emphasizing collectivization was of course fundamentally correct, he argued, collectivization abroad could only be achieved after the victory of the proletarian revolution. At the moment, however, the peasants in the West were not ready for it and talking about collectivization would be counterproductive. Experience had shown that for now, it was important to turn the peasantry in the West against the capitalist system, through calls for the expropriation of landowners or by agitating against taxes, Manuilsky continued.[4]

As shown previously, Germany continued to play a key role in the plans of Stalin and the communist leadership, and remained the most important economic and political partner of the Soviet Union. On 21 January 1933, Molotov once again re-affirmed the extraordinary position of Germany: "A special place in these [international] relations is taken up by Germany. With Germany, we had and still have the strongest economic ties. This is no coincidence. It is the result of the interests of both countries."[5] Molotov then continued to shower Germany with praise: "Trade relations between the Soviet Union and Germany are an example of how economic relations between the Soviet Union and a capitalist country can develop in a positive way, when the interests of both countries are properly understood, to the mutual benefit of their people."[6]

According to the data Molotov cited, German exports to the Soviet Union grew from 266 million mark, or 5.5% of total exports in 1926, to 762 million mark or 11.9% of total exports in 1932. Not only was the quantity of the German exports important, but also the quality. In the first half of 1932, 92% of hydraulic presses the Soviet Union imported came from Germany, as did 88% of lifting cranes, 80% of all steam engines and 75% of metalworking machinery.[7] The entire Soviet industrialization and armaments effort was based on imported German machines.

However, close cooperation did not mean that Stalin had abandoned his plans to Sovietize Germany and expropriate or even kill the industrial magnate he was trading with. On the contrary: the Sovietization of Germany remained Stalin's most important strategic goal, since gaining access to Germany's vast industrial potential would solve most of the Soviet Union's problems and also allow it to dominate all of Europe – and then the world. Within Germany, it was the KPD that carried out his orders, which he gave either through the Comintern or simply directly. Given its extraordinary importance, the KPD was given special instructions which were quite different from those received by communist parties in other countries. Most importantly, the KPD did not call for a communist or proletarian revolution, but for a national revolution.

The idea of having the German communists advocate for a national revolution came from Stalin himself. In July 1930, he had Manuilsky, Kuusinen, and Sokolnikov – none of them Germans – flesh out the idea of a KPD-led national revolution, which was then confirmed by the political secretariat of the Comintern on 23 July 1930, thereby being included in the guidelines for the KPD. When the KPD received these instructions, its Central Committee immediately began to work out its new program of the national and social liberation of the German people, which was then published on 24 August 1930 by *Rote Fahne*, its flagship paper. With this new program, Stalin hoped to capitalize on the widespread discontent in Germany, even trying to attract "members of the urban middle class, poor peasants, clerks, housewives."[8]

In its new program, the KPD thus claimed to be the sole, true defender of not only the "working masses" but also the national interests of the German nation. It openly rejected the payment of reparations and demanded the return of lands Germany lost at Versailles, while also campaigning about the plight of Germans living abroad – excluding the USSR, of course. Hitler's NSDAP had used similar slogans to great success and Stalin aimed to win that electorate over for the KPD.[9] In its "Manifesto for the National and Social Liberation of the German People" from 24 August 1930, the Central Committee of the KPD declared, among other things:

The fascists (national socialists) claim that they are fighting for the liberation of the German people. They act as if they are against the Young Plan, which brings the working masses of Germans hardship and hunger. These assertions of the fascists are deliberate lies. [...] Only we communists are fighting against the Young Plan as well as against the Versailles Robbery-Peace, as well as against all international treaties, agreements and plans (Locarno Treaty, Dawes Plan, Young Plan, German-Polish Convention, etc.) that emerged from the Versailles Peace Treaty. [...] We will tear up the rapacious Versailles "Peace Treaty" and the Young Plan, which keep Germany down, we will annul all debts and reparations imposed on the workers of Germany by the capitalists. We communists will advocate for the full right of self-determination of all nations and in agreement with the revolutionary workers of France, England, Poland, Italy, Czechoslovakia, etc. we will secure the possibility of accession to Soviet Germany of all German regions that express the desire for it.[10]

Of course, the slogan of the national revolution was nothing more than a tactical trick – the true goal remained the creation of a "Soviet Germany or a free socialist Germany" that would aid the Soviet Union.[11] The above mentioned manifesto thus also included this passage: "We communists will establish a firm political and economic alliance between Soviet Germany and the Union of Soviet Socialist Republics, on the basis of which the factories of Soviet Germany will deliver industrial goods to the Soviet Union in return for food and raw materials from the Soviet Union."[12]

The success of such a national revolution in Germany would have undoubtedly caused serious conflict with virtually all of Germany's neighbors, with Czechoslovakia over the Sudetenland, with Poland over Danzig, the Polish Corridor and Upper Silesia, and with France over Alsace-Lorraine. A major war in the center of Europe would have been on the cards again, a possibility Stalin and his comrades welcomed and for which they had been preparing intensely for the past few years.

Stalin was quite explicit in this regard. On 22 August 1932, Stalin sent a letter to Kaganovich in which he criticized the content of a Comintern resolution: "The phrase 'against national wars' is wrong and scandalous. We are not against, but for national wars of liberation."[13] Naturally, this did not apply to the peoples of the Soviet Union, whose aspirations for independence were drowned in blood.

For Stalin and the KPD, the NSDAP may have been its greatest German rival, but it was far from its greatest enemy. Indeed, the goal was and remained the destruction of the Weimar Republic, and in this struggle, the NSDAP was a tactical ally. As the chief pillar of the Weimar Republic, it was the Social Democrats that were the KPD's greatest enemy. In the manifesto from 24 August 1930, the Central Committee of the KPD elaborated: "Every action of the treasonous, corrupt social democracy is continued high treason against the vital interest of the working masses of Germany."[14] The attacks on the German Social Democrats continued and even intensified the next year. On 10 May 1932, Stalin was sent a report which stated: "After consultations with the Russian delegation in November 1931, when a series of mistakes of the KPD leadership in its treatment of social democracy had been revealed, the party [KPD] focused its agitation against social democracy as the primary social pillar of support of the bourgeoisie.[15]

It is difficult to overstate the devastating role the KPD's uncompromising fight against the SPD played in the collapse of the Weimar Republic. When elections were held in Germany on 14 September 1930, the SPD gained 24.5% of the vote, the KPD 13.1% and the NSDAP 18.3%. Together with the Catholic Center Party which had gained 11.8% of the vote, the KPD and SPD could have supported a functional government. Even after 6 November 1932, when the NSDAP became by far the strongest party with 33.1% of the vote, the SPD (21.6%), KPD (16.9%) and the Center Party (11.9%) still would have held a slight majority.[16] Had the KPD supported the democratic factions of the Weimar Republic, Hitler probably would have never risen to power, especially since the NSDAP's appeal would have most likely waned with the onset of the economic recovery as it did in the mid-1920s. The KPD – on Stalin's personal orders – thus played a vital role in Hitler's rise to power.

However, Stalin had completely misjudged the situation. Already in September 1930, immediately after the embrace of the national revolution by the KPD, Stalin's great rival, Trotsky, had warned: "this very underestimation of fascism [i.e. the NSDAP] by the present leadership of the Communist Party, may lead the revolution to a more severe crash for many years to come."[17] Trotsky was right.

Hitler's Rise to Power

After weeks of maneuvering, Germany's President Hindenburg tasked Hitler with forming a new government. Hitler seized this golden opportunity to rapidly solidify his grip on power, turning Germany into a dictatorship. In late 1932, the first signs of an economic upturn were noticeable in Germany and throughout 1933, Germany enjoyed a rapid recovery that benefited all sectors of society. Between February 1933 and March 1934, unemployment fell by 2.6 million and continued to fall over the coming years. By 1939, Germany had effectively reached full employment. GDP also rebounded, surpassing pre-crisis levels in 1935.[18] This great recovery earned Hitler the broad popular support he needed to establish and sustain his dictatorship.

His popularity was further bolstered by a series of triumphs, both at home and abroad. Hitler successfully defied the Western powers by rebuilding the Wehrmacht, reintroducing conscription, and even marching his revived army into the demilitarized Ruhr area. In 1938 alone, he managed to reintegrate Austria and take the Sudetenland – both without bloodshed. In the span of just a few years, Hitler had managed to once again turn Germany into a confident, great power.

These were successes the previous German governments could not even have dreamed of and "to a large part of the German population, traumatized by inflation and the Great Depression, [...] Hitler appeared as a hero, a secularized 'savior'."[19] Drowned out by a general feeling of reawakened optimism and enthusiasm, the increasing persecution of the political opposition, most notably the social democratic and communist activists, as well as Germany's well-integrated Jewish minority – around half a million people – went largely ignored. This was made even easier by the fact that many Germans directly profited from the marginalization of the Jews in public life, taking over Jewish businesses and positions held by Jews.

In 1933, Germany did indeed see a revolution - not a national or even proletarian revolution, but a national socialist revolution. Hitler and his men immediately began to destroy the KPD. Leading activists were thrown into the newly-established concentration camps or had to flee to the Soviet Union, while much of the rank and file went on to join the NSDAP. On 17 May 1944, Stalin and Molotov met with Oskar Lange, a Polish economist of German origin who was also a Soviet agent.[20] In the course of the conversation, Lange asked Stalin what he thought about the state of Marxism in Germany. Stalin replied that "there had been Marxist cadres in Germany, however, these people had been destroyed and the masses that had marched with them dissipated, because they had been guided by the atmosphere [as opposed to ideology, B.M.]"[21]

It was only in 1933 that Stalin realized that he had been wrong about Hitler. He immediately ordered the KPD to change its approach and join forces with the SPD in 1933, but by then it was already too late.[22] By spring 1934, he had all but given up his dream of a communist revolution in Germany. On 7 April 1934, Stalin met with Dimitrov, the future chief of the Comintern, and told him to change the strategy of communist parties in the West. From now on, communists were to tone down their attacks on parliamentary democracy. At the same time, he emphasized that fascism would emerge victorious in all capitalist countries.[23] The debacle was not Stalin's fault, but an iron rule of history.

At the same meeting, Dimitrov blamed mistaken propaganda for the fact that European workers preferred social democracy or even National Socialism like in Germany. Stalin, who was responsible for the propaganda, disagreed. In his opinion, the real reason was the special historical pathway European countries had taken, where the working class had traditionally strong ties to bourgeois democracy. Furthermore, European countries did not have sufficient raw materials at home and therefore had to get them from their colonies, without which they would collapse. European workers were well aware of this, Stalin surmised, and were thus afraid of losing their colonies, which made them hostile to Soviet anti-imperialism and thus pushed them into an alliance with the bourgeoisie. In other words, it was the workers who were wrong. The communist had to fight hard to convince the European workers, but for this, they needed time, Stalin continued. He then criticized Manuilsky, who had always followed Stalin's directions, for not understanding this issue.[24]

A few days later, on 24 April 1934, Dimitrov then met with Manuilsky, noting afterwards: "We did not take advantage of the greatest crisis in the world."[25] The two men met the next day. Manuilsky told Dimitrov that he had thought a lot about the latter's meeting with Stalin. He believed that it had been very important politically, signifying a great turning point in the history of the Comintern, which could only be achieved by Dimitrov on account of his great authority and his direct access to Stalin.[26]

In the coming months and years, the Comintern and the communist parties under its influence began to relentlessly attack fascism. Social democrats and other democratic parties were from now on not regarded as communism's chief enemies anymore and in some cases they even became allies. This strategy was to last throughout much of the 1930s, until the Hitler-Stalin Pact in the summer of 1939.

Hitler had thus single-handedly overturned Stalin's earlier ideological and geopolitical strategy. No longer did he believe in an imminent social or communist revolution abroad, and his concept of a national revolution had failed spectacularly as well. Nevertheless, Stalin and his comrades continued to believe that the total victory of the revolution was inevitable – it would just take a bit longer than expected. Following the new round of revolutionary failures, Lenin's words of spreading the revolution by force of arms seemed like the only feasible way ahead, and to make this possible, the Soviet Union needed its capitalist enemies to engage in a fratricidal imperialist war – helped on by the Bolsheviks themselves if need be. On 2 September 1935, Stalin wrote to Kaganovich and Molotov:

Kalinin has reported that the People's Commissariat of Foreign Affairs has raised doubts regarding as to whether the export of grain and other products from the USSR to Italy is permissible due to the conflict in Abyssinia or not. I think that the doubts of the People's Commissariat of Foreign Affairs stem from a lack of understanding of the international situation. This conflict is not only between Italy and Abyssinia, but also between Italy and France on the one side, and England on the other. The old entente does not exist anymore. Instead, two ententes are emerging: The entente between Italy and France on the one hand, and the entente between England and Germany on the other, the worse the scuffles between them get, the better for the USSR. We can sell grain to both sides so they can fight each other. It is not advantageous for us that one side smashes the other already now. For us it is advantageous if the scuffles between them continue for as long as possible, but without a quick victory of one over the other.[27]

This was the guiding principle of Stalin's foreign policy. To weaken the capitalists, the Soviet Union had to fuel if not outright stir up conflict between their countries, so that they weakened themselves while the Soviet Union readied itself for a grand revolutionary war. Stalin did not have peace in mind, or even defense for that matter.

When the Soviet Union launched its first great armament program in 1927/8, it was not threatened military by any of its neighbors. Likewise, the expansion of plans at the onset of the Great Depression happened during a moment of profound capitalist weakness, when invasion had become even less likely than it had already been. At the same time, the completely refurbished army was designed to fight in Central and Western Europe, and was not particularly suited for fighting on terrain controlled by the Soviet Union. Some historians seek to explain the armament plans of 1931/2 by the threat from Japan, following its occupation of Manchuria in September 1931.[28] Robert Service even wrote that "the Kremlin was concerned that this [the Japanese invasion of Manchuria] could become the prelude to an attack on the USSR in Siberia."[29]

This thesis does not hold up, however, and Stalin followed an aggressive, not defensive policy in regards to Manchuria, extensively meddling in its affairs and even going so far as sending troops there in November 1929. He also ordered to instigate a rebellion in Manchuria, take the key city of Harbin, install a "revolutionary government" as well as to "massacre landowners".[30] More importantly, there had been no talk about a Japanese threat at the turn of 1930-31, when Stalin had approved Tukhachevsky's grandiose plans to rebuild the Red Army. On the contrary, while the Soviet Union was involved in Manchuria, the theater in general was not considered to be all that important, with only around 5% of its troops – 42,000 men, 353 artillery pieces, 88 aircraft and 16 tanks – being stationed there.[31]

Internal discussions also make clear that while the Kremlin was concerned about Japan's actions, it did not particularly care about what Japan was doing. On 14 September 1931, Stalin wrote to Kaganovich: "One has to be careful with Japan. One has to hold onto one's position firmly and unshakably, but the tactics have to be elastic and prudent. [...] The time for an attack has not come yet."[32] A week later, on 23 September 1931, Stalin wrote to Molotov and Kaganovich: "Our military involvement [in the Japanese-Chinese War] is of course out of the question, and diplomatic involvement is not expedient now either, because it will only unify the imperialists, when it is in our interests that they quarrel amongst themselves."[33]

At the same time, Tukhachevsky's new Red Army was completely unsuited for a war in the Far East. The Soviet armaments industry was concentrated in the West, with only the Trans-Siberian Railroad connecting the factories to the Far East. As a result, transferring even a fraction of the planned 50,000 tanks, 40,000 aircraft and millions of soldiers to the Far East, and keeping them supplied would cause significant logistical issues.[34] Even worse, the thick forests, hills, and the lack of roads made the large-scale deployment of tanks unfeasible in the Soviet Far East.

But that was not a problem at all, since Tukhachevsky explicitly wrote in his memorandum from 11 January 1930 that it was the West that was the intended target, not the East: "This memorandum is oriented primarily against our Western neighbors and the great imperialists of Europe, who stand behind them."[35] The goal was to dominate the heart of Europe – Germany. In order to get there, the Red Army had to destroy Poland, but for that task, the 50,000 tanks, 40,000 aircraft and 1 million men were far too much considering that Poland had a much smaller army. The Red Army's main purpose was not to beat Poland or even a demilitarized Germany, but to defeat Europe's dominant land power, France and its allies, who would likely not tolerate the destruction of Poland and the Sovietization of Germany. It was considerations such as these that guided the armaments plans of 1931/32, not fear of Japan.

Hitler's rise to power did not change the calculations in a meaningful way. In spite of the many frustrating setbacks, the gigantic armaments program continued, as did the preparations for an offensive war. After one of the usual government meetings in early 1930s, Moscow, Semyon Budyonny, now the Inspector of Cavalry, handed his friend Kliment Voroshilov a slip of paper: "E[fremovich] K[liment]. What is this supposed to be? Three years ago it was said that we would need two to three years, then we could attack on our own. And now we are asking for five years. From what is being reported here about our readiness, I think that we will be less able to do so each year. S.B."[36]

The impact of Hitler's rise to power on Stalin's strategic plans was also softened by Stalin's mistaken belief that Hitler would not last long. It was only after the Night of the Long Knives in which Hitler had Ernst Röhm, the leader of the SA, the powerful and relatively leftwing, armed wing of the NSDAP, murdered alongside his closest associates.[37] Indeed, this purge had impressed Stalin and according to Mikoyan, Stalin went on to repeatedly praise Hitler: "He [Hitler] is a great guy, that is correct – said Stalin, one has to admit that."[38]

Nevertheless, the Soviet Union cancelled German-Soviet military cooperation as early as 1933.[39] This was most likely done because Soviet leadership feared that Germany could use this opportunity to spy on the Red Army, in the process learning about the gigantic armaments program and the enormous setbacks it suffered. Things looked quite different in the field of economic cooperation, however. Despite the ideological enmity, German-Soviet economic ties continued to flourish for a while, and on 20 March 1935, Germany issued a 200 million Reichsmark loan to the Soviet Union, which it used to purchase German machinery and industrial equipment. This was a notable success for Moscow as it had been trying to reach such a deal earlier, but had been rebuffed by Hitler's predecessors.

On 17 April 1935, the Politburo assigned the 200 million Reichsmarks it had just borrowed to individual departments: around 100 million were to be used on purchases for heavy industry, 10.64 million went to the transport sector, 10.64 to the timber industry, while the People's Commissariat of Defense received 10 million directly. The remaining 53.762 million Reichsmark were to be saved for future purchases.[40] This loan thus helped Moscow continue expanding the Soviet armaments industry and the Red Army, and it is likely not a coincidence that just a few weeks later, on 10 May 1935, the Politburo decided to expand the Red Army from 1,094,000 men on 23 March 1935 to 1,513,400 men by 1 January 1938.[41]

Hitler had other plans, however, and soon moved to ban the sale of crucial military goods to the Soviet Union. In February 1935, mere weeks after signing the loan agreement, the German Ministry of Economics announced its right to amend the Soviet order list and even veto the export of certain military goods. In January 1936, Hitler went even further and prohibited the export of all kinds of military goods to the Soviet Union. Unfortunately for the Kremlin, Hitler continued to restrict trade with the Soviet Union, even cutting both the export and import of non-military goods.[42]

Stalin had misjudged Hitler once again, and he would continue to do so. Curiously enough, he had read Hitler's *Mein Kampf*, but apparently did not take it seriously. When the not-yet-disgraced Tukhachevsky presented

Stalin with his newest memorandum titled "Hitler's War Plans", Stalin heavily edited it, adding comments, highlighting sentences, even deleting entire paragraphs while adding his own. Thanks to Stalin's extensive edits, one can catch a glimpse of how Stalin viewed Hitler and his plans.

First of all, Stalin changed the title. He thus crossed out the word "Hitler" and replaced it with "today's Germany", rechristening the document as "War Plans of Today's Germany". Apparently, Stalin sought to highlight that Hitler's policies were widely popular in Germany and that he himself enjoyed broad popular and institutional support, especially when it came to the question of war reparations. Aside from the title, Stalin did not make any changes to the first part of the script, in which Tukhachevsky wrote about the rearmament of Germany under Hitler and the country's great military-industrial potential.[43]

In the second part of the script, Tukhachevsky analyzed the debate surrounding the future military doctrine of Germany, which he thought was more or less fleshed out already: "The new German military doctrine is emerging and is now being secured with materiel." According to him, the Germans were now arming and organizing their military in such a way that it would be able to crush the main force of an enemy while at the same time disrupting the enemy's mobilization efforts and destroying its vital centers of power. The use of tanks and aircraft was key in this respect, but Tukhachevsky also noted that the rest of the army was not neglected either and that Germany was in the process of building a powerful invasion army.[44] In other words, Tukhachevsky thought that Hitler was more or less doing what the Soviets had been trying to do for the past half-decade.

Tukhachevsky continued by pointing out that Germany put a lot of emphasis on the creation of a strong air force, with a special focus on bombers, as well as the expansion of the aviation industry in general. The new German army was also highly mechanized, with new armored corps being created and outfitted with the most modern tanks. At the same time, Tukhachevsky pointed out that at least 15 infantry divisions had been fully motorized already. Furthermore, Germany also had a great number of private motor vehicles that could be mobilized for the Wehrmacht in times of war, including 661,000 cars, 12,500 buses, 191,000 trucks and 983,000 motorcycles. The German infantry was therefore highly mobile.[45]

After examining the military potential of Hitler's Germany, he dedicated the next chapter "Hitler's Anti-Soviet Plans" to the question of what Hitler could use that army for. This evidently did not sit well with Stalin who changed the title to "Hitler's Anti-Soviet *and Revanchist* Plans", emphasizing Germany's threat to its neighbors as opposed to the Soviet Union. In the introduction of the chapter, Tukhachevsky cited a passage from *Mein Kampf*, in which Hitler wrote about his idea of Lebensraum:

We National Socialists thus consciously draw a line through the foreign policy direction of our pre-war era. We begin where we stopped six centuries ago. We stop the eternal Germanic migration to the south and west of Europe and turn our gaze towards the lands of the East. We finally end the colonial and trade policy of the pre-war era and turn towards the policy of the soil of the future. But when we talk today about new ground and soil, we can primarily only think about Russia and the peripheral countries subject to it. Fate itself seems to want to give us a hint here.[46]

Stalin underlined the last sentence with his black pen and left a comment: "the entire quote in italics". While Tukhachevsky noted that Hitler had his eyes on the East in the long term, he also emphasized that for the time being, Hitler had no concrete plans to go after the Soviet Union. According to intelligence reports, Hitler had even expressed that he wanted to keep his options open regarding the USSR, and that for now, the Germans only sought to weaken the western borders of the USSR and to prevent a Franco-Soviet alliance. Tukhachevsky also pointed to a public statement by Hitler, in which he reassured the French that he had no intention of revising the Franco-German border and that he was prepared to issue a guarantee. Tukhachevsky believed that he did this because "Hitler does not want the growth of French armament". Stalin edited this sentence as follows: "Hitler *lulls France because he does not want to provide a reason for* French armament."[47]

Tukhachevsky also warned that the anti-Soviet front was growing stronger with each passing day. He counted Poland, the USSR's largest Western neighbor, to be part of that group and suggested that Poland could very well enter an alliance with Germany against the Soviet Union. Stalin clearly did not agree with that assessment and crossed it out in its entirety.[48] The deleted section also includes a passage that Stalin had extensively edited first, with the edits shown in italics:

> It is self-evident that Hitler's imperialist designs do not only have an anti-Soviet direction. *That direction is a cover to disguise the revanchist plans in the West (Belgium, France) and in the South (Posen, Czechoslovakia, Anschluss [of Austria]. Nevertheless, one cannot deny that Germany needs French iron ore.* Germany also needs to expand its fleet. The experiences of the war of 1914-1918 have shown with all clarity that without the harbors of Belgium and Northern France, Germany cannot build up its naval power.[49]

The text corrected by Stalin was finally published in *Pravda* on 29 March 1935. As shown by his edits, Stalin was acutely aware that Hitler's public assurances towards France were bald-faced lies. However, he misinterpreted Hitler's anti-Soviet rhetoric as a deceptive maneuver designed to trick his neighbors about his revisionist aims.

Even though Stalin was ultimately wrong, the following years seemed to prove him right, which only strengthened his faith in this regard. Four years later, on 19 March 1939, he claimed that the Anti-Comintern rhetoric of Germany, Italy, and Japan was but a feint; their real goal was to "infringe upon the interests of the non-aggressive states, primarily England, France and the USA." To prove this, Stalin pointed at Germany which had in to meantime "seized Austria and the Sudeten region", while Japan had "seized a vast stretch of territory in China", Italy – Abyssinia, and Italy and Germany together – Spain.[50] Stalin was far from alone in his belief. On 3 March 1939, Andrey Zhdanov gave a speech in Leningrad in which he explained that Hitler wanted to wage war on the West and not the Soviet Union.[51] In the summer of 1939, he wrote down some thoughts which evidently came from Stalin: "[German] Push towards the East – English invention. […] They [the British] want to shift the war to the East in order to save their own skin."[52]

Throughout the 1930s, Stalin did not feel threatened at all by Hitler's Germany, and completely dismissed Hitler's vision of Lebensraum, like many others in the West. If anything, Stalin assumed, Hitler could only dream of laying claim to the Lebensraum in the East after he had managed to revise Germany's borders to the west, south and east. In 1935, nobody thought that Hitler would be able to do that without triggering a great war. On 16 April 1934, Stalin elaborated in a speech:

Germany's withdrawal from the League of Nations [on 14 October 1933] and the spectre of revanchism have further added to the tension and have given a fresh impetus to the growth of armaments in Europe. [...] Once again, as in 1914, the parties of bellicose imperialism, the parties of war and revanchism are coming to the foreground. Quite clearly things are heading for a new war. [...] As is well known, during the first imperialist war it was also intended to destroy one of the great powers, i.e. Germany, and to profit at its expense. But what was the upshot of this? They did not destroy Germany; but they sowed in Germany such a hatred of the victors, and created such a rich soil for revenge, that even to this day they have not been able to clear up the revolting mess they made, and will not, perhaps, be able to do so for some time. On the other hand, the result they obtained was the smashing of capitalism in Russia, the victory of the proletarian revolution in Russia, and – of course – the Soviet Union. What guarantee is there that a second imperialist war will produce "better" results for them than the first? Would it not be more correct to assume that the opposite will be the case?[53]

Hitler unleashing Germany's revanchist desires made another great "imperialist" war in Europe much more likely, which was exactly what Stalin needed. Indeed, this had been the idea behind the KPD's "national revolution", which had been formulated by Stalin and his associates, after all. Hitler was thus unwittingly executing Stalin's will, or so Stalin thought.

This all stands in stark contrast to what is being written in many Russian but also Western accounts, which claim that in the 1930s, Stalin and the Soviet Union were striving for peace and did their best to avert the looming war. The story of the Soviet love of peace may have been the official Soviet narrative, but it was far from the truth. Despite the "pacifist propaganda", as Zhdanov formulated it on 6 June 1941, the Soviet Union was looking forward to war.[54]

Chapter 18

1938/39 – The Turning Point

Germany's rapid expansion at the expense of its neighbors in 1938 and 1939 seemed to confirm Stalin's assessment. The fact that the Soviet Union and Germany were actively supporting opposite sides in the Spanish Civil War (1936-1939) did not change things, since the impoverished southwestern fringe of Europe was not seen as crucial in the Soviet bid for European domination. While Stalin did send aid to the Republicans, he nevertheless doubted that a proletarian revolution could succeed in Spain. In a conversation with two Spanish writers, Rafael Alberti and Maria Teresa Leon, on 20 March 1937, Stalin is said to have explained:

> The Spanish people are currently not able to carry out a proletarian revolution. – The internal and international situation for that is not favorable. (It was different in 1917 Russia – region, wartime, conflicts of opinion between capitalist states, within the bourgeoisie, etc.) The creation of Soviets in Spain would unify all capitalist states, and fascism would win.[1]

While the Spanish Civil War was not really promising from the Soviet perspective, the events of 1938 definitely were. On 12 March 1938, German troops marched into Austria and the country was annexed by Germany, without bloodshed. This had been explicitly forbidden at Versailles, and even though France and Great Britain reacted with diplomatic protests, it was clear that the post-war order was on its way out.

Shortly after annexing Austria, Germany turned towards Czechoslovakia, demanding the Sudetenland, a key border region with a German majority. Czechoslovakian security may have been guaranteed by France and Britain, but neither were ready or willing to fight, especially since Czechoslovak defensive lines had effectively been outflanked by the annexation of Austria in the South. On 30 September 1938, Great Britain, France, Italy, and Germany thus signed the Munich Agreement in which Germany was given the Sudetenland in return for respecting the borders of the Czechoslovak rump state. The Czechoslovak government was not present during the negotiations at Munich and was presented with a fait accompli, which it begrudgingly accepted.

With the Sudetenland falling without a shot, Czechoslovakia's other neighbors turned on their weakened neighbor. Hungary took southern Slovakia with its sizable Hungarian population, while Poland took the Cieszyn region, a majority-Polish region in Silesia that Czechoslovakia had taken by force of arms in 1919 when Poland was preoccupied with other conflicts. However, this was not the end of Czechoslovakia's troubles and on 15 March 1939, Hitler broke his promise of respecting Czechoslovak independence and annexed the rest of Bohemia and Moravia, while turning Slovakia into a German puppet state. Czechoslovakia was no more. Two weeks later, on 3 April, Hitler then ordered the Wehrmacht to prepare for war against Poland.[2]

In the immediate aftermath of Munich, Hitler was not entirely sure how to expand next, but the Polish unwillingness to give in to German demands did not give him much room to maneuver. On 23 November 1939, Hitler had this to say to his assembled generals: "The decision to invade Bohemia had been taken. Then came the establishment of the protectorate, and thus the basis for the conquest of Poland had been laid, but to this point in time it was not quite clear to me whether I should move first against the East and then against the West, or the other way around. [...] Inevitably, the war against Poland came first."[3]

As the Wehrmacht was preparing for the invasion of Poland, Britain and France launched a diplomatic offensive to build up a broad anti-German front. Following the Italian invasion of Albania on 7 April, Britain and France extended their military and political guarantees to Romania, Greece and then Turkey, thereby reshaping the strategic situation in Central and Eastern Europe.[4]

However, many doubted the veracity of the Franco-British guarantees for Poland or Romania. Since 1933, Germany had rearmed to such an extent that a quick German victory seemed likely. The Soviet ambassador to London, Ivan Maisky, was one of those who shared that belief: "What can Great Britain (or even Great Britain and France together) truly do for Poland and Romania in case of a German attack on these countries? Very little. By the time the British blockade against Germany grows into a serious threat to the latter, Poland and Romania will have ceased to exist."[5]

A fair number of influential British politicians thought so as well and pointed out that the only realistic way of getting military aid to Poland was through the Soviet Union. This was not without reason, for Poland's sea access was exclusively through the Polish Corridor, a tiny sliver of land flanked by Germany on both sides. If war was to break out, it was clear that the Western powers could only help Poland with the support or at least the consent of the Soviet Union.[6]

Hitler was more than aware of this and thus sought to pre-empt any such efforts. He needed the Soviet Union to block all Western aid to Poland, and perhaps even have it support Germany in the conflict. While he did not fear the Polish army at all and did not think he needed any military help from the Soviets, Hitler wanted to defeat Poland as soon as possible, before Britain and France could intervene militarily. Soviet support for Germany would significantly speed up the anticipated German victory over Poland while also making sure that the Soviet Union was on Germany's side in case France and Britain did indeed intervene militarily.

For Stalin, this was a golden opportunity. The former pariah state he ruled over was now being aggressively courted by both the Western powers and Germany, with each trying to do their best to buy Soviet support. In this contest, it was Germany that had the better cards. In its quest to upend the old European order, Hitler simply had more to offer – namely new territories and entire countries – than the Western Allies, who sought to maintain the status quo. At the same time, while the Western Allies frantically tried to prevent another great war, it was clear that Hitler was intent on provoking it – which was exactly what Stalin had been hoping for all of those years.

Still, it was the Western Allies that made the first move. Already in April 1939, France and Britain began to negotiate with the Soviet Union with the intent of creating an alliance to keep Germany in check. The Kremlin did not show much enthusiasm and in late May 1939, Molotov reported to the Central Committee: "The English proposed that the Soviet Union should protect Poland, Romania and other countries from attack, without these countries assuming any obligations towards the Soviet Union. *Litvinov suggested to accept. We declined.*"[7]

This was the erstwhile end of Litvinov's career as the People's Commissar for Foreign Affairs. On 3 May 1939, he was removed and replaced by none other than Molotov. Litvinov immediately tried to apologize, but Stalin mocked him instead with "the ironic remark that Litvin[ov] as the 'specialist' for international issues did not consider the Politburo competent enough in these questions!"[8] Over recent decades, many scholars have interpreted the dismissal of Litvinov – who was Jewish – as a signal to Hitler that Stalin was ready for talks with Germany. However, this does not seem to be the case – the problem was his completely different outlook.[9]

Had the Soviet Union accepted the Franco-British proposal, it would have seen the creation of a "cordon sanitaire" on its western and southern border in Europe, creating much-needed distance between itself and Germany. Had the Soviet Union felt genuinely threatened by Hitler, it would have accepted this proposal as Litvinov had suggested. However, the Politburo had other plans, as Molotov told the plenum of the Central Committee:

We demanded the signing of a defense pact between England, France and the Soviet Union, with the later inclusion of Poland and Romania. Romania must renounce the pact with Poland, which is directed against the Soviet Union. Likewise the creation of a pact with the Baltic states. The English have declared – after much vacillation – that they accept our proposals but they formulated it in such a way that the pact would be concluded on the basis of Article 16 of the League of Nations, which means that the League of Nations (i.e. states like Bolivia) has to decide if there has been an aggression and who the aggressor is. We have of course declined.[10]

The rejection of that proposal seems incomprehensible at first glance, but it begins to make sense in the context of the Soviet war plans against Germany. A few weeks later, on 10 July 1939, the Chief of Staff of the Red Army, Shaposhnikov, wrote a memorandum in which he laid out the various possibilities of Soviet military action if the Soviet Union were to join France and Britain; Voroshilov read the memorandum and forwarded it to Stalin. In it, Shaposhnikov envisaged four different scenarios: (1) a German attack on France and England, (2) a German attack on Poland; (3) a Hungarian and Bulgarian attack on Romania, with German support; (4) a German attack on the Soviet Union via Estonia, Latvia and Finland.[11]

What is striking about this memorandum is that all four different scenarios are focused on the offensive and ignore defense, even though the fourth scenario was explicitly about a German attack on the Soviet Union. Furthermore, the offensive operations were to occur according to the same blueprint, regardless of how the war actually unfolded. In each case, England and France were to mobilize immediately, amassing 110 infantry divisions, 15,000 artillery pieces, 6,000 tanks and 7,000 aircraft at the Franco-German and Belgo-German borders by the fifteenth day of the operation. From there, they were to strike at the vital Ruhr Area and Cologne, before continuing east towards Magdeburg. While the allied navies would blockade Germany's ports, the French and English air forces were to bomb industrial centers and cities such as Kiel, Hamburg, and Berlin.[12]

As France and Britain were advancing from the west, the Red Fleet would contest control over the Baltic Sea against the German Kriegsmarine. At the same time, the Red Army would attack East Prussia with 30% of its forces. Unlike the plans for England and France, Shaposhnikov had no set date for the Soviet attack, but it was clear that it could only occur after the Western Allies managed to convince Poland to join the war and give the Soviet Union military access. Likewise, Romania and the Baltic states had to grant the Soviets military access as well. Polish consent to the plan was key, however.[13]

A month later, on 11 August 1939, Shaposhnikov prepared a second, very similar memorandum ahead of the talks with France and Britain, which Stalin read attentively, judging by the many written remarks he left on the document.[14] Looking at both memoranda – as well as Stalin's notes – it is clear that the Soviet Union was imagining its war against Germany to be a largely offensive war. Even if Germany were to shy away from making the first move, an incident could always be manufactured, which is exactly what the Soviet Union did with Finland just three months later, in November 1939. Furthermore, the war was to be fought primarily by France, Britain, and Poland, while the Soviet Union would only use 30%

of its forces, and only against East Prussia, which was neither particularly important strategically nor difficult to attack. In return, the Soviet Union wanted the Western powers to recognize Poland, Romania, and the Baltic states as part of the Soviet sphere of influence, for this is what having the Soviet Union station troops there would have inevitably led to.

With the Soviet Union holding back, the resulting war would likely be long and bloody, devastating Western and Central Europe. This was precisely what the Bolsheviks had hoped for from the beginning. For example, on 3 March 1939, Zhdanov held a speech in Leningrad, in which he talked about recent political events and the looming threat of war. In this context, he emphasized that the Soviet Union would seek to bide its time "until we can settle things with Hitler and Mussolini and at the same time with Chamberlain."[15] As written earlier, Stalin had said similar things in the past as well.

On 12 August 1939, the negotiations for a possible French, British, and Soviet alliance began in earnest. On the third day of the talks in Moscow, Voroshilov demanded military access through Polish territory in the west (Vilnius/Wilno) and in the south (Galicia), as well as military access through Romania in case of war. Neither the French nor the British delegation could guarantee this, but they did assume that at least Poland would accept. After all, the head of the British delegation, Admiral Drax, noted that if Poland and Romania were to reject Soviet military aid, they would soon turn into German provinces. Nevertheless, Voroshilov announced that the negotiations should be paused for as long as the Polish government did not accept the Soviet demands.[16]

Voroshilov had ample reason for this. Over the previous months, the Polish government had made it clear that it did not want to let Soviet troops into its territory. The British and the French tried to get the Polish government to change its mind after 14 August, but on the 19th, the Polish government again reiterated its opposition to such a deal.[17] In the eyes of the Poles, letting Soviet troops march through their lands would directly lead to Poland's subjugation by the Soviet Union.[18] These concerns were not unfounded, and later events in the Baltic states would confirm Poland's fears, when the Soviet Union took control over Estonia, Latvia, and Lithuania within months of being granted military access.

Despite Poland not accepting Soviet demands, negotiations continued on 15 August, and the last regular round of negotiations occurred on 22 August. Negotiations were broken off on 25 August, a day after Germany and the Soviet Union had announced that they had just signed a non-aggression treaty.[19]

Chapter 19

The Hitler-Stalin Pact

On 24 August 1939, Europe awoke to a completely changed geopolitical reality – the great antagonists, Nazi Germany and the communist Soviet Union, announced that they had signed a non-aggression pact just the night before. Countless works have been written about the circumstances and motivations that led both sides to sign the Hitler-Stalin Pact. In particular, the motivations of the Soviet side are still hotly debated, and it is not entirely clear how exactly the treaty came about.[1] Recent discoveries in Moscow's archives illuminate things here as well.

Modern scholarship generally assumes that it was Germany that initiated the treaty, which is backed up by the documents from Moscow. Already in late January 1939, after Poland once again declined to join an anti-Russian alliance, the German foreign minister Ribbentrop is said to have exclaimed that "the only way out for us is to come to an agreement with Russia if we do not want to be completely encircled." Following the final Polish refusal on 26 April, Hitler told his general, von Brauchitsch: "Do You know what my next step will be? Better sit down before I tell you: A state visit to Moscow." At that point, Hitler had already lost all hope that Poland would submit without a fight, and on 23 May, he told his generals: "A repeat of Czechia is not likely. There will be a fight. The task is to isolate Poland."[2]

In early May 1939, the German foreign ministry thus produced an analysis of Soviet foreign policy over the preceding months. In it, the authors concluded: "If there has to be a war, a war over foreign policy interests, ignoring all ideological questions, why would it have to be a war with Poland against Germany, which requires an outrageous, unprofitable effort, while a reverse war, [with] Germany against Poland, would be much less risky and could see the return of the old, lost Belarusian and Ukrainian territories."[3]

The German diplomats were now given the task to prepare German-Soviet negotiations. However, this was much easier said than done, for both sides deeply mistrusted each other.[4] The breakthrough came in June and July, after Gustav Hilger, the Second Secretary of the German embassy in Moscow, personally met with Anastas Mikoyan, the People's Commissar for Internal and External Trade, whom he had known for years at that point. Under instructions from Berlin, he met Mikoyan on three separate occasions, on 2, 10 and 17 June, where he tried to convince him that Germany was genuinely interested in friendly relations with the Soviet Union. At the same time, he asked that the diplomat Karl Schnurre be received as a German representative in order to initiate German-Soviet trade negotiations.[5]

The Hilger-Mikoyan talks were a breakthrough and on 20 June 1939, Mikoyan wrote to Stalin about the Germans' willingness to talk.[6] On 21 July 1939, the Soviet government publicly announced the beginning of trade and credit negotiations with Germany. On the Soviet side, they were led by Babarin, the Soviet deputy trade representative in Berlin who had also attended the Hilger-Mikoyan talks and took notes; his German counterpart was Schnurre.[7]

Parallel to the economic talks, secret political negotiations began as well. Aside from Schnurre, only the secretary of state Ernst von Weizsäcker, the father of the later Western German president Richard von Weizsäcker, knew about these negotiations in the German foreign ministry.[8] Despite – or because of – the strict secrecy of these talks, the negotiators soon reached concrete results. On 3 August 1939, the German ambassador to Moscow, Count von der Schulenburg, thus came to an agreement with Molotov that both sides would soon begin to negotiate about spheres of influence. The German proposal arrived five days later: Germany signaled that aside from Lithuania, it did not have much interest in the fate of the Baltic states, as well as Bessarabia and most of the formerly Russian areas of Poland, with the exception of some parts of Polish Ukraine. In return, the Germans asked the Soviets to show little interest in Danzig, the formerly German parts of Poland, as well as Galicia. Naturally, this precluded a Franco-British-Soviet military alliance.[9]

Stalin hesitated, but the Germans pushed for a quick decision, since they planned to attack Poland on 25 August. On 15 August, Berlin sent another offer to Moscow, suggesting a non-aggression treaty as well as another deal on spheres of influence. This time, Stalin accepted the offer and the next few days saw intense negotiations take place in Moscow. With the talks going well, Hitler sent a telegram to Stalin on 20 August, asking for Ribbentrop to be received in Moscow on 22 or 23 August at the latest: "The Foreign Minister has the complete general mandate to draft and sign the non-aggression treaty and the protocol." A few hours after Hitler's message, the draft of the treaty was sent to Berlin.[10]

On the evening of 21 August, Stalin agreed to Hitler's request and on the 23rd, at 13:00 local time, Ribbentrop landed in Moscow. Stalin and Molotov immediately began negotiations with their guest, which continued until after midnight. At around 02:00 on 24 August 1939, Molotov and Ribbentrop signed the treaty, dated the previous day.[11] The pact was to last for 10 years, with a possible extension by another 5 years, and was to come into effect immediately (Art. 7). While the non-aggression treaty was highly significant on its own, the most important part of the treaty was its secret additional protocol, which divided Eastern Europe into German and Soviet spheres of interest, giving each side a green light to annex the still-independent countries lying between them. Regarding Poland, Point 2 of the protocol states:

> In case of a territorial-political reorganization of the territories belonging to the Polish state, the spheres of interest of Germany and the USSR will be approximately delimited by the rivers Narew, Vistula and San. The question of whether the preservation of an independent Polish state seems desirable or not, and how such a state should be delimited, can only be answered conclusively only in the course of further political developments. In any case, both governments shall solve this issue by means of friendly understanding.[12]

As the initial negotiations had occurred under the guise of trade talks, the treaty also contained a comprehensive German-Soviet credit agreement. The Soviet Union was now allowed to buy 200 million Reichsmarks worth of German goods at 5% interest. In return, it was to export great amounts of key resources, mainly wheat and oil, without which Germany stood little chance of defeating the Western Allies.

Even though the agreement on the division of Poland and the rest of Eastern Europe would remain secret for years to come, news of the non-aggression treaty shocked the world and with one blow shattered the Franco-British hopes of getting the Soviet Union on their side. With the failed Allied containment of Germany, war was inevitable. Within a week, Germany attacked Poland. The Second World War had begun.

Chapter 20

Stalin Triumphant

Signing the Hitler-Stalin Pact was the culmination of over a decade of Soviet foreign policy, as Stalin made repeatedly clear. In the summer of 1939, during the negotiations with Germany, Andrei Zhdanov wrote down a series of notes that had most likely been formulated by Stalin himself. One of them read: "To destroy the enemies with their own hands and to be strong at the end of the war."[1] On 7 September 1939, Stalin met with a few of his closest associates – Molotov, Zhdanov, and Dimitrov – and, among other things, explained why he had decided to side with Nazi Germany over the Western Allies. In his diary, Georgi Dimitrov summarized his talk as follows:

> The war is being waged between two groups of capitalist states [...].-
> We have nothing against them beating each other up energetically and weakening each other. It is not bad if Germany were to shake up the situation of the richest capitalist countries (above all England). [...] Hitler himself is, without understanding or intending to, destroying and undermining the capitalist system. [...] We can maneuver and rile up one side against the other, so that they fight each other even more. *The non-aggression treaty helps Germany to a certain extent. The next step is to encourage the other side.*[2]

As shown earlier, Stalin had repeatedly said such things over the past decade. Nothing had changed. At the same meeting with Molotov, Zhdanov, and Dimitrov, Stalin also brought up the failed negotiations with the Western Allies: "We had preferred treaties with the so-called democratic states and had therefore conducted negotiations. But the English and the French wanted to have us as servants and *without paying anything for it.*"[3] This was the reason these talks failed. It was not the Polish refusal to grant military access,[4] but the fact that the Western Allies did not want to "pay" Stalin by giving him the right to conquer vast tracts of land in Eastern Europe.

Stalin was far from the only one in the Kremlin who thought that way. In a secret speech at a session of the Comintern in June 1939, Manuilsky had brought up the ongoing negotiations, gushing over the fact that "they now woo us, like a rich Moscow bride before (laughter in the auditorium), but we know the price of our beauty (applause), and if we marry, then with a receipt [*po raschetu*] (laughter, applause)."[5] Hitler was very generous and freely offered Stalin much of Eastern Europe, intending to take them for himself at a later point anyway, of course. Meanwhile, the Western Allies could only pay with the hope of preserving peace, something Stalin was not interested in at all.

What Stalin wanted was to have a great imperialist war in Europe that plunged the capitalist countries into utter chaos, while the Soviet Union waited on the sidelines until it could overwhelm its weakened foes. As Zhdanov had said on 3 March 1939, months before the negotiations, the Soviet Union wanted to preserve its strength "until we can settle matters with Hitler and Mussolini and at the same time with Chamberlain as well".[6] At the meeting with his closest associates on 7 September 1939, Stalin had outlined the goal: "Under the conditions of the imperialist war lies the question of the destruction of slavery!"[7] By slavery, Stalin was of course referring to the capitalist system, not his system of forced labor in the kolkhozes and concentration camps.

Hitler gave Stalin what he wanted. By striking a deal with Stalin, Hitler managed to isolate Poland, allowing him to overwhelm it before an Allied intervention. Speed was of the essence in this operation, as current scholarship agrees that the Germans bet on the Western Allies not intervening in the war if it was concluded fast enough. The pact with Stalin allowed him to do just that, and also dispelled any fears – or hopes – of a potential Soviet intervention.

On the morning of 1 September 1939, Germany launched its invasion of Poland. Using its overwhelming military superiority to its advantage, Germany handily defeated its Polish enemy before the Western Allies could invade Germany. However, contrary to German hopes, they did in fact declare war on 3 September 1939, crushing Hitler's hopes of a limited war against Poland. While bad for Hitler, this was great news for Stalin. The much-anticipated imperialist war had finally broken out and the Soviet Union was not directly involved.

Stalin waited until 17 September when he ordered his army to invade Eastern Poland. By then, the Polish army had already been more or less destroyed by Germany and the Western Allies had all but given up on Poland, and did not declare war on the Soviet Union. With the outnumbered, weakened, disoriented, and demoralized Polish troops offering only token resistance, the Red Army advanced 250-300 km on a broad front in just 12 days. In the course of this campaign, the Polish army lost around 6,000-7,000 dead and 10,000 wounded, while the Red Army claimed to have only lost 737 dead and 1,862 injured.[8]

On 28 September, Molotov and Ribbentrop then signed a border and friendship treaty, in which the division of Poland was finalized, with the new border running along the rivers San and Bug. The Soviet Union received 201,000 km^2 of land, a bit over half of Poland's pre-war territory. With it, came around 13.2 million people who had to be subdued as soon as possible. Thus the Soviets immediately moved to Sovietize the region with violence and terror.[9]

The quick and easy victory over Poland sent the political and military leadership of the Soviet Union into a triumphant frenzy. Some went too far, however. On 13 November 1939, the commander of the 4th Army, Vasily Chuikov, the later hero of Stalingrad, gave a speech that was also transmitted over radio. In it, he said: "If the party issues the order, then we will do it like in the song: To Warsaw, to Berlin." Horrified, Ponomarenko notified Stalin of this incident, who noted on the margins of the document: "To Comrade Voroshilov. Chuikov is obviously an idiot, if not a hostile element."[10] Luckily for Chuikov, the Red Army purges had ended a year prior. Stalin and his comrades took great care to not unsettle their newfound German friends. After all, they still had a war to fight against the Western Allies.

While the operation seemed like a great success on paper, a closer analysis revealed serious problems. Polish troops only offered sporadic resistance, but when they did fight, the Red Army did not perform well. For example, the mobilization of artillery troops went poorly and in the course of the invasion, they were plagued by organizational chaos, while their tractors broke down and great amounts of artillery shells were simply left lying around as the troops advanced.[11] The performance of the railroad forces was even worse, and Soviet reports complained they had been caught unprepared and therefore failed in the operation.[12]

The performance of frontline troops also gave cause for concern. Coordination between individual units was very poor and the advancing troops regularly panicked when coming under hostile fire.[13] In battles with the enemy, Soviet troops thus suffered high casualties in both personnel and material. In military terms, the invasion was far from a spotless affair.[14]

However, the military and political leadership of the Soviet Union was swept away by euphoria over their easy victory and ignored the warning signs, much to their detriment. In April 1940, Stalin looked back: "The Polish campaign has hurt us terribly, it spoiled us. We wrote entire articles, held speeches that our army was invincible, that there was no army as powerful as ours, that we had everything, that there had been no shortcomings and that there are none. [...] Our army did not realize [...] that the war against Poland had been a military walk in the park and not a war."[15]

Issues regarding Soviet military performance notwithstanding, the de-facto alliance with Germany had paid off immediately. Eastern Poland had been conquered with minimal losses, and more territorial acquisitions – the Baltic states, Bessarabia, and Finland – were more or less guaranteed to happen in the near future. Furthermore, the great imperialist war had begun, with the Soviet Union standing on the sidelines, ostensibly neutral. At the same time, the economic cooperation with Germany gave the Soviet Union access to the modern industrial equipment and machinery it needed to further expand and improve its armaments industry. And finally, after over two decades of futile attempts by Lenin, Trotsky and Stalin, the Soviet Union had established a direct land border with Germany, the heart of industrialized Europe.

In the autumn of 1939, the Kremlin was filled with optimism. Nineteen years after the defeat at Warsaw had prevented the breakthrough into Central Europe, the Polish barrier had been dismantled. Once again, the Soviet Union went on the offensive, carrying the flames of revolution abroad, by force of arms. On 4 June 1941, Zhdanov looked back during a session of the Chief War Council: "The wars with Poland and Finland were no defensive wars. We have taken the path of offense. [...] We have begun to realize Lenin's guiding principle." Zhdanov then went on to state the Leninist principle he had in mind: "If necessary, the victorious proletariat will act against the capitalist states with military means" to spread the revolution.[16]

Chapter 21

The Attack on Finland –
The Moment of Truth

Energized by the victory over Poland, Stalin turned his gaze towards Finland. Already in September 1939, he demanded the Karelian Isthmus from Finland, offering other territories in Soviet Karelia as compensation. Finland rejected that offer, in part because its intelligence services did not believe the Red Army to be ready for war.[1]

Moscow was not pleased with Helsinki's recalcitrance and gradually increased the pressure on Finland. Germany attempted to mediate, but was unsuccessful and Finland continued to refuse Soviet demands. In early November 1939, Stalin thus gave the order to prepare for the invasion of Finland in what was supposed to be another quick and easy war. On 26 November, the Soviet Union staged a border incident, which it quickly used to break off relations with Finland and to cancel the non-aggression treaty from 1931. A few days later, on 30 November 1939, the Red Army began its attack on Finland, without Moscow issuing a formal declaration of war.[2]

Finland was much smaller than the Soviet Union and also had a much smaller population. As a result, it could only field 160,000 men, who were also poorly equipped. At the beginning of the war, the country only had 100 anti-tank guns and 100 aircraft, as well as 36 obsolete artillery pieces per division. However, it had highly motivated soldiers and excellent military leadership. At the same time, the Finns had correctly assessed the Soviets' desire for expansion years earlier and had thus massively fortified the Karelian Isthmus with the formidable Mannerheim Line.[3]

On the other side, the Soviets sought to overwhelm their outnumbered foe with an attack from four different armies. The 7th Army was tasked with breaking through the Mannerheim Line and then taking Helsinki with 200,000 men and 150 tanks. Further north, the 8th Army was to bypass the Mannerheim Line and outflank its defenders with 140,000 men and 400 tanks, while the 9th Army together with the 14th were ordered to open a secondary front just north of the advancing 8th Army. The Finnish army was outnumbered 3:1, for every Finnish artillery piece, there were 5 Soviet ones, while the Red Army fielded 80 times as many tanks as the Finns.[4]

Against all odds, however, the Finns' managed to hold out for several months thanks to their excellent defensive tactics, which stalled the poorly-led Soviets. To make matter worse for the Red Army, its soldiers were not adequately equipped for winter warfare and many thousands fell victim to ice and disease.[5] The leadership in Moscow was anything but pleased with this development. On 21 January 1940, nearly two months into the war, Stalin raised the following toast at a reception: "To the fighters of the Red Army, who were insufficiently prepared, poorly clothed and shoed, who we only now provide with clothes and shoes, who are fighting for their honor – albeit a tarnished honor – and for their share of glory."[6]

Unsurprisingly, troop morale was also low. On 10 May 1940, Mekhlis, chief of the political administration of the Red Army, complained that the troops did not care much about "liberating" the Finnish people at all. Many did not understand the idea, and many of those who did, were not on board with it. Therefore, Mekhlis continued, the propaganda had to be changed. Instead of trying to "liberate" the Finns from capitalist oppression, the attack on Finland was to be presented as a necessary step to guarantee the safety of Leningrad and northwestern Russia. "The entire army understood this slogan", claimed Mekhlis.[7] And not just the army – Mekhlis' propaganda slogan is still being taken seriously in Western historiography.[8]

On 22 December 1939, Gorokhov, the chief of the political administration of the 7th Army, reported on the state of his army, which was leading the primary attack on Finland. Roughly a month into the war, Gorokhov lamented the poor discipline and training of his soldiers; entire units abandoned their positions without orders, and many soldiers tried to leave the frontlines under all kinds of pretenses. There were also serious issues with reconnaissance and the military staff did not work well at all.[9] On 13 and 14 April 1940, shortly after the war had been concluded, a session of the Chief War Council Commission on Military Ideology took place, in which the chief of the administration of the air force, a certain

Smushkievich, stated: "In the first phase of the war, we could observe a lot of cowardice and a lot of panic in the Red Army, including among the air force personnel. […] With democratic exhortations at meetings, it is impossible to ensure discipline."[10]

Zhdanov, who was a member of the War Council of the 8th Army, wrote in his notes: "Fear mongers are to be shot."[11] He was not the only one to think so. On 26 January 1940, the People's Commissar of Defense ordered the creation of blocking detachments behind the frontlines. These blocking detachments were made up of operative troops of the NKVD and had the task of liquidating deserters and rooting out hostile elements in the areas behind the front. In a short amount of time, 27 blocking detachments were established, numbering 100 men each, and soon they prowled the rear areas for deserters who were immediately court martialed and executed without further investigation.[12]

Throughout the winter of 1939/40, Stalin closely followed the progress of the war. He even directly intervened in the fighting, calling frontline commanders and giving them orders. On 7 January 1940, for example, he and Voroshilov called the commander of the 8th Army, Shtern. Shtern complained about a dire need of supplies caused by a breakdown of the transport system. Many trucks simply froze in the cold Finnish winter, while many tractors lacked proper rubber tires and came to a halt on the icy roads. At the same time, there was a lack of spare parts for cars, as a result of which over 1,000 cars had been rendered unusable already. There were also not enough fuel trucks to supply the Red Army's cars, aircraft and tanks.[13] Shtern's report unsettled Stalin and Voroshilov, and on the night of 7/8 January, they called Mekhlis. He also complained about the organizational chaos on the frontlines, and the lack of grenades and grenade launchers. Even worse, many grenades were of poor quality and some exploded at low temperatures. Furthermore, Mekhlis reported that there was a general lack of warm clothing and tents for the soldiers, who suffered terribly because of it. Stalin was taken aback, but reassured him that help was on its way; the supplies would start flowing again soon and the faulty grenades were to be replaced also.[14]

In the first few weeks, Finland had managed to grind the advance of the Red Army to a halt. However, Moscow did not give up. Fresh units were ferried to the frontlines, along with much-needed equipment and supplies. With renewed vigor, the Red Army thus launched a fresh offensive on 1 February 1940. This time, the Soviets met more success and the exhausted Finns were forced to retreat. On 3 March, the Red Army put into motion another great offensive, which put the Finnish army under even more pressure. With the Finns facing insurmountable odds, Helsinki was forced to initiate ceasefire talks with Moscow on 8 March. On 12 March 1940, the war was over. In the peace treaty, Finland lost most of Karelia to the Soviet Union and 450,000 Finns had to abandon their homes, a significant portion of the Finnish population. In addition, 27,000 Finnish soldiers had been killed. Though defeated in battle, Finland managed to retain its independence. Meanwhile, the victorious Red Army lost around 127,000 men, around 20% of whom died from the cold and lack of medical treatment. The war was also extremely costly in terms of materiel: of the 3,000 Soviet aircraft that saw use in the war, up to 40% had been destroyed.[15]

The heavy losses shocked the Kremlin and exposed the weakness of the Red Army to the entire world. Andrey Zhdanov wrote down in his notes: "Had the enemy had a bigger army, he would have smashed [the Red Army] into pieces."[16] This assessment likely came from Stalin himself, for he had stated in a speech on 17 April 1940: "It is good that our army has had this experience not against the German Luftwaffe, but in Finland, with God's help."[17]

This stood in stark contrast to Stalin's position after the initial failures in January 1940, when he played the role of the self-assured, resolute leader who had everything under control. In his diary, Dimitrov noted that during a reception on 21 January 1940, Marshal Kulik delivered such "unpleasant news" on the course of the war that Stalin felt it necessary to tell him: "You are panicking. I shall give you Chelpanov's book about the basics of psychology. The Greek priests were smart men. When they received bad news, they went into the sauna, bathed and washed themselves, before they assessed the events and made decisions."[18]

With the war over, the necessity of warding off panic was gone and the time for self-criticism had come. On 27 March 1940, the Winter War was discussed at the Plenum of the Central Committee. Marshal Voroshilov, who would not be People's Commissar of Defense for much longer, was particularly critical if not entirely honest regarding his own performance: "Not sufficiently prepared for such a war. – A number of commanders are unfit. – The army is poorly equipped. – In the course of the war, the deficiencies were eliminated. – Our losses are at 233,000 men, including 52,000 killed [in reality 127,000] – Finns – 70,000 dead [in reality 27,000] and 200,000 injured."[19] In truth, the entire Finnish army, which had supposedly taken over 270,000 casualties, numbered only 160,000 men.

With these manipulated casualty numbers, Voroshilov tried to save the last shred of his professional reputation, which had been more or less destroyed by the disastrous war. He even went on to state that the Red Army needed to be turned into a truly professional army. This was an admission of total failure. After all, it had been Voroshilov himself as People's Commissar for Defense who had been in charge of the Red Army since 1925, without interruption. He further suggested to expand the Red Army as well as to reduce "fluctuation within the commander corps" – clearly a reference to the devastating Red Army purges –, to improve railway transport and to increase the number of reserves. The Mannerheim Line, which had caused the Red Army so much trouble, was to be studied as well, now that it had fallen into Soviet hands.[20]

The next day, the Central Committee discussed Voroshilov's report. Dimitrov noted that Voroshilov was openly attacked by his comrades, but Stalin came to the defense of his disgraced marshal: "It is not often here that a People's Commissar openly talks about his mistakes." Stalin also put much of the blame on the commanders: "*Of the commanders, 60% are good, 40% are wimps, without character, cowards, etc.* [...] Everything depends on the commanders. A good commander can deal with a weak division, a poor commander can wreck even the best division. [...] If the People's Commissariats are doing better work, we will have the best army in the world."[21]

Between 14 and 17 April 1940, the Central Committee organized another conference to discuss the experiences of the Winter War. On the last day, Stalin gave a speech, in which he focused on the weakness of Soviet military doctrine, which, according to him, had consisted of trying to "bury" the enemy "with caps". In Stalin's mind, the reason for the debacle was that the Red Army was not prepared to wage a modern war with massed use of aircraft, tanks, and artillery. Instead, he criticized that the commanders drew on their experiences from the Civil War, which had not been a truly modern war, seeing very limited use of artillery and virtually no tanks and aircraft. Stalin also lambasted the lack of grenade launchers, which he felt were essential. He then went on to again attack the low quality of the commander corps and called for "the creation of a cultivated, qualified and educated commander corps. We do not have such commanders, if we do, we only have a few." The military staff system did not work properly either, he complained, and the soldiers were of poor quality as well: "Our soldier shows little initiative. He is poorly developed as an individual. He is poorly trained, and when a man is bad at his trade, how can he show initiative, because of that he is poorly disciplined."[22]

The debacle of the Winter War triggered a serious rethinking in Moscow. Once the initial waves of criticism had washed over, the Chief War Council set up a great number of commissions and sub-commissions that dealt with all kinds of questions, from weaponry to the organizational structure of the Red Army and various combat arms, military training, logistics, railway transport, strategy and military doctrine, and the system of military maneuvering. Under the close personal supervision of Stalin himself, these commissions reviewed the Red Army and proposed a series of changes, many of which were later adopted as orders, guidelines and resolutions by the People's Commissariat of Defense, the Chief War Council or the Politburo itself.[23]

Chapter 22

The Ideology of the Revolutionary War

While the Winter War had deeply shaken Stalin and his comrades, the shock was nowhere near as great as to effect a major rethinking of their "offensive policy". The goal was and remained to launch a grand revolutionary war of aggression, and the reforms initiated after the end of the Winter War were geared towards that purpose. Already on 21 April 1940, Stalin had this to say regarding the training of commanders: "We shall educate our commanders in the spirit of active defense, which also includes the attack. This idea needs to be popularized under the slogan of security, of defending our homeland, our borders."[1] Defense was a mere pretext for aggression, like against Finland a few months prior.

Also telling is the work of the commission dealing with the training of commanders and military doctrine. On 10 May 1940, Lev Mekhlis gave a speech in front of the commission in which he formulated the existing and future military doctrine of the Red Army:

The Red Army is, like any other army, an instrument of war. […] Our war with the capitalist world will be a just, progressive war. The Red Army will operate actively, seek the destruction and annihilation of the enemy, shift the military action onto enemy territory. Therefore, we have to educate our entire army and our entire country in such a spirit that every war that is being waged by the army of socialism, will be a progressive war, the most just of all wars ever to have been waged. Regarding this, Lenin said unequivocally: 'That would be a war for socialism, for the liberation of other peoples from the bourgeoisie. Engels was completely right when he openly admitted the possibility of a defensive war of already *victorious* socialism in the letter to Kautsky on 12 December 1882. He had in mind the defense of the victorious proletariat against the bourgeoisie of other countries.' [...] This speech is about the active measures taken by the victorious proletariat and the working peoples of the capitalist countries against the bourgeoisie, about such active measures *in which the initiative for this just war is taken by our state and its workers' and peasants' Red Army*. In this spirit we have to educate our Red Army and the entire proletariat, so that they know that each of our wars, wherever it is being waged, is a progressive and just war.[2]

In his speech, Mekhlis had made more than clear that the entire Soviet Union – army, state and populace alike – was to remain absolutely devoted to the ideology of the revolutionary war. With all of its traditional enemies to the west gone, and interest in the Far East and the south being relatively low, there could only be one target of that revolutionary war: Germany. It is notable that on 10 May, the day Mekhlis held his speech, Germany launched its long-awaited invasion of France and the Low Countries. While the Wehrmacht would go on to achieve a complete victory over its enemies on the continent within a few weeks, Moscow – and indeed most observers – believed that this war would surely devolve into a costly war of attrition, which would greatly weaken the Wehrmacht and Germany as a whole.

The ideology of the just and progressive revolutionary war continued to be the ideological foundation of the ever-ambitious Soviet armament program, which Stalin further intensified with the help of modern German machinery and equipment. As with his previous efforts, Stalin primarily relied on weaponry that was key to leading a modern offensive war, namely tanks, aircraft, and artillery.

Until then, the Soviets had habitually underestimated the importance of artillery. Immediately after the conclusion of the Winter War, on 28 March 1940, Stalin elaborated at a plenum of the Central Committee: "The artillery plays the decisive role, the tanks clear the way for the riflemen."[3] On 17 April, he talked in detail about the role of individual combat arms in a modern offensive war, in which he specifically highlighted the role of artillery in breaking through heavily fortified defensive lines. He stated: "First, comes the artillery. Second, the air force, massed air force, not hundreds but thousands of aircraft. Whoever wants to wage a modern war, whoever wants to prevail in a modern war, cannot say that he wants to save on bombs. This is nonsense, comrades, one has to throw more bombs onto the enemy, to stun him, to turn his cities into rubble, that is how we win."[4]

Stalin continued: "Third, tanks, also of decisive importance, vital are massive numbers of tanks, not hundreds, but thousands. […] Third, grenade launchers, no modern war without grenade launchers, masses of grenade launchers. […] Furthermore, automatic small arms. […] Infantry, equipped with semi-automatic rifles and machine pistols – essential."[5] A year later, on 5 May 1941, Stalin once again highlighted the importance of offensive combat arms:

> The most important thing is a well-equipped infantry. – But the main role is played by the artillery (guns, tanks). – To fulfill this role, the artillery needs the air force. – The air force does not decide the outcome of the battle on its own, but in conjunction with infantry and artillery, it plays a particularly important role. – […] The cavalry has not lost its importance in modern warfare. - It is especially important in pursuing the enemy who has been driven out of his positions and to not give him the opportunity to entrench himself in new positions.[6]

The military reforms Stalin initiated following the Winter War were the greatest changes to the Red Army since the beginning of the 1930s, when Tukhachevsky first tried his hand at turning the Red Army into a modern attacking force. Naturally, this included personal consequences for the people who had overseen the disaster of the Winter War. Despite being one of Stalin's closest and most loyal associates, Marshal Voroshilov, who had been the Soviet Union's People's Commissar for Military and Navy Affairs since 1925 (People's Commissar for Defense since 1934), had to leave his post on 8 May 1940. His replacement was Marshal Semyon Timoshenko. Other personnel changes followed down the line, in the Chief War Council and the Military Districts, and on 15 August, General Kirill Meretskov replaced Shaposhnikov as the Chief of the General Staff.[7]

Unlike after previous failures, however, Stalin shied away from arrests, show trials, and executions. Instead, officers that had been imprisoned since

1937/38 were released and allowed to rejoin the Red Army. In April 1940 alone, 4,000 higher-ranking commanders were pardoned and re-entered military service that way.[8] At that point, Stalin realized that the previous purges had been rather counterproductive, having led to the dismissal, arrest and execution of many thousands of experienced commanders, while also undermining the authority of the remaining commanders.[9] At the session of the commission of the Chief War Council on 13 April 1940, the chief of the administration of the armored units, Dmitri Pavlov summed up the problem with the purges: "It turned out that there had been so many peoples' enemies in our ranks that I doubt that all of them had been enemies. And here I have to say that the operation of the years 1937/38, before Comrade Beria came, hit us so hard that we, in my opinion, only narrowly avoided complete disaster at the hands of an enemy like Finland."[10]

Stalin apparently took this to heart and aside from refraining from another wave of purges, he also began to restore the authority of the commanders he himself had seriously damaged a few years ago. On 7 May 1940, he reintroduced generals' ranks into the Soviet armed forces and by 4 June, the Soviet Union had 982 generals and 74 admirals. A few months later, non-commissioned officer ranks were reintroduced as well.[11] Both had been abolished as a relic of the old Tsarist order after the Bolshevik Revolution. Timoshenko, the new People's Commissar for Defense, also quickly moved to raise the level of discipline in the Red Army, issuing several orders aimed at this.[12] On 12 August 1940, the Presidium of the Supreme Soviet issued a decree strengthening the unified command of the Red Army and the Red Fleet. This was done by improving the position of the commanders while limiting the authority of the political commissars. The commissars had been given wide-ranging power on 15 August 1937, at the beginning of the Red Army purges; they even had the authority to override orders the commanders had already given. Many commissars made frequent use of their newfound authority, which threw the military chain of command into chaos. After this change, the political commissars were now relegated once again to dealing with propaganda. Unified command had thus been restored.[13]

Chapter 23

Hitler's Victory in the West – Stalin's Dilemma

While Stalin was busy dealing with the fallout of the worst Soviet military debacle since the Battle of Warsaw in 1920, Hitler waged war on the Western Allies. Following the German attack on their ally, Poland, Great Britain and France declared war on Germany, but refused to go on the offensive, waiting for the expected German attack on their side of the border, protected by the formidable Maginot Line. At the same time, the Germans refused to attack the Western Allies before they were ready for their own grand offensive. With both sides reluctant to attack, the so-called Phony War unfolded on the Western front, lasting from September 1939 until the German campaign in May 1940.

A month before it began, however, on 9 April 1940, Germany launched a surprise attack on Denmark and Norway to forestall the landing of an Allied expeditionary corps. Attacking with nine divisions, and overwhelming naval and aerial support, the Wehrmacht almost immediately received the surrender of the Danish government within hours. Norway, meanwhile, fought back, but was soon crushed as well. Only in the north of the country did Norwegian and Allied troops manage to stop the German advance for a while. Following the evacuation of Allied forces on 8 June, the Norwegian army surrendered two days later.[1]

Despite the ongoing fighting in northern Norway, Germany launched its long-awaited offensive against France and the neutral Low Countries on 10 May 1940. On paper, this was an unequal fight. In terms of manpower, the Germans' 135 divisions with nearly 3 million men were slightly outnumbered by the 151 Allied divisions with around 3.5 million men. In terms of materiel, the Allied advantage was much larger. Whereas Germany fielded 7,378 artillery pieces, the Allies had 13,947. Likewise, the Allies also had considerably more tanks – 4,204 against the Germans' 2,439, and aircraft – 4,469 against 3,578.[2]

Germany attacked France via the neutral Low Countries, which were quickly overrun. While this move had been anticipated by the Allies, a surprise attack through the Ardennes Forest threw the Allied forces into confusion, and after just 10 days, Germany had reached the English Channel. The British Expeditionary Force was cut off and barely managed to escape at Dunkirk, leaving behind virtually all of its equipment, including 2,472 artillery pieces and 63,897 vehicles. Over the coming weeks, France failed to put a stop to the German advance, and on 10 June, Italy declared war and attacked southern France. Paris was declared an open city and was taken by Germany on 14 June. On 20 June, the French government asked for a ceasefire, which was signed two days later. In the words of the German historian Rolf Müller: "What had remained out of reach for four years in the First World War, Hitler's Wehrmacht had achieved in four weeks. France, the strongest military power on the continent in the 1920s and 1930s, had been defeated."[3]

Over the decades, much has been written about this outright shocking victory. What is often forgotten, however, is that the German triumph was only possible thanks to Soviet support. Ostensibly neutral, the Soviet Union helped engineer the entire situation by entering a de-facto alliance with Hitler, which allowed him to focus entirely on the West. Furthermore, Stalin had provided Hitler with the additional petroleum and grain shipments he desperately needed for that campaign, and which were greenlit by Stalin precisely for that purpose. Consequently, in May 1940, Germany received 61,000 tons of oil and 76,000 tons of grain from the Soviet Union. In June 1940, Germany was sent another 102,000 tons of oil and 167,000 tons of grain.[4]

Even though Stalin and his comrades enabled Hitler's victory over France, they were still surprised by the swiftness of the victory. On 16 May 1940, Köstring, the German military attaché in Moscow, wrote to Colonel Kurt von Tippeiskirch, the chief quartermaster of the general staff of the German army, that despite all "congratulations, praise" he had noticed "a noticeable apprehension". The victorious German advance had left the Soviets speechless, he continued.[5]

Ever-opportunistic, Stalin immediately moved to capitalize on the German invasion of France. As the world was preoccupied with events in the West, Stalin demanded the annexation of the Baltic states and parts of Romania. With the respective governments unable to face off against the Red Army, these regions fell into Soviet hands without a fight and were quickly – and violently – Sovietized. Germany did not oppose Soviet expansion, for it had agreed for them to be included in the Soviet sphere of influence in the Hitler-Stalin Pact, just a few months earlier, in August 1939. Nevertheless, Hitler was outraged at Stalin's latest round of expansion, especially against Romania, where Stalin had taken areas such as Northern Bukovina, which had not been mentioned in the Hitler-Stalin Pact.[6]

Romania played quite an important role in German strategic considerations, largely because of its vast oil reserves. On 27 May 1940, Germany and Romania concluded an oil treaty. Romania's oil exports to Great Britain, accounting for nearly 40% of its oil production, ceased immediately. Instead, Romania now provided Germany with oil, around 200,000 to 300,000 tons per month, and so became the main source of oil for the German war machine.[7]

Chapter 24

Preparing for the Attack on Germany

Instead of preparing for defense and forging an alliance against Germany, Stalin focused on further conquests and readied himself to attack his German ally. The annexations of summer 1940 had only awakened his appetite for easy conquests and during that summer, the Soviet Union once again made territorial claims against Romania and Finland, even going so far as to prepare for another war against Finland in order to finally Sovietize the entire country.[1] Stalin also set his sights on Turkey and the Balkans.

On 12 November 1940, Molotov travelled to Berlin to find out what other countries could be acquired with Germany's blessing. Stalin was interested in the following: Finland, Romania, Bulgaria, Hungary, Greece, Yugoslavia, Turkey, and Iran. This time, however, the two parties could not come to an agreement, and Molotov left Berlin on 14 November without having achieved anything other than strengthening Hitler's resolve to attack the Soviet Union as soon as possible.[2]

Back in Moscow, Stalin also realized that further compromises would not happen and any further expansion into Europe would be met with German resistance. As a result, concrete measures needed to be taken in order to prepare explicitly for the attack on Germany. As early as the summer of 1940, Stalin had the Comintern's mode of action modified. Communists in the German-occupied countries were instructed to remain neutral, i.e. to support neither the German occupiers nor their own governments in exile or Britain. Until then, the communists in Western countries had been obeying their orders to act against their own governments and support Germany.[3] It went so far that even Jewish communists in the ghettos of German-occupied Poland advocated cooperation with the German occupiers, because that was the directive they had received from Moscow.[4] From the summer of 1940, however, the Comintern headquarters gave their instructions an increasingly strident, anti-German edge, certainly with Stalin's approval.[5] The aim was to undermine the numerous German occupation authorities.

On 25 November 1940, Dimitrov discussed the current foreign policy goals of the Soviet Union with Molotov. Molotov was complaining about the failure of the talks in Berlin and about German activities in Turkey and the Balkans. In response, Dimitrov interjected: "We are striving to break up the German occupation forces in various countries, and we intend to even escalate these activities without making a big fuss about it. Will this not hinder Soviet policy?" To this Molotov replied, "Of course it must be done. We would not be communists if we did not follow this course. But it must be done silently."[6]

After the conversation with Molotov, Dimitrov went to Comintern headquarters and was immediately summoned to see Stalin, where he again met Molotov and also Vladimir Dekanozov, the Soviet ambassador in Berlin. In the conversation, Stalin described his plans regarding Bulgaria and Turkey. He wanted to impose a mutual assistance pact on Bulgaria and urge Turkey to assent to a military base at the Turkish Straits, which would give the Soviet Union unfettered access to the Mediterranean. At the same time, Stalin also cautioned: "Our relations with the Germans are outwardly polite, but there is serious friction between us."[7]

In August 1940, it was decided to set up a one-year Comintern school in Moscow leading party functionaries of various "communist brother parties" currently staying in the Soviet Union and who were to be deployed in their countries of origin in the future.[8] The preparations dragged on for months, and it was not until the spring of 1941 that things got moving. On 5 February 1941, Dimitrov noted in his diary: "Discussed school matters. [...] Agreement on setting up three training institutions: 1. a general party school (65 participants), 2. a Spanish school (60 participants plus 40 older students for a 6-month special course, and 3. a German-Austrian school (35 participants). For the other nationalities (Bulgarians, Poles, Rumanians, etc.) individual training is to be organized."[9]

On 27 February, Dimitrov again discussed "school matters" with Zhdanov, Andreyev, and Malenkov. Dimitrov then noted: "The aim is to train primarily the cadres from the Slavic countries (Bulgaria, Yugoslavia, Poland, Czechoslovakia). - The main points of the training program are the study of one's own country, one's own party, its problems and the question of how to defeat the enemy in one's own country." Zhdanov referred to the discussion of the new Comintern mode of operation: "Proletarian internationalism should be combined with the healthy national feeling of the respective people."[10] In short, Moscow sought to exploit the resistance against the German occupations in their future attack.

On 20 April 1941, Stalin reaffirmed this line in a conversation with Dimitrov and his other close confidants: "They [the communist parties] must become national communist parties with different names – workers' party, Marxist party, etc. The name is not important. What is important is that they gain a foothold among their people and concentrate on their own specific tasks. [...] Now, national tasks for each country are coming to the fore."[11]

What also attested to Stalin's plan to attack Germany in the near future was the reorientation of his policy towards Poland. On 29 June 1940, Stalin received Wanda Wasilewska, a Soviet writer and communist of Polish origin, in his Kremlin office; the conversation lasted 45 minutes. Stalin held Wasilewska in high esteem and often discussed Polish affairs with her. Wasilewska claimed after the war that in the conversation of 29 June 1940, Stalin spoke about the end of German-Soviet cooperation and the imminent liberation of Warsaw. In July 1940, Kazimierz Bartel, a Polish professor from Lviv and former Polish prime minister, was also summoned for talks to Moscow. Bartel was likely to become the head of a future Polish government.[12] Yet, after German troops entered Lviv, Bartel was murdered by an SS task force.

On 30 July 1940, Georgi Dimitrov addressed Malenkov on the matter of the Polish Communist Party (KPP), which had been disbanded in 1938 and its members either killed or imprisoned in Soviet camps and prisons. Dimitrov wrote that among the imprisoned there were many honest comrades loyal to the revolutionary movement. They were the cadre reserve for future work.[13] The summer of 1940 also saw a change in the course of cultural policy in the occupied eastern Polish territories. Polish culture and language in the former eastern Polish territories were no longer subject to eradication but were instead Sovietized, similar to what was happening with the Belarusian and Ukrainian cultures and languages.[14]

At the end of 1940, after Molotov's visit to Berlin, a reception for mid-level Polish communists was held, the host being Panteleimon Ponomarenko, the head of the Communist Party in Belarus. According to a report by Jakub Berman, a Polish Communist of Jewish origin, who was present at the reception, Ponomarenko declared to the assembled Communists: "You still have great tasks ahead of you, the war can pass into the next phase, the question of Poland will be on the agenda, and new prospects will open up for the Polish communists." "We haven't heard such a tone since the dissolution of the party," commented Berman.[15]

No later than autumn 1940, before Molotov's journey to Berlin, Stalin considered creating Polish and Czech formations in Soviet territory, consisting of Polish and Czech prisoners of war, to fight against Germany in the future German-Soviet war. He instructed Beria to handle this issue. On 2 November 1940, Beria reported to Stalin on the results achieved so far. There were still 18,297 Polish prisoners of war in the NKVD camps on 1 November 1940, including two generals, 39 colonels and lieutenant colonels, 222 majors and captains, 601 lieutenants and first lieutenants, 4,022 non-commissioned officers, and 13,321 soldiers of lower ranks. In addition, there were 3,303 military men who had been interned in Lithuania and Latvia and later handed over to the Soviets, as well as 22 officers who had been arrested in the Soviet-occupied eastern Polish territories as members of the Polish resistance. Most of them came from the territories that were under German occupation.[16]

It should be noted here that most of the Polish officers who had fallen into Soviet captivity in the autumn of 1939 were shot on Stalin's orders in April and May 1940. In total, the Soviet communists murdered 14,587 Polish professional and reserve officers and police at that time. In addition, there were 7,285 people who had been arrested after the campaign against Poland who were also shot. These were resistance fighters and officers who had not fallen into Soviet captivity in September 1939, as well as landowners, factory owners, state officials, and other "hostile elements". Ordinary soldiers, on the other hand, were in most cases released immediately.[17]

On Stalin's orders, the NKVD reviewed personnel and investigation files of the Polish officers still alive in prison, interviewed some of them, and selected 26 senior Polish officers. Among them were three generals, one colonel, eight lieutenant colonels, six majors and captains, as well as six lieutenants and first lieutenants. They all declared to the NKVD staff that they absolutely wanted to fight alongside the Soviet Union against Germany. They were also firmly convinced that there would be a German-Soviet war. Some of them had also asserted that only the USSR could solve the Polish question.[18]

In addition, groups NKVD operative staff were sent to the camps where Polish soldiers and officers were imprisoned in order to determine the atmosphere among the detainees. It was found that the vast majority of them could be used for the "organization of Polish troops". With this in mind, Beria proposed that a Polish division be set up first, with utmost secrecy. For the selection of cadres, the staff and location of the future division were to be organized in one of the sovkhozes in the southeast USSR. This division was to be subordinated to the General Staff of the Red Army, and the special divisions of the NKVD were to ensure "internal discipline".

Czech prisoners of war, on the other hand, were far less numerous in Soviet camps, totaling 507 Czechs and 76 Slovaks. Among them were 47 officers, 176 non-commissioned officers and 354 ordinary soldiers. Thirteen officers declared themselves ready to fight the Germans, on the condition, however, that they would still be considered Czech prisoners of war, regarding Beneš, the president of the Czechoslovak government-in-exile in London, as their supreme commander. If necessary though, they were prepared to accept Colonel Ludvík Svoboda as their superior. Since Svoboda remained outside Soviet borders, Beria stated in his report, "he shall be summoned by us from abroad."[19]

Among the senior Polish officers, only five were ultimately selected and placed in a mansion in Malakhovka near Moscow. There, the NKVD subjected them to intensive ideological "conditioning" up to the point of acceptance of Poland as a future Soviet republic. Colonel Zygmunt Berling, one of the five officers, was proposed to command a Polish armored division in the future. However, the formation of the Polish division dragged on for months. It was not until 4 June 1941, that the Politburo confirmed the proposal of the People's Commissar for Defense to transform the 238th Infantry Division into a Polish-speaking one. The

238th Division, which was stationed in the Central Asian Military District, was to be staffed with Poles and Polish-speaking Red Army soldiers. The strength of the division was 10,298 men.[20] However, the German invasion on 22 June prevented the implementation of this decision.

The fact that in the autumn of 1940 Stalin was in the process of creating Polish and Czech formations to fight alongside the Red Army against Germany, can only be interpreted as further evidence that Stalin was preparing for an attack on Germany. Yet, the Red Army was still far from ready, a fact that, much to his horror and anger, Stalin had to realize time and time again.

On 7 November 1940, a reception was held in the Kremlin after a military parade in Red Square, to which Stalin had invited his closest associates. At the end, when everyone was about to leave, an angry, irritated Stalin took the floor. He gave a lengthy speech in which he talked himself into a rage, insulting and threatening his confidants:

History has spoiled us. We have achieved numerous successes relatively easily. This has created complacency among many, a dangerous complacency. [...] The lessons of the war with Finland, the lessons of the war in Europe have not been learned. [...] If our armed forces, transportation, etc., are not as strong as those of our opponents (and these are all capitalist states, even those who pretend to be our friends!), they will eat us up. [...] We are currently restructuring the infantry, the cavalry has always been good, now you have to seriously look at the air force and air defense. This is what I am now concerned about on a daily basis. I receive constructors and other specialists. But I am the only one who deals with all these questions. None of you is even thinking about it. I stand alone... If I can learn, read, devote every day; why can't you do that? You don't like to learn, you live complacently. You are squandering Lenin's legacy with both hands.[21]

Mikhail Kalinin, Politburo member and Chairman of the Presidium of the Supreme Soviet, made the mistake of trying to excuse himself and his comrades by saying that there was "somehow a lack of time". This remark infuriated Stalin: "No, that is not the point! People want a carefree life, do not want to learn and gain new skills. You listen to me, but everything remains the same. But I will show you when I explode. You already know I can do that. I'm going to beat these fat paunches so hard it will be heard from afar."[22]

This time no one dared to say a word. Dimitrov noted: "(Everyone) stood and listened in silence, obviously not expecting such a 'sermon' from J[oseph] V[issarionovich] [Stalin]. Tears came to Voroshilov's eyes. – During his speech J.V. had addressed Kaganovich and Beria in particular). – I have never seen and heard J.V. as he was that evening – a memorable evening."[23] Voroshilov, who until a few months earlier had been in charge of national defense, likely cried because he feared – not without reason – that his dear friend Stalin would have him tortured and murdered.

Stalin's outburst of rage can only be understood in the context of the state of Soviet war preparations, which despite all the reforms, reorganizations, and other measures taken after the war against Finland, remained abysmal. As already pointed out, Soviet fighter planes and tanks were obsolete, and the rest of the military was plagued by serious issues as well. In late 1940 and early 1941, Stalin and his comrades made a series of decisions to organize and begin mass production of new types of tanks and aircraft to provide the Red Army with modern equipment. However, the Germans attacked before these changes had been fully implemented.

The situation was no different in other areas. In September 1940, the People's Commissariat for State Control was established under the leadership of Lev Mekhlis in place of the dissolved Commission of Soviet Control of the Council of People's Commissars and the Main Military Control. The State Control investigated all economic and military spheres, checked the implementation of plans, investigated problems and shortfalls and reported them to the party and state leadership. State Control reports thus provide unvarnished insights into the condition of the entire Soviet economy, including the Red Army and the defense industry.

Mekhlis went to work immediately and on 31 January 1941, he reported to Stalin and Molotov on the inspection results in seven infantry divisions and one air force division base. The report speaks of the disastrous supply of uniforms and shoes for the soldiers. Overall, the storage, issuance, and inventory of uniforms, footwear, linen, food, and military equipment was in an extremely neglected state, Mekhlis noted in the report.[24] For example, soldiers of the 43rd and 123rd Infantry Divisions of the Leningrad

Military District were sometimes left without uniforms and footwear, and others were issued the wrong sizes. It happened that soldiers could not stand guard because they were barefoot.[25]

On 12 February 1941, Marshal Timoshenko, the People's Commissar for Defense, commented on Mekhlis's report of 31 January 1941, and had to admit: "The military economy of the Red Army is even now in an extremely difficult situation."[26] In the spring of 1941, officials of the State Control reviewed the condition of naval artillery. The results were devastating: new artillery systems had not been adopted, artillery ammunition was rusting and improperly stored in the open. Accidents and shortages had either been reported too late or not at all.[27]

Numerous other State Control reports from late 1940 and the first half of 1941 indicated the catastrophic conditions of the army's supply of uniforms, food, and fuel in the transportation sector, and elsewhere. These reports all ended up on both Stalin's and Molotov's desks.[28]

In spite of such news, the Soviet leader had evidently recovered from his outburst of November 1940. In the spring of 1941, production of new types of tanks and aircraft began, and the army and armaments was steadily growing, regardless of the numerous setbacks and grievances. Foreign policy also seemed to be developing according to Stalin's wishes. He rejoiced at the easy and large territorial gains of the previous year and a half, with the exception of the Finnish case. At the same time, the Anglo-German war dragged on with no end in sight, and blockaded Germany was in desperate need of Soviet raw materials. Against this background, Stalin thought he still had enough time in the spring of 1941 to calmly build up the largest invasion army in world history.

On 4 February 1941, a reception was held in the Kremlin to celebrate Voroshilov's 60th birthday. Present were Politburo members, senior military officers, and People's Commissars including Stalin and Dimitrov. The latter noted in his diary:

Two or three times Stalin made a toast. - To the Red Army and the Fleet. - 'With our foreign policy we have managed to enjoy and also benefit from the achievements of peace (we buy low and sell high!). [...] We have been lucky. "God" has helped us. There have been many easy successes, so today there is a danger of being taken in by deception. But you must not become arrogant, you must persistently work and learn. – We have already raised an army of 4 million, prepared for any possibility.'[29]

On 22 April 1941, during another reception, Stalin gave a toast to Lenin and proclaimed: "Lenin has made us who we are, toughened us, organized, armed, and showed us the goal [i.e., the world revolution]. He created the party of the Bolsheviks, which fears no hardships, knows no fear in struggle."[30]

A day later, on 23 April, Dimitrov had a meeting with Comintern on the international situation, in which he explained, among other things: "a) The events in the Balkans do not precipitate the end of the war, but rather prolong and escalate it. A world war is a protracted war. b) The flame of war is approaching more and more the frontiers of the Soviet Union, which must prepare itself as best it can for all possible 'surprises'. c) The Soviet Union is getting more and more hands free with regard to the West [i.e., Germany]."[31] Certainly, Dimitrov was presenting Stalin's thoughts and guidelines here.

Stalin's Secret Speech of 5 May 1941: "Now the Time has Come to Move from Defense to Attack."

On 5 May the ceremonial meeting of graduates from the Military Academy took place in the Kremlin, followed by a reception.[32] At this event, Stalin gave a speech, which would become his last before the German invasion. During the reception that followed, he took the floor one more time. Stalin spoke freely and asked the audience not to take notes. Nevertheless, a short transcript of his speech as well as of the speeches during the reception (nine and three pages, respectively) appeared. Also, Georgi Dimitrov summarized Stalin's speech in his diary.[33]

Dimitrov's concise summary agrees with the aforementioned transcript, in places almost word for word. Furthermore, after 5 May, Moscow proceeded to actually implement the directives that Stalin had formulated during the reception. Moreover, several Soviet officers who had been taken captive by the Germans after 22 June 1941, confirmed independently of each other that such a speech by Stalin had indeed taken place.[34] There exist, therefore, no sources that could substantiate any reason to doubt the authenticity of the transcript,[35] which is persuasive enough to be reproduced here in greater detail.

At the beginning of his speech, Stalin discussed the condition of the Red Army, which had undergone a fundamental transformation in the past three to four years. Before that, the Red Army had consisted mainly of infantry equipped with simple rifles, backed up with light and heavy machine guns, howitzers, and cannons. Aircraft had a maximum speed of 400-450 km/h and tanks were only protected with thin armor. "Now," Stalin said, "we have rebuilt our army, equipped it with modern war technology." Previously, there would have been 120 divisions (18-20,000 men each); now, he said, there are 300 divisions (15,000 men each), one-third of them mechanized. Of the 100 mechanized divisions, two-thirds were armored and one-third motorized. This year, he continued, the Red Army will have 500,000 tractors and trucks. "Our tanks" now have armor three to four times stronger than before, he said. "We have tanks of the first squadron that will tear up the front. There are second and third squadron tanks – these are tanks to support infantry. Their firepower has also been increased."[36]

Furthermore, Stalin emphasized the importance of modern artillery, which would be used primarily in the fight against fortifications and enemy tanks. "We have a sufficient number of and produce large quantities of aircraft with a maximum speed of 600 to 650 km/h." In reality, mass production of new types of aircraft was only just beginning. Stalin also pointed out that the Red Army now fielded motorcycle troops, which had not existed before; they were the motorized cavalry. At the same time, however, Stalin complained that the military schools were lagging behind the development of the army. This, he said, was caused by the fact that the military schools trained future officers, such as aviators, using old military equipment.[37]

Stalin then lectured on the causes of the French defeat and Germany's victory in the West. After its defeat in the First World War, Germany had looked for new ways and learned from the past, whereas the French rested on their laurels. At the same time, Stalin emphasized that there were no invincible armies, nor was the German army invincible. "A large part of the German army is now losing the momentum it had at the beginning of the war. Moreover, conceit, smugness and arrogance are spreading in the German army. Military thinking is not progressing, war technology is lagging, not only behind ours, as concerns the air force, America is about to overtake Germany."[38]

Stalin also attributed the Wehrmacht's victories to the fact that Germany had started the war under the slogan of "Liberation from Versailles":

And it could count on the approval of those nations who had been suffering under the Treaty of Versailles. But now Germany continues the war under the banner of *subjugation, oppression of other nations*, under the banner of *hegemony*. This is a great drawback for the German army. It can no longer enjoy the previous approval of a number of countries and peoples, but on the contrary, it has turned many of the countries it occupies against itself. An army which has to fight on hostile ground and has hostile territories and masses in its rear is exposed to serious dangers.[39]

After the celebration, the reception for the top party, state, and military leadership took place. Stalin gave a few toasts. "He was clearly in a good mood," Dimitrov noted. According to the transcript, Stalin took the floor three times. The third speech is reproduced here in full:

Third speech by Comrade Stalin during the reception. A Major General of the armored troops makes a toast to Stalin's peaceful foreign policy. *Comrade Stalin:* 'Allow me to make a correction. Peaceful policy secured peace for our country. Peaceful policy is a good thing. We have so far, until this time, followed the line of defense – until now, until we have re-equipped our army, until we have provided the army with modern means of war. But now that we have reconstructed our army, supplied it sufficiently with technology for modern combat, as we have become strong – *now we must move from defense to attack*. In the defense of our country, we are obliged to take the offensive. From defense we must move towards the war policy of offensive operations. We must remodel our education, our propaganda, agitation, our press in the spirit of attack. The Red Army is a modern army and a modern army is an offensive army.'[40]

Dimitrov reproduced Stalin's speech much more succinctly: "*Our policy of peace and security is at the same time a policy of preparation for war. There is no defense without attack. One must educate the army in the spirit of attack. One must prepare for war.*"[41]

These remarks can only be interpreted one way: Stalin was planning to attack Germany in the near future. It should be emphasized that Stalin made these remarks spontaneously, feeling challenged by the Major General's toast to correct talk of "peaceful foreign policy". This exchange prompted Stalin to drop the pacifist propaganda in the army; after 5 May, the propaganda apparatus of the Red Army began to work on new propaganda guidelines and materials based on Stalin's speech of 5 May. By the beginning of June 1941, two drafts of new directives for political work in the ranks of the Red Army had been prepared.[42]

On 4 June 1941, the Chief War Council convened to discuss the new guidelines for "party-political work in the ranks of the Red Army". Among the participants were Marshal Timoshenko, People's Commissar for Defense, and Budyonny, as well as Zhdanov and Malenkov, a Politburo member and close confidant of Stalin's.[43] During the briefing, Zhdanov stated, among other things:

1.) Why do we need a new type of propaganda? It is war. It is necessary to explain why France perished and why Germany triumphed. The legend about the invincibility of the German army must be exposed. 2.) The power of the USSR has increased. [...] We have become stronger, we can face more offensive tasks. The wars against Poland and Finland were not defensive wars. We have already embarked on the path of offensive policy. 3.) Between peace and war there is one step. And that is why our propaganda must not be peaceful. The propaganda should have a corresponding pace. Right now we cannot plan political education for two years in advance and have a political textbook prepared from which these two years would be taught. The army should be ready at any time. Hence the task of reorganizing propaganda in such a way that it meets the new goals. [...] This is not a transition from one policy to another. It was already Lenin who, during World War I, stated in the essay 'On the slogan of the United States of Europe', if it is necessary, the victorious proletariat will also fight against the capitalist states by means of war. We have also earlier applied the policy of the offensive. This policy was established by Lenin. We're only changing the slogan now. We have taken the first steps to make Lenin's guiding principle come true.[44]

Malenkov confirmed what Zhdanov had said by adding: "Change in the propaganda and not in the policy", and at the same time criticized the drafts presented: "The document should contain factual answers to all questions; explain all queries in order to provide concrete help for the propaganda, while all the explanation that you provide in the draft directive is limited to quoting Lenin that we will grab all capitalism by the collar. The document is written in a primitive way, as if we were to wage the war tomorrow." Zhdanov agreed with Malenkov: "But then it becomes incomprehensible why we are maneuvering with diplomacy if we are going to wage war tomorrow," and reiterated the "change in propaganda and not in the policy."[45]

This and the other points show that the Soviet Union had been preparing for an ideologically motivated war of aggression for years. Zhdanov's statement in the meeting is clear here: "We have also earlier applied the policy of the offensive. This policy was established by Lenin. We're only changing the slogan now. We have taken the first steps to make Lenin's guiding principle come true," which stood for spreading the "proletarian revolution" by force of arms.

Stalin had long since ceased to believe that the communist parties in the West would be able to stage a successful communist revolution. The Bolsheviks had seen the greatest chances for this in Germany, and yet they were repeatedly disappointed. On 7 November 1939, in a small circle of his confidants (Kaganovich, Molotov, Mikoyan, Budyonny, Kulik, Dimitrov), Stalin stated,

> *That the slogan of the transformation of an imperialist war into a civil war (in the first imperialist war) applied only to Russia, where the workers were united with the peasants and could, under the conditions of Tsarism, rise against the bourgeoisie.* For the European states, this slogan was unsuitable, since the workers there had enjoyed certain democratic reforms thanks to the bourgeoisie and clung to them, they were not ready for a civil war (revolution) against the bourgeoisie.

(The European workers had to be approached differently). One had to take into account this specificity of the European worker and pose the question in a different way, using some different slogans with him.[46]

Although these considerations refer to the events at the end of the First World War and immediately afterwards, they did apply all the more to the 1930s and the beginning of the 1940s. From the late 1920s onwards, Stalin put his trust in the Red Army as the only instrument of spreading the world revolution. On 21 January 1940, Stalin stated to a close circle: *"The world revolution as a single act is nonsense. It takes place at different times in different countries. The operations of the Red Army are also within the scope of the world revolution."*[47]

When Did Stalin Intend to Attack Germany?

The question now arises as to when Stalin planned to attack Germany, since in 1941 it was only Germany that was a viable target. Unlike what some authors argue, Moscow did not plan to attack in the coming weeks or even months. On 4 June 1941, Malenkov stated that the attack would not take place "tomorrow," and Zhdanov concurred. An indication of the possible date of the attack can be found in Zhdanov's remarks during the same meeting, who justified the changeover of the previous "pacifist" propaganda to the one of aggressive war as follows: "The propaganda should have a corresponding pace. Right now we cannot plan political education for two years in advance and have a political textbook prepared from which these two years would be taught."[48]

These statements may be interpreted as a hint that Stalin was planning the war of aggression against Germany in two years' time (1943), for Zhdanov and Malenkov were close confidants of his and acted on Stalin's order in drafting the new directives. This hypothesis is supported by further evidence. When, on 7 November 1940, during the reception in the Kremlin, Stalin insulted his comrades and complained that the Red Army was not prepared for war, Molotov reminded him: "We will not be in a position to face the Germans on an equal footing until 1943."[49] Stalin himself is also said to have later told Molotov that "Only in 1943 will we be ready for Germany."[50]

However, these statements are circumstantial evidence, not proof of the date of the planned attack, especially since the planned course of the war preparations points rather to spring 1942. Still, the year 1941, be it summer or autumn, can be ruled out.

The elimination of a long list of deficiencies and weaknesses of the Red Army, which had been identified repeatedly in 1940, as well as the restructuring and re-equipping of the armored and air forces, required enormous efforts. It is not surprising, therefore, that in May 1941, the Red Army was not ready for war. On 8 May 1941, a meeting of the Red Army's Supreme Military Council was held, at which it was stated: "Overall, combat readiness, although increased in comparison with 1940, still does not meet the current requirements to conduct operations and fight. It [combat readiness] is characterized by the failure to fulfill the tasks specified in the order No. 30 of the People's Commissar for Defense."[51]

There are numerous other documents from the spring of 1941 in which senior military leaders alerted the party leadership about the difficulties of preparing for war. On 15 April 1941, the Chief of the General Staff, Zhukov, complained that the army had not been adequately equipped with ammunition, especially artillery shells.[52] On the same day, the Supreme Military Council of the Red Army passed a resolution that the government should see to it that the army was adequately supplied with ammunition of all calibers by the end of 1941, so that stocks could be built up to fight a three-month war.[53] For example, the units of Brest Fortress had been equipped with a large number of modern cannons by June 1941, but the ammunition for them did not arrive before 22 June 1941.[54]

On 14 May 1941, Lieutenant General Fedorenko informed the People's Commissar for Defense that the motorized corps was not quite ready for combat because of insufficient supply of tanks with cannons and machine guns.[55] For example, the 208th Motorized Division, formed in early 1941 and stationed at Hajnówka near Bialystok, had only 70-80% of its equipment in June 1941. On paper, Regiment 128 had 250 tanks but did not receive even a single one before 22 June 1941.[56] This was no exception. In spring 1941, the major Soviet tank formations were in the phase of deep restructuring and refitting, and their full combat readiness was not scheduled until the spring of 1942.[57]

The situation was no different with respect to the air force. Its comprehensive restructuring and its equipment reform had only been initiated only in the spring of 1941. Fighter squadrons 41, 124, 126, and 129 of the 8th Air Division stationed in Belarus received 240 new MiG-1 and MiG-3 fighters in the spring of 1941 as part of the restructuring of the air force. By 12 June 1941, 53 "incidents" had occurred with ten planes totally destroyed and five so seriously damaged that they had to be repaired in aircraft factories, 38 more needed major repairs in aircraft workshops. In addition, because of various production defects in the planes and their engines, more than 100 aircraft were not airworthy. Instead of the scheduled 240 aircraft, the 8th Air Division thus had only 85 to 90 operational aircraft on 17 June 1941.[58]

On 10-11 June 1941, Marshal Timoshenko, then the People's Commissar for Defense, and General Zhukov, Chief of the General Staff, reported to Stalin about the unsatisfactory progress in the development of railroads, which formed the backbone of the Soviet supply system: "The works on the extension of the eleven new railroad lines in the western section began at the end of April [1941], and to this day they have not yet reached their full scope. As of 1 June, only 8% of the annual plan had been completed on these lines. [...] The annual plan for bridge construction in these sections [the western and southern sections] was, as of 1 June [1941], completed from 18% to 20%."[59]

According to the report, the main cause of the difficulties was a shortage of building materials (cement, wood, and construction steel). The aim of the project was to construct and expand the railroad lines leading to the German-Soviet and Romanian-Soviet borders, as well as to the Baltic Sea (Baltic countries). The Politburo ordered that expansion on 14 February 1941, and a total of 57,000 workers were employed for this purpose starting in March/April 1941.[60]

Ponomarenko alerted Stalin on 30 May and Beria on 7 June that the construction and expansion of airfields along the German-Soviet border was also proceeding slowly. Although considerable progress had been made on earthworks in the meantime, the more extensive works (runways, airfield facilities, etc.) could hardly be carried out because the construction machinery ordered had either only been delivered in part or not at all. The situation was similar with regard to construction materials, primarily cement for laying the runways.[61]

On 24 March 1941, the Politburo ordered the construction of 20 new airfields and the expansion of 231 airfields for the needs of the armed forces in 1941. Sixty-two of these airfields were located in the Western Military District (present-day Belarus and northeastern Poland), most of them at a distance of up to about 100 km from the then German-Soviet border. Another 63 airfields were located in the Kyiv Military District, most of them close to the German-Soviet border. In addition, there were 23 airfields in the Baltic countries, 22 in the Leningrad Military District, and 20 in the Odessa Military District (along the Soviet-Romanian border), with the remainder in other regions of the USSR.[62]

The decision on the construction and expansion of railroads and airfields along the German-Soviet border adopted for 1941 is an indication of the preparations for a war of aggression in 1942. A similar indication is also the decision by the Politburo of 6 June 1941, to stockpile large quantities of fuel and raw materials, food, fodder, articles of daily use for soldiers, uniforms, and underwear by 1 January 1942. Here are some examples: 13.5 million tons of coal were to be maintained in a state of reserve by 1 January 1942. On 1 January 1941, it still amounted to 7.6 million tons; 6.5 million tons of petroleum products were also to be stored by that deadline (on 1 January 1941: they amounted only to 1.5 million tons).[63]

In terms of grain and food for the needs of the Red Army, on 6 June 1941 the Politburo ordered that the following stocks be accumulated by 1 January 1942): 346,800 tons of rye (on 1 January 1941: 273,000 tons), 140,800 tons of wheat (65,000 tons), 738,800 tons of flour (538,800 tons), 381,000 tons of barely (281,000 tons), 1,181,000 tons of oats (1,216,000 tons), 51,606 tons of meat (39,406 tons), and 23,869 tons of fish (16,169 tons). In addition, large quantities of other foodstuffs and beverage products such as canned meat, bacon, butter, sugar, tea, coffee, etc. were also to be stored.[64]

In parallel with the massive buildup, rearmament, expansion, and reconstruction of the Red Army, the expansion of the railroad system and the massive buildup of supplies were featured in the General Staff's drafted plans in 1940/41 for an attack west, i.e., on the German troops. The last known plans are from May 1941.[65] The current state of research and the sources presented here demonstrate that in 1941 the Red Army was under no circumstances prepared for a war against such a strong opponent as Germany was at that time, and Moscow knew it.

Chapter 25

A Pre-Emptive War?

In spring 1941, the Soviet Union was in the process of assembling a great army at the border with Germany. It was not there to beat back a German invasion but to rush forward and spread the revolution to the rest of Europe, and move closer to the goal of world revolution. The German attack of 22 June 1941 surprised this invasion army in the midst of its preparations.

The Soviet war preparations are nevertheless not proof of the so-called preemptive war thesis, according to which Hitler invaded the Soviet Union in order to forestall an imminent Soviet attack.[1] In the 1990s, the preventive war controversy "developed into a kind of political-ideological war of faith". Its supporters were and are accused, often enough justifiably, of wanting to portray the German invasion of the USSR as a war defensible under international law. "All the more, anti-revisionist historians consider it an urgent act of public enlightenment to prove the complete absurdity of the preventive war thesis."[2] In their understandable anti-revisionist zeal, however, some authors take the Soviet propaganda of the Soviet Union's peaceful foreign policy at face value and even go as far as to portray the Soviet attack on Finland as a defensive measure.[3]

Although Stalin was indeed preparing for the invasion of Germany, the German invasion was no preemptive war. First of all, the Red Army was not ready for a war of aggression under any circumstances in the summer of 1941. This fact is ignored by the supporters of the preventive war thesis, while they claim exactly the opposite, pointing to the enormous amounts of war material and troops that Stalin had undeniably concentrated along the German-Soviet borders, preparing for the future offensive.[4]

More importantly, however, Germany had no knowledge of the state of the Soviet armed forces, let alone of its extensive war preparations. Thus, there was no immediate reason for a preventive war from the German point of view, as had been the case for the Polish army in April 1920 which had received countless intelligence reports warning of an imminent Bolshevik attack. On the contrary, Hitler and his generals not only grossly underestimated the military strength and armament potential of the Soviet Union, but also misjudged the fighting capabilities of the Red Army, which, given their own military successes and Soviet failures in the war against Finland, should hardly be considered a surprise.

As late as the beginning of May 1941, a few weeks before the German invasion, the opinion prevailed in the High Command of the Wehrmacht that the Red Army had "not improved significantly" and did not have "a good leader corps."[5] When Hitler decided to invade the Soviet Union, he assumed that the Wehrmacht would crush the Red Army within a few weeks.[6] "We are on the verge of an unparalleled triumphal march," Goebbels noted in his diary after a conversation with Hitler on 16 June 1941, six days before the invasion.[7]

In the first weeks of the Eastern campaign, the expectations for a quick victory seemed to come true. On 9 July 1941, Hitler told Goebbels "that the war in the East has been more or less won. We will still have a number of difficult battles to fight, but from the defeats suffered thus far the armed forces of Bolshevism will not be able to recover." Soon, however, the atmosphere at the Führer's headquarters changed radically. Goebbels wrote in his diary on 1 August 1941: "It is now openly admitted that there was some mistake in the assessment of the Soviet fighting strength. The Bolsheviks are showing stronger resistance than we suspected, and above all the material means at their disposal are greater than we had assumed.[8]

Ten days later, on 10 August Goebbels stated: "It will still take tough and bloody fighting until the Soviet Union lies shattered at our feet."[9] The initial euphoria had faded. Hitler suffered from severe diarrhea, which Goebbels described in politically correct terms as a "dysentery attack," because the military events in the east had taken such a toll on the Führer, as the Minister of Propaganda knew to report. Goebbels continued: "It is also explainable that the military events of the last few weeks have made him [Hitler] very irritable. [...] We had not expected the military difficulties to such an extent. It has been a decidedly bad time in the last four weeks."[10] Goebbels further noted in his diary on 19 August 1941:

We apparently completely underestimated the Soviet offensive power and, above all, the equipment of the Soviet army. Nor did we have anywhere near a clear picture of what was available to the Bolsheviks. That is where our misjudgments came from. For example, the Führer estimated the number of Soviet tanks at 5,000, while in reality they possessed close to 20,000. Aircraft, we believed, they had around 10,000; in reality they possessed over 20,000. [...] It may have been a good thing that we were not so clear about the potential of the Bolsheviks. Perhaps we would have shied away from tackling the now due question of the east and Bolshevism. [...] The Führer is very displeased with himself that he has allowed himself to be so deceived about the potential of the Bolsheviks by the reports from the Soviet Union.[11]

A year later, on 4 June 1942, Hitler conversed with Marshal Mannerheim, the Finnish commander-in-chief, on his special train. Hitler paid a surprise visit to Mannerheim on the occasion of his 75th birthday. By chance, the first eleven minutes of this conversation were recorded, for which a Finnish tape technician was responsible.[12] In the recorded conversation, Hitler stated:

We did not know ourselves exactly how tremendously armed this state [the Soviet Union] was. [...] They have the most monstrous armament imaginable. [...] If someone had told me that a state could deploy 35,000 tanks, I would have said: You have gone insane! [...] If a general of mine had told me that here's a state with 35,000 tanks, then I would have said: You, sir, see everything double or tenfold, you are insane; you are seeing ghosts. I did not think that to be possible. [...] If I had suspected it, my heart would have been even harder, but then I would have taken the decision even more, because there was no other possibility. It was already clear to me in the winter of '39 and '40 that the conflict had to come.[13]

In reality, in June 1941 Soviet forces had at their disposal 25,508 tanks, 18,700 aircraft, and 5,774,000 soldiers.[14] Hitler and his generals had no idea of the Soviet Union's actual war potential, nor did they know that Soviet preparations for an aggressive war had been in full swing for years. They were not "in the know" and underestimated their opponent "completely," as Goebbels put it.

Yet, it is also a fact that Hitler spoke of a general threat from the Soviet Union before 22 June 1941. On 16 July, 1941, Goebbels had a conversation with Hitler, after which he noted down in his diary Hitler's arguments for the invasion of the Soviet Union: "We must act. Moscow will stay out of the war until Europe is tired and bled dry. Then Stalin wants to act, Bolshevize Europe, and impose his own rule. He will be thwarted in this calculation. [...] Russia would attack us if we became weak, and then we would have the two-front war which we are avoiding by this preventive action."[15]

With this assessment, Hitler hit at the core, the basic principles and goals of Stalin's foreign policy towards Europe in general and Germany in particular. Here, however, one must agree with Bernd Wagner, who asks in this context "where does the line run in such statements between personal conviction and propagandistic calculations to legitimize taking action."[16]

In the already quoted, recorded conversation with Mannerheim, Hitler also claimed that he had feared that the Soviet Union would invade Romania in 1940/41: "Because I was always afraid that Russia would suddenly invade Romania in late autumn and take possession of the petroleum sources, and we had not yet been ready in late autumn of 1940. If Russia had occupied the Romanian petroleum sources, Germany would have been lost."[17] This was no outlandish claim; after all, Stalin made no secret to Hitler that he wanted all of Romania.

It is also a fact that Germany was in an extremely precarious situation with regard to fuel, raw materials and food during this period. Oil supplies were particularly critical, with Germany relying exclusively on Romanian and Soviet supplies. The difficult situation concerning raw materials even called into question the consolidation of Germany's power in Europe. A successful invasion of the Soviet Union would solve all these problems, especially since Hitler was sure of victory.[18] After the victory against the Soviet Union, Germany would have raw materials and food (the Ukrainian "granary") in abundance, Hitler believed. On 18 September 1941, Hitler explained, in a small circle of his confidants, the economic-strategic importance of the Soviet Union for Germany: "The struggle for hegemony in the world is decided for Europe by possession of the Russian land; it makes Europe the most blockade-proof place in the world."[19]

Naturally, such considerations are completely unrelated to the idea of a preemptive strike. Indeed, the German invasion was prepared in advance and was primarily motivated by ideology. The military-economic and strategic aspects facilitated Hitler's decision for the attack and at the same time served as a pretext. For Adolf Hitler was obsessed throughout his life with the idea that history meant the "struggle for Lebensraum" according to the rules of "racial determinism". As early as the 1920s, he attacked German foreign policy pursued up to that time, which he defined as "border politics" for being short-sighted and anachronistic. He himself advocated "space politics," by which he understood the conquest of a "living space" for the German people in Eastern Europe.[20]

After taking power in 1933, Hitler elevated the Lebensraum idea to the state ideology of the new Germany. On 3 February 1933, Hitler explained to German generals the purpose of the new armed forces to be built up as follows: "Conquest of new Lebensraum in the East and its ruthless Germanization."[21] Already ten years earlier, in 1923, Hitler had written the following on the subject:

> [...] We, the National Socialists, [must] unalterably adhere to our foreign policy goal, namely to secure for the German people the territory on this earth which it deserves. And this action is the only one which, before God and our German posterity, justifies the sacrifice of blood. [...] But when we speak of a new territory in Europe today, we can think first and foremost only of Russia and the peripheral states subject to it.[22]

In a conversation with his closest associates on 16 July 1941, Hitler stated that in the war against the Soviet Union all will be finally settled: "Basically it is [...] a matter of dividing up this gigantic cake conveniently so that we can first of all dominate it, secondly administer it, and thirdly exploit it. [...] We must make a Garden of Eden out of the newly won eastern territories; they are vital for us."[23]

There is no doubt that the German invasion of the USSR was ideologically motivated and occurred independently of Soviet war preparations. The claims of the Soviet threat to Germany, which was real but of which Hitler was in fact entirely unaware, served only as a pretext before his generals and allies. This is nothing unusual; even the Soviets had claimed to have felt threatened by tiny Finland in 1939. Both Stalin and Hitler were only interested in concealing from the public the true motives for their expansion at first.

Fundamentally, the German-Soviet war was unavoidable on account of the ideologies that motivated both systems. Hitler saw the Soviet territories as the future Lebensraum for the German people, and a prerequisite for German rule over the world. Stalin, on the other hand, saw Germany as the key to controlling Europe and thus, the world. With Germany's economic and human potential, the Soviet Union hoped to dominate and Sovietize the entire continent. The war in Russia brought total defeat to Hitler, while the Soviet Union was able to extend its rule and the communist system all the way to the Elbe - with the added halo of liberator from the fascist reign of terror.[24]

Final Remarks

Communist expansionism was not merely a historical accident, but lay at the very heart of the state the Bolsheviks had built upon the ruins of the Russian Empire, and which formed the very core of the international communist movement. From the beginning, the Bolshevik leaders saw the triumph of their revolution in Russia as but a stepping stone on the path to the – in their mind – inevitable world revolution. With Russia secured, the Bolsheviks immediately turned towards Europe, where they quickly identified centrally-placed Germany with its great industrial and human potential as the key to dominating the continent. Believing that they needed to control Germany to bring about the world revolution, the Bolsheviks did their best to bring about a revolution in Germany, even planning to support its revolutionaries with the Red Army.

However, following setback after setback, Moscow finally gave up its hopes for a successful revolution in Germany by 1924, and new strategies began to be discussed. In the power struggle that followed Lenin's death, it was Stalin who prevailed, championing the idea of Socialism in One Country, which Lenin himself had drawn up in 1915. According to this idea, the Soviet Union would spread the sparks of the world revolution on its own, by force of arms. Once his power had been fully secured in 1927, Stalin and the Politburo drew up ambitious plans to arm the Soviet Union and turn the Red Army into the most powerful invasion army the world had ever seen. However, these plans failed due to the poor and backward state of Soviet industry.

Despite the early failures, the beginning of the Great Depression energized Stalin and motivated him to accelerate his project of arming the country. Beginning in 1930, all of Soviet society and the economy were mobilized for this purpose. At the same time, Stalin relentlessly persecuted everyone who "sabotaged" these preparations or could endanger the Soviet hinterland in the coming revolutionary war. Primarily, this meant the peasants who desperately resisted forced collectivization and grain requisitions, which in effect turned them into serfs without any rights.

It was in large parts precisely through collectivization and the export of grain that the Soviet Union was able to gather the funds necessary for the exceedingly costly expansion of its military, its armaments industry, as well as the import of Western technology and machinery. In order to finance his grand project, Stalin also intensified the export of other raw materials such as wood and increased the sale of vodka domestically.

Through collectivization and the gulag system, Stalin and his comrades – as well as the entire Soviet state apparatus – effectively turned the Soviet Union into a gigantic forced labor camp. While the newly-created industry did succeed in quickly producing vast quantities of war materiel, the quality was terrible: aircraft and tanks were outdated and were delivered with severe production flaws. The soldiers' equipment was likewise lacking; they were poorly fed, clothed, trained, led, and generally unwilling to sacrifice their lives on the altar of world revolution. Together with the poor quality of equipment, this also contributed to countless breakdowns and accidents, which in turn were interpreted as acts of sabotage and punished accordingly.

It was among these setbacks that the Great Terror of the 1930s was conceived. Starting out as an effort to root out saboteurs and wreckers, it soon developed its own dynamic and affected all sectors of the state and society; even the Red Army, the party, the state economy and the NKVD itself were ruthlessly purged. Once again, however, the main victim was the rural population that had just been re-enserfed by the Bolsheviks, while the rural elites, wealthy peasants, clergy, religious, political and other non-communist activists were systematically annihilated – as was the intelligentsia of the national minorities. Millions were arrested, sent to concentration camps or outright executed, while others were deported to the remote, inhospitable regions in the empire's north and east, together with their families.

Contrary to what the Bolsheviks had expected, the Great Depression did not immediately result in an imperialist war. To make matters worse, Hitler's rise to power in Germany in 1933 permanently dashed the hopes of a communist revolution there – the Soviet Union thus continued to be doomed to political isolation. This only changed with the signing of the Hitler-Stalin Pact on 24 August 1939, in which the two past and future enemies lay aside their differences to divide Poland and the rest of Eastern Europe. Even better for Stalin, Hitler's war against Poland led to France and Britain declaring war on Germany, but not the Soviet Union – the long-sought imperialist war had finally arrived.

The success of the Soviet invasion of already mostly defeated Poland on 17 September 1939 triggered an outright frenzy in Moscow and the Bolsheviks immediately moved to their next target – Finland. However, the Finnish-Soviet Winter War of 1939/40 quickly turned into a military disaster that shocked both Stalin and his comrades. Realizing the gravity of the situation, Stalin once again spearheaded and personally oversaw a wide range of radical reforms that reorganized and rearmed the battered Red Army. With confidence restored, the Red Army began to explicitly prepare for its own invasion of Germany by early 1943 at the very latest. It was precisely in the midst of these preparations that Hitler launched his attack on the Soviet Union on 22 June 1941, which caught the Soviet leadership completely by surprise.

The devastating Soviet defeats in the summer of 1941 were in large part the result of the Soviet Union's exceedingly offensive orientation that led its leaders to discount the danger of a German attack and left the Red Army ill-prepared for a defensive war. In contrast, the Bolsheviks' aggressive industrialization and armament programs of the 1930s and early 1940s had left the country with a gigantic military-industrial base that allowed it to outproduce and in the end defeat Germany, albeit at an incredible cost.[1] At the same time, the mass terror had broken the back of the anti-communist resistance of both the peasantry and national minorities, and the great rebellions in the hinterland that Stalin and his comrades had feared so much failed to materialize in 1941. On the contrary, the Soviet bureaucracy, the NKVD, and the militia managed to keep order throughout.

Finally, it has to be said that the Soviet war preparations, the massive armament and industrialization program, and the mass terror were intrinsically tied to the person of Stalin and his emergence as dictator with unlimited authority. It was Stalin who turned the Soviet Union into a gigantic forced labor camp which the Soviet bureaucracy lorded over with an iron fist, while the NKVD cracked down on any opposition, real or imagined. Throughout his reign, Stalin was like a cult leader whose visions of a proletarian paradise on earth attracted the blind devotion of millions of fanatic communists at home and abroad, who were more than eager to carry out mass murder or at the very least welcome it.[2] To this day, former Stalinist perpetrators and their modern-day ideological successors in Moscow and abroad downplay or even outright deny their crimes without remorse.

Although his empire would crumble before the end of the century, through his actions, Stalin was undoubtedly one of the most impactful people in the history of the 20th century. Under his iron fist, the Soviet Union became a world power, easily outmatching the Russian Empire in both size and sheer might. For that, the peoples of Eastern and Central Europe but also of Siberia and Central Asia paid a steep price, with millions killed, enslaved and many more turned into serfs. Furthermore, Stalin also personally reconfigured the ethnic makeup of these regions: on his orders, Poland was moved west by 200 kilometers, while Kazakhstan suddenly became a European-majority country and roughly sixteen million Germans were expelled from Eastern Europe following the war.[3]

Even though his crimes rivaled those of Hitler, Stalin's bloody legacy, to this day, is not anchored in historical memory; on the contrary, it is being ignored or even met with tacit approval in many respects. This book hopes to shed a critical light on one of the areas where old Stalinist propaganda still has a noticeable effect – the myth of the pacifist Soviet Union.

Abbreviations

BA-MA	Bundesarchiv-Militärarchiv, Freiburg
BSSR	Byelorusskaya Sovyetskaya Sotsialisticheskaya Respublika (Byelorussian Soviet Socialist Republic)
d.	delo (file)
ECCI	Executive Committee of the Communist Internationale
f.	fond (archival holding)
f./ff.	On the following page/pages
FN	Footnote
GARF	Gosudarstvenny Arkhiv Rossiyskoy Federatsii (State Archive of the Russian Federation)
GPU	Glavnoye Politicheskoye Upravleniye (State Political Directorate) = OGPU
GVPU	Glavnoye Voienno-Promyshlennoye Upravleniye (Chief Administration of the Armaments Industry)
IfZ	Institut für Zeitgeschichte
KGB	Komitet Gosudarstvennoy Bezopasnosti (Committee for State Security)
Komsomol	Kommunisticheskiy Soyuz Molodyozhi (Young Communist League)
Comintern	Communist International
KPD	Comunist Party of Germany

CPC	Komissiya Partiynogo Kontrolya (Commission for Party Control)
KPP	Polish Communist Party
CSC	Komissiya sovietskogo kontrolya (Commission for Soviet Control)
MTS	Mashinno-Traktornaya Stantsiya (Machine-Tractor Station)
NARB	Natsionalny Arkhiv Respublik Belarus (National Archives of the Republic of Belarus in Minsk)
NKGB	Narodnyy Komitet Gosudarstvennoy Bezopasnosti (People's Commissariat for State Security)
NKO	Narodnyy Komissar/ Komissariat Oborony (National Commissar/Commissariat for Defense)
NKVD	Narodnyy Komissariat Vnutrennikh Del (People's Commissariat for Internal Affairs)
NEP	New Economic Policy
OGPU	Obyedinyonnoye Gosudarstvennoye Politicheskoye Upravleniye (Joint State Political Directorate) = GPU
OO	osobiy otdel (special detachment)
op.	Opis (archival inventory)
RGASPI	Rossiyskiy Gosudarstvenny Arkhiv Sotsialno-Politicheskoi Istorii (Russian State Archive of Socio-Political History in Moscow)
RGVA	Rossiyskiy Gosudarstvenny Voiennyy Arkhiv (Russian State Military Archive)
RSFSR	Rossíyskaya Sovietskaya Federatívnaya Socialistícheskaya Respublika (Russian Soviet Federative Socialist Republic)

RS STO	Rasporyaditelnojye Zassedaniye STO (Administrative Session of the Council for Labor and Defense)
RVS	Revolutsyonny Voienny Soviet (Revolutionary War Council)
RVSR	Revolutsyonny Voienny Soviet Respubliki (Revolutionary War Council of the Republic)
SNK, SovNarKom	Soviet Narodnykh Kommissarov (Council of People's Commissars)
SSSR	Soyuz Sovetskikh Sotsialisticheskikh Respublik (USSR)
STO	Soviet Truda i Oborony (Council for Labor and Defense)
USSR	Union of Soviet Socialist Republics
v.	Verso
VfZ	Vierteljahrshefte für Zeitgeschichte
VChK (VeCheKa)	Vserossiyskaya Chrezvychaynaya Komissiya (All-Russian Extraordinary Commission); short = Cheka
VCP(b)	Vsesoyuznaya kommunisticheskaya partiya (bol'shevikov) (All-Union Communist Party [Bolsheviks])
VSNKh	Vyzhshy Soviet Narodnogo Khozyaystva (Chief Economic Soviet)
ZAMO	Central Archives of the Russian Ministry of Defense (ZAMO)
TsIK	Tsentralny Ispolnitelny Komitet (Central Executive Commitee)

Notes

Introduction

1. Overy, *Die Diktatoren*, p. 585; Similarly argue.: Gabriel Gorodetsky, *Grand Delusion: Stalin and the German Invasion of Russia*, Yale University Press, New Haven, Connecticut 1999; Geoffrey Roberts, *Stalin's Wars. From World War to Cold War, 1939-1953*, New Haven and London 2006; and Jonathan Haslam, *The Soviet Union and the Struggle for Collective Security in Europe, 1933-1939*, London 1984.
2. Cf. Dunn, The Soviet Economy and the Red Army. Basedon published Soviet statistics, Dunn argues that the Soviet Union prepared for war intensely beginning in 1933; Musial (author), Sowjetische Partisanen in Weißrussland, p. 16; Overy, Russlands Krieg, pp. 67-122; Ennker, »Stalin-Regime 1939-1941«, p. 142 ff.
3. Wegner, »Präventivkrieg 1941?«, pp. 214, 219; Wegner devotes an entire chapter to Hitler's knowledge of the Soviet war preparations in depth.
4. Suvorov, Icebreaker; Suvorov continued to publish other books in which he defended and expanded his original theses, such as M-Day.
5. For example, Politbyuro CK RCP(b) - VCP(b) i Komintern (Politburo und Komintern); Politbyuro CK RCP(b) - VCP(b) i Evropa (Politboro und Europe).
6. *Tragediya sovietskoi derevnii*; Sovietskaya derevnya glazami VCC-OGPU-NKVD; Istoriya stalinskogo gulaga (The history of the Stalinist gulag); Lubjanka. Stalin i VCC-GPU-OGPU-NKVD. yanvar 1922 - dekabr 1936 (henceforth: Lubyanka. 1922-1936); »Zimnyaya voina«: robota nad oshibkami, aprel-mai 1940 g; Lubyanka. Stalin i glavonoye upravienie gosbezopasnosti NKVD 1937-1938; Glavny voienny Soviet RKKA. 13 marta 1938 g. - 20 iyunya 1941 g; Voienny Soviet pri Narodnom Komissare Oborony SSSR - 1938, 1940.
7. In Germany, there is a slow forgetting of the genesis of the Hitler-Stalin Pact. An example is the book Claudia Weber, *Der Pakt. Stalin, Hitler und die Geschichte einer mörderischen Allianz 1939-1941*, München 2019. Among others, the author grossly underestimates the importance of the German-Soviet economic alliance signed on 19 August 1939, which, albeit well-documented, is frequently overlooked by both historians and publicists. Tragically so, considering the extensive German-Russian economic cooperation that enabled Putin to strike at Ukraine. At the same time, the author, like many others, did not conduct archival research in Russian archives and also neglected to analyze translated sources, such as Dimitrov's diaries.
8. For example, in 2015, the diaries of Ivan Maisky, the Soviet ambassador to London between 1932 and 1943, were published: *The Maisky Diaries. Red Ambassador to the Court of St. James's 1932-1943*, ed. Gabriel Gorodetsky. While touted as a breakthrough, these diaries did not in fact bring anything new to the table as Maisky, in far-off London, was not part of the key decision-making group in the Kremlin. Luckily, however, others

do take into account the latest research, such as Roger Moorhouse, *The Devil's Alliance: Hitler's Pact with Stalin 1939-1941*, London 2014; or Sean McMeekin, *Stalin's War: A New History of World War II*, New York 2021.

9. Vladimir Putin, *The Real Lessons of the 75th Anniversary of World War II*, in: *The National Interest*, 18 June 2020: https://nationalinterest.org/feature/vladimir-putin-real-lessons-75th-anniversary-world-war-ii-162982?page=0%2C5. [Accessed 09.05.2022]

Chapter 1

1. This is how Lenin referred to the Bolshevik revolution in Russia. Examples include Lenin's speech at the Seventh All-Russia Congress Of Soviets, printed in: Lenin, *Works*, Vol. 30: September 1919 - April 1920, Moscow 1974, pp. 205-252, here: p. 209; Wladislaw Subok and Konstantin Pleschakow, *Der Kreml im Kalten Krieg. Von 1945 bis zur Kubakrise*, Hildesheim 1997, pp. 19 f.

2. Lenin, Speech At A Joint Plenum Of The Moscow Soviet Of Workers', Peasants' And Red Army Deputies, The Moscow Committee Of The R.C.P.(B.) And The Moscow City Trade Union Council, Dedicated To The Third Anniversary Of The October Revolution, 6 November 1920, printed in: Lenin, *Works*, Vol. 31: April - December 1920, Moscow 1974, pp. 397-402, here: p. 397.; a few days later, on 21 November 1920, Lenin declared: "For victory to be lasting, we must achieve the victory of the proletarian revolution in all, or at any rate in several, of the main capitalist countries." (Speech Delivered at the Moscow Gubernia Conference of the R.C.P.(B.) Our Foreign and Domestic Position and the Tasks of the Party, 21 November 1920, printed in: ibid., pp. 408-426., here: p. 411); and 5 days later: "We have, however, always said that we are only a single link in the chain of the world revolution, and have never set ourselves the aim of achieving victory by our own means." (Speech Delivered At A Meeting of Cells' Secretaries Of The Moscow Organisation Of The R.C.P.(B.), November 26, 1920, printed in: ibid., pp. 430-429, here: 433).

3. Lenin, Speech Delivered at the First All-Russia Congress of Working Cossacks, on 1 March 1920, printed in: Lenin, *Works: September 1919 - April 1920, Works*, Vol. 30: *September 1919 - April 1920*, Vol. 30, pp. 380-400, here: p. 380.

4. Cf. Lenin, Ninth Congress of the R.C.P.(B.), Speech Closing The Congress, 5 April 1920, printed in: Lenin, *Works*, Vol. 30, pp. 485-490, here: p. 486; also cf. Lenin, Speech Delivered At A Conference Of Chairmen Of Uyezd, Volost And Village Executive Committees Of Moscow Gubernia, 15 October 1920, printed in: Lenin, *Works*, Vol. 31, pp. 318-333, here: p. 324.

5. I. Lenin, *State and Revolution*, Postscript to the First Edition, printed in: Lenin, *Works*, Vol. 25 (June-September 1917), 1972, p. 497.

6. Trotsky to Lenin, no date, before 23 November 1921: RGASPI, p. 325, op. 1, d. 480, p. 1.

7. Lenin to Trotsky, 23 November 1921: ibid.

8. Firsov, "Ein Oktober, der nicht stattfand", p. 36.

9. "Der I. Kongress der Kommunistischen Internationale"

10. Zinoviev, »Perspektiven der proletarischen Revolution«, in: *Die Kommunistische Internationale* (1919), No. 1, pp. 41-42, as cited in Firsov, »Ein Oktober, der nicht stattfand«, p. 36

11. Zinoviev: Theses on the coming "German Revolution" and the tasks of the Russian communists, presented on 21 September 1923 at the Plenum of the Central Committee and with amendments by the commission of the Politburo, approved on 22 September 1923: RGASPI, f. 558, op. 11, d. 139, pp. 22-30.

12. Geyer: »Sowjetrussland und die deutsche Arbeiterbewegung«, p. 5.

13. Lenin, Speech Delivered at the First All-Russia Congress of Working Cossacks, on 1 March 1920, printed in: Lenin, *Works: September 1919 - April 1920*, Vol. 30, pp. 380-400, here: p. 391.

14. Cf. Zinoviev: Theses on the coming "German Revolution" and the tasks of the Russian communists, presented on 21 September 1923 at the Plenum of the Central Committee and with amendments by the commission of the Politburo, approved on 22 September 1923: RGASPI, f. 558, op. 11, d. 139, pp. 22-30.

15. Telegram from Karl Liebknecht from 3 November 1918 to the VI. All-Russian Extraordinary Congress of Councils: RGASPI, f. 325, op. 1, d. 50, p.4.

16. Short overview of the current strategic-military situation of the Russian Soviet Republic and the future tasks of the Red Army from 23 February 1919, Commander-in-Chief of the Armed Forces of the Republic: RGASPI, f. 325, op. 1, d. 409, pp. 1-11, here: p. 3 g.

17. Draft of the note of the Soviet delegation in Great Britain to British Prime Minister Lloyd George, regarding the conditions for a truce with Poland, from 8 August 1920: RGASPI, f. 5, op. 1, d. 2002, pp. 1 f.

18. Short overview of the current strategic-military situation of the Russian Soviet Republic and the future tasks of the Red Army from 23 February 1919, Commander-in-Chief of the Armed Forces of the Republic: RGASPI, f. 325, op. 1, d. 409, pp. 1-11, here: p. 4.

19. Report on the state of the fronts on 17 April 1919, from 18 April 1919: RGASPI, f. 325, op. 1, d. 50, pp. 120-123, here: p. 123.

20. Report on the surrender of Vilnius (Wilno) on behalf of the All-Russian Extraordinary Commission for the Fight against Counterrevolution and Speculation (Cheka) from 19 June 1919, authored by Michin: RGASPI, f. 17, op. 109, d. 59, pp. 1-38, here: p. 10.

21. Davies, *White Eagle, Red Star*, pp. 19-61; Davies, *White Eagle, Red Star*, pp. 19-61; Stalin, Letter to V. I: Lenin about the Situation on the Western Front, 11 August 1919, printed. in: Stalin, *Works*, Vol. 4, Moscow 1953, pp. 282-284.

22. Davies, *White Eagle, Red Star*, pp. 19-61; Ziemke, *Red Army*, pp. 101-116; Roszkowski, *Najnowsza Historia Polski*, pp. 57 ff.

23. Ziemke, *Red Army*, pp. 101-116.

24. "Strategic situation", excerpt from a report for the month of November 1919: RGASPI, f. 325, op. 1, d. 50, p. 22.

25. Lenin, Seventh All-Russia Congress Of Soviets, Report of the All-Russia Central Executive Committee and the Council of People's Commissars, December 5, printed. in: Lenin, *Works*, Vol. 30, pp. 207-231, here: pp. 208, 219 (emphasis in the original).

26. Lenin, Report On The Work Of The All-Russia Central Executive Committee And The Council Of People's Commissars Delivered At The First Session Of The All-Russia Central Executive Committee, Seventh Convocation, 2 February 1920, published in: ibid., pp. 315-336, quote on p. 316.

27. Lenin, Speech Delivered at the First All-Russia Congress of Working Cossacks, on 1 March 1920, printed in: Lenin, *Works: September 1919 - April 1920*, Vol. 30, pp. 380-400, here: pp. 398 f.

28. Lenin, Speech Delivered at a Congress of Leather Industry Workers, October 2, 1920, in: Lenin, *Works*, Vol. 31, pp. 300-313, here: pp. 304.

29. Lenin, Ninth Congress of the R.C.P.(B.), Opening Speech, 29 March 1920, published in: Lenin, *Works*, Vol. 30, p. 441 f.

30. Lenin – Report of the Central Committee of 29.03.1920, delivered during the IXth Party Congress of the RKP(b), published in: ibid., pp. 435-454, here: p.444.

Chapter 2

1. Davies, *White Eagle,* p. 60 (maps with frontlines).
2. Protocol and consultative reports by members of the intelligence agencies convened by the registration administration on 8 December 1919: RGASPI, f. 17, op. 109, d. 64, pp. 2-6. The protocol lists the following points which military intelligence had to take under consideration: "1.) Military policy and stance [of Poland] towards Soviet Russia, 2.) Policy regarding the Whites (Denikin, Yudenich), 3.) towards Germany, Czechoslovakia, etc., 4.) Composition of army and armament of the field army, reserve troops, etc., 5.) the human resources, how mobilization proceeds, the system of mobilization, already mobilized cohorts, measures to attract volunteers, 6.) Military units in the war zone and in the interior of the country. In this context, the identification of troop movements from one front to another are particularly important."
3. Julian Marchlewski was born in 1866 in Leslau (Włocławek). In Germany, he was one of the founders of the Marxist Spartakusbund, a precursor of the KPD. In 1918, he was extradited from Germany and remained in Moscow before illegally entering Germany again a year later, where he joined the headquarters of the KPD. From 1922 until his death in 1925, he was the first head of International Red Aid, a communist "charity organization" active in Europe and the rest of the world.
4. Marchlewski to the Central Committee of the RCP(b) on 24 December 1919: RGASPI, f. 63, op. 1, d. 186, pp. 1 ff.
5. Ibid.
6. Nowak, "Rok 1920".
7. Protocol No. 90 of the Session of the Revolutionary and War Council of the Republic (RWCR from now on), 5 January 1920, printed in: *Revvoyensoviet Respubliki,* pp. 13-20, here: p. 16; protocol No. 93 of the session of the RWCR, 27 January 1920, printed in: ibid., pp. 27-29, here: p. 27.
8. Polish Bureau to the Central Committee of the RCP (b) on 17 February 1920: RGASPI, f. 17, op. 109, d. 74, p. 9 f.
9. Lenin, In Reply To Questions Put By Karl Wiegand, Berlin Correspondent of Universal Service. First published on 21 February 1920 in the *New York Evening Journal,* No. 12671, printed in: Lenin, *Works,* Vol. 30, pp. 365-367, here: p. 365.
10. Encrypted telegram from Trotsky to Lenin, sent from a train on 27 February 1920, received on 28 February 1920: RGASPI, f. 17, op. 109, d. 79, p. 12.
11. Session Protocol of the Politburo of the Central Committee of the RCP(b) from 28 February 1920 (point 22): RGASPI, f. 17, op. 3, d. 63, pp. 1-5, here: p. 4 f. Present: Lenin, Kamenev, Krestinsky, Kalinin, Bukharin, Serebyakov, Lugovinov, Ishchenko, Schmidt, Vinokurov, Rosengolts.
12. Lenin, Speech Delivered at the First All-Russia Congress of Working Cossacks, on 1 March 1920, printed in: Lenin, *Works: September 1919 – April 1920,* Vol. 30, pp. 380-400, here: p. 394.
13. Encrypted telegram from Trotsky to Lenin from 1 March 1920: RGASPI, f. 17, op. 109, d. 79, p. 13.
14. Lenin, Speech Delivered at a Meeting of the Moscow Soviet of Workers' and Red Army Deputies, 6 March 1920, printed in: Lenin, *Works,* Vol. 30, pp. 410-416, here: p. 411.
15. Protocol No. 101 of the session of the RWCR, 8 March 1920, printed in: *Revvoyensoviet Respubliki,* pp. 48-51, here: p. 49; protocol No. 102 of the session of the RWCR, 15 March 1920, printed in: ibid., pp. 53-59, here: p. 54 f.

16. Encrypted telegram from Unszlicht to Lenin from 12 March 1920: RGASPI, f. 17, op. 109, d. 79, pp. 14.

17. Session protocol of the Politburo of the Central Committee of the RCP from 17 March 1920 (point 6): RGASPI, f. 17, op. 3, d. 66, pp. 1 ff.

18. Report on the activities of the military organization abroad at the Revolutionary War Council of the Western Front from 9 July 1920, Unszlicht: RGASPI, f. 17, op. 109, d. 101, pp. 20-25.

19. Protocol No. 103 of the session of the RWCR, 19 March 1920, printed in: *Revvoyensoviet Respubliki,* pp. 59-63, here: pp. 59, 61.

20. Protocol No. 104 of the session of the RWCR, 26 March 1920, printed in: *Revvoyensoviet Respubliki,* pp. 64-69.

21. Protocol No. 105 of the session of the RWCR, 8 April 1920, printed in: ibid., pp. 69-74, here: p. 71.

22. Telegram from Trotsky to Dzerzhinsky from 13 October 1918: RGASPI, f. 17, op. 109, d. 21, p. 16.

23. Report of the Political Administration of the Republic, not dated (after 1 October 1919): RGASPI, f. 5, op. 1, d. 2529, pp. 21-35, here: p. 23 f.

24. Expansion of the Red Army from November 1918 to December 1919, table, not dated (December 1919): RGASPI, f. 325, op. 1, d. 50, p.117.

25. Protocol No. 49 of the Politburo session from 9 March 1920 (point 19b): RGASPI, f. 17, op. 3, d. 65, pp. 1-4, here: p. 3.

26. Report on the activities of the military organization abroad at the Revolutionary War Council of the Western Front from 9 July 1920, Unszlicht: RGASPI, f. 17, op. 109, d. 101, pp. 20-25.

27. Protocol of the Politburo session from 9 March 1920 (points 18 and 19): RGASPI, f. 17, op. 3, d. 65, pp. 1-4.

28. In early May 1920 at the latest, Soviet Russia proposed to the Lithuanian government to divide up the northeastern territories of Poland. In return for joining in the war against Poland, the Bolsheviks would leave Wilno, the Wilno region, the Lida and Oszmiana districts and parts of the Grodno district to Lithuania. Lithuania refused that offer, demanding also the Molodeczno and Wilejka districts as well as the entire Grodno district. Cf. the report from Yoffe to Trotsky on the progress of the talks with the Lithuanian delegation from 15 May 1920: RGASPI, f. 325, op. 2, d. 26, p. 73; encrypted telegram from Trotsky to Chicherin from 8 May 1920 (copy): RGASPI, f.17,op.3,d.76, p. 3.

29. Koenen, *Der Russland-Komplex,* p. 294.

30. Units of the Red Army and opposing forces on the Polish front according to data from 16 April 1920 (map) RGASPI, f. 5, op. 1, d. 3018, p. 1.

31. Telegram from Trotsky to the Political Administration of the Republic, the Central Committee of the RCP and the Moscow Committee of the RCP from 23 April 1920: RGASPI, f. 17, op. 109, d. 79, p. 19.

32. Nowak, *Zanim złamano »Enigme,«,* pp. 34-39; Davies, *White Eagle,* pp. XV-XVIII.

33. Nowik, *Zanim złamano »Enigme«,* pp. 359-510.

34. Ibid., pp. 511-664

35. Ibid., pp. 734-739; Davies, *White Eagle,* pp. 105-129.

36. Nowik, *Zanim złamano »Enigme,«,* pp. 738 f., 766 f.

37. Ibid., pp. 734-739; Davies, *White Eagle,* pp. 105-129.

38. Nowik, *Zanim złamano »Enigme,«,* pp. 738 f., 766 f.

39. Ibid., pp. 767-799.

40. Telegram from Trotsky to Chicherin, from his armored train on 10 August 1920: RGASPI, f. 17, op. 3, d. 76, p.3.

41. Appeal from Trotsky to the Central Committee of the RCP(b) from 9 May 1920: RGASPI, f. 17, op. 109, d. 79, p. 39.

42. Encrypted telegram from Trotsky to the Central Committee from 10 May 1920: RGASPI, f. 17, op. 109, d. 79, p. 41.

43. Three telegrams from Danilov to the Cheka headquarters in Moscow from 16 May 1920: RGASPI, f. 17, op. 109, d. 79, p. 61.

44. Roszkowski, *Najnowsza historia Polski*, p. 64 f.

45. Nowik, *Zanim złamano »Enigme,«*, pp. 767-842, 911-914; Davies, *White Eagle*, p. 141.

46. Ziemke, *Red Army*, pp. 122-126; Davies, *White Eagle*, pp. 130-157.

47. Telegram from Yegorov, commander of the South-Western Front, to the High Command from 11 July 1920: RGASPI, f. 325, op. 1, d. 479, p. 234.

48. Ziemke, *Red Army*, pp. 118, 124.

49. People's Commissariat for Foreign Affairs to the Politburo of the Central Committee of the RCP on 30 July 1920: RGASPI, f. 17, op. 3, d. 99, p. 3; some conditions for ceasefire negotiation between the RFSR and Poland, decided by the RWCR, not dated (before 30 July 1920), amended by Chicherin on 30 or 31 July 1920: RGASPI, f. 17, op. 3, d. 99, pp. 4-11. The Politburo approved these conditions on 31 July 1920: Protocol No. 32 of the session of the Politburo from 31 July 1920 (point 8): RGASPI, f. 17, op. 3, d. 99, p. 1 f.

50. Encrypted telegram from Trotsky to Stalin and Smilga, copies to Rakovsky, Skiyansky, High Command, Central Committee on 17 July 1920: RGASPI, f. 325, op. 1, d. 479, p. 361 f. author's emphasis.

51. Protocol of Politburo session No. 29 from 23 July 1920, point 2: RGASPI, f. 17, op. 3, d. 96, p. 1 f.; Roszkowski, *Najnowsza historia Polski*, p. 66 f.

52. Davies, *White Eagle*, pp. 134-195; Roszkowski, *Najnowsza Historia Polski*, pp. 64 ff.

53. Quoted according to: "Das Wunder an der Weichsel", *Der Standard* from 10/11 February 2001 (http://derstandard.at/?url =/?id = 474592).

54. Quoted according to Koenen, *Der Russland-Komplex*, p. 283; Koenen mistakenly dated the statement to September 1920. Instead, Lenin made it on 19 July 1920 (e-mail from Gerd Koenen to Bodgan Musial on 30 March 2007).

55. Protocol No. 32 of the Politburo session from 31 July 1920 (point 6): : RGASPI, f. 17, op. 3, d. 99, p. 1 f.

56. Chicherin to Yoffe on 5 August 1920: RGASPI, f. 5, op. 1, d. 2000, p. 3.

57. Koenen, *Der Russland-Komplex*, pp. 285, 290-294.

58. Quoted according to: Ibid., p. 290.

59. In more detail, cf. Ibid., p. 290 f.

60. Quoted according to: Ibid., p. 285.

61. Telegram No. 745, Trotsky to Chicherin, copy to Krestyansky and Zinoviev, not dated, before 10 August 1920: RGASPI, f. 17, op. 109, d.74, p.32.

62. Davies, *White Eagle*, pp. 182-186; Albrecht, *Najnowsza historia Polski*, p. 69.

63. Session protocol No. 36 of the Politburo of the Central Committee of the RCP(b) from 13 August 1920 (Point 3): RGASPI, f. 17, op. 3, d. 102, pp. 1 ff.

64. Session protocol No. 35 of the Politburo of the Central Committee of the RCP(b) from 10 August 1920 (Point 4): RGASPI, f. 17, op. 3, d. 101, pp. 1 f.

65. Encrypted radio letter from Unszlicht to the Central Committee of the RCP and Trotsky from 13 August 1920: RGASPI, f. 17, op. 109, d. 79, p. 133.

66. Lenin, Speech Delivered at the Ninth All-Russia Conference of the Russian Communist Party (Bolsheviks), September 22, 1920, in: Lenin, *Works*, Vol. 31, pp. 275-279, here: p. 276.

67. Encrypted radio letter from Smilga to Lenin and Trotsky from 12 August 1920: RGASPI, f. 5, op. 1, d. 2429, p. 51.

68. Report by Yury Pyatakov on the defeat at Warsaw and the reasons for that defeat, addressed to the Central Committee of the RCP, copy to Lenin and Trotsky, from 4 September 1920: RGASPI, f. 17, op. 109, d. 79, pp. 161-167, quote p. 163; Smilga to Lenin (telegram) on 19 August 1920: RGASPI, f. 5, op. 1, d. 2429, p. 52. In the telegram, Smilga claims that there was still hope (albeit not much) for a revolution in Poland. The state of the troops was so poor, however, that an attack on all fronts was not possible any longer. According to Smilga, the defeat had not been due to fresh Polish troops but due to the lack of ammunition and supplies.

69. 76th Radio letter of Tukhachevsky, the commander of the Western Front, to the commander-in-chief, copy to the command of the South-Western Front, from 8 August 1920 (copy): RGASPI, f. 325, op. 1, d. 479, p. 348.

70. Telegram to the command of the 12th and 14th Armies and the 1st Cavalry Army from 13 August 1920 (copy): Ibid.: p. 356; the commander of the South-Western Front, Yegorov, to the commander of the 12th Army on 12 August 1920 (copy): Ibid., p. 355.

71. Shorthand notes of the telephone conversation between Kamenev, Stalin, Yegorov and Bersin (member of the Revolutionary War Council of the South-Western Front) from 13 August 1920 (copy): RGASPI, f. 558, op. 11, d. 445, p. 8 f.; cf. also Davies, *White Eagle*, pp. 213 ff.; Ziemke, *Red Army*, p. 126 f.

72. Cf. Davies, *White Eagle*, pp. 188-225; and Ziemke, *Red Army*, p. 128 f.

73. Session Protocol No. 37 of the Politburo of the Central Committee of the RCP from 19 August 1920: RGASPI, f. 17, op. 3, d. 103, p. 1 f.

74. Ziemke, *Red Army*, p. 126 f.

75. Session Protocol No. 37 of the Politburo of the Central Committee of the RCP from 19 August 1920: RGASPI, f. 17, op. 3, d. 103, p. 1 f.

76. Encrypted telegram from Smilga to Lenin and Trotsky from 20 August 1920: RGASPI, f. 17, op. 109, d. 79, p. 139.

77. Session Protocol No. 39 of the Politburo of the Central Committee of the RCP from 26 August 1920: RGASPI, f. 17, op. 3, d. 105, p. 1.

78. Session Protocol No. 40 of the Politburo of the Central Committee of the RCP from 1 September 1920 (Points 6, 7, 12, 19, 24): RGASPI, f. 17, op. 3, d. 106, pp. 1-5.

79. Ibid.

80. Ibid.

81. Nowik, *Zanim złamano »Enigme«*; »Bolszewik zlamany«, Interview with Grzegorz Nowik in: *Gazeta Wyborcza* from 7 August 2006.

82. Report by Yury Pyatakov on the defeat at Warsaw and the reasons for that defeat, addressed to the Central Committee of the RCP, copy to Lenin and Trotsky, from 4 September 1920: RGASPI, f. 17, op. 109, d. 79, pp. 161-167.

83. Attachment 1 to Yury Pyatakov's report from 4 September 1920: Ibid., p. 168.

84. Message regarding losses among the communists of the 16th Army between 15 August and 10 September 1920, not dated: Ibid., p. 174.

85. Report of the former chief of the political administration of the 27th Division from 15 September 1920 to Trotsky an the Central Committee of the RCP: Ibid., pp. 186 ff., here: p. 187.

86. Davies, *White Eagle,* pp. 226-233.
87. Ibid.
88. Peace Treaty between Russia and Ukraine on one side and Poland on the other side, signed on 18 March 1921 in Riga: RGASPI, f. 5, op. 1, d. 2036, pp. 1-51; Albrecht, *Najnowsza Historia Polski,* p. 71 f.
89. Lenin, Speech Delivered at the Ninth All-Russia Conference of the Russian Communist Party (Bolsheviks), September 22, 1920, in: Lenin, *Works,* Vol. 31, pp. 275-279, here: p. 276 (emphasis by the author).
90. Lenin, Speech Delivered at a Congress of Leather Industry Workers, October 2, 1920, in: Ibid., pp. pp. 300-313, here: p. 304.
91. Lenin's speech at the Moscow Governorate Conference of the CPR(b) on 21 November 1920 on "Our Foreign and Domestic Situation and the Tasks of the Party", printed in: Ibid., pp. 402-422, here: pp. 405,407 f.
92. Stalin, Report on National Factors in Party and State Affairs, published in: Stalin, *Works.* Vol. 5 (1921-1923), Moscow 1953, pp. 241-269, here: pp. 241 f.
93. Interview with Roman Werfel, Polish-Jewish Communist, in 1983, in: Torańska, *Oni,* pp. 272-311, here: p. 286.
94. *Pravda* No. 56,15.03.1923, Printed in: Stalin, *Sochinenija,* Vol. 5, *1921-1923,* Moskau 1947, pp. 160-180, here: p. 167; emphasis by the author.
95. Report by Comrade Manuilsky on the question of nationalities during the congress of the CPP on 31 January 1925: RGASPI, f. 523, op. 1, d. 72, pp. 24-62, here: p. 51.
96. Intelligence report: Poland – Training and tactical preparations of the army by 1 January 1922, documents of strategic intelligence, administration of intelligence of the staff of the Red Army: RGASPI, f. 5, op. 1, d. 2508, pp. 1-114.
97. Grigori Zinoviev: Theses on the coming "German Revolution" and the Tasks of the Russian Communists, presented on 21 September 1923 at the Plenum of the Central Committee and with amendments of the commission of the Politburo approved on 22 September 1923: RGASPI, f. 558, op.ll, d. 139, pp. 22-30, here: p. 25; (emphasis by the author).
98. Lenin, Speech Delivered at a Congress of Leather Industry Workers, October 2, 1920, in: Lenin, *Works,* Vol. 31, pp. 300-313, here: pp. 304, 306.
99. Lenin's paper on the concessions, delivered at the meeting of the CPR(b) faction of the VIII Soviet Congress on 21 December 1920, published in: Ibid., pp. 459-482, here: pp. 471 f.
100. Lenin's speech at the meeting of the Moscow organization of the CPR(b) on 6 December 1920, published. in: Ibid., pp. 434-454, here: p. 445 f.
101. Lenin's paper on the concessions, delivered at the meeting of the CPR(b) faction of the VIII Soviet Congress on 21 December 1920, published. in: Ibid., pp. 459-482, here: p. 471.
102. Lenin's speech on the 3rd anniversary of the October Revolution at the session of the Moscow Soviets of Workers', Peasants' and Red Army Deputies of 6 November 1920, published. in: Ibid., pp. 391-396, here: p. 393.
103. Stalin, The Communist Party of Poland. Speech Delivered at a Meeting of the Polish Commission of the Comintern, July 3, 1924, published in: Stalin, *Works,* Vol. 6, pp. 276-284, here: p. 279.
104. Viktor Kopp, the Soviet Russian representative for matters of prisoners of war, to Trotsky on 6 November 1920: RGASPI, f. 325, op. 2, d. 45, pp. 6-7.
105. Ibid.
106. Cf. Koenen, *Der Russland-Komplex,* pp. 294-298; Gorlov, »Geheimsache Moskau-Berlin«, pp. 133-169; Zeidler, *Reichswehr und Rote Armee.*

Chapter 3

1. Lenin, Speech Delivered at a Congress of Leather Industry Workers, October 2, 1920, in: Lenin, *Works,* Vol. 31, Moscow 1959, pp. 300-313, here: p. 311.

2. Lenin, Speech Delivered at a Meeting of Activists of the Moscow Organisation of the R.C.P.(B.), December 6, 1920, printed. in: ibid., pp. 438-459, here: p. 454 f.

3. Ziemke, *Red Army,* p. 135

4. Ibid., pp. 130-135.

5. Trotsky's speech on the 9th Conference of Councils: RGASPI, f. 325, op. 1, d. 72, pp. 17-56, here: p. 17.

6. Table: Reduction of the Red Army Between December 1920 and December 1921, Excluding Troops for Special Use, Troops of the Cheka and the Fleet, not dated, (December 1921): Ibid., p.143.

7. Report on the state of the Red Army from Shtrodakh, member of the staff of the 15th Army, from 17 November 1920: RGASPI, f. 17, op. 109, d. 128, pp. 1-2.

8. Table: Reduction of the Red Army Between December 1920 and December 1921, Excluding Troops for Special Use, Troops of the Cheka and the Fleet, not dated, (December 1921): RGASPI, f. 325, op.1,d.72, p. 143.

9. Lenin, Report On Concessions Delivered To The R.C.P.(B.) Group At The Eighth Congress Of Soviets, 21 December 1920, printed in: Lenin, *Works,* Vol. 31, pp. 463-486, here: p. 480.

10. Lenin, Speech Delivered at a Meeting of Activists of the Moscow Organisation of the R.C.P.(B.), 6 December 1920, printed in: Ibid., pp. 438-459, here: pp. 455, 459.

11. Lenin, Report On Concessions Delivered To The R.C.P.(B.) Group At The Eighth Congress Of Soviets, 21 December 1920, printed in: Ibid., Vol. 31, pp. 463-486.

12. Yu. P. Bokarev, "NEP kak samoorganizuyushchaisya i samorasru-shayushchaisya sistema", in: NEP; *Ekonomicheskiye, politicheskiye i soziokulturnye aspekty,* pp. 121-133, here: p. 123 f.

13. Yu. Muchin, "Sovietskaya aviapromyshlennost' w gody NEPa 'Gadkiy Utenok' 'Oboronki'", in: ibid., pp. 202-223, here: p. 204.

14. Samuelson, *Krasny Koloss,* p. 43 f.

15. Trotsky's memorandum "Theses on Industrialization" from 16 February 1923: RGASPI, f. 325, op. 1, d. 509, pp. 70-86, here: pp. 71, 75.

16. Response by Dzerzhinsky to Trotsky's memorandum from 16 February, 4 March 1923: RGASPI, f. 325, op. 1, d. 511, pp. 15-20, here: p. 15.

17. Ibid., here: p. 16.

18. Resolution of the Politburo from 25 February 1930 XXX on dealing with concessionaires, attachment no. 2 to the session protocol from 25 February 1930, Point 14: RGASPI, f. 17, op. 162, d. 8, pp. 81 f., 92 f.

19. Excerpt from the report of the district committee of the party in Pugachev, Samara Governement, 18 January 1921, printed. in: *Krestyanskoye dvisheniye v Povolzhiye,* p. 627.

20. Cf. similar documents for the Volga region (ibid.) and for the entirety of Soviet Russia in: *Sovietskaya derevniya glazami VChK-OGPU-NKVD.*

21. B. Orlov, »NEP v regionalnom rakurze: ot usrednennych otsenok k mnogoobrasiyu«, in: NEP; *Ekonomicheskiye, politicheskiye i soziokulturnye aspekty,* pp.33-54; Werth, »Ein Staat gegen sein Volk«, pp. 136-141.

22. Lenin, On Cooperation, Part II, January 06, 1923, printed in: Lenin, *Works,* Vol. 33, pp. 472-475.

23. Ibid., here: p. 472.

24. N. Suvorova, "NEP: Ekonomicheskiye problemy", in: NEP; *Ekonomicheskiye, politicheskiye i soziokulturnye aspekty,* pp.. 96-120; Bokarev, » NEP kak samoorganizuyushchaisya i samorasru-shayushchaisya sistema «, in: ebd., pp. 121-133 (growth figures on p.127).

Chapter 4

1. Lenin, Five Years of the Russian Revolution and the Prospects of the World Revolution. Report to the Fourth Congress of the Communist International, November 13, 1922, printed in: Lenin, *Works,* Vol. 33, pp. 418-432, here: p.421.

2. Lenin, Concluding Remarks at a Conference of Chairmen of Uyezd, Volost and Village Executive Committees of Moscow Gubernia, October 15, 1920, printed in: Lenin, *Works,* Vol. 31, pp. 334-338, here: p. 337.

3. Telegram from Frunze to Lenin on the breakthrough in combat against Ukrainian banditry, from 7 February 1921, printed in: *Nestor Machno,* p. 585 f.

4. Protocol No. 1 of the session of the Commission for the Combat against Banditry in Ukraine from 29 December 1920: RGASPI, f. 76, op. 3, d. 70, p. 32; order regarding the command of all armed forces in Ukraine and representatives of the RVSR in Ukraine from 29 December 1920: Ibid., p. 33; encrypted telegram to the commander of the troops in Ukraine, Comrade Frunze, from Sklayansky, S. Kamenev, Lebedev and Dzerzhinsky from 4 January 1921: Ibid., p. 36; report of the RVSR from 23 August 1921 on the state of the Red Army: RGASPI, f. 17, op. 109, d. 128, pp. 12-13.

5. Telegram from Frunze to Lenin on the breakthrough in the combat against Ukrainian banditry, from 7 February 1921, printed in: *Nestor Machno,* p. 585 f.

6. Cf. numerous other documents and reports from 1921 in the document collection: *Nestor Machno.*

7. Werth, »Ein Staat gegen sein Volk«, p. 125

8. Ibid., pp. 126 f.

9. Ibid., pp. 126 f., 133.

10. Ibid., pp. 133 f.

11. Tukhachevsky to Lenin on 16 July 1921, Report on Banditry in the Tambov Governorate: RGASPI, f. 325, op. 1, d. 482, pp. 219-221.

12. For example, Bolshevik authorities in the Tyumen Governorate in Western Siberia were fighting over 40,000 rebels in February/March 1921. *Za Soviety bez komunistov. Krestyanskoye vosstanie v Tyumenskij gubernii 1921. Sbornik dokumentov,* Nowosibirsk 2000, p. 17.

13. Cf. Werth, »Ein Staat gegen sein Volk«, pp. 124-135; numerous documents regarding the fight against "banditry" in the eastern Volga region in 1921 can be found in the anthology *"Krestyanskoye Dvisheniye v Povolzhe"* and *"Sovietskaya Derevniya"* Vol. 1 for all of Soviet Russia.

14. Werth, »Ein Staat gegen sein Volk«, pp. 128-131.

15. Ibid.

16. Report of the RVSR on the state of the Red Army from 23 August 1921: RGASPI, f. 17, op. 109, d. 128, pp. 12-13.

17. Resolution of the Central Committee of the RCP on detachment for special use of the RFSR, from 24 March 1921: RGASPI, f. 17, op. 87, d. 30, pp. 13 f.

18. Two-week situation report No. 5 of the intelligence administration of the staff of the Red Army on the activities of Russian White guards abroad and on the domestic front, from 1 September 1921: RGASPI, f. 17, op. 87, d. 332, pp. 18-33, here: p. 22.

19. Ibid., pp. 18-33.

20. Two-week situation report No. 5 of the intelligence administration of the staff of the Red Army on the activities of Russian Whites abroad and on the domestic front, from 1 September 1921: Ibid., pp. 96-111.
21. Trotsky's speech on the 9th Soviet conference from 27 December 1921: RGASPI, f. 325, op. 1, d. 72, pp. 17-56, here: p. 33.
22. Directory of cities, districts, governorates, oblasts and autonomous republics which were under martial law on 5 August 1922, from 11 August 1922: RGASPI, f. 17, op. 87, d. 169, pp. 1 ff.; Directory of cities, districts, governorates, oblasts and autonomous republics which were under martial law on 15 October 1922: Ibid., pp. 11 f.; Directory of cities, districts, governorates, oblasts and autonomous republics which were under martial law on 15 December 1922: Ibid., pp. 14 f.
23. From the report of the information department of the OGPU on anti-Soviet occurrences in the countryside between 1925 and 1927, not dated, after 1 March 1928, printed in: *Sovietskaya derevnya*, Vol. 2, pp. 626-641, here: p. 626.

Chapter 5

1. Lenin, 'Five Years of the Russian Revolution and the Prospects of the World Revolution.' Report to the Fourth Congress of the Communist International, 13 November 1922, printed in: Lenin, *Works*, Vol. 33, pp. 418-432, here: pp. 424 f.
2. Lenin on 6 March 1922: "Of what value are our meetings and commissions? Very often they are just make-believe [...] Our worst internal enemy is the bureaucrat – the Communist who occupies a responsible (or not responsible) Soviet post and enjoys universal respect as a conscientious man. [...] He is very conscientious, but he has not learnt to combat red tape, he is unable to combat it, he condones it. *We must rid ourselves of this enemy, and with the aid of all class-conscious workers and peasants we shall get at him.* [...]All those who run all these commissions and conferences and talk but do no practical work would do better to go into the field of propaganda, agitation and other useful work of that kind.": The International and Domestic Situation Of The Soviet Republic Speech Delivered To A Meeting Of The Communist Group At The All-Russia Congress Of Metalworkers, 6 March 1922, printed. in: Lenin, *Works*, Vol. 33, pp. 212-226, here: pp. 224-226. (emphasis in the original); Lenin on the state apparatus, from 2 March 1923: "Better Fewer, But Better" and "our state apparatus is so deplorable, not to say wretched, that we must first think very carefully how to combat its defects": printed in: Ibid., pp. 487-502, here: p. 487; on 17 October 1921, Lenin listed the three main enemies of the NEP: "Communist conceit", i.e. the tendency to rule by decree, "illiteracy" and "bribery": The New Economic Policy And The Tasks Of The Political Education Departments Report To The Second All-Russia Congress Of Political Education Departments 17 October 1921, printed. in: ibid., pp. 60-80, here: pp. 77 f.
3. Lenin, Five Years of the Russian Revolution and the Prospects of the World Revolution. Report to the Fourth Congress of the Communist International, November 13, 1922, printed in: ibid., pp. 418-432, here: p. 425.

Chapter 6

1. Table: Reduction of the Red Army between December 1920 and December 1921, not including troops for special use, troops of the Cheka and the fleet, not dated (December 1921): RGASPI, f. 325, op. 1, d.72, p. 143.
2. Information on the strength of the Red Army on 1 December 1921, from 26 December 1921: Ibid., p. 147.

3. Excerpt from session protocol No. 328 of the Council for Labor and Defense from 28 June 1922: RGASPI, f. 76, op. 3, d. 306, p. 84.

4. Excerpt from protocol No. 5 of the session of the Plenum of the Central Committee of the VCP from 8 August 1922: RGASPI, f. 82, op. 1, d. 799, p. 7.

5. Report on the state of the army, not dated, handwritten date on the margins: 5 May [1923], unknown author: RGASPI, f. 76, op. 2d. 17, pp. 23-38.

6. Excerpt from session protocol No. 328 of the Council for Labor and Defense from 28 June 1922: RGASPI, f. 76, op. 3, d. 306, p. 84.

7. Excerpt from the resolution of the Council for Labor and Defense from 27 September 1922: Ibid., p. 87.

8. Trotsky on the state of the Red Army, not dated, after 3 February 1924: RGASPI, f. 325, op. 1, d. 522, pp. 22-25.

9. Information on the armed forces of foreign countries from 26 July 1924, chief of the Department for Information and Statistics of the Red Army: RGASPI, f. 325, op. 1, d. 524, p. 20.

10. Ibid.

11. Ibid.

12. Report on the state of the army, not dated, handwritten date on the margins: 5 May [1923], unknown author: RGASPI, f. 76, op. 2,d. 17, pp. 27-30.

13. Report on the Defects of the Red Army which directly affect its Combat Readiness as of 1 April 1923, authored by the chief of the 1st Department of the OO of the GPU, Lavrovsky, from 17 May 1923: RGASPI, f. 76, op. 2, d. 17, pp. 48-68, here: p. 50.

14. Ibid., here: pp. 50 ff., 60 ff.

15. Ibid., pp. 52 f.

16. Report on the state of the army, not dated, handwritten date on the margins: 5 May [1923], unknown author: RGASPI, f. 76, op. 2, d. 17, pp. 23-38.

17. Report on the Defects of the Red Army which directly affect its Combat Readiness as of 1 April 1923, authored by the chief of the 1st Department of the OO of the GPU, Lavrovsky, from 17 May 1923: RGASPI, f. 76, op. 2, d. 17, pp. 48-68, here: p. 54.

18. Report of the Political Administration of the Revolutionary War Council of the Republic No. 122 from 24 August 1922: RGASPI, f. 17, op. 87, d. 334, pp. 22-23, here: p. 22.

19. Report of the Political Administration of the Revolutionary War Council of the Republic No. 24 from 30 August 1922: Ibid., pp. 36-37, here: p. 36.

20. Report of the Political Administration of the Revolutionary War Council of the Republic No. 17 from 3 August 1922: Ibid., pp.36-37, here: p. 40.

21. Report on the state of the army, not dated, handwritten date on the margins: 5 May [1923], unknown author: RGASPI, f. 76, op. 2, d. 17, pp. 23-38.

22. Letter from Voroshilov, Moralov, Lashkevich and others to the members of the Central Committee of the RCP(b) and the Central Control Committee on the catastrophic state of the barracks and the horrible supply with fuel within the Red Army, from 2 July 1923: RGASPI, f. 82, op. 2, d. 799, pp. 13 f.

23. Report of the Political Administration of the Revolutionary War Council of the USSR for the month of February 1924, not dated (on the margins: 17 March 1924): RGASPI, f. 17, op. 87, d. 346, pp. 100 ff.

24. Report of the OO of the GPU, Yagoda, on the shortcomings in the Red Army and military agencies, 22 May 1923: RGASPI, f. 76, op. 2, d. 17, pp. 86-96 (emphasis in the original).

25. Report on the Defects of the Red Army which directly affect its Combat Readiness as of 1 April 1923, authored by the chief of the 1st Department of the OO of the GPU, Lavrovsky, from 17 May 1923: RGASPI, f. 76, op. 2, d. 17, pp. 48-68, here: pp. 64 f.

26. Report of the Political Administration of the Revolutionary War Council of the USSR for the month of February 1924, not dated (on the margins: 17 March 1924): RGASPI, f. 17, op. 87, d. 346, pp. 100 ff.

27. Ibid., here: p. 102.

28. GPU situation report on the political atmosphere in the USSR in the month of December 1924, Yagoda, Prokofiev: RGASPI, f. 17, op. 87, d. 181, pp. 2-8, here: pp. 6 f.

29. Cf. GPU reports on the political situation in the USSR for the year 1925: RGASPI, f. 17, op. 87, d. 182,183.

30. Situation report of the Political Administration of the RKKA (Red Army) and the RKKF (Red Fleet) for the month of May 1924: RGASPI, f. 17, op. 87, d. 346, pp. 1-2.

31. Report of the Political Administration of the Revolutionary War Council of the USSR for the month of April 1924: Ibid., pp. 36 ff.

32. Report of the Political Administration of the Revolutionary War Council of the USSR No. 214, from 29 February 1924: Ibid., pp. 103-105, here: p. 104.

33. Report on the political situation in the USSR for the month of October 1925: RGASPI, f. 17, op. 87, d. 183, pp. 32-67, here: p. 38.

34. Report of the Political Administration of the Revolutionary War Council of the USSR No. 214, from 29 February 1924: Ibid., pp. 103-105, here: p. 104.

35. Report of the Political Administration of the Revolutionary War Council of the USSR No. 212, from 25 February 1924: Ibid., pp. 110-112, here: p. 110.

36. Table: National composition of the troops of the Red Army in November 1921: RGASPI, f. 17, op. 87, d. 330, p. 4.

37. Report of the Political Administration of the Revolutionary War Council of the USSR for the month of February 1924, not dated (on the margins: 17 March 1924): RGASPI, f. 17, op. 87, d. 346, pp. 100 ff., here: p. 102.

38. Cf. *CC RCP(b) – VCP (b) i natsionalny vopros*, Vol. 1, *1918-1933* gg, p.402(FN2).

39. Report of the Political Administration of the Revolutionary War Council of the USSR No. 210, from 19 February 1924: RGASPI, f. 17, op. 87, d. 346, pp. 116-117, here: pp. 116 f.

40. Situation report of the Political Administration of the RKKA (Red Army) and the RKKF (Red Fleet) for the month of May 1924: RGASPI, f. 17, op. 87, d. 346, pp. 1-2, here: p. 1.

41. Report of the Political Administration of the RVS of the USSR No. 233, from 10 May 1924: RGASPI, f. 17, op. 87, d. 346, pp. 26 ff., here: p. 26.

42. Memorandum by Tukhachevsky to the Central Committee of the RCP from 23 January 1924: RGASPI, f. 558, op. 11, d. 446, pp. 2-4 (emphasis in the original).

43. Ibid.

44. Trotsky on the state of the Red Army, not dated, after 3 February 1924: RGASPI, f.325, op. 1, d. 522, pp. 22-25, here: p. 22 (emphasis in the original). In the Tsarist military and in the Red Army, demobilized soldiers took home their uniforms.

45. Excerpt from the session protocol of the Plenum of the Central Committee of the RCP No. 17 from 30 March 1923: RGASPI, f. 76, op. 2, d. 17, p. 1.

46. Excerpt from the session protocol of the Plenum of the Central Committee of the RCP from 3 May 1923: Ibid., p. 22.

47. Statement by Danilov to the members of the Central Committee of the RCP(b) regarding the report by Gusev on the state of the Red Army from 3 February 1924, on 28 April 1924: RGASPI, f. 82, op. 2, d. 799, pp. 15-25.

48. Session protocol No. 2 of the Commission for the Development of Measures necessary for the Restoration and Strengthening of the Army, from 19 February 1924, recorded by Trotsky: RGASPI, f. 325, op. 1, d. 522, pp. 8 f.

49. Memorandum by the chief of the OGPU, Felix Dzerzhinsky, on the economic situation, addressed to the Politburo of the Central Committee of the RCP(b), from 9 September 1924, printed in: *Sovietskaya derevnya*, Vol. 2, pp. 223-227, here: p. 226.

50. Resolution of the Revolutionary War Council of the USSR from 17 August 1924; RGASPI, f. 325, op. 1, d. 99, pp. 5 f.

51. Mikhail Frunze, Chief of Staff of the Red Army, to the chief of the RVS of the USSR, Trotsky, from 5 July 1924: RGASPI, f. 325, op. 1, d. 524, pp. 8-9.

52. Tukhachevsky's response to the criticism from the staff of the RKKA regarding his memorandum from 8 March 1930 on the reorganization of the Red Army, from 19 June 1930, addressed to Stalin, copy to Voroshilov: RGASPI, f. 558, op. 11, d. 446, pp. 6-11, here: p. 10.

53. Documents regarding the rehearsed mobilization of 1925, not dated (late 1925 or early 1926): RGASPI, f. 76, op. 2, d. 182, pp. 104-110.

54. Ibid.

55. Protocol of the Operative Conference of the Authorized Representatives from 8 July 1926: RGASPI, f. 76, op. 3, d. 364, pp. 64-69.

56. Ibid.

57. Ibid.

58. Ibid.

59. From the report of the Secret Unit of the OGPU "Anti-Soviet Movement in the Countryside", October 1928, published in: *Sovietskaya derevnya*, pp. 780-817, here: pp. 812 ff.

60. Memorandum of Military Industry and National Defense, Smirnov, member of the Central Committee for National Defense, not dated, early June 1923: RGASPI, f. 76, op. 2, d. 17, pp. 98 f.

61. Ibid.

62. Attachment "Handguns" from Smirnov's memorandum from early June 1923: Ibid., pp. 99-104.

63. Ibid.

64. Attachment "Ammunition for Handguns" from Smirnov's memorandum from early June 1923: Ibid., pp. 105-108.

65. Attachment "Artillery" from Smirnov's memorandum from early June 1923: Ibid., pp. 109-115.

66. Attachment "Explosives and Associated Equipment Elements" from Smirnov's memorandum from early June 1923: Ibid., pp. 116 f.

67. Attachment "Aircraft and engines" from Smirnov's memorandum from early June 1923: Ibid., pp. 118-121.

68. Attachment "Fleet" table "Five Year Production Plan of the Armaments Industry 1923-1928" from Smirnov's memorandum from early June 1923: Ibid., pp. 122-125.

69. Attachment "Five Year Production Plan of the Armaments Industry 1923-1928" from Smirnov's memorandum from early June 1923: Ibid., p. 125.

70. Resolution of the Revolutionary War Council of the USSR from 17 August 1924: RGASPI, f. 325, op. 1, d. 99, pp. 5 f.

71. Summary of Trotsky's speech "Our Military Tasks", held at the Military Academy of the Red Army on 7 May 1924: RGASPI, f. 325, op. 1, d. 87, pp. 10-18, here: pp. 11,13.

72. Cf. Ziemke, *Red Army*, pp. 149 ff.

73. Trotsky's speech at the yearly congress of the "Society of Friends of Chemical Defense" on 19 May 1924: RGASPI, f. 325, op. 1, d. 92, pp. 1-23, here: pp. 8 f.

74. Memorandum of the chief of the Council of the Association of Chemical Industry, unreadable signature, not dated (1925): RGASPI, f. 76, op. 2, d. 203, pp. 2-8, here: p. 3.

75. Dzershinsky to Kraval and Shtern on 28 May 1926: RGASPI, f. 76, op. 2, d. 182, p. 99.

76. Dzerzhinsky to the Politburo of the Central Committee of the RCP(b), copy to Frunze, 8 March 1925: Ibid., p. 64. In the letter, Dzerzhinsky criticized the project of the resolution on the Commission for Defense at the Politburo of the Central Committee of the RCP(b) (sent on 4 March 1925, No. 4328). Dzerzhinsky criticized that this was not a party commission but a pure Soviet commission – a new secretive STO [Council for Labor and Defense], with greater powers. This project thus handed over powers from the Politburo and the STO to the commission. According to him, this would not work and the secretiveness of the commission would only create confusion. Despite Dzerzhinsky's opposition, the commission began to operate soon after. On 5 July 1926, the 13th session of the commission took place, during which it was composed of: Rykov (chairman), Dzerzhinsky, Voroshilov, Kuznetsov, Unszlicht, Bubnov, Rudsutak. Protocol No. 13 of the Commission of Comrade Rykov at the Politburo of the Central Committee of the VKP(b) from 5 July 1926: Ibid., pp. 175 f. That it was the Rykov commission which was the secret Commission for Defense is proven by the following reports (ibid., pp. 176-188).

77. Report on the State of the Armaments Industry, not dated (late June/ early July 1926), author name unreadable: RGASPI, f. 76, op. 2, d. 182, pp. 176-188.

78. Project of the Resolution of the Commission for Defense from 5 July 1926: Ibid., pp. 210-214.

79. Ibid.

80. Excerpt from the session protocol No. 39 of the Politburo from the 8th of July 1926: Ibid., p. 229.

Chapter 7

1. Lenin, Speech at a Meeting of the Moscow Soviet in Celebration of the First Anniversary of the Third International, 6 March 1920, printed in: Lenin, *Works*, Vol. 30, pp. 417-425, quote on pp. 424, author's emphasis.

2. Lenin, Report On Concessions Delivered To The R C.P.(B.) Group At The Eighth Congress Of Soviets, 21 December 1920, printed in: Lenin, *Works*, Vol. 31, pp. 463-486, here: p. 472.

3. Stalin, The October Revolution and the Tactics of the Russian Communists. *Preface to the Book "On the Road to October"*, published. in: Stalin, *Works*, Vol. 6 (1924), pp. 374-420.

4. Stalin, Political Report of the Central Committee, *December 3*. The Fifteenth Congress of the C.P.S.U.(B.), *December 2-19, 1927*, published. in: Stalin, *Works*, Vol. 10, pp. 275-363, here: pp. 280, 282.

5. Cf. Schwabe, "Der Weg der Republik", pp. 95-133.

6. G. Zinoviev: Theses on the Coming "German Revolution" and the Tasks of the Russian Communists, presented on 21 September 1923 at the Plenum of the Central Committee and with amendments from the commission of the Politburo approved on 22 September 1923: RGASPI, f. 558, op. 11, d. 139, pp. 22-30, and: RGASPI, f. 17, op. 2, d. 101, pp. 5-13.

7. Quoted according to Firsov "Ein Oktober, der nicht stattfand", pp. 38 f.

8. Ibid., excerpt from the protocol No. 27 of the Politburo session from 22 August 1923, published in: *Deutscher Oktober 1923*, pp. 130 f.

9. Protocol No. 27 of the Politburo session of 22 August 1923: RGASPI, f. 17, op. 162, d. 1, pp. 4 f.; excerpt from the protocol No. 27 of the Politburo session from 22 August 1923, published in: *Deutscher Oktober 1923*, S. 130 f.

10. Bessedovsky, *Im Dienste der Sowjets*, pp. 151 f. Bessedovsky was in Moscow until September 1923, when he was sent to Warsaw as a Soviet representative. His claims are by and large supported by the Politburo protocols, in particular those of the Politburo sessions No. 29 on 30 August 1923, No. 31 on 6 September 1923, No. 33 on 18 September 1923: RGASPI, f. 17, op. 162, d. 1, pp. 7-9, 12.

11. Protocol No. 30 of the Presidium session of 23 August 1923, published in: *Deutscher Oktober 1923*, pp. 132 f.; Firsov, "Ein Oktober, der nicht stattfand".

12. From the stenographic protocol of the secret Moscow conference of the Russian members of the executive with the delegations of the KPD and the communist parties of France and Czechoslovakia, Moscow, 25 September 1923, published in: *Deutscher Oktober 1923*, pp. 162-178, here: S.163.

13. G. Zinoviev: Theses on the Coming "German Revolution" and the Tasks of the Russian Communists, presented on 21 September 1923 at the Plenum of the Central Committee and with amendments from the commission of the Politburo approved on 22 September 1923: RGASPI, f. 558, op. 11, d. 139, pp. 22-30, and: RGASPI, f. 17, op. 2, d. 101, pp. 5-13.

14. Letter from Stalin to August Thalheimer, 20 September 1923: RGASPI, f. 558, op. 11, d. 139, p. 18; published as facsimile in: *Deutscher Oktober 1923*, p.212.

15. Georgij Cicerin (Chicherin), Grigorij Zinov'ev (Zinoviev), Lev Trockij (Trotsky), Nikołaj Bucharin, Karl Radek, Iosif Stalin: "Konspekt der Debatte des Politbüros des ZK der RKP(b) über die 'deutsche Revolution'", Moscow, 21 August 1923, co-authored by Bazanov (Bazhanow), published in: *Deutscher Oktober 1923*, pp. 116-128, here: pp. 123 f.

16. Firsov, "Ein Oktober, der nicht stattfand".

17. Iosif Stalin, "Anmerkungen zum Charakter und zu den Perspektiven der deutschen Revolution", 19.08.1923, published in: *Deutscher Oktober 1923*, pp. 110-112, here: p. 112.

18. Georgij Cicerin (Chicherin), Grigorij Zinov'ev (Zinoviev), Lev Trockij (Trotsky), Nikołaj Bucharin, Karl Radek, Iosif Stalin: "Konspekt der Debatte des Politbüros des ZK der RKP(b) über die 'deutsche Revolution'", Moskau, 21.08.1923, co-authored by Bazanov (Bazhanow), published in: *Deutscher Oktober 1923*, pp. 116-128, here: pp. 124.

19. On 3 March 1921, Poland and Romania signed a military alliance aimed against Soviet Russia. In case of a Bolshevik attack on one of the countries, the other would be required to offer military aid.

20. Notice from Guzev to Zinoviev from 1923 (no specific date): RGASPI, f. 558, op. 11, d. 139, p. 32.

21. Commentary by Stalin regarding Guzev's proposal, not dated: Ibid., p. 33.

22. Session protocol No. 45 of the Politburo of the Central Committee of the RCP(b) from 13 November 1923: RGASPI, f. 17, op. 162, d. 1, p. 28; on 18 October 1923, the Politburo set up a commission to tackle this issue, which came up with measures that were adopted on 13 November 1923. The commission was composed of Chicherin, Frunze, Unszlicht and Skripnik: Session protocol No. 40 of the Politburo from 18 October 1923: RGASPI, f. 17, op. 3, d. 388, pp. 1-7, here: p. 2.

23. Trotsky to the members of the Politburo and the Presidium of the Central Control Committee regarding the Polish question on 3 October 1923: RGASPI, f. 325, op. 1, d. 518, pp. 68 ff.

24. Iosif Stalin, "Notes on the Character and Perspective of the German Revolution, 20 August 1923", published in: *Deutscher Oktober 1923*, pp. 110 ff., here: p. 112.

25. Kopp, "Report Regarding the Polish Question" addressed to the Politburo of the Central Committee of the RCP from 9 October 1923: RGASPI, f. 325, op. 2, d. 52, pp. 34 f.;

file notice by Kopp regarding the conversation with Knoll (addressed to members of the Collegium of the People's Commissariat for Foreign Affairs, Comrade Obolensky and the members of the Politburo) from 13 October 1923: RGASPI, f. 325, op. 2, d. 52, p. 42.

26. Protocol No. 40 of the Politburo session from 18 October 1923: RGASPI, f. 17, op. 3, d. 388, pp. 1-7, here: p. 2.

27. Bessedovsky, *Im Dienste der Sowjets*, pp. 171 ff.

28. Ibid.

29. Trotsky to Chicherin, copy to Stalin, from 22 November 1923: RGASPI, f. 325, op. 1, d. 520, p. 4.

30. Bessedovsky, *Im Dienste der Sowjets*, pp. 171 ff.

31. Ibid., pp. 169-175.

32. Cf. Schwabe, "Der Weg der Republik".

33. Firsov, "Ein Oktober, der nicht stattfand", pp. 48 ff.; *Deutscher Oktober 1923*, pp. 234-237.

34. Report on the "Hamburg Uprising" by the military chief at the headquarters of the KPD, Valdemar Roze, from 26 October 1923, published in: *Ibid.*, pp. 247-251, here: p. 250.

35. Ibid., pp. 52 f.

36. Ibid., pp. 54-57; cf. Stalin blaming his rivals on 15 January 1924: "Die deutsche Revolution und die Fehler des Genossen Radek. Aus dem Bericht auf dem Plenum des ZK der RKP(b), 15.01.1924" as well as "Resolutionsentwurf des Plenums des ZK der RKP(b) zur 'Deutschen Frage'" from the same day, published in: Ibid., pp. 433-451.

37. Quoted according to: *Deutscher Oktober 1923*, S. 104.

38. Trotsky's speech "Questions of Civil War" from 29 September 1924, held during a session of the Board of the Society for Military Studies (published as a brochure): RGASPI, f. 325, op. 1, d. 278, pp. 27-48, here: p. 36.

39. Stalin, The Communist Party of Poland. *Speech Delivered at a Meeting of the Polish Commission of the Comintern, July 3, 1924*, published in: Stalin, *Works*, Vol. 6, pp. 276-284, here: p. 279.

40. Stalin, "The International Situation and the Tasks of the Communist Parties," printed in: Stalin, *Works*, Vol. 7, pp. 51-57, here: p. 51.

41. Bessedovsky, *Im Dienste der Sowjets*, S. 180 f.

42. Stalin, "The International Situation and the Tasks of the Communist Parties," printed in: Stalin, *Works*, Vol. 7, pp. 51-57, here: pp. 52 f.

43. Chang/Halliday, *Mao*.

Chapter 8

1. Trotsky's speech at the Third Moscow Conference of the All-Russian Association of Metalworkers from 19 October 1923: RGASPI, f. 325, op. 2, d. 80, pp. 87-92, here: p. 91 (author's emphasis).

2. Cf. Michałka, "Deutsche Außenpolitik 1920-1933", pp. 311 f.

3. Quoted according to: Dębski, *Między Berlinem a Moskwą*, p. 59, FN 11.

4. Letter from P. Lapichinsky to Dzerzhinsky from 11 August 1924: RGASPI, f. 76, op. 3, d. 339, pp. 1 f.

5. Protocol No. 20 of the Politburo session from 28 August 1924: RGASPI, f. 17, op. 162, d. 2, pp. 30 f.

6. Protocol No. 43 of the Politburo session from 3 January 1925: Ibid., pp. 54 f.

7. This is evident from the correspondence regarding the question of national minorities between Manuilsky and Stalin in the 1920s: RGASPI, f. 558, op. 11, d. 763.

8. Speech by Manuilsky regarding the question of national minorities at the Congress of the KPP on 30 January 1925: RGASPI, f 523, op. 1, d. 72, pp. 24-62, here: pp. 49, 52, 53, 55 (author's emphasis).

9. Even though Germany won the contentious plebiscite in Upper Silesia with 59.8% of the vote, it did not receive the entirety of the region. On 20 October 1921, it was decided at an ambassadors' conference in Paris that the region was to be divided, with the heavily Polish industrial centers going to Poland. As a result, Poland received around 90% of Upper Silesia's coal reserves as well as the zinc, lead and silver smelters. Cf. Kazimierz Popiołek, *Historia Sląska. Od pradziejów do 1945 roku,* Katowice 1984; Karl C. von Loesch, *Wie Ostgebiete des Reiches verlorengingen.*

10. Speech by Manuilsky regarding the question of national minorities at the Congress of the KPP on 30 January 1925: RGASPI, f 523, op. 1, d. 72, pp. 24-62, here: p. 58.

11. G. Zinoviev: Theses on the Coming "German Revolution" and the Tasks of the Russian Communists, presented on 21 September 1923 at the Plenum of the Central Committee and with amendments from the commission of the Politburo approved on 22 September 1923: RGASPI, f. 558, op. 11, d. 139, pp. 22-30, here: p. 25.

12. Roszkowski, *Najnowsza Historia Polski,* pp. 155-165.

13. Excerpt from the Politburo protocol No. 17 from 25 March 1926: RGASPI, f. 76, op. 2, d. 58, p. 2.

14. Protocol of the session of the Polish Commission of the Politburo of the VCP(b) from 30 March 1926: Ibid., p. 3.

15. Dzerzhinsky to Bogucki on 17 April 1926: Ibid., p.4.

16. Official Communication of the Secretariat of the Head of the Komintern, Comrade Zinoviev to Comrade Tovstukh from 19 May 1926: RGASPI, f. 76, op. 3, d. 364, pp. 39-41, here: p. 39.

17. Cf. Roszkowski, *Najnowsza Historia Polski,* pp. 162-168.

18. Cf. Stalin, The International Situation and the Defense of the USSR *Speech Delivered on August 1,* printed in: Stalin, *Works,* Vol. 10, pp. 3-62, here: pp. 3-5.

19. Protocol of the session of the Politburo from 20 May 1926: RGASPI, f. 17, op. 162, d. 3, pp. 74 f.

20. Western communist academics such as Grover C. Furr described Piłsudski as the "prewar fascist dictator of Poland" (Grover C. Furr, »The AFT, The CIA, and Solidarnosc«, in: *Comment* [Montclair State College, NJ], vol. 1, no. 2 (Spring 1982), pp. 31-34, here: p.32); other instances include: Alex Ravda, »Review of Native Fascism in the Successor States, 1918-1945, by Peter F. Sugar«, *The American Political Science Review,* vol. 70, no. 3 (Sept. 1976), pp. 1002 f.; more recently, American historian Prof. Beth A. Griech-Polelle wrote: "In 1936, Europe was a land of upheaval and displacement, grappling with economic depression and a fear of fleeing foreigners. Many Germans, Austrians, and Italians fled Hitler and Mussolini, Romanians hid from the Iron Guard, Poles feared their military dictator, General Piłsudski, and Hungarians suffered under Admiral Horthy's oppressive rule." Beth A. Griech-Polelle, "The Impact of the Spanish Civil War upon Roman Catholic Clergy in Nazi Germany", in: *Antisemitism, Christian Ambivalence, and the Holocaust,* published by Kevin P. Spicer, Bloomington/Ind. 2007, pp. 121-135, here: p. 121. It has to be noted that Piłsudski died in May 1935, meaning that he was not a military dictator in 1936 anymore. At the same time, there is no mention of the repressive and bloody colonial regimes of Britain, France, the Netherlands and Belgium, let alone of the Soviet terror regime that claimed millions of lives in the 1930s.

21. Cf. Roszkowski, *Najnowsza Historia Polski,* pp. 168-179.

22. Dzerzhinsky to Yagoda on 25 June 1926: RGASPI, f 76, op. 3, d. 364, pp. 55-56, here: p. 55.

23. The claim that Poland prepared for an attack on the Soviet Union in 1926 or later is entirely baseless. Had there been concrete plans, Soviet and communist Polish party historians would have found them after 1945; they would surely have published it in order to discredit Piłsudski's supposedly fascist government. Indeed, the "fascism" of Piłsudski had been one of the favorite themes of communist party historians such as Jerzy Tomaszewski and Andrzej Garlicki.

Chapter 9

1. Stalin, Political Report of the Central Committee, 18 December. The Fourteenth Congress of the C.P.S.U.(B.), 18-31 December, 1925, published in: Stalin, *Works*, Vol. 7 (1925), pp. 265-361, here: pp. 269-271.

2. Cf. Melvin P. Leffler, "1921-1932: Expansionist Impulses and Domestic Constraints", in: *Economics and World Power*. An Assessment of American Diplomacy since 1789, hg. von William H. Becker und Samuel F. Wells, Jr., New York 1984, pp. 225-276.

3. Stalin, Political Report of the Central Committee, *December 18*. The Fourteenth Congress of the C.P.S.U.(B.), *December 18-31, 1925*, published in: Stalin, *Works*, Vol. 7 (1925), pp. 265-361, here: pp. 272 f.

4. Lenin, "Better Fewer, But Better" on 2 March 1923, printed in: Lenin, *Works*, Vol. 33, pp. 487-502, pp. 498 f.

5. Ibid., p. 489.

6. Trotsky's speech at the Third Moscow Conference of the All-Russian Association of Metalworkers from 19 October 1923: RGASPI, f. 325, op. 2, d. 80, pp. 87-92, here: p. 91.

7. Trotsky's speech at the Conference of Metalworkers of the Moscow Governorate, from 5 July 1923: ibid., pp. 47-64, here: p. 54.

8. Stalin, Political Report of the Central Committee, *December 18*. The Fourteenth Congress of the C.P.S.U.(B.), *December 18-31, 1925*, published in: Stalin, *Works*, Vol. 7 (1925), pp. 265-361, here: p. 320.

9. Stalin, "On the Grain Front." From a Talk to Students of the Institute of Red Professors, the Communist Academy and the Sverdlov University, 28 May 1928, printed in: Stalin, *Works*, Vol. 11, pp. 85-101, here: pp. 86 f.

10. Before the war, Russian agriculture produced around 5 billion pud of grain, of which around 1.3 billion were sold outside the village. Around half of the 5 billion pud were produced by estate owners and wealthy peasants, the rest by medium and small-scale peasants. Of the 1.3 billion pud sold outside of the village, however, 47% was sold by landowners, 34% by wealthy peasants, and only 14.7% by medium and small-scale peasants. In 1926/27, grain production in the Soviet Union stood at 4.749 billion pud, of which only 630 million pud – roughly half of the pre-war amount – was sold outside the village. The new sovkhozes and kolkhozes produced only 80 million pud, of which they sold 37.8 million pud outside of the village. In contrast, wealthy peasants produced 617 million pud of grain, of which 20 million was sold outside of the village. Small and medium-scale peasants accounted for the vast majority of grain production now, with 4.052 billion pud, but only 466.2 million pud, or 11.2% of total production, made it out of the village. (ibid., here: p. 89.).

11. Ibid., here: p. 88.

12. Stalin, Political Report of the Central Committee, *December 3*. The Fifteenth Congress of the C.P.S.U.(B.), *December 2-19, 1927*, published. in: Stalin, *Works*, Vol. 10, pp. 275-363, here: p. 312.

13. Memorandum on the Results of the Industrialization and the Theses of the Central Committee regarding the Five Year Plan, signed by 14 members of the inner opposition (L. Emeylanov, et. al.), 04.11.1927: RGASPI, f. 84, op. 2, d. 35, pp. 6-53, here: p. 31.

14. "Grain Collection Policy in the Context of the General Economic Situation", theses of the report by Mikoyan, unanimously approved by the commission of the Politburo, not dated, before 30 June 1928: RGASPI, f. 84, op. 2, d. 6, pp. 43-51, here: p. 45.

15. Gross product of agriculture and industry in the years 1913 to 1926/27: RGASPI, f. 74, op. 2, d. 142, p. 234; Stalin, Political Report of the Central Committee, *December 3*. The Fifteenth Congress of the C.P.S.U.(B.), *December 2-19, 1927*, published. in: Stalin, *Works*, Vol. 10, pp. 275-363, here: p. 300.

16. Stalin, Political Report of the Central Committee, *December 3*. The Fifteenth Congress of the C.P.S.U.(B.), *December 2-19, 1927*, published. in: Stalin, *Works*, Vol. 10, pp. 275-363, here: p. 301.

17. Trotsky's speech at the Conference of the Metalworkers of the Moscow Governorate, from 5 July 1923: RGASPI, f. 325, op. 2, d. 80., pp. 47-64, here: pp. 54 f.

18. Dzerzhinsky to Stalin on 3 December 1925, note on the margins: "Not sent, 6.XII": RGASPI, f. 76, op. 2, d. 270, pp. 6-10.

19. Ibid.

20. Ibid.

21. Dzerzhinsky to Kuibyshev on 3 July 1926: RGASPI, f. 76, op. 2, d. 270, p. 31 ff.

22. Note by Felix Dzerzhinsky to "V. V." (apparently Valerian Vladmirovich Kuibyshev), not dated (before 20 July 1926.): RGASPI, f. 76, op. 2, d. 270, pp. 63 f.

23. Felix Dzierżyński. *Biography*, pp. 454 ff., 552.

24. Cf. documents such as the session protocols of the Politburo (RGASPI, f. 17, op. 3) or the documents to price policy in the year 1928: RGASPI, f. 84, op. 2, d. 6 (document inventory Mikoyan).

25. Stalin, "On the Bond between the Workers and Peasants and On State Farms." From a Speech Delivered on July 11, 1928, printed in: Stalin, *Works*, Vol. 11, pp. 197-205, here: pp. 197 f.

26. Table in the memorandum of the chief of the OGPU, Felix Dzerzhinsky, on the economic state of the country, addressed to the Politburo of the Central Committee of the RCP(b) from 9 July 1924, printed in: *Sovietskaja derevnya*, Vol. 2, pp. 223-227.

27. "Bukharin in the Fight against the Opposition Bloc", documents spread by the inner opposition in Moscow and the Moscow district, not dated, after 24 July 1926: RGASPI, f. 84, op. 2, d. 25, pp. 180-210, here: pp. 188 f.

28. Memorandum on the Results of the Industrialization and the Theses of the Central Committee regarding the Five Year Plan, signed by 14 members of the inner opposition (L. Emelyanov, et. al.), 4 November 1927: RGASPI, f. 84, op. 2, d. 35, pp. 6-53, here: pp. 7f.

29. Cf. Report No. 34 of the Information Department of the OGPU for the time between 23 October and 25 November 1925, printed in: *Sovietskaja derevnya*, Vol. 2, pp. 358-365; Situation Report of the Governorate Division of the TULA OGPU on the Progress of Grain Collection and the Commodity Market from 10 January 1928, printed in: ibid., pp. 643-647; "Bukharin in the Fight against the Opposition Bloc", documents spread by the inner opposition in Moscow and the Moscow district, not dated, after 24 July 1926: RGASPI, f. 84, op. 2, d. 25, pp. 185-210 (on the hunger for goods pp. 189 f.).

30. Cf. Margolina, Wodka.
31. Trotsky on Stalin, to the Politburo on 28 January 1931: RGASPI, f. 325, op. 1, d. 508, p. 27.
32. Report of the OGPU division of the Pskov Governorate until 2 September 1924, from 15 September 1924, printed in: *Sovietskaja derevnya*, Vol. 2, pp. 246-248.
33. Ibid., p. 247.
34. Lenin, Tenth All-Russian Conference of the R.C.P.(B.), Summing-Up Speech On The Tax In Kind 27 May, 27 May 1921, printed in: Lenin, *Works*, Vol. 32, pp. 417-432, here: p. 426.
35. Lenin, Eleventh Congress Of The R.C.P.(B.), Closing Speech On The Political Report Of The Central Committee Of The R.C.P.(B.) 28 March 1922, printed in: Lenin, *Works*, Vol. 33, pp. 310-324, here: p. 312.
36. Trotsky to Pyatakov on 23 July 1923: RGASPI, f. 325, op. 1, d. 518, pp. 10 f.
37. Trotsky to Semeshko on 13 August 1923: ibid., pp. 31 f.
38. Ibid.
39. Trotsky to Pyatakov, 23 July 1923: ibid., pp. 10 f.
40. Trotsky to Serebryakov on 23 July 1923: ibid., p. 16.
41. Trotsky an Rykov on 26 July 1923: ibid., p. 15.
42. Session protocol No. 53 of the Politburo of the Central Committee of the RCP(b) from 18 March 1925 (point 9): RGASPI, f. 17, op. 162, d. 2, pp. 89 f.
43. Criticism of the Five Year Plan from 10 November 1927 by the Opposition, signed by Bakayev, Evdohimov, Pterson, Zinoviev, Kanenev, Muralov, Rakovsky, Smilga, Trotsky: RGASPI, f. 84, op. 2, d. 35, pp. 53-102, here: p. 98.
44. Stalin, Political Report of the Central Committee, *December 18*. The Fourteenth Congress of the C.P.S.U.(B.), *December 18-31, 1925*, published in: Stalin, *Works*, Vol. 7 (1925), pp. 265-361, here: p. 349.
45. The Genoa Conference took place between 10 April and 19 May 1922. Among others, the representatives of Great Britain, France, Italy, Japan and other capitalist states demanded that Soviet Russia pay off all Russian wartime and pre-war debts, return nationalized property to foreign owners. The Soviet delegation refused.
46. Stalin, Letter to Shinkevich, 20 March 1927, printed in: Stalin, *Works*, Vol. 9, pp. 194 f.
47. Stalin, Political Report of the Central Committee, *December 3*. The Fifteenth Congress of the C.P.S.U.(B.), *December 2-19, 1927*, published. in: Stalin, *Works*, Vol. 10, pp. 275-363, here: p. 320; *Pravda* No. 279 and 282 on 6 and 9 December 1927.
48. Criticism of the Five Year Plan from 10 November 1927 by the Opposition, signed by Bakayev, Evdohimov, Pterson, Zinoviev, Kanenev, Muralov, Rakovsky, Smilga, Trotsky: RGASPI, f. 84, op. 2, d. 35, pp. 53-102, here: p. 73.
49. Stalin an Molotow, 01.09.1930, published in: Stalin, *Briefe an Molotow*, pp. 226 f.
50. Resolution of the Politburo from 15 September 1930, Session protocol No. 8: RGASPI, f. 17, op. 162, d. 9, p. 31; published also in: Stalin, *Briefe an Molotow*, p. 227. However, there the date of the Politburo decision is mistakenly given as 15 December 1930, the correct date is 15 September 1930.
51. Resolution on the Distillation of Spirits, approved by the Politburo on 30 October 1930: RGASPI, f. 17, op. 162, d. 9, pp. 65 f.
52. Session Protocol No. 15 of the Politburo of the Central Committee of the VCP(b) from 15 November 1930, point 11/17: RGASPI, f. 17, op. 162, d. 9, pp. 68-72.
53. Report of the OGPU Division in the Penza Governorate, from 16 September 1924, published in: *Sovietskaja derevnya*, Vol. 2, pp. 245 f.
54. Report of the OGPU Division in the Pskov Governorate, from 2 September 1924, published in: ibid., pp. 246 ff.

55. Report No. 5 of the Informational Division of the OGPU regarding economic differentiation and the political situation in the village between 24 and 31 January 1925, published in: ibid., pp. 271-287, here: pp. 286 f.

56. "Grain Collection Policy in the Context of the General Economic Situation", theses of the report by Mikoyan, unanimously approved by the commission of the Politburo, not dated, before 30 June 1928: RGASPI, f. 84, op. 2, d. 6, pp. 43-51, here: p. 50.

57. Stalin, First Results of the Procurement Campaign and the Further Tasks of Party. *To All Organisations of the C.P.S.U.(B.)*, printed in: *Stalin*, Works, Vol. 11, pp. 12-22, here: p. 17.

58. Report of the OGPU on the political situation in the USSR for October 1925: RGASPI, f. 17, op. 87, d. 183, pp. 32-67, here: p. 35 v.

59. Criticism of the Five Year Plan from 10 November 1927 by the Opposition, signed by Bakayev, Evdohimov, Pterson, Zinoviev, Kanenev, Muralov, Rakovsky, Smilga, Trotsky: RGASPI, f. 84, op. 2, d. 35, pp. 53-102, here: p. 98.

60. Lev Trotsky, "The Situation of the Working Class", not published manuscript, June 1927: RGASPI, f. 325, op. 1, d. 590, pp. 1-72, here: pp. 68, 70.

61. "Bukharin in the Fight against the Opposition Bloc", documents spread by the inner opposition in Moscow and the Moscow district, not dated, after 24 July 1926: RGASPI, f. 84, op. 2, d. 25, pp. 180-210, here: pp. 188, 204; The total number of workers and clerks stood at 6,326,000 in 1923/24, not counting railway and inland navigation workers, at 7,257,000 in 1924/25 and at 8,592,000 in 1925/26. Numbers from: P. N. Avdeyev, *Trudovye konflikty v SSSR*, Moscow 1928, p. 68 (RGASPI, f. 613, op. 3, d. 93, pp. 67-100, here: p. 86).

62. *Vsesoyusnayaperepis naseleniya 1937 goda*, pp. 42-53.

63. Lev Trotsky, "The Situation of the Working Class", unpublished manuscript, June 1927: RGASPI, f. 325, op. 1, d. 590, pp. 1-72.

64. Ibid., p. 4 (emphasis in the original).

65. Ibid., p. 8.

66. Ibid., pp. 12 f., 48 f.

67. Ibid., pp. 10 ff., 50.

68. Memorandum on the Results of the Industrialization and the Theses of the Central Committee regarding the Five Year Plan, signed by 14 members of the inner opposition (L. Emeylanov, et. al.), 4 November 1927: RGASPI, f. 84, op. 2, d. 35, pp. 6-53, here: p. 31.

69. OGPU report on the political situation in April 1925, June 1925: RGASPI, f. 17, op. 87, d. 182, pp. 1-12.

70. Cf. RGASPI, f. 17, op. 87, d. 181,182,183; Simonov "Strengthen the Defence". Simonov also examines the attitudes of the workers who, according to the OGPU reports he analyzed, were anti-Soviet and complained that they were in a worse situation than under the Tsars.

71. Lev Trotsky, "The Situation of the Working Class", upublished manuscript, June 1927: RGASPI, f. 325, op. 1, d. 590, pp. 1-72, here: p. 18.

72. Ibid., pp. 18 f.; P. N. Avdeyev, *Trudovye konflikty v SSSR*, Moscow 1928, p. 68 (RGASPI, f. 613, op. 3, d. 93, pp. 67-100, here: pp. 85-96).

73. From the report of the Information Division of the OGPU on anti-Soviet Occurances in the village between 1925 and 1927, not dated, after 1 March 1928, published in: *Sovietskaja derevnya*, Vol. 2, pp. 626-641.

74. Ibid., p. 626.

75. Ibid., pp. 626 f.

76. Ibid., pp. 628 f.

77. Simonov, "'Strengthen the Defence'".

78. From the report of the Information Division of the OGPU on anti-Soviet Occurrences in the village between 1925 and 1927, not dated, after 1 March 1928, published in: *Sovietskaja derevnya*, Vol. 2, pp. 626-641, here: pp. 628 f.

79. Ibid., pp. 692 f; From the report of the secret unit of the OGPU "Anti-Soviet Movement in the Village" from October 1928, printed in: *Sovietskaja derevnya*, Vol. 2, pp. 780-817, here: pp. 806 f.

80. From the report of the secret unit of the OGPU "Anti-Soviet Movement in the Village" from October 1928, printed in: *Sovietskaja derevnya*, Vol. 2, pp. 780-817, here: pp. 786 f.

81. From the report of the Information Division of the OGPU on anti-Soviet Occurrences in the village between 1925 and 1927, not dated, after 1 March 1928, published in: *Sovietskaja derevnya*, Vol. 2, pp. 626-641, here: pp. 630 f.

82. Ibid.

83. Ibid., pp. 632 f.; From the report of the secret unit of the OGPU "Anti-Soviet Movement in the Village" from October 1928, printed in: *Sovietskaya derevnya*, Vol. 2, pp. 780-817, here: pp. 785-794.

84. From the report of the Information Division of the OGPU on anti-Soviet Occurrences in the village between 1925 and 1927, not dated, after 1 March 1928, published in: *Sovietskaja derevnya*, Vol. 2, pp. 626-641, here: pp. 633 f.

85. Ibid., pp. 637, 640; From the report of the secret unit of the OGPU "Anti-Soviet Movement in the Village" from October 1928, printed in: *Sovietskaya derevnya*, Vol. 2, pp. 790, 809.

86. From the report of the Information Division of the OGPU on anti-Soviet Occurrences in the village between 1925 and 1927, not dated, after 1 March 1928, published in: *Sovietskaya derevnya*, Vol. 2, pp. 626-641, here: pp. 636 ff.; From the report of the secret unit of the OGPU "Anti-Soviet Movement in the Village" from October 1928, printed in: *Sovietskaya derevnya*, Vol. 2, pp. 808 f.

87. From the report of the secret unit of the OGPU "Anti-Soviet Movement in the Village" from October 1928, printed in: *Sovietskaya derevnya*, Vol. 2, pp. 780-817, here: p. 812; From the report of the Information Division of the OGPU on anti-Soviet Occurrences in the village between 1925 and 1927, not dated, after 1 March 1928, published in: *Sovietskaya derevnya*, Vol. 2, pp. 626-641, here: pp. 640 f.

88. From the report of the secret unit of the OGPU "Anti-Soviet Movement in the Village" from October 1928, printed in: *Sovietskaja derevnya*, Vol. 2, pp. 780-817, here: pp. 810 f; From the report of the Information Division of the OGPU on anti-Soviet Occurrences in the village between 1925 and 1927, not dated, after 1 March 1928, published in: *Sovietskaja derevnya*, Vol. 2, pp. 626-641, here: pp. 638 ff.

89. Ibid.

90. From the report of the secret unit of the OGPU "Anti-Soviet Movement in the Village" from October 1928, printed in: *Sovietskaya derevnya*, Vol. 2, pp. 780-817, here: pp. 811 f; from the report of the Information Division of the OGPU on anti-Soviet Occurrences in the village between 1925 and 1927, not dated, after 1 March 1928, published in: *Sovietskaya derevnya*, Vol. 2, pp. 626-641, here: pp. 639 f.

91. From the decision of the Revolutionary War Council of the USSR "On the Political-Moral Condition of the Red Army" from 28 June 1928, signed by Voroshilov and Lutunovsky, printed in: *Reforma v Krasnoi Armii*, Book 2, pp. 223-231, here: p. 224.

92. Cf. From the report of the secret unit of the OGPU "Anti-Soviet Movement in the Village" from October 1928, printed in: *Sovietskaya derevnya*, Vol. 2, pp. 780-817, here: pp. 812 ff.

93. Stalin, Industrialisation and the Grain Problem. *Speech Delivered on July 9, 1928*, printed in: Stalin, *Works*, Vol. 11, pp. 165-178, here: p. 185 (author's emphasis).

94. Bessedovsky, *Den Klauen der Tscheka entronnen*, p. 178.

95. Ibid.

96. From the report of the Information Division of the OGPU on anti-Soviet Occurrences in the village between 1925 and 1927, not dated, after 1 March 1928, published in: *Sovietskaya derevnya*, Vol. 2, pp. 626-641, here: p. 629.

97. Nationalities in the USSR according to the census of 1937 (including data for 1926), published in: *Vsesoyusnaya perepis naselenyja 1937 goda*, pp. 86 f.

98. Service, *Lenin*, pp. 583 ff.; Service, *Stalin*, pp. 207-218.

99. Service, *Stalin*, pp. 216 f.

100. Stalin's theses on the ethnic factor in the build-up of the party and the state, not dated, sent to Trotsky on 17 March 1923: RGASPI, f. 325, op. 1, d. 511, pp. 90-99.

101. Ibid.

102. Ibid.

103. Trotsky to the members of the Politburo on 10 June 1923: RGASPI, f. 325, op. l, d. 513, p. 112.

104. The Chief of Staff of the Red Army to the Chief of the RVS of the USSR on 5 July 1924: RGASPI, f. 325, op. 1, d. 524, pp. 8-9, here: p. 9.

105. Summary of the Main Administration of the RKKA on the State of the Red Army in the Years 1927/28, from 30/31 October 1928, printed in: *Reforma v Krasnoi Armii*, Book 2, pp. 261-318, here: p. 277. Among them were Ukrainian, Belarusian, Georgian, Armenian, Azeri, Uzbek, Turkmen and Kazakh units. In 1927, the national units numbered 29,489 men with a planned 56,043 men. Report of the deputy chief of staff of the Red Army, Pugachev, from 30 April 1927 on national units in the RKKA, printed in: ibid., pp. 63-70.

106. Resolution of the Politburo of the Central Committee of the VKP(b) on the state of defense of the USSR from 15 July 1928, attachment No. 1 to the session protocol No. 89 of the Politburo from 18 July 1929: RGASPI, f. 17, op. 162, d. 7, pp. 101 ff., here: p. 103, in it, the combat strength of the national units was to be increased while their numbers should remain at the current level; on 25 November 1938, Lev Mekhlis reported at the session of the War Council at the People's Commissar for Defense: "The liquidation of national units had progressed well. The nationals need help with learning the Russian language. There are still remnants of national units (34th Infantry Division – Georgian artillery, 92nd Infantry Division – Armenian section, 57th Corps – Car Battalion). In some units [...] the formation of section occurs along national lines. This is wrong." (protocol of the morning session of the War Council, printed in: *Voienny Soviet pri Narodnom Komissare Oborony SSSR -1938,1940*, pp. 158-167, here: p. 166.

107. Manuilsky to Stalin on 4 September 1922 RGASPI, f. 558, op. 11, d. 763, pp. 1 ff.

108. From the report of the secret unit of the OGPU "Anti-Soviet Movement in the Village" from October 1928, printed in: *Sovietskaja derevnya*, Vol. 2, pp. 780-817, here: pp. 814 f.

109. Ibid., p. 815.

110. Ibid., p. 816.

111. Ibid., p. 816.

112. Ibid., pp. 816 f.

113. From the report of the Information Division of the OGPU on anti-Soviet Occurrences in the village between 1925 and 1927, not dated, after 1 March 1928, published in: *Sovietskaya derevnya*, Vol. 2, pp. 626-641, here: p. 628.

114. On the atmosphere in the Tatar Republic cf. Resolution of the Bureau of the Tatar Oblast Committee on the Islamic-Religious Movement, 10.08.1926, printed in: *ZK RKP(b) - WKP(b) i natsionalny vopros*, pp.417-421. The resolution mentions among others: "Regarding the question of the religious movement in the Tatar part of the population, the oblast committee reports strong growth of this movement in the past year and notes: a) The strengthening of the religious movement is a result of the activities of the national bourgeoisie under the conditions of the NEP (NEP-elements in the cities and kulaks in the village). They support intensively, with moral and material means, the Islamic clergy who are conducting a broad religious campaign under the working Tatars, especially in the villages." Religious schools in mosques were considered to the basis of this religious movement, and Russian-Orthodox clergy also campaigned to be given the same rights, and called for the faithful to demand equal treatment. The religious movement was seen to go against the party. On the situation in the Northern Caucasus, cf. Report of the chief of the Information Division of the OGPU to the Central Committee of the VCP(b) from April 1928, published in: ibid., pp. 541-561; on the situation in Uzbekistan, cf. Report of the OGPU to the Central Committee of the VCP(b) on the Political Atmosphere in Uzbekistan from 31 May 1928, published in: ibid., pp. 574-592.

115. Report on the Fight against Antisemitism from 26 August 1926, S. M. Dimantsteyn, Subdivision National Minorities, Division for Agitation and Propaganda of the Central Committee of the VCP(b), printed in: ibid., pp. 425 ff.

Chapter 10

1. Stalin, The Results of the Work of the Fourteenth Conference of the R.C.P.(B.); *Report Delivered at a Meeting of the Active of the Moscow Organisation of the R.C.P.(B.)*, May 9, 1925, published in: Stalin, *Works*, Vol. 7, pp. 90-134, here: pp. 91-93.

2. Stalin, The International Situation and the Defense of the USSR *Speech Delivered on August 1*, printed in: Stalin, *Works*, Vol. 10, pp. 3-62, here: p. 7.

3. Mikoyan's notice from 17 August regarding his conversation with Kamenev (copy in Mikoyan's biography): RGASPI, f. 84, op. 3, d. 116, p. 156 (»My idem k katastroficheskoi rasvvyaske revolyutsii«).

4. Cf. Service, *Lenin*, pp. 562-618.

5. Cf. Service, *Stalin*, pp. 196-206, 219-229; Mikoyan's autobiography, manuscript, written in the 1960s: RGASPI, f. 84, op. 3, d. 116, pp. 1-265, here: p. 109.

6. Service, *Stalin*, pp. 235 f.

7. Dimitrov, *Tagebücher*, pp. 161-193 (entry from 7 November 1937).

8. Isaac Don Levin: "Bolshevik Political Machinery" from 6 September 1924, on the takeover of power by the troika following Lenin's death: RGASPI, f. 82, op. 2, d. 1498, pp. 9-14.

9. Cf. Service, *Stalin*, pp. 230-241, 253-264.

10. Mikoyan's autobiography, manuscript, written in the 1960s: RGASPI, f. 84, op. 3, d. 116, pp. 1-265, here: p. 112.

11. Lev Trotsky, "The Situation of the Working Class", not published manuscript, June 1927: RGASPI, f. 325, op. 1, d. 590, pp. 1-72, here: pp. 70 f.

12. Stalin, The October Revolution and the Tactics of the Russian Communists. *Preface to the Book "On the Road to October"*, published. in: Stalin, *Works*, Vol. 6 (1924), pp. 374-420, here: p. 414.

13. Stalin, Reply to the Discussion on the Report on "The Social-Democratic Deviation in our Party," *November 3, 1926*, in: Stalin, *Works*, Vol. 8 (1926), pp. 311-372, here: p. 328.

14. Mikoyan's autobiography, manuscript, written in the 1960s: RGASPI, f. 84, op. 3, d. 116, pp. 1-265, here: p. 112.

15. Lenin, "On the Slogan for a United States of Europe", printed in: Lenin, *Works*, Vol. 21, pp. 339-343, here: p. 342 (author's emphasis). The article first appeared in *Sotsial-Demokrat* No. 44 on 23 August 1915.

16. This is how Stalin referred to Lenin's slogan on 3 November 1926, in the closing remarks of his lecture: Stalin, Reply to the Discussion on the Report on "The Social-Democratic Deviation in our Party," November 3, 1926, in: Stalin, *Works*, Vol. 8 (1926), pp. 311-372, here: pp. 333 f.

17. Musial, "'Kapitalismus am Kragen packen'", pp. 58 ff.

18. For example, Stalin also cited the section on the use of armed force in this context in his article "Concerning Questions of Leninism" from 25 January 1926, published in: Stalin, *Works* Vol. 8, pp. 11-96, here: pp. 73; on 3 November 1926, Stalin energetically argued with Trotsky and Kamenev, who were arguing that Lenin had not meant Russia, but one of the capitalist countries when he wrote about the possibility of building communism in one country, cf. Stalin's closing remarks at his lecture "Reply to the Discussion on the Report on 'The Social-Democratic Deviation in our Party'" *November 3, 1926*, in: ibid., pp. 311-372; on 7 November 1926, Stalin vehemently opposed Trotsky's claim that Stalin and Bukharin only brought up the question of building socialism in 1925, pointing again at Lenin's article from 1915 and citing the section about using armed force against capitalist countries, cf. Once More on the Social-Democratic Deviation in Our Party. *Report Delivered on December 7*, in: Stalin, *Works*, Vol. 9, pp. 3-64, here: pp. 30-37; weeks later, on 13 December 1926, Stalin again attacked Trotsky, claiming that Trotsky had called the thesis of building socialism "some unknown 'theory' of Stalin's" when in reality it had been Lenin's idea. Cf. Reply to the Discussion, *December 13*, in: Ibid., pp. 65-155, here: pp. 120-131, here: p. 121.

19. Stalin, The Social-Democratic Deviation in our Party. *Report Delivered at the Fifteenth All-Union Conference of the C.P.S.U.(B.), November 1, 1926*, published in: Stalin, *Works*, Vol. 8, pp. 245-310, here: p. 358.

20. Resolution of the Fifteenth Party Congress on the Oppositon in the VCP(b) and on Building of Socialism in One Country, sent at Stalin's behest to members and candidates of the Central Committee and members of the Central Control Committee on 7 August 1927: RGASPI, f. 84, op. 2, d. 32, pp. 89-105, here: pp. 91 f.

21. Ibid., pp. 92 f.

22. Ibid., p. 96.

23. Cf. McDermott, *Stalin*, p. 60; Robert Service likewise rejects this thesis (Service, *Stalin*, p. 405).

24. Stalin, On the Death of Lenin. A Speech Delivered at the Second All-Union Congress of Soviets, 26 January 1924, printed in: Stalin, *Works*, Vol. 6, pp. 47-53.

25. Ibid., here: p. 51.

26. Baberowski, *Der rote Terror*, p. 92.

27. Dimitrov, *Tagebücher*, pp. 315 ff. 193 (entry from 7 November 1940).

28. Dimitrov, *Tagebücher*, pp. 340 ff., here: p. 342. 193 (entry from 4 February 1941).

29. Mikoyan's autobiography, manuscript, written in the 1960s: RGASPI, f. 84, op. 3, d. 116, pp. 1-265, here: p. 208.

Chapter 11

1. Ken, *Mobilitsatsyonnoye planirovaniye*, pp. 156 f.

2. The archival inventory of the Committee for Defense at the Council of the People's Commissars of the USSR has only been opened since 2004 (GARF f. 8418), but a significant portion still remains inaccessible.

3. Dzerzhinsky to the Politburo of the Central Committee of the RCP(b), copy to Frunze, 8 March 1925: RGASPI, f. 76, op. 2, d. 182, p. 64.

4. Quoted according to Ken, *Mobilitsatsyonnoye planirovaniye*, p. 21.

5. Session protocol No. 78 of the Politburo from 13 January 1927: RGASPI, f. 17, op. 162, d. 4, pp. 42-46, here p. 42; Samuelson, *Krasny koloss*, p. 51.

6. Samuelson, *Krasny koloss*, pp. 51 f., 251. The commission included Rykov, his deputy Tsyurup, Voroschilov, Unszlicht, Ordzhonikidze, Kuibyshev, Krzhizhanowsky, Rudsutak, Bryuchanov, Menshinsky and Mikoyan.

7. This is supported by the documents of the Committee for Defense at GARE f. 8418.

8. Session protocol No. 81 of the Politburo from 17 March 1927: RGASPI, f. 17, op. 162, d. 4, pp. 80 ff., here: p. 80.

9. Session protocol No. 94 of the Politburo from 7 April 1927 (point 1): RGASPI, f. 17, op. 162, d. 4, pp. 97-101, here: p. 97.

10. Session protocol No. 100 of the Politburo from 5 May 1927 (Point 1): Ibid., pp. 123 ff.; the documents on the project, which was approved, remain closed, as well as Point 1 of the session protocol. However, Point 1 and 1g from the attachment to the project were – perhaps accidentally – published in *Lubyanka, 1922-1936*, p. 129.

11. Samuelson, *Krasny koloss*, p. 52.

12. Ibid., p. 54.

13. Ibid.

14. Ibid., pp. 54 ff.

15. Report on the Fundamental Measures of the Leadership for the Preparation of the Country for Defense, presented on 15 July 1929: GARF, f. 8418, op. 18, d. 26, pp. 55-61.

16. From the report of the deputy chief of the Main Administration of the RKKA, Levichev, on the results of the reorganization of the Red Army from 3 May 1927, printed in: *Reforma w Krasnoj Armii*, Book 2, pp. 71-80; from the report of the deputy chief of the Main Administration of the RKKA, Levichev, on the state of the RKKA (army and air force) from August 1927, printed in: Ibid., pp. 99-116; memorandum of the People's Commissar for Defense and Navy, Voroshilov, to the RZ STO from 10 April 1928: Ibid., pp. 198-201 (2.6 million soldiers in case of mobilization following the decision of the political leadership in 1927); Samuelson, *Krasny koloss*, p. 85; Ken, *Mobilitsatsyonnoye planirovaniye*, p. 456 (Table 4 A).

17. Svirin, *Bronya krepka*, pp. 34-64.

18. Stenographic report of the Plenum of the Central Committee and the Central Control Committee of the VCP(b) from 7-12 January 1933: RGASPI, f. 17, op. 2, d. 514 (Part 1), pp. 1-70, here: pp. 62-66.

19. Report on the Fundamental Measures of the Leadership for the Preparation of the Country for Defense, presented on 15 July 1929: GARF, f. 8418, op. 18, d. 26, pp. 55-61.

20. Ken, *Mobilitsatsyonnoye planirovaniye*, pp. 26 ff.; session protocol of the Central Committee and of the VCP(b) from 21 July 1927, Point 3: RGASPI, f. 17, op. 162, d. 5, pp. 72 f.

21. Excerpt from the session protocol No. 6 (Point 34) of the Council of the People's Commissars of the BSSR from 21 March 1928: GARF, f. 8418, op. 18, d. 16, pp. 47 f.

22. Session protocol No. 1 of the Politburo of the Central Committee of the VCP(b) from 7 January 1926, Point 9: RGASPI, f. 17, op. 162, d. 3, pp. 1 ff.

23. Session protocol No. 117 of the Politburo of the Central Committee of the VCP(b) from 14 July 1927, Point 4: RGASPI, f. 17, op. 162, d. 5, pp. 67-71.

24. Session protocol No. 133 of the Politburo of the Central Committee of the VCP(b) from 3 November 1927, Point 2: Ibid., p. 123.

25. Session protocol No. 136 of the Politburo of the Central Committee of the VCP(b) from 28 November 1927, Point 1: Ibid., pp. 125 ff.

26. Session protocol No. 138 of the Politburo of the Central Committee of the VCP(b) from 28 November 1927, Point 22: Ibid., pp. 130 f.

27. Cf. J. V. Stalin, Works, Vol. 7, pp. 277-78, 279-80.

28. Stalin, Political Report of the Central Committee, *December 3. The Fifteenth Congress of the C.P.S.U.(B.), December 2-19, 1927*, published. in: Stalin, *Works*, Vol. 10, pp. 275-363, here: p. 286.

29. Stalin, Results of the July Plenum of the C.C., C.P.S.U.(B.). *Report to a Meeting of the Active of the Leningrad Organisation of the C.P.S.U.(B.), July 13, 1928*, printed in: Stalin, *Works*, Vol. 11, pp. 206-227, here: p. 209.

30. N. S. Simonov, "Strengthen the defence of the land of Soviets": The 1927 'war alarm' and its consequences, in: Europe-Asia Studies, December 1996, Vol. 48, pp. 1355-1365.

31. Ibid., p. 1355.

32. Note from Stalin from 1923, in response to Guzev's proposal to attack Poland in Galicia and advance into Czechoslovakia in case of a German revolution: RGASPI, f. 558, op. 11, d. 129, p. 32.

33. Stalin to Molotov, 1 September 1930, published in: Stalin, *Briefe an Molotow*, pp. 226 f. (emphasis in the original).

34. Dzerzhinsky to Stalin on 11 July 1926: RGASPI, f. 76, op. 3, d. 364, p. 58; printed in: *Lubyanka. 1922-1936*, p. 118.

35. Ibid.

36. Resolution Project of the Commission of the United Plenum of the Central Committee and the Central Control Committee Regarding the Violation of Party Discipline by Comrades Zinoviev and Trotsky, from 8 August 1927: RGASPI, f. 84, op. 2, d. 32, pp. 120-128, here: p. 125.

37. Stalin, The International Situation and the Defence of the USSR Speech Delivered on August 1, printed in: Stalin, *Works*, Vol. 10, pp. 3-62, here: p. 62.

38. Stalin to Kaganovich on 11 August 1932: RGASPI, f. 81, op. 3, d. 99, pp. 144-151; printed in: *Stalin i Kaganovich. Perepiska*, pp. 273 ff.

39. Stalin, Notes on Contemporary Themes, printed in: Stalin, *Works*, Vol. 9, pp. 328-370, here: pp. 328, 355; *Pravda*, No. 169 from 28 July 1927.

40. Stalin, The Entente's New Campaign against Russia, *Pravda* from 20 May 1920, published in: Stalin, *Works*, Vol.4, pp. 331-340, here: p. 335.

41. Stalin, Political Report of the Central Committee, *December 3. The Fifteenth Congress of the C.P.S.U.(B.), December 2-19, 1927*, published. in: Stalin, *Works*, Vol. 10, pp. 275-363, here: p. 288.

42. Stalin, The Work of the April Joint Plenum of the Central Committee and Central Control Commission. *Report Delivered at a Meeting of the Active of the Moscow Organisation of the C.P.S.U.(B.), April 13, 1928*, printed in: Stalin, *Works*, Vol. 11, pp. 30-68, here: p. 53.

43. Ibid., pp. 57-67.

44. Stalin, To the Members of the Political Bureau of the Central Committee. *Reply to Frumkin. (With Reference to Frumkin's Letter of June 15, 1928)*, printed in: Stalin, *Works*, Vol. 11, pp. 121-132, here: p. 123.

45. Ibid.

46. Stalin, The Trotskyist Opposition Before and Now. *Speech Delivered at a Meeting of the Joint Plenum of the Central Committee and Central Control Commission of the C.P.S.U.(B.), October 23, 1927*, printed in: Stalin, *Works*, Vol. 10, pp. 177-211, here: pp. 203 f.

47. Stalin, Industrialisation and the Grain Problem. *Speech Delivered on July 9, 1928*, printed in: Stalin, *Works*, Vol. 11, pp. 165-196, here: p. 185.

48. Stalin, The International Situation and the Defence of the USSR *Speech Delivered on August 1*, printed in: Stalin, *Works*, Vol. 10, printed in: Stalin, *Works*, Vol. 10, pp. 3-62, here: p. 45.

49. Information of the Administration for Inventory and Military Service at the Main Administration of the RKKA Regarding the Social Composition of the Red Army on 1 April 1926, from 19 February 1927, printed in: *Reforma v Krasnoj Armii*, pp. 49 f.

50. Table: Armament and Ammunition Stores of the Countries of Poland, Romania, Finland, Estonia and Latvia, attachment to Tuhachevsky's memorandum on the reconstruction of the Red Army from 11 January 1930: RGASPI, f. 558, op. 11, d. 447, p. 57.

51. Memorandum by Tukhachevsky, Chief-of-Staff of the Red Army, regarding the status and plans of the mobilization of the economy, not dated (1926): RGASPI, f. 76, op. 2, d. 182, pp. 157-169; Samuelson, *Krasny koloss*, pp. 67-75.

52. Ken, *Mobilitsatsyonnoye planirovaniye*, pp. 26 ff.

53. Session protocol No. 91 of the Politburo of the Central Committee of the VCP(b) from 27 June 1927, Point 5: RGASPI, f. 17, op. 162, d. 5, pp. 52 f.

54. Session protocol No. 119 of the Politburo of the Central Committee of the VCP(b) from 11 July 1927, Point 54: Ibid., pp. 74-79.

55. Rykov to Molotov on 15 July 1927: RGASPI, f. 82, op. 2, d. 799, pp. 32 f.

56. Rykov to Molotov on 15 July 1927 and the attached instructions for the members of the special institute (not dated): RGASPI, f. 82, op. 2, d. 799, pp. 32 ff.; Postinov, chief of the administration of the mobilization planning, to Molotov, authorized representative of the RZ STO for the mechanical engineering works "Komintern": Ibid., pp. 39 f.

57. RZ STO, Rykov, Report on the Results of the Work of the Group of Comrades Delegated to the Leningrad Factories, from 9 February 1928: RGASPI, f. 82, op. 2, d. 799, pp. 42 ff.

58. The project of the RZ STO on the creation of a commission to investigate war preparations, March 1929: GARF, f. 8418, op. 3, d. 30, pp. 78 f.; Political Administration of the RKKA, Chief of the 3rd Department, Rybaov, to Bubnov, Chief of the Political Administration of the RKKA, on 27 April 1929: Ibid., p. 81.

59. The Politburo intensively dealt with the state of war preparations in the first half of July. The resolutions cited below summarize the discussions. In more detail, cf. *Krasny koloss*, pp. 97-104.

60. Resolution of the Politburo of the Central Committee of the VCP(b) from 15 July 1929 Regarding the Armaments Industry, Attachment No. 2 for session protocol No. 89 of the Politburo: RGASPI, f. 17, op. 162, d. 7, pp. 113-121.

61. Ibid.

62. Ibid.

63. Ibid.

64. Voroshilov to Stalin on 13 July 1929: RGASPI, f. 17, op. 166, d. 319, p. 20.

65. Session protocol No. 89 of the Politburo of the Central Committee of the VCP(b) from 18 July 1929, Point 22: RGASPI, f. 17, op. 162, d. 7, pp. 97-100; Report/Theses on Fundamental Measures for the Preparation of the Country for Defense, presented at the Politburo session from 15 July 1929: GARF, f. 8418, op. 18, d. 26, pp. 55-61.

66. Resolution of the Politburo of the Central Committee of the VCP(b) on the State of Defense of the USSR from 15 July 1928, attachment No. 1, for session protocol No. 89 of the Politburo: RGASPI, f. 17, op. 162, d. 7, pp. 101-112, here: p. 102.

67. Ibid.

68. Ibid., p. 103.

69. Ibid., pp. 104 f.
70. Litunovsky to Voroshilov, not dated, summer 1929: RGASPI, f. 74, op. 2, d. 101, pp. 107 f.
71. Resolution of the Politburo of the Central Committee of the VCP(b) on the State of Defense of the USSR from 15 July 1928: RGASPI, f. 17, op. 162, d. 7, pp. 101-112, here: p. 105.
72. Ibid.
73. Litunovsky to Voroshilov on 10 August 1929: RGASPI, f. 74, op. 2, d. 101, pp. 105-106, here: p. 105.
74. Resolution of the Politburo of the Central Committee of the VCP(b) on the State of Defense of the USSR from 15 July 1928: RGASPI, f. 17, op. 162, d. 7, pp. 101-112, here: pp. 106 f.
75. Ibid., p. 107.
76. Ibid., pp. 108-111.

Chapter 12

1. Baberowski, *Der rote Terror*, p. 114.
2. Ibid., pp. 112-116.
3. Session protocol No. 89 of the Politburo from 3 March 1927, Point 3: RGASPI, f. 17, op. 162, d. 4, pp. 70-74.
4. Session protocol No. 93 of the Politburo from 31 March 1927, Point 3: Ibid., pp. 89-93.
5. Resolution of the Politburo of the Central Committee of the VCP(b) from 31 March 1927 on Measures in the Fight against Sabotage, Fires, Explosions, Accidents and other Harmful Acts: Ibid., pp. 94 ff.
6. Ibid.
7. Encrypted telegram from Stalin to Molotov, from 8 June 1927: RGASPI, f. 558, op. 11, d. 71, pp. 2 f.; printed in: *Lubyanka. 1922-1936*, p. 133.
8. Session protocol No. 109 of the Politburo of the Central Committee of the VCP(b) from 8 June 1927, Point 1: RGASPI, f. 17, op. 162, d. 5, p. 35; printed also in: *Lubyanka. 1922-1936*, pp. 133 f. The Politburo also ordered additional protection for central agencies and individual leading comrades.
9. Session protocol No. 91 of the Politburo of the Central Committee of the VCP(b) from 27 June 1927, Point 5: RGASPI, f. 17, op. 162, d. 5, pp. 52 f.
10. Special report by Yagoda (OGPU) on "wrecking activities" in the Donugla system (Donets Coal Basin), addressed to Stalin, from 12 March 1928, printed in: *Lubyanka. 1922-1936*, pp. 148-152.
11. On 2 March 1928, the Politburo set up a commission to investigate the Shakhty Affair, which was composed of Stalin, Ordzhonikidze, Molotov, Kuibyshev and Rykov (session protocol No. 14 of the Politburo from 8 March 1928, Point 12: RGASPI, f. 17, op. 162, op. 6, pp. 36 ff.); Stalin, The Work of the April Joint Plenum of the Central Committee and Central Control Commission. *Report Delivered at a Meeting of the Active of the Moscow Organisation of the C.P.S.U.(B.), April 13, 1928*, printed in: Stalin, *Works*, Vol. 11, pp. 30-68, here: pp. 57-67; regarding the propagandistic exploitation of the Shakhty Affair, cf. Baberowski, *Der rote Terror*, pp. 121 f.
12. Cf. The letter from Stalin to the members and candidates of the Politburo from 12 May 1928, regarding a group of specialists in the armaments industry, printed in: *Lubyanka 1922-1936*, p. 187; Bericht von Jagoda an Stalin, Ordschonikidse, Woroschilow und Rykow regarding the case of Mikhailov from 8 May 1928 (until late 1926, Mikhailov led the main administration of the armaments industry), printed in: Ibid., pp. 161 ff.;

Resolution of the Politburo Regarding the OGPU Report on Wrecking in the Transport Sector, from 14 June 1928: RGASPI, f. 17, op. 162, d. 6, p. 105.

13. Stalin to the members and candidates of the Politburo, secretaries of the Central Committee of the VCP(b) and members of the Presidium of the Central Control Committee regarding the OGPU Report on Wrecking in the Transport Sector, from 16 June 1928, printed in: *Lubyanka 1922–1936*, p. 166; attached was Report No. 2 of the OGPU (Yagoda, Blagnonravov) to Stalin Regarding the Wrecking Activities of Counterrevolutionary Organizations in the Railway Transport Systems and the Consequences Thereof, not dated (before 16 June 1928), printed in: Ibid., pp. 166-171.

14. Werth, "Ein Staat gegen sein Volk", p. 162.

15. Excerpt from the Resolution of the Politburo Regarding the Use for Labor of Criminal Prisoners, from 27 June 1929, printed in: *Gulag. 1918–1960*, p. 62; Project of the Commission of the Politburo Regarding the Transfer of Prisoners Sentenced to Three Years or more to the Camps of the OGPU and Regarding the Organization of New Concentration Camps, attachment No. 3 to Point 11 of the session protocol No. 86 of the Politburo, printed in: Ibid., p. 63; Resolution of the Council of People's Commissars of the USSR Regarding the Use for Labor of Criminal Prisoners, printed in: Ibid., pp. 64 f.

Chapter 13

1. Stalin, The Economic Situation of the Soviet Union and the Policy of the Party. *Report to the Active of the Leningrad Party Organisation on the Work of the Plenum of the C.C., C.P.S.U.(B.), April 13, 1926*, in: Stalin, *Works*, Vol. 8 (1926), pp. 123-156, here: pp. 128 f.

2. Ibid., p. 129.

3. Ibid., p. 131.

4. Mikoyan's report to the Politburo regarding the loan negotiations with Germany, 16 April 1929: RGASPI, f. 84, op. 2, d. 10, pp. 101-109.

5. Mikoyan's autobiography, manuscript, written in the 1960s,: RGASPI, f. 84, op. 3, d. 116, pp. 1-265, here: pp. 128 f.

6. The amended import/export plan for 1928/29, Lezhava, Council for Economy, to Rykov, from 26 March 1929, with attachments: RGASPI, f. 84, op. 2, d. 10, pp. 71-80.

7. Mikoyan's report to Molotov on the import/export plan for the fiscal year of 1930/31, from 19 August, with attachments: RGASPI, f. 84, op. 2, d. 15, pp. 83-90.

8. "Policy of Grain Collection in the Context of the General Economic Situation", theses of Mikoyan's lecture, unanimously approved by the commission of the Politburo, before 30 June 1928: RGASPI, f. 84, op. 2, d. 6, pp. 44-51, here: p. 44; Stalin sent the memorandum to all members and candidates of the Politburo, members of the Central Control Committee and select Central Committee members (accompanying letter from 30 June 1928: Ibid., p. 43).

9. Ibid., pp. 45 ff.

10. Stalin, Political Report of the Central Committee, *December 3*. The Fifteenth Congress of the C.P.S.U.(B.), *December 2-19, 1927*, published. in: Stalin, *Works*, Vol. 10, pp. 275-363, here: pp. 312 f.

11. "Policy of Grain Collection in the Context of the General Economic Situation", theses of Mikoyan's lecture, unanimously approved by the commission of the Politburo, before 30 June 1928: RGASPI, f. 84, op. 2, d. 6, pp. 44-51, here: p. 47; Werth, "Ein Staat gegen sein Volk", p. 160. Three years later, Stalin claimed that the crisis had been caused by the

failure of the winter crop: "Noticeable is the drop in the grain crop area in 1927-28. This drop is to be explained not by a retrogression of grain farming such as the ignoramuses in the Right opportunist camp have been chattering about, but by the failure of the winter crop on an area of 7,700,000 hectares (20 per cent of the winter crop area in the USSR)." Stalin, Political Report of the Central Committee to the Sixteenth Party Congress of the C.P.S.U. (B.), 27 June 1930, printed in: Stalin, *Works*, Vol. 12, pp. 242-385, here: p. 282.).

12. Werth, "Ein Staat gegen sein Volk", pp. 160 f.; Lynne, *Peasant Rebels under Stalin*, pp. 21-24.

13. Stalin, Results of the July Plenum of the C.C., C.P.S.U.(B.). *Report to a Meeting of the Active of the Leningrad Organisation of the C.P.S.U.(B.), July 13, 1928*, printed in: Stalin, *Works*, Vol. 11, pp. 206-227, here: p. 215.

14. *Kak lomali NEP*, Vol. 1, pp. 5-14 (introduction by V. P. Danilov).

15. Stalin, Grain Procurement and the Prospects for the Development of Agriculture. *From Statements Made in Various Parts of Siberia in January 1928. (Brief Record)*, printed in: Stalin, *Works*, Vol. 11, pp. 3-11, here: p. 7.

16. On 13 April 1928, Stalin declared in a speech: "[…] we must do our utmost to develop in the countryside large farms of the type of the collective farms and state farms and try to convert them into grain factories for the country organised on a modern scientific basis." Stalin, The Work of the April Joint Plenum of the Central Committee and Central Control Commission. *Report Delivered at a Meeting of the Active of the Moscow Organisation of the C.P.S.U.(B.), April 13, 1928*, printed in: Stalin, *Works*, Vol. 11, pp. 30-68, here: pp. 44 f).

17. Stalin, On the Bond between the Workers and Peasants on State Farms, From a Speech Delivered on 11 July 1928, printed in: Ibid., pp. 197-205, here: pp. 199-202.

18. Stalin, The Programme of the Comintern. *Speech Delivered on July 5, 1928*, printed in: Ibid., pp. 147-164, here: p. 152.

19. Cf. *Kak lomali NEP.*

20. Stalin, Political Report of the Central Committee, *December 3.* The Fifteenth Congress of the C.P.S.U.(B.), *December 2-19, 1927*, published. in: Stalin, *Works*, Vol. 10, pp. 275-363, here: p. 314.

21. Fitzpatrick, *Stalinskiye Krestyane*, pp. 56 f.

22. Ibid., p. 56.

23. Notification of the People's Commissariat for Agriculture on the State of Collectivization in the Oblasts and Regions of the USSR on 15 December 1929, not dated (after 15 December 1929), printed in: *Tragediya sovietskoi derevnii*, Vol. 2, *Noyabr 1929 - Dekabr 1930*, Moscow 2000, pp. 52-60.

24. From the report of the secret-operative unit of the OGPU "Preliminary Results of the Fight against the Counterrevolution in the Villa in the Year 1929" from 15 January 1930, published in: *Sovietskaya derevnya*, Vol. 2, pp. 1016-1021; data for 1930 from the OGPU report on counterrevolutionary activities of the kulaks between 1 January and 1 May 1930, not dated, published in: *Sovietskaya derevnya*, Vol. 3, Part 1, pp. 327-332, here: p. 329.

25. The number is for the years 1926 and 1927 taken together.

26. From the report of the secret-operative unit of the OGPU "Preliminary Results of the Fight against the Counterrevolution in the Village in the Year 1929" from 15 January 1930, published in: *Sovietskaya derevnya*, Vol. 2, pp. 1016-1021.

27. Ibid., Vol. 2, pp. 1016-1021.

Chapter 14

1. Stalin, The International Situation and the Defence of the USSR *Speech Delivered on August 1*, printed in: Stalin, *Works,* Vol. 10, pp. 3-62, here: p. 7.

2. Purman to the Central Committee of the VCP(b) on the 14 January 1929: RGASPI, f. 82, op. 2, d. 799, p. 74.

3. Voroshilov to Molotov on 31 January 1929: ibid., p. 72 ; Mogilny to Voroshilov, on Molotov's request on 15 January 1929: ibid., p. 73.

4. Session protocol No. 105 of the Politburo of the Central Committee of the VCP(b) from 25 October 1929, Point 9: RGASPI, f. 17, op. 162, d. 7, pp. 185-188, here: p. 185.

5. Stalin's letter to Molotov from 7 October 1929, published in: Stalin, *Briefe an Molotow,* pp. 198 f. (emphasis in the original).

6. Stalin, Political Report of the Central Committee, *December 3. The Fifteenth Congress of the C.P.S.U.(B.), December 2-19, 1927,* published. in: Stalin, *Works,* Vol. 10, pp.275-363, here: p. 180.

7. Stalin, The Trotskyist Opposition Before and Now. *Speech Delivered at a Meeting of the Joint Plenum of the Central Committee and Central Control Commission of the C.P.S.U.(B.), October 23, 1927,* printed in: Stalin, *Works,* Vol. 10, pp. 177-211, here: p. 206.

8. Stalin, Political Report of the Central Committee, *December 3. The Fifteenth Congress of the C.P.S.U.(B.), December 2-19, 1927,* published. in: Stalin, *Works,* Vol. 10, pp. 275-363, here, here: p. 280.

9. Ibid., p. 289.

10. On 19 December 1928, Stalin proclaimed at the session of the presidium of the ECCI: "The Comintern holds that the present capitalist stabilisation is a temporary, insecure, shaky and decaying stabilisation which will become more and more shaken as the capitalist crisis develops." (The Right Danger in the German Communist Party. *Speech Delivered at a Meeting of the Presidium of the E.C.C.I., December 19, 1928,* printed in: Stalin, *Works,* Vol. 11, pp. 307-324, here: p. 308); two weeks earlier, Stalin had declared: "Stabilisation is giving rise to a new revolutionary upsurge." (Stalin, Political Report of the Central Committee, *December 3. The Fifteenth Congress of the C.P.S.U.(B.), December 2-19, 1927,* published. in: Stalin, *Works,* Vol. 10, pp. 275-363, here: p. 291). The statement of the Comintern regarding the future crisis of capitalism is thus based on Stalin's words. Cf. Stalin's letter to Bukharin, Rykov, Molotov on the project of the Comintern program from 24 March 1928: RGASPI, f. 558, op. 11, d. 136, pp. 8 ff.; published in: *Politbyuro i Komintern,* pp. 515 f.

11. Session protocol No. 113 of the Politburo of the Central Committee of the VCP(b) from 15 January 1930, Point 50: RGASPI, f. 17, op. 162, pp. 39-42, here: p. 41 (The Politburo ordered the supreme court to charge Bessedovsky only with fraud and embezzlement, not treason).

12. Bessedovsky, *Den Klauen der Tscheka entronnen,* pp. 259 ff.

13. Möller, *Europa zwischen den Weltkriegen,* p. 83.

14. Ibid., p. 82.

15. *Die Weimarer Republik,* p. 637.

16. Cf. Funke, "Republik im Untergang", pp. 505-531.

17. Pyatnitsky to Stalin on 26 October 1929, published in: *Politbyuro i Komintern,* pp. 615 f.

18. *Politbyuro i Komintern,* pp. 615 f.

19. Ibid., p. 620.

20. Session protocol No. 112 of the Politburo of the Central Committee of the VCP(b) from 5 January 1930, Point 54: RGASPI, f. 17, op. 3, d. 771, pp. 1-11, here: p. 9.

21. Cf. documents from: *Politbyuro i Komintern* such as the protocol No. 3 of the session of the Bureau of Delegates of the VCP(b) and the ECCI from 18 July 1930 regarding the theses for the planned Fifth Congress of the Profintern, where it was planned to discuss questions such as "how strikes should be organized" (ibid., pp. 626-629).

22. Stalin, Political Report of the Central Committee to the Sixteenth Party Congress of the C.P.S.U. (B.), June 27, 1930, printed in: Stalin, *Works*, Vol. 12, pp. 242-385, here: pp. 242 f.

23. Ibid., here: pp. 254-257.

24. Ibid., here: pp. 259, 261 f.

25. Secretary of the RZ STO, Appoga, to Shaposhnikov, Chief-of-Staff of the RKKA, 5 November 1922: GARF, f. 8418, op. 3, d. 30, pp. 84 f.

26. Resolution of the Politburo Regarding the Mobilization Readiness of the Industry, 15 January 1930: RGASPI, f. 17, op. 162, d. 8, pp. 43-46; in Point 11, the Politburo noted that among others, the government resolutions regarding the armaments industry from July 1929 had not been fulfilled to a large extent.

27. Session protocol No. 107 of the Politburo of the Central Committee of the VCP(b) from 25 November 1929, Point 25: ibid., pp. 4-7.

28. Session protocol No. 108 of the Politburo of the Central Committee of the VCP(b) from 5 December 1929, Point 11: ibid., pp. 13-17.

29. Resolution of the Politburo from 5 December 1929 Regarding the Fulfillment of the Tank and Tractor Program: ibid., pp. 18 f.

30. Ibid.

31. Session protocol No. 123 of the Politburo of the Central Committee of the VCP(b), 15 April 1930, Point 30: RGASPI, f. 17, op. 162, d. 8, p. 133; excerpt from the session protocol No. 123 of the Politburo from 15 April 1930: ibid., p. 134; session protocol No. 14 of the Politburo of the Central Committee der VCP(b) from 5 November 1930, Point 8: RGASPI, f. 17, op. 162, d. 9, pp. 57-60; Resolution of the Politburo from 5 November Regarding Tank Production: Ibid., p. 61; Svirin, *Bronya krepka*, pp. 162-210.

32. Session protocol No. 108 of the Politburo of the Central Committee of the VCP(b) from 5 December 1929, Point 37, 53: RGASPI, f. 17, op. 162, d. 8, pp. 13-17.

33. Resolution of the RZ STO from 11 November 1929 Regarding the Allocation of Funds for Defense for the Year 1929/30: GARF, f. 8418, op. 3, d. 173, pp. 2-8.

34. Resolution of the RZ STO from 1 March 1930: ibid., p. 1.

35. Session protocol No. 109 of the Politburo of the Central Committee of the VCP(b) from 15 December 1929, Point 49: RGASPI, f. 17, op. 162, d. 8, pp. 22 f.

36. Session protocol No. 110 of the Politburo of the Central Committee of the VCP(b) from 20 December 1929, Points 8,15: ibid., pp. 26 f.; Mikoyan's message to Stalin from 14 November 1930: RGASPI, f. 84, op. 2, d. 15, pp. 165 ff.

37. Session protocol No. 113 of the Politburo of the Central Committee of the VCP(b) from 15 January 1930, Point 52: RGASPI, f. 17, op. 162, op. 8, pp. 39-42; guidelines for Ossinsky for the negotiations: ibid., p. 48.

38. Session protocol No. 114 of the Politburo of the Central Committee of the VCP(b) from 20 January 1930, Point 4: ibid., pp. 49 f.

39. Session protocol No. 112 of the Politburo of the Central Committee of the VCP(b) from 5 January 1930, Point 30: ibid., pp. 29-32.

40. Session protocol No. 113 of the Politburo of the Central Committee of the VCP(b) from 15 January 1930, Points 1,11: ibid., pp. 39-42.

41. Resolution of the Politburo Regarding the Mobilization Readiness of the Industry, approved by the Politburo on 15 January 1930: ibid., pp. 43-46.

42. Ibid.

43. Ibid.

44. Session protocol No. 113 of the Politburo of the Central Committee of the VCP(b) from 15 January 1930, Point 11: RGASPI, f. 17, op. 162, op. 8, pp. 39-42.

45. Session protocol No. 2 of the Revolutionary War Council of the USSR from 23 January 1930: GARF, f. 8418, op. 16, d. 11, pp. 1-5.

46. Report on the air force, addressed to Ordzhonikidze, not dated, before 5 March 1930: GARF, f. 8418, op. 18, d. 26, pp. 2-16.

47. Ibid.

48. Resolution of the Central Committee of the VCP(b)Regarding the Question of the Aviation Industry, approved by the Politburo on 5 March 1930: RGASPI, f. 17, op. 162, d. 8, pp. 106 ff.; Session protocol No. 117 of the Politburo of the Central Committee of the VCP(b) from 5 March 1930, Point 2 a: ibid., pp. 103 ff.

49. Session protocol No. 115 of the Politburo of the Central Committee of the VCP(b) from 25 January 1930, Point 5: RGASPI, f. 17, op. 162, d. 8, pp. 51-55; resolution of the STO on the Export-Import-Plan for the second quarter of 1929/30, approved by the Politburo on 25 January 1930: ibid., pp. 56 f.

50. Session protocol No. 115 of the Politburo of the Central Committee of the VCP(b) from 25 January 1930, Point 33: RGASPI, f. 17, op. 162, d. 8, pp. 51-55; Resolution of the Politburo Regarding Purchases from America from 25 January 1930: ibid., p. 58.

51. Directive for Bogdanov (he was to lead the negotiation with the USA), approved by the Politburo on 30 January 1930: ibid., pp. 70-73.

52. Session protocol No. 117 of the Politburo from 15 February 1930, Point 12: RGASPI, f. 17, op. 162, d. 8, pp. 76-80; protocol of the conversation between Mikoyan and the German ambassador, Dirksen, from 15 December 1929: RGASPI, f. 84, op. 2, d. 14, pp. 27-33; accompanying letter from Mikoyan to Stalin and Litvinov from 3 January 1930: Ibid., p. 27.

53. Session protocol No. 118 of the Politburo of the Central Committee of the VCP(b) from 25 February 1930, Point 4: RGASPI, f. 17, op. 162, d. 8, pp. 81-84.

54. Attachment No. 1 to the session protocol No. 118 of the Politburo "On the Progress of the Liquidation of Wrecking Activities in the Factories of the Armaments Industry", approved by the Politburo on 25 February 1930: RGASPI, f. 17, op. 162, d. 8, pp. 85-91, here: pp. 85 f. (emphasis in the original).

55. Ibid., p. 86 (emphasis in the original).

56. Ibid., pp. 86 f.

57. Report regarding the air force, addressed to Ordzhonikidze, not dated, before 5 March 1930: GARF, f. 8418, op. 18, d. 26, pp. 2-16, here: pp. 3 f.

58. For example, on 25 May 1930, the Politburo authorized the OGPU to execute supposed wreckers in the paper industry, forestry, road building, postal and telegraph system: Session protocol No. 127 of the Politburo of the Central Committee of the VCP(b)from 25 May 1930, Point 9,11 ff.: ibid., pp. 157 ff.

59. Resolution of the Central Committee of the VCP(b) regarding the aviation industry, approved by the Politburo on 5 March 1930: RGASPI, f 17, op. 162, d. 8, pp. 106 ff.

60. Attachment No. 1 to the session protocol No. 118 of the Politburo "On the Progress of the Liquidation of Wrecking Activities in the Factories of the Armaments Industry", approved by the Politburo on 25 February 1930: ibid., pp. 85-91, here: pp. 86 f.

61. Zhuravlyov, *Das Moskauer Elektrokombinat;* Erler, *Terror gegen deutsche Polit- und Wirtschaftsemigranten.*

62. Litunovsky to Voroshilov on 11 August 1930: RGASPI, f. 74, op. 2, d. 101, pp. 126-139, here: pp. 134 f.

63. Session protocol No. 54 of the Politburo of the Central Committee of the VCP(b) from 5 August 1931, Point 3: RGASPI, f. 17, op. 162, d. 10, pp. 138-142. This applied at first to specialists in the metallurgy (gold and non-ferrous metals) and transportation, a process that was to be overseen by the OGPU. On 15 Septermber 1930, the Politburo also allowed for the rehabilitation of railway workers. (Session protocol No. 62 of the Politburo of the Central Committee of the VCP(b) from 15 September 1931, Point 1: ibid., d. 11, pp. 7 f.).

64. Report from I. A. Akulov to Stalin regarding the handover of specialists convicted by the OGPU to the economic agencies, from 26 November 1931, published in: *Lubyanka 1922-1936*, pp. 287 f.

65. Lenin, Speech Delivered at a Meeting of the Moscow Soviet of Workers' and Red Army Deputies, 6 March 1920, printed in: Lenin, *Works*, Vol. 30, pp. 410-416, here: p. 413.

66. From the session protocol No. 108 of the Politburo from 5 December 1929: RGASPI, f. 17, op. 3, d. 1876, p. 8, printed in: *Tragediya sovietskoj derevnii*, Vol. 2, p. 35; from the protocol No. 66 of the combined session of the Executive Committee of the Volga Region and the Commission of the Deputy Head of the SNK of the RSFSR, Ryskulov, regarding the collectivization in the Volga Region, from 24/25 November 1929, printed in: ibid., pp. 33 ff.

67. Stalin's letter to Molotov from 5 December 1929, published in: Stalin, *Briefe an Molotow*, pp. 199 f.

68. Resolution draft of the Central Committee of the VCP(b) regarding the speed of establishing kolkhozes, 18 December 1929, printed in: *Tragediya sovietskoj derevnii*, Vol. 2, pp. 61-66; Yakovlev's message to the Politburo regarding the work of the commission from 22 December 1929, printed in: ibid., p. 75; Stalin's letter to Molotov from 25 December 1929; published in: Stalin, *Briefe an Molotow*, pp. 201 f.

69. Telegram from Molotov to Stalin, not dated, from 1 January 1930 at the latest, published in: *Tragediya sovietskoj derevnii*, Vol. 2, p. 76; Stalin's telegram to Molotov from 1 January 1930, published in: ibid., p. 76.

70. Telegram from Stalin to the Secretary of the Committee of the Lower Volga Region, Zheboldayev, 4 January 1930, printed in: ibid., p. 84.

71. Session protocol No. 112 of the Politburo of the Central Committee of the VCP(b) from 5 January 1930, Point 13: RGASPI, f. 17, op. 3, d. 771, pp. 1-11, here: p. 3; published in: *Tragediya sovietskoj derevnii*, Vol. 2, p. 84.

72. Resolution of the Politburo regarding the speed of the collectivization and state aid for kolkhoz expansion, 5 January 1930: RGASPI, f. 17, op. 3, d. 771, pp. 21 ff.; *Tragediya sovietskoj derevnii*, Vol. 2, pp. 85 f.

73. Memorandum of the Sub-Commission on Kulaks in the Rayons of Complete Collectivization, under the leadership of K. Bauman, not dated, before 15 December 1929, printed in: *Tragediya sovietskoj derevnii*, Vol. 2, pp. 37-40.

74. Ibid.; report from M. Khatayevich on the work of Yakovlev's commission, 21 December 1929, printed in: ibid., pp. 67-74; table of the special detachment of the OGPU regarding the dekulakization and deportation of those dekulakized between 1 January and 1 July 1931, from 15 July 1931, published in: *Sovietskaya derevnya*, Vol. 3, Book 1, pp. 716 f.

75. Resolution draft of the Central Committee of the VCP(b) regarding the speed of establishing kolkhozes, 18 December 1929, printed in: *Tragediya sovietskoj derevnii*, Vol. 2, pp. 61-66.

76. Letter of the deputy chief of the OGPU, Yagoda, to leading employees of the OGPU, from 11 January 1930, printed in: ibid., pp. 103 f.
77. Ibid. (emphasis by the author).
78. Ibid.
79. Ibid.
80. OGPU directive to all agencies of the OGPU, from 11 January 1930, printed in: *Tragediya sovietskoj derevnii*, Vol. 2, pp. 104 f.
81. Session protocol No. 113 of the Politburo of the Central Committee of the VCP(b) from 15 January 1930, Point 16: RGASPI, f. 17, op.3, d. 772, p.3; also in: *Tragediya sovietskoj derevnii*, Vol. 2, p. 116.
82. Session protocol No. 116 of the Politburo of the Central Committee of the VCP(b) from 30 January 1930, Point 36: RGASPI, f. 17, op. 162, d. 8, pp. 59-61. The preparation phase of the resolution is well documented (first drafts, additional proposals, etc.) in the document collection: *Tragediya sovietskoj derevnii*, Vol. 2, pp. 117-126.
83. Resolution of the Politburo of the Central Committee of the VCP(b) from 30 January 1930 "On Measures for the Liquidation of Kulak Farms in the Rayons of Complete Collectivization": RGASPI, f. 17, op. 162, d. 8, pp. 64-69; printed in: *Tragediya sovietskoj derevnii*, Vol. 2, pp. 126-130.
84. Ibid.
85. Ibid.
86. Yagoda's report on the measures for the liquidation of the kulaks as a class from 2 February 1930: *Tragediya sovietskoj derevnii*, Vol. 2, pp. 163-167; cf. numerous similar documents from the same time period, published in: ibid., pp. 105-204.
87. Service, *Stalin*, p. 286; the term "25,000-ers" comes from the number of workers who were to mobilized for that purpose. Resolution draft of the Central Committee of the VCP(b) regarding the speed of establishing kolkhozes, 18 December 1929, printed in: *Tragediya sovietskoj derevnii*, Vol. 2, pp. 61-66, here: 64; report from M. Khatayevich on the work of Yakovlev's commission, 21 December 1929, printed in: ibid., pp. 67-74, here: p. 71; Reese, *Stalin's Reluctant Soldiers*, p. 92.
88. Report of the information department of the OGPU on the state of and the atmosphere among the "25,000ers" in the village by 21 February 1931, from 26 February 1931, published in: *Sovietskaya derevnya*, Vol. 3, Book 1, pp. 626-636.
89. Cf. Applebaum, *Der Gulag*, pp. 81-94.
90. Report of the information department of the OGPU, not dated, after 5 January 1930, printed in: *Tragediya sovietskoj derevnii*, Vol. 2, pp. 99 f.
91. Ibid.
92. Report of the information department of the OGPU, not dated, after 5 January 1930, printed in: *Tragediya sovietskoj derevnii*, Vol. 2, pp. 99 f.
93. Ibid.
94. Ibid.
95. Report from Yagoda to Stalin regarding excesses during collectivization and dekulakization from 7 March 1933, with relevant attachments, published in: *Tragediya sovietskoj derevnii*, Vol. 2, pp. 292-302, here: p. 302.
96. Report of the chief of the operative group of the authorized representatives of the OGPU, Pusinsky, on the results of the deportation of the kulaks of the second category, from 6 May 1930, published in: *Istoriya stalinskogo gulaga*, Vol. 5, pp. 107-124.
97. Ibid.
98. OGPU report on the results of the deportation of the kulaks of the second category, 9 February 1931: ibid., pp. 136-140.

99. Report of the chief of the operative group of the authorized representatives of the OGPU, Pusinsky, on the results of the deportation of the kulaks of the second category, from 6 May 1930, published in: *Istoriya stalinskogo gulaga*, Vol. 5, pp. 107-124, here: pp. 121 ff.

100. Excerpt from a letter in a survey of the information department of the OGPU on the letters of the kulaks who were deported to the North, not dated, after 1 July 1930, published in: *Tragedija sowjetskoj derewni*, Vol. 2, pp. 521-523.

101. Ibid.

102. Special notification from Yagoda to Stalin regarding the completion of the kulak deportation operation, from 15 October 1931, published in: *Lubyanka, 1922-1936*, p. 267.

103. Letter from Tomachev to Lebed, not dated (between 15 and 21 April 1930), published in: *Istoriya stalinskogo gulaga*, Vol. 5, pp. 103-107; accompanying letter from Lebed to Stalin from 21 April 1930, published in: ibid., p. 103.

104. OGPU report on the results of the deportation and resettlement of the kulaks of the second category, published in: *Istoriya stalinskogo gulaga*, Vol. 5, pp. 136-140; Werth, "Ein Staat gegen sein Volk", pp. 174 f.

105. OGPU report on the internal resettlement of the kulaks of the third category from 19 February 1931, published in: *Sovietskaja derevnya, 1932-1934*, Vol. 3, Book 1, pp. 613-620.

106. Table: Number of Refugee-kulaks of the Second Category, 7 February 1931, published in: ibid., p. 612, as well as *Istoriya stalinskogo gulaga*, Vol. 5, p. 135; in early 1932, the OGPU reported the presence of 456 settlements of kulaks of the third class in which 28,356 families (117,048 persons) were living (table: Directory of the Settlements of the Kulaks of the Third Category according to data from 5 March 1932 by the secret political unit of the OGPU, published in: *Sovietskaya derevnya*, 1932-1934, Vol. 3, Book 2, p. 56).

107. Report of the Special Detachment of the OGPU Regarding the Progress of the Kulak Deportation Operation from 17 November 1930, published in: *Sovietskaya derevnya*, Vol. 3, Book 1, pp. 519-527; data from the central registration department of the OGPU on the number of persons of the first category arrested by the OGPU in the course of the Kulak Operation, not dated, after 1 October 1930, published in: ibid., p. 484. Of the 140,724 persons who had been arrested between January and 15 April 1930, 50,920 were sent to concentration camps, 17,632 were deported, 9333 liberated and 2877 received suspended sentences. The fate of the remaining 59,962 was unclear as of October 1930 (ibid.).

108. Telegram No. 13,422 of the leadership (Yagoda and Evdokimov) of the OGPU to all local OGPU agencies, 25 November 1930, 1930, published in: *Sovietskaya derevnya*, Vol. 3, Book 1, p. 509.

109. OGPU report on the character and dynamic of anti-Soviet mass-occurrences in the village between 1 January and 1 October 1931, from 13 October 1931, published in: ibid., pp. 774-779.

110. Documents regarding the question of the kulak counterrevolution from 1 February 1931, not dated (after the 1st of February 1931), published in: ibid., pp. 589-595.

111. Excerpt from the resolution of the Politburo of the Central Committee of the VCP(b) from 15 March 1931, published in: *Lubyanka 1922-1936*, p. 264; session protocol No. 30 of the Politburo of the Central Committee of the VCP(b) from 25 March 1931, Point 31/44: RGASPI, f. 17, op. 162, d. 9, pp. 172-175; On Kulaks. Session Protocol of the Commission of Comrade Andreyev, 18 March 1931: ibid., pp. 176 ff.; published also in: *Lubyanka 1922-1936*, pp. 264 ff.

112. Special report from Yagoda to Stalin from 15 October 1931, published in: *Lubyanka 1922-1936*, p. 267.

113. Table of the special detachment of the OGPU regarding the number of resettled kulaks in 1930/31, not dated, after 30 September 1931, published in: *Sovietskaya derevnya*, Vol. 3, Buch 1, p. 771; table of the special detachment of the OGPU regarding the number of kulaks resettled within the oblasts, not dated, after 30 September 1931, published in: ibid., p. 771.

114. Protocol of the Politburo commission for special settlers from 26 January 1932, approved by the Politburo on 28 January 1932: RGASPI, f. 17, op. 162, d. 11, pp. 167 ff.

115. Report of the Politburo regarding the economic development of the special settlers in the Norymsk region from 23 December 1932: RGASPI, f. 17, op. 162, d. 11, pp. 103-106; protocol of the Politburo commission for special settlers from 26 January 1932, approved by the Politburo on 28 January 1932: ibid., pp. 167 ff.

116. Question of the chief of the secret political detachment of the OGPU, Molchanov, to the deputy chief of the OGPU, Akulov, from 27 January 1932, published in: *Sovietskaya derevnya*, Vol. 3, Book 2, p. 53; information of the secret political detachment of the OGPU regarding the registered kulak farms from 25 January 1932, published in: ibid., p. 54; information of the secret political detachment of the OGPU regarding the registered kulak farms from 10 March 1932, published in: ibid., p.58.

117. Session protocol of the Commission of the Central Committee of the VCP(b) for Special Settlers from 10 April 1932, approved by the Politburo on 13 April 1932: RGASPI, f. 17, op. 162, d. 12, pp. 104-107.

118. Session protocol of the commission of the Central Committee of the VCP(b) for special settlers from 26 April 1932, approved by the Politburo on 4 May 1932: ibid., pp. 126 f.; operative register of the secret political detachment of the OGPU regarding the resettlement of kulak farms in 1932, April 1932, published in: *Sovietskaya derevnya*, Vol. 3, Book 2, pp. 98 f.

119. Session protocol No. 100 of the Politburo of the Central Committee of the VCP(b) from 6 May 1932, Point 14: RGASPI, f. 17, op. 162, d. 12, pp. 132-137.

120. Information of the secret-political detachment of the OGPU regarding the number of resettled counterrevolutionary kulak elements between October 1932 and May 1933, 21 April 1933, published in: *Sovietskaya derevnya*, Vol. 3, Book 2, p. 389.

121. *Istoriya stalinskogo gulaga. Naselenie gulaga*, pp.35, 573 (FN 7); memorandum of the People's Commissar for Internal Affairs of the RSFSR, V. N. Tolmachev, to the Politburo of the Central Committee of the VCP(b) from 1 July 1929, ibid., pp. 61 f.; Applebaum, *Der Gulag*, pp. 57-78.

122. Resolution of the Politburo of the Central Committee of the VCP(b), 30 January 1930 "Regarding Measures for the Liquidation of Kulak Farms in the Rayons of Complete Collectivization": RGASPI, f. 17, op. 162, d. 8, pp. 64-69.

123. *Istoriya stalinskogo gulaga, Naselenie gulaga*, p. 35.

124. Ibid., p. 35; table by the chief administration of the camps (gulags) regarding the numer of prisoners in the USSR, not dated, 1935, published in: *Istoriya stalinskogo gulaga. Naselenie gulaga*, pp. 68 f. On 8 May 1933, Stalin and Molotov ordered to reduce the number of prisoners from 800,000 to 400,000: Order to all Party and Soviet Functionaries as well as all Agencies of the GPU and Courts and Prosecutors from 8 May 1933, signed by Stalin (Central Committee) and Molotov (SNK): RGASPI, f. 17, op. 3, d. 922, pp. 58 f.

125. Stenographic report of the Plenum of the Central Committee und Central Control Committee of the VCP(b) between 7 and 12 January 1933, the 8th section on 11 January 1933: RGASPI, f. 17, op. 2, d. 514 (Part 2), pp. 4-6.

126. Order to all Party and Soviet Functionaries as well as all Agencies of the GPU and Courts and Prosecutors from 8 May 1933, signed by Stalin (Central Committee) and Molotov (SNK): RGASPI, f. 17, op. 3, d. 922, pp. 58 f.

127. Ibid.

128. Orientation plan of the OGPU regarding the resettlement of kulaks from 12 May 1933, published in: *Sovietskaya derevnya*, Vol. 3, Book 2, pp. 419 f.

129. Report of the NKVD regarding the resettlement of kulaks and anti-Soviet elements in the first half of 1935, from 15 July 1935, published in: *Tragediya sovietskoj derevnii*, Vol. 4, pp. 550 f.

130. Fitzpatrick, *Stalinskyje Krestyane*, pp. 91-95, 221-222; cf.: *Lubyanka 1922-1936*, *Sovietskaya derevnya*, Vol. 3, Book 2; *Tragediya sovietskoj derevnii*, Vol. 4, 5, 6.

131. Resolution No. 579 of the Central Executive Committee of the USSR from 27 May 1934, cited in: *Istoriya stalinskogo gulaga*, Vol. 5, pp. 734, FN 64.

132. Yagoda to Stalin on 17 January 1935, published in: *Istoriya stalinskogo gulaga*, Vol. 5, pp. 209 f.; Newsletter of the NVKD of the USSR No. 36 from 15 March 1935, published in: ibid., pp. 210 f.

133. Protocol No. 51, resolutions of the Politburo of the Central Committee of the VCP(b) from 20 June to 31 July 1937, Point 94: RGASPI, f. 17, op. 162, d. 21, pp. 86-119, here: p. 89.

134. Resolution from 9 July 1937, Point 187: ibid., p. 95; Resolution from 10 July 1937, Point 199, 206; Resolution from 11 July 1937, Point 212: ibid., p. 99.

135. Accompanying letter from Frinovsky to the Politburo for the Operative NKVD Order No. 00477, published in: *Lubyanka 1937-1938*, pp. 273-281.

136. NKVD report on arrests and convictions on the basis of the Operative NKVD Order No. 00477 from 30 July 1937, not dated, after 1 January 1938, published in: *Tragediya sovietskoj derevnii*, Vol. 5, Book 1, pp. 387-393.

137. Protocol No. 57, decisions of the Politburo between 25 January and 9 February 1938, Point 48 (31 January): RGASPI, f. 17, op. 162, d. 22, pp. 112-120, here: p. 113.

138. Protocol No. 58, decisions of the Politburo between 11 February and 23 February, Point 67 (17 February): Ibid., pp. 124-133, here: p. 127.

139. Werth, "Ein Staat gegen sein Volk", p. 213.

140. Stalin, Report to the Seventheenth Party Congress on the Work of the Central Committee of the C.P.S.U. (B.), *January 26, 1934*, published in: Stalin, *Works*, Vol. 13, pp. 288-388, here: p. 329.

141. Information of the State Plan of the USSR Regarding the Progress of Collectivization 1933-1934, from 14 November 1934: published in: *Tragediya sovietskoj derevnii*, Vol. 4, pp.300 ff.; *Vsesoyusnaya perepis naselenya 1937 goda*, p. 5.

142. Zelenin, *Stalinskaya "revolutsiya sverkhu"*, pp. 188 f.

143. Social Composition of the Population of the USSR in the Year 1937, published in: *Vsesoyusnaya perepis naselenya 1937 goda*, pp. 124 f.

144. The Politburo decision from 15 November 1932 as well as the implementation guidelines have been published in: *Istoriya stalinskogo gulaga. Massovye repressii v SSSR*, pp. 149,650 f.; Session protocol No. 126 of the Politburo of the Central Committee of the VCP(b) from 16 December 1932: RGASPI, f. 17, op. 3, d. 911, p. 2.

145. In contrast, sovkhoz peasants employed as agricultural laborers in large state-owned agricultural enterprises received passes, cf. ibid.

146. Memorandum "Return to the Party Program, to the Soviet Constitution, to Leninism (Our Tasks)", not dated, 1932, unknown author published in: *Lubyanka 1922-1936*, pp. 327-334, here: p.331; accompanying letter from Balitsky (OGPU) to Stalin from 11 October 1932 published in: ibid., p. 326.

147. Stalin to Molotov, undated, not before 23 August 1930, published in: *Briefe an Molotow*, pp. 220 f (empasis in original).

148. Stalin to Molotov on 24 August 1930, published in: ibid., pp. 222 f.

149. Session protocol No. 6 of the Politburo of the Central Committee of the VCP(b) from 5 September 1930, Point 11/17: RGASPI, f. 17, op. 162, d. 9, pp. 21 f.

150. Letter from Mikoyan to Stalin regarding the use plan for grain for the year 1930/31 from 23 November 1930: RGASPI, f. 84, op. 2, d. 15, pp. 179-182.

151. Attachment No. 1 to the letter from Mikoyan to Stalin regarding the use plan for grain for the year 1930/31 from 23 November 1930: ibid., p. 183.

152. Message from Mikoyan on the progress of the grain collection program from 23 November 1930: ibid., pp. 168-175.

153. Report from Rosenholz on the economic position of the USSR in England, Italy and Germany, from 4 November 1930: ibid., pp. 154-158; Mikoyan to Molotov on the planned export and imports for the year 1930/31, with attachments, from 19 August 1930: ibid., pp. 83-90.

154. Mikoyan to Molotov regarding the planned exports and imports for 1930/31, including attachments, from 19 August 1930: ibid., pp. 83-90; import plan for the year 1932 including attachment with data on imports in the year 1931, authored by Kuibyshev, 28 November 1931, RGASPI, f. 17, op. 162, d. 11, pp. 87-93.

155. Ibid.; Session protocol No. 79 of the Politburo from 8 December 1931, Resolution from 29 November 1931: ibid., pp. 80-84.

156. Directives for the talks with Germany regarding the expansion of Soviet exports, approved by the Politburo on 15 October 1931: ibid., pp. 28 f.

157. Kaganovich to Stalin on 6 September 1931, published in: *Stalin i Kaganovich*, pp. 83-86.

158. Session protocol No. 61 of the Politburo of the Central Committee of the VCP(b) from 10 November 1931, Point 40/5: RGASPI, f. 17, op. 162, d. 11, pp. 1-5.

159. Kaganovich to Stalin on 6 September 1931, published in: *Stalin i Kaganovich*, pp. 105 ff.; Kaganovich to Stalin on 26 July 1931: ibid., pp. 119 f.; Kaganovich to Stalin, 5 October 1931: ibid., pp. 127 f.

160. Protocol of the Discussions Regarding Grain Collection with the Participation of Comrade Molotov on 29 December 1931, authored by Friedman: RGASPI, f. 82, op. 2, d. 137, pp. 21-24; things were similar in the years prior, cf.: Message from Mikoyan regarding the progress of the grain collection campaign from 23 November 1930 (table): RGASPI, f. 84, op. 2, d. 15, pp. 168-175, here: p. 173.

161. Session protocol No. 77 of the Politburo of the Central Committee of the VCP(b) from 25 November 1931, Point 54/33: RGASPI, f. 17, op. 162, d. 11, p. 68.

162. Session protocol No. 78 of the Politburo of the Central Committee of the VCP(b) from 1 December 1931, Point 25: ibid., pp. 69-74; Session protocol No. 81 of the Politburo of the Central Committee of the VCP(b) from 23 December 1931, Point 11: ibid., pp. 99-102.

163. Resolution of the Politburo on 16 January 1932 regarding the export, foreign exchange and import plan for the year 1932: ibid., d. 11, pp. 131-154; session protocol No. 86 of the Politburo of the Central Committee of the VCP(b) from 28 January 1931, Points 12, 24: ibid., pp. 159-163; resolution regarding the export and import plan for the first quarter of 1932, approved by the Politburo on 28 January 1932: ibid., pp. 164 f.; supply plan for wheat for the first half of 1932, approved by the Politburo on 28 January 1932: ibid., p.172.

164. Protocol of the Discussions Regarding Grain Collection with the Participation of Comrade Molotov on 29 December 1931, authored by Friedman: RGASPI, f. 82, op. 2, d. 137, pp. 21-24.

165. Travel Itinerary of Comrade Molotov in Ukraine for Purposes of Grain Collection between 28 December 1931 and 3 January 1932: ibid., p. 1; resolution of the Politburo of the Central Committee of the CP(b)U from 29 November 1931 regarding measures for the acceleration of grain collection: ibid., pp. 4-7.

166. Resolution of the Politburo of the Central Committee of the CP(b)U regarding grain collection with the collection plans for the respective operative groups, not dated (29 December 1931): ibid., pp. 8-20.

167. Telegram from Stronganov to Molotov from 31 December 1931: ibid., pp. 114.

168. Stenogram of the Conference on Grain from 2 January 1932: RGASPI, f. 82, op. 2, d. 137, pp. 49-92, quote from pp. 50 f., 64, 91 f.

169. Special report of the secret-political unit of the OGPU on negative occurrences and the political situation in the individual regions of the USSR, not dated, after 1 April 1932, published in: *Sovietskaya derevnya*, Vol. 3, Book 2, pp. 64-91, here: p. 64.

170. Ibid., pp. 65 f.

171. Ibid., pp. 64-91.

172. Session protocol No. 93 of the Politburo of the Central Committee of the VCP(b) from 23 March 1932, Point 38/1,41/4: RGASPI, f. 17, op. 162, d. 12, pp. 30 f.

173. Session protocol No. 94 of the Politburo of the Central Committee of the VCP(b) from 1 April 1932, Point 55/18: ibid., pp. 32-40; Session protocol No. 95 from 8 April 1932, Point 41/6, 45/10: ibid., pp. 81-86; Session protocol No. 97 from 23 April 1932, Point 29/6: ibid., pp. 107-110; Session protocol No. 98 from 4 May 1932, Point 33/9: ibid., pp. 113-117.

174. On 20 March, the Politburo approved the shipment of 2500 tons of oats to the Lower Volga region; 270,000 pud of barley and 130,000 pud of wheat to sovkhozes and kolkhozes in the Northern Caucasus and Bashkiria on 26 March; 2000 tons of millet, 1500 tons of linen seeds and 7500 tons of oats for the Tatar Republic on 1 April; 27800 quintals of wheat and 300,000 pud of millet to Bashkiria on 5 April; 16,000 tons of rye and wheat, as well as 8000 tons of millet to kolkhozes in Western Siberia on 21 April; 500 tons of barley and 530 tons of buckwheat to Belarus on 3 May. All these shipments were "seed loans" that were be "repaid" from the harvest of 1932: (Lower Volga Region) Session protocol No. 93 of the Politburo of the Central Committee of the VCP(b) from 20 March 1932, Point 44/7: RGASPI, f. 17, op. 162, d. 12, pp. 30 f.; (Northern Caucasus, Bashkiria, Tatar Republic) Session protocol No. 94 from 1 April1932, Point 41/4,32: ibid., pp. 32-40; (Bashkiria) Session protocol No. 95 from 8 April 1932, Point 41/6, 46/11: ibid., pp. 81-86; (Ural) Session protocol No. 96 from 16 April 1932, Point 34/3: ibid., pp. 92-97; (Western Siberia) Session protocol No. 97 from 23 April 1932, Point 37/14: ibid., pp. 107-110; (Belarus) Session protocol No. 98 from 4 May 1932, Point 39/15: ibid., pp. 113-117.

175. Special report of the secret-political unit of the OGPU on the spring sowing campaign from 28 April 1932, published in: *Sovietskaya derevnya*, Vol. 3, Book 2, pp. 101-104.

176. Session protocol No. 102 of the Politburo of the Central Committee of the VCP(b) from 1 June 1932, Point 58/1: RGASPI, f. 17, op. 162, d. 12, pp. 151-156.

177. Stalin to Kaganovich on 15 June 1932, published in: *Stalin i Kaganovich*, pp. 168 ff.

178. Report of the Politburo of the Central Committee of the VCP(b) from 16 March 1932 regarding the export/import and foreign exchange plan for March 1932: RGASPI, f. 17, op. 162, d. 12, pp. 11-16.

179. Export-Import and Foreign Exchange Plan for the Second Quarter of 1932, approved by the Politburo on 1 April 1932: ibid., pp. 41-64 ; Export Plan for the Third Quarter of

1932, approved by the Politburo on 17 June 1932: ibid., pp. 198 ff. ; Session protocol No. 113 of the Politburo of the Central Committee of the VCP(b) from 25 August 1932, Point 47/4: RGASPI, f 17, op. 162, d. 13, pp. 75-80.

180. Grain Usage Plan for the Year 1932/33, approved by the Politburo on 9 December 1932: RGASPI, f. 17, op. 162, d. 14, p. 34; session protocol No. 125 of the Politburo of the Central Committee of the VCP(b) from 10 December 1932, Point 56/50: ibid., pp. 24-29.

181. Grain Usage Plan for the Harvest of 1933 approved by the Politburo on 7 August 1933: RGASPI, f. 17, op. 162, d. 15, p. 38; session protocol No. 151 of the Politburo of the Central Committee of the VCP(b) from 20 December 1933, Point 100/75: ibid., pp. 151-157.

182. Stalin to Molotov on 19 July 1932, Stalin, *Briefe an Molotow,* pp. 248 f.; Stalin to Kaganovich on 1 July 1932, published in: *Stalin i Kaganovich,* p. 205; Stalin to Kaganovich and Stalin on 18 June 1932, published in: ibid., pp. 179 f.; Kaganovich to Stalin on 28 June 1932, published in: ibid., p. 201; Kaganovich to Stalin on 1 July 1932, published in: ibid., pp. 207 f.

183. Werth, »Ein Staat gegen sein Volk«, pp. 181 f.

184. Resolution of the Politburo on Grain Collection in Ukraine, the Northern Caucasus and the Western Oblast from 14 December 1932: RGASPI, f. 17, op. 3, d. 911, pp. 11,42 f.; published in: *Central Committee RKP(b) - WKP(b) i natsionalny vopros,* pp. 696 ff.

185. Cf. various OGPU reports, published in: *Sovietskaya derevnya,* Vol. 3, Book 2, pp. 293-301 (report from 1 March of 1933), pp. 305-308 (report from 5 March of 1933), pp. 334-338 (reports from 9 and 14 March 1933), pp. 354-363 (report from 28 March of 1933).

186. Report of the secret-political unit of the OGPU regarding the supply crisis in a number of rayons in Ukraine, 23 June 1933, published in: ibid., pp. 427 ff.

187. Ibid.

188. Ibid.

189. Conquest, *Harvest of Sorrow,* pp. 304 f.

190. Werth, »Ein Staat gegen sein Volk«, p. 185.

191. Table according to data from: Eberhard, *Przemiany,* p. 132.

192. During the First Five Year Plan, the population had grown by 14.1 million – an average of 2.8 million per year – and stood at 165.7 million in late 1932 (Population of the USSR, excerpt from the documents of the State Plan of the USSR Regarding the Fulfillment of the First Five Year Plan, not dated: RGASPI, f. 82, op. 2, d. 258, p. 54). It is possible that these are numbers "corrected" in the early 1930s in order to hide the demographic catastrophe.

193. Eberhard, *Przemiany,* pp. 131 f.

194. Stalin, Report to the Seventheenth Party Congress on the Work of the Central Committee of the C.P.S.U. (B.), *January 26, 1934,* published in: Stalin, *Works,* Vol. 13, pp. 288-388, here: p. 343.

195. In early June 1929, the OGPU had reported a famine in the Russian provinces, Belarus, Ukraine and the Volga Region, cf. Report of the Information Unit of the OGPU Regarding the Supply Situation on the Countryside on the Basis of Data from 1 June 1929, published in: *Sovietskaya derevnya,* Vol. 2, pp. 875-887.

196. Eberhard, *Przemiany,* pp. 132 f.

197. Cf. the Report on the Basis of the Deputy Chiefs for Political Affairs of the MTS (Engines-Tractors-Stations) from 15 July 1934, published in: *Sovietskaya derevnya,* Vol. 3, Buch 2, pp. 586-589.

198. Golotik/Minayev, *Naseleniye i Vlast,* p. 49.

199. Protocol No. 43 of the Politburo of the Central Committee of the VCP(b), resolutions from 2 September to 11 October 1936, Point No. 226: RGASPI, f. 17, op. 162, d. 20, pp. 66-97, here: p. 81.

200. Protocol No. 49, decisions of the Politburo of the Central Committee of the VCP(b) from 17 April to 15 June 1937, Point 234.251: RGASPI, f. 17, op. 162, d. 21, pp. 26-63, here: pp. 41 f.

201. Analysis of population movement between the censuses of 17 December 1926 and 6 January 1937 by the deputy chief of the population and health department, Kurman, from 14 March 1937 published in: *Vsesoyusnaya perepis*, pp. 285-288.

202. Baberowski, *Der rote Terror*, p. 200; between 1930 and 1936, just over 40,000 death sentences were handed out in cases brought before court by state security (Overy, *Die Diktatoren*, pp. 267).

203. Golotik/Minayev, *Naseleniye i Vlast*, pp. 65-68.

204. Eberhard, *Przemiany*, p. 133.

205. Population numbers in the USSR on 17 December 1926 and on 6 January 1937, published in: *Vsesoyusnaya perepis*, pp. 42-47; report of the secret-political unit of the GPU of the Ukrainian SSR on the progress of the resettlement of kolkhoz peasants from the RSFSR and Belarus from 3 January 1934, published in: *Sovietskaya derevnya*, Vol. 3, Book 2, pp. 500-504.

206. Nationalities in the Soviet Union based on the censuses of 1926 and 1937, not dated, published in: *Vsesoyusnaya perepis*, pp. 110 f.; Eberhard, *Przemiany*, p. 90.

207. Eberhard, *Przemiany*, pp. 142 f.

208. Stalin to Kaganovich and Molotov on 11 August 1932, published in: *Stalin i Kaganovich*, pp. 273 ff.

209. Service, *Stalin*, p. 388.

210. Dimitroff, *Tagebücher*, p. 259 (entry from 28 May 1939).

211. Fitzpatrick, *Stalinskiye Krestyane*, p. 96.

212. Cf. Service, *Stalin*, pp. 330 f.; Baberowski, *Der Rote Terror*, pp. 134 f.

213. Politburo report regarding collectivization and the fight against kulak-dom in the national, economically backward regions, 20 February 1930: RGASPI, f. 17, op. 162, d. 8, pp. 94-101.

214. Cf. Iwanow, *Pierwszy Naród Ukarany*.

215. Baberowski, *Der rote Terror*, pp. 196 f.

216. Report of the Politburo Regarding the Polish Settlements in the Border Oblasts, from 5 March 1930, RGASPI, f. 17, op. 162, d. 8, pp. 109 f.; session protocol No. 117 of the Politburo of the Central Committee of the VCP(b) from 5 March 1930, Point 5: ibid., pp. 103 ff.

217. Ibid.

218. Ibid.

219. Politburo resolution on measures for the cultural and economic development of the border regions in 1929/30, not dated (20 April 1930): RGASPI, f. 17, op. 162, d. 8, pp. 141 f.; session protocol No. 124 of the Politburo of the Central Committee of the VCP(b) from 25 April 1930, Point 80: ibid., pp. 136-139.

220. Session protocol No. 120 of the Politburo of the Central Committee of the VCP(b) from 15 March 1930, Point 72 "On Ukraine and Belarus": ibid., pp. 111-115; published also in: *Lubyanka 1922-1936*, pp. 235 f.

221. From the report of the operative group of the OGPU regarding the results of the deportation of kulaks of the second category from 6 May 1930, published in: *Tragediya*

sovietskoi derevni, Vol. 2, pp. 409-432, here: p.413, 423 f.; according to an OGPU report from 17 September 1930, 3309 persons were deported from the BSSR in the course of the Polish Action, published in: ibid., pp. 702-709, here: p. 706.

222. Session protocol No. 14 of the Politburo of the Central Committee of the VCP(b) from 5 November 1930, Point 9/11: RGASPI, f. 17, op. 162, d. 9, pp. 57-60; published in: *Lubyanka 1922-1936*, p. 257.

223. Resolution of the Politburo Regarding the Political and Economic Situation in the Border Regions of the Ukrainian SSR and the BSSR from 1 December 1931: RGASPI, f. 17, op. 162, d. 11, pp. 76-79; session protocol No. 78 of the Politburo of the Central Committee of the VCP(b) from 1 December 1931, Point 60/32: ibid., pp. 69-74.

224. Report by Prokofiev to Stalin regarding the results of the purge action of the western border from 8 August 1933, published in: *Lubyanka, 1922-1936*, pp. 460-463; Balitsky to Stalin on the progress of the investigation into the Polish Military Organization from 8 August 1933: ibid., p. 460; telegram from Sakovsky to Stalin on the topic of the Polish Military Organization from 4 October 1933, published in: ibid., pp. 467 f.

225. Report by S. Kosior to Stalin on the consolidation of the border regions from 23 December 1934, published in: *Lubyanka, 1922-1936*, pp. 582 ff.

226. NKVD report on the deportation of kulaks and anti-Soviet elements in the first half of 1935, from 15 July 1935, published in: *Tragediya sovietskoj derevnii*, Vol. 4, pp. 550 f.

227. Protocol No. 39, Resolutions of the Politburo of the Central Committee of the VCP(b) between 22 April and 20 May 1936, Point 57 (28 May 1926): RGASPI, f. 17, op. 162, d. 19, pp. 153-173, p. 159; resolution regarding to deport 15,000 Polish and German farms from the Ukrainian SSR to the Karaganda Oblast, Kazakhstan: ibid., pp. 174 ff.; 36,045 Poles were deported from Ukraine in 1936 alone. The Politburo allocated 23 million rubles for the operation; however, this was too little and the NKVD and the party leadership in Karaganda asked for additional funds. The Politburo refused this request on 4 September 1936 and instead ordered the NKVD to adhere to the planned number of deportees while staying within the budget: Eberhard, *Przemiany*, p. 145; cf. Protocol No. 43 of the Politburo of the Central Committee of the VCP(b), resolutions between 2 September and 11 October 1936, Point Nr. 18: RGASPI, f. 17, op. 162, d. 20, pp. 66-97, here: p. 66.

228. Baberowski, *Der rote Terror*, p. 198; Yezhov and Stalin on 27 July 1937, published in: *Lubyanka, 1937-1938*, p. 270; Operative Order No. 00439 of the People's Commissar for Domestic Affairs of the USSR from 25 July 1937, published in: ibid., pp. 271 f.

229. Nationalities in the USSR on the basis of the censuses of 1926 and 1937, not dated, published in: *Vsesoyusnaya perepis*, pp. 110 f.

230. Secret letter from Yezhov to the the People's Commissars for Domestic Affairs in the various Soviet republics and the chiefs of administration of the NKVD in the autonomous republics, oblasts and regions from 11 August 1937 regarding the fascist, insurrectionist, spying, sabotaging, wrecking and terrorist activities of Polish counterintelligence in the USSR, published in: *Lubyanka, 1937-1938*, pp. 303-321.

231. Yezhov to Stalin on 14 September 1937, published in: *Lubyanka, 1937-1938*, pp. 352-359.

232. Cf. reports from 19 September 1937 (ibid., pp. 373 ff.) and 22 March 1938(ibid., pp. 500-503).

233. Cf. Pietrow, "Polska operacja NKWD"; Aleksander Gurjanov, "Sowieckie represje wobec Polaków i obywateli polskich w latach 1936-1956 w świetle danych sowieckich", in: *Europa Nieprowincjonalna. Przemiany na ziemiach wschodnich dawnej Rzeczpospolitej (Bialourś, Litwa, Łotwa, Ukraina, wschodnie pogranicze 111 Rzeczpospolitej Polskiej w latach 1772-1999)*, published by Krzysztof Jasiewicz, Warsaw, London 1999, pp. 972-982.

234. Eberhard, *Przemiany,* p. 144.

235. Ibid., pp. 145 ff.

236. Ponomarenko to Stalin on 3 August 1938: GARF, f. 8418, op. 22, d. 561, pp. 15-20.

237. Kiselev, Chairman of the Council of People's Commissars of the BSSR, to Molotov on 18 August 1938: GARF, f. 8418, op. 22, d. 561, pp. 12 f; as late as November 1938, it had not been decided whether to deport these families or not; Note from 22 November 1938: ibid., p. 10; Yezhov mentioned a letter to Molotov 27 October 1938 regarding difficulties in carrying out mass deportations that had prevented the March decision of the Politburo to deport hostile elements from the Ukrainian borderlands to be implemented: ibid., pp. 13 f.

238. Bericht über die Lage im Bereich der Sich.-Div. 221 vom 19.09. 1941: Bundesarchiv-Militärarchiv Freiburg (fortan BA-MA), RH 24-221/84 (no pagination).

239. For this piece of information I thank Andrej Zamojski who has spent years studying the history of collectivization in Belarus.

240. Baberowski, *Der rote Terror,* pp. 197-200.

241. Eberhard, *Przemiany,* pp. 145 f.

Chapter 15

1. Data from: Meltyukho, *Upushchenny Shans Stalina,* p. 358 f.

2. Data from: Ibid., pp. 598 ff.; Samuelson, *Krasny Koloss,* p. 160 (tank production in 1932).

3. Data from: Samuelson, *Krasny Koloss,* p. 207.

4. Ken, *Mobilizatsyonnoye Planirovaniye,* p 456 (table 4 A).

5. Table from: Ibid., p. 457 f.

6. Samuelson, *Krasny Koloss,* pp. 160, 202, 207.

7. Tukhachevsky to Stalin on 30 December 1930: RGASPI, f. 558, op. 11, d. 446, pp. 66–71.

8. Memorandum by Tukhachevsky on air transport from 17 August 1929: ibid., pp. 26-29.

9. Letter by Tukhachevsky to Antonov from 23 August 1929: ibid., p. 31f.

10. Memorandum by Tukhachevsky on rebuilding of the railway network from 19 October 1929, addressed to Voroshilov, People's Commissar for Military Affairs and the Fleet: ibid., pp. 47-57 v.

11. Memorandum by Tukhachevsky on rebuilding of the Red Army from 11 January 1930, addressed to Voroshilov: ibid., pp. 12-18 v, here p. 12; the same document with attachments appears in: RGASPI, f. 558, op. 11, d. 447, ppl. 33–53.

12. Memorandum by the Commander of the Leningrad Military District Tukhachevsky rebuilding of the Red Army from 11 January 1930, addressed to Voroshilov: RGASPI, f. 558, op. 11, d. 446, pp. 12–18 v, here pp. 13v-14.

13. Ibid., p. 16 v f.

14. Ibid., p. 18f.; statement by Shaposhnikov regarding the memorandum by Tukhachevsky (01.11.1930) from 13 February 1930: RGASPI, f. 558, op. 11, d. 447, pp. 19–32, here p. 21.

15. Samuelson, *Krasny Koloss,* p. 130.

16. Statement by Shaposhnikov regarding the memorandum by Tukhachevsky (01.11.1930) from 13 February 1930: RGASPI, f. 558, op. 11, d. 447, pp. 19–32, here p. 21.

17. Ziemke, *Red Army,* p. 165.

18. Statement by Shaposhnikov regarding the memorandum by Tukhachevsky (01.11.1930) from 13 February 1930: RGASPI, f. 558, op. 11, d. 447, pp. 19–32, here p. 21.

19. Statement by the General Staff of the Red Army regarding the memorandum by Tukhachevsky (01.11.1930), undated (before 03.05.1930): Ibid., pp. 10-18.

20. Voroshilov to Stalin on 5 March 1930: Ibid., p. 9.

21. Stalin to Voroshilov on 23 March 1930: Ibid., 8 (emphasis in the original).

22. Memorandum by Tukhachevsky regarding the mobilization of the industry from 23 February 1930: RGASPI, f. 558, op. 11, d. 446, pp. 58–63 v.

23. Memorandum by Tukhachevsky, commander of the Leningrad Military District, regarding the production of artillery pieces and shells from 8 March 1930, to Voroshilov, to Shaposhnikov: Ibid., pp. 19-25.

24. Memorandum by Tukhachevsky regarding combat engineers from 16 March 1930: Ibid., pp. 34-43.

25. Memorandum by Tukhachevsky regarding the ad-hoc roads made out of pre-fabricated materials from 26 May 1930: Ibid., pp. 44-46 v.

26. Response by Tukhachevsky from 19 June 1930 to the criticism levied against his memorandum regarding the reorganization of the Red Army from 8 March 1930 by the staff of the RKKA, to Stalin, copy to Voroshilov: Ibid., pp. 6–11 v.

27. Ibid.

28. Tukhachevsky to Stalin on 30 December 1930: Ibid., pp. 66-71.

29. Response by Tukhachevsky from 19 June 1930 to the criticism levied against his memorandum regarding the reorganization of the Red Army from 8 March 1930 by the staff of the RKKA, to Stalin, copy to Voroshilov: Ibid., pp. 6–11 v.

30. Protocol of the Politburo Commission of the Central Committee of the VKP(b) from 29 November 1930: RGASPI, f. 17, op. 162, d. 9, pp. 84, 88–92.

31. Resolution of the Politburo regarding the tank building program from 20 February 1931: Ibid., pp. 151-156.

32. Tukhachevsky to Stalin on 30 December 1930: RGASPI, f. 558, op. 11, d. 446, pp. 66–71.

33. Ken, *Mobilizatsyonnoye planirovaniye*, p. 171.

34. Stalin to Tukhachevsky on 7 May 1932, copy sent to Voroshilov: RGASPI, f. 558, op. 11, d. 447, pp. 2 f.

35. Ibid.

36. Resolution of the Politburo regarding the tank building program from 20 February 1931: RGASPI, f. 17, op. 162, d. 9, pp. 151–156.

37. Tukhachevsky to Stalin on 30 December 1930: RGASPI, f. 558, op. 11, d. 446, pp. 66–71.

38. Ibid.

39. Ibid.

40. Samuelson, *Krasny Koloss*, p. 136.

41. Resolution regarding the tank building program passed, by the Politburo on 20 February 1931: RGASPI, f. 17, op. 166, d. 387, pp. 34–77.

42. Ibid.

43. Resolution of the Politburo regarding the Commanders in the Red Army from 25 February 1931: RGASPI, f. 17, op. 166, d. 387, pp. 4–7.

44. Resolution of the Central Committee of the VKP(b) regarding the Commanders and political workers in the Red Army from 5 July 1931: RGASPI, f. 17, op. 162, d. 10, pp. 72 ff.

45. Svirin, *Bronya krepka*, pp. 138 f.

46. Samuelson, *Krasny Koloss*, pp. 138 f.

47. Ibid., p. 156

48. Ibid., pp. 156 f., 186 ff.

49. Report by Voroshilov on the results of the war preparations of the Red Army in the years 1931-1932 from 16 November 1932: GARF, f. 8418, op. 6, d. 168, pp. 26–42, here p. 26 f.

50. Ibid., p. 28.
51. Ibid., pp. 29 ff.
52. Ibid., pp. 33 ff.
53. Ibid., p. 36 f.
54. Ibid., p. 40 f.
55. Samuelson, *Krasny Koloss*, pp. 157-161.
56. Table from: Ibid., p. 160.
57. Ibid., pp. 159, 162.
58. Ibid., pp. 158-161.
59. Ibid., p. 207.
60. Ibid., p. 166.
61. Table from: Meltyukhov, *Upushchtenny Shans Stalina*, p. 601.
62. Voroshilov to Stalin, Ordzhonikidze and Kaganovich from 2 August 1936: GARF, f. 8418, op. 11, d. 46, pp. 8–12, here p. 8.
63. Special OGPU report on the delivery of defect weapons to the Red Army and on the work of the Office for Military Procurement and Quality Control in Factories from 1 August 1933, signed by Yagoda and Mironov: GARF, f. 8418, op. 8, d. 175, pp. 34–40, here p. 36 f.
64. Ibid.
65. Resolution by the Council for Labor and Defense regarding the organization of the procurement of military production from November 1933, signed by Molotov and Bazilevich: GARF, f. 8418, op. 8, d. 175, pp. 87–90.
66. Khalepsky to Kuibyshev on 1 December 1933: GARF, f. 8418, op. 9, d. 42, pp. 19 f.
67. Golodel [Chair of the Council of the People's Commissars of the BSSR] and G. Goncharov [Advisor for Military Affairs at the Council of People's Commissars of the BSSR] to Molotov on 16 March 1935: GARF, f. 8418, op. 9, d. 42, pp. 141 f.
68. Report regarding the causes for the non-fulfilment of the plans for the general overhaul of military machinery in the first half of 1935 from 19 July 1935: GARF, f. 8418, op. 9, d. 42, pp. 210 ff.
69. Khalepsky to Rukhimovich [Deputy People's Commissar for Heavy Industry] from 1 November 1936: GARF, f. 8418, op. 11, d. 46, pp. 56 f.
70. On 7 September 1936, the Politburo ordered the People's Commissariat for Foreign Trade to import an additional amount of ball bearings for 2,383,000 rubles. Protocol No. 43 of the Politburo of the Central Committee of the VKP(b), resolutions from 2 September to 11 October 1936, point 77: RGASPI, f. 17, op. 162, d. 20, pp. 66–97, here p. 70.
71. Report on the general overhaul of military machinery in industrial plants in the first half of 1936 from 14 July 1936, signed by Olshansky: GARF, f. 8418, op. 11, d. 45, pp. 12–15. In the first half of 1936, the targets for repairs had been achieved to varying extent: 84% of BT tanks, 106.2% of T-26, 96.2% of T-27, 66.7% of T-37, 13.3% of T-26 motors and 64.1% of M-5 (ibid.).
72. Report on the general overhaul of military machinery in industrial plants in the first quarter of 1936 from 14 April 1936: GARF, f. 8418, op. 11d. 45, pp. 29 ff.
73. Cf. related resolutions and orders issued by the Economic Council from 7 April 1939. 13 May 1939, 4 July 1939: GARF, f 8418, op. 23, d. 515, pp. 1 ff., pp. 26 ff., pp. 30 f.
74. Voroshilov to Stalin, Ordzhonikidze and Kaganovich on 2 August 1936: GARF, f. 8418, op. 11, d. 46, pp. 8–12, here p. 8.
75. Ibid.

76. Tukhachevsky to Stalin on 9 July 1936: Ibid., pp. 22 f.

77. Ibid.

78. Ibid.

79. Resolution by the Committee for Defense on the usage regulations and the creation of a fleet of tanks for training purposes from 1 August 1937, signed by Molotov and Bazilevich: GARF, f. 8418, op. 12, d. 93, p. 1; Voroshilov to Molotov on 5 July 1937: GARF, f. 8418, op. 12, d. 93, pp. 5 f.

80. Report by Pavlov at the session of the Chief War Council in early 1938, published in: Glavny woyenny soviet RKKA, p. 47 f. (FN 2).

81. Transcripts of the reports and presentations of the participants of the session of the war council at the NKO SSSR, evening session on 21 November 1937, published in: Woyenny soviet, 1937, pp. 24–86, here p. 51.

82. Transcript of the reports and presentations of the participants of the session of the war council at the NKO SSSR, evening session on 22 November 1937, presentation by Gorodovkov published in: Ibid. pp. 144-211, here p. 167.

83. Concluding speech by Voroshilov at the session of the war council at the NKO SSSR, 27 November 1937, presentation by Gorodovkov published in: *Woyenny soviet*, 1937, pp. 308-328, here pp 313 f.

84. Protocol No. 4 of the session of the Workers' and Peasants' Red Army on 20 April 1938, published in: *Glavny voienny soviet RKKA*, p. 36-41.

85. Ibid.

86. Svirin, Bronevoy Shchit Stalina, pp. 102-105, 148-158: Armiya Pobedy, pp. 325–328, 341–348; Meltyukhov, *Upushchenny shans Stalina*, p. 601.

87. Ibid.

88. Protocol No. 30, decisions of the Politburo of the Central Committee of the VKP(b) from 2 to 9 April 1941, decision from 7 April 1941, point 87: RGASPI, f. 17, op. 162, d. 33, pp. 99–122, here pp. 103–107.

89. Decision of the Politburo from 15 March 1941 regarding the production of the "KV" tank for the year 1941 (point 236): RGASPI, f. 17, op. 162, d. 32, pp. 129–138.

90. Decision of the Politburo of the Central Committee of the VKP(b) on the production of T-34 tanks for the year 1941, from 5 May 1941, signed by Stalin and Molotov: RGASPI, f. 17, op. 162, d. 34, pp. 179–188.

91. Resolution of the SNK of the USSR regarding the military procurement plan for the NKO, the fleet and the NKVD for the 2nd quarter of 1941, approved by the Politburo on 12 April 1941: RGASPI, f. 17,op. 162, d. 34, pp. 44–52; decision of the Central Committee of the VKP(b) regarding the production of T-50 tanks in the Factory No. 174 from 16 April 1941: Ibid., pp. 57–64; *Armiya Pobedy*, pp. 311–314 (specifications of the T-40 und T-50 tanks).

92. Danchenko to Molotov on 3 August 1940: RGASPI, f. 82, op. 2, d. 572, pp. 8 ff.

93. Meltyukhov, *Upushchenny Shans Stalina*, p. 601.

94. Memorandum by Rydakov regarding the production of tanks and the necessity of the creation of a People's Commissariat for Tank and Tractor Production, addressed to Stalin, Molotov, Voroshilov and Zhdanov, from 9 December 1940: RGASPI, f. 82, op. 2, d. 572, pp. 14 ff.; during the Soviet-Finnish War, a single tank brigade lost 96 of its 145 T-28 tanks (*Armiya Pobedy*, p. 322).

95. Report on the state of the air force, addressed to Ordzhonikidze, not dated, before 5 March 1930: GARF, f. 8418, op. 18, d. 26, pp. 2–16.

96. Bystrova, *Sovyetsky Woyenno-Promyshlenny Kompleks*, pp. 91–101.

97. Samuelson, *Krasny Koloss*, pp. 186 f.

98. Transcript of the report of the conference of the Central Committee and the Central Control Commission of the VKP(b) from 7-12 January 1933: RGASPI, f. 17, op. 2, d. 514 (part I), pp. 3–9 v, 62–66.

99. The exact number of planes in the Soviet air force in January 1933, has eluded the author. However, it has to be noted that between 1930 and 1932, the Soviet Union's aviation industry is reported to have produced over 5100 planes (Meltyukhov, *Upushchenny Shans Stalina*, p. 600).

100. Chief of the head office of the aviation industry, Korolev, to the STO on 25 September 1933: GARF, f. 8418, op. 8, d. 64, pp. 27–30.

101. Report of the OGPU regarding the fulfilment of the program for the production of aircraft and motors for the first 9 months of 1933, from 9 October 1933: Ibid., pp. 69–79.

102. Excerpt from the transcript of the meeting No. 14 of the Committee for Defense of the USSR, from 9 October 1933:: Ibid., pp. 23 f.

103. Resolution No. 103 of the STO regarding the measures taken to implement the aircraft program for the year 1933, signed by Molotov (chairman of the STO) and Bazilevich (for the secretary of the STO): Ibid., pp. 2–7.

104. Ibid.

105. Ibid.

106. Stalin to the members of the Committee of Defense as well as the comrades Tukhachevsky, Alksin, N. Kuibyshev, Khakhanyan, on 16 June 1934: RGASPI, f. 82, op. 2, d. 820, p. 6.

107. Memorandum by Kurchevsky, addressed to Stalin and Ordzhonikidze, on 9 June 1934: Ibid., pp. 6–9.

108. Ibid.

109. Report by the chief of the head office of the aviation industry, Korolyov, regarding the progress in refitting the air force of the Red Army from 14 October 1935: GARF, f. 8418, op. 10, d. 31, pp. 38–57, here p. 52. The R-5 was a Soviet-built biplane that entered production in 1928. It was armed with three light 7.62 mm machine guns and had a range of 800 km as well as a speed of 225 km/h at 3700 m. It could reach heights of up to 5940 m and had a load capacity of up to 500 kg. Between 1931 and 1937, 7000 R-5 planes were built, making it the main type of combat aircraft in the Soviet air force. The U-2 biplane was also produced domestically beginning in 1927. It was armed with a single 7.62 mm machine gun, had a range of 450 km and could carry up to 350 kg in ordnance. The U-2's could reach speeds of up to 134 km/h and heights of only up to 1500 m. Both the R-5 and the U-2 biplanes saw use in the Second World War and beyond. Cf. *Armiya Pobedy*, pp. 436–440; The I-5 interceptor was a biplane as well and entered production in 1930. It could reach speeds of up to 280 km/h and heights of up to 7500 m. It was armed with two 7.62 mm machine guns and had a range of 620 m (I. Kolesnikov, *Initsyativa v Vozdushnom Boyu*, in: http://www.mkmagazin.almanacwhf.ru/avia/i_5.htm). In 1933 alone, 1675 R-5 and 1280 U-2 planes were to be built (Korolyow to the STO, 25 September 1933 [receipt stamp]: GARF, f. 8418, op. 8, d. 64, pp. 27–30).

110. Report by the chief of the head office of the aviation industry, Korolyov, regarding the progress in refitting the air force of the Red Army from 14 October 1935: GARF, f. 8418, op. 10, d.31, pp. 38–57.

111. Report on the implementation of the plan for the production of modern aircraft and engines from 5 October 1935, authored by Khakhanyan (Chief of the War Control of the KSK) and Berezin (Deputy Chief of the naval group of the KPK) to Stalin and Molotov: GARF, 8418, op. 10, d. 31, pp. 13–24.

112. Ibid.

113. Ibid., here: p. 14.

114. Ibid., here: p. 19.

115. Report by the chief of the head office of the aviation industry, Korolyov, regarding the progress in refitting the air force of the Red Army from 14 October 1935: GARF, f. 8418, op. 10, d. 31, pp. 38–57, here p. 52; Meltyuchow, *Upushchenny Shans Stalina*, p. 600.

116. Samuelson, *Krasny Koloss*, p. 207.

117. Shaposhnikov to Voroshilov, March 1936: GARF, f. 8418, op. 10, d. 31, pp. 179 ff.

118. Meltyukhov, *Upushchenny Shans Stalina*, p. 600.

119. Dimitrov, *Diaries*, pp. 315 ff. (entry from 7 November 1940).

120. *Armyja Pobedy*, pp. 421–424; W. Radinger und W. Schick, *Messerschmitt Me 109, alle Varianten von Bf 109 A bis 109 E*, Munich 1997.

121. Protocol No. 1 of the session of the commission of the Chief War Council from 4 May 1940, published in: »*Zimnyaya Voyna*«, üü. 215–221, here p. 216.

122. Dimitrov, *Diaries*, pp. 315 ff. (entry from 7 November 1940). Emphasis in the original.

123. In the folder RGASPI, f. 558, op. 11, d. 151 there are several documents on this topic that were either addressed to Stalin or written by him.

124. Stalin and Molotow to the management of the Factory No. 22 on 2 December 1940: RGASPI, f. 558, op. 11, d. 151, p. 15. Stalin personally wrote this letter, which was later typed out by Molotov. Molotov signed it as well (Ibid.: p. 16).

125. Protocol No. 31, decisions of the Politburo of the Central Committee of the VKP(b) from 10 to 26 April 1941: RGASPI, f. 17, op. 162, d. 34, pp. 1–38, here pp. 1 ff., 12–21; decision of the Central Committee of the VKP(b) from 19 April 1941 (Pe-2 bomber): Ibid., pp. 81–88; decision of the Central Committee of the VKP(b) from 23 April 1941 (LaGG-3): Ibid., pp. 135–138.

126. Protocol No. 31, decisions of the Politburo of the Central Committee of the VKP(b) from 10 to 26 April 1941: Ibid., pp. 12–21; Protocol No. 32, decisions of the Politburo of the Central Committee of the VKP(b) from 28 April to 14 May 1941: Ibid., pp. 145–158, here: pp. 145 f., 151–153.

127. Protocol No. 31, decisions of the Politburo of the Central Committee of the VKP(b) from the 10 to 26 April 1941: Ibid., pp. 1–38, here pp. 33 f.; decision of the SNK and the Central Committee regarding the reorganization of the rear areas of the air force from 10 April 1941: Ibid., pp. 39 ff.

128. Cf. the extensive correspondence on this issue from February 1941, replete with personal edits and notes by Stalin: RGASPI, f. 558, op. 11, d. 439.

129. Litunovsky to Voroshilov on 11 August 1930: RGASPI, f. 74, op. 2, d. 101, pp. 126–139, here pp. 130 ff.

130. Resolution of the Central Committee of the VKP(b) and the SovNarKom of the USSR regarding the "Accidents in the Units of the Air Force of the Red Army" from 5 July 1932: RGASPI, f. 17, op. 162, d. 13, pp. 18–36.

131. Ibid; Protocol No. 107 of the session of the Politburo from 10 July 1932, point 3: Ibid. pp. 11–15.

132. Protocol No. 116 of the Politburo of the Central Committee of the VKP(b) from 16 September 1932, point 60: Ibid., pp. 96–102.

133. Resolution of the Central Committee of the VKP(b) regarding accidents in the air forces of the Red Army, not dated (16 September 1932): Ibid., pp. 103–111.

134. Order of the People's Commissar for Defense of the Soviet Union, Voroshilov, from June 1936: GARF, f. 8418, op. 11, d. 60, pp. 11–22, here p. 11.

135. Report by the NKVD on the accidents of the aerial forces of the Red Army between 1934 and May 1936, Commissar for State Security of second rank, Gay, not dated (receipt stamp: 7 June 1936): GARF, f. 8418, op. 11, d. 60, pp. 93–119.

136. On 27 July 1936, Molotov in his position as the chief of the STO issued a decree ordering a number of measures to be taken in the fight against accidents in the air forces of the Red Army: Ibid., pp. 7–10; on 13 August 1936, the STO issued another decree to lower the number of accidents among air force units stationed in the Far East: Ibid., pp. 1–5.

137. Final speech by Voroshilov on 29 November 1938 at the yearly conference of the War Council at the People's Commissariat for Defense (21 to 29 November 1938), published in: *Woyenny Sowiet, 1938, 1940*, pp. 235–264, here pp. 252 ff.

138. Ibid. (Information for the time between 1936 and October 1938); the report of the NKVD on the accidents of the air forces … (cf. note 135 for the numbers for 1934 and 1935).

139. Final speech by Voroshilov on 29 November 1938 at the yearly conference of the War Council at the People's Commissariat for Defense (21 to 29 November 1938), published in: *Woyenny Sowiet, 1938, 1940*, pp. 235–264, here pp. 254 f.

140. Oder No. 070 of the People's Commissar for Defense regarding the measures taken to prevent accidents in the Air Forces of the Red Army from 4 July 1939, published in: *Prikazy NKO SSSR, 1937–1941*, pp. 102–110.

141. Protocol of the session of the War Council, authored by Colonel V. Kondashov on 1 December 1938, published in: *Woyenny Soviet, 1938, 1940*, pp. 168–205, here p. 176.

142. Final speech by Voroshilov on 29 November 1938 at the yearly conference of the War Council at the People's Commissariat for Defense (21 to 29 November 1938), published in: Ibid., p. 253.

143. Order No. 0109 of the NKO of the USSR from 14 December 1937, published in: *Voyenny Sowiet, 1937*, pp. 329–340, here p. 333.

144. Protocol of the session of the Chief War Council of the Red Army from 16 to 17 May 1939, published in: *Glawny Voyenny Sowiet*, pp. 202–216, hier p. 204.

145. Ibid., p. 206.

146. Resolution of the Central Committee of the VKP(b) and the SNK of the USSR "On accidents and catastrophes in the Air Forces of the Red Army" from 9 April 1941: RGASPI, f. 17, op. 163, d. 1308, pp. 208 ff.; published in: *Lubyanka, 1939–1946*, pp. 261 f.

147. Capital investments in the aviation industry made up around a third of all investments into the armaments industry, in 1936: 499 million out of 1.6 billion rubles, in 1937: 721.8 million out of 2.2 billion rubles, in 1938: 1.49 billion out of 2.78 billion rubles; for the following years, these investments were planned – 1939: 1.85 billion out of 5.9745 billion rubles, 1940: 1.6 billion out of 5 billion rubles, 1941: 1.2 billion out of 4 billion rubles; Samuelson, *Krasny Koloss*, pp. 220 f. (charts 8.5 and 8.6).

148. Among them is the inventory of the Committee for Defense in the GRAF (f. 8418). All files that deal with chemical weapons remain closed.

149. Trotsky's presentation on the yearly congress of the "Society of the Friends of Chemical Defense" on 19 May 1924: RGASPI, f. 325, op. 1, d. 92, pp. 1–23, here pp. 8 f. Stalin likewise recognized the need for chemical warfare. In March 1923, he complained about the – in his view – inadequate strategy and tactics of the Russian communists: "The organizational forms of armies, the types of troops and the service arms are usually adapted to the forms and methods of warfare. [...] In a war of movement, victory is usually achieved by the massed use of cavalry. In a war of position, cavalry either plays no role at all or just a minor role: Heavy artillery and aircraft, poison gas and tanks decide everything." ("Regarding the Question of Strategy and Tactics of the Russian

Communists", published in: *Pravda* on 14 March 1923, printed in: Stalin, *Works*, Vol. 5, pp. 90–99, here p. 94.)

150. Report on the state of and the perspectives for the development of the armed forces of the USSR between May 1927 and June 1929, not dated (June 1929), Voroshilov sent this report to Rudsutak: GARF, f.8418, op. 18, d. 26, pp. 144–210, here p. 207.

151. Transcript of the plenary session of the Central Committee and the Central Control Commission of the VKP(b) between 7 and 12 January 1933: RGASPI, f. 17, op. 2, d. 514 (Part I), pp. 3–9, 62–66, here p. 63.

152. Report by Voroshilov on the results of the war preparations of the Red Army in the years 1931-1932, from 16 November 1932: GARF, 8418, op. 6, d. 168, pp. 26–42, here: p. 36.

153. Samuelson, *Krasny Koloss*, pp. 202 ff.; Bystrova, *Sovietsky Woyennopromyshlenny Kompleks*, p. 122.

154. Directory of arms factories with special hiring regulations for workers, approved by the Politburo on 4 May 1934: RGASPI, f. 17, op. 162, d. 16, pp. 51–54.

155. Litunovsky to Voroshilov on 11 August 1930: RGASPI, f. 74, op. 2, d. 101, pp. 126–139, here pp. 128 f.

156. Bystrova, *Sovietsky Woyennopromyshlenny Kompleks*, pp. 115–118.

157. Report by Yagoda and Mironov to Stalin regarding the "spy organization" in the artillery and weapons industries from 7 August 1933, published in: *Lubyanka, 1922–1936*, pp. 454 ff.

158. Chart with data from Samuelson, *Krasny Koloss*, pp. 202, 207, 221.

159. Special report of the OGPU on the delivery of defective weapons to the Red Army and the work of the offices for military procurement and the quality control in the factories from 1 August 1933, signed by Yagoda and Mironov: GARF, f. 8418, op. 8, d. 175, pp. 34–40.

160. Report by Tukhachevsky to Voroshilov regarding the 45 mm anti-tank projectiles from 26 July 1935: RGASPI, f. 558, op. 11, d. 447, pp. 147–150.

161. Order No. 113 of the NKO on the military and political training of the troops for the training year of 1939, from 11 December 1938, published in: *Voyenny Soviet 1938, 1940*, pp. 295–318, here pp. 309 f.; Transcript of the Lectures and Presentations given by the Participants of the Session of the War Council at the NKO SSSR, evening session on 21 November 1937 (lecture by Fedko), published in: *Voyenny Soviet 1937*, pp. 24–86, here pp. 48–56; Lecture by Sedyakin at the Session of the War Council of the NKO of the USSR on 22 November 1937, published in: Ibid., p. 171.

162. Letter by M. Galaktinov to Molotov regarding a conference of leading logistics troops officers of the Red Army from 17 July 1935: RGASPI, f. 82, op. 2, d. 800, pp. 1 f.

163. Reese, *Stalin's Reluctant Soldiers*, pp. 41–46.

164. Final speech by Voroshilov on 29 November 1938 at the yearly conference of the War Council at the People's Commissariat for Defense (21 to 29 November 1938), published in: *Voyenny Soviet, 1938, 1940*, pp. 235–264, here pp. 260 f.

165. Reese, *Stalin's Reluctant Soldiers*, pp. 49–51.

166. Transcript of the morning session on 26 November 1938, published in: *Voyenny Soviet, 1938, 1940*, pp. 158–167, here: p. 164 f.

167. Reese, *Stalin's Reluctant Soldiers*, pp. 71–74.

168. Simin, a member of the War Council of the North Caucasian Military District at the session of the War Council at the NKO of the USSR between 21 and 29 November 1938, published in: *Voyenny Soviet, 1938, 1940*, p. 197. The accident rate for cars was at 11.2%

among artillery units, at 6.1% in the cavalry, at 5.2% in the infantry, at 5% among tank troops and at 4.4% in the navy; it was at 2% in the air force (ibid.).

169. The Chief of the Administration of Automobiles and Tanks in the Red Army, Bokis at the session of the War Council at the NKO of the USSR, between 21 and 27 November 1937, published in: *Voyenny Soviet, 1937*, p. 177.

170. Transcripts of the reports and presentations of the participants of the session of the war council at the NKO SSSR, evening session on 21 November 1937, published in: Voyenny Soviet, 1937, pp. 24–86, here pp. 48-56.

171. *Voyenny Soviet*, 1937, pp. 5 ff.

172. Transcript of the morning session on 26 November 1938, published in: *Voyenny Soviet, 1938, 1940*, pp. 158–167, here: pp. 164 f.

173. Final speech by Voroshilov on 29 November 1938 at the yearly conference of the War Council at the People's Commissariat for Defense (21 to 29 November 1938), published in: *Woyenny Sowiet, 1938, 1940*, pp. 235–264, here: pp. 258 f.

174. *Voyenny Soviet*, 1937, pp. 4, 8.

175. Final speech by Voroshilov on 29 November 1938 at the yearly conference of the War Council at the People's Commissariat for Defense (21 to 29 November 1938), published in: *Woyenny Sowiet, 1938, 1940*, pp. 235–264, here p. 262. (Emphasis by the author).

176. Transcript of the morning session on 26 November 1938, published in: *Voyenny Soviet, 1938, 1940*, pp. 158–167, here: p. 164.

177. Interjection by Rogachev during the final speech by Voroshilov on 29 November 1938 at the yearly conference of the War Council at the People's Commissariat for Defense (21 to 29 November 1938), published in: *Woyenny Sowiet, 1938, 1940*, pp. 235–264, here p. 257.

178. Litunovsky to Voroshilov on 28 August 1930: RGASPI, f. 74, op. 2, p.101, p. 159 f.

179. RVS of the Caucasian Army of the Red Flag to the Chief of the RVS of the USSR on 1 April 1930: RGASPI, f. 74, op. 2, d. 95, pp. 36–37 v.

180. Yagoda's order regarding the measures taken in the liquidation of the kulaks as a class from 2 February 1930: *Tragediya Sovietskoi Derevnii*, Bd. 2, pp. 163–167, here: p. 166.

181. Report pf the political administration of the RKKA regarding the political mood in the Red Army from 22 May 1932: RGASPI, f. 82, op. 2, d. 799, pp. 75–79.

182. Ibid., here: p. 76.

183. Report by H. I. Dobroditsky on negative occurrences in the Independent Far-Eastern Army of the Red Flag from 4 May 1933, addressed to Yagoda and Stalin, published in: *Lubyanka, 1922–1936*, pp. 429–435.

184. Report on extraordinary occurrences in the navy from 29 July 1932: RGASPI, f. 82, op. 2, d. 799, pp. 84–87.

185. Budyonny to Voroshilov, not dated: RGASPI, f. 74, op. 2, d. 97, p. 157.

186. Transcript of the evening session of the war council at the NKO SSSR on 21 November 1938, here: Remarks by A. I. Zaproshes, division commissar and member of the war council of the Moscow Military District, published in: *Voyenny Soviet, 1938, 1940*, pp. 33–89, here: p. 50; Transcript of the morning session of the war council at the NKO SSSR on 26 November 1938, here: Remarks by Lev Mekhlis, published in: Ibid., pp. 158–167, here p. 164.

187. Reese, *Stalin's Reluctant Soldiers*, pp. 56–52; at the session of the war council at the NKO of the USSR that was held between 21 and 27 November 1938, the attendees complained about the abysmal discipline, "extraordinary events" and manifestations of

amoral behavior in the ranks of the Red Army. Voroshilov reacted to several reports by exclaiming "Disgrace and dishonor", in: *Voyenny Soviet, 1938, 1940*, pp. 196–200.

188. Final speech by Voroshilov on 29 November 1938 at the yearly conference of the War Council at the People's Commissariat for Defense (21 to 29 November 1938), published in: *Woyenny Sowiet, 1938, 1940*, pp. 235–264, here pp. 258 f.

189. Order No. 0219 of the People's Commissar for Defense on the Battle against Drunkenness in the Red Army from 28 December 1938, published in: *Prikazy NKO SSSR, 1937–1941*, pp. 84 f.

190. Bogdan Musial, "Erbarmungslose Abrechnung mit Deserteuren".

Chapter 16

1. For example, in March 1933, the OGPU arrested 16 leading personnel in the petroleum industry on charges of participating in a counterrevolutionary spying and wrecking organization. Some of the arrested belonged to the old elite, while others were allegedly the sons of Tsarist officers and "wealthy Cossacks"; among them was also a former member of the Bund, a secular Jewish socialist movement in Tsarist Russia (Report from Yagoda to Stalin Regarding the Arrest of Specialists in the Petroleum Industry from 16 March 1933, published in: *Lubyanka, 1922-1936*, pp. 414 f.).

2. Report from Yagoda and Mironov to Stalin on the "espionage organization" in the artillery and weapons industry, 7 August 1933, published in: *Lubyanka, 1922-1936*, p.454 ff.

3. Ibid.

4. Session protocol No. 1 Politburo of the Central Committee of the VCP(b) from 20 February 1934, Point 4: RGASPI, f. 17, op. 3, d. 939, pp. 1-22, here p. 2

5. *Lubyanka, 1922-1936* (FN 128). For example, in summer 1936 a group of operative agents of the economic department of the NKVD were sent to Voronezh to investigate six armaments factories in secret (ibid.).

6. Memorandum by I. A. Akulov to Stalin and Kaganovich on the reorganization of the OGPU and the creation of the NKVD from 22 February 1934, published in: *Lubyanka, 1922-1936*, pp. 487 ff.; Akulov argued to limit the juridical powers of the OGPU/NKVD; among others, the wanted to limit the agency's sentencing to 3 or 5 years of deportation and making imposing the death penalty a privilege of ordinary courts as in the past, the OGPU troikas had imposed many death penalties that could not be confirmed later on.

7. Session protocol No. 4 of the Politburo of the Central Committee of the VCP(b) from 29 March 1934, Point 6: RGASPI, f. 17, op. 162, d. 16, pp. 25-29.

8. Session protocol No. 4 of the Politburo of the Central Committee of the VCP(b) from 4 May 1934, Point 2: ibid., pp. 45-50.

9. Directory of armaments factories with the special hiring order, approved by the Politburo on 4 May 1938: ibid., pp. 51-54.

10. Excerpts from Order No. 004 are published in: *Lubyanka, 1922-1936*, pp.814f. (FN 133).

11. Yagoda's report from 14 June 1935 and excerpts from Order No. 0012 are published in: *Lubyanka, 1922-1936*, pp. 815 f. (FN 135).

12. Ibid.

13. Ibid.

14. Resolution of the Central Committee and Central Control Committee of the VCP(b) Regarding the Purge of the Party from 28 April 1933: RGASPI, f. 17, op. 3, d. 922, pp. 50-55.

15. Baberowski, *Der rote Terror*, pp. 156-160.

16. Abramov, *Smersh*, pp. 45-58.

17. Cf. Wieczorkiewicz, *Łańcuch Śmierci*, pp. 31-69 (data on: p.69).
18. Stenograph of Zhdanov's speech at the Conference of the Leningrad Oblast Committee of the Party on 25 December 1936: RGASPI, f. 77, op. 1, d. 634, pp. 1-4.
19. Stalin and Zhdanov to Kaganovich and Molotov on 25 September 1936, published in: *Stalin i Kaganovich*, pp. 682 f.; resolution of the Politburo from 11 October 1936, published in: *Lubyanka, 1922-1936*, p. 767; the document collection *Lubyanka, 1922-1936* includes several documents showing that Yezhov was a key leading participant in the earlier purges; Baberowski, *Der rote Terror*, pp. 164 f.
20. Baberowski, *Der rote Terror*, p. 165.
21. Project draft from Ordzhonikidze, Kaganovich and Stalin from early February 1937: RGASPI, f. 84, op. 2, d. 46.
22. Project draft from Ordzhonikidze regarding wrecking activities in the industry, not dated, (early February 1937): RGASPI, f. 84, op. 2, d.46, pp. 42-59.
23. Ibid.
24. Werth, "Ein Staat gegen sein Volk", p. 204; Baberowski, *Der rote Terror*, pp. 130 ff., 183-186.
25. Project draft from Ordzhonikidze regarding wrecking activities in the industry, not dated, (early February 1937): RGASPI, f. 84, op. 2, d. 46, pp. 42-59, here p. 46.
26. Ibid., pp. 48-57.
27. Kaganovich on the lessons from the wrecking activities, sabotage and espionage of the Trotskyist-Japanese-German sabotage and espionage organizations in the railway transport system, not dated (early February 1937): ibid., pp. 60-77.
28. Draft project from Stalin Regarding the Political Education of Party Functionaries and Measures in the Fight against Trotskyists and other Two-Face Ones in the Party Organizations, not dated (early February 1937): ibid., pp. 126-143.
29. Dimitrov, *Tagebücher*, p. 152 (entry from 3 March 1937).
30. Mikoyan's autobiography, manuscript, written in the 1960s: RGASPI, f. 84, op. 3, d. 116, pp. 1-265, here: pp. 49-104; regarding the relationship between Stalin and Ordzhonikidze cf. Chlewnjuk, *Das Politbüro*, pp. 221-245.
31. Dimitrov, *Tagebücher*, p. 165 f. (entry from 11 November 1937).
32. Petrov, "Die Kaderpolitik des NKWD", p. 21
33. Dimitrov, *Tagebücher*, p. 149 (entry from 11 February 1937).
34. Cf. Baberowski, *Der rote Terror*, pp. 183-204; Werth, "Ein Staat gegen sein Volk", pp. 206-225; Service, *Stalin*, pp. 367-378.
35. Wieczorkiewicz, *Łańcuch Śmierci*, pp. 61 f. (quote on: p. 62).
36. Quoted according to: Ibid.
37. Protocol No. 47, decisions of the Politburo of the Central Committee of the VCP(b) between 19 March and 7 April 1937, Point 102: RGASPI, f. 17, op. 162, d. 21, pp. 1-15, here p. 9.
38. Wieczorkiewicz, *Łańcuch Śmierci*, pp. 63-69; report from Yezhov to the members of the Politburo on 27 April 1937, published in: *Lubyanka, 1937-1938*, p.135.
39. Protocol No. 49, decisions of the Politburo of the Central Committee of the VCP(b) between 17 April and 16 June 1937, Point 37: RGASPI, f. 17, op. 162, d. 21, pp. 26-63, here p. 29.
40. People's Commissar of Defense, Voroshilov, to Comrade Stalin (Politburo of the Central Committee of the VCP(b)) and Molotov, (SNK of the USSR) on 10 May 1937: RGASPI, f. 82, op. 2, d. 800, p. 27.
41. Order No. 85 of the NOK of the USSR from 11 May 1937 regarding the notification of the resolution of the Presidium of the TsIK of the USSR regarding the dismissal of

M. N. Tukhachevsky from the post of Deputy People's Commissar of Defense on 10 May 1937, published in: *Prikazy NKO, 1937-1941*, p. 12.

42. Wieczorkiewicz, *Łańcuch Śmierci*, pp. 70-74.
43. Ibid.; *Voyenny Soviet, 1938,1940*, p. 3.
44. Wieczorkiewicz, *Łańcuch Śmierci*, pp. 892.
45. *Voyenny Soviet*, 1938,1940, pp. 3 f.
46. Wieczorkiewicz, *Łańcuch Śmierci*, pp. 908 f.; regarding the debate on the casualties of Stalinist terror in the Soviet military cf. ibid., pp. 897-921; Overy, *Russlands Krieg*, p. 61.
47. Wieczorkiewicz, *Łańcuch Śmierci*, pp. 1078 f.
48. Overy, *Russlands Krieg*, p. 61.
49. Wieczorkiewicz, *Łańcuch Śmierci*, pp. 1077-1092.
50. Report from Shchadenko, Deputy People's Commissar of Defense, at the session of the War Council at the NKO of the USSR on 25 November 1938, protocol of the evening session, published in: *Voyenny Soviet, 1938, 1940*, pp. 149-157, here pp. 155 ff.
51. *Voyenny Soviet, 1937*, pp. 8 f.
52. Wieczorkiewicz, *Łańcuch Śmierci*, pp. 1070 f.; cf. Stocker, "Tönerner Koloß ohne Kopf".
53. Protocol of the evening session of the War Council at the NKO of the USSR on 25 November 1938, published in: *Voyenny Soviet, 1938,1940*, pp. 33-89, here p. 60.
54. Protocol of the morning session of the War Council, published in: ibid., pp. 158-167, here p. 160.
55. Ibid.
56. Introduction, *Voyenny Soviet, 1938, 1940*, p. 6.

Chapter 17

1. Dimitrov, *Tagebücher*, p. 98 (entry from 7 April 1934).
2. Bogolepov to Stalin on 2 March 1931: RGASPI, f. 558, op. 11, d. 763, pp. 65-69.
3. On the margins of Bogolepov's letter, Stalin wrote: "Comrade Manuilsky! Can You read the letter by Comrade Bogolepov and comment on it? J. Stalin.": Ibid.
4. Manuilsky to Stalin on 19 March 1931: ibid., pp. 70 f.
5. Manuscript of Molotov's lecture on the results of the Five Year Plan, held on 21 January 1933 at the Third Session of the Central Executive Committee of the USSR (with remarks from Molotov and Stalin): RGASPI, f. 82, op. 2, d. 257, pp. 1-61, here p. 52.
6. Manuscript of Molotov's lecture "The Most Important Aspects of the International Situation of the USSR in the Year 1932", not dated (January 1933): RGASPI, f. 82, op. 2, d. 258, pp. 131-153, here pp. 145.
7. Ibid., pp. 145.
8. Session protocol No. 3 of the Delegate Bureau of the VCP(b) and the ECCI from 18 July 1930; report by Knorin, Manuilsky an Pyatnitsky to Stalin and Molotov regarding the political guidelines of the ECCI for the KPD for the year 1931 from 28 October 1931, published in: Politbyuro i Komintern, pp. 647-652 (quote: p. 648).
9. Ibid.
10. Ernst Thälmann: "Programmerklärung zur nationalen und sozialen Befreiung des deutschen Volkes", Proklamation des ZK der KPD vom 24.08.1930, in: *Die Rote Fahne* from 24 August 1930.
11. Pyatnitsky to Stalin on 10 May 1932 regarding the state of the KPD and the guidelines for the upcoming consultation with the German comrades (attachment), published in: *Politbyuro i Komintern*, pp. 655-660, here: p. 659.

12. Ernst Thälmann: "Programmerklärung zur nationalen und sozialen Befreiung des deutschen Volkes", Proklamation des ZK der KPD vom 24.08.1930, in: *Die Rote Fahne* from 24 August 1930.

13. Stalin to Kaganovich on 22 August 1932, printed in: *Stalin i Kaganovich*, p. 295.

14. Ernst Thälmann: "Programmerklärung zur nationalen und sozialen Befreiung des deutschen Volkes", Proklamation des ZK der KPD vom 24.08.1930, in: *Die Rote Fahne* from 24 August 1930.

15. Pyatnitsky to Stalin on 10 May 1932 regarding the state of the KPD and the guidelines for the upcoming consultation with the German comrades (attachment), published in: *Politbyuro i Komintern*, pp. 655-660, here: p. 657.

16. Election results in the Empire 1919-1933, published in: *Die Weimarer Republik 1918-1933*, pp. 628 f.

17. Leo Trotzki, "The Turn in the Communist International and the Situation in Germany", 26 September 1930, published in: Bulletin of the Opposition, no. 17–18, November–December 1930.

18. Tooze, *Ökonomie der Zerstörung*, pp. 59-92.

19. Möller, *Europa zwischen den Weltkriegen*, p. 9.

20. Sławomir Cenckiewicz, »Oskar Lange po stronie Sowietow«, *Rzeczpospolita* on 16/17 December 2006; Wieczorkiewicz, *Historia polityczna Polski*, p. 381.

21. Protocol of the conversation between Stalin, Molotov and Oskar Lange from 11 May 1944, written by Pavlov: RGASPI, f. 558, op. 11, d. 354, pp. 58-69; three months later, on 9 August 1944, Stalin told Stanislaw Mikołajczyk, the Prime Minister of the Polish government in exile, that "Communism fits onto Germany like a saddle onto a cow." (Protocol of the conversation between Stalin and the members of the delegation of the Polish government headed by Mikołajczyk, from 9 August 1944, written by Pavlov, printed in: Sovietsky factor, Vol. 1, pp. 84-89, here p. 87).

22. Stalin to the Central Committee of the VCP(b), Kaganovich und Molotov on 26 October 1933, published in: *Stalin i Kaganovich*, pp. 405 f.

23. Dimitrov, *Tagebücher*, pp. 97 f. (entry from 7 April 1934).

24. Ibid.

25. Ibid., p. 102 (entry from 24 April 1934).

26. Ibid., pp. 102 f. (entry from 25 April 1934).

27. Stalin to Kaganovich and Molotov on 2 September 1935: RGASPI, f. 558, op. 11, d. 89, p. 2 f.; published in: *Stalin i Kaganovich*, p. 545.

28. Cf. Bystrowa, *Sovietsky voyenno-promyshlenny kompleks*, p. 68.

29. Service, *Stalin*, p. 409.

30. Chang/Halliday, *Mao*, pp. 101 f., 136.

31. Ken, *Mobilisatsionnoye planirovaniye*, pp. 203 f.

32. Stalin to Kaganovich on 14 September 1931, published in: *Stalin i Kaganovich*, pp. 103 f.

33. Stalin to Molotov and Kaganovich on 23 September 1931, published in: ibid., pp. 116 f.

34. In early 1944, Stalin told a group of Polish communists: "Kuropatkin [the Russian commander during the Russo-Japanese War of 1904/05] lost the war against Japan because he did not have reinforcements. He asked the Tsar for the increase of transport trains from 4 to 7 per day on the Eastern Line [Trans-Siberian Railroad]. The Tsar was unable to do that. The Soviet Union built the new, second tracks and set the plans to 35 per day. However, it emerged that the plan had been formulated so poorly that only 17 trains drive per day. Other factors [aside from tracks] had not been sufficiently considered and therefore, the transport plan could not be fulfilled." (Session protocol of the Central

Committee of the PPR from 22 October 1944: Archiwum Akt Nowych, (Warschau), PPR 295/V-1, pp. 23-31, here: p.27).

35. Tukhachevsky's memorandum on the reconstruction of the Red Army from 11 January 1930, addressed to Voroshilov: RGASPI, f. 558, op. 11, d. 446, pp. 12-18, here p. 12.

36. Note from Semyon Budyonny to Kliment Voroshilov, not dated, likely 1933: RGASPI, f. 74, op. 2, d. 97, p. 145.

37. Cf. Slutsch, "Stalin und Hitler 1933-1941".

38. Mikoyan's autobiography, manuscript, written in the 1960s: RGASPI, f. 84, op. 3, d. 116, pp. 1-265, here: p. 256.

39. *Politbyuro i Evropa*, pp. 315 f.; Excerpts from the Politburo protocol from 15 June 1930, published in: ibid., p. 225; Slutsch, "Stalin und Hitler 1933-1941".

40. Session protocol No. 25 of Politburo of the Central Committee of the VCP(b) from 13 May 1935, Point 4: RGASPI, f. 17, op. 162, d. 18, pp. 18-25, here: p. 18; attachment to Point 4 of the Politburo resolution of 17 April 1935 (Registry of Purchases for the Individual Departments): ibid., p. 26-34.

41. Session protocol No. 25 des Politburo of the Central Committee of the VCP(b) from 13 May 1935, Point 102: ibid., p. 24; attachment to Point 104 of the Politburo resolution of 10 May 1935 (Organizational Measures and Expansion of the Red Army in the Years 1936 and 1937): ibid., pp. 35-37.

42. Slutsch, "Stalin und Hitler 1933-1941".

43. Tukhachevsky's memorandum "Hitler's War Plans" from 29 March 1935: RGASPI, f. 558, op. 11, d. 447, pp. 130-145.

44. Ibid.

45. Ibid., pp. 134-139.

46. Ibid., pp. 139 f.; quote in the original: Adolf Hitler, *Mein Kampf,* München 1942, p. 742.

47. Ibid., pp. 140 f.

48. Ibid., p. 143.

49. Ibid.

50. Stalin, Report on the Work of the Central Committee to the Eighteenth Congress of the C.P.S.U.(B.) *(Delivered March 10, 1939.)*, published in: Stalin, *Works*, Vol. 14, pp. 355-431, here p. 364.

51. O'Sullivan, *Stalins "Cordon sanitaire"*, p. 67.

52. Note by Andrey Zhdanov, not dated (likely August 1939): RGASPI, f. 77, op. 1, d. 896, p. 2; O'Sullivan, *Stalins "Cordon sanitaire"*, p. 78.

53. Stalin, Report to the Seventeenth Party Congress on the Work of the Central Committee of the C.P.S.U. (B.), *January 26, 1934*, published in: Stalin, *Works*, Vol. 13, pp. 288-388, here: pp. 298, 301.

54. Cf. Pietrow-Ennker, "Mit den Wölfen heulen..." Stalinistische Außen- und Deutschlandpolitik 1939-1941, *Präventivkrieg?*, pp. 77-94; or Yurii Gorkov, "22. Juni 1941: Verteidigung oder Angriff? Recherchen in russischen Zentralarchiven", in: ibid., pp. 190-207.

Chapter 18

1. Dimitrov, *Tagebücher*, p. 155 (entry from 20 March 1937).

2. Fleischhauer, *Der Pakt*, pp. 127 ff.; Weisung »Fall Weiß« vom 03.04.1939, published in: *Hitlers Weisungen*, pp. 17 ff.

3. Besprechung beim Führer am 23.11.1939. Anwesend: alle Oberbefehlshaber, published in: Jacobsen, *Der Weg zur Teilung der Welt*.

4. Cf. Fleischhauer, *Der Pakt,* pp. 128 ff.
5. Quoted according to: Ibid., p. 131.
6. Ibid., pp. 131 ff.
7. Dimitrov, *Tagebücher,* pp. 259 f. (entry from 28 May 1939).
8. Ibid., p. 260.
9. Cf. Fleischhauer, *Der Pakt,* pp. 160-166; O'Sullivan, *Stalins "Cordon sanitaire",* pp. 70 ff.
10. Dimitrov, *Tagebücher,* pp. 259 f. (entry from 28 May 1939).
11. Memorandum from Shaposhnikov from 10 July 1939: RGASPI, f. 558, op. 11, d. 220, pp.3-9.
12. Ibid.
13. Ibid.
14. Memorandum from Shaposhnikov from 11 August 1939: ibid., pp. 10-20.
15. O'Sullivan, *Stalin's "Cordon sanitaire",* p. 67.
16. Protocol of the Session of the Military Missions of England, France and the USSR, 14 August 1939: RGASPI, f. 558, op. 11, d. 220, pp. 51-65.
17. Fleischhauer, Der Pakt, pp. 187 f., 331.
18. On 20 August 1939, the Inspector General of the Polish Armed Forces, Rydz-Smigły, is supposed to have told the French ambassador to Warsaw: "With the Germans we risk our freedom, with the Russians we lose our soul." Quoted according to: Fleischhauer, *Der Pakt,* p. 339.
19. Cf. the Soviet protocols for the negotiations: RGASPI, f. 558, op. 11, d. 220, pp. 21-138.

Chapter 19

1. Cf. Fleischhauer, *Der Pakt,* pp. 9-35; cf. auch O'Sullivan, *Stalins "Cordon sanitaire",* pp. 25-36.
2. Quoted according to: Fleischhauer, *Der Pakt,* pp. 98, 129, 199 f.
3. Report "Russlands Neuorientierung", not dated (between 5 and 10 May 1939), Political Department V, Russia, quoted according to: Dębski, *Między Berlinern a Moskwą,* p. 82.
4. There had been several failed attempts to initiate Soviet-German economic and political talks beforehand. Cf. Fleischhauer, *Der Pakt,* pp. 100-217.
5. Protocols of the talks between Mikoyan and Hilger in the presence of Babarin on 2, 8 and 17 June 1939: RGASPI, f. 84, op. 1, d. 146, pp. 1-9; Fleischhauer describes the negotiations from the German perspective (*Der Pakt,* pp. 260 ff.).
6. Mikoyan to Stalin on 20 June 1939: RGASPI, f. 84, op. 1, d. 146, p. 10.
7. Fleischhauer, *Der Pakt,* p. 264.
8. Ibid., pp. 264-275.
9. Ibid., pp. 290-292; O'Sullivan, *Stalin's "Cordon sanitaire",* pp. 75 f.
10. Cf. Fleischhauer, *Der Pakt,* pp. 314-342 (quote: p.342).
11. Cf. Ibid., pp. 336-403.
12. Secret Supplementary Protocol to the Non-Aggression Treaty of 23 August 1939, in: *Sowjetstern und Hakenkreuz,* p. 232.

Chapter 20

1. Note from Andrey Zhdanov, not date (likely August 1939): RGASPI, f. 77, op. 1, d. 896, p. 2; cf. also O'Sullivan, *Stalin's "Cordon sanitaire",* pp. 78 f.
2. Dimitrov, *Tagebücher,* pp. 273 f. (entry from 7 September 1939), emphasis in the original.
3. Ibid. (emphasis by the author).

4. Cf. Fleischhauer, *Der Pakt*, p. 331.

5. Quoted according to: O'Sullivan, *Stalins "Cordon sanitaire"*, p. 75.

6. Ibid., p. 67.

7. Dimitrov, *Tagebücher*, pp. 273 f. (entry from 7 September 1939).

8. War Losses of the Belarusian and Ukrainian Fronts in the Course of the Operation Between 17 September and 1 October 1939, Colonel Bychkov, Department of the Rear Areas of the Operative Administration of the General Staff of the Red Army, 20 October 1939: ZAMO, f. 13, op. 137145, d. 30, p. 379; Musial, *"Konterrevolutionäre Elemente"*, p. 25; Grzelak, *Kresy w czerwieni*, pp. 480 f.

9. Musial, *"Konterrevolutionäre Elemente"*, pp. 25-97.

10. Telegram from Ponomarenko to Stalin from 13 November 1939: RGASPI, f. 558, op. 11, d. 66, p. 13.

11. Report on the deployment of rear area artillery units in the Polish campaign, 3 November 1939: ZAMO, f. 81, op. 28329, d. 5748, pp. 179-189.

12. Report on the deployment of railway troops in the Polish campaign by Smokachev, member of the War Council of the Belarusian Front, 19 October 1939: ZAMO, f. 32, op. 65584, d. 12, pp. 177-180.

13. Report on the Deployment of the Southern Group of the Ukrainian Front during the Crushing of the Polish Troops and the Liberation of Western Ukraine, I. V. Tyulenev, Commander of the 12th Army, 14 October 1939: RGVA, f. 35084, op. 1, d. 188, pp. 302-310.

14. Cf. Grzelak, *Kresy w czerwieni*, pp. 228-481.

15. Stalin's speech during the conference of the Central Committee of the VCP (b) regarding the experience of the fighting with Finland (14 to 17 April 1940), from 17 April 1940: RGASPI, f. 17, op. 165, d. 77, pp. 178-212; published in: *"Zimnyaya voina"*, pp. 31-42.

16. Quoted according to: Musial, *"'... Kapitalismus am Kragen packen'"*, p. 59.

Chapter 21

1. van Dyke, *The Soviet Invasion of Finland*, pp. 19 f.

2. Ibid., pp. 20-27, 42.

3. Trotter, *A Frozen Hill*, p. 47; Upton, *Finland 1939–40*, pp. 51-67.

4. van Dyke, *The Soviet Invasion of Finland*, pp. 42-53.

5. Cf. van Dyke, *The Soviet Invasion of Finland*.

6. Dimitrov, *Tagebücher*, pp. 280 f. (entry from 21 January 1940).

7. Lecture by the Chief of the Political Administration of the Red Army, Lev Mekhlis, on military ideology, on 10 May 1940: RGVA, f. 9, op. 36, d. 4252, pp. 114a-195; published in: *"Zimnyaya voina"*, pp. 329-343, here: p. 335.

8. For example, Stoecker writes regarding the Stalin's motives: "In the case of Finland, it was Stalin's intention to keep the country out of German reach, because he did not trust Germany. In 1938, Stalin initiated talks with the Finnish government with the goal of receiving the guarantee that Germany would not be allowed to use Finnish territory as a springboard for an attack against the USSR." (Stoecker, *Tönerner Koloß*, p. 150).

9. Report of the Political Administration of the 7th Army for 21 December 1939, from 22 December 1939, Gorokhov: RGASPI, f. 77, op. 4, d. 45, pp. 49-57.

10. Session protocol of the commission of the Chief War Council on the question of military ideology, on 13 and 14 April 1940, published in: *"Zimnyaya voina"*, pp. 344-389, here: p. 368.

11. Note from Andrey Zhdanov during the time of the Finnish campaign: RGASPI, f. 77, op. 3, d. 162, pp. 91, 295.

12. Wesołowski, "'Sztrafniki'", pp. 109-127, here: pp. 111 f.

13. Telephone call from Stalin and Voroshilov to Shtern, the commander of the 8th Army, from 7 January 1940: RGASPI, f. 558, op. 11, d. 445, pp. 12-17.

14. Telephone call from Stalin and Voroshilov to Mekhlis in the night of 7/8 January 1940: ibid., pp. 17 ff.

15. van Dyke, *The Soviet Invasion of Finland;* Dimitrov, *Tagebücher,* pp. 296 (entry from 28 March 1940).

16. Note from Andrey Zhdanov during the time of the Finnish campaign: RGASPI, f. 77, op. 3, d. 163, p. 264.

17. Stalin's speech during the conference of the Central Committee of the VCP (b) regarding the experience of the fighting with Finland (14 to 17 April 1940), from 17 April 1940: RGASPI, f. 17, op. 165, d. 77, pp. 178-212; published in: *"Zimnyaya voina",* pp. 31-42.

18. Dimitrov, *Tagebücher,* p. 290 (entry from 21 January 1940).

19. Ibid., pp. 295 f. (entry from 27 March 1940).

20. Ibid.

21. Ibid., pp. 296 f. (entry from 28 March 1940) (emphasis in the original).

22. Stalin's speech during the conference of the Central Committee of the VCP (b) regarding the experience of the fighting with Finland (14 to 17 April 1940), from 17 April 1940: RGASPI, f. 17, op. 165, d. 77, pp. 178-212; published in: *"Zimnyaya voina",* pp. 31-42.

23. Cf. various documents such as: various Politburo resolutions between March and July 1940: RGASPI, f. 17, op. 162, d. 27, 28; proposals and sessions of the individual commissions, sessions of the Chief War Council, orders of the People's Commissar for Defense between April and July 1940, published in: *"Zimnyaya voina";* orders of the People's Commissar for Defense published in: *Prikazy NKO, 1937-1941.*

Chapter 22

1. Records of the Orders of Comrade Stalin at the Session of the Commission of the Chief War Council in the Kremlin on 21 April 1949: RGVA, f. 4, op. 14, d. 2768, pp. 64 f.; published in: *"Zimnyaya voina",* p. 154.

2. Lecture by the Chief of the Political Administration of the Red Army, Lev Mekhlis, on military ideology, on 10 May 1940: RGVA, f. 9, op. 36, d. 4252, pp. 114a-195; published in: *"Zimnyaya voina",* pp. 329-343, here: pp. 331 f. (emphasis by the author).

3. Dimitrov, *Tagebücher,* pp. 296 ff. (entry from 28 March 1940).

4. Stalin's speech during the conference of the Central Committee of the VCP (b) regarding the experience of the fighting with Finland (14 to 17 April 1940), from 17 April 1940: RGASPI, f. 17, op. 165, d. 77, pp. 178-212; published in: *"Zimnyaya voina",* pp. 31-42, here: pp. 36 ff.

5. Ibid.

6. Dimitrov, *Tagebücher,* pp. 381 ff. (entry from 5 May 1940).

7. *Komandny i nachalstvuyushchi,* pp. 73-109.

8. Fleischhauer, *Diplomatischer Widerstand,* p. 146.

9. Cf. Wieczorkiewicz, *Łańcuch Śmierci,* pp. 1070-1079.

10. Session protocol of the commission of the Chief War Council on the question of military ideology, on 13 and 14 April 1940, published in: *"Zimnyaya voina",* pp. 344-389, here: p. 346.

11. Order No. 112 of the NKO regarding the introduction of higher military ranks in the Red Army, 8 May 1940, published in: *Prikazy NKO, 1937-1941,* pp. 133 f.; Order No. 1391 of the NKO regarding the introduction of military ranks for privates and lower-ranking

commanders in the Red Army, 2 November 1940, published in: ibid., pp. 188 f.; Timoshenko to Molotov regarding the introduction of non-commissioned officer ranks on 22 July 1940 and the draft order: RGASPI, f. 82, op. 2, d. 801, pp. 108 f.; Ziemke, *Red Army*, p. 237.

12. On 13 July 1940, Timoshenko issued an order regarding punitive battalions for soldiers and lower-ranking commanders who had been sentenced to prison sentences of between 6 months and 2 years (Order No. 214 of the NKO from 15 July 1940, published in: *Prikazy NKO 1937-1941*, p. 157); on 12 October 1940, Timoshenko the order to implement the new disciplinary rules of the Red Ary (Order No. 356 of the NKO from 12 October 1940, published in: ibid., pp. 180-183); cf. also Wesołowski, "Sztrafniki", pp. 112 ff.

13. NKO Order No. 262 from 14 August 1940 regarding the announcement of the decree of the Highest Soviet of the USSR "On the Strengthening of the Unified Command in the Red Army and Red Fleet" from 12 August 1940, published in: ibid., p. 163.

Chapter 23

1. Cf. Müller, *Der letzte deutsche Krieg*, pp. 40-43.
2. Müller, Der letzte deutsche Krieg, p. 46.
3. Ibid., pp. 44-55, quote from: p. 52.
4. Fleischhauer, *Diplomatischer Widerstand*, pp. 151 f., 198 f.
5. Quoted according to: ibid., p. 154.
6. Ibid., pp. 161-190.
7. Tooze, *Ökonomie der Zerstörung*, p. 443.

Chapter 24

1. Besymenski, "Molotows Berlin-Besuch", p. 122.
2. Fleischhauer, *Diplomatischer Widerstand*, pp. 230–257; O'Sullivan, *Stalin's "Cordon sanitaire"*, pp. 86–89; Besymenski, "Molotows Berlin-Besuch".
3. O'Sullivan, *Stalin's "Cordon sanitaire"*, p. 85 f.
4. Hausner, *Justice at Jerusalem*, p. 184.
5. O'Sullivan, *Stalin's "Cordon sanitaire"*, p. 85 f.
6. Dimitrov, *Tagebücher*, p. 320 f. (entry from 24 November 1940).
7. Ibid.
8. Dimitrov's letter to the Secretariat of the CC of the CPSU, A. A. Andreiev, from 30. 08. 1940, published in: *Politbyuro und Komintern*, p. 788 f.
9. Dimitrov, *Tagebücher*, p. 342 (entry from 5 February 1941) (emphasis by the author).
10. Ibid., p. 351 f. (Entry from 27 February 1941) (emphasis by the author).
11. Ibid., p. 374 f. (Entry from 20 April 1941) (emphasis in the original).
12. Dębski, *Między Berlinem a Moskwą*, p. 384 f.
13. Dimitrov to Malenkov on 30 July 1940, published in: *Komintern i vtoryja mirovaya voina*, Sheet 1, p. 399 f.
14. Dębski, *Między Berlinem a Moskwą*, p. 385 f.
15. Torańska, *Oni*, p. 22.
16. Beria to Stalin on 2 November 1940, published in: *Lubyanka 1939–1946*, p. 191 ff.; Sokolov, "Pokhvalnoye slovo Viktoru Suvorovu", pp. 24–27.
17. Cf. Musial, *Konterrevolutionäre Elemente*, p. 34 ff. In total, about 250,000 Polish soldiers and officers became Soviet prisoners of war in the autumn of 1939. (Ibid.).
18. Beria to Stalin, 2 November 1940, published in: *Lubyanka 1939–1946*, p. 191 ff.
19. Ibid.

20. Protocol no. 33, Decisions of the Politburo of the CC of the CPSU from 15 May to 12 June 1941, item 183: RGASPI, f. 17, op. 162, d. 35, pp. 1–29, p. 13; Wieczorkiewicz, *Historia polityczna Polski*, pp. 203–206; Sokolow, "Pokhvalnoye slovo Viktoru Suvorovu".

21. Dimitrov, *Tagebücher*, p. 315 ff. (Entry from 7 November 1940) (Emphasis in the original).

22. Ibid.

23. Ibid. (Emphasis in the original).

24. Report of the People's Commissar for State Control, Mekhlis, to Stalin and Molotov on control of storage, inventory and issue of material and financial goods in seven Infantry Divisions and one air base of the Red Army from 31 January 1941: RGASPI, f. 82, op. 2, d. 803, pp. 10–67.

25. Chief of the Administration for Grenade Launcher Weapon Systems, Colonel Borisov, to People's Commissar for State Control, Mekhlis, on 27 December 1940: RGASPI, f. 82, op. 2, d. 809, pp. 19 f.

26. Statement of the People's Commissar for Defense, Tymoshenko, on the report of the People's Commissar for State Control, Mekhlis, to the CC of the CPSU and SNK of the USSR from 01. 2. 1941, 12. 02. 1941: RGASPI, f. 82, op. 1, d. 803, pp. 68–80, quote p. 68.

27. 29 Results of the revision of the administration of artillery and the storage of ammunition in artillery stores, on warships and in navy troops, People's Commissar for State Control, Mekhlis, to Stalin and Molotov., 11. 04. 1941: RGASPI, f. 82, op. 2, d. 809, pp. 29–73.

28. Numerous State Control reports from the autumn of 1940 and spring of 1941 can be found i.a. in: RGASPI, f. 84, op. 1, d. 81.

29. Dimitrov, *Tagebücher*, p. 341 f. (Entry from 4 February 1941).

30. Ibid., p. 375 f. (Entry from 22 April 1941).

31. Ibid., p. 376 f. (Entry from 23 April 1941).

32. Cf. Besymenski, "Tschto sche skasal Stalin 5 maja 1941"; Neweschin, "Retsch Stalina 5 maja 1941"; Joachim Hoffmann, *Stalins Vernichtungskrieg*, pp. 34–38; Bonwetsch, "Die Forschungskontroverse"; Service, *Stalin*, p. 434 ff.

33. Besymenski, "Tschto sche skasal Stalin"; id., *Stalin und Hitler*, pp. 373–397; Dimitrov, *Tagebücher*, p. 380 f. (Entry from 5 May 1941).

34. Besymenski, *Stalin und Hitler*, p. 378; Neweshin, "Politiko-ideologicheskie kampanii Kremlya", p. 316 f.; Hoffmann, *Stalins Vernichtungskrieg*, p. 36 ff.

35. Cf. Bonwetsch, "Die Forschungskontroverse", p. 176 f.

36. Brief summary of Comrade Stalin's address during the ceremonial meeting of graduates of the Military Academy in the Kremlin on 5 May 1941, recorded by K. Semenov: RGASPI, f. 558, op. 1, d. 3808, pp. 1-9; Semenov was an employee of the People's Commissariat of Defense (Neveshin, "Rech Stalina 5 maya 1941").

37. Ibid.

38. Ibid., pp. 5–8.

39. Dimitrov, *Tagebücher*, p. 380 f. (Entry from 05. 05. 1941). Dimitrov reproduced this section of Stalin's speech in more detail.

40. Addresses by Comrade Stalin during the reception on 5 May 1941 (brief shorthand, recorded by K. Semenov): RGASPI, f. 558, op. 1, d. 3808, pp. 10 ff. (emphasis in the original, italics added).

41. Dimitrov, *Tagebücher*, p. 382 (entry from 5 May 1941, emphasis in the original).

42. Neveshin, "Politiko-ideologicheskie kampanii Kremlya", pp. 317–324.

43. Upcoming tasks regarding political work of the Party in the Red Army: (Short protocol of discussion of the draft directive of the Main War Council of the Red Army of 4 June 1941), reprinted in: *Glawny wojenny sowjet RKKA*, p. 490 f.

44. Ibid.

45. Ibid.

46. Dimitrov, *Tagebücher*, p. 281 (entry from 7 November 1939, emphasis in the original).

47. Ibid., p. 289 (entry from 21 January 1940, emphasis in the original).

48. Musial, "… Kapitalismus am Kragen packen", p. 59.

49. Quoted after Service, *Stalin*, p. 433.

50. Quoted after Sebag Montefiore, *Stalin*, p. 397.

51. Minutes of Meeting No. 3 of the Main War Council of the Red Army, 8 May 1941, reprinted in: Glawny voienny soviet RKKA, pp. 303-307, here: p. 304. Order by the People's Commissariat of Defence No. 30 on Combat and Political Preparation and Training of the Army for 1941 was issued on 21 Janury 1941, published in: *Prikazy 1937–1941*, pp. 206–224.

52. Minutes of Meeting No. 1 of the Chief War Council of the Red Army, 15 April 1941, reprinted in: *Glavny voienny soviet RKKA*, p. 296 f.

53. Decision No. 1 of the Main War Council of the Red Army of 15 April 1941, reprinted in: Ibid., p. 298.

54. Secretary of the Brest Oblast Committee, T. Novikova, to the CC of the CPB on 19 July 1941: RGASPI, f. 17, op. 88, d. 480, pp. 27–33.

55. Meltyukhov, *Upushchenny shans Stalina* p. 348.

56. Minutes of the conversation with Colonel Nichiporovich, the (former) commander of the 208th Motorized Division, dated 15 September 1942: NARB, f. 3500, op. 4, d. 89, pp. 3–16.

57. Cf. the subchapter "Building Tanks and Expanding the Armored Corps" in this book; but also Irinarkhov, *Zapadny osoby*, p. 62 ff., 69–79; Stoecker, *Tönerner Koloß*, p. 166.

58. Report of the Chief of the 3rd Department of the Special Warfare District West (Belarus), Begma to Ponomarenko, Secretary of the CC of the CPB, on production deficiencies in the MiG-1 and MiG-3 aircraft from 17. 06. 1941: NARB, f. 4p, op. 21, d. 2470, pp. 1–7.

59. Report of the USSR People's Commissar for Defense, S. K. Timoshenko, and the Chief of the General Staff of the Red Army, G. K. Zhukov, to Stalin, 10-11 June 1941, reprinted in: *Glavny voienny soviet RKKA*, p. 491 ff.

60. Minutes No. 27, decisions of the Politburo from 5 to 22 February 1941, here decision of the Politburo of 14. 02. 1941, promulgated as a decision of the CC of the CPSU and SNK USSR "On the construction plan of railroad lines in the southwest, west and northwest of the USSR of 14 February 1941, item 75: RGASPI, f. 17," op. 162, op. 32, pp. 58–67.

61. Ponomarenko to Stalin on 30 May 1941: NARB, f. 4p, op. 21, d. 2333, pp. 68-77; Ponomarenko to Beria on 07.06.1941: Ibid., d. 2336, pp. 92 ff.; both documents published in: *Nakanune*, p. 371 f., 375 ff.

62. 64 Politburo decision of 24 March 1941 on measures to build 251 airfields for the People's Commissariat of Defense in 1941 (item 171): RGASPI, f. 17, op. 162, d. 33, pp. 11-20; list of airfields on which concrete runways are to be built in 1941: Ibid., pp. 42–50.

63. Plan of replenishment of state reserves of hard coal for 1941, Annex No. 3 to Politburo decision of 6 June 1941: RGASPI, f. 17, op. 162, d. 35, pp. 104-109; Plan of replenishment of state reserves of petroleum products, Annex No. 4 to Politburo decision of 6 June 1941: Ibid., p. 110.

64. Plan of replenishment of the mobilization reserves of the Red Army and the war fleet of grain and cereal products, foodstuffs and luxury articles, Annex 7 to the Politburo decision of 6 June 1941: RGASPI, f. 17, op. 162, d. 35, pp. 129 ff.

65. In detail about the plans and about the debate about them: Meltyukhov, *Upushchenny shans Stalina*, pp. 370–414, Roberts, *Stalin's Wars*, pp. 70–81.

Chapter 25

1. In the meantime, numerous works and articles have been published on the controversy surrounding the so-called preventive war, cf. i. a. *Der deutsche Angriff auf die Sowjetunion 1941*; Pietrov-Ennker (Hg.), *Präventivkrieg?*; Wegner, "Präventivkrieg 1941?"; Rainer F. Schmidt, "Appeasement oder Angriff".
2. Wegner, "Präventivkrieg 1941?", p. 214.
3. For example, Sally W. Stoecker writes about Stalin's motives for the war against Finland: "Im Falle Finnlands war es Stalins Absicht, das Land vom deutschen Zugriff fernzuhalten." (Stoecker, *Tönerner Koloß*, p. 150).
4. Likewise Hoffmann, *Stalins Vernichtungskrieg*, pp. 57 f; Scheil, *1940/41*, pp. 257–262; Magenheimer, *Entscheidungskampf 1941*, pp. 77–82, 90–118.
5. *Kriegstagebuch des Oberkommandos der Wehrmacht 1940–1945*, Volume 1/II, p. 393 (entry from 8 May 1941).
6. Cf.: Arnold, *Die Wehrmacht und die Besatzungspolitik*, pp. 62–74.
7. *Die Tagebücher von Joseph Goebbels: Sämtliche Fragmente*, Volume 4, p. 695.
8. *Die Tagebücher von Joseph Goebbels*, Part II, *Diktate 1941–1945*, Volume 4, pp. 35, 161.
9. Ibid., p. 208.
10. Entry from 19 August 1941, in: Ibid., p. 258.
11. Entry from 19 August 1941, in: Ibid., p. 259 ff.
12. Wegner, "Hitlers Besuch in Finnland".
13. Ibid., p. 130 ff.
14. Meltyukhov, *Upushchenny shans Stalina*, pp. 446, 601.
15. *Die Tagebücher von Joseph Goebbels: Sämtliche Fragmente*, Volume 4, p. 695.
16. Wegner, *Präventivkrieg 1941*, p. 216.
17. Wegner, *Hitlers Besuch in Finnland*, p. 134.
18. Müller, *Der letzte deutsche Krieg*, pp. 81–90.
19. Hitler, *Monologe im Führerhauptquartier*, p. 62.
20. Cf. Hitler, *Mein Kampf*, S. 741 ff.; *Hitlers zweites Buch*, p. 78 f., 163.
21. Records by Gen. d. Inf. a.D. Liebemann, in: *VfZ*, 2 (1954), p. 435.
22. Hitler, *Mein Kampf*, pp. 739, 742.
23. Bormann's notes on a conversation Hitler had with his associates about the objectives in the war against the USSR, 16 July 1941, reprinted in.: *Vom Generalplan Ost zum Generalsiedlungsplan*, pp. 61–64.
24. Cf. Subok/Pleshakov, *Der Kreml im Kalten Krieg*; zur Debatte darüber vgl. Gibianskij, "Osteuropa".

Final Remarks

1. In 1941, Soviet heavy industry delivered 6662 tanks, the majority of which were modern tanks such as the KV (1038 tanks between July and December) and T-34 (1898 tanks between July and December); the next year, the Soviet industry was able to produce 24,446 tanks. In comparison, the German industry was only able to produce 3790 tanks in 1941 and 6180 in 1942: Malyshev to Stalin on 4 January 1942: RGASPI, f. 82, op. 2, d. 572, pp. 19-24; Davies, *Europe at War*, p. 33 f.
2. Subok/Pleschakow, *Der Kreml im Kalten Krieg*, p. 33.
3. B. Musial, "Die Rechnung Stalins ging auf", *Frankfurter Allgemeine Zeitung, 10 March 2007*, p. 6.

Archival Sources

Russian Federation

Russian State Archive of Socio-Political History in Moscow (RGASPI), among others:
Secret protocols of the Politburo of the Central Committee of the VCP(b) (f. 17, op. 3) Documents of the party leadership regarding questions of defense of the republic.
1917–1922 (f. 17, op. 109) Situation reports of the GPU and by military agencies (f. 17, op. 87) Party control (f. 613) Lenin secretariat (f. 5) Lazar Kaganovich (f. 81) Georgy Malenkov (f. 83) Vyacheslav Molotov (f. 82) Aleksandr Shcherbakov (f. 88) Stalin (f. 558). Kliment Voroschilov (f. 74) Andrei Zhdanow (f. 77) Felix Dzerzhinsky (f. 76) Lev Trotsky (f. 325) Anastas Mikoyan (f. 84) Dmitri Manuilsky (f. 523) Komintern (f. 485).

State Archive of the Russian Federation (GARF): *Committee for Defense (f. 8418) People's Commissariat for State Control (f. 8300).*

Central Archives of the Russian Ministry of Defense (ZAMO):
Reports regarding the Polish campaign.

Russian State Military Archive (RGVA), among others:
Session protocols of the Chief War Council.

Republic of Belarus
National Archives of the Republic of Belarus in Minsk (NARB):
Central Committee of the CP(b)B (f. 4).

Selected Bibliography

Abramov, Vadim, *Smersch. Sovietskaya voiennaya kontrraswedka protiv raswedku Tretego Reikha*, Moscow, 2005.

Albert, Andrzej (= Wojciech Roszkowski), *Najnowsza Historia Polski, 1918-1980*, Warsaw, 1989.

Applebaum, Anne, *Der Gulag*, Berlin 2003.

Armiya Pobedy v Velikoi Otechestvennoi Voine 1941-1945, Moscow/Minsk 2005.

Arnold, Klaus Jochen, *Die Wehrmacht und die Besatzungspolitik in den besetzten Gebieten der Sowjetunion. Kriegführung und Radikalisierung im "Unternehmen Barbarossa"*, Berlin 2005.

Baberowski, Jörg, *Der rote Terror. Die Geschichte des Stalinismus*, München 2003.

Bessedowski, Grigori, *Im Dienste der Sowjets. Erinnerungen*, Leipzig 1930.

-, *Den Klauen der Tscheka entronnen. Erinnerungen*, Leipzig, Zürich 1930.

Besymenski, Lew, *Stalin und Hitler. Das Pokerspiel der Diktatoren*, Berlin 2002.

-, "Wjatscheslaw Molotows Berlin-Besuch vom November 1940 im Licht neuer Dokumente", in: Pietrov-Ennker, *Präventivkrieg?*, pp. 113-127.

-, "Chto zhe skazal Stalin 5 maja 1941 goda?" in: *Novoye Vremiya*, 1991 (No. 19), pp. 36-40.

Bonwetsch, Bernd, "Die Forschungskontroverse über die Kriegsvorbereitungen der Roten Armee 1941", in: Pietrow-Ennker, *Präventivkrieg?*, pp. 170-189.

Bystrowa, I. W., *Sovietski voyenno-promyshlenny kompleks: problemy stanowienia i rasvitya (1930-1980-e gody)*, Moscow 2006.

Chang, Jung, und Jon Halliday *Mao. Das Leben eines Mannes, das Schicksal eines Volkes*, München 2005.

Chlewnjuk, Oleg W., *Das Politbüro. Mechanismen der Macht in der Sowjetunion der dreißiger Jahre*, Hamburg 1998.

Chiari, Bernhard, "'Nationale Renaissance' Belorussifizierung und Sowjetisierung: Erziehungs- und Bildungspolitik in Weißrussland 1922-1944", in: *Jahrbücher für Geschichte Osteuropas*, 42 (1994), 4, pp. 521-540.

Conquest, Robert, *Harvest of Sorrow. Soviet Collectivization and the Terror-Famine*, New York 1986.

Davies, Norman, *White Eagle, Red Star. The Polish-Soviet War 1919-1920 and the "Miracle on the Vistula"*, London 2003.

-, *Europe at War 1939-1945. No Simple Victory*, London 2006.

Dębski, Sławomir, *Między Berlinem a Moskwą. Stosunki niemiecko-sowieckie 1939-1941*, Warsaw 2003.

Der deutsche Angriff auf die Sowjetunion 1941. Die Kontroverse um die Präventivkriegsthese, published by Gerd R. Ueberschär und Lev A. Bezymenskij, Darmstadt 1998.

Deutscher Oktober 1923. Ein Revolutionsplan und sein Scheitern, published by: Bernhard H. Bayerlein, Leonid G. Babicenko, Fridrich I. Firsov und Alexander Ju. Vatlin, Berlin 2003.

Dimitroff, Georgi, *Tagebücher 1933–1943*, published by Bernhard H. Bayerlein, Berlin 2000.

Dunn, Walter S., *The Soviet Economy and the Red Army, 1930-1945*, Westport, Conn., 1995.

Dyke, Carl van, *The Soviet Invasion of Finland 1939-1940*, London, Portland/Or, 1997.

Eberhard, Piotr, *Przemiany narodowościowe na Ukrainie XX wie/cM*, Warsaw 1994.

Economics and World Power. An Assessment of American Diplomacy since 1789, published by William H. Becker und Samuel F. Wells, Jr, New York 1984.

Ennker, Benno, "Stalin-Regime 1939-1941: Politische Lähmung im Angesicht der kommenden Katastrophe", in: Bianka Pietrow-Ennker (publisher), *Präventivkrieg?*, pp. 131-145.

Peter Erler, *Terror gegen deutsche Polit- und Wirtschaftsemigranten*, in: Wladislaw Hedeler (publisher), *Stalinistischer Terror 1934–41*, Berlin 2002, pp. 239-258.

Europa Nieprowincjonalna. Przemiany na ziemiach wschodnich dawnej Rzeczpospolitej (Białoruś, Litwa, Łotwa, Ukraina, wschodnie pogranicze 111 Rzeczpospolitej Polskiej w latach 1772-1999), published by Krzysztof Jasiewicz, Warsaw, London 1999.

Feliks Dzierżyński. Biographie, Autorenkollektiv unter Leitung von S. S. Chromov, Berlin 1981.

Firsov, Fridrich I., "Ein Oktober, der nicht stattfand. Die revolutionären Pläne der RKP(b) und der Komintern", in: *Deutscher Oktober 1923*, pp. 35-58.

Fitzpatrick, Sheila, *Stalinskiye Krestyane. Sotsyalnaya istoriya Sovietskoi Rossii v 30-e gody: Derevnya*, Moscow 2001.

Fleischhauer, Ingeborg, *Der Pakt. Hitler, Stalin und die Initiative der deutschen Diplomatie 1938-1939*, Berlin, Frankfurt/Main 1990.

-, *Diplomatischer Widerstand gegen "Unternehmen Barbarossa". Die Friedensbemühungen der Deutschen Botschaft Moskau 1939-1941*, Berlin, Frankfurt/Main 1991.

Funke, Manfred, "Republikim Untergang. Die Zerstörung des Parlamentarismus als Vorbereitung der Diktatur", in: *Die Weimarer Republik*, pp. 505-531.

Vom Generalplan Ost zum Generalsiedlungsplan, published by Czesław Ma-dajczyk, München et al. 1994.

Geyer, Dietrich: "Sowjetrussland und die deutsche Arbeiterbewegung", in: *Vierteljahrshefte für Zeitgeschichte* XXIV (1976), Nr. 1, pp. 2-37.

Gibianskij, Leonid, "Osteuropa: Sicherheitszone der UdSSR, sowjetisiertes Protektorat des Kreml oder Sozialismus 'ohne Diktatur des Proletariats'? Zu den Diskussionen über Stalins Osteuropa-Politik am Ende des Zweiten Weltkrieges und am Anfang des Kalten Krieges", *Forum für osteuropäische Ideen- und Zeitgeschichte*, 8. Jg. 2004, H. 2, pp. 113-137.

Glavny voienny Soviet RKKA. 13 marta 1938 g. - 20 iyunya 1941 g. Dokumenty i materialy, Moscow 2004.

Golotik, S. I., und W. W. Minayev, *Naselenie i Wlast. Ocherki demografícheskoj istorii SSSR 1930-kh godov*, Moscow 2004.

Gorkow, Juri: "22. Juni 1941: Verteidigung oder Angriff? Recherchen in den russischen Zentralarchiven", in: Pietrow-Ennker (publisher): *Präventivkrieg 1941?*, pp. 190-207.

Gorlov, Sergej, "Geheimsache Moskau-Berlin. Die militärische Zusammenarbeit zwischen der Sowjetunion und dem Deutschen Reich 1920-1933", V/Z44 (1996), pp. 133-169.

Grzelak, Czesław K., *Kresy w czerwieni. Agresja Związku Sowieckiego na Polskę, w 1939 roku*, Warsaw 2001.

Gulag. 1918-1960. Dokumenty, published by A. I. Kukurin und N. W. Petrow, Moscow 2002.

Handbuch der Geschichte Weißrusslands, published by Dietrich Beyrau und Rainer Lindner, Göttingen 2001.

Hausner, Gideon, *justice at Jerusalem*, New York 1966.

Historische Debatten und Kontroversen im 19. und 20. Jahrhundert, published by Jürgen Elvert und Susanne Krauß, Wiesbaden 2003.

Hitler, Adolf, *Mein Kampf*, München 1942.

Monologe im Führerhauptquartier 1941-1944, aufgezeichnet von Heinrich Heim, published by Werner Jochmann, München 2000.

Hitlers Weisungen für die Kriegführung 1939-1945, published by Walther Hubatsch, Bonn 1983.

Hitlers zweites Buch. Ein Dokument aus dem Jahre 1928, eingeleitet und kommentiert von Gerhard L. Weinberg, Stuttgart 1961.

Hoffmann, Joachim, *Stalins Vernichtungskrieg 1941-1945, Planung, Ausführung und Dokumentation*, 5., revised and supplemented new edition, München 1999.

Irinarkhov, R. S., *Zapadyi osohyj*, Minsk 2002.

Istoriya stalinskogo gulaga. Massovye repressii v SSSR, Vol. 1, published by Yu. N. Afanasev, R Gregori et al., Moscow 2004.

Istoriya stalinskogo gulaga. Naselenie gulaga: chislennost i uslowiya soderzhaniya, Vol. 4, published by A. B. Besobrodov, B. M. Khrustalev, Moscow 2004.

Istoriya stalinskogo gulaga. Konets 1920-kh -pervaya polovina 1950-kh godov, Vol. 5, *Spetsprezelentsy v SSSR*, published by T. B. Tsarevskaya-Dyakina, Moscow 2004.

Iwanow, Mikołai, *Pierwszy Naród Ukarany. Polacy w Związku Radzieckim. 1921-1939*, Warsaw/Wroclaw 1991.

Jacobsen, Hans Adolf, *Der Weg zur Teilung der Welt*, Koblenz, Bonn 1997.

Kok lomali NEP. Stenogramy plenumov TsK VCP(b) 1928-1929, 5 Vol., published by V. P. Danilov, O. W. Khlewniuk, A. Yu. Watlin, Moscow 2000.

Kazlou, L., und A. Ciau, *Belarus na siami ruhiashakh*, Minsk 1993.

Ken, Oleg N., *Mobilizatsionnoye planirowaniye i politicheskie resheniya. Konets 1920 - seredina 1930-ck gg*, St. Petersburg 2002.

Koenen, Gerd, *Der Russland-Komp ex. Die Deutschen und der Osten 1900-1945*, München 2005.

Komandny i nachalstvuyushchi sostav Krasnoi Armii v 1940-1941 gg. Struktura i kadry tsentralnogo apparata NKO SSSR, voiennych okrugow i obshchevoiskovykh armij. Dokumenty i materialy, Moscow 2005.

Komintern i vtoraja mirovaya voina, published by N. S. Lebedeva und M. M. Narski, Moscow 1994.

"Der I. Kongress der Kommunistischen Internationale. Protokoll der Verhandlungen in Moskau vom 2. bis zum 6. März 1919", *Bibliothek der Kommunistischen Internationale*, Vol. VII, Verlag der Kommunistischen Internationale, Hamburg 1921.

Kostyrchenko, G. W., *Tainaya politika Stalina. Wlast i antisemitism*, Moscow 2003.

Krestyanskoye Dwiszhenie w Powolzhye: 1919-1922. Dokumenty i materialy, published by V. Danilova und T. Shanina, Moscow 2002.

Kriegstagebuch des Oberkommandos der Wehrmacht, 1940-1945, Vol. I/II: *1. August 1940 bis 31. Dezember 1941*, published by Hans-Adolf Jacobsen et al., München 1982.

Lenin, V. I., *Works*, 45 Volumes, Moscow 1974. Accessed from: https://www.marxists.org/archive/lenin/works/cw/index.htm

Lubyanka. Stalin i VchK-GPU-OGPU-NKVD. janvar 1922 - dekabr 1936. Dokumenty, published by V. N. Khaustow, V. P. Naumov und N. S. Plotnikova, Moscow 2003.

Lubyanka. Stalin i glawonoye uprawieniye gosbesopasnosti NKVD 1937-1938, published by V. N. Khaustow, V. P. Naumov und N. S. Plotnikova, Moscow 2004.

Lubyanka. Stalin i NKVD-NKGB-GUKR "Smersh" 1939 - mart 1946. Dokumenty, published by V. N. Khaustow, V. P. Naumov und N. S. Plotnikova, Moscow 2006.

Lynne, Viola, *Peasant Rebeis under Stalin, Collectivisation and the Culture of Peasant Resistance*, New York, Oxford 1996.

Magenheimer, Heinz, *Entscheidungskampf 1941. Sowjetische Kriegsvorbereitungen, Aufmarsch, Zusammenstoß*, Bielefeld 2000.

The Maisky Diaries. Red Ambassador to the Court of St. James's 1932-1943, ed. Gabriel Gorodetsky. Yale University Press, 2015.

Margolina, Sonja, *Wodka. Trinken und Macht in Russland*, Berlin 2004.

-, *Das Ende der Lügen. Rußland und die Juden im 20. Jahrhundert*, Berlin 1992.

McDermott, Kevin, *Stalin: Revolutionary in an Era of War*, New York 2006.

McMeekin, Sean, *Stalin's War: A New History of World War II*, New York 2021.

Meltyuchov, Mikhail, *Upushchenny shans Stalina. Sovietski soyus i borba za Evropu: 1939-1941*, Moscow 2000.

Merridale, Catherine, *Iwans Krieg. Die Rote Armee 1939-1945*, Frankfurt/Main 2006.

Michalka, Wolfgang, "Deutsche Außenpolitik 1920-1933", in: *Die Weimarer Republik*, pp. 303-326.

Möller, Horst, *Europa zwischen den Weltkriegen*, München 1998.

Moorhouse, Roger, *The Devil's Alliance: Hitler's Pact with Stalin 1939-1941*, London 2014.

Müller, Rolf-Dieter, *Der letzte deutsche Krieg 1939-1945*, Stuttgart 2005.

Musial, Bogdan, *"Konterrevolutionäre Elemente sind zu erschießen". Die Brutalisierung des deutsch-sowjetischen Krieges im Sommer 1941*, München 2000.

- (publisher), *Sowjetische Partisanen in Weißrussland. Innenansichten aus dem Gebiet Baranovici 1941-1944. Eine Dokumentation*, München 2004.

-, "Wir werden den ganzen Kapitalismus am Kragen packen". Sowjetische Vorbereitungen zum Angriffskrieg in den dreißiger und Anfang der vierziger Jahre', *Zeitschrift für Geschichtswissenschaft* 2006/1, pp. 45-65.

Musial, Bogdan, *Stalins Beutezug; Die Plünderung Deutschlands und der Aufstieg der Sowjetrunion zur Weltmacht*, Propyläen, München 2010.

Musial, Bogdan, *Sowjetische Partisanen 1941-1944: Mythos und Wirklichkeit*, Schöningh Verlag, Paderborn 2009.

Nakanune. Zapadny osoby voienny okrug (konets 1939 g. -1941 g.j. Dokumenty i materialy, Minsk 2007.

NEP; *Ekonomicheskiye, politicheskiye i sotsiokulturnye aspekty*, published by A. S. Senyavsky, V. B. Zhiromskaya, S. V. Zhuravlev et al, Moscow 2006.

Nestor Makhno. Krestyanskoye Dvishenie na Ukrainie 1918-1921. Dokumenty i Materialy, published by V. Danilova und T. Shanina, Moscow 2006.

Neveshin, Vladimir, "Rech Stalina 5 maja 1941 godai apologijanastu-patelnoj voiny", *Omtechestvennaaa istoriya*, 1995 (No. 2), pp. 54-69.

-, "Politiko-ideologicheskie kampanii Kremlja (1939-1941 gg)", in: *Mezhdunarodny krisis 1939-1941 gg: Ot Sovietsko-germańskich govorov 1939 goda do napadenija Germanii na SSSR*, Moscow 2006, pp. 307-325.

Nowak, Andrzej, "Rok 1920: pierwszy plan ofensywy sowieckiej przeciw Polsce", *Niepodległość* 1997 (49), pp. 7-19.

Nowik, Grzegorz, *Zanim złamano "Enigme".. Polski radiowywiadpodczas wojny z bolszewicką Rosją 1918-1920*, Warsaw 2005.

O'Sullivan, Donald, *Stalin's "Cordon sanitaire". Die sowjetische Osteuropapolitik und die Reaktionen des Westens 1939-1949*, Paderborn 2003.

Overy, Richard, *Russlands Krieg 1941-1945*, Reinbek 2003.

-, *Die Diktatoren. Hitlers Deutschland, Stalins Russland*, München 2005.

Pietrow, N. W., und K. W. Skorokin, *Kto rukowodil NKWD 1934-1941. Sprawotschnik*, Moscow 1999.

Pietrow, Nikita, "Die Kaderpolitik des NKWD während der Massenrepressalien 1936-39", in: Wladislaw Hedeler (publisher), *Stalinistischer Terror 1934–41. Eine Forschungsbilanz*, Berlin 2002, pp. 11-32.

-, "Polska operacja NKWD", *Karta* 1993 (11), pp. 24-44.

Pietrow-Ennker, Bianka (publisher), *Präventivkrieg? Der deutsche Angriff auf die Sowjetunion*, Frankfurt/Main 2000.

Politbyuro TsK RCP(b) - VCP(b) i Evropa. Reshenija "osoboj papki" 1923-1939, published by G. Adibekov et al., Moscow 2001.

Politbyuro TsK RCP(b) - VCP(b) i Komintern. 1919-1943. Dokumenty, published by G. M. Adibekov et al., Moscow 2004.

Prikasy Narodnogo Komissara Oborony SSSR: 1937-21 iyunya 1941 g. T. 13 (2-1), Moscow 1994.

Protko, Tatyana S., *Stanowienie Sovietskoj totalitarnoj sistemy w Belarussi (1917-1944 gg.)*, Minsk 2002.

Putin, Vladimir, *The Real Lessons of the 75th Anniversary of World War II*, in: *The National Interest*, 18 June 2020: https://nationalinterest.org/feature/vladimir-putin-real-lessons-75th-anniversary-world-war-ii-162982?page=0%2C5

Reese, Roger R., *Stalin's reluctant soldiers. A social history of the Red Army 1925-1941*, Lawrence/Kans. 1996.

Reforma v Krasnoi Armii. Dokumenty i materialy 1923-1928 gg., Book 1 and 2, Moscow 2006.

Revvoiensoviet Respubliki. Protokoly 1920-1923. Sbornik dokumentov, Moscow 2000.

Roberts, Geoffrey, *Stalin's Wars. Prom World War to Cold War, 1939-1953*, New Häven/Conn., London 2006.

Samuelson, Lennart, *Krasny koloss. Stanowieniye voienno-promyshlennogo kompleksu SSSR. 1921-1941*, Moscow 2001.

Scheil, Stefan, *1940/41. Die Eskalation des Zweiten Weltkrieges*, München 2005.

Schmidt, Rainer F., "Appeasement oder Angriff". Eine kritische Bestandsaufnahme der sog. 'Präventivkriegsdebatte' über den 22. Juni 1941", in: *Historische Debatten und Kontroversen im 19. und 20. Jahrhundert*, pp. 220-233.

Schwabe, Klaus, "Der Weg der Republik vom Kapp-Putsch 1920 bis zum Scheitern des Kabinetts Müller 1930", in: *Die Weimarer Republik 1918-1933*, pp. 95-133.

Sebag Montefiore, Simon, *Stalin. Am Hof des roten Zaren*, Frankfurt/ Main 2005.

Service, Robert, *Lenin. Eine Biographie*, München 2000, *Stalin. A Biography*, London 2004.

Shurawljow, Sergej, "Das Moskauer Elektrokombinat. Arbeit und Alltag deutscher Wirtschaftsemigranten", in: Wladislaw Hedeler (publisher), *Stalinistischer Terror 1934–41*, Berlin 2002, pp. 229-238.

"Zimnyaya voina": robota nad oshibkami, aprel-mai 1940 g. Materialy komissi Glavnogo voiennogo sovieta Krasnoj Armii po obobshchniyu opyta finskoj kampanii, Moscow 2004.

Simonov, N. S., "'Strengthen the defence of the land of Soviets: The 1927 'war alarm' and its consequences", *Europe-Asia Studies*, December 1996, vol. 48, pp. 1355-1364.

Slutsch, Sergej, "Stalin und Hitler 1933-1941. Kalküle und Fehlkalkulationen des Kreml", in: Jürgen Zarusky (publisher), *Stalin und die Deutschen*, München 2006.

Sokolow, Boris, "Pokhvalnoye slovo Viktorom Suvorovu i epitafiya katynskim polyakom", in: *Gotovil Ii Stalin nastupatelnuyu voinu protiv Gitlera? Nezaplanirowannaya diskussiya. Sbornik materialov*, published by G. A. Borbyugayev und V. A. Neweshin, Moscow 1995, pp. 24-27.

Sovietskiaja derewnya glazami VChK - OGPU - NKVD. Dokumenty i materialy, Vol. 1-3: *1918-1939*, Moscow 2000-2005.

Sovietskyi faktor v vostochnoi Evropye 1944-1953, Vol. 1:1944-1948, published by T. V. Volkotina et al., Moscow 1999.

Sowjetstern und Hakenkreuz 1938-1941. Dokumente zu den deutschsowjetischen Beziehungen, published by Kurt Pätzold und Günter Rosenfeld, Berlin 1990.

Stalin i Kaganowich. Perepiska. 1931-1936 gg., published by Oleg Khlewnyuk, R. U. Devis, L. R. Kosheleva, E. A. Ris, L. A. Rogowaya, Moscow 2001.

Stalin, J. W., *Briefe an Molotow, 1925-1936*, published by Lars T. Lih, Oleg Naumow und Oleg Chlewnjuk, Berlin 1996.

-, *Works*, 18 Volumes, Moscow 1953. Accessed from: https://www.revolutionarydemocracy. org/Stalin/

Stalinistischer Terror 1934-41. Eine Forschungsbilanz, published by Wladislaw Hedeler, Berlin 2002.

Stoecker, Sally W., "Tönerner Koloß ohne Kopf. Stalinismus und Rote Armee", in: Pietrov-Ennker (publisher), *Präventivkrieg? Der deutsche Angriff auf die Sowjetunion*, pp. 148-169.

Subok, Wladislaw, und Konstantin Pleschakow, *Der Kreml im Kalten Krieg. Von 1945 bis zur Kubakrise*, Hildesheim 1997.

Suworow, Viktor, *Der Eisbrecher. Hitler in Stalins Kalkül*, Stuttgart 1989.

-, *Der Tag M*, Stuttgart 1995.

-, *Stalins verhinderter Erstschlag. Hitler erstickt die Weltrevolution*, Selent 2000.

Svirin, Mikhail, *Bronya krepka. Istoriya Sovietskogo tanka 1919-1937*, Moscow 2005.

-, *Bronyewoi shchit Stalina, Istoriya Sovietskogo tanka 1937-1943*, Moscow 2006.

Die Tagebücher von Joseph Goebbels. Sämtliche Fragmente, published by Elke Fröhlich, 4 Vol., München 1987 -, Teil II, *Diktate 1941-1945*, published by Elke Fröhlich, München et al. 1995.

Tooze, Adam, *Ökonomie der Zerstörung. Die Geschichte der Wirtschaft im Nationalsozialismus*, München 2007.

Torańska, Teresa, *Oni*, London 1985.

Tragediya sovietskoi derevnii. Kolektivizatsya i raskulachivaniye. Dokumenty i materialy. 1927-1939, Vol. 1-5, Moscow 2000-2002.

Trotter, William, *A Frozen Hill*, Chapel Hill/N. C. 1991.

Upton, Anthony, *Finland 1939-40*, Newark/N. J. 1979.

Wegner, Bernd, "Hitlers Besuch in Finnland. Das geheime Tonprotokoll seiner Unterredung mit Mannerheim am 4. Juni 1942", *VfZ* 1993 (43), pp. 117-137.

-, "Präventivkrieg 1941? Zur Kontroverse um ein militärhistorisches Scheinproblem", in: *Historische Debatten und Kontroversen im 19. und 20. Jahrhundert*, pp. 206-219 *Die Weimarer Republik 1918-1933. Politik, Wirtschaft, Gesellschaft*, published by K. D. Bracher, M. Funke und H.-A. Jacobsen, Bonn 1987.

Weber, Claudia, *Der Pakt. Stalin, Hitler und die Geschichte einer mörderischen Allianz 1939-1941*, Beck Verlag, München 2019.

Werth, Nicolas, "Ein Staat gegen sein Volk. Gewalt, Unterdrückung und Terror in der Sowjetunion", in: *Das Schwarzbuch des Kommunismus. Unterdrückung, Verbrechen und Terror*, published by Stephane Courtois et al., München 1998, pp. 45-295.

Wesołowski, Tomasz, "'Sztrafniki' - Jednostki karne Armii Czerwonej w latach 1940-1945", in: *Studia Podlaskie*, Białystok 2000 (Band X), pp. 109-127.

Wieczorkiewicz, Paweł, *Łańcuch Śmierci. Czystka w Armii Czerwonej 1937-1939*, Warsaw 2001 -, *Historia polityczna Polski 1939-1945*, Warsaw 2006 *Voyenny Soviet pri Narodnom Kommissare Oborony SSSR. Noyabr 1937g. Dokumenty i materialy*, published by 1.1. Basik, V. L. Vorontsow et al., Moscow 2006 *Voienny soviet pri Narodnom Komissare Oborony SSSR - 1938,1940. Dokumenty i materialy*, Moscow 2006.

Vsesoyusnaya perepis naseleniya 1937 goda: Obshchie itogi. Sbornik dokumentov i materialov, Moscow 2007.

Za Soviety bez komunistov. Krestyanskoye vosstaniye w Tyumenskoi gubernii 1921. Sbornik dokumentov, Nowosibirsk 2000.

Zeidler, Manfred, *Reichswehr und Rote Armee 1920–1933,* München 1994.

Tselenin, I.E., *Stalinskaya "revolucija svercku" posle "velikogo pereloma". 1930–1939. Politika, ossushchestvleniye, rezultaty,* Moscow 2006.

Ziemke, Earl F., *The Red Army 1918–1941: Prom vanguard of world revolution to U. S. ally,* London, New York 2004.

TsK RCP(b) – VCP(b) i natsionalny vopros, Book 1, *1918–1933 gg,* published by L. S. Gatagova, L. P. Kosheleva, L. A. Rogovaya, Moscow 2005.

Index